Essential
CPA Law Review

Seventh Edition

Essential
CPA Law Review

George C. Thompson
Graduate School of Business, Columbia University

Gerald P. Brady
Graduate School of Business, Columbia University

Kent Publishing Company
A Division of Wadsworth, Inc.
Boston, Massachusetts

Executive Editor: Richard C. Crews
Production Editor: Rachel Hockett/Cobb-Dunlop Publisher Services, Inc.
Interior Designers: Marsha Cohen, Andrea DaRif
Cover Designer: Margaret Tsao
Production Coordinator: Linda Siegrist

Kent Publishing Company

A Division of Wadsworth, Inc.

Printed in the United States of America

2 3 4 5 6 7 8 9 — 90 89 88 87 86

Library of Congress Cataloging in Publication Data

Thompson, George C.
  Essential CPA law review.

  Includes index.
  1. Commercial law—United States—Examinations,
questions, etc. I. Brady, Gerald P. II. Title.
KF889.5.T46 1986   346.73'07'076   85-18218
ISBN 0-534-06192-3   347.3067076

To the instructors and CPA candidates
who have found the book to be helpful
in coping with the CPA examination

Preface

Since the sixth edition of *Essential CPA Law Review,* published in 1984, there have been additional major changes which impact upon the business law part of the CPA examination. The most important change by far was the wholesale revision of the original *Business Law Content Specification Outline,* adopted in 1981 and effective November 1983. The *Revised Specifications* were adopted in September 1984 and effective with the May 1986 examination. From the candidate's standpoint, the revision is a beneficial change, since it represents a major reduction in size of the body of law for which the CPA candidate is responsible. Antitrust, consumer protection, administrative law, and bulk transfers have been eliminated in their entirety. Furthermore, federal securities regulation, government regulation of employment, and the "other forms" of doing-business category included under the "business organizations" designation have been substantially shortened. As a result, there has been a shift in the percentages allocated to Area 2 (Business Organizations), which has been increased by 5%, and a reduction by 5% of Area 5 (Government Regulation of Business). Area 2 thus moves up to 20 from 15%, and Area 5 is decreased from 15 to 10%. This reallocation of percentages should also make the examination less onerous since the business organization area topics (Agency, Partnership, Corporations, and Trusts) are mainstream areas and are covered in depth in business law courses and texts.

The other major development results from a change in the AICPA's policy regarding the use of the copywritten examinations and unofficial answers. Heretofore, the AICPA had granted unlimited use of their examinations and answers without charge to anyone, including your authors. The current policy is to allow instructors to use the materials in their business law courses given in the various universities and colleges without charge. Examination questions and answers used by authors of CPA review books and by those giving CPA review courses may be obtained by paying a percentage royalty based upon sales or enrollment fees. The net effect upon the cost of a book to the candidate who uses a book containing this material is obvious—an increase in price. However, at least insofar as this book is concerned, this will not occur. Instead, the review book need not include the AICPA questions and answers of recent examinations. This prior practice has been rendered obsolete as a result of a new publication by the AICPA designed to aid the candidate in his or her preparation for the examination. The first such edition appeared in 1984 and contained an anthology of examination questions and unofficial answers, indexed according to the *Business Law Content Specification Outline*. This was followed by a second edition covering the years 1980–1984. The second book includes the examinations and unofficial answers from May 1980 to November 1984. Once again this would certainly appear to be a plus factor for the candidates since the book undoubtedly consists of the better questions from the 10 examinations covered. This book currently sells at a modest price to students (about $8 plus postage and handling).

Taking all the above factors into consideration, it is obvious that our prior reprinting of the 10 or more most recent examinations and answers is no longer desirable. Instead, we include the best examination questions and unofficial answers from examinations prior to 1981. In addition, we include a section of questions without answers which will be appropriate for use by the instructor or for self-testing. This practice is also resorted to in the last part of the book, which contains a complete examination with answers and one without answers.

Of course, there have also been major changes in several of the substantive areas of law covered in the book. These have been reflected in the outlines. The most notable changes are contained in the Bankruptcy and The CPA and the Law chapters. In 1984 the Bankruptcy Code was amended to correct certain deficiencies, problems, and oversights which experience revealed were present in the 1978 Bankruptcy Code. The CPA liability area has been changed by two significant United States Supreme Court decisions. The first involves the question of privileged communication in respect to the accountant's tax accrual workpapers. In the second case the Supreme Court held that Civil RICO is applicable to businesses and thus to accountants without prior criminal conviction of the defendant.

The basic purposes of this book remain the same:

1. To present a brief yet comprehensive review of business law.
2. To enable CPA candidates to prepare effectively for the business law examination. The outline form shortens the time necessary for review; it is logical and relatively easy to remember.
3. To build candidates' confidence by providing questions and answers to test themselves.
4. To provide an approach to the examination. The introduction discusses common pitfalls as well as the proper mechanics and method of writing examination answers.
5. To help make studying for the law part of the CPA exam a gratifying, once-in-a-lifetime experience.

This book is designed primarily for CPA business law review courses, or it can be used for individual review. It can also be used as supplemental material in business law courses.

We extend our special thanks to Robert G. Harvey, a recent Columbia Law School graduate, who contributed invaluable research assistance.

The excellent introduction was originally drafted by the late Louis A. Sigaud for use in the first edition of this book, published in 1959. It has been substantially revised, rewritten, and expanded to reflect the extensive changes in the AICPA examination since 1958. Mr. Sigaud was, until his retirement in 1958, the Assistant Director of Examinations of the AICPA, specializing in the law part of the examination.

George C. Thompson
Gerald P. Brady

Contents

INTRODUCTION

Preparation for the Business Law Examination

Background Information

Logically, any meaningful review for the business law part of the AICPA examination must begin at the source; that is, with the description of the Uniform CPA Examination, in particular the Business Law Section and relevant discussion contained in the newly revised *Content Specification Outlines,* which was adopted on September 25, 1984. These are now contained in the AICPA's *Information for CPA Candidates* (Seventh Edition, 1985).* The importance of the general description of the exam and the Business Law Section cannot be overstated, for this is the language of the Board of Examiners of the AICPA, whose responsibility it is to prepare the Uniform CPA Examination. Of greatest importance in this publication is the *Revised Content Specification Outline.* This appears throughout our book at the beginning of each of the substantive area designations (Areas 1 to 7). Let us now turn briefly to the words of the President of the AICPA; "The information provided in this booklet [*Information for CPA Candidates*] *is intended to help candidates* prepare for and write the Uniform CPA Examination. . . . I urge those interested in becoming CPAs to *read this booklet carefully*" (emphasis added).

There are two important statements in the *Information* booklet which might be overlooked or their significance underestimated. The first is from the introductory discussion preceding the *Business Law Content Specifications:*

> This section deals with federal and widely adopted uniform laws. Where there is no federal or appropriate uniform law on a subject, the questions are intended principally to test candidates' knowledge of the majority rules. Federal tax elements may be covered where appropriate in the overall context of a question.

Note that the candidate's answer should be stated in terms of the majority rule established by the decisions rendered in the state courts. The restatements (torts, contracts, and agency) are helpful in this respect. Next, taxation to the extent previously covered in the Business Law part of the examination is retained. These outlines contain an adequate

---

*AICPA, *Information for CPA Candidates* (7th ed., 1985). The Revised Content Specification Outlines appear in the appendix of this publication.

coverage of taxation as it applies to the relevant chapters (e.g., partnerships, corporations, social security, and trusts).

The second statement is taken from the "background information" portion of the *Revised Content Specifications,* as follows:

> The content specification outlines are considered to be complete as to the subjects to be tested on an examination, including recent professional developments as they affect these subjects. Candidates should answer examination questions, developed from these outlines, in terms of the most recent developments, pronouncements, and standards in the accounting profession. When new subject matter is identified, the outlines will be amended to include it and this will be communicated to the profession.

Again, two important points are presented for your edification. First, the *Content Specifications* represent the entire scope of the examination. The chapters of this, the seventh edition, have been revised in accordance with this policy statement, and they contain nothing more and nothing less than is necessary. Finally, there is an indication that recent developments will be included. This warning applies largely to the other parts of the examination with one notable exception—The CPA and the Law. It is expected that the candidate will be aware of United States Supreme Court decisions or any important statutory changes in this area. The Journal of Accountancy for the recent years preceding the exam should be examined for such developments.

The Tools for Essential Review

In addition to this book, the following are mandatory:
* AICPA, *Information for CPA Candidates* (cited above)
* AICPA, *Business Law, Selected Questions and Unofficial Answers,* Indexed to Content Specification Outlines, edited by James Blum and Mark Goldstein. The latest edition covers examination questions and unofficial answers from May 1980 to November 1984. There undoubtedly will be a third edition which will appear in early 1986 and will cover examinations through November 1985.
* Any widely used business law text which covers the areas included in the *Content Specifications.*
* The chapter on Accountant's Liability contained in a standard auditing text. For a more *extensive* and *lively* treatment of the subject matter, see Miller and Brady, *Accountant's Liability: Meeting the Challenge* (John Wiley, 1986).

The Goal

Although you may be aware of the exam's overall content and format, you must also have sufficient knowledge in order to pass it. Mere acquisition of knowledge, however, is not enough. The acquired knowledge must be qualitative and selective—yet comprehensive. It must have a realistic relation to the specific subject as well as to the scope, content, and depth of past examinations.

When an examination is intended to test not only the existence of adequate knowledge but also the ability to make effective use of it at a professional level, several other requirements must be met. These are (1) the ability to recall quickly and accurately the principles applicable to specific problems and situations; (2) the ability to apply these principles with good judgment; and consequently (3) the ability to express logical decisions and solutions clearly.

The outlines in this book are purposely designed to meet all these needs. Candidates who have used the standard textbooks in a course in business law will find these outlines extremely effective for essential review. The vital importance of intensive and effective review is dramatically illustrated by the fact that inadequate review is a major cause of failure of the CPA examination.

There are various methods of reviewing fundamentals and of ensuring their effective retention. Candidates may compile and consult their own notes. Textbook writers include well-organized and useful digests and other review materials in their works. Special review courses and books are also available. Each of these methods has both distinct advantages and limitations. The outlines in this book have a particular merit that makes them especially effective. They are based not on the particular organization, content, and treatment of a single textbook, but on the area descriptions of the AICPA *Content Specifications,* past examinations, and the overall content of the standard textbooks on business law. They are also related to past examinations in that they are based on the general nature and relative frequency of questions that have already appeared in different areas.

Coverage of the Examination

The need for review is imperative, but there are other significant matters that should not be overlooked in taking CPA examinations. The nature of the examination must be clearly understood in advance. More particularly, the most effective answers must be given to the questions. Papers cannot be graded on the basis of the knowledge candidates may actually possess. They must be graded on the basis of the knowledge the candidates express in their answers to the examination questions. Clarity, certainty, and responsiveness are potent aids in expressing that knowledge.

The CPA examination is meant to test overall competence to practice accountancy. Specifically, as to knowledge of business law, the CPA examination is meant to have particular application to points of law that are apt to present themselves in the general practice of accounting and in situations typically encountered in auditing. The basic purpose of requiring such knowledge is to enable accountants dealing with accounting matters to recognize readily the existence of legal problems and the possible need for solution or action by competent legal or other appropriate authorities.

Business is organized and functions with due regard for principles of law applicable to its organization and operation. Ignorance of the law is no excuse for errors, and lack of knowledge can cause economic disaster. One need only read the current court decisions in order to appreciate this statement. Furthermore, the accountant's legal responsibility is sharply increasing. In view of the special nature of the professional services they render their clients, accountants must have an adequate knowledge of law. They must be able to see that a legal question or situation may exist under specific circumstances that might require preventive, remedial, or other action.

The law part of the examination seeks to test, through essay and objective questions, the ability of candidates (1) to recognize the existence of a legal problem from consideration of certain indicated facts, the general nature of the problem, and the basic legal principles applicable, and (2) to grasp, in a general way, the possible outcome of applying these legal principles to the situation. Accountants need an adequate knowledge of *business law,* and examination questions largely fall within the scope of standard textbooks on this subject, applicable federal law, and the appropriate Uniform Acts where they have been widely adopted.

It is impossible, of course, to learn in advance what will be specifically covered in any CPA examination. But those who are intelligently and thoroughly prepared to deal with the subject are as well equipped as if they were gifted with foresight. The basic subject, business law, consists of a definitely limited number of topics, each of which is composed of a limited number of subdivisions. Each primary subdivision can be broken down into several subordinate parts with legal principles or rules that may be concisely stated. Such a breakdown constitutes a compact summary of the area in a systematic outline form. When accountants master and retain the more important principles in each, they can relate them effectively to most situations, whether they occur in actual experience or in examination questions.

Because certain areas are more significant than others, they play a proportionately larger role in the examinations. The problem (subjective) questions are invariably drawn from these areas. Although it is impossible to foresee the particular pattern of the forthcoming test, two very helpful clues are available. First, the *Content Specifications* provide the percentage allocation by area of law tested. Each exam will cover all areas. Furthermore, the CPA and the Law and Contracts will account for 25% of the exam. Next, past examinations reveal a general pattern, and the areas in which most questions have been asked are likely to be equivalent in future exams. At the very least, this analysis furnishes a guide to the relative amount of review that each subject may warrant.

Unfortunately, candidates who have the requisite knowledge often fail to communicate it. It is essential to organize one's ideas at the beginning of the examination in order to state them clearly and concisely.

Although it takes a little more time, some candidates read all of the subjective questions at the beginning of a particular part of the examination in order to obtain an overall picture of what is required. This results in a better understanding of each question. It also allows the candidates to determine which question is easiest for them. That question should be answered first. Other candidates prefer to read one question at a time and then answer it. All candidates, of course, should read the rules and suggestions preceding the questions, noting how much time is allowed.

Whatever method you use, be sure to read each question in its entirety before writing. Furthermore, since the questions are issue-seeking and analysis-oriented, take time to think before writing. You should fully understand the facts given in each question before you attempt to answer it; only then should you apply your knowledge of legal principles to the facts and reach an appropriate conclusion. It is only after careful analysis that you are prepared to support your answer with clear, orderly, and definite reasons. It is suggested that you allocate from 40 to 50% of your time to thinking about the questions. Answers that do not reflect this procedure indicate to the grader that the candidates have failed to grasp the question or its factual content; that they have answered without adequate preliminary organization; or that they do not know the related principles of law.

Though all parts of a question should be read and considered in relation to the entire question, each part should subsequently be considered and answered separately. A single all-inclusive answer for several parts is neither in line with stated requirements nor properly informative. This often presents an insoluble grading problem, since the grader cannot sort out the statements relating to the various parts from those dealing with the general problem. If there are four parts to a question, there should be answers to all four. If one part is further subdivided, the answer should also be subdivided. Follow the structure of the requirements part of the question, it is intended to guide you and can only help you. When each answer is completed, candidates should make sure that they have answered all the parts. This checking should be included in the time allowed for each question. You *must* under all circumstances *answer all parts of all questions.* Your knowledge of the area may be limited and your response may be weak, but you will undoubtedly gain some valuable grading points.

Answers that offer alternative possibilities but fail to state a conclusion on the validity of either are unresponsive. Intentionally or not, they reveal the candidate's unwillingness or inability to make a decision. Many answers ramble on, contain contradictory statements, and ultimately limp to a conclusion. This reflects an attempt to think through the conclusion and supporting reasons while writing, rather than deciding on an answer before writing. Obviously, such rambling and hesitant answers deserve less credit than a concise and well-organized statement.

A "responsive" answer is of paramount importance. "Responsiveness" demands that the answer be relevant, and in the particular form required. If a conclusion is asked for, it should be expressly stated; when an explanation is required, an unsupported conclusion clearly has no merit.

It is unnecessary to theorize further. The characteristics of responsiveness are shown by the unofficial answers, published regularly in a supplement to the *Journal of Accountancy* and in a five-year collection of selected business law questions published yearly after the examinations for the most recent year have been given. This book contains the questions and answers from those examinations not covered by this AICPA publication. The publication containing the most recent five years is available from the AICPA. These answers are prepared not only to give the correct and adequate solutions and explanations, but also to be directly responsive to the specific requirements of each question. Candidates who review the questions and answers of several past examinations will benefit in various ways. First, they train themselves to answer responsively and to make their answers brief, explicit, and comprehensive. Second, they learn to allocate their time properly and to apply their general knowledge of principles to specific facts and conditions. Third, they broaden their general knowledge of law in strategic areas.

Since CPA examinations are given semiannually and cover a specified number of general topics in business law, general problems presented in the past may recur in other forms. The same ideas can be made the subject of questions posed in significantly different ways. On the other hand, a change in the factual content of a question can transform it into a new problem requiring the application of completely different principles.

The ever-increasing number of candidates, the growing cost of grading, and the influence of the testing experts have all brought about a greater emphasis on objective questions. In addition, they make it possible to cover all areas of the *Content Specifications* and provide the proper percentage allocations. The CPA examination currently contains one objective question consisting of 60 parts and four problem (essay) questions for a total of five questions. The multiple choice questions are worth 60%.

Anxieties and Attitudes

Tension is at the root of many problems and difficulties. Some temporary nervousness is understandable, but those who are adequately prepared will usually settle down quickly. As a confidence builder you should select the question which is the easiest for you despite the fact you will be answering out of sequence. This should settle you down, reassure you, and possibly save some time for other, more difficult questions. Your attitude should be one of justified assurance. Candidates should be sure that they have adequately prepared for the examination by an appropriate course of study backed by recent review. Your state of preparedness should be comparable to a hot knife ready to cut through butter.

Accounting is not a closed profession. It is constantly broadening its range of activities and is seriously undermanned in relation to both current and future needs. These two facts impose specific responsibilities. One is to bring the profession up to appropriate numerical strength to meet fully the increasing demands society is making on it. The other is to establish and maintain standards of competence so as to ensure that services required of professional accountants will be performed with requisite professional skill, judgment, and care. The consequence is that the profession and those who establish the requirements for admission welcome all those who can qualify; however, it is their duty to the public and to the candidates to admit only those who are demonstrably qualified.

The "Note to the Candidates" at the beginning of each examination sets forth the time limitations. For each question there is an estimated minimum and maximum time for "adequate answers." It is urged that these estimates be used as a guide and that no more time

Frequency of Areas Covered on CPA Business Law Examination (P = problem; M = multiple choice)

CHAPTERS	5/85	11/84	5/84	11/83	5/83	11/82	5/82	11/81	5/81	11/80
1. The CPA and the Law	10%P	10M	10P	10M	10P	10P	10P	10P	6M	10P
2. Agency	5M	2M	4M	2M	2M	5P	3M	5M	6M	6M
3. Partnerships	5M	3M	5P	4M	3M	5P	4M	7M	10P	6M
4. Corporations	5M	10P,5M	6M	6M	10P	0	3M	4P	8M	5P
5. Estates and Trusts	1M	0	10P	5P	0	0	3M	4M	3M	4M
6. Contracts	3P,12M	5P,10M	10P,5M	10P,4M	15M	15M	10P,5M	11M	10P,5M	10P
7. Bankruptcy	10P	3M	4M	5P	4M	4M	5M	10P	5M	5P
8. Suretyship	0	5P	0	5P	3M	5M	4M	0	5M	5P
9. Employer-employee relationship	3M	4M	2M	3M	2M	4M	4M	1M	3M	3M
10. Federal securities regulation	5P,2M	5M	7M	4M	5P	5P,6M	10P	6P	2M	6M
11. Commercial paper	7M	7M	10M	5P	5P	11M	9M	10M	10P	10M
12. Documents of title and investment securities	1M	0	1M	4M	4M	1M	2M	0	0	1M
13. Sales	7P,3M	4M	10M	11M	5P,5M	5M	10P	5P	8M	7M
14. Secured transactions	2M	10P,4M	4M	5P	6M	7M	5M	6M	10P	8M
15. Property	3P,4M	5P	0	5P	3M	5P	4M	0	1M	4M
16. Mortgages	3M	5P	0	0	5M	0	2M	0	3M	0
17. Insurance	3M	0	0	0	1M	5P	3M	6M	4M	5M

*The first exam to which the original AICPA *Content Specification Outlines* applied was the November 1983 exam. Prior exams also largely conformed with the business law outline. The *Content Specifications* required that the exam contain set percentages for each of the seven designated areas. Prior examinations did not require this literal percentage approach. It was possible that an area might not be covered at all or was not assigned the designated content specification percentage. We have analyzed the results in the chart in terms of percentages for all exams. Note that the total percentage for an exam may not equal 100% since only the current (May 1986) *Content Specification* Areas and Groups are listed as Chapters 1–17 in the left-hand column of the chart.

than the *estimated maximum* be spent on any one question *until* all other questions have been answered.

These suggestions are so simple that they cannot be misunderstood. When candidates cannot finish the examination within the allotted time, it may be that they have insufficiently prepared in one or both of the following ways: They may have insufficient command of the general subject to answer promptly; or they may not be able to express their conclusions and explanations readily. The basic preparation, therefore, relates directly to the time element. We reiterate again—you must answer all parts of all questions.

When well-prepared candidates have an appreciable number of minutes left over, they can use this time to great advantage. They should use it to make certain that they have answered all questions, and have followed the general instructions in all other particulars. They can also use their extra minutes to expand some answer that might warrant it. Maximum time for a 3½-hour period is 210 minutes. Minimum estimated time for adequate answers is typically as low as 170 minutes. The difference of 40 minutes represents time that candidates may have available to review their papers in full or in part before turning them in.

Using This Book

Some comments on studying the outlines that follow will be of value. Each substantive area of this review outline should be gone over separately and finished before another is begun. Divisions and subdivisions of an outline that are immediately clear should cause no further concern. Their immediate recognition and comprehension assure practically instantaneous recall in pertinent situations.

The time spent on each outline should be determined by the relative weight assigned to each area by the revised *Content Specification Outlines* and the frequency distribution in recent exams (see chart above). Each examination will cover all areas indicated in the *Specifications* with the percentages indicated. Four or five topics are covered in the subjective questions. As you can see from the chart, more time should certainly be devoted to the outline for Contracts than to that for Estates and Trusts. The chart indicating the frequency with which areas are covered and the length of the respective outlines and questions will furnish a useful guide. It is desirable, naturally, to be well grounded in all areas. But it is more important to be particularly well qualified in the areas in which the questions were weighted more heavily in past examinations. An area designated with a 0 on the chart contains three or fewer objective questions, or is a minor point insofar as the subjective questions are concerned.

Another valuable feature of these outlines is the inclusion of related questions and answers and test questions without answers to provide the candidate with an opportunity to test himself or herself. Their inclusion accomplishes three purposes: (1) There are numerous instances where the questions or the concepts tested in the questions have been revised and presented in substantially the same form. (2) like the outline itself, they serve as a comprehensive review of fundamentals; and (3) they indicate to the students whether their grasp of the outline is as good as they think it is. In effect, students must prove it. Furthermore, the large number of objective questions and answers provide an excellent review and a unique opportunity for candidates to solidify their knowledge.

Conclusion

It may well be that the *Specifications* provide a tactical advantage for teachers and candidates. First and foremost is the assigning of specific percentages to each of the seven major areas [e.g., "I. The CPA and the Law (10%)"]. The percentages for the entire examination are all stated "up front," and guessing is limited to the percentages for each of the components within an area. Based upon 25 years of experience with the law part of the CPA exam, we venture to predict that the major areas and emphasis of the exam will continue in our opinion to be based substantially upon the subjects previously emphasized.

Subject	Our Estimated Weight
• The CPA and the Law	10%
• Agency	5%
• Partnerships	5%
• Corporations	6%
• Contracts	15%
• Bankruptcy	6%
• Federal Securities Acts	8%
• Commercial Paper	9%
• Sales	9%
• Secured Transactions	5%
• Property and Mortgages	7%
Total	85%

*AICPA *Information for CPA Candidates*, 7th ed. 1985.

This leaves approximately 15% for the balance of the *Specifications'* coverage. Except in the areas for which the full percentage is included (e.g., The CPA and the Law, Contracts), the foregoing table represents our conclusion as to the probable breakdown for the remaining *major substantive areas*. Time will tell. This breakdown gives a more manageable view of what is still important overall insofar as attaining the magic 75% necessary to pass the exam. Obviously, we urge thorough preparation for each area, group, and topic; however, we hope that this discussion and analysis will help to put the *Content Specification Outline* in proper focus.

One final point about the *Specifications:* They represent the whole "ball of wax." If it's not included within the *Specifications,* it should not appear on the examination. Once again, in the words of the Board of Examiners: "The *Content Specification Outlines* are considered to be complete as to the subjects tested on the exam. . . ."

Essential
CPA Law Review

PART

I

Business Law Areas for the CPA Examination

THE CPA
AND THE LAW (10%)

Chapter 1. The CPA and the Law

1

The CPA and the Law

AICPA Content Specification Outline*

Common Law Liability to Clients and Third Persons
Federal Statutory Liability

Securities Acts
Internal Revenue Code

Workpapers, Privileged Communication, and Confidentiality

Contents

*Source: AICPA, *Information for CPA Candidates* (7th ed., 1985).

Note   If you have not read the preface and introduction, go back and do so. It contains an abundance of important and vital information that will undoubtedly improve your chances of passing the business law part of the CPA exam.

   I. Common Law Liability to Clients: General Considerations, Negligence, and Fraud

   A. Imposed by state law and predominantly judge-made law:

   1. Basis: a contractual relationship. Much of the relationship is often implied rather than explicitly stated in the contract. Certainly better practice would be to have a clearly drafted "engagement" (or as it is also known an "arrangement-engagement") letter signed by the parties. Generally, an accountant is a professional agent and is considered an independent contractor in relation to the client (see Agency, p. 41).

   a. Duty may be express, e.g., to perform specifically defined services for the client, or implied, e.g., to do what is customary in a competent manner. Thus, the CPA must perform the undertaking in a nonnegligent manner or face a legal action by the client for negligence (malpractice). The client can state a cause of action based upon breach of contract or for the tort of negligence. Common practice is to assert both.

   2. Relationship to other areas of law: In general, the major legal concepts governing accountants were drawn from contracts, negligence, fraud, agency, and partnerships. Where the accountant's legal responsibility is not defined in this topic, the general rules set forth in those topics apply.

3. Nature of the standard imposed.
   a. Similar to that imposed upon all professional men. May be phrased in terms of requiring the CPA to have such superior skill and knowledge as the professional CPA has or holds himself or herself out as having.
   b. Must possess average degree of learning and skill as accountants in the particular area and exercise same with reasonable care.
   c. In effect, the law imposes upon the accountant the profession's generally accepted standards of competence and care.

4. Sources of guidance for the CPA in respect to his or her legal liability.
   a. The contractual undertaking as defined in the agreement with the client. The contract is normally referred to as an engagement letter. This should be explicitly and carefully defined.
   b. The standards established by the profession, i.e., generally accepted accounting principles and auditing procedures (GAAP and GAAS). Such standards are called the "custom of the industry" in general negligence law.
   c. Court decisions defining and interpreting the accountant's contractual and tort liability.
   d. The special standards established by federal and state regulatory agencies (e.g., the SEC).

5. Scope of liability.
   a. Responsibility is limited to the usual standard for an audit engagement unless a greater responsibility is assumed or unless a lesser responsibility is expressly indicated. An accountant is not an insurer or guarantor. Strict liability does not apply to the accountant's performance; fault must be established.
   b. Greater responsibility may be assumed by express provision in the contract's terms or by the wording of the audit report, e.g., a defalcation engagement.
   c. To ensure limitation of responsibility for unaudited work and any other limitation on the usual standard or scope, a disclaimer is used. The courts are likely to construe the disclaimer narrowly and resolve any doubt or ambiguity in the attempted limitation in favor of the client. Judicial dislike for disclaimers is apparent.
   d. Accountant is not liable for honest errors in judgment as long as he or she acted with reasonable care and was not fraudulent. Again, the accountant is not an insurer.
   e. The accountant will invariably plead GAAP and GAAS (the custom of the industry) if there has been compliance with same. Meeting the custom of the industry is a positive factor for the accountant and is entitled to due evidentiary weight. However, the courts have not always accepted the custom of the industry as sufficient either because the circumstances dictate a greater amount of care or the industry's custom is found not to be reasonable. However, one thing is crystal clear: Failure to meet the custom of the industry (GAAP and GAAS) will invariably be fatal.

6. Liability for undiscovered defalcations.
   a. Most legal actions by clients involve claims based upon shortages often resulting from management fraud, defalcations, or irregularities not un-

covered, and in such actions the general responsibility of accountants to their audit clients has been most clearly defined by the profession. The standards for unaudited engagements are still developing.

   b. The usual audit is intended to express a professional opinion as to financial position and operating results, not primarily to uncover irregularities or embezzlements. However, although the ordinary audit is not especially designed to disclose irregularities, their discovery frequently results as a consequence of such audit.

   c. In an ordinary audit, the accountant does not insure or guarantee the clients against losses through irregularities. As indicated below, such an audit is not even especially designed to do so.

   d. In examining the statements and reporting thereon, the accountant is obligated to exercise ordinary or reasonable care (i.e., he or she will be liable if negligent).

   e. Responsibility for failure to discover an irregularity or embezzlement in an ordinary audit for the examination of statements results only when the examination itself has been performed with a lack of reasonable care and the irregularity would have been discovered had the audit been made with average professional skill and related reasonable care.

   f. Greater responsibility can be assumed if the accountant is specifically engaged to perform a defalcation audit. Additional procedures, tests, and checks are resorted to. This type of audit goes well beyond the usual or typical audit. Although it is aimed at detecting defalcations, liability is not absolute. That is, the accountant is not an insurer. For example, if the type of embezzlement was unique and virtually undetectable even though the accountant performed the defalcation audit in a careful and competent manner, the accountant will *not* be liable.

7. A firm of public accountants may not escape liability to clients or third persons by reason of the fact that whatever wrong was committed was not the personal act of the accountants, but instead was that of their subordinates. The partners in the firm (principals) are liable for the wrongful acts of their fellow partners and their subordinates (agents) if committed within the scope of the employment.

8. Insurance.

   a. The CPA may acquire malpractice insurance to cover possible negligence liability caused by the CPA or his or her employees. Malpractice insurance doesn't cover fraud by the CPA or the employees.

   b. If the client has insurance covering the loss (e.g., defalcations) and the client's insurance company pays for a loss which the accountant's negligence facilitated, the insurance company is subrogated to the client's right against the accountant. The privity defense is nonapplicable since the insurer-surety company has the same standing as the client. The insurer is said "to stand in the shoes of" the client.

B. Liability to the client for negligence:

1. Where the action is based on negligence, the degree of care required is reasonable care by a professional CPA under the circumstances. This is more specifically defined above in I.A.3.

2. Listed below are some common examples or descriptions of negligent conduct by the CPA. These are taken from the leading cases which considered the negligence issue.

   a. Failure to follow GAAP or GAAS.

   b. An important and substantial divergence from the CPA's own audit program because of time or cost.

   c. Lack of at least a rudimentary understanding of the law, (e.g., contracts, real property) and a failure to appreciate when legal counsel should be obtained.

   d. Almost blind acceptance of management's explanations and false documentation when there are suspicious circumstances present.

   e. Last-minute entries of unverified accounts receivables.

   f. A major part of accounts confirmations being sent to post office boxes.

   g. An unusually high percentage of nonresponding confirmations.

   h. Negligent nonfeasance in the form of failure to further investigate when there were missing shipping numbers, customer's invoice numbers, and other suspicious features.

   i. Deposits of cash to bank accounts just before close of the audit and withdrawal immediately after the date of the financial statements and a failure to use a cash cutoff statement.

   j. Disregard of warnings or suspicions raised by staff members of the audit team by the auditor in charge.

3. Contributory negligence of the client may be a defense if the client was also at fault and thereby contributed to the loss. That is, the client failed to exercise reasonable care. There are not many cases wherein the accountant has been able to prevail on this theory. First, the accountant is hired to discover deficiencies in the client's internal controls, to discover errors, and to point them out to the client. Next, the client's duty of care is relatively low as compared with that of the expert CPA. Furthermore, with the advent of comparative negligence, even if the client is also negligent, this will only diminish the amount recoverable rather than result in a total bar to recovery.

   a. In a *pure comparative* negligence jurisdiction, the plaintiff may recover even though the plaintiff was more negligent than the defendant.

   b. In a *modified* comparative negligence jurisdiction, the plaintiff must not be more than 50% negligent.

4. The privity defense has no application to the accountant's liability to the client since the client is a party to the contract.

C. Liability to the client for fraud:

1. The elements necessary to establish a cause of action based upon fraud (deceit) against the defendant-accountant are:

   a. A material misrepresentation of fact

   b. Knowledge of falsity (scienter)

   c. An intent that the misrepresentation be relied upon by the plaintiff

   d. Actual reliance by the plaintiff

   e. Damages suffered by the plaintiff

2. These same elements are used in common law, federal securities law, and criminal cases.

3. When the action is based on fraud, the fraud may be *actual* or *constructive* (see Contracts, pp. 152–153, IV.D). The *key element is scienter*.
   a. In constructive fraud there need not be *actual* intent to deceive (scienter). Such intent may be inferred when statements meant to be relied on are made with reckless disregard, or an insincere statement of opinion, as to their truth. Thus, scienter may be established by use of an objective standard rather than the subjective (guilty knowledge) scienter required to establish actual fraud.
   b. Lack of even slight care constitutes gross negligence and indicates a reckless disregard of the truth. Hence, while negligence does not of itself constitute constructive fraud, it may be possible to infer fraud reasonably from evidence of gross negligence.
   c. Punitive damages for common law fraud may be assessed for fraud, constructive fraud, or gross negligence. The Federal Securities Acts do not so provide.
   d. The following diagram is presented for further clarity. Assume you have a silo with a capacity or scale of 1 to 10 and the plaintiff must reach or attain various levels of evidence in order to prevail. The various levels indicate the quantity of evidence for measuring culpability. We begin with a zero level which indicates faultless conduct; hence no liability. The lowest level for plaintiff to factually establish fault is negligence. Next is the level for grossly negligent conduct, followed by the level for establishing reckless conduct. Finally, the highest level of proof is reached when the plaintiff has established a knowing or actual intent to defraud.

Amount of Evidence Required

10	Actual intent to deceive (Fraud established, defendant lied.)
	Constructive fraud (Reckless conduct, such that "intent" is implied.)
	Gross negligence (Inference of fraud)
	Negligence (Negligence only)
1	Faultless conduct (No liability)
0	

II. Common Law Civil Liability to Third Parties

A. Negligence and the privity defense:
   1. Privity. The accountant as already indicated is liable to the client for negligence in performance of the engagement. However, the third party's standing to sue is an entirely different case since third parties are not parties to the contract and therefore are not in privity with the accountant. Creditors, investors, and purchasers of the business audited are common examples of third parties who may be barred by privity which prevents them from suing. They may not even

know the accountant and have given no legal consideration for the accountant's services.

2. The *current* status of the privity defense. There are three competing rules which may apply depending on the jurisdiction:

    a. The older rule (1931) as stated in *Ultramares v. Touche*. In this most famous of all accounting cases, privity was challenged by a creditor of the client who sued the CPA firm for negligence and fraud in performance of the audit. The case was sent back to the trial court to be tried on the fraud theory since privity does not apply to fraud, including constructive fraud and the possible inference of fraud, if gross negligence was found to be present. However, privity was retained insofar as the negligence cause of action was concerned. *Ultramares* represents the high water mark for the use of the privity defense by accountants. Currently, it represents a minority rule applicable in a decreasing number of jurisdictions.

    b. The *Restatement of Torts, 2nd,* rule. The prevailing or majority rule appears to be the rule stated in the *Restatement of Torts, 2nd*. Under this rule the plaintiff will not be barred by privity if the plaintiff is within a known intended class of beneficiaries.

    c. Total rejection of *Ultramares* and application of generally prevailing negligence rules to the accountant. The generally prevailing negligence rule is phrased in terms of whether there is any foreseeable harm to the plaintiff or the class of people of which the plaintiff is a member. When the third rule is applicable, the courts simply apply generally prevailing tort law. These jurisdictions have completely rejected the privity defense. Instead, general common law rules apply which preclude only such third parties to whom there is no foreseeable harm. In an accounting–real world context, privity is dead under this approach.

3. The third-party beneficiary exception:

    a. Accountants may be held liable for *ordinary negligence* (lack of reasonable care) by certain third parties despite the lack of *privity* when the accountant knows that the services for a client are primarily for the benefit of a third party. This exception to the privity rule treats the third party as if he were a party to the contract. This approach, if established, will allow the plaintiff to sue no matter which of the above three privity rules apply.

    b. When the services are primarily for the benefit of a known third party, the third party is, in effect (even though not in actuality), a party to the contract between the accountant and client (*a third-party beneficiary*—see Contracts, p. 157, VI.C.). This is one method of overcoming a lack of privity by a third party even if privity in its original full applicability is present in the particular jurisdiction (state).

    c. Consider the following diagram:

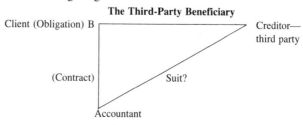

The Third-Party Beneficiary

Client (Obligation) B   Creditor— third party

(Contract)   Suit?

Accountant

In a typical accounting context, the client seeks to borrow money from the creditor. The creditor insists that audited financial statements be submitted to it by the client before the loan is made. The client agrees or has no choice but to supply the audited financials. Client proceeds to engage a CPA firm to satisfy the obligation. In doing so, the client indicates who is the real party in interest (the creditor) and that the purpose of the engagement is to satisfy this obligation. The CPA and the client enter into a contract for the performance of the requisite services which are performed negligently and the creditor loses a substantial amount of money as a result. At this point, the question is not whether the accountant was negligent or what the client has lost. The question is whether the creditor, who was not a party to the contract or gave any consideration, can sue. The answer is yes, if the creditor qualifies as a third-party beneficiary. Here the creditor clearly does. There was a clear indication of who the real party of interest was, who the primary beneficiary was, a clear intent to benefit this party, and the intent of the client to benefit the creditors is clear.

    d. When services by accountants for clients are primarily for the benefit of the clients as a convenient instrumentality for use in developing their businesses or obtaining funds, and only incidentally or collaterally for the use of third parties to whom the accountant's reports may be exhibited, such third parties are incidental beneficiaries and the accountants have no liability to such third parties for ordinary negligence (lack of reasonable care) in the limited number of jurisdictions which retain the original privity rule as a bar to third-party suits and in those following the *Restatement of Torts, 2nd*.

B. Fraud:

    1. Accountants owe a duty to all third parties to make their reports without fraud, whether such reports are intended primarily for the benefit of third parties or primarily for the benefit of clients. Privity is unnecessary.

    2. Constructive fraud and gross negligence amounting to a "reckless disregard for the truth." This provides an objective standard which the plaintiffs will resort to if actual fraud cannot be established. It will also result in liability to third parties if present despite a lack of privity. **See the diagram on p. 13 (III.A.4) which summarizes all the various theories or methods whereby privity has been diminished or abolished.**

    3. Damages: Party suing must show causal relationship between accountant's breach of duty and the damages or losses:

        a. Punitive damages are allowed if the accountant was held to have had fraudulent intent.

        b. The fraud in question may also be the basis for a separate criminal action by the federal or state government.

III. Liability to Third Parties Created by Federal Statutes

A. Securities Act of 1933:

    1. The Act regulates *public* offerings of securities through the mails or in interstate commerce. Liability in general under the federal securities acts is covered in

Chapter 10. The accountant's liability fits into this broader context. Therefore, it is suggested that a final review should cover these two chapters as a whole.

2. The Act requires that a registration statement be filed with the SEC prior to the offering, which discloses all material facts regarding the securities to be offered. The Act is known as the "truth in securities law" and is aimed at protecting the investing public. (See Federal Securities Regulation, p. 239.)

3. The registration statement must include financial statements audited by independent public accountants (invariably CPAs).

4. Any person acquiring securities covered by the registration statement may sue the accountant. This, of course, includes third parties (the investing public) who are not clients of the accountant and *who are not* and need not be in privity with the accountants. The investing public at large is protected by the Act. Thus, it renders much of the privity limitation contained in the *Ultramares* case obsolete. *Ultramares* was decided prior to the 1933 Act. The 1934 Act also rejects privity where the transaction involves the purchase or sale of securities in interstate commerce. Consider the summary presentation of the limits on the once powerful privity defense shown in Figure 1.

Accountants' Privity Defense

1. Third-party beneficiary status
2. Actual fraud
3. Constructive fraud
4. Gross negligence
5. The Federal Securities Acts
6. The Restatement 2d rule
7. Judicial overrule and rejection

Figure 1: THE DECLINE OF THE CITADEL OF PRIVITY.

5. The basis for the claim is an alleged false statement or omission of a material fact in the audited financial statements.

   a. Such a claim by the party suing (the plaintiff) establishes a *prima facie* case, i.e., one which will suffice unless contradicted by other evidence.

   b. Thus, the plaintiff does not have the added burden of proving that the accountants were negligent or fraudulent in auditing the financial statements.

   c. Plaintiff need not prove reliance upon the financial statement or that the loss suffered was the proximate result of the false statement or misleading omission. However, if it can be shown he had actual knowledge and could not have relied, recovery will be denied.

   d. In effect, much of the burden of proof, typically required of a plaintiff, has been shifted to the accountant (defendant). There is an old saying in the law, "He who has the burden of proof loses more often than not." The shift is significant.

   e. The courts and SEC regulations define "material" information to be that about which "an average, prudent investor ought reasonably to be informed before purchasing the security registered."

6. The accountant has the burden of proving he was neither negligent nor fraudulent in auditing the financial statements, and that he acted with **due diligence.**
   a. He may satisfy this burden by showing that he made a reasonable investigation, had a reasonable basis for his belief, and did believe the financial statements to which he audited and gave his opinions did fairly represent the financial condition of his client on the day or for the time period involved.
   b. His duty as to the truth of the audited statements is *as of the time when the registration statement becomes effective,* and not the typical time, which is as of the date of the financial statements. Thus, once again, potential liability has been increased, by responsibility for subsequent events.

7. Differences between generally accepted accounting principles (GAAP) and fair disclosure in a prospectus will be resolved in favor of the disclosure requirements of the securities law.

8. The accountant may also avoid or reduce liability by showing that the plaintiff's loss was caused in whole or in part by factors other than the false statements or omissions of material facts in the financial statements.

9. Generally, recovery, where a registration containing a false statement or omission has been filed and becomes effective, is based upon the difference between the amount paid for the security (not exceeding the price at which the security was offered to the public) and
   a. The value at the time of suit, or
   b. The value at the time the security was disposed of prior to suit, and
   c. In no event may recovery exceed the price at which the security was offered to the public.

10. In addition to the above liability, the Act provides:
    a. That any person who offers or sells a security in violation of the Act's registration requirement by failing to file a required registration statement; (see p. 245, I.G.6) shall be liable to the person suing for:
       (1) The amount paid, plus interest, less the amount of income received upon tender of the security (rescission).
       (2) Damages if the party no longer owns the security.
    b. The same liability indicated above in a. (rescission) applies to offers or sales of securities (whether or not exempted) in interstate commerce or by use of the mails, by the means of a prospectus or oral communications that contains an untrue statement or omission of a material fact.

11. The Act also contains an antifraud provision (Section 17) which applies to all fraudulent offers to sell or sales of securities in interstate commerce. Because of the popularity of Section 10b of the 1934 Act, Section 17 has been overshadowed (see p. 15).

12. The Act contains a short two-part statute of limitations, which bars actions under its provisions.
    a. First, any action must be brought within 1 year after discovery of the untrue statement or omission, or after such discovery should have been made by the exercise of reasonable diligence.
    b. Second, in no event can an action be brought more than three years after the security was offered in good faith to the public.
    c. The rationale for this short statute of limitations is based upon the need for tranquility and certainty in the securities industry or markets.

B. Securities Exchange Act of 1934:

1. The Act contains two bases for liability; these are *fraud* and *Section 18* liability. Section 18 is a strange and difficult basis for establishing liability and is rarely invoked against accountants because of its onerous requirements and liberal defenses. It does not strictly apply negligence standards and seems to be just the reverse of the unfavorable approach to defendants taken in respect to liability for negligence under the 1933 Act.

2. The *antifraud provision* (Section 10(b)). This section of the Act is extremely broad in scope and has been liberally construed by the courts. Furthermore, the SEC's Rule 10b-5 which interprets and expands Section 10b is much feared and is a widely used basis for liability. For a more complete discussion of the antifraud provisions, see pp. 250–253.

   a. The section is based upon fraud although it is easier to establish than common law fraud, e.g., a specific intent to injure need not be proved. However, in one of the most important and favorable recent decisions in respect to CPAs, *(Ernst & Ernst v. Hochfelder),* the Supreme Court of the United States rejected plaintiff's attempt to recover under Section 10b without establishing knowledge of falsity (scienter). The court held that an accountant is not liable under Section 10(b) for fraud for false or misleading statements or omissions in absence of scienter. The decision also indicated that *scienter includes recklessness* as well as actual intent to deceive and knowledge of falsity.

   b. Scope. The section is not limited to false statements or omissions contained in filings with the SEC. However, the CPA's liability will invariably arise from the 1934 Act's **reporting requirements** since financial statements are required to accompany most filings by the reporting corporation (see below).

3. Issuers of securities listed and traded on national exchange must report. In addition, most provisions of the Act apply to companies whose securities are traded over the counter and have in excess of $3 million in total assets and a class of equity securities held by 500 or more persons as of the last day of the fiscal year. (See Chapter 10, Federal Securities Acts, p. 249.) The Act also regulates securities exchanges.

4. The SEC requires each reporting corporation subject to the Act to file an annual report (form 10-K) within 120 days after the close of the fiscal year.

   a. Form 10-K is subject to specific SEC information requirements and to provisions governing the form and content of the financial statements that must accompany the report (see Federal Securities Regulation, p. 250).

   b. Recently the form 10-K annual report, along with amendments to the proxy rules and regulations, was changed to require that summary audited financial data and management discussions of financial statements (unaudited) required by form 10-K appear also in a registered and reporting corporation's annual report to shareholders and be either incorporated or duplicated in the form 10-K report.

   c. The accountant's chief source of liability under the Act results from the required filing of audited financial statements that must accompany the annual report or other filings required by the SEC (e.g., proxy statement).

5. Section 18 liability. The Act also imposes civil liability upon any person (including the auditing accountant) who in any application or report *filed* with the SEC makes a statement that is false or misleading in respect to any material fact.

6. Any buyer or seller of the security to which the false statement relates may sue, provided he can prove that he:

    a. Bought or sold at a price affected by the false or misleading statement.

    b. Relied upon the statement, and

    c. Did not know of its falsity.

7. The accountant may avoid liability if she proves that she:

    a. Acted in good faith, and

    b. Had **no** knowledge that the statement was false or misleading.

    c. However, constructive knowledge may be found where the CPA's performance amounts to a "reckless disregard for the truth."

8. An auditor has a duty to anyone still relying on his or her report to disclose subsequently discovered errors in the report even when the discovery arises from the performance of management studies.

9. **A comparison** of the major features of both Acts makes it apparent that the 1933 Act is much stiffer in respect to the imposition of liability on accountants. The most obvious differences are:

    a. In the burden of proof of the respective parties,

    b. The requirements necessary to establish the defense of exercise of due diligence, and

    c. The time at which the statements are to be tested as to truth (the 1933 Act goes beyond the date of the financial statements to the time the registration statement becomes effective). Consequently, the 1934 Act makes it much more difficult to successfully sue for negligence than does the 1933 Act.

10. The Securities Exchange Act has the same short statute of limitations (1 or 3 years) for bringing an action as discussed above in relation to the Securities Act of 1933. See p. 14, III.A.12.

11. There is no implied private cause of action for negligence against a CPA for damages due to an improper audit of a broker-dealer under Section 17(a) of the 1934 Act; that section merely requires broker-dealers to keep records and file certain reports accompanied by audited financial statements as requested by the SEC.

C. Tax Preparer Liability: Revenue Acts of 1976 and 1978, Tax Act of 1982 (TEFRA) and the Deficit Reduction Act of 1984.

1. If the preparer prepares a return (a claim for refund) for compensation for one other than his employer or employs one or more persons to prepare returns or claims for refund for compensation, he must sign it as preparer and enter his identifying number and address. The preparer must manually sign the return; a signature stamp or label is unacceptable. If the return is for the employer, the preparer must sign it and enter the employer's name, identifying number, and address.

2. The preparer must furnish the taxpayer with a copy of the prepared return and he must also retain a copy of the return or a list of the names and addresses of taxpayers for whom returns were prepared. The preparer need not sign the taxpayer's copy of the return.

3. A record must be retained by the employer of return preparers for three years, listing the name, taxpayer identification number, and place of work of each preparer employed. A return preparer who is self-employed or an independent contractor must retain his own record.

4. A return preparer is liable for a $100 penalty if his understatement of taxpayer liability on a return is due to negligent or intentional disregard of rules or regulations.

5. A return preparer is liable for a $500 penalty if his understatement of taxpayer liability on a return is due to a willful attempt in any manner to understate liability. An employer or partnership of such a preparer is not subject to the penalty unless it also participated in the willful attempt.

   a. An example of willful understatement is where the preparer ignores information given him by the taxpayer so that the preparer may understate his client's tax liability.

6. Other penalties:

   a. $25 for failure to sign a return, to furnish identifying number, or failure to furnish the taxpayer with a copy of the prepared return.

   b. $50 for failure to retain a copy of prepared returns or a list of taxpayers for whom returns were prepared.

   c. $100 for failure to retain for three years a record of the name, identification number, and place of work of each preparer employed during a return period; $5 for each item missing on such record.

   d. $500 for endorsing or negotiating another person's income tax refund check.

   e. A criminal penalty is provided in order to preserve the confidentiality of information provided by taxpayers to other persons preparing individual, corporate, and fiduciary income tax returns; to prevent disclosure of information furnished by taxpayers for preparation of a return or declaration; or for use of such information for any purpose other than preparation of the return or declaration.

   f. Taxpayers may also commence a civil suit against any person who knowingly or negligently makes an unauthorized disclosure of returns or return information.

7. The IRS has the power to seek an injunction prohibiting an income tax preparer from the following practices:

   a. Conduct subject to disclosure requirement penalties and understatement-of-taxpayer-liability penalties.

   b. Conduct subject to criminal penalties under the Internal Revenue Code.

   c. Misrepresentation of:

      (1) Return preparer's eligibility to practice before the IRS, or

      (2) His experience or education as an income tax preparer.

   d. Guarantee of payment of a tax refund or of allowance of a tax credit.

    e. Other fraudulent or deceptive conduct that substantially interferes with proper administration of the internal revenue law.

8. Return preparer may avoid possible injunctive action by filing a $50,000 surety bond with the IRS office in his district.

9. The 1982 Tax Act (TEFRA) added:

    a. Certain liability for tax return preparers, e.g., where the preparer **knowingly** aids in the preparation of a return which results in an understatement of taxpayer's liability. The fine is $1,000.

    b. Penalties for persons who promote abusive tax shelters.

10. The 1984 Deficit Reduction Act (effective for 1985) provides as follows:
A return preparer is:

    a. Required to advise taxpayers of the requirements that adequate contemporaneous records must be kept in order to substantiate certain business expenses.

    b. Required to obtain a written confirmation from the taxpayer that the requirements are met.

    c. Subject to $25 penalty for failure to comply.

IV. Criminal Liability

A. Federal Statutes:

1. The Federal Securities Acts of 1933 and 1934: Any person convicted of a willful violation of any provision of the Acts or their regulations, willful falsification of any material fact in a registration statement, or willful omission of any material fact required to be stated therein or necessary to make the statements therein not misleading is **subject to a fine of not more than $10,000, or imprisonment for not more than five years, or both.**

    a. Proof that certified information is in compliance with generally accepted accounting principles is very persuasive, but not conclusive evidence that the auditor acted in good faith.

2. The Internal Revenue Code provides fines or imprisonment for any person violating its provisions. For example:

    a. Willfully making a statement, return, or other document that contains a written declaration that is made under the penalties of perjury, and that the preparer does not believe to be true and correct as to every material matter; or

    b. Willfully aiding in the preparation of any matter arising under internal revenue law that is fraudulent or false in any material matter, whether or not such falsity or fraud is with the knowledge or consent of the person authorized or required to present such matter; or

    c. Fraudulently executing documents required by provisions of the internal revenue law or procuring the false execution thereof, e.g., back dating of records and documents; or

    d. Removing or concealing goods with intent to evade any tax imposed by the internal revenue law; or

    e. Willfully delivering documents that are known to the preparer to be fraudulent or false.

    f. The burden of proof for conviction is "beyond a reasonable doubt," which is generally believed to have rendered resort to the fraud sections ineffective except in the grossest of cases; hence the 1976 and subsequent Acts were adopted.

3. *Criminal and Civil RICO (Racketeer Influenced and Corrupt Organizations)* The RICO statutes prohibit a person who is affiliated with an "enterprise" which affects, or is engaged in interstate commerce, from engaging in any of the following types of conduct: A person employed by or associated with an "enterprise" may not conduct the affairs of the enterprise through a "pattern of racketeering."

    a. An *enterprise* includes any association in fact or law and includes any individual, partnership, corporation, association, or other legal entity.

    b. *Pattern of racketeering* is defined as a course of conduct which involves the commission of at least two "acts of racketeering activity" during a 10-year period. *Racketeering activity* is defined by statute to include: fraud which is actionable under the federal mail fraud statute and fraud which is actionable under the federal securities laws.

    c. Although aimed at organized crime, criminal RICO has been used to supplant the use of mail fraud and securities act fraud indictments. The criminal penalties under criminal RICO are substantial and include a fine of not more than $25,000 and imprisonment of not more than 20 years. In addition, the RICO statues provide for forfeiture of any financial interest, assets, or earnings that the defendant has acquired through the "pattern of racketeering activity."

    d. Criminal RICO has been used against accounting practitioners. An accountant who is affiliated with an accounting firm or associated with a business concern, such as being the auditor for a company, may satisfy the requirement of being associated with an enterprise engaged in or affecting interstate commerce. To the extent the accountant engages in two or more acts of mail fraud or securities Act fraud in connection with his or her activities relating to the "enterprise," the ground work for criminal RICO has been laid.

    e. Civil RICO. In order to provide an additional means of enforcement, an incentive was added in the form of treble damages to a private litigant. It is not necessary that there have been either an indictment or conviction for civil RICO to apply. The United States Supreme Court so held in July 1985. This aspect of the RICO statute is the most controversial and "hottest" issue facing the accounting profession. One federal court of appeals (Illinois) had previously decided that civil RICO applies to accountants without a prior criminal conviction. The case is awaiting trial.

V. Accountant's Working Papers

A. Common law:

    1. In the absence of express agreement that working papers of accountants are to belong to clients or to be held for them, ownership of such working papers is held to rest in the accountants.

    2. Common law recognition of ownership by the accountants is judge-made law in most jurisdictions.

B. State Statutes:

    1. In a minority of jurisdictions, it is provided expressly by statute that, in the absence of express or written agreement to the contrary, ownership of working papers rests in the accountants.

C. Limitation of Ownership

    1. Ownership of working papers by accountants is actually restricted in several respects so as to be partially custodial, with the dual purpose of permitting the accountants to retain them as evidence of the nature and extent of the services rendered, and to prevent confidential information therein from being transmitted to others (including other accountants) without the actual consent of clients. Accountants may, in general, render services to competing clients.

    2. It has been held that an accountant (a sole proprietor) could not dispose of his working papers by will and that they must be destroyed unless needed to protect the estate against claims.

    3. Ownership of working papers by accountants is not a valid ground for refusing to testify regarding matters covered thereby or to produce them in evidence when such testimony or production is required by legal process.

    4. Accountant must keep information in working papers confidential.

    5. Accountant must produce working papers for the government or for an agency if served with an enforceable subpoena or IRS summons.

VI. Privileged Communications

A. Common law: **At common law no status of privileged communication exists** between an accountant and his or her client, and, therefore, privilege is not available as a valid ground for refusing to testify as to such communications when such testimony is required by legal process.

B. State Statutes: In a distinct minority of jurisdictions (approximately one-third), the status of privileged communication has been given by statute to confidential communications between an accountant and the client. **Such privilege does not apply to federal law,** but only to cases based upon state law tried in a federal court where there is diversity of citizenship as to the litigants and $10,000 in damages is involved. Such cases are based upon state common law torts or contracts, i.e., the federal courts hearing such case will apply state law including the state privilege rule.

C. Waiver of privilege: Since the status of privilege is established for the benefit of clients, waiver of such privilege in any instance can normally only be by the client.

D. No confidential accountant-client relationship exists under federal law, and no state-created privilege has been recognized in cases *involving federal law*. Hence, a privilege is available in a federal court only when state law applies and there is a privilege statute.

E. The IRS has successfully gained access to the auditor's tax accrual working papers. In a recent case, *United States v. Arthur Young & Company* (1984), the Supreme Court of the United States held that no accountant-client privilege exists as to tax accrual files. That opinion was unanimous in rejecting establishment of such a privilege and is written in a manner which it is believed forecloses the successful assertion of such a privilege in the future by accountants. This is the leading case on the subject.

VII. Evidentiary Considerations and Problems

A. Accountant's records may be subpoenaed by a court of law.

B. Disclosure of confidential client data is prohibited unless:

   1. Client consents.
   2. Disclosure is necessary to comply with GAAP and/or GAAS.
   3. Disclosure is in compliance with an enforceable subpoena.
   4. Disclosure is necessary for a voluntary quality review under AICPA authorization.
   5. Disclosure is in response to an AICPA trial board.

C. The Federal Rules of Discovery will generally govern what CPA must disclose and what he need not disclose.

Selected CPA Examination Questions and Answers on the CPA and the Law

Introductory Note to Examination Questions*

Each substantive section in this book will be followed by questions from examinations given prior to the November 1981 examination of Uniform CPA Examinations in Business Law. These examinations are administered under the auspices of the AICPA. As previously indicated, these pre-1981 questions are being used in lieu of the ten most recent past examination questions and answers because the AICPA is now publishing a five-year anthology of the *better* questions from these examinations. This inexpensive paperback is available from the AICPA if it is not sold in your bookstore or distributed as a part of the materials used in the CPA review course you take. Each question in our first group of subjective questions is followed by the unofficial AICPA answer. The second group of selected subjective questions are not answered and are intended for self-testing or class discussion. Finally, a number of multiple choice questions are included at the end of the subjective questions.

   Part II *infra,* p. 411, contains two entire illustrative examinations, one with answers and the other without answers, which are intended to provide a model and to permit the candidate to test himself or herself.

---

*Prepared by the Board of Examiners of the American Institute of Certified Public Accountants (AICPA) and adopted by the examining boards of all states, territories, and the District of Columbia. Permission to use same is gratefully acknowledged. These questions have been selected almost exclusively from the Business Law examinations for the years May 1973 –May 1981.

Subjective Questions and Answers

Q. 1. Millard & Hans, CPAs, has been engaged for several years by Happy Toys, Inc., to perform the "usual" examination of its financial statements and provide other accounting services. The understanding was oral, and the fee was based on an annual retainer.

    Millard & Hans regularly prepared unaudited quarterly financial statements and examined and reported on Happy Toys' annual financial statements. During the current year's examination, Happy Toys decided to go public and requested that Millard & Hans assist in preparing all the necessary financial statements and other financial information and supply the independent auditor's reports as necessary for inclusion in a registration statement to be filed with the Securities and Exchange Commission (SEC). Millard & Hans is independent in accordance with SEC rules and regulations. Millard & Hans complied with Happy Toys' request and subsequently submitted a bill to Happy Toys for $15,000 for the additional work performed in connection with the SEC filing. Happy Toys refused to pay, claiming that the additional work was a part of the "usual" engagement and was covered by the annual retainer.

Required
1. If Millard & Hans sues Happy Toys for its $15,000 fee, who is likely to prevail? Explain.
2. Discuss how Millard & Hans can avoid similar problems in the future with Happy Toys and other clients.

A. 1. Millard & Hans will prevail if the $15,000 fee is reasonable in relation to the extra work involved. The requirements and work involved in an SEC registration would undoubtedly not be considered to be within the scope of the "usual" examination of financial statements. In fact, a strong argument can be made that it is an extraordinary undertaking. This is especially the case in light of the increased potential liability involved in the "certification" of financial statements to be used in connection with a public offering of securities. Hence, the fee for the additional work required for the registration statement would probably be collectible.

    The court would be required to determine the meaning of the word "usual" as used in the context presented in the question. In doing so, the court would look to the "custom of the trade," that is, what does the typical or normal undertaking include, viewed objectively. Furthermore, it would seem that the court would also look to the scope of the duties previously performed under the existing oral retainer. Since this did not include SEC work, it would seem that this fact has a high evidentiary value in relation to Millard & Hans' claim.

    2. Millard & Hans should avoid relying only on oral understandings with its clients. Understandings should be stated in writing in what is ordinarily referred to as an engagement letter. Furthermore, if doubts should arise as to the scope of an engagement, the questions should be discussed with the client and resolved in advance, including additional fees that may be involved. Where appropriate, the sense of these discussions should be put in writing to avoid future misunderstandings.

5/75

Q. 2. Barney & Co., CPAs, has been engaged to perform an examination of the financial statements of Waldo, Inc., for several years. The terms of the engagement have been set out in an annual engagement letter signed by both parties. The terms of each engagement included the following:

> This being an ordinary examination, it is not primarily or specifically designed, and cannot be relied upon, to disclose defalcations and other similar irregularities, although their discovery may result.

    Three years ago Harold Zamp, head cashier of Waldo and an expert in computer operations, devised a previously unheard-of method of embezzling funds from his employer. At first, Zamp's thefts were small, but they increased as time went on. During the current year, before Barney began working on the engagement, the thefts became so large that serious variances in certain accounts came to the attention of the Controller.

When questioned about the variances, Zamp confessed and explained his unique embezzlement scheme. Investigation revealed that Zamp had stolen $257,550. Zamp has no assets with which to repay the thefts.

Waldo submitted its claim for $257,550 to Multi-State Surety Company in accordance with the terms of the fidelity bond covering Zamp. Fulfilling its surety obligation, Multi-State paid the claim and now seeks to recover its losses from Barney.

In defense, Barney asserts, in the alternative, the following defenses:

1. Multi-State has no standing in court to sue because it was not a party to the contract (i.e., lacking in privity) between Barney and its client, Waldo.

2. Even if Multi-State had the standing to sue, its claim should be dismissed because Barney's engagements with Waldo did not specifically include the discovery of defalcations other than those that might arise in the process of an ordinary examination.

3. Even if Barney's contract had made it responsible for discoverable defalcations, it could not have discovered Zamp's defalcations with the exercise of reasonable care. Zamp's technique was so new, unique, and novel that no accounting firm could have discovered the defalcations in any event.

Required

In separately numbered paragraphs, discuss the validity of each of Barney's defenses.

A. 1. Multi-State has the standing to sue Barney. Having settled the claim on the fidelity bond, Multi-State is subrogated to the rights of Waldo.

2. An engagement to perform an ordinary examination of financial statements does not require the auditors to undertake special procedures to discover defalcations. Barney's engagement letters covered this point specifically; hence, Barney was responsible for performing its examinations in a careful and competent manner. If Barney's examinations were performed in a careful and competent manner, it would not be liable even though the defalcations were not discovered.

3. Even if Barney had agreed to a special undertaking regarding defalcations, it would appear that Zamp's defalcations could not have been discovered in any event because of Zamp's new, unique, and novel technique. Therefore, as long as Barney used due care in performing its special undertaking, Barney would not be liable. Auditors are not insurers in regard to defalcations unless the contract is so worded as to create this type of strict liability.

11/74

Q. 3. Jackson was a junior staff member of an accounting firm. He began the audit of the Bosco Corporation which manufactured and sold expensive watches. In the middle of the audit he quit. The accounting firm hired another person to continue the audit of Bosco. Due to the changeover and the time pressure to finish the audit, the firm violated certain generally accepted auditing standards when they did not follow adequate procedures with respect to the physical inventory. Had the proper procedures been used during the examination they would have discovered that watches worth more than $20,000 were missing. The employee who was stealing the watches was able to steal an additional $30,000 worth before the thefts were discovered six months after the completion of the audit.

Required

Discuss the legal problems of the accounting firm as a result of the above facts.

A.   The firm is undoubtedly liable for negligence. The failure to follow generally accepted auditing standards indicates negligence in the conduct of the audit. Although the courts do not always recognize adherence to the custom of the profession (generally accepted auditing standards) as a defense, they invariably hold that the failure to follow customary practice constitutes negligence. The fact that Jackson left in the middle of the audit and caused a problem for the firm is of no consequence. The firm, by reason of the negligence of its agents, will be liable for the actual loss up to at least the $30,000 worth of watches stolen after the completion of the audit.

This loss would not have occurred if the audit had been conducted properly. In addition, the firm may also be liable on the initial $20,000 of thefts to the extent that prompt discovery in the course of the audit would have permitted recovery of this loss.

5/76

Q. 4. The CPA firm of Martinson, Brinks, & Sutherland, a partnership, was the auditor for Masco Corporation, a medium-sized wholesaler. Masco leased warehouse facilities and sought financing for leasehold improvements to these facilities. Masco assured its bank that the leasehold improvements would result in a more efficient and profitable operation. Based on these assurances, the bank granted Masco a line of credit.

The loan agreement required annual audited financial statements. Masco submitted its 1975 audited financial statements to the bank which showed an operating profit of $75,000, leasehold improvements of $250,000, and net worth of $350,000. In reliance thereon, the bank loaned Masco $200,000. The audit report which accompanied the financial statements disclaimed an opinion because the cost of the leasehold improvements could not be determined from the company's records. The part of the audit report dealing with leasehold improvements reads as follows:

> Additions to fixed assets in 1975 were found to include principally warehouse improvements. Practically all of this work was done by company employees and the cost of materials and overhead were paid by Masco. Unfortunately, fully complete detailed cost records were not kept of these leasehold improvements and no exact determination could be made as to the actual cost of said improvements. The total amount capitalized is set forth in note 4.

In late 1976 Masco went out of business, at which time it was learned that the claimed leasehold improvements were totally fictitious. The labor expenses charged as leasehold improvements proved to be operating expenses. No item of building material cost has been recorded. No independent investigation of the existence of the leasehold improvements was made by the auditors.

If the $250,000 had not been capitalized the income statement would have reflected a substantial loss from operations and the net worth would have been correspondingly decreased.

The bank has sustained a loss on its loan to Masco of $200,000 and now seeks to recover damages from the CPA firm, alleging that the accountants negligently audited the financial statements.

Required
Answer the following, setting forth reasons for any conclusions stated.

1. Will the disclaimer of opinion absolve the CPA firm from liability?
2. Are the individual partners of Martinson, Brinks, & Sutherland, who did not take part in the audit, liable?
3. Briefly discuss the development of the common law regarding the liability of CPAs to third parties.

A. 1. No. The disclaimer of opinion will not absolve the CPA firm from liability. The auditor was negligent by failing either to take adequate measures to determine whether the leasehold improvements existed or to give notice that their existence had not been verified. As a result of such negligence and the bank's reliance upon the report, the CPA firm would be liable to the bank.

An auditor generally will not be held responsible for limitations on the audit if the auditor's report gives adequate notice of them. A disclaimer of opinion is the means used by the auditor to give adequate notice of limitations. Although the CPA firm attempted to disclaim an opinion on the financial statements, the wording in the auditor's report was sufficiently unclear that it is doubtful a court would find the report accomplished its intended purpose. The disclaimer said only that the "actual cost" of the improvements could not be determined, and the explanation strongly implied that the improvements actually existed and had substantial value (by use of such phrases as "were found" and "work was done") when in fact they did not exist. Consequently, the report was misleading.

2. Yes. The individual partners of the CPA firm are liable even though they did not take part in the audit. A partnership is an entity that is an association of two or more persons as co-owners to carry on a business for profit. All partners are jointly and severally liable and therefore personally responsible for the firm's liability to the bank. The individual partners may have to satisfy the bank's claim from their personal assets, even though they did not personally take part in the audit.

3. Determination of the liability of a CPA to third parties requires balancing two conflicting recognized interests of the law:

    (a) The CPA's reasonable right to self-protection from claims of unknown persons whom the CPA has no reason to suspect would rely on his report, and

    (b) The important public policy of protecting third parties who rely upon financial statements from the adverse effects of incompetent performance by professionals.

    The *Ultramares* case in 1931 firmly established the doctrine of privity of contract leaving a CPA liable for simple or ordinary negligence only to a client. However, the opinion in that case indicated that a CPA could be liable to third parties if the conduct of the examination or preparation of the auditor's report involved fraud or negligence so gross as to permit an inference of fraud.

    An additional basis upon which a third party could recover is as a third-party beneficiary. This relationship would be found in cases where it was clearly indicated that the engagement was undertaken for and was intended to benefit the third party, typically a lender.

    The position of courts in upholding the doctrine of privity of contract began to change in the 1950s and 1960s. Court decisions began to reflect the view that CPAs owe a duty of care not only to their own clients but also to those whom they *should* know will rely on their reports in the transactions for which these reports are prepared. The courts began to rule that the CPA is liable for negligence for careless financial misrepresentations relied upon by foreseen and limited classes of persons. This extended the CPA's liability to third parties for simple or ordinary negligence to *reasonably* limited and *reasonably* definable classes of persons whom the CPA might *reasonably* expect would rely upon his report.

5/77

Q. 5. Gordon & Groton, CPAs, were the auditors of Bank & Company, a brokerage firm and member of a national stock exchange. Gordon & Groton examined and reported on the financial statements of Bank which were held with the Securities and Exchange Commission.

    Several of Bank's customers were swindled by a fraudulent scheme perpetrated by Bank's president who owned 90% of the voting stock of the company. The facts establish that Gordon & Groton were negligent but not reckless or grossly negligent in the conduct of the audit and neither participated in the fraudulent scheme nor knew of its existence.

    The customers are suing Gordon & Groton under the antifraud provisions of Section 10(b) and Rule 10b-5 of the Securities Exchange Act of 1934 for aiding and abetting the fraudulent scheme of the president. The customers' suit for fraud is predicated exclusively on the nonfeasance of the auditors in failing to conduct a proper audit, thereby failing to discover the fraudulent scheme.

Required

Answer the following, setting forth reasons for any conclusions stated.

1. What is the probable outcome of the lawsuit?

2. What other theory of liability might the customers have asserted?

A. 1. The case should be dismissed. A suit under Section 10(b) and Rule 10b-5 of the Securities Exchange Act of 1934 must establish fraud. Fraud is an intentional tort and as such requires more than a showing of negligence. Although the audit was admittedly improper and performed in a negligent manner, the CPAs neither participated in the fraudulent scheme nor did they know of its existence. The element of scienter or guilty knowledge must be present in order to state a cause of action for fraud under Section 10(b) of the Securities Exchange Act of 1934.

2. The plaintiffs might have stated a common law action for negligence. However, they may not be able to prevail due to the privity requirement. There was no contractual relationship between the defrauded parties and the CPA firm. Although the exact status of the privity rule is unclear, it is doubtful that the simple negligence in this case would extend Gordon & Groton's liability to the customers who transacted business with Bank. However, the facts of the case as presented in court would determine this.

11/78

Q. **6.** A CPA firm was engaged to examine the financial statements of Martin Manufacturing Corporation for the year ending December 31, 1977. The facts revealed that Martin was in need of cash to continue its operations and agreed to sell its common stock investment in a subsidiary through a private placement. The buyers insisted that the proceeds be placed in escrow because of the possibility of a major contingent tax liability that might result from a pending government claim. The payment in escrow was completed in late November 1977. The president of Martin told the audit partner that the proceeds from the sale of the subsidiary's common stock, held in escrow, should be shown on the balance sheet as an unrestricted current account receivable. The president was of the opinion that the government's claim was groundless and that Martin needed an "uncluttered" balance sheet and a "clean" auditor's opinion to obtain additional working capital from lenders. The audit partner agreed with the president and issued an unqualified opinion on the Martin financial statements which did not refer to the contingent liability and did not properly describe the escrow arrangement.

The government's claim proved to be valid, and pursuant to the agreement with the buyers, the purchase price of the subsidiary was reduced by $450,000. This adverse development forced Martin into bankruptcy. The CPA firm is being sued for deceit (fraud) by several of Martin's unpaid creditors who extended credit in reliance upon the CPA firm's unqualified opinion on Martin's financial statements.

Required

Answer the following, setting forth reasons for any conclusions stated.

Based on these facts, can Martin's unpaid creditors recover from the CPA firm?

A. Yes. The CPA firm is guilty of a common law *deceit,* commonly referred to as "fraud." The CPA firm was associated with financial statements that were not in conformity with generally accepted accounting principles because of the failure to disclose the restriction on the cash received, as well as the contingent liability. This association constitutes the commission of an actionable tort (deceit) upon the creditors. The fact that there was no privity of contract between the creditors and the accountants is immaterial in relation to an action based on deceit. Where *deceit* is involved, the defense of lack of privity is not available. Deceit is an intentional tort, and those who engage in it must bear the burden of their wrongdoing, even though they may not have intended harm to those affected.

The common law elements of deceit in general are—

1. A false representation of a material fact made by the defendant.
2. Knowledge or belief of falsity, technically described as "scienter."
3. An intent that the plaintiff rely upon the false representation.
4. Justifiable reliance on the false representation.
5. Damage as a result of the reliance.

Clearly, the elements of deceit are present. The only element that needs further elaboration is the "scienter" requirement. About the only defense available to the CPA firm would be that it honestly believed that the government's claim was groundless based upon the president's statement. However, even if this were true, the CPA firm did not have a sufficient basis to express an unqualified opinion that the financial statements were fairly presented. The law includes not only representations made with actual knowledge or belief of falsity but also those made with a reckless disregard for the truth. The fact that the CPA firm did not intend to harm anyone is irrelevant. The CPA firm must be considered liable in light of its training, qualifications, and responsibility and its duty to those who would read, and might act upon, financial statements with which the firm is associated.

Q. 7. The partnership of Watkins, Miller, & Fogg, CPAs, was engaged for the first time recently to examine the financial statements of Flinco Corporation. Flinco is the largest manufacturing concern in the locale. It is engaged in a multistate business, and its stock is traded on the over-the-counter market. The Watkins firm has enjoyed considerable stature in the business community but has traditionally served small to medium-sized businesses. The firm has never audited a publicly held corporation before.

Required
1. State the general guidelines that a CPA firm may look to in assessing its legal liability when assuming the responsibility for a publicly held client.
2. Discuss the significant additional potential liabilities imposed by federal statutes and related regulations that the Watkins firm is assuming in accepting the Flinco engagement.

A. 1. The following are the general guidelines which a CPA firm may look to in assessing its legal liability:
  a. Its contractual undertaking as defined in the agreement with the client.
  b. The standards established by the profession.
  c. Court decisions interpreting and amplifying the above.
  d. Special standards established by state and federal statutes and the regulations promulgated thereunder by the regulatory agencies pursuant to their statutory authority; e.g., the Securities and Exchange Commission.

  2. Now that Watkins, Miller, & Fogg will be handling a client subject to SEC regulation, the firm must thoroughly digest reporting requirements and liability imposed by the Securities Act of 1933 and related regulations and releases. Any public offering of securities by the client will require certified financial statements as an integral part of the proposed offering. Liability based upon negligence and fraud is defined by the Act and is greater for the CPA undertaking this type of engagement as compared with traditional, nongovernment regulated engagements. There is also the possibility of criminal liability.

  The Securities Exchange Act of 1934 and related regulations and releases may also apply to Flinco, whose stock is traded over the counter, if it has assets in excess of 3 million dollars and a class of equity securities held by 500 or more persons as of the last day of the fiscal year. Numerous reports are required by the Act, including an annual audited report (form 10-K) to the SEC. Again, liability for negligence or fraud of a CPA is defined under the Act and regulations. These represent expanded exposure to liability for the CPA. There are also criminal provisions which are applicable to the CPA.

Q. 8. Whitlow and Wyatt, CPAs, has been the independent auditor of Interstate Land Development Corporation for several years. During these years, Interstate prepared and filed its own annual income tax returns.

  During 1974, Interstate requested Whitlow and Wyatt to examine all the necessary financial statements of the corporation to be submitted to the Securities and Exchange Commission in connection with a multistate public offering of 1 million shares of Interstate common stock. This public offering came under the provisions of the Securities Act of 1933. The examination was performed carefully, and the financial statements were fairly presented for the respective periods. These financial statements were included in the registration statement filed with the SEC.

  While the registration statement was being processed by the SEC but prior to the effective date, the Internal Revenue Service (IRS) subpoenaed Whitlow and Wyatt to turn over all its working papers relating to Interstate for the years 1971–1973. Whitlow and Wyatt initially refused to comply for two reasons. First, Whitlow and

Wyatt did not prepare Interstate's tax returns. Second, Whitlow and Wyatt claimed that the working papers were confidential matters subject to the privileged communication rule. Subsequently, however, Whitlow and Wyatt did relinquish the subpoenaed working papers.

Upon receiving the subpoena, Wyatt called Dunkirk, the chairman of Interstate's board of directors and asked him about the IRS investigation. Dunkirk responded, "I'm sure the IRS people are on a fishing expedition and that they will not find any material deficiencies."

A few days later Dunkirk received written confirmation from the IRS that it was contending that Interstate had underpaid its taxes during the period under review. The confirmation revealed that Interstate was being assessed $800,000 including penalties and interest for the three years.

This $800,000 assessment was material relative to the financial statements as of December 31, 1974. The amount for each year individually exclusive of penalty and interest was not material relative to each respective year.

Required
1. Discuss the additional liability assumed by Whitlow and Wyatt in connection with this SEC registration engagement.
2. Discuss the implications to Whitlow and Wyatt and its responsibilities with respect to the IRS assessment.
3. Could Whitlow and Wyatt have validly refused to surrender the subpoenaed materials? Explain.

A. 1. The Securities Act of 1933 has significantly changed the duty and liability of CPAs who examine financial statements used as a part of a registration statement. The CPA has the burden of proving he was neither negligent nor fraudulent in examining the financial statements. The CPA may satisfy his burden of proof by showing that he made a reasonable investigation, had a reasonable basis for his belief, and did believe the financial statements he examined were fairly presented. The above duty is required at the date the registration becomes effective, not at the date of the financial statements.

Thus, Whitlow and Wyatt must continue to examine the financial statements after the date of its report thereon. The fact that the CPA's performance was faultless as of the date of these statements does not excuse the CPA from the continuing obligation to investigate until the time of the effective date of the registration statement in order to determine whether any significant events have occurred subsequently which would materially affect the validity of these financial statements.

Since no privity requirement exists under the Securities Act of 1933, the CPA's potential liability is extremely broad. The CPA firm faces potential liability to the purchasers of the one million shares to the extent that the omitted disclosure of the tax assessment causes purchasers to lose money on their investment.

2. The CPA should investigate matters affecting the financial statements until the effective date of the registration. Whitlow and Wyatt should, therefore, investigate the potential additional tax liability and not merely rely on Dunkirk. This investigation should include reviewing Interstate's tax returns for the periods in question. Whitlow and Wyatt should also review correspondence between the IRS and Interstate to ascertain the area(s) causing the assessment and to judge the possible validity of the assessment. Furthermore, the CPA firm should confirm with Interstate's legal counsel the implications of the IRS assessment. Whitlow and Wyatt should discuss the situation with Interstate's management to determine whether Interstate intends to contest the IRS assessment.

Whitlow and Wyatt should insist that Interstate disclose these facts to the SEC and that amended financial statements disclosing the tax liability or contingent liability, depending on the circumstances, be filed with the SEC.

3. No. Although a minority of state courts apply the privileged-communication rule to the CPA-client relationship, the federal courts do not follow this rule of evidence where federal law applies. [In fact, in 1984 the United States Supreme Court specifically ruled such tax workpapers are not privileged.] Hence, the CPA firm had no choice but to honor the subpoena even though it did not prepare the client's tax returns.

Practice Questions*

Q. 1. Donald Sharpe recently joined the CPA firm of Spark, Watts, and Wilcox. He quickly established a reputation for thoroughness and a steadfast dedication to following prescribed auditing procedures to the letter. On his third audit for the firm, Sharpe examined the underlying documentation of 200 disbursements as a test of purchasing, receiving, vouchers-payable, and cash-disbursement procedures. In the process, he found 12 disbursements for the purchase of materials with no receiving reports in the documentation. He noted the exceptions in his working papers and called them to the attention of the in-charge accountant. Relying on prior experience with the client, the in-charge accountant disregarded Sharpe's comments, and nothing further was done about the exceptions.

Subsequently, it was learned that one of the client's purchasing agents and a member of its accounting department were engaged in a fraudulent scheme whereby they diverted the receipt of materials to a public warehouse while sending the invoices to the client. When the client discovered the fraud, the conspirators had obtained approximately $70,000, $50,000 of which was after the completion of the audit.

Required

Discuss the legal implications and liabilities to Spark, Watts, and Wilcox as a result of the above facts.

Q. 2. The partnership of Porter, Potts, & Farr, CPAs, was engaged by Revolutionary Products, Inc., to examine its financial statements for the year ended June 30, 1973. The contract said nothing about the CPA firm's responsibility for defalcations. Porter, Potts, & Farr performed its examination in a careful and competent manner, following generally accepted auditing standards and using appropriate auditing procedures and tests under the circumstances.

Subsequently, it was discovered that the client's chief accountant was engaged in major defalcations. However, only an audit specifically designed to discover possible defalcations would have revealed the fraud. Revolutionary Products asserts that Porter, Potts, & Farr is liable for the defalcations.

Required

Is Porter, Potts, & Farr liable? Explain.

Q. 3. Factory Discount Prices, Inc., is a chain store discount outlet which sells women's clothes. It has an excessively large inventory on hand and is in urgent need of additional cash. It is bordering on bankruptcy, especially if the inventory has to be liquidated by sale to other stores instead of the public. Furthermore, about 15% of the inventory is not resalable except at a drastic discount below cost. Faced with this financial crisis, Factory approached several of the manufacturers from whom it purchases. Dexter Apparel, Inc., one of the parties approached, indicated a willingness to loan Factory $300,000 under certain conditions. First, Factory was to submit audited financial statements for the express purpose of providing the correct financial condition of the company. The loan was to be predicated upon these financial statements and Factory's engagement letter with Dunn & Clark, its CPAs, expressly indicated this.

The second condition insisted upon by Dexter was that it obtain a secured position in all unsecured inventory, accounts, and other related personal property. In due course a security agreement was executed and a financing statement properly filed and recorded.

In preparing the financial statements, Factory valued the inventory at cost which was approximately $100,000 over the current fair market value. Also, Factory failed to disclose two secured creditors to whom substantial amounts are owed and who take priority over Dexter's security interests.

Dunn & Clark issued an unqualified opinion on the financial statements of Factory which they believed were fairly presented.

*Prepared by the Board of Examiners of the American Institute of Certified Public Accountants (AICPA) and adopted by the examining boards of all states, territories, and the District of Columbia. This applies to the practice and practice objective questions following each chapter.

Six months later Factory filed a voluntary bankruptcy petition. Dexter received $125,000 as its share of the bankrupt's estate. It is suing Dunn & Clark for the loss of $175,000. Dunn & Clark deny liability based upon lack of privity and lack of negligence.

Required

Answer the following, setting forth reasons for any conclusions stated.

Is Dexter entitled to recover its loss from Dunn & Clark?

Q.   4. The CPA firm of Blank, Miller & Tage prepares a significant number of individual and corporate income tax returns. Jones is a newly hired junior accountant. This is Jones' first job since graduation from school. Jones' initial assignment is to work with the tax department in the preparation of clients' 1978 income tax returns.

Required

Answer the following, setting forth reasons for any conclusions stated.

1. What is the principal legal basis for potential liability of the CPA firm and Jones to clients in connection with the preparation of income tax returns?
2. Give some examples of performance which would result in such liability.
3. What is the basis for determining the amount of damages to be awarded to the client?

Q.   5. Smith, CPA, is the auditor for Juniper Manufacturing Corporation, a privately owned company which has a June 30 fiscal year. Juniper arranged for a substantial bank loan which was dependent upon the bank receiving, by September 30, audited financial statements which showed a current ratio of at least 2 to 1. On September 25, just before the audit report was to be issued, Smith received an anonymous letter on Juniper's stationery indicating that a five-year lease by Juniper, as leasee, of a factory building which was accounted for in the financial statements as an operating lease was in fact a capital lease. The letter stated that there was a secret written agreement with the lessor modifying the lease and creating a capital lease.

Smith confronted the president of Juniper who admitted that a secret agreement existed but said it was necessary to treat the lease as an operating lease to meet the current ratio requirement of the pending loan and that nobody would ever discover the secret agreement with the lessor. The president said that if Smith did not issue his report by September 30, Juniper would sue Smith for substantial damages which would result from not getting the loan. Under this pressure and because the working papers contained a copy of the five-year lease agreement which supported the operating lease treatment, Smith issued his report with an unqualified opinion on September 29.

In spite of the fact that the loan was received, Juniper went bankrupt within two years. The bank is suing Smith to recover its losses on the loan.

Required

Answer the following, setting forth reasons for any conclusions stated. Is Smith liable to the bank?

Q.   6. A CPA firm has been named as a defendant in a class action by purchasers of the shares of stock of the Newly Corporation. The offering was a public offering of securities within the meaning of the Securities Act of 1933. The plaintiffs alleged that the firm was either negligent or fraudulent in connection with the preparation of the audited financial statements which accompanied the registration statement filed with the SEC. Specifically, they allege that the CPA firm either intentionally disregarded, or failed to exercise reasonable care to discover, material facts which occurred subsequent to January 31, 1978, the date of the auditor's report. The securities were sold to the public on March 16, 1978. The plaintiffs have subpoenaed copies of the CPA firm's working papers. The CPA firm is considering refusing to relinquish the papers, asserting that they contain privileged communication between the CPA firm and its client. The CPA firm will, of course, defend on the merits irrespective of the questions regarding the working papers.

Required
Answer the following, setting forth reasons for any conclusions stated.

1. Can the CPA firm rightfully refuse to surrender its working papers?
2. Discuss the liability of the CPA firm in respect to events which occur in the period between the date of the auditor's report and the effective date of the public offering of the securities.

Q. 7. The partnership of Smith, Frank, & Clark, a CPA firm, has been the auditor of Greenleaf, Inc., for many years. During the annual examination of the financial statements for the year ended December 31, 1972, a dispute developed over whether certain disclosures should be made in the financial statements. The dispute resulted in Smith, Frank, & Clark's being dismissed and Greenleaf's engaging another firm. Greenleaf demanded that Smith, Frank, & Clark turn over to it all working papers applicable to the Greenleaf audits or face a lawsuit. Smith, Frank, & Clark refused. Greenleaf has instituted a suit against Smith, Frank, & Clark to obtain the working papers.

Required
1. Will Greenleaf succeed in its suit? Explain.
2. Discuss the rationale underlying the rule of law applicable to the ownership of working papers.

Practice Objective Questions

Introduction
The instructions below are the standard instructions for the multiple choice questions currently in use. They appear as an introduction to question 1 of the exam. They have been used for the past several years and will continue to be used in the foreseeable future. Currently, there are 60 objective questions worth 60% of the grade and they are exclusively multiple choice, and you are to select the *best* answer. This is the only type of objective question you will be exposed to.

Instructions 1–12
Select the *best* answer for each of the following items. Mark only one answer for *each* item. Answer all items. Your grade will be based on your total correct answers.

1. Magnus Enterprises engaged a CPA firm to perform the annual examination of its financial statements. Which of the following is a correct statement with respect to the CPA firm's liability to Magnus for negligence?
   a. Such liability *cannot* be varied by agreement of the parties.
   b. The CPA firm will be liable for any fraudulent scheme it does *not* detect.
   c. The CPA firm will *not* be liable if it can show that it exercised the ordinary care and skill of a reasonable man in the conduct of his own affairs.
   d. The CPA firm must *not* only exercise reasonable care in what it does, but also must possess at least that degree of accounting knowledge and skill expected of a CPA.

2. Martinson is a duly licensed CPA. One of his clients is suing him for negligence, alleging that he failed to meet generally accepted auditing standards in the current year's audit, thereby failing to discover large thefts of inventory. Under the circumstances:

    a. Martinson is *not* bound by generally accepted auditing standards unless he is a member of the AICPA.

    b. Martinson's failure to meet generally accepted auditing standards would result in liability.

    c. Generally accepted auditing standards do *not* currently cover the procedures that must be used in verifying inventory for balance sheet purposes.

    d. If Martinson failed to meet generally accepted auditing standards, he would undoubtedly be found to have committed the tort of fraud.

3. Martin Corporation orally engaged Humm & Dawson to audit its year-end financial statements. The engagement was to be completed within two months after the close of Martin's fiscal year for a fixed fee of $2,500. Under these circumstances what obligation is assumed by Humm & Dawson?

    a. None, because the contract is unenforceable since it is *not* in writing.

    b. An implied promise to exercise reasonable standards of competence and care.

    c. An implied obligation to take extraordinary steps to discover all defalcations.

    d. The obligation of an insurer of its work which is liable without fault.

4. The Apex Surety Company wrote a general fidelity bond covering defalcations by the employees of Watson, Inc. Thereafter, Grand, an employee of Watson, embezzled $18,900 of company funds. When his activities were discovered, Apex paid Watson the full amount in accordance with the terms of the fidelity bond, and then sought recovery against Watson's auditors, Kane & Dobbs, CPAs. Which of the following would be Kane & Dobbs' best defense?

    a. Apex is *not* in privity of contract.

    b. The shortages were the result of clever forgeries and collusive fraud which would *not* be detected by an examination made in accordance with generally accepted auditing standards.

    c. Kane & Dobbs were *not* guilty either of gross negligence or fraud.

    d. Kane & Dobbs were *not* aware of the Apex-Watson surety relationship.

5. Winslow Manufacturing, Inc., sought a $200,000 loan from National Lending Corporation. National Lending insisted that audited financial statements be submitted before it would extend credit. Winslow agreed to this and also agreed to pay the audit fee. An audit was performed by an independent CPA who submitted his report to Winslow to be used solely for the purpose of negotiating a loan from National. National, upon reviewing the audited financial statements, decided in good faith *not* to extend the credit desired. Certain ratios, which as a matter of policy were used by National in reaching its decision, were deemed too low. Winslow used copies of the audited financial statements to obtain credit elsewhere. It was subsequently learned that the CPA, despite the exercise of reasonable care, had failed to discover a sophisticated embezzlement scheme by Winslow's chief accountant. Under these circumstances, what liability does the CPA have?

    a. The CPA is liable to third parties who extended credit to Winslow based upon the audited financial statements.

    b. The CPA is liable to Winslow to repay the audit fee because credit was *not* extended by National.

    c. The CPA is liable to Winslow for any losses Winslow suffered as a result of failure to discover the embezzlement.

    d. The CPA is *not* liable to any of the parties.

6. The traditional common law rules regarding accountant's liability to third parties for negligence:

    a. Have remained substantially unchanged since their inception.

    b. Were less favorable to the accountant than the rules currently applicable.

    c. Are of relatively minor importance to the accountant.

    d. Have been substantially changed at both the federal and state levels.

7. A CPA is subject to *criminal* liability if the CPA

    a. Refuses to turn over the working papers to the client.

    b. Performs an audit in a negligent manner.

    c. Willfully omits a material fact required to be stated in a registration statement.

    d. Willfully breaches the contract with the client.

8. Josephs & Paul is a growing medium-sized partnership of CPAs. One of the firm's major clients is considering offering its stock to the public. This will be the firm's first client to go public. Which of the following is true with respect to this engagement?

    a. If the client is a service corporation, the Securities Act of 1933 will *not* apply.

    b. If the client is *not* going to be listed on an organized exchange, the Securities Exchange Act of 1934 will *not* apply.

    c. The Securities Act of 1933 imposes important additional potential liability on Josephs & Paul.

    d. As long as Josephs & Paul engages exclusively in intrastate business, the federal securities laws will *not* apply.

9. An investor seeking to recover stock market losses from a CPA firm, based upon an unqualified opinion on financial statements which accompanied a registration statement, must establish that

    a. There was a false statement or omission of material fact contained in the audited financial statements.

    b. He relied upon the financial statements.

    c. The CPA firm did *not* act in good faith.

    d. The CPA firm would have discovered the false statement or omission if it had exercised due care in its examination.

10. A third-party purchaser of securities has brought suit against a CPA firm, based upon the Securities Act of 1933. The CPA firm will prevail in the suit brought by the third party even though the CPA firm issued an unqualified opinion on materially incorrect financial statements if:

    a. The CPA firm was unaware of the defects.

    b. The third-party plaintiff had *no* direct dealings with the CPA firm.

    c. The CPA firm can show that the third-party plaintiff knew of misstatements in the financials, did *not* rely upon the audited financial statements.

    d. The CPA firm can establish that it was *not* guilty of actual fraud.

11. The CPA firm of Knox and Knox has been subpoenaed to testify and produce its correspondence and working papers in connection with a lawsuit brought against Johnson, one of its clients. Regarding the attempted resort to the privileged communication rule in seeking to avoid admission of such evidence in the lawsuit, which of the following is correct?

    a. Federal law recognizes such a privilege if the accountant is a Certified Public Accountant.

    b. The privilege is available regarding the working papers since the accountant is deemed to own them.

    c. The privilege is as widely available as the attorney-client privilege.

    d. In the absence of a specific statutory provision, the law does *not* recognize the existence of the privileged communication rule between an accountant and his client.

12. The partnership of Maxim & Rose, CPAs, has been engaged by their largest client, a limited partnership, to examine the financial statements in connection with the offering of 2,000 limited-partnership interests to the public at $5,000 per subscription. Under these circumstances, which of the following is true?

    a. Maxim & Rose may disclaim any liability under the federal securities acts by an unambiguous, bold-faced disclaimer of liability on its audit report.

    b. Under the Securities Act of 1933, Maxim & Rose has responsibility only for the financial statements as of the close of the fiscal year in question.

    c. The dollar amount in question is sufficiently small so as to provide an exemption from the Securities Act of 1933.

    d. The Securities Act of 1933 requires a registration despite the fact that the client is *not* selling stock or another traditional "security."

2

BUSINESS ORGANIZATIONS (20%)

2

Agency

AICPA Content Specification Outline

Formation and Termination
Liabilities of Principal
Disclosed and Undisclosed Principals
Agent's Authority and Liability

Contents

I. Formation of the Agency Relationship

A. Agency defined: It is a consensual fiduciary relationship between one person (the agent) who agrees to act for and under the control of the principal.

    1. Control is the key distinguishing characteristic.

    2. It must be consensual, i.e., the agent must agree to act *for* the principal. It need not involve remuneration, but invariably does.

    3. The agent owes a fiduciary duty to the principal.

    4. Consider the following diagram:

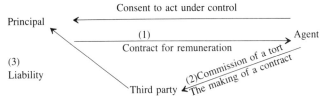

In the balance of the outline, the most important and fascinating questions arise in regard to (3), liability of the principal to the third party either for tort or contract when the agent is acting wrongfully. The agent has the **power** to impose liability upon the principal to third parties even though the agent is acting outside the scope of the employment or the scope of authority. Although the rights and duties in relation to (1) and (2) are important, they are relatively minor and straightforward when compared with the liability question posed by (3).

B. Capacity of the parties:

    1. To be a principal, i.e., to appoint an agent, one must have the legal capacity to contract (see Contracts, p. 148):

        a. The fact that the agent has the legal capacity to contract is irrelevant in determining whether the principal is bound. Look to the capacity of the principal, not the agent. In a majority of states an infant may appoint an agent. Appointment of an agent, where not for purposes of obtaining necessaries, is voidable at infant's option, as are the contracts for nonnecessaries made by the agent.

   b. Marriage is not a bar for either spouse to be a principal or agent.

   c. Corporations: act exclusively through their agents.

   d. Partnerships: act through the partners who are their agents; can appoint agents in addition to the partners.

2. To act as an agent:

   a. The capacity of the principal not the agent is the test. Only general capacity to exercise the authority is needed to act as an agent.

   b. Whether the agent has the capacity to contract for himself or herself is irrelevant.

   c. Infants may be agents and even persons lacking mental capacity have been found to be acting legally as agents.

C. Manner of formation or creation of the agency:

1. Express agency: created by written contract or oral appointment; needs an agreement between principal and agent.

   a. One common type of appointment is made by a power of attorney, an instrument authorizing another to act as one's agent.

   (1) Whatever a principal cannot do, he may not delegate to be done by an agent through a power of attorney. (E.g., a minor cannot delegate conveyance of real estate or confession of judgment against himself, since he may repudiate a conveyance of real estate and he has no capacity to confess judgment against himself.)

   (2) Attorney in fact: An agent whose authority to do a type of transaction is conferred by a written instrument, such as a power of attorney.

   b. Statute of Frauds (see Contracts, p. 148, III.E): If agent's duties involve the making of a contract governed by this statute, some states require agency to be in writing (e.g., agency for the sale of real property).

2. Implied agency: one created by acts or deduced from circumstances evidencing an intention to create the relationship. (E.g., an agent with possession of an authority to sell personal property would have implied authority to do whatever is reasonably necessary to carry out agency, including power to make usual representations and warranties and receive payment, but not including unusual powers such as the power to mortgage, exchange, or pledge goods or give credit or sell at an auction.)

3. Agency by ratification: Approval after the fact of an unauthorized act done by an agent, or acts done by one who was not an agent.

   a. Principal may ratify an act, if it is not unlawful. Hence a tort may be ratified and subject the person so ratifying to liability; a crime, however, may not be ratified.

   b. Principal must be competent to have appointed agent in order to be able to ratify act done by agent (see p. 38, I.B.I.).

   c. Act must be purported to have been done in name and on behalf of the person ratifying.

   d. Principal must have full knowledge of the facts.

   e. Ratification must cover the entire act; principal cannot ratify in part and reject in part. Ratification is retroactive, but not retractable.

  f. Ratification may be express (written or oral) or by implication, as by accepting the benefits of an act with full knowledge of facts. Even silence may amount to ratification.

  g. A person seeking to ratify an act must have been in existence at the time when the act was done. (E.g., a corporation cannot ratify acts of promoters done on its behalf prior to incorporation. However, it can adopt them and become liable—see Corporations, p. 89, II.A.3.)

  h. Ratification requires the same formalities as authorization.

  i. Ratification doctrine does *not* apply to unauthorized acts by an undisclosed principal.

  4. Agency by estoppel: created by operation of law; prevents party from denying the existence of an agency where a third person relies on circumstances that would reasonably lead to the conclusion that one exists. (E.g., X permits Z to pose as his agent, and Y acts on the belief that there was an agency and relies thereon to his detriment in dealing with Z.)

  5. Apparent or ostensible agency: based upon principal's manifestations to third party; differs from estoppel in that reliance (change of position) is not necessary.

  6. Agency by necessity: implied in law where a situation exists or an emergency arises, that makes it necessary to presume an agency as a matter of public policy. (E.g., a wife is an agent of necessity of her husband when he fails to provide her with necessaries and she obtains them; or an agency is implied in emergencies to contract for medical, hospital, or first-aid expenses.)

II. Principal's Tort Liability and Liability to Agent

A. Principal's tort liability (a very important and costly area):

  1. General rule:

   a. Principal is liable for all torts committed within scope of *employment* by *servant-agent*.

   b. Principal is liable only for torts committed within scope of *authority* by *nonservant-agent*.

   c. Principal is *not* liable for the torts of *independent contractor*.

  2. This type of liability is often referred to as vicarious liability. It is a form of strict liability from the principal's standpoint. That is, the principal may have taken every precaution in hiring and training the agent-servant, but cannot avoid liability even though personally not at fault. Liability insurance seems to be the only answer to the principal's risk.

  3. Although this area of law is to a large extent readily understandable and predictable, there is some definitional confusion. Terms causing confusion are:

   a. *Agent.* As used in the *Restatement of Torts, 2nd*, this is the broad term which encompasses all types of agents, including servant-agents and nonservant-agents.

   b. *Servant-agents.* Control is the key determinative. Does the principal actually control or have the right or ability to control the agent's performance of the job? A servant-agent is usually a supervised worker (laborer, factory worker, chauffer) who does not have the power to bind the principal contractually with third parties.

(1) With regard to a servant, the principal is known as "master."

(2) Under the doctrine of *Respondeat Superior,* a master may be liable for the torts of his servants committed within the scope of employment (almost anything while on the job).

c. *Nonservant-agent.* Nonservant-agents are highter-level persons, (e.g., a bank manager), and they often have extensive power to bind the principal contractually, although they have less power to impose tort liability upon the principal. The test for determining whether an agent is a servant or a nonservant agent is the degree of control. The principal's liability for the torts of nonservant-agents is limited to those torts committed within the scope of authority, that is, those acts which are his duty to perform.

d. *Independent contractor.* One whose work is not subject to control and supervision of one who employs him, often the agent of an independent party. The CPA and attorney-at-law are classic examples. The employer is generally not liable to third parties for torts committed by the independent contractor.

(1) Independent contractor often does work for many different employers.

(2) Employer seeks results only, the contractor controls the method.

(3) In certain cases an independent contractor may become an agent, e.g., where she submits herself to the detailed control of the employer and so changes the normal relationship.

e. *Employee.* This is the term which causes the most confusion in a candidate's mind since it is the term we all use and think of automatically when we consider a work relationship. However, an employee can be a nonservant, a servant-agent, or an independent contractor. The amount of control by the principal is the key factor. A Detroit assembly-line worker might be hostile if you called him "servant," but for the purposes of agency law, he is probably just that. Adding to the confusion is the fact that most employment legislation, (e.g., workers' compensation) uses the term "employee," but uses agency concepts to define the scope of the term (see Chapter 9, p. 228). The term ''employee'' is not a functional term in the law of agency.

f. What constitutes *control?* The courts define requisite control sufficient to find servant status as follows:

(1) Relates to control of the physical conduct of the person in question.

(2) Includes not only actual control or supervision but more importantly includes employment relationships where the principal has the right to control.

4. Principal is liable for agent's torts if they are within the scope of his employment and committed during the course of his duties. This rule is known as *Respondeat Superior.* The type of tort liability we are primarily concerned with here is bodily injury as a result of personal contact (e.g., negligent operation of machinery or assualt). The courts talk in terms of foreseeable harm to the third party by the servant. As to the agents who are not servants, the principal is liable for such agents' torts if committed within the scope of the agent's authority.

a. Rule applies even though servant-agent violated principal's instructions in committing the tort.

b. Most states presume that the driver of an auto (other than the owner) is the agent for the owner and thus impose liability on the owner for torts of the driver. This is an alternate basis for imposition of liability. The principal-owner could be held liable under either theory if the permitted user of the auto is also a servant.

5. Principal's liability for agent's crimes: principal is not *criminally* liable for agent's crimes unless he planned, directed, ordered, or acquiesced in their commission. However, even if the tort committed by a servant is also a crime (e.g., an assault-battery) the principal will or at least may have liability. Was the tort-crime committed within the scope of employment (during work hours and while on duty) and was it a foreseeable type of conduct by such a servant (was the servant a bouncer?)? If the answers are yes, then the principal will have civil liability for the tort even though it also constituted a criminal act.

B. Duties of principal to agent:

1. To compensate agent, unless there is an express agreement to the contrary:
   a. Amount ordinarily a matter of contract; or if there is no agreement, the reasonable value of services will be inferred.
   b. Drawing account: deemed to be agent's salary unless specifically provided that it is a loan.
2. To reimburse agent: Agent is entitled to expenses expressly or implicitly authorized and incurred during course of agency.
3. To indemnify agent against loss and liability for acts performed at principal's direction when said acts are not manifestly illegal or known to be wrong.
4. Agent's lien: attaches to principal's money or property in agent's hands in connection with which agent made advances, incurred expenses, or sustained losses.
5. Not to discredit the agent or interfere with his work.
6. To inform agent of risks involved.

III.   Disclosed and Undisclosed Principal's Liability on Contracts

A. Types of principals:

1. Disclosed: when third party knows, or should know, that the agent is acting for a principal and who the principal is.
2. Partially disclosed: when third party knows, or should know, that the agent is acting for a principal but does not know the principal's identity.
3. Undisclosed: when third party has no notice that agent is acting for a principal, i.e., the third party believes agent is the principal.

B. Disclosed principal is liable on contract made by his agent when contract was:

1. Authorized (either expressly or implicitly). However, where agent has no authority, express or implied, third party deals with him at his peril. (E.g., a third party paying an agent who has no authority to collect funds remains liable to principal for purchase price.)
2. Unauthorized initially but subsequently ratified.
3. Made under circumstances where principal is deemed to have clothed his agent with certain **apparent authority.** An act performed by an agent within the usual scope of authority is binding upon the principal, for his agent has apparent

authority even though the particular act has been forbidden. An innocent third party will be protected if the act done by the agent is the usual practice, and the principal has not taken steps to make the third person aware of his agent's disability to contract in this area. (E.g., where an agent is properly appointed to sell personal property, he has implied authority to make usual warranties of title and to collect the purchase price when he delivers the goods.)

C. **Undisclosed principal:** where third party has no notice that the agent is acting for a principal.

    1. Principal is liable on a contract which agent was authorized to make unless:

        a. Contract is fully performed by agent.

        b. Contract is a negotiable instrument.

        c. Contract specifically excluded an undisclosed principal as a party thereto or where personal performance is important.

        d. Third party, later ascertaining the existence of the undisclosed principal, has elected to hold agent exclusively.

    2. Principal is liable on contract that general agent was not authorized to make, but that was usual or necessary to a transaction that agent was authorized to conduct.

    3. Principal has benefit of election theory. Third party, upon ascertaining the existence of an undisclosed principal, may elect to hold either the agent or the undisclosed principal.

        a. This election is irrevocable in some jurisdictions:

            (1) If, after disclosure of agency, the third party proceeds to judgment against agent with knowledge of principal's identity, only agent is liable, but

            (2) If he proceeds to judgment against principal, principal is liable and agent is not.

        b. In a few jurisdictions a third party may proceed to judgment against both principal and agent, but may obtain only one satisfaction.

    4. The undisclosed principal can *not* ratify unauthorized contracts made by his agent

D. Partially disclosed principal is generally treated the same as undisclosed principal, with the following exceptions:

        a. A partially disclosed principal, unlike an undisclosed principal, may ratify an unauthorized contract.

        b. Agent of a partially disclosed principal may be personally liable in some cases where the agent has not made adequate disclosure as to nature of agency.

IV. Agent's Authority and Liability

A. Classification of agents:

    1. Scope of authority:

        a. General agent has broad authority to represent his principal.

        b. Special agent has authority limited to a specific task or series of routine tasks.

        c. Agent's specific authority is determined by the principal.

        d. Generally, agent has authority to bind the principal as regards third parties.

2. Special types of agents.
    a. Attorneys at law: qualified by admission to the bar to represent other persons in matters of a legal nature.
    b. Auctioneer: authorized and licensed by the state to conduct a public sale of property; agent for thc seller until fall of the gavel, and then agent for both parties.
    c. Factor or commission merchant: a commercial agent employed by principal to sell or dispose of goods.
        (1) Factor is entrusted with possession of goods; however, title remains in principal, the factor being merely a bailee for the purpose of the agency.
        (2) Compensation is called factorage or commission.
        (3) Having possession of principal's goods, he is the ostensible owner of them; thus, he can sell them in his own name, and collect the proceeds subject to his duty to account to his principal.
        (4) Factor can convey better title than he has to the goods. (I.e., a third party who buys goods in good faith and for value, from factor who has exceeded his authority, gets title as against principal.)
        (5) Factor has duty to give principal full accounting.
        (6) Factor has a general lien on goods for expenses incurred in his capacity of factor for the principal and for any unpaid amounts due him from the principal (e.g., advances made by factor to principal).
    d. Exclusive agency: agreement by owner that during the life of the contract she (or he) will not sell the property to a purchaser procured by another agent. Agreement does not preclude owner from selling to a purchaser she procures.
    e. Exclusive sale: agent given exclusive rights to act for principal in sale of his property during the duration of the agency, with no right of sale remaining with owner.
    f. *Del credere* agent: a sales agent who has assumed, generally for a higher commission, an obligation to pay his principal what the purchaser fails to pay (i.e., he guarantees the accounts of his customers).
        (1) If debt is not paid when due, action will at once lie against *del credere* agent.
        (2) Although his guaranty is a promise to answer for the debt of another (see Contracts, p. 150, III.E.3.b), it is considered as having been given primarily for his own benefit and, therefore, not within the Statute of Frauds.
    g. Real estate broker: authorized to negotiate for purchase or sale of real property.
        (1) Must usually be licensed to qualify as agent and earn commissions.
        (2) Entitled to commissions only when there is an express or implied contract with principal.
        (3) Hiring usually subject to automatic termination in case of a prior sale.
        (4) Broker not entitled to commission unless buyer he produces is ready, willing, and able to meet seller's terms.
    h. **Agency coupled with an interest or obligation: the only agency relationship that courts generally enforce specifically** in that the agent has a property or security interest in the thing to be disposed of or managed under

the power created by the agency. It is referred to as an "irrevocable agency" relationship as principal cannot terminate the agency relationship. (E.g., X owes Y $100 and Z owes X $500; X makes Y his agent for collection from Z with instructions to pay himself out of the proceeds and remit the surplus to X.)

    i. Gratuitous agent: one who assumes the role of an agent without expectation of compensation. He is not bound to perform even though he promises to do so; but once he does begin performance he must perform in a nonnegligent manner. He is not subject to as high a degree of care as a compensated agent.

    j. Promoter: person who attempts to form a corporation; generally held liable for his preincorporation contracts with third parties, even if corporation does come into being.

3. Agent distinguished from:

    a. Independent contractor: work not subject to control and supervision of one who employs him.

        (1) Employer seeks results only; contractor controls the methods.

        (2) Employer generally not liable for torts committed by independent contractor.

        (3) In certain cases an independent contractor may be an agent, e.g., where he submits himself to the detailed control of the employer and so changes normal relationship.

    b. Trustee: acts in his own name; has legal, but not equitable title to property, and retains authority until purpose of trust is fulfilled; he can be removed only for cause.

    c. Servant: a type of agent who is usually a supervised employee (laborer, factory worker, chauffeur), as opposed to a general agent whose primary task involves the power to bind the principal legally in relationships with third parties (sales representatives, executives).

        (1) Principal is known as "master."

        (2) Under the doctrine of *Respondeat Superior,* a master may be liable for the torts of his servants.

    d. Subagent: derives authority not from the principal, but from an agent, who is expressly or implicitly authorized to appoint subagents.

        (1) Intent to allow agent the power to delegate may be gathered from:

            (A) Expressions of the principal.

            (B) Character of the business.

            (C) Usages or prior conduct of the parties.

            (D) Necessity of meeting an emergency.

            (E) Character of acts committed to subagent, being ministerial only.

        (2) If agent is authorized only to employ for his principal, the second agent is also an agent of the principal and not a subagent; otherwise second agent is a subagent.

4. Agency distinguished from:

    a. Sale: The buyer is not usually the seller's agent.

    b. Assignment: is irrevocable; agent's authority can be withdrawn at will if not coupled with an interest.

    c. Lease: is an interest in land; tenant is not the agent of the landlord.

B. Duties of agent to principal:

   1. Utmost loyalty and good faith: *agency is a fiduciary relationship.*
      a. Agent cannot represent two principals with conflicting interests unless they consent.
      b. Dealing for agent's own interest absolutely prohibited.
      c. Agent must not engage in business competing with principal's unless with principal's knowledge and consent.
      d. Violation of the above duty deprives agent of the right to compensation, reimbursement, indemnification, or to agent's lien, and subjects him or her to liability for damages resulting therefrom.
   2. Obedience.
      a. When duties are routine in nature, agent must adhere to instructions in all cases in which they can be obeyed by the exercise of reasonable and diligent care.
      b. When duties involve use of discretion, agent must act competently and carefully, and is liable for failure to use reasonable care.
   3. To use necessary skill, care, and diligence to perform task properly; however, agent is not an insurer (i.e., will not be liable without fault) of services he renders unless he guarantees the result by express contract.
   4. Not to make a delegation or substitution: Agency relationship normally involves trust and confidence and therefore cannot be delegated without consent—see p. 161, I.C.4.d(1).
   5. Duty to account: duty to render unto principal that which is, or in good faith should be, the principal's.
      a. All profits and advantages gained by the agent in the execution of the agency belong to the principal, regardless of whether the profit results from strict performance or from violation of the agent's duty.
   6. Not to commingle funds. If agent commingles funds and they are somehow lost (e.g., a bank fails), agent will be strictly liable.
   7. Right of employee (agent) to use the fruits of his employment: employee is entitled to his own invention even though made on his employer's time and with use of his employer's equipment.
      a. Called the "shop rights doctrine."
      b. This license (i.e., right to use the invention) is irrevocable, nonassignable, and nonexclusive.
   8. After termination, must cease acting as agent but may still have duty not to reveal secrets of the principal.

C. Effect of notice given to agent will constitute notice to principal unless:

   1. Disclosure to the principal would be adverse to the agent's personal interest.
   2. Notice was given prior to commencement of the agency relationship, except where agent remembers the notice while he is acting for principal and is under no duty to a prior principal to keep it secret.

D. Agent's liability to third parties: Although generally not liable, an agent becomes liable to third parties when he:

1. Acts for nonexistent or incompetent principal, i.e., one under contractual disability (e.g., where a promoter acts for a corporation yet to be formed), and he:
   a. Knows of the principal's lack of capacity.
   b. Knows that third party is ignorant of principal's disability or nonexistence, or
   c. Represents to third parties that principal is competent or in existence.
2. Acts for undisclosed principal and third party elects to hold him liable.
3. Signs a negotiable instrument in his own name. (Only agent is liable, not principal; agent should always sign negotiable paper: "P, Principal, by A, Agent.")
4. Contracts in his own name.
5. Misrepresents his scope of authority to third party, who is thereby misled and who is unable to hold principal liable.
6. Wrongfully receives money on behalf of principal and has not delivered it to principal (agent is also responsible to principal).
7. Personally guarantees certain acts of his principal.
8. Commits a tort, even if it is in the course of discharging his duties. (If tort was committed within course of employment, principal will also be liable to third party.)
9. Third party's liability to principal and agent. Third party has no contractural liability to agent unless agent is a party to the contract or has an interest in the contract.

V. Termination of the Agency

A. Termination by act of parties:

1. The principal may reserve the right to terminate the agency. The agreement may also provide for the termination of the agency after a certain date, the accomplishment of a stipulated objective, the occurrence of a specific event, or by mutual agreement.
2. The parties may generally terminate the relationship unilaterally even if the agreement does not provide for that.
   a. The principal may generally revoke agency.
      (1) Principal may rightfully revoke when the agent violates his duties to his principal.
      (2) If the principal wrongfully revokes agency, he is liable to the agent for damages (e.g., if he revokes a valid contract for an "irrevocable" agency of fixed duration).
      (3) Where the agency is coupled with an interest or obligation, the principal may not revoke the agency.
   b. Agent may renounce or abandon agency, but if he does so wrongfully, he is liable to principal for damages for breach of the agreement unless:
      (1) Principal violates agency agreement, or
      (2) Agency is gratuitous, or
      (3) Agency is terminable at the will of either party.

B. Termination by operation of law results when there is:

1. Illegality of subject matter. Relationship is therefore void.
2. Impossibility (e.g., destruction or loss of subject matter).
3. Death or disability of parties. Some states, however (e.g., New York), provide that the agency may continue after disability or incompetency of the principal provided that the statutory language is used in the power of attorney.
4. Bankruptcy or insolvency of principal. But bankruptcy of agent will not terminate the agency unless it is a matter of consequence to the principal and affects the agency relationship.

C. Notice of termination:

1. Reasonable notice of revocation by principal or renunciation by agent must be given to third persons in order to avoid continued apparent agency relationship.
   a. Notice by letter takes effect when received and read.
   b. Where authority has been given to perform several different acts, principal may terminate authority as to some without impairing agent's authority as to others. However, where performance of one act is dependent on performance of another, termination of authority to perform one will terminate authority to perform the other.
2. **Third parties who have dealt with the agent must receive actual notice,** or they may act as though agency continued, and thus hold principal for acts of former agent, if they had prior dealings with the agent.
3. As to third parties who have had no prior dealings with agent, constructive notice by publication in a local paper will be sufficient.

Selected Problems from CPA Examinations on Agency

Subjective Questions and Answers*

Q. 1. John Barry, a world-famous golfer, represents Golf Cart Company, Inc., as a sales agent to promote sales of the Company's product, a golf cart. The Company sells a new type of golf cart, which it has named the "Barry Golf Cart," and it has commenced an extensive marketing campaign. As a part of this campaign the Company sends letters advertising the cart to presidents of golf clubs. In its letter the Company represents that the new cart "can be driven a full 18 holes of golf under any conditions" and that "the cart will not require any major repair for 2 years." Also in the letter, which is signed by John Barry as vice president in charge of sales promotion, there is a statement by John Barry that he "personally tested the cart and was delighted with its performance." Jones, a president of a golf club, bought a golf cart after reading the letter and corresponding with the Company to determine the model that best suited his needs. He now finds that the cart is totally unsatisfactory, since it continually breaks down when it is driven on the golf course. He has informed Barry that he intends to bring a suit for damages against both the Company and Barry in his individual capacity. However, he further states that if he could be sure that Golf Cart Company, Inc., is solvent, he would not sue Barry individually but would sue only the Company. To determine the Company's financial status, he asks Barry to secretly allow him access to the Company's financial records. Barry suspects that Jones may have other motives for wishing to secretly view the Company's records.

*See Introductory Note to Examination Questions, p. 21. This procedure is followed in all succeeding chapters.

Required

1. Explain the legal relationship that exists between Barry and Golf Cart Company, Inc.
2. What should Barry do with regard to arranging for Jones to secretly examine the Company's financial records to avoid a suit against himself individually?
3. What legal theory would support a suit brought by Jones against Golf Cart Company, Inc.? Describe the necessary elements to be proved to justify a recovery.
4. In the event that Barry is sued individually by Jones, what defense(s) is (are) available to him? Explain.

A. 1. The legal relationship which exists between Barry and Golf Cart Company, Inc. as a result of his acting as sales agent for the Company is an agency relationship. The relationship is consensual whereby Barry (the agent) has been authorized by the Company (the principal) to act for the Company and represent it in connection with its sales promotion campaign and Barry has agreed to do this. Although Barry is an employee of the Company, he is not merely a servant whose responsibility is restricted to routine work. Rather, he was hired to represent the Company as an agent and act on its behalf. Therefore, he has the power to act for the Company so long as he performs his duties within the scope of his authority and under the control of the Company.

2. Barry should not aid Jones. As an agent, Barry is a fiduciary and owes to his principal the duty of good faith and loyalty. He is prohibited from acting in any manner which would be contrary to the interests of his principal. Since Jones wishes to review the Company's books in secret and may have hidden motives for wanting to do this, helping him with such plans would be a breach of the duty which Barry owes to the Company. Barry should report the entire incident to the Company official who would have jurisdiction over this matter because an agent owes his principal the duty of conveying to him all information which may affect the principal.

3. The theory of warranty could support a suit brought by Jones against Golf Cart Company, Inc. The statements in the Company's letter concerning the durability of the cart could be found to be express representations concerning merchantability and fitness which were relied upon by the buyer and which became part of the basis of the bargain. In this case, such statements would be construed as express warranties made by the seller. To be express warranties, the statements must have been intended by the seller as warranties to induce the purchaser to purchase and the purchaser must have relied upon the statements. Mere statements of opinion or seller's puffing will not suffice. Whether or not the statements in the letter constituted express warranties will be determined from a reasonable interpretation of the language used in the seller's letter and in the light of all of the circumstances. However, even if an express warranty did not exist, an implied warranty of fitness would exist since the golf cart was sold for a particular purpose. Apparently Jones, the buyer, relied on the seller's judgment and the seller knows the purpose for which Jones intends to use the golf cart. A warranty that the cart will be fit for use on the golf course therefore exists. An implied warranty of merchantability would also exist because the seller is a merchant with respect to the goods being sold. The seller warranted that the golf cart was merchantable and free of latent defects.

4. Barry would have a defense if he were sued individually. Barry signed the letter as an agent for the Company so that his agency was disclosed. An agent will not be personally bound to a contract he signs on behalf of his company so long as the contract relates to the matter of the agency and is within the authority conferred upon the agent. It can be argued that there was no evidence of any intention to substitute or add the personal individual liability of Barry to that of the Company, his principal. In order to prevent himself from becoming a party to a contract, it is only necessary that an agent make it clear that he is acting solely in a representative capacity for a disclosed principal. The fact that the cart was named after Barry and that Barry stated in the letter that he "personally tested the cart and was delighted with its performance" should not have caused a reader of the letter to believe that he could rely on Barry individually as well as the Company if he was unsatisfied with the performance of the cart.

11/67

Q. 2. Harold Watts was employed by Superior Sporting Goods as a route salesman. His territory, route, and customers were determined by Superior. He was expected to work from 9:00 AM to 5:00 PM, Monday through

Friday. He received a weekly salary plus time and one-half for anything over 40 hours. He also received a small commission on sales which exceeded a stated volume. The customers consisted of sporting goods stores, department stores, athletic clubs, and large companies which had athletic programs or sponsored athletic teams. Watts used his personal car in making calls or, upon occasion, making a delivery where the customer was in a rush and the order was not large. Watts was reimbursed for the use of the car for company purposes. His instructions were to assume the customer is always right and to accommodate the customer where to do so would cost little and would build goodwill for the company and himself.

One afternoon while making a sales call and dropping off a case of softballs at the Valid Clock Company, the personnel director told Watts he was planning to watch the company's team play a game at a softball field located on the other side of town, but that his car would not start. Watts said, "Don't worry, it will be my pleasure to give you a lift and I would like to take in a few innings myself." Time was short and while on the way to the ballpark, Watts ran a light and collided with another car. The other car required $800 of repairs and the owner suffered serious bodily injury.

Required
Answer the following, setting forth reasons for any conclusions stated.

1. What is Superior's potential liability, if any, to the owner of the other car?
2. What is Valid's potential liability, if any, to the owner of the other car?

A. **1.** Superior Sporting Goods is liable for the negligence of its servant-agent Watts. The requisite control of his activities is apparent from the facts. Furthermore, based upon the instructions Watts received, it would appear that he was acting within the scope of his employment. In fact, one could conclude from the facts that Watts had express authority to make a trip such as the one he made when the accident occurred. He specifically was told to generally accommodate the customer where to do so would cost little and would build goodwill for the company and himself. This appears to be exactly what he did. Superior will undoubtedly attempt to assert the "independent frolic" doctrine and claim that Watts had abandoned his employment in order to pursue his own interests or pleasures. However, the deviation was not great, it took place during normal working hours, and, most importantly, was at the request of a customer and was a type of conduct Superior specifically encouraged.

2. Valid Clock Company has no liability. Its agent was not at fault, nor can it be reasonably argued that an agency relationship was created between itself and Watts because its personnel director accepted the ride offered by Watts. The requisite control of Watts' physical activities by Valid is not present.

11/78

Q. **3.** During your examination of the financial statements of the Ace Equipment Company you discover a problem relating to a sale.

Charles Jackson was one of Ace's best salesmen. The Company had placed him on a special incentive payment plan whereby he could double his salary if he doubled his sales volume. Jackson was very aggressive and used hard-sell techniques. He had an opportunity to sell 15 fork lifts to a cargo handling company, a sale that would put him over the top in his incentive plan. The cargo company insisted upon an express warranty that the particular fork lifts would handle 8,000 pounds safely. Jackson, without authority and knowing the lifts were only guaranteed to handle 7,000 pounds, represented that the equipment had an 8,000-pound capacity. He thought that the lifts probably were adequate. Ace Equipment neither authorized this express warranty nor was aware of Jackson's misrepresentation.

Two weeks after delivery of the fork lifts one of them gave way and dropped a carton containing computer equipment weighing 7,800 pounds. The cargo company seeks to return the fork lifts to Ace and to recover for the damage caused to the computer equipment. Ace refuses to refund the money for the fork lifts and denies liability for Jackson's misrepresentation.

Required

What are the rights of the cargo company against Ace Equipment? Explain.

A.   The cargo company can rescind the contract for a breach of warranty and/or fraud and obtain damages for injury to the computer equipment. A principal is liable for the misrepresentation made by his agent either on a warranty theory, in which case knowledge of falsity need not be proved, or on the tort of fraud where the agent has the requisite knowledge that his representation is false. Under both theories the cargo company may recover damages and rescind the contract.

11/70

Q. 4. Your examination of Fantastic Fan Co's financial statements discloses a problem relating to accounts payable.

James Williamson was one of Fantastic Fan's general purchasing agents. On August 11 the president of Fantastic Fan sent Williamson a lengthy memorandum indicating that storage space had become so costly that the Company was no longer prepared to purchase and store a large inventory of fans during the winter. The president stated that no further purchases were to be made. The Company had previously made such purchases when it could buy manufacturer close-outs at bargain prices.

Williamson glanced hurriedly at the memo but did not pay serious attention to it at the time. Unfortunately, he called upon one of the Company's leading suppliers of fans later on the same day and was offered 500 large fans at a substantial reduction. Williamson promptly accepted and signed an order for the 500 fans on Fantastic Fan's behalf. Williamson had made such purchases in previous years. Fantastic Fan, upon learning of the purchase, promptly notified the manufacturer that it canceled the order and denied liability, since Williamson had no authority to make the purchase.

Required

Is Fantastic Fan correct in its denial of liability? Explain.

A.   No. Although Williamson had no actual authority to make the contract, Fantastic Fan is liable on the basis of Williamson's apparent authority. This authority is based upon Williamson's position as a general purchasing agent and the fact that similar purchases had been made by Williamson in prior years. Limitations on an agent's usual authority are not binding on third parties who deal with the agent without knowledge or notice of such limitations.

11/70

Q. 5. Duval was the agent for Sunshine Pools, Inc. He sold pools, related equipment, and accessories for Sunshine. Holmes, president of Tilden Sporting Equipment, Inc., approached Duval and offered him an excellent deal on a commission basis if he would secretly sell their brand of diving boards and platforms instead of the Sunshine products. Duval agreed. The arrangement which was worked out between them was to have Duval continue to act as a general sales agent for Sunshine and concurrently act as the agent for an "undisclosed" principal in respect to Tilden diving boards. He could then sell both lines to new pool customers and go back to prior customers to solicit sales of the Tilden boards. Duval was not to mention his relationship with Tilden to the prospective customers, and of course, no mention of these facts would be made to Sunshine. Duval was told to use his discretion insofar as effectively misleading the prospective customers about whose diving board they were purchasing.

Things went smoothly for the first several months until Tilden began to manufacture and ship defective diving boards. Subsequently, Tilden became insolvent, and Holmes absconded with advance payments made by purchasers including those who had purchased from Duval.

Required

Answer the following, setting forth reasons for any conclusions stated.

1. What are the rights of the various customers against Duval?
2. What are the rights of the various customers against Tilden and/or Holmes?
3. What rights does Sunshine have against Duval?
4. What rights does Sunshine have against Tilden and/or Holmes?

A. 1. Duval has potential liability based upon two separate legal theories: the undisclosed principal doctrine and the theory of fraud. Duval led the customers to believe that the diving boards were Sunshine products. Thus, at a minimum, he would not be disclosing his true principal, or he may have been intentionally misstating the facts so as to make it appear that the purchaser was obtaining all Sunshine products. The rule is clear that an agent is personally liable on the contracts when acting for an undisclosed principal. Thus, the customers can sue Duval and recover on this basis. Alternatively, fraud may be asserted, and if proved, liability will attach in that the agent is responsible for his torts even though committed in an agency capacity.

2. Tilden, an undisclosed principal, is liable for the contracts made for and on its behalf even though its identity was not initially disclosed. Furthermore, Tilden would be liable for the tort of conversion committed by Holmes who absconded with advance payments made by purchasers. Tilden also would be liable for breach of warranty with respect to defective goods delivered to the various customers. Finally, Holmes would be personally liable for the conversion of the customers' advance payments.

3. Duval has breached his fiduciary duty by selling a competing item without his principal's knowledge and consent. Therefore, he can be dismissed, and he can be required to account for any profits he has realized as a result of his breach of contract and trust.

4. Sunshine could proceed against Tilden based upon Tilden's intentional interference with a contractual relationship. This well-recognized tort occurs, as it did here, when a party intends to induce the breach of a contract or interfere with the performance of a contract (here the Sunshine-Duval contract) with the knowledge of the existence of that contract and the belief that such breach or interference will follow. In addition, Sunshine would have an action against Holmes personally as a result of his tortious conduct even though Holmes acted in his capacity as president of Tilden.

11/77

Practice Questions*

Q. 1. Peter, a minor, engaged his brother-in-law, Allen, as his agent for the purchase of a used sports car from Tom. Allen knew that Peter was a minor, and that Tom did not know this, but made the purchase to accommodate Peter. He acted without compensation and with a written authorization to make the purchase. At the time of the sale Allen exhibited the authorization to the seller and signed the contract in such a way as to clearly indicate he was acting in an agency capacity. Peter, after driving the car for several days, decided he could obtain a better deal elsewhere. He disaffirmed the contract, stopped all payments, and returned the car to Tom.

Required

Tom seeks to hold Peter or Allen to the contract. May he do so? Explain.

Q. 2. Rapid Delivery Service, Inc., hired Dolson as one of its truck drivers. Dolson was carefully selected and trained by Rapid. He was specifically instructed to obey all traffic and parking rules and regulations. One day while

---

*See Introductory Note to Practice Examination Questions, p. 29.

making a local delivery, Dolson double parked and went into a nearby customer's store. In doing so, he prevented a car legally parked at the curb from leaving. The owner of the parked car, Charles, proceeded to blow the horn of the truck repeatedly. Charles was doing this when Dolson returned from his delivery. As a result of a combination of several factors, particularly Charles' telling him to "move it" and that he was "acting very selfishly and in an unreasonable manner," Dolson punched Charles in the nose, severely fracturing it. When Charles sought to restrain him, Dolson punched Charles again, this time fracturing his jaw. Charles has commenced legal action against Rapid.

Required

Answer the following, setting forth reasons for any conclusions stated.

1. Will Charles prevail?
2. What liability, if any, would Dolson have?

Q. 3. On October 1 Great Puppet Shows, Inc., hired Mandrake as its new purchasing agent. The Company knew that Puppetland Corp. was interested in selling certain stage scenery and props, but it believed that it could purchase the property for less money if it did not disclose its identity. Therefore, it instructed Mandrake to drive over to Puppetland's office the next day and negotiate for the purchase of the property in his own name, without disclosing the Company's identity. Mandrake was authorized to spend up to $5,000.

On October 2 Mandrake negotiated and signed a contract with Puppetland for the purchase of the property for $4,500 and for delivery and payment on October 15.

After signing the contract, Mandrake began to drive back to the Company office. On the way he stopped at a bar for a few drinks, which he knew was in violation of a Company policy, which prohibited drinking of alcoholic beverages during working hours. After becoming intoxicated, he left the bar and began driving to the office. En route he negligently struck and killed a pedestrian. Upon learning these facts, the Company immediately discharged Mandrake, who then advised Puppetland that when he signed the contract in his own name he was really doing so for his former employer's benefit and that he wanted nothing more to do with the contract.

Required

1. Does Puppetland have the right to enforce the contract against the Company? State "yes" or "no" and discuss.
2. Does Puppetland have the right to enforce the contract against Mandrake? State "yes" or "no" and discuss.
3. Does the Company have the right to enforce the contract against Puppetland? State "yes" or "no" and discuss.
4. Does the pedestrian's estate have a right to recover against Mandrake and Great Puppet? State "yes" or "no" and discuss.
5. Does the Company have a right to recover against Mandrake if it incurs any liability to the pedestrian's estate? State "yes" or "no" and discuss.

Q. 4. In the course of your examination of the financial statements of Higgins Electronics, Inc., for the year ended March 31, 1971, you learned of a claim for $75,000 that James Ladd had made against the Company. Your investigation disclosed that the Company wanted to purchase some valuable used electronic equipment from Ladd, a competitor. The Company hired Lemmon to make the purchase in his name and instructed him not to disclose that he was acting for the Company. Lemmon signed a contract in his own name to purchase the equipment from Ladd for $75,000, with delivery and payment to be made 30 days later. Before the payment date the Company learned of a major technological breakthrough in electronic equipment and decided to buy new equipment that incorporated the discovery. Lemmon was instructed immediately to neither pay for nor accept delivery of the used equipment. When Ladd learned subsequently that the Company was Lemmon's principal, he sued the Company for breach of contract. The Company defended, contending that it was not liable to Ladd because (a) Ladd intended to contract with Lemmon only and (b) recovery was barred because Ladd discovered the identity of the Company after the contract was executed.

Required
1. Discuss the validity of each defense asserted by your client, Higgins Electronics, Inc.
2. Discuss the extent of Lemmon's liability to Ladd

Q. 5. On January 1, 1963, Baker loaned Able $1,000. Able owned a painting for which the X Museum had offered $2,000. On January 20, 1963, Able gave Baker a writing by which Baker is given the authority, in case of nonpayment of the loan by March 31, 1963, to sell the painting to the X Museum for $2,000 and to retain out of the proceeds the amount of the loan. He was to pay the surplus to Able. On April 1, 1963, Able informed Baker that at that time he could not repay the loan and that the authority to sell the painting was revoked. On the same day, Able informed the curator of the X Museum that the painting was not for sale. On April 4, 1963, Baker showed the written authorization to the curator, and they executed a sale of the painting for $2,000.

Required
1. Does Able have any remedy against Baker for selling the painting? Explain.
2. Does Able have any remedy against the Museum for buying the painting? Explain.

Practice Objective Questions

Instructions 1–10
Select the *best* answer for each of the following items. Mark only one answer for *each* item. Answer all items. Your grade will be based on your total correct answers.

1. Dolby was employed as an agent for the Ace Used Car Company to purchase newer model used cars. His authority was limited by a $3,000 maximum price for any car. A wholesaler showed him a 1938 classic car which was selling for $5,000. The wholesaler knew that Ace only dealt in newer model used cars and that Dolby had never paid more than $3,000 for any car. Dolby bought the car for Ace, convinced that it was worth at least $7,000. When he reported this to Williams, Ace's owner, Williams was furious but he nevertheless authorized processing of the automobile for resale. Williams also began pricing the car with antique car dealers who indicated that the current value of the car was $4,800. Williams called the wholesaler, told him that Dolby had exceeded his authority, that he was returning the car, and that he was demanding repayment of the purchase price. What is the wholesaler's *best* defense in the event of a lawsuit?
   a. Dolby had apparent authority to purchase the car.
   b. Dolby's purchase was effectively ratified by Ace.
   c. Dolby had express authority to purchase the car.
   d. Dolby had implied authority to purchase the car.

2. Halliday engaged Fox as her agent. It was mutually agreed that Fox would *not* disclose that he was acting as Halliday's agent. Instead he was to deal with prospective customers as if he were a principal acting on his own behalf. This he did and made several contracts for Halliday. Assuming Halliday, Fox, or the customer seeks to avoid liability on one of the contracts involved, which of the following statements is correct?
   a. The third party may choose to hold either Fox or Halliday liable.
   b. The third party can avoid liability because he believed he was dealing with Fox as a principal.
   c. Halliday must ratify the Fox contracts in order to be held liable.
   d. Fox has *no* liability once he discloses that Halliday was the real principal.

3. Futterman operated a cotton factory and employed Marra as a general purchasing agent to travel through the southern states to purchase cotton. Futterman telegraphed Marra instructions from day to day as to the price to be paid for cotton. Marra entered a cotton district in which she had not previously done business and represented that she was purchasing cotton for Futterman. Although directed by Futterman to pay no more than 25 cents a pound, Marra bought cotton from Anderson at 30 cents a pound, which was the prevailing offering price at that time. Futterman refused to take the cotton. Under these circumstances, which of the following is correct?

    a. The negation of actual authority to make the purchase effectively eliminates any liability for Futterman.

    b. Futterman is *not* liable on the contract.

    c. Marra has *no* potential liability.

    d. Futterman is liable on the contract.

4. Wilcox works as a welder for Miracle Muffler, Inc. He was specially trained by Miracle in the procedures and safety precautions applicable to installing replacement mufflers on automobiles. One rule of which he was aware involved a prohibition against installing a muffler on any auto which had heavily congealed oil or grease or which had any leaks. Wilcox disregarded this rule, and as a result an auto caught fire causing extensive property damage and injury to Wilcox. Which of the following statements is correct?

    a. Miracle is *not* liable because its rule prohibited Wilcox from installing the muffler in question.

    b. Miracle is *not* liable to Wilcox under the workmen's compensation laws.

    c. Miracle is liable irrespective of its efforts to prevent such an occurrence and the fact that it exercised reasonable care.

    d. Wilcox does *not* have any personal liability for the loss because he was acting for and on behalf of his employer.

5. Star Corporation dismissed Moon, its purchasing agent. Star published a notice in appropriate trade journals which stated: "This is to notify all parties concerned that Moon is no longer employed by Star Corporation, and the corporation assumes no further responsibility for his acts." Moon called on several of Star's suppliers with whom he had previously dealt, and when he found one who was unaware of his dismissal, he placed a substantial order for merchandise to be delivered to a warehouse in which Moon rented space. Star had rented space in the warehouse in the past when its storage facilities were crowded. Moon also called on several suppliers with whom Star had never dealt and made purchases from them on open account in the name of Star. The merchandise purchased by Moon was delivered to the warehouse. Moon then sold all the merchandise and absconded with the money. Which of the following most accurately describes the legal implications of this situation?

    a. Moon had apparent authority to make contracts on Star's behalf with suppliers with whom Moon was currently dealing as Star's agent if they had *no* actual knowledge of his dismissal.

    b. The suppliers who previously had *no* dealings with Star can enforce the contracts against Star if the suppliers had *no* actual knowledge of Moon's lack of authority.

    c. Star is liable on the Moon contracts to all suppliers who had dealt with Moon in the past as Star's agent and who have *not* received personal notice, even though they had read the published notice.

    d. Constructive notice by publication in the appropriate trade journals is an effective notice to all third parties regardless of whether they had previously dealt with Moon or read the notice.

6. Brian purchased an electric typewriter from Robert under a written contract. The contract provided that Robert retained title until the purchase price was fully paid and granted him the right to repossess the typewriter if Brian failed to make any of the required ten payments. Arthur, an employee of Robert, was instructed to repossess the machine on the basis that Brian had defaulted in making the third payment. Arthur took possession of the typewriter and delivered it to Robert. It was then discovered that Brian was not in default. Which of the following conclusions is supported by the above facts?

    a. Arthur is *not* liable to Brian.

    b. Brian can sue either or both Arthur and Robert for damages, but can collect only once.

    c. Neither party is liable since it was apparently an honest mistake.

    d. If Arthur is sued and must pay the judgment obtained against him, he has *no* rights against Robert.

7. Harper was employed as a carpenter by the Ace Construction Company. He negligently constructed a scaffold at one of Ace's construction sites. The scaffold collapsed and injured Dirks (a fellow employee), Franklin (a supplier), and Harper.

    a. Ace Construction Company is *not* liable to Franklin if Harper disobeyed specific instructions regarding construction of the scaffold.

    b. Ace Construction Company is liable to Franklin even though Harper was grossly negligent.

    c. Harper is *not* personally liable to Dirks or Franklin.

    d. Harper *cannot* obtain workmen's compensation.

8. Under which of the following circumstances will an agent acting on behalf of a disclosed principal *not* be liable to a third party for his actions?

a. He signs a negotiable instrument in his own name and does *not* indicate his agency capacity.

b. He commits a tort in the course of discharging his duties.

c. He is acting for a nonexistent principal which subsequently comes into existence after the time of the agent's actions on the principal's behalf.

d. He lacks specific express authority but is acting within the scope of his implied authority.

9. In order to hold the principal liable under the ratification doctrine for the unauthorized act of a party purporting to act as his agent

   a. The principal need *not* have been in existence at the time the contract was made.

   b. The purported agent must have been acting for an undisclosed principal.

   c. The principal must have full knowledge of the facts regarding the action taken on his behalf.

   d. The ratification must be in writing and made within a reasonable time after the unauthorized action was taken on his behalf.

10. Badger Corporation engaged Donald Keller as one of its sales representatives to sell automotive parts. Keller signed an employment contract that required him to obtain home-office approval on any contract in excess of $500 entered into by Keller on Badger's behalf. The industry custom and most of Badger's agents had authority to make such contracts if they did *not* exceed $1,000. Keller signed a contract on Badger's behalf with Zolar Garages, Inc., for $850. Badger rejected the contract and promptly notified Zolar of its decision. Under these circumstances:

    a. Keller is a *del credere* agent.

    b. Keller did *not* have express authority to make the Zolar contract.

    c. Keller had the implied authority to make the contract.

    d. Badger's prompt disaffirmance of Keller's action retroactively terminated any liability it might have had.

CHAPTER

3

Partnerships and Joint Ventures

AICPA Content Specification Outline

Formation and Existence
Liabilities and Authority of Partners and Joint Owners
Allocation of Profit or Loss
Transfer of Interest
Termination, Winding Up, and Dissolution

Contents

I. Formation, Existence, and Characteristics
   A. Partnership defined
   B. Types of partnership
   C. Methods for creation and determination of partnership existence
   D. Distinctive features of a partnership
   E. Comparison of partnership and corporation
   F. Capacity to be a partner

I. Formation, Existence, and Characteristics

A. Partnership defined: The Uniform Partnership Act (UPA) is a uniform statute adopted by virtually all states. The UPA defines partnership as "an association of two or more persons to carry on as co-owners a business for profit." To carry on a business covers almost every trade, occupation, or profession, but does not include passive co-ownership of property. Parts I to VI of this chapter deal exclusively with the UPA's rules applicable to a general partnership unless otherwise specifically indicated.

B. Types of partnerships:

1. General: created for usual partnership purposes. Older law made a distinction between trading and nontrading partnerships in relation to the partner's apparent authority to bind the partnership. Whatever remains of this distinction is today based upon commercial versus professional or service partnerships. The scope of apparent authority would be based upon this distinction rather than the trading versus nontrading status since the older distinction has been all but obliterated by modern business practice. The nontrading or now the professional or service partner is said to have less apparent authority than the general partner of a commercial partnership.

2. Limited partnership (see VII, p. 68).

3. Joint ventures (see VII, p. 69).

4. Partnership liability by estoppel (see below, C.3).

C. Methods for creation and determination of partnership existence:

1. By express contract

a. May be written or oral. A writing is needed only when the Statute of Frauds applies. (See Contracts, p. 149, III.E.2). Such is not generally the case except for contracts, "which by their terms cannot be performed within one year from the date of the making thereof." Most partnerships do not have a fixed duration. Further, the partnership may be dissolved as a result of numerous factors which may occur within less than a year. Hence, a written agreement is not usually required.

b. Articles of partnership or the partnership agreement. Obviously, it is best to have an express written agreement between or among the partners. It should be express in order to determine the partners' rights and duties, to avoid UPA presumptions, and for tax purposes. It should be written in order to avoid disputes and for proof purposes in the event of such disputes.

2. Implied from the facts and actions of the parties involved (e.g., sharing profits and losses and joint management).

a. Under the UPA, receipt of a share of the profits of a business by a person raises a presumption that he is a partner. However, if payments are for services rendered, interest on loans, payment of debts, as annuity to a widow of a deceased partner, as rent to a landlord, and so on, the presumption of a partnership no longer holds.

      b. Receipt of gross returns does not in itself establish a partnership.

      c. To be protected against liability, an employee should request provisions in her contract for employment which make her legal status clear. For example, she should clearly be designated as an employee, indicate that payments or remuneration is salary no matter what form it takes and employee is in no way to be held out as a partner.

   3. By estoppel: The UPA contains an alternate method to the above methods of determination of partnership liability. The key difference between the above determinations of partnership and partner status is that in the above [(1) and (2)] the parties are, in fact, partners for sharing in profits and loss and other legal incidents of partnership participation; whereas here there is no such relationship. The party labeled a partner by estoppel (or ostensible partner) is treated as such only for the purpose of imposition of liability.

      a. Partnership by estoppel is an equitable doctrine to prevent injustice to one who has relied upon a misrepresentation by not allowing the misrepresentor to deny the truth of the assertion he has expressly or implicitly made.

      b. May be liable as partners regardless of whether or not they have an actual interest in the business.

      c. The relationship will be imposed upon a party where such party either misrepresents his status as a partner or expressly or impliedly "consents" to another holding such person out as a partner, such as by allowing his name to be used.

D. Distinctive features of a general partnership:

   1. Voluntary association of persons as individuals; not considered a separate entity for most purposes.

   2. Organized by simple agreement without governmental sanction; must be for a legal purpose and licensed if this is required.

   3. Fiduciary relationship among the partners.

   4. Co-ownership: Each partner has a proprietary interest in the subject matter of the partnership (tenancy in partnership).

   5. Association must be for profit.

   6. Mutual agency of partners: Each partner is agent for the others and for the partnership in respect to all transactions "within the scope of the partnership business." Agreement can also be inferred from conduct.

   7. Joint and several liability for partner's tortious acts and breach of trust, e.g., misapplication of funds; joint liability for all other debts and obligations of the partnership, e.g., breach of contract.

E. Comparison with the corporation regarding:

   1. Initial expense. (Corporations' initial charges and fees may be greater.)

   2. Liabilities for debts of the business. (Stockholders of corporations have limited liability.)

   3. Liability of owners of the business for the acts of one another. (Corporations normally have no liability for the acts of individual stockholders, nor stockholders for each other.)

4. Continuity of existence and effect of death, bankruptcy, or sale of one's interest in business. (Corporation, being a separate legal entity, is not affected by the death, bankruptcy, or transfer of stockholder's interest.)

5. Necessity of obtaining permission to do business from governmental agencies. (Corporation cannot come into existence without state approval; normally, however, approval is routinely granted.)

6. Right to practice a profession. Special statutes in most states permit professional corporations, e.g., medicine, law, and accounting.

7. Advantages of partnership:
   a. Less formality necessary for partnership action; normally greater equality and control of business by partners.
   b. Possibly a lighter tax burden in that the partnership is not itself a taxable entity and the income (or loss) is reported and taxed via inclusion in the individual partner's return.
   c. Relative freedom from public supervision.
   d. Freedom to unite professional skills in fields forbidden to corporations in some states (e.g., to practice law).
   e. Theoretically greater borrowing power in that partners are personally liable for firm debts.

F. Capacity to be a partner:
   1. Generally, any person who is competent to make a contract (see Contracts, p. 147).
      a. Infants: May become partners; however, have right to disaffirm; but may not withdraw investment after debts are incurred unless remaining assets are sufficient to pay such debts. Only liability to amount of capital contribution.
      b. Corporations:
         (1) A corporation may serve as a general partner in most jurisdictions; this right has been conferred on corporations in those jurisdictions by a grant of specific authority.
         (2) Capacity, in absence of specific authority conferred by state corporation laws, is lacking.
         (3) May be liable as a partner by estoppel.

II. Partnership Property

A. Firm name:
   1. May consist of actual names of partners.
   2. May consist of fictitious or assumed names; however, statutes will usually require filing of certificate that discloses the true names of the partners.
   3. May not be such as to mislead the public. Statutes provide:
      a. That no person may conduct business in the name of a partner not associated with the firm, except where an established business continues in existence and the name of a former partner is retained.
      b. That when the designation "and Company," "and Co.," or similar designation is used, it must represent an actual partner, except where a preexisting firm or corporation discontinuing business consents to the use of its name.

    4. In most states partners must sue or be sued in their individual names.

        a. Common Law so provides, and a partnership is not a legal entity for this purpose.

        b. Statutes in some states permit partnership to sue or be sued in the firm name or in the name of a specified officer.

    5. Firm can hold property in the firm name and is considered a legal entity for this particular purpose. This is the Uniform Partnership Act rule, which is contrary to the common law.

B. Good will: reputation for honesty, efficiency, and fairness that a firm builds up in the eyes of the business world.

C. Capital contributions:

    1. Aggregate of individual contributions in money or property contributed by partners to the partnership.

    2. Distinguished from partnership property in regard to:

        a. Amount: Capital is an agreed amount whereas property continually varies in amount.

        b. Undivided profits. Capital does not necessarily include them, while property does.

        c. Distribution upon dissolution: Capital is repayable in proportion to amounts contributed; property is not necessarily so distributed.

D. Partnership property includes:

    1. All property originally brought into the partnership or subsequently acquired on account of the partnership.

    2. Property acquired with partnership funds unless a contrary intent appears.

    3. Undivided profits.

III. Rights, Duties, and Liabilities of Partners to One Another

A. Partnership Act presumptions. Unless the partnership agreement provides otherwise, the following rules apply:

    1. Profits and losses are shared equally by the parties.

    2. Partners are indemnified for payments made, or personal liability reasonably assumed, in behalf of the partnership.

    3. A partner who makes an advance beyond his or her agreed contribution is entitled to interest from the date of the advance; on the capital contribution, however, he or she is only entitled to interest from the date when repayment thereof should have been made.

    4. Partners have equal rights in management and conduct of partnership business.

    5. No partner is entitled to salary for acting in partnership affairs.

B. Other rights and duties:

    1. A partner is accountable as a fiduciary to the partnership and must exercise good faith and loyalty to the firm interests.

    2. Partners must exercise reasonable skill and enterprise in conducting firm business.

3. Right to be informed: Whether he takes an active part or not, a partner has a right to be informed particularly as to firm's operations.

4. Right to an accounting: A partner is entitled to a formal accounting as to partnership affairs whenever circumstances render an accounting just and reasonable.

   a. A demand for an accounting is usually, but not necessarily, joined with a demand for a dissolution. However, one cannot have a dissolution without an accounting, because dissolution is followed by distribution, which requires an accounting.

   b. Generally available when partnership agreement so provides, when a partner is excluded from partnership business or when some other irregularity occurs, an accounting is a comprehensive investigation of partnership transactions and a determination of the rights of partners.

5. A partner has a right of access to firm's books and records, which, in absence of a contrary agreement, are kept at principal place of business.

6. A partner has the right to return of capital upon dissolution after partnership property has been applied to partnership debts.

C. Property rights of a partner in specific partnership property. The partner is a co-owner of specific property. This type of ownership is called a **tenancy in partnership,** and it has the following legal incidents:

1. Right to possess and use property for partnership purposes.

2. Right to participate in management not assignable without consent of all partners. However, partner's right to share in profits and receive a share upon dissolution of partnership is assignable. Dissolution only occurs if both the assignee and assignor withdraw; until withdrawal the assignor remains liable as a partner.

3. Partner's right to specific partnership property is not subject to attachment or execution on the basis of partner's personal liability to third persons.

4. Remaining partners have survivorship rights in a deceased partner's interest in specific partnership property. However, remaining partners must account to the deceased partner's estate for his partnership interest, which consists of his share of profits and capital.

   a. Although rights to profit and capital pass to deceased partner's estate, right of management does not.

   b. Partner's interest in partnership's real or personal property is considered to be personal property.

IV. Liability to Third Parties

A. Mutual agency of partners:

1. **Each partner is an agent** of the partnership and for every other partner, and **while acting within actual or apparent scope of partnership business,** he or she binds the other parties. (E.g., a partner who receives payment, although misapplying funds, binds partnership to payment.) **Agreements among partners limiting their powers are not binding on third parties unless they have knowledge of them.**

a. (1) Any partner in a trading partnership may purchase a customary amount of goods on credit and bind the partnership regardless of his or her actual authority.

(2) Agents or employees hired by a partner may assume that the partner was authorized to hire them.

(3) Partnership is liable to an innocent party from whom a partner borrowed money on behalf of the firm.

b. Acts of a partner that are not apparently for the carrying on of the partnership business in a usual way do not bind the partnership unless authorized by the other partners.

(1) No partner has power to bind the firm on accommodation paper or contracts of suretyship or guaranty unless expressly authorized, or in furtherance of firm business.

(2) No partner has power to make a gift of partnership property.

(3) A conveyance made by one partner of real property held in the firm name may be rescinded by the firm unless it has been subsequently resold to a *bona fide* purchaser for value. However, where there is a conveyance of firm property that has only the name of the conveyor on record (with no indication of rights of partnership), title passes to an innocent purchaser for value.

c. Liability of partnership begins when it is actually formed, although articles of partnership are not executed until later.

d. Majority of partners can control ordinary decisions of business, but fundamental changes (e.g., change from retail to wholesale selling) require unanimous consent. Also, the following acts require unanimous consent unless there is an abandonment of the firm business.

(1) Assigning partnership property in trust for creditors.

(2) Confessing a judgment.

(3) Submitting a claim to arbitration.

(4) Disposing of good will of the business.

(5) Doing any act that makes it impossible to carry on ordinary business of partnership (e.g., selling out entire stock).

(6) Admission of a new partner.

(7) Partnership agreement may change the above (e.g., management voice determined by amount of capital contribution).

2. Tort liability of partners: **General partners are liable for torts committed during the course of the partnership.**

3. Criminal liability of partners: Partners are not liable for crimes committed by other partners unless they themselves participated, planned, aided, or acquiesced in their commission.

4. A deceased partner's estate is liable for firm debts incurred while she was a partner.

5. An incoming partner, under the Uniform Partnership Act, is liable for pre-existing firm obligations only to the extent of his capital contribution. At common law he would not be liable even to this extent.

a. He may, however, become personally liable by assumption or novation.

6. A retiring partner is liable to creditors for existing debts of the partnership, but not for those incurred after retirement, so long as creditors had notice of the retirement before extending the credit.

7. No person can become a member of a partnership without the consent of all the partners unless the partnership agreement provides otherwise.

8. **Partner's liability is personal; extends to all personal assets, not just investment in partnership, for all debts and liabilities of the partnership.**

9. Partnership assets must be exhausted before partner's individual assets may be reached by creditors.

V. Transfer of Partnership Interest

A. In general. At common law, any change in the membership of the partnership resulted in the dissolution of the partnership. Any addition, loss, or substitution of a partner dissolved the partnership. Under the UPA, or under the partnership agreement, current law provides for different ways of treating dissolutions.

B. Incoming partner: brought about by any one of three methods:
   1. By negotiation with the full partnership, without the loss of a partner, with an appropriate contribution of capital by the new partner.
   2. By a new partner who purchases the interest of an old partner.
      a. Any partner may sell his interest at any time under the Uniform Partnership Act.
      b. However, the purchaser does not become a partner until full consent is given by the partnership.

C. Liability of the new partner.
   1. Unless otherwise agreed, a new partner is not liable for prior debts of the partnership, except to the extent of his investment in the partnership.
   2. Occasionally, someone who is a new partner will be held under an estoppel theory to be liable to prior creditors as if he were already a partner, because of his past dealing with the creditors as if a partner, or use of his name in the name of the partnership.

D. Outgoing partner. There are two usual ways by which a partner leaves a partnership:
   1. Sale or disposal of his interest in the partnership to a new partner, or to the partnership as a whole.
   2. Death or disability of the partner.

E. Liability of outgoing partner upon sale or other disposition.
   1. New creditors after the disposal: Outgoing partner is not personally liable to *new creditors* under the UPA if he places a notice as to his departure in an appropriate local newspaper.
   2. Existing creditors of the partnership.
      a. The existing creditors continue to have a claim against the assets of the partnership and the other partners.
      b. The personal liability of the outgoing partner continues for debts incurred before his departure, and for debts after his departure unless there is actual notice.

    c. Typically, the party acquiring the outgoing partner's interest agrees as a condition of the sale of the interest to assume the obligations of the outgoing partner.

    d. The outgoing partner may seek a release from existing creditors.

VI. Dissolution, Termination, and Winding Up of the Partnership

A. Definition: The UPA defines "dissolution" as "the change in relation of the partners caused by any partner ceasing to be associated in the carrying on, as distinguished from the winding up, of the business." Note that dissolution generally does not result in the termination of the partnership's business. Usually, a new partnership is formed, with the remaining partners carrying on the same business. However, in some circumstances, the partners may decide to terminate or "wind up" the business of the partnership.

B. Voluntary dissolution: brought about by agreement of partners, either in original agreement or by subsequent agreement.

    1. Where partnership provided for a definite term, which has expired, partners may continue in partnership for an indicated term by agreement, or, if the parties continue without agreement, it is a partnership at will.

C. Dissolution by operation of law (involuntary) occurs:

    1. Upon death of a partner. Unless partnership agreement specifically provides to the contrary there will also be a winding up of partnership affairs.

    2. Upon bankruptcy of a partner or of the partnership.

    3. When partnership enterprise becomes illegal or participation by a partner becomes illegal.

    4. When, upon the outbreak of war, partners are citizens of enemy countries.

    5. Upon the withdrawal and retirement by a partner either in accordance with the term fixed or before the time fixed by agreement; however, if withdrawal is before time fixed, the partner is liable for breach of contract.

        a. Assignment of interest in a partnership by one partner will not dissolve the partnership since the assignee does not become a partner nor displace the liability of the assigning partner.

        b. When a new partner is admitted into an existing partnership, business may be continued without liquidation of the affairs of the previous partnership, but the former partnership is dissolved.

    6. Upon application by a partner, a judicial decree of dissolution must be granted when:

        a. A partner is shown to be of unsound mind, or

        b. A partner is shown to be permanently incapacitated so that he cannot conduct his duties, or

        c. There is misconduct sufficiently serious so as to affect prejudicially the success of the business, or

        d. The business is a failure (i.e., conducted at a heavy loss so that further activities would be futile), or

        e. There is any situation that would make it equitable to do so (e.g., such lack of harmony as to jeopardize the partnership profitability).

D. Expulsion: Unless otherwise provided by agreement, no partner can be expelled; however, a similar result may be achieved by dissolving the partnership and forming a new one excluding the undesirable partner.

E. Death or disability of a partner:

1. When a partner dies, the partnership is automatically dissolved.
2. If a partner becomes disabled, the partnership may be dissolved by court order.
3. However, since the remaining partners generally wish to continue the business, the partnership agreement often provides for procedure in case of dissolution by death or disability.
   a. The partnership agreement may provide that the survivors take all, and the business continue.
   b. The agreement may provide that the remaining partners purchase the deceased partner's share, either at a price set by the agreement, or by appraisal.
   c. The agreement may provide that the deceased partner's estate will remain in the partnership as a sort of limited partner, liable only to the extent of the assets invested.

F. Effect of dissolution:

1. Dissolution generally does not lead to termination of the enterprise and winding up.
2. Dissolution is more like a signal that an event has occurred that *could* lead to termination and winding up, but need not.
3. Generally, the partnership agreement contains provisions which will apply in case of dissolution, under which the remaining partners may elect to make any settlements necessary and continue the enterprise, or terminate and wind up the enterprise.

G. Effect of termination and winding up:

1. Partners have no authority to conduct new business.
2. Partners are trustees for the purpose of winding up affairs of the firm and should proceed to:
   a. Discharge the firm debts, and
   b. Distribute remaining assets, or
   c. Court may appoint a receiver when partners disagree as to proper distribution.
3. Disposition of the firm name on dissolution.
   a. If there is no provision, any partner may use it, so long as public is not misled (see p. 61, II.A.3.a).
   b. Right to use the firm name may be sold as a business asset.
   c. Retiring partner may give or sell the right to continue to use his or her name in the firm name.
   d. Court may order sale of assets upon death of partner, and the firm name must then be accounted for.

H. Order of distribution of firm assets of a general partnership (order is different for limited partnership). Do not confuse them (see p. 69, VII.E):

1. Firm (i.e., partnership) assets in order of priority:
   a. To firm creditors other than partners.
   b. To partners for liabilities other than for capital and profits.
   c. To partners for liabilities arising from capital contributions made by them after allocation of losses, if any.
   d. To partners for liabilities arising from undistributed profits of the firm.
2. Where there are insufficient firm assets, **partners are personally liable for firm debts.**
   a. Each partner must contribute toward the losses (including capital loss) according to his share in profits.
      (1) Profits and surplus in absence of agreement will be distributed in equal proportions after all liabilities, including those to partners, are satisfied.
   b. Marshaling of assets (equitable doctrine):
      (1) Firm assets must first be made available for payment of firm debts; surplus, if any, goes toward payment of individual partner's debts to the extent of his partnership interest.
      (2) Personal assets of a partner are applied to his personal debts; surplus, if any, goes toward payment of firm debts.

I. Where business is conducted after dissolution, a new partnership is formed and old creditors become creditors of the new partnership.

VII. Limited Partnership

A. Definition: a partnership formed pursuant to a statute (not recognized at common law) and consisting of one or more general partners, jointly and severally liable as ordinary partners, and by whom the business is conducted and one or more special or limited partners who contribute capital to the common fund, *but who do not manage the firm business,* and who are not liable for debts of the partnership beyond the amount they contributed.

B. The Uniform Limited Partnership Act (ULPA), adopted in a majority of states, requires that:

1. A certificate signed and sworn to by all parties must be filed, recorded, and published, and must contain:
   a. The name of the firm and the address of its principal place of business.
   b. The general nature of the partnership business and its duration.
   c. The names, residences, and capital contributions of each partner.
   d. The method for determining changes of personnel and continuance of business in the event of death or retirement of general partners.
2. There must be at least one general partner.
3. Contributions of limited partners can be in cash or property, but cannot consist of services.
4. Firm name cannot contain name of limited partner unless it is the same as that of a general partner.

5. In absence of statutory restriction, the limited partnership may carry on any business that a general partnership may carry on.

C. Rights of limited partner: in general, the same rights (except in management) as a general partner. He has the right:

1. To receive profits and compensation as provided in the agreement.
2. To have books kept at principal place of business, to inspect the books and formal accounts, and to make copies of them.
3. To demand a formal accounting whenever the circumstances warrant.
4. To obtain return of capital contribution upon withdrawal, subject to creditors' rights.
5. To have a dissolution and winding up by a decree of a court of competent jurisdiction.

D. Restrictions on limited partner (determined by statute):

1. Limited partner will be held liable as a general partner:
  a. Where she takes an active part in the business.
  b. Where she interferes in management.
  c. Where she permits her name to be used in the firm name.
  d. In some states, as a result of the withdrawal of any part of the sum contributed by a limited partner, either as dividends, profits, or otherwise, at any time during the continuance of partnership. In most states, such withdrawal merely renders limited partner liable to restore the sums withdrawn with interest.

E. Order of distribution of assets after dissolution provided for by the ULPA:

1. To creditors in order of priority as provided by law.
2. To limited partners in respect to their share of undistributed profits and other compensation by way of income on their contributions.
3. To limited partners in respect to their capital contributions.
4. To general partners other than for capital and profits.
5. To general partners in respect to profits of the firm.
6. To general partners in respect to capital contributions.

F. The utility of a limited partnership:

1. It secures the advantages of corporate liability for investors in business organizations that cannot conveniently incorporate.
2. Certain tax advantages: treated the same as a general partnership for tax purposes, i.e., not recognized as a separate taxable entity.
3. Firm name need not disclose that there is a limited partnership.

VIII. Joint Ventures

A. General observations:

1. The overwhelming opinion by commentators and judges who have considered the question of whether joint ventures are partnerships is affirmative.
2. Extensive text coverage of the joint venture is not readily available since it is treated the same as any other partnership for most purposes. However, recent

notoriety and use of this vehicle for multimillion dollar undertakings have apparently caused accountants to come in contact with the joint venture which, therefore, requires a rudimentary knowledge of this business organization.

3. In the popular sense, joint venture is not limited to use of the partnership as the *modus operandi*. The term is also used in connection with the use of a "subsidiary" corporation formed by two or more corporations or other participants to carry out a combined adventure.

B. Definitions:

1. "The joint venture is an association of two or more persons (including entities) to carry out one or more transactions for profit or for commercial gain or benefit."*

2. "A joint venture is an association created by co-owners of a business undertaking, differing from partnership (if at all) in having a more limited scope. In all important respects, the joint venture is treated as a partnership."†

C. Garden variety examples:

1. One of the earliest joint ventures or adventures was used in the sailing ship days wherein the participants (joint venturers) joined for the purpose of purchasing, transporting, and selling the cargo of a particular ship. The venture ended upon disposition of the ship's cargo.

2. The joining together for mutual profit of a landowner with capital and a building contractor to build residential homes or a motel to be sold or leased or to construct a shopping mall.

3. An oil company and an exploration company participate in a joint venture for the purpose of exploration of a given tract of land to which the oil company has mineral rights.

4. A chemical company and an oil company join for the purpose of testing a newly developed petrochemical process.

5. In any of the above examples where corporations are involved as participants, the joint venture may take the form of a jointly owned subsidiary corporation. Undoubtedly, the type and number of participants, local law, and tax considerations will determine the form of joint venture to be used.

D. Joint ventures—distinquishing characteristics: Although as indicated, they take many varied forms, we are concerned here with the distinquishing characteristics between a joint venture which is categorized as a partnership and the general partnership which it resembles.

1. Partnerships may be used for either ventures encompassing a single transaction, or a continuing limited enterprise.

2. Corporations may participate as partners in joint ventures. In fact, although there was once a prohibition against corporations becoming general partners in a partnership, they could validly participate in a joint venture. This was a stimulus for use of the joint venture. Today in most jurisdictions a corporation is permitted by state law to participate as a partner of a general partnership.

3. General principles of partnership law apply, including

---

*Steffen, *Agency—Partnership in a Nutshell* (West, 1977), p. 211.
†Crane and Bromberg, *Law of Partnership* (West, 1968), p. 189.

> **a.** Joint and several liability for torts and contracts,
> **b.** Fidiciary relation between parties.

4. Perhaps the most significant difference between the two is that the participant in the joint venture has less apparent authority than a partner in a general partnership. This is so because of the limited scope of the joint venture.

5. Joint ventures using the partnership form will also be treated as partnerships for tax purposes.

6. If there are a sufficient number of participants who are in essence investors, the joint-venture participation agreement may constitute a "security" offered to the public and therefore is subject to the 1933 Security Act's registration requirements (see Federal Securities Acts, p. 240, I.C.2).

IX. Federal Income Taxation of Partnerships and Partners

A. Introduction:

On page xi of the Introduction to this book the AICPA, in discussing the examinations content, states, "Federal tax elements may be covered where appropriate in the overall context of a question." The exact dimension of this change is not 100% predictable; however, based upon the evidence and practice to date, the scope of federal income taxation has been and will in all probability continue to be rather minor and will be aimed at fundamentals. Many of the existing texts cover this aspect of partnership and corporation law in that manner. Next, separate coverage is afforded taxation on a regular basis in the Accounting Practice part of the CPA examination. Finally, with the exception of Part a.5, of the May 1973 examination, the subjective part of the examination has not asked specific questions on taxation nor has much attention to this subject been manifested in the objective questions. Occasionally, one will find an objective question on taxation, but more often the examination contains only a couple of objective questions with one of the four responses relating to taxation. The tax questions are mainly from the partnership and corporate areas, and we have added tax materials to the outlines in both the Partnerships, Corporations, Trusts and Social Security topics.

B. Partnerships:

1. A *bona fide* partnership or limited partnership is *not* recognized as a taxable entity; it pays no taxes. The partnership does file a tax return for reporting purposes, i.e., to show each partner's share of the income (or loss), and each partner will be personally taxable thereon whether it is distributed or not. A penalty for failure to file was added in 1978.

2. Only recognized as an entity for limited purposes under the Internal Revenue Code (e.g., for filing purposes, in respect to the treatment of a partner's guaranteed salary, insofar as partner's buying property from or selling property to the partnership).

3. Can under certain limited circumstances have a tax year that differs from that of the partners.

C. Partners:

1. The character of the income received by the partnership passes through to the partners because the partnership is not a taxable entity but an aggregate of individuals. Contrast this with a corporation, which is a distinct entity for legal and tax purposes. Thus, in a partnership each partner reports his share of the income or loss. To the extent that he does not receive his share of the income, it increases his partnership investment; consequently, losses have the opposite effect. In the reporting of income, items which have special tax treatment are shown separately, e.g., capital gains or tax-exempt interest, as are deductions which have a special tax treatment, e.g., investment interest, depletion, or capital losses. Thus the special tax status of such items is passed through and allocated to each partner. This tax treatment follows the conduit theory of partnerships.

Even though a partnership may characterize a distribution to a partner as a "salary," it is considered a distribution of profit and is not a tax deduction to the partnership in determining its distributable taxable income, unless it is a "guaranteed payment." Contrast this position with that of the corporation, where a salary paid to a shareholder-employee is usually considered a deduction in computing the taxable income of the corporation.

2. The individual partner combines his partnership income according to its tax character (e.g., ordinary income, ordinary loss, capital gain, or capital loss) with the corresponding tax items on his personal income tax return. In the case of an ordinary loss from the partnership, each partner can use it to offset his other income.

3. The agreed-upon sharing of partnership profits, losses, and credits as contained in the partnership agreement or according to the Uniform Partnership Act presumption (equally if not otherwise agreed upon) applies (see p. 62, III.A.1). However, the above is subject to a limitation phrased in terms of requiring that the particular partner receiving a favorable tax allocation show that the allocation has a "substantial economic effect."

4. Partnerships, other than real estate partnerships, are subject to the general "at-risk rules." Thus, in the absence of special circumstances, limited partners, other than in real estate, will not be able to deduct losses in excess of their investment. The "at-risk rules" were added in 1976 and amended subsequently in order to curb abuses in connection with tax shelters. The limited partnership was the most widely used vehicle in which to operate in order to shelter their income from tax.

5. The IRS is attacking limited partnerships which are deemed to be "abusive," i.e., those limited partnerships which lack economic substance. The IRS treats them as corporations for tax purposes, thereby preventing the pass through of losses from such abusive tax shelters.

Selected Problems from CPA Examinations on Partnerships

Subjective Questions and Answers

Q. 1. Arms, Balk, and Clee formed a partnership to operate a retail drug and sundries store under the name Drug Shop. Arms and Balk each contributed $25,000, and Clee contributed the store building in which the business was to be carried on. Clee was credited with a contribution of $50,000, the fair value of the property. Clee retained title in his own name. It was agreed that Arms would have the sole right to purchase merchandise on credit. The partners agreed that Balk was to act as manager of the store. The firm hired Dell, a pharmacist, for a five-year term and agreed to pay him a fixed annual salary plus 10% of the profits.

Following are events which occurred subsequent to the formation of the partnership.

- Fricke, a supplier of fixtures, indicated to the partners that he would sell fixtures to the firm on credit only if Dell, the pharmacist and a wealthy man, was a partner. Dell, who was present, said that he was a partner, and the sale on credit was made. Dell, however, later notified all others dealing with the firm that he was not a partner.
- Balk ordered merchandise, for resale by the store, on credit from a wholesaler in the firm name.
- Else was admitted as a partner with a ⅕ interest in the partnership and in profits and losses upon payment of $40,000.
- Clee, who was generally known to be a partner in the firm, (a) guaranteed in writing and in the firm name a note executed by a customer in purchasing a car for the customer's own use, and (b) conveyed in his own name the store building to Sweeney.

Required

1. Prior to admitting Else as a partner, if the partnership agreement was silent about sharing profits and losses, how should the partners share a remaining profit of $30,000 after all payments to Dell? Explain.
2. If the partnership becomes insolvent, may creditors hold Dell liable as a partner? Explain.
3. Can the wholesaler hold the firm to the contract? Explain.
4. Will Else have any liability to creditors of the firm for obligations which arose prior to his admission? Explain.
5. Discuss the liability of the firm on the customer's note in the event of default.
6. Discuss whether Sweeney would obtain good title to the building.

A. 1. The three partners would share the profit equally in the absence of an agreement to the contrary despite the fact that capital contributions were unequal.

2. As a partner by estoppel, Dell would be held liable to Fricke on the obligation because Dell actively held himself out as a partner. He cannot be so held by others who knew that he was not a partner. In spite of the fact that he shared in profits and absent a finding of partnership by estoppel, Dell would not incur partnership liability by virtue of his sharing in profits. While a sharing in profits is evidence of partnership, the Uniform Partnership Act provides that no such inference of partnership shall be drawn if such profits were received in payment as wages of an employee.

3. The wholesaler can hold the firm to the contract unless the wholesaler knew of the restriction on Balk's authority. Balk was acting within his apparent authority as an agent of the partnership in carrying on a normal activity. If the wholesaler knew of the restriction, the firm would not be bound.

4. Under the Uniform Partnership Act, a person admitted as a partner into an existing partnership is liable for all the obligations of the partnership arising before his admission as though he had been a partner when such obligations were incurred, but this liability may only be satisfied out of partnership property, and his liability is limited, therefore, to his share of the partnership property.

5. On the facts given, it seems quite unlikely that the partnership would be liable if the maker of the note defaults. While every partner is an agent of the partnership for the purpose of its business, a partner's act that is not for carrying on the partnership's business in the usual way does not bind the partnership unless authorized by the other partners. Of course, if they had authorized the action, or ratified it, the partnership would be bound. The fact that Clee may have incurred personal liability does not create a partnership obligation.

6. Whether Sweeney obtained good title depends on the circumstances. Where the title to real property of a partnership is in the name of one of the partners, a purchaser for value and in good faith, receiving a conveyance from the partner with record title, obtains the interest of the partnership, provided he had no knowledge of the partnership interest.

Q. **2.** Millard rented office space in a building owned by Burbank. Millard was in the import-export business and was desperately in need of additional cash. Therefore, he decided to use Burbank's name in conjunction with his own as if they were partners in order to obtain credit from several lenders. He placed a nameplate on his door with the legend "Millard & Burbank" and had the same name listed on the directory in the lobby. In addition, he had business cards and stationery printed with the same title. Finally, he placed an announcement in the local paper that Burbank had joined him in the newly-created partnership of Millard & Burbank. Burbank's rental agent saw the partnership named on the door, saw the listing in the lobby directory, and informed Burbank of the situation. Burbank read the notice in the local paper. In response to this misrepresentation, Burbank told his rental agent to remove the listing in the lobby and to tell Millard to stop the nonsense. These instructions were not followed. In the interim, Millard was negotiating a $10,000 loan with Easy Credit Corporation, one of the other tenants in the office building. Dunlop, one of Easy's officers, had seen the "partnership" nameplate on Millard's door, the listing in the lobby, and the notice in the paper. Therefore, based exclusively upon the credit standing of Burbank, the loan was made. Millard defaulted on the loan and is hopelessly insolvent. Easy demanded payment from Burbank who refused to pay and denied any liability as Millard's partner.

Required

Answer the following, setting forth reasons for any conclusions stated.

1. Are Millard and Burbank partners in fact?
2. Under what legal theory could Easy prevail?

A. **1.** No. The Uniform Partnership Act provides the criteria for determining whether a partnership exists between two or more parties. Although there are several other factors, such as sharing in losses, joint ownership of property, and exercise of management functions, the most important single factor is whether the parties share in profits. Under the facts of the case presented, there is a total lack of any of the factors necessary to establish the existence of an actual partnership between Millard and Burbank.

   2. Since Millard and Burbank are not in fact partners, the only legal theory upon which Easy might recover is that Burbank is a "partner by estoppel." This theory is contained in Section 16 (1) of the Uniform Partnership Act:

> When a person, by words spoken or written or by conduct, represents himself, or consents to another representing him to anyone, as a partner in an existing partnership or with one or more persons not actual partners, he is liable to any such person to whom such representation has been made, who has, on the faith of such representation, given credit to the actual or apparent partnership, and if he has made such representation or consented to its being made in a public manner he is liable to such person, whether the representation has or has not been made or communicated to such person so giving credit by or with the knowledge of the apparent partner making the representation or consenting to its being made.

The central issue is apparent from a reading of the facts and the statute. Did Burbank "consent"? There is a split of authority on the question of whether Burbank's inaction constituted consent. It has been held that persons are liable if they have been held out as partners and know that they are being so held out, unless they prevent it, even if to do so they have to take affirmative action. On the other hand, the partnership act takes the position that to be held as a partner, one must consent to the holding out and that consent is a matter of fact to be proven as any other fact. Since "consent" is to be proven as any other fact, it can be inferred from circumstantial evidence, that is, the conduct of one held out taken in light of all the surrounding circumstances. Based upon Burbank's failure to do virtually anything under the circumstances, it would not be surprising if Burbank were held to have consented.

5/78

Q. **3.** **Part a.** Charles Meskill has decided to invest $600,000 in a new business venture. Meskill will be joined by two, possibly three, former business associates. He has purchased the patent rights to a revolutionary adhesive substance known as "sticko." In connection with the transaction, he is considering the various forms of business organization he might use in establishing the business. You have been engaged to study the accounting and business problems he should consider in choosing to operate as a general partnership, limited partnership, or corporation. Meskill requests specific advice on the following aspects as they relate to the operation of a business as one of these three forms of business organization: (a) personal liability in the event the venture proves to be a disaster; (b) the borrowing capacity of the entity; (c) requirements for doing a multistate business; (d) the liability of the entity for the acts of its agents; and (e) the recognition of the entity for income tax purposes and major income tax considerations in selecting one of the three forms of business organization.

Required

Discuss the various legal implications of each specific aspect for which Meskill seeks advice for operating a business in the above-mentioned forms of business organization.

A. 1. **(a)** The corporation's key characteristic is the limited liability for its owners. Except in a limited number of cases, an investor will not have liability beyond his capital investment. An exception is made in cases where less than par is paid for stock issued by the corporation. The limited partnership provides the same type of insulation from liability for limited partners as found in the corporate form. A limited partner may lose his protected status, however, if he participates in the partnership management or allows his name to be held out as a partner. However, the general partners in a limited partnership have unlimited joint and several liability. The regular general partnership does not afford the partners any protection against liability for firm debts.

(b) Based upon the general partners' personal liability for debts of the entity, a general partnership or a limited partnership, to the extent of the general partners' assets, can ordinarily obtain a greater amount of credit, other things being equal. However, in the event the financial position of the corporation is such that it will not justify a given loan, it is usually possible to increase the borrowing capacity of the corporation by having the principal stockholders and/or officers guarantee the loan.

(c) Any corporation doing business in a foreign jurisdiction (i.e., state other than the state in which it was incorporated) must qualify to do business in a foreign jurisdiction. Partnerships, on the other hand, are generally not subject to such requirements. Therefore, it is usually less complicated to carry on a multistate business in the partnership form, limited or general.

(d) General partners of a regular partnership or a limited partnership have broad authority to bind the entity by the usual contracts they make or by torts committed in the course of their responsibilities. Limited partners normally have no such power. The corporation, on the other hand, is liable for those contracts which are made by its agents within the scope of their express, implied, and apparent authority. In this instance the stockholders would undoubtedly be directors and employees of the corporation and would thus have comparable authority to that of general partners to bind the corporation. Their authority would flow from their roles as officers and/or employees, however, not as stockholders.

(e) The major difference between taxation of a partnership as compared with a corporation is that the partnership is not recognized as a taxable entity, whether general or limited, while the corporation is a separate taxable entity.

The partnership pays no taxes. Instead, the income or loss is passed through the partnership to the individual partners in accordance with the partnership agreement regarding the sharing of income and losses. Furthermore, the individual income and loss items retain their same tax status in the hands of the partners as in the partnership, e.g., capital gains or losses are passed to the partners as capital gains or losses. The income and loss items are included in the individual partners' returns and taxed at the appropriate individual rates.

Q. 4. In the above (question 3), selecting the general partnership versus the corporation as a form of business organization requires consideration of (a) the right to compensation for services rendered, (b) the fiduciary duty, and (c) management prerogatives.

Required

Compare and contrast the rights and responsibilities of a common stockholder with a general partner for each of the three areas states above.

A. 1. (a) The rights of both stockholders and partners concerning compensation for services rendered are similar. Unless there is an agreement to the contrary, stockholders and partners serve without compensation. The underlying rational is that the owners are "contributing" their efforts to enhance the value of the entity; hence, they serve for nothing. Their rewards come from the profits of the respective entities. However, it is common practice to expressly provide for compensation for partners or stockholder-employees who serve the partnership or the corporation.

   (b) Given the facts presented, if a corporation were formed, the corporation would undoubtedly be closely held and the stockholders would also be officers-employees. Under these circumstances the legal fiduciary responsibility of a stockholder-officer-employee and a partner is essentially the same. A stockholder-officer-employee (including directors) owes a fiduciary duty to the corporation he represents; a partner owes the same duty to his partnership. That is, each must act in utmost good faith in all his dealings with and for the entity which each serves or represents.

   Normally, in a larger corporation, a stockholder has no fiduciary responsibility to other stockholders or to the corporation. Only in the event a stockholder becomes a director, officer, or employee does the fiduciary relationship come into play. There is an exception for stockholders classified as insiders of corporations under the jurisdiction of the Securities and Exchange Commission.

   (c) A stockholder has no management prerogatives except to the extent he may control management through his stockholder voting rights. Stockholder-officer-employees (including directors) have management prerogatives, but these prerogatives arise from their capacity as directors, officers, or employees, not from their capacity as stockholders. On the other hand, a partner, unless expressly provided otherwise, has the right to share equally with his fellow partners in the managerial decisions of the partnership.

   In choosing between the partnership and corporate forms of business organization, investors who also intend to operate the business should consider the tax rates of a corporation in relation to the individual tax rates of the investors. Except for reasonable compensation for services rendered, investor/operators often retain all income in the business for expansion. If the corporate tax rate(s) is less than the investors' personal rates, it may be possible to pay less taxes in the short run, having more retained income for business expansion. In these situations dividends are often not contemplated, even though the accumulated earnings tax problem must be considered and dealt with appropriately. For stockholders of some corporations, the potential double taxation resulting from adopting the corporate form of business may be deferred through a nontaxable merger or minimized through a taxable sale of the business with the gain taxed at the capital gain rate.

   The corporation, on the other hand, pays a tax on its ordinary income at the applicable corporate rate. Capital gain is taxed separately at the corporate capital gain rate. Capital losses are deductible only from capital gains. Operating losses and capital losses in a given year may be carried back and forward and are applicable to prior or successive years of the corporation; i.e., the stockholders receive no operating or capital loss benefits. (A corporation which has appropriately elected to be taxed under the provisions of subchapter S of the Internal Revenue Code is significantly different; these characteristics apply only to corporations who do not qualify or who have not elected to be taxed under the provisions of subchapter S.) Distributions by the corporation are normally ordinary income to the individual stockholders. They do receive a dividend exclusion, currently a maximum of $100, which is offset against the dividends received.

5/73

Q. 5. Elwynn, Mitchell, and Grady formed a partnership to assemble and market lamps. After renting delivery trucks for several years the partnership was able to accumulate sufficient cash to purchase three delivery trucks. The title to the trucks was placed in the partnership name. Six months after the trucks were purchased, Grady sold one of the trucks and retained the proceeds on the basis that one of the three trucks belonged to him. The other partners disagreed and sought to regain title to the truck from the buyer or recover the proceeds from Grady.

Required

Answer the following, setting forth reasons for any conclusions stated.

1. Discuss the distinction between "partnership property" and a "partnership interest." Include in your discussion reasons for the legal importance of the distinction.
2. Under what circumstances will the partnership succeed in regaining title to the truck from the buyer?
3. If the partnership does not regain title to the truck from the buyer, may it recover the proceeds from Grady?

A. 1. Partnership property is property originally contributed to the partnership or subsequently acquired with partnership funds. It may be real property or personal property. As such, it belongs to the partnership directly (title is vested in the partnership) or indirectly, and as such, it is held in a "tenancy in partnership" which is a form of joint tenancy borrowed from real property law and adapted to partnership needs. The main legal characteristic of such joint ownership is the right of survivorship in the remaining partners upon the death of one of the partners. Another important rule regarding partnership property is that partners have equal rights to possess partnership property for partnership use unless otherwise agreed. According to section 26 of the Uniform Partnership Act, "A partner's interest in the partnership is his share of the profits and surplus, and the same is personal property."

   The distinction between partnership property and partnership interest is important because a partner's right in specific partnership property is neither assignable nor attachable unless for a partnership debt. Finally, it is not inheritable, and heirs, widows, and next of kin cannot validly claim rights to specific partnership property. On the other hand, a partner's interest in the partnership is assignable, inheritable, and attachable.

   2. Since the trucks were purchased with partnership funds and title was placed in the partnership name, the trucks were in fact partnership property, and Grady did not own any of the three partnership trucks. Consequently, the partnership will prevail in two differing sets of circumstances. First, if the buyer had actual notice that Grady had no authority to sell the truck, the partnership could reclaim the truck. An express limitation on Grady's authority if known to the other party will be paramount. The only factual information given is that the truck was registered in the partnership name; however, this would not normally be sufficient in and of itself to give the buyer notice of the fact that Grady could not sell it on behalf of the partnership.

   Second, the partnership will prevail if there is no express authority and the sale exceeds the partner's apparent authority to enter into the contract. The truck was held in the partnership's name and is not an inventory asset. That is, it is not an asset that one would expect to be sold by such a partnership in the ordinary course of its business. If the average buyer dealing with the partnership would have reason to know that such sales are not made by a single partner without the consent of the other partners, then the buyer does not obtain good title.

   3. Yes. Grady has acted wrongfully in respect to his obligations to the partnership and to his fellow partners. Grady did not own the asset and thus his sale is wrongful. He has in fact committed the tort of conversion and is liable to the partnership. Other theories might be an implied obligation to return the money on the basis of money wrongfully had or received, or that he merely holds the money in trust for the benefit of the partnership. Under any of the above theories, recovery of the proceeds by the partnership would be proper.

5/77

Q. 6. The Minlow, Richard, and Jones partnership agreement is silent on whether the partners may assign or otherwise transfer all or part of their partnership interests to an outsider. Richard has assigned his partnership interest to Smith, a personal creditor, and as a result the other partners are furious. They have threatened to remove Richard as a partner, not admit Smith as a partner, and bar Smith from access to the firm's books and records.

Required

Answer the following, setting forth reasons for any conclusions stated.

Can Minlow and Jones successfully implement their threats? Discuss the rights of Richard and Smith and the effects of the assignment on the partnership.

A.   Unless there is an express prohibition against the assignment of a partner's partnership interest stated in the partnership agreement, it is assignable. This rule applies whether all or part of the partnership interest is assigned. Probably the most common situation in which a partner assigns his partnership interest is in connection with collateralizing a personal loan. Therefore, barring an express prohibition or a clause requiring the consent of the other partners, Richard may assign his interest.

As a result of the above assignment, Richard remains a partner. Although Richard has assigned his partnership interest he still remains a partner and retains all of the rights, privileges, perquisites, duties, and liabilities he formerly had vis-à-vis the partnership and his fellow partners. The assignee (Smith) has only the right to Richard's share of the profits in the event of a default. He would succeed to Richard's rights, in whole or in part, upon the dissolution and winding up of the partnership or upon its bankruptcy. Smith does not, however, succeed to Richard's right to access to the partnership's books and records.

5/77

Q.   7. Dowling, a partner of Lazor, Bassett, Dowling, & Lamb, died on February 2, 1976. The four partners were equal partners in all respects (i.e., capital accounts, profit and loss sharing, etc.). The partnership agreement was silent on the question of the rights of a deceased partner upon his death. Dowling's Last Will and Testament bequeathed his entire estate to his "beloved wife." His widow is now claiming the right to 25% of all partnership property.

Required

1. What rights does Dowling's widow have in respect to specific partnership property or against the partnership or surviving partners? Explain.
2. How would a "buy-out" agreement affect your answer to 1? Explain.

A.   1. Mrs. Dowling has no rights to any particular partnership property nor to a share thereof. Pursuant to the Uniform Partnership Act, the surviving partners have a right of survivorship in all partnership property, and such property is not subject to the surviving spouse's award. The property passes according to this law regardless of any provisions contained in a deceased partner's last will and testament.

However, Mrs. Dowling does have the right to compensation for her husband's partnership interest. At a minimum, this would consist of a return of his capital contribution plus accumulated and current profits to the date of death. However, if the partners wish to continue the firm without a "winding up" and under its existing name, then the aspect of goodwill and the fair market value of the decedent's interest becomes more complex. If the problem cannot be solved amicably by negotiation between the remaining partners and the widow, then an independent appraisal or litigation or both would be necessary.

2. A "buy-out" agreement would provide for the automatic continuation of the firm, usually under the original name, despite the legal or technical dissolution caused by death. Also, it would eliminate the requirement and need for a "winding up." Finally, it would solve most of the valuation problems, because the price or method of determining the value of the decedent's partnership interest would be established by specific terms in the agreement.

5/76

Q.   8. Fletcher, Dry, Wilbert, and Cox selected the limited partnership as the form of business entity most suitable for their purpose of investing in mineral leases. Fletcher, the general partner, contributed $50,000 in capital. Dry,

Wilbert, and Cox each contributed $100,000 capital and are limited partners. Necessary limited-partnership papers were duly prepared and filed clearly indicating that Fletcher was the sole general partner and that the others were limited partners.

Fletcher managed the partnership during the first two years. During the third year, Dry and Wilbert overruled Fletcher as to the type of investments to be made, the extent of the commitments, and the major terms contained in the leases. They also exercised the power to draw checks on the firm's bank account. Finally, Fletcher withdrew and was replaced by Martin, a new and more receptive general partner. Cox did not join his fellow partners in these activities. However, his name was used without qualification and with his general knowledge and consent on the partnership stationery as part of the firm's name.

Required

Discuss the legal liability of Martin, Dry, Wilbert, and Cox, as individuals, to creditors of the partnership.

A.   Martin, Dry, Wilbert, and Cox are all liable as general partners. Martin is an incoming general partner, and, as such, he would have the same liability as a general partner in an ordinary partnership. In effect, the law states that he has unlimited joint and several liability. However, as to obligations incurred prior to his entry into the partnership, his liability cannot exceed his capital contribution.

Dry and Wilbert are liable as general partners because, in addition to the exercise of their rights and powers as limited partners, they also took part in the control of the business.

Cox's liability as a general partner rests upon the doctrine of estoppel or a specific provision under the Uniform Limited Partnership Act. The act provides that a limited partner whose name appears in the partnership name is liable as a general partner to partnership creditors who extend credit to the partnership without actual knowledge that he is not a general partner. Hence, unless a creditor knows of Cox's true status, Cox has unlimited liability to that creditor.

5/76

Practice Questions

Q.   1.   Idaho Mining & Minerals was formed 10 years ago by five individuals as a general partnership. After several years of losses the partnership finally began to show a modest profit from its operations which has increased steadily. The current picture is one of justified optimism. The most recent year showed a profit in excess of $250,000, and realistic projections indicate profits in excess of $1 million within five years. The partners are considering incorporating the business and going public sometime in the future. The partners are concerned about the implications of incorporating from the standpoint of (1) their liability after incorporation, with particular emphasis on possible liability for claims against the corporation and preexisting claims against the partnership, and (2) the tax implications to them of a transfer of the business to a newly created corporation.

Their concern is predicated upon the following facts. There is a significant lawsuit against the partnership which is believed to be baseless but which could nevertheless result in serious liability. Furthermore, the tax basis of their respective partnership interests is low in relation to the current fair market value of the partnership's assets.

Required

Answer the following, setting forth reasons for any conclusions stated.

1. Explain the legal liability and implications of the proposed incorporation to the partners and the corporation.
2. What are the federal income tax implications to the partners as to recognition of gain or loss as a result of a transfer of the partnership assets to a newly created corporation?

Q.   2. Taylor, Polk, and Buchanan are partners doing business as Famous Autographs. Their partnership agreement provides that they are to continue their partnership for 10 years, that all partners are to be active in the management, and that Taylor is to act as sales manager while Polk and Buchanan are to purchase autographs for the firm. Taylor and Polk each contributed $20,000 to the firm and Buchanan contributed $10,000. The partnership agreement is silent as to how profits and losses are to be shared. During the first year the partnership had income of $15,000. During the next three years the firm incurred losses of $8,000, $12,000, and $15,000, respectively, and conditions in the industry were such that the firm could not continue except at a loss. Taylor, a well-to-do businessman, asked the other partners to dissolve the firm at the end of the fourth year, but Polk and Buchanan, although personally insolvent, were optimistic about the future and refused to do so.

Required
1. How should the first year's income be divided? Discuss.
2. Does Taylor have a right to have the partnership dissolved at the end of the fourth year: If so, how must he proceed? Discuss.
3. What is the firm's liability, if any, on a contract that was made by Taylor in violation of the partnership agreement for the purchase of an autograph from Skinner? Discuss.
4. Discuss the legal effect on the partnership of Polk's assignment of his interest in the partnership to Barron.
5. Assume the firm failed at the end of the fourth year. For what portion of the firm's debts, that remained after the firm's assets were applied to firm debts, would Taylor be personally liable to firm creditors? Discuss.
6. Would your answer to 5 be the same under all of the facts stated in the problem except that a certificate of limited partnership had been duly filed and published designating Polk and Buchanan as general partners and Taylor as a limited partner? State "yes" or "no" and discuss.

Q.   3. Palmer is a member of a partnership. His personal finances are in a state of disarray, although he is not bankrupt. He recently defaulted on a personal loan from the Aggressive Finance Company. Aggressive indicated that if he did not pay within one month, it would obtain a judgment against him and levy against all his property including his share of partnership property and any interest he had in the partnership. Both Palmer and the partnership are concerned about the effects of this unfortunate situation upon Palmer and the partnership.

Required
Answer the following, setting forth reasons for any conclusions stated.

1. Has a dissolution of the partnership occurred?
2. What rights will Aggressive have against the partnership or Palmer concerning Palmer's share of partnership property or his interest in the partnership?
3. Could Palmer legally assign his interest in the partnership as security for a loan with which to pay off Aggressive?

Q.   4. Strom, Lane, and Grundig formed a partnership on July 1, 1974, and selected "Big M Associates" as their partnership name. The partnership agreement specified a fixed duration of 10 years for the partnership. Business went well for the partnership for several years and it established an excellent reputation in the business community. In 1978, Strom, much to his amazement, learned that Grundig was padding his expense accounts by substantial amounts each month and taking secret kick-backs from certain customers for price concessions and favored service. Strom informed Lane of these facts and they decided to seek an accounting of Grundig, a dissolution of the firm by ousting Grundig, and the subsequent continuation of the firm by themselves under the name, "Big M Associates."

Required

Answer the following, setting forth reasons for any conclusions stated.

1. Were there any filing requirements to be satisfied upon the initial creation of the partnership?
2. What will be the basis for the accounting and dissolution and should such actions be successful?
3. Can Strom and Lane obtain the right to continue to use the firm name if they prevail?

Practice Objective Questions

Instructions 1–12

Select the *best* answer for each of the following items. Mark only one answer for *each* item. Answer all items. Your grade will be based on your total correct answers.

1. For which of the following purposes is a general partnership recognized as an entity by the Uniform Partnership Act?
   a. Insulation of the partners from personal liability.
   b. Taking of title and ownership of property.
   c. Continuity of existence.
   d. Recognition of the partnership as the employer of its members.
2. In the course of your audit of Harvey Fox, doing business as Harvey's Apparels, a sole proprietorship, you discovered that in the past year Fox had regularly joined with Leopold Morrison in the marketing of bathing suits and beach accessories. You are concerned whether Fox and Morrison have created a partnership relationship. Which of the following factors is the *most* important in ascertaining this status?
   a. The fact that a partnership agreement is *not* in existence.
   b. The fact that each has a separate business of his own which he operates independently.
   c. The fact that Fox and Morrison divide the net profits equally on a quarterly basis.
   d. The fact that Fox and Morrison did *not* intend to be partners.
3. A general partner will *not* be personally liable for which of the following acts or transactions committed or engaged in by one of the other partners or by one of the partnership's employees?
   a. The gross negligence of one of the partnership's employees while carrying out the partnership business.
   b. A contract entered into by the majority of the other partners but to which the general partner objects.
   c. A personal mortgage loan obtained by one of the other partners on his residence to which that partner, without authority, signed the partnership name on the note.
   d. A contract entered into by the partnership in which the other partners agree among themselves to hold the general partner harmless.
4. Wilcox & Wyatt, a general partnership, and Wyatt, individually, are insolvent in the bankruptcy sense. Wilcox has sufficient assets to satisfy all her personal creditors as well as the obligations of the firm. Under these circumstances
   a. Wilcox will be liable to partnership creditors to the extent that their claims exceed partnership assets.
   b. Wilcox has joint and several personal liability for the debts incurred by Wyatt to his personal creditors.
   c. Firm creditors *cannot* resort to Wilcox's personal assets beyond her proportionate profit and loss sharing ratio.
   d. Wyatt *cannot* escape personal liability to Wilcox for any additional amounts Wilcox has to pay for and on behalf of firm debts by filing a voluntary petition in bankruptcy and obtaining a discharge.
5. Concerning the order of distribution for satisfying firm debts upon the dissolution and winding up of a general partnership, which of the following is a correct statement?
   a. General creditors, including partners who are also general creditors, are ranked first.
   b. Profits are distributed only after all prior parties, including partners, have had their various claims satisfied.
   c. Secured obligations are disregarded entirely insofar as the order of distribution.
   d. Capital contributions by the partners are distributed before unsecured loans by the partners.

6. Grand, a general partner, retired, and the partnership held a testimonial dinner for him and invited 10 of the partnership's largest customers to attend. A week later a notice was placed in various trade journals indicating that Grand had retired and was no longer associated with the partnership in any capacity. After the appropriate public notice of Grand's retirement, which of the following *best* describes his legal status?
   a. The release of Grand by the remaining partners and the assumption of all past and future debts of the partnership by them via a "hold harmless" clause constitutes a novation.
   b. Grand has the apparent authority to bind the partnership in contracts he makes with persons who have previously dealt with the partnership and are unaware of his retirement.
   c. Grand has *no* liability to past creditors upon his retirement from the partnership if they all have been informed of his withdrawal and his release from liability, and if they do *not* object within 60 days.
   d. Grand has the legal status of a limited partner for the three years it takes to pay him the balance of the purchase price of his partnership interest.

7. Berg is the founder and senior partner of Berg Associates, a consulting firm. He is now 75 years old and wants to retire. The other partners have agreed to purchase Berg's partnership interest for $250,000; the amount includes $50,000 for goodwill. The agreement also provides for the right of the other partners to continue the business and the right to use Berg's name. Berg is to receive $100,000 upon his retirement and an additional $50,000 per year for three years. The remaining partners agreed to hold Berg harmless for any past or future debts of the partnership and release him from all liability. If Berg accepts this offer to sell his partnership interest, it means that
   a. The existing firm (Berg Associates) has *not* been dissolved because the business is to be carried on by the remaining partners.
   b. The remaining partners may *not* use the original firm name, but may only indicate the newly named firm formerly was known as "Berg Associates."
   c. The payment of $50,000 for the goodwill of Berg has important tax consequences to him and the firm.
   d. Berg as a retired partner has the right to attend and vote in the year-end partnership meeting.

8. Kimball, Thompson, and Darby formed a partnership. Kimball contributed $25,000 in capital and lent the partnership $20,000; he performed no services. Thompson contributed $15,000 in capital and part-time services, and Darby contributed only his full-time services. The partnership agreement provided that all profits and losses would be shared equally. Three years after the formation of the partnership, the three partners agreed to dissolve and liquidate the partnership. Firm creditors, other than Kimball, have *bona fide* claims of $65,000. After all profits and losses have been recorded, there are $176,000, assets to be distributed to creditors and partners. When the assets are distributed:
   a. Darby receives nothing since he did not contribute any property.
   b. Thompson receives $45,333 in total.
   c. Kimball receives $62,000 in total.
   d. Each partner receives one-third of the remaining assets after all the firm creditors, including Kimball, have been paid.

9. Bonanza Real Estate Ventures is a limited partnership created pursuant to the law of a state that has adopted the Uniform Limited Partnership Act. It has 3 general partners and 1,100 limited partners living in various states. The limited partnership interests were offered to the general public at $5,000 per partnership interest. Johnson purchased a limited-partnership interest in the Bonanza Real Estate Ventures. As such, he:
   a. *Cannot* assign his limited-partnership interest to another person without the consent of the general partners.
   b. Is entitled to interest on his capital contribution.
   c. Is a fiduciary vis-à-vis the limited partnership and its partners.
   d. Must include his share of the limited-partnership taxable profits in his taxable income even if he does not withdraw anything.

10. A limited partner
   a. May *not* withdraw his capital contribution unless there is sufficient limited-partnership property to pay all general creditors.
   b. Must *not* own limited-partnership interests in other competing limited partnerships.
   c. Is automatically an agent for the partnership with apparent authority to bind the limited partnership in contract.

    d. Has *no* liability to creditors even if he takes part in the control of the business as long as he is held out as being a limited partner.

11. Absent any contrary provisions in the agreement, under which of the following circumstances will a limited partnership be dissolved?

    a. A limited partner dies and his estate is insolvent.

    b. A personal creditor of a general partner obtains a judgment against the general partner's interest in the limited partnership.

    c. A general partner retires and all the remaining general partners do *not* consent to continue.

    d. A limited partner assigns his partnership interest to an outsider and the purchaser becomes a substituted limited partner.

12. Jack Gordon, a general partner of Visions Unlimited, is retiring. He sold his partnership interest to Don Morrison for $80,000. Gordon assigned to Morrison all his rights, title, and interests in the partnership and named Morrison as his successor partner in Visions. In this situation:

    a. The assignment to Morrison dissolves the partnership.

    b. Absent any limitation regarding the assignment of a partner's interest, Gordon is free to assign it at his will.

    c. Morrison is entitled to an equal voice and vote in the management of the partnership, and he is entitled to exercise all the rights and privileges that Gordon had.

    d. Morrison does *not* have the status of a partner, but he can, upon demand, inspect the partnership accounting records.

4

Corporations

AICPA Content Specification Outline

Formation, Purposes, and Powers
Stockholders, Directors, and Officers
Financial Structure, Capital, and Dividends
Merger, Consolidation, and Dissolution

Contents

III. Corporate Purposes, Powers, and Liabilities
    A. Corporate rights as a legal entity
    B. Scope of corporate powers
    C. Laws
    D. Corporate liability
IV. Rights of Stockholders
    A. Stockholder
    B. When stockholder's rights commence
    C. Rights and privileges of a stockholder
    D. Stockholder's limited liability
V. Directors
    A. Principal duties and powers of directors
    B. Delegation of duties by directors
    C. Meetings of directors
    D. Compensation of directors
    E. Tenure of office
    F. Liability of directors
    G. Indemnification of directors and others
VI. Officers
    A. Distinquished from directors
    B. Selection and tenure
    C. President
    D. Compensation
    E. Liability to the corporation
    F. Indemnification
VII. Financial Structure, Capital, and Dividends
    A. Capital
    B. Shares of capital stock
    C. Classes of stock
    D. Stock subscriptions
    E. Contract to purchase stock
    F. Corporate bonds
    G. Dividends
VIII. Mergers and Consolidations
    A. Forms
    B. Asset purchase
    C. Stock purchase
    D. Laws governing
IX. Dissolution
    A. Definition
    B. Not resulting from
    C. Voluntary dissolution
    D. Involuntary dissolution
X. Federal Income Taxation of Corporations
    A. The corporate tax entity
    B. Normal tax rates
    C. Net long-term capital gains

I. Basic Characteristics and Types of Corporations

A. Definition: an artificial person or *legal entity* created by or under the authority of an act of the legislature to accomplish some purpose that is authorized by the charter or governing statute.

B. Governing law:

    1. State statutes regulate activities (e.g., formation, powers, liabilities, management) of corporations they charter.

    2. State statutes conform to a general pattern but vary from state to state as to particulars.

    3. Uniform statutes dealing with corporations:

        a. Model Business Corporation Act (adopted in whole or in part in over two-thirds of the states and represents the majority rule insofar as the corporations area is concerned. This chapter follows the Act wherever appropriate). The Act is also cited as the Model Act.

        b. UCC Article 8 (Investment Securities). See Documents of title, and Investment Securities, p. 302.

C. Attributes:

    1. Creation and regulation by the state.

    2. Existence as a legal entity.

        a. Corporation exists separate and distinct from its stockholders, directors, officers, and employees.

            (1) Corporate property belongs to the corporation, not to the stockholders.

            (2) Corporate liabilities are liabilities of the corporation, not of its stockholders (limited liability for stockholders).

            (3) Corporate contractual rights and obligations are separate and distinct from those of its shareholders.

        b. Separate legal entity normally respected even if one stockholder owns all the shares.

  c. However, where legal entity is used to perpetrate a fraud or merely as the "agent" or "instrumentality" of its individual owner or owners or its parent corporation, the courts may disregard the rule of limited liability (i.e., "pierce the corporate veil").

3. Continuity of existence.

  a. Existence continues, regardless of death or incapacity of any of its directors, officers, or employees, and regardless of transfer of stock by shareholders.

  b. Existence continues forever unless the charter provides otherwise.

4. Operates through its board of directors, officers, and other human agents.

5. Purposes for which corporation may be formed: generally for any lawful purpose; professional corporations now allowed in most states under special acts, e.g., to practice law, medicine, and accounting.

6. Corporations have power to do all things reasonably necessary to enable them to carry out their purposes, absent conflicting state statutes or provisions in articles of incorporation.

7. Advantages of corporate form of business:

  a. Limited liability (see p. 98, IV.D).

   (1) Stockholder is generally not liable for corporate debts.

   (2) Stockholder is not personally liable for acts of a corporation's directors, officers, or employees.

  b. Flexibility of financing: can issue common and preferred stocks and bonds in varying amounts to suit its needs and to conform to its investors' demands.

  c. Continuity of existence despite death or incapacity of directors, stockholders, or officers.

  d. Transferability of shareholders' interests, i.e., shares of stock may be sold, traded, given away, etc.

  e. Relative attractiveness to investors; due to the above advantages, the corporation is generally favored by investors over other forms of business entities.

  f. Concentration of business strength through right to act as a legal entity.

  g. Professional management. While partnerships are generally managed by the investors in the partnership, corporations may hire professional business managers who need not have an investment in the corporation.

  h. The corporation may offer unique tax benefits, e.g., reorganizations.

8. Disadvantages of corporate form of business:

  a. Expense: fees for incorporating and other organization costs.

  b. Taxation:

   (1) State franchise tax, stock issuance, and transfer taxes.

   (2) Federal and state income tax burden may be heavier for corporations than for individuals in the lower tax brackets.

   (3) Double taxation as distributed earnings (dividends) are taxed first as income to the corporation and then as income to shareholder.

  c. Scope of authority: limited by express powers contained in charter.

   (1) When a corporation is acting beyond its powers, it is said to be acting *ultra vires* (alleged very seldom today).

(2) This problem has been diminished by the current practice of drafting the corporate charter so broadly as to permit the corporation to do anything within reason.

(3) Model Business Corporation Act has almost entirely abolished the doctrine.

    d. Right to do business in other states is subject to limitations imposed on foreign corporations by individual states (see p. 91, II.E).

    e. Greater governmental supervision.

    f. May still not be allowed to practice some professions in some states, e.g., law.

  9. Comparison with other associations (partnerships, joint ventures, joint stock associations, business trusts, and limited partnerships). See Partnerships, p. 60, I.E.

D. Types of corporations:

  1. Public corporation: corporation created as an agency of the state for governmental purposes.

    a. Municipal corporation: includes any county, town, school district, village, city, or other territorial division of the state established by law with powers of local government.

    b. Public-benefit corporation: any corporation organized to construct or operate a public improvement in which the profits inure to the benefit of the government (e.g., a state-operated bridge). Its stock is typically owned entirely or largely by the government.

  2. Quasi-public corporation (public utility): engaged in rendering service of such general public importance as to justify privilege of eminent domain and amenability to public regulation under public power.

  3. Private: organized for nongovernmental purposes.

    a. Stock corporation: one having shares of stock and authorized by law to distribute dividends to holders.

    b. Nonstock corporation (membership corporation: includes every other private corporation (e.g., athletic clubs, co-op apartments).

    c. States also provide for the formation of charitable, educational, social, and other nonprofit corporations.

  4. Domestic: A corporation is a domestic corporation in the state wherein it was incorporated.

  5. Foreign: A corporation doing business in any state other than that in which it was incorporated is a foreign corporation in all such states.

  6. Close corporation: one whose stock is closely held by a limited number of persons. Normally, restrictions are placed upon the transfer of stock in closely held corporations in order to prevent outsiders from becoming shareholders.

  7. Subchapter S corporation: closely held corporation that elects to have its income taxed directly to its shareholders. (See p. 107, X.G.)

  8. Holding company: corporation that owns or controls such a dominant interest in one or more other corporations that it may dictate their policies through voting control.

9. Professional corporations: Majority of states have statutes permitting the practice of professions, e.g., medicine, by duly licensed individuals under corporate status, using letters P.A. (Professional Association), P.C. (Professional Corporation), or S.C. (Service Corporation) after corporate name.
   a. Licensed professional is personally liable for own professional conduct, e.g., a doctor who negligently performs an operation.
   b. Permits various tax advantages that don't pertain to individuals or partnerships, e.g., more advantageous pension plans.
   c. Enabling statute may limit ownership of shares of stock to licensed professionals.

II. Promotion, Formation, and Organization

A. Promotion:
   1. Relates to plans and steps that precede and determine the formation, purpose, and structure of a corporation and the way its shares and interests are to be issued and distributed.
   2. Promoter.
      a. Definition: the person who takes the preliminary steps to organize a corporation, such as securing a charter, issuing its prospectus, procuring stock subscriptions, and raising capital.
      b. Responsibility: The promoter is in a fiduciary relationship to the corporation and is not permitted to make secret profits at the expense of the corporation or its subscribers. He must exercise good faith in dealing with the corporation and shareholders.
   3. Corporate liability for promoter's contracts.
      a. *Promoter is not the agent for the corporation, since one cannot be the agent for a nonexistent principal.*
      b. *Corporation not bound unless and until it approves* and thereby adopts the contracts of the promoter upon coming into corporate existence.
      c. Until corporation's approval, promoter alone is bound, unless contrary intent was clearly understood; in such a case no one is bound.
      d. Adoption of contract, if it occurs, should be reflected in corporate minutes. However, adoption may also be inferred from corporate conduct (i.e., acceptance of the benefits).
   4. Corporation's liability for promoter's services: no liability for preincorporation services unless the board of directors approves payment after the corporation comes into existence. Approval may be express or implied from its acts.

B. Formation:
   1. Relates to the legal steps by which a corporation is brought into existence.
   2. Source of authority:
      a. Sovereign power to grant corporate charters vested in states.
      b. Federal government can grant charters only as an incident to the conduct of its own business (e.g., Federal Bank, TVA).

      c. Charters are granted subject to the right of the state at any time to repeal, alter, or amend.

      d. *De jure* corporation: one duly and properly formed under the law.

      e. *De facto* corporation: see below.

      f. Corporation by estoppel: an equitable doctrine to prevent injustice wherein a party has acted to his detriment in reliance on corporate existence; therefore, a corporation will be deemed to exist for the purpose of a specific transaction.

  3. Qualifications of incorporators:

      a. Vary from state to state. Incorporators must look to state law in crder to insure fulfillment of any particular state's requirements.

      b. Most states require one or more natural persons of 21 years or over (now lowered to 18 years or more in many states) who are U.S. citizens; often a domestic or foreign corporation may also act as incorporator.

  4. Contents of certificate of incorporation:

      a. Proposed name (must not have the same name as, or bear too close a resemblance to, the name of another corporation incorporated within the state, and must indicate its corporate status, with "Co.," "Inc.," etc.)

      b. Purpose, objects, and powers (current practice is to draft these as broadly as possible).

      c. Capital structure (description of shares authorized, including amount, types, par or no-par, etc.).

      d. Location of principal office.

      e. Duration, which may be perpetual.

      f. Directors.

      g. Subscribers to stock.

      h. Designation of agent for service of process (usually secretary of state where incorporated, in addition to any other agent).

C. Organization:

  1. First meeting of incorporators.

      a. "Dummies" (persons used for convenience in incorporating and who have no real interest in the corporation), if they are used in incorporating, assign their stock subscriptions to the true stockholders in interest.

      b. Bank designated as depository of money received via subscriptions or loans.

  2. First meeting of directors.

      a. Usually follows immediately after first meeting of incorporators.

      b. Directors select officers. (Corporation is now ready to do business.)

      c. Bylaws adopted.

      d. Issuance of stock that was authorized.

  3. Bylaws.

      a. Govern conduct of corporation and are binding upon the directors and officers.

      b. Generally, are adopted by the incorporators or directors at the first meeting, subject to any bylaws stockholders may adopt; bylaws can be altered by the board if the charter so provides.

D. *De facto* corporations. The Model Act has all but abolished the *de facto* corporation doctrine. It provides that:

1. Upon the issuance of the certificate of incorporation by the State, the corporate existence shall begin, and such certificate of incorporation shall be conclusive evidence that all conditions precedent have been complied with.

2. The above conclusive presumption applies to all parties except the State in a proceeding to cancel or revoke the certificate of incorporation or for involuntary dissolution of the corporation.

E. Foreign corporations:

1. Authorization required in order to qualify to "do business" in a state other than that of incorporation:

   a. Depend on the laws of the particular state where the corporation is doing business.

   b. The Model Act requires a filing similar in many regards to an incorporation and a payment of a registration fee.

2. What constitutes "doing business":

   a. To constitute "doing business," there must be a more or less permanent and continuous business, e.g., a permanent facility such as a store.

   b. Isolated transactions normally do not constitute "doing business."

3. Penalties and deprivations for "doing business" without a license:

   a. Foreign corporation may be deprived of right to sue in such state.

   b. Corporation is liable to the state in an amount equal to all fees and franchise taxes which would have been imposed for the period in question and which would have been paid had it obtained a certificate of authority, plus interest and penalties.

III. Corporate Purposes, Powers, and Liabilities

A. Corporate rights as a legal entity:

1. To buy, own, hold, and sell property.
2. To make contracts through its human agents in the corporate name.
3. To sue and be sued in its own name.
4. To have exclusive use of its corporate name in the jurisdiction.
5. To have a corporate seal.

B. Scope of corporate powers:

1. Those expressly conferred by its charter, and
2. Those that may be reasonably implied therefrom in order to carry out the corporate objects and purposes.

   a. Acts within its express or implied powers are *intra vires*.

   b. Acts outside its express or implied powers are *ultra vires* (see p. 93, III.D.2).

3. General powers that every corporation is deemed to possess:

   a. Power to have succession or continued existence. The Model Act provides perpetual life unless charter provides otherwise.

   b. Power to take, hold, sell, and convey real and personal property for corporate purposes.

   c. Power to make bylaws not inconsistent with law:

(1) For management of the business.

(2) For transfer of stock.

(3) For regulation of its affairs.

    d. Power to appoint such officers and agents as are necessary and to fix their compensation.

C. Laws limit corporation in the following rights, powers, and functions:

    1. Right to become a partner: The Model Act permits the corporation to enter into a partnership; a minority of states deny this right. However, all states recognize that a corporation may be estopped to deny that it is a *de facto* partner.

    2. Right to buy its own stock: Even without express authorization in the charter, a corporation may acquire and hold its own stock provided:

        a. Transaction is fair and made in good faith.

        b. Transaction is not fraudulent.

        c. Rights of creditors and stockholders will not be prejudiced by the purchase.

        d. Purchase is made out of existing, earned, and/or capital surplus as provided by the Model Act. The corporation cannot vote this stock.

        e. Purchase will not cause the corporation to become insolvent.

        f. Corporation is not in the process of dissolution.

    3. Right to buy stock in other corporations:

        a. Generally, corporation may buy stock in another corporation.

        b. May be restricted by antitrust laws.

    4. Power to lend money:

        a. Corporation may lend money if it is necessary to do so as an incidental part of its normal functions and powers.

        b. As to loans to officers and directors, see p. 100, V.F.2.d.

    5. Power to guarantee obligations: ordinarily no such power unless:

        a. Guaranty and surety bonds are issued by a company engaged in such business.

        b. If the corporation owns negotiable paper, it may indorse it.

        c. The corporation is the parent corporation (i.e., owns over 50% of another corporation); then the parent may guarantee an obligation of the subsidiary.

    6. Power to indorse for accommodation: Corporation cannot indorse negotiable paper for another's accommodation, and one who accepts a negotiable instrument with such an indorsement cannot hold the corporation liable.

    7. Right to practice most professions in corporate form is now permitted, by special statute (e.g., law, medicine, and accounting).

D. Corporate liability:

    1. Contracts:

        a. A corporation is liable for contracts made by its agents within the scope of their express authority. Apparent authority of officers to make binding contracts is strictly construed so that those dealing with officers of corporations should make sure of their authority.

        b. Corporation is not liable on contracts made in its behalf prior to incorporation, unless such contracts are expressly or implicitly adopted (see p. 89, II.A.3).

      c. Corporation not liable on illegal contracts.

   2. *Ultra vires* acts:

      a. No act of a corporation and no conveyance or transfer of real or personal property to or by a corporation shall be invalid by reason of the fact that the corporation was without capacity or power to do such act or to make or receive such conveyance or transfer.

      b. However, such lack of capacity or power may be asserted:

         (1) By a shareholder in a proceeding against the corporation to enjoin the doing of any act or the transfer of real or personal property by or to the corporation if the unauthorized act or transfer sought to be enjoined is executory. The court may if it is equitable to do so set aside the performance of the *ultra vires* contract.

         (2) By the corporation, whether acting directly or through a receiver, trustee, or other legal representative, or through shareholders in a representative suit, against the incumbent or former officers or directors of the corporation.

         (3) By the Attorney General in a proceeding to dissolve the corporation, or in a proceeding by the Attorney General to enjoin the corporation from the transaction of unauthorized business.

   3. Unauthorized acts of officers:

      a. Corporation is liable for such acts, provided they are customarily delegated to such officers.

      b. The board of directors and officers who engage in unauthorized acts are personally liable to the corporation for any loss.

   4. Torts:

      a. Corporation is liable for all torts committed by its officers, agents, or employees during course and within the scope of their corporate duties.

      b. It is no defense that the acts or transactions in connection with which such torts occurred were unauthorized.

   5. Crimes:

      a. Corporations are capable of committing some crimes (e.g., violating labor or antitrust statutes).

      b. Punishment typically is in the form of fines or forteiture of charter, since the corporation, a fictitious being, cannot be imprisoned. The recent Foreign Corrupt Practices Act provides for a maximum fine of $1 million.

IV. Rights of Stockholders

  A. Stockholder: one recognized as the true owner of stock:

   1. At law: one who holds the stock directly or in the "street" name.

   2. In equity: one for whose benefit stock is held by another (e.g., beneficiary of a trust holding stock).

   3. Methods of acquiring stock:

      a. By original issue.

      b. By purchase of treasury stock.

      c. By stock transfer from an existing stockholder.

B. Stockholder's rights commence:

    1. When one becomes the true owner of the stock either at law or in equity.

        a. In the case of a present subscription, when said subscription has been accepted by the corporation.

        b. In the case of a contract to purchase, upon payment of the purchase price and delivery of the certificate.

    2. As between old and new stockholder: as soon as new stockholder buys the stock.

    3. As between corporation and new stockholder:

        a. Latter not recognized as a stockholder until transfer is registered on corporate books.

        b. Stockholder may institute suit to compel corporation to make the transfer on the corporate books.

C. Rights and privileges of a stockholder:

    1. Right to a stock certificate.

    2. Right to transfer stock.

        a. By delivering certificate duly indorsed.

        b. By delivering certificate accompanied by a separate assignment.

        c. In a and b above, a transfer on the books of the corporation is not required to validly transfer legal title; however, a *bona fide* payment of dividends by the corporation to the holder of record will be good as against the real owner.

        d. A stock certificate is a negotiable instrument, but may be rendered nonnegotiable by restrictive provisions as to transfer.

        e. Limitations upon right to transfer stock may be imposed by charter, bylaw, or special contract.

            (1) Restrictions must be reasonable.

            (2) Restrictions may be placed upon holders of unpaid stock, or a stockholder may not be allowed to sell his stock to a third party without first giving the corporation or the other stockholders the option of buying it.

            (3) The Uniform Commercial Code requires that any restriction or transfer be conspicuously noted on the certificate if such restrictions are to bind an innocent third party.

            (4) A statement on the stock certificate to the effect that the stock is "transferable only on the books of the corporation" does not prevent transfer as between old and new stockholders in a or b above, even though the transfer has not been made on the corporate books.

            (5) Limitations are often imposed in the case of close corporations.

            (6) The articles of incorporation or the bylaws of a corporation often include restrictions requiring shareholder approval of certain transactions, or even supermajorities (e.g., two-thirds approval) of the board or shareholders for extraordinary decisions (sale of assets, merger, expanding power of board).

    3. Right to vote.

        a. Governed by the charter.

            (1) If the charter is silent on the rights of the different classes of stock, both preferred and common have equal voting rights.

            (2) Usual provision is that only common may vote.

      (3) If dividends remain unpaid for specified period on the preferred stock, preferred stockholders may be given the right to vote and participate in control of the corporation or to take over control.

      (4) Normally, one vote is allowed for each director for each share of stock held.

      (5) Cumulative voting is optional under the Model Act. It may be provided for in the charter. Uniformity is lacking in this area.

          (A) Each stockholder may multiply the number of shares he owns by number of directors to be elected, and the total may be cast for a single director or a number of directors. (E.g., X has 100 shares of stock and five directors are to be elected. X has a total of 500 votes, all of which may be cast for one or split among several of the candidates.)

          (B) By the use of cumulative voting the minority is given an opportunity to place one or more of its members on the board of directors.

b. Governed by the bylaw provisions: Bylaws may require that certain corporate acts be authorized or approved by the stockholders or they will be invalid.

c. Model Business Act provides

      (1) If a charter or bylaw provision conflicts with a statutory provision regarding the stockholder's right to vote, the statute governs.

      (2) At a duly called meeting of shareholders, a majority vote is required to amend the articles of incorporation, e.g., change corporate name, increase or decrease the par value of the authorized shares.

      (3) At a duly called meeting of shareholders, a majority vote is also required to approve the merger or consolidation with another corporation, or the dissolution of the corporation, or selling substantially all its assets.

d. Minority stockholders must abide by a decision of majority but may seek to restrain the majority from exercising control when the proposed action is:

      (1) To the detriment of the corporation, or

      (2) *Ultra vires,* or

      (3) In violation of the charter, bylaws, or statute, or

      (4) Illegal or fraudulent (as to suits brought by stockholders—see p. 97, IV.C.9).

e. Usually, shareholders exercise the right to vote via proxy—an assignment of voting rights, normally to the members of the board of directors who will attend the annual shareholders' meeting.

4. Right to have and participate in shareholders' meetings.

  a. Regular: annual meeting as fixed in the bylaws.

  b. Special: additional meetings called to handle matters requiring special attention.

  c. Minutes: records of meetings, which must be kept in the minutes book.

  d. Quorum: the number of votes necessary to validate a meeting, normally a majority of the entire body.

  e. Proxy: power of attorney given by a stockholder authorizing a designated person to cast the stockholder's ballot; proxies may not be redelegated without express permission.

      f. Voting trust: agreement by which stockholders surrender their stock certificates and voting power and transfer them irrevocably into the hands of others to vote as they see fit; approved by public policy, but statutes considerably limit their operations particularly as to duration (e.g., 10 years).

  5. Right to dividends.

      a. Payment of dividends (except liquidating dividends) must not impair capital as defined in corporation statutes. The Model Act primarily limits payments to unrestricted earned surplus.

      b. Except where dividends are somehow guaranteed, a stockholder has no inherent right to a dividend until one is declared.

      c. When stockholders may compel the declaration of a dividend:

        (1) Normally, determination of whether to declare a dividend is within the exclusive discretion of the board of directors.

        (2) However, when there is a surplus together with adequate cash, stockholders may be able to compel declaration of dividends if directors are withholding the dividends dishonestly, or out of spite, or for their own private purposes, or for some other reason that is a *clear abuse of discretion.*

      d. Dividends normally will be made payable to the stockholders of record on a given date.

      e. Corporation may refuse to recognize a stockholder of record if his stock is not fully paid for.

      f. Dividends illegally declared and paid may be recovered by the corporation, a stockholder in the name of the corporation, judgment creditors of the corporation, or by a trustee in bankruptcy.

      g. Dividends become a *debt* of the corporation as soon as declared, provided they are properly declared and public notice is given; dividends are irrevocable and cannot be recalled except when:

        (1) The declaration is illegal, *ultra vires,* in fraud of creditors, or

        (2) It is revoked at the same meeting in which it was declared, or

        (3) It is payable in the future and the declaration has not been made public or communicated to the stockholders, or

        (4) A stock dividend is declared and the stock has not been issued.

  6. Right to inspect the books, records, and stocklists.

      a. Most jurisdictions have enacted statutes specifically defining which books, records, and stocklists must be kept for the purpose of permitting inspections by shareholders; it is both necessary (e.g., for tax purposes) and desirable that the following books be maintained at the corporation's principal place of business:

        (1) Minute books of the directors' meetings.

        (2) Stockholder lists.

        (3) General books of account.

        (4) Other records and files containing accurate records of corporate affairs. (Under the "business entry" rule, all the above books and records are admissible in evidence if kept by the corporation in the regular course of business, although, ordinarily, evidence not given under oath is not permitted.)

    b. A stockholder had a common law right and the Model Act provides a statutory right to inspect the books of account, records, stockholder lists, etc., for any legitimate purpose. The right may not be denied unless the corporation can show that the stockholder's motive in seeking to inspect the books is for an unwarranted purpose (e.g., to obtain a stocklist for its commercial value), for a purpose hostile to corporation (e.g., to aid a competitor), or to gratify idle curiosity.

    c. If the corporate officers wrongfully refuse to allow an inspection, the stockholder may obtain an injunction from the court ordering the corporation to open its books to the shareholder; some states also provide for fines against those parties who wrongfully deny the right of inspection.

    d. A stockholder may bring an attorney and an accountant to aid him in the inspection, and transcripts may be made.

    e. Directors, unlike shareholders, have an absolute right of inspection.

7. Right to financial statements.

    a. The Model Act requires that each domestic corporation and foreign corporation doing business in the state file a report with data to enable a franchise tax to be determined, e.g., value of assets.

    b. Each shareholder may request in writing a copy of the most recent financial statement, which must be sent.

    c. Annual report required for all corporations registered under the SEC. See Federal Securities Regulations, p. 250.

8. Preemptive right.

    a. Right to subscribe at fair market value or less to newly issued stock in proportion to stockholder's existing holdings, before such stock is offered to the public to prevent dilution of the stockholder's proportion of the stock.

    b. Right does not generally attach to treasury stock sold to the public.

    c. Preferred stockholders generally do not have preemptive rights.

    d. The Model Act denies the preemptive right unless the Articles of Incorporation expressly grants this right.

    e. In the event of a reduction of capital stock outstanding, the shareholders would have their proportionate number of shares reduced on a pro rata basis.

9. Right to sue.

    a. A shareholder in his own right may be able to obtain injunctive relief in the nature of an order prohibiting a transaction that is fraudulent, *ultra vires,* or detrimental to the continued existence of the corporation.

    b. A derivative action may be brought by a shareholder in the name of, and for the benefit of, the corporation against directors, officers, and others to recover damages. Any recovery goes to the corporation or is held by the stockholder in trust for the corporation's benefit.

    c. Before a shareholder may sue derivatively, he must first make a demand on the directors or officers to sue unless such demand would be useless, in which case he is excused from this requirement.

10. Rights on dissolution: A stockholder is entitled to a pro rata distribution of net assets after payment of debts. Preferred stock, however, is usually given a preferential, but limited, right on distribution.

11. Right to the fair market value of stock from the corporation: This right is available to dissenting stockholders when a fundamental corporate change is undertaken, such as a merger or consolidation.

D. Stockholder's limited liability:

1. Stockholders have no general personal liability for the corporation's debts; the extent of loss is, thus, normally limited to capital investment.
2. Stockholders may be liable to creditors or victims of torts under extreme circumstances. This is known as "piercing the corporate veil."
   a. Where the corporation is severely or fraudulently undercapitalized.
   b. Where an important or sole stockholder uses the corporation fraudulently, or so commingles his personal and corporate finances that it is impossible to distinguish between them.

V. Directors

A. Principal duties and powers of directors:

1. Establish and guide policies of the corporation.
2. Select officers of the corporation.
   a. Furnish authority for officers' major acts.
   b. Supervise officers' conduct generally.
3. Determine whether to declare dividends.
4. Act when meeting as a board (i.e., usually must act as a unit), with the requisite number of directors present so as to constitute a quorum. A director acting in his individual capacity as a director has no power to bind the corporation.
5. Have implied power to do what is required for full discharge of their duties.
6. Directors are guided and limited by the charter, bylaws, and governing statutes.
7. One who continuously exercises the powers and duties of a director and who holds or purports to hold office under some colorable claim of an election, appointment, or a holding over in office is a *de facto* director.

B. Delegation of duties by directors:

1. May not vote by proxy in relation to discretionary powers but may delegate ministerial (routine) duties to others.
2. Executive committee: a device that, unless prohibited, permits a part of the entire board to act in designated matters. Full board delegates some of its powers to an executive committee.

C. Meetings of directors:

1. May be held outside state of incorporation per the Model Act.
2. Parliamentary usage generally governs.
3. Usually meet as a unit and conform to the procedures required by law and as set forth in the charter and bylaws, (e.g., there must be a quorum of the board present, which usually means a majority) unless restricted by charter or bylaws, board meeting may be held by conference telephone if all can hear each other.
4. Action may be taken by the board without a meeting unless prohibited by

the articles of incorporation or bylaws and if there is unanimous written consent to the action by members of the board.

D. Compensation of directors:

1. The board has authority to fix the compensation of its members unless prohibited by articles of incorporation or bylaws.
2. Entitled to compensation if services are rendered in a capacity other than that of director (e.g., if X, a director, renders services as a lawyer).
3. A retroactive voting of compensation for directors is voidable.

E. Tenure of office:

1. Directors are elected by shareholders at annual meeting.
2. A director may be removed with or without cause at a meeting called especially for that purpose by a majority of the shares then entitled to vote.
3. The Model Act limits tenure so as to require periodic reelection.
4. Directors whose terms have expired hold over until their successors are chosen, or until they resign or are removed.
5. It is against public policy to contrive to perpetuate directors in office by agreement or by dispensing with elections; however, it is not illegal for stockholders to unite upon a common policy for the election of certain directors (e.g., a voting trust).
6. Even though a statute or the corporate charter or a bylaw provides that tenure shall continue until a qualified successor is duly elected or appointed, a director may, nevertheless, resign at any time.
7. Personal bankruptcy of a director does not disqualify him from holding office.

F. Liability of directors:

1. Transactions with the corporation:
   a. Formerly, almost any transaction between a corporation and a director or a firm in which a director has a financial interest was void or voidable because of conflict of interest, even if the director was excluded from voting on the transaction. Now, however, it is extremely difficult to void such a transaction, even if the interested director participates in the vote for it, *if*
   (1) The director's relationship is disclosed to the board and the board approves the transaction by a vote sufficient without counting the vote of the interested director; or
   (2) The relationship is disclosed to the shareholders who vote to approve the transaction; or
   (3) The transaction is fair and reasonable to the corporation.
2. Liability of directors in other common situations:
   a. For negligence:
   (1) Not responsible for mistakes of judgment made in a manner the director reasonably believes to be in the best interests of the corporation.
   (2) Test is whether a director acted with such care as an ordinary prudent person would act in similar circumstances.
   (3) Directors may be negligent in failing to detect and prevent wrongs by co-directors.

       (4) Negligence must be proximate cause of corporation's loss.

   b. Directors of a nonexistent or defectively formed corporation (i.e., one which is neither *de jure* nor *de facto*), are personally liable when acting for such a body.

   c. For transactions involving a conflict of interest in which the corporation is harmed, the responsible directors are liable.

   d. For loans to directors and employees: A corporation shall not lend money to or use its credit to assist its directors without authorization in the particular case by its shareholders, but may lend money to and use its credit to assist any employee of the corporation or of a subsidiary, including any such employee who is a director of the corporation, if the board of directors decides that such loan or assistance may benefit the corporation.

   e. In connection with the acquisition of treasury stock, directors are personally liable if stock is improperly acquired, e.g., the corporation is rendered insolvent or as otherwise provided by the Model Act.

   f. For declaring dividends that impair the capital of the corporations, directors are personally liable.

   g. For *ultra vires* acts of the corporation, directors are personally liable unless they have indicated their dissent to such acts.

  3. Additional liability for directors is imposed by the Securities Acts.

G. Indemnification of directors and others:

  1. A corporation has the power to indemnify any person (director, officer, employee, or agent) who is sued or threatened with a suit whether civil, criminal, administrative, or investigative by reason of the fact that he was acting on behalf of the corporation in his representative capacity (e.g., as a director) as follows.

  2. To the extent that a director, officer, employee, or agent of a corporation has been successful on the merits or otherwise in defense of any suit, action or proceeding, he shall be indemnified for expenses (including attorneys' fees) actually and reasonably incurred by him.

  3. In the event the director, officer, employee, or agent loses or settles the matter, he shall be entitled to expenses (including attorneys' fees) judgments, fines, and amounts actually paid and reasonably incurred by him, if he acted in good faith and in a manner reasonably believed to be in the best interests of the corporation, and, with respect to any criminal action or proceeding, he had no reasonable cause to believe his conduct was unlawful. A conviction or plea of *nolo contendere* shall not, of itself, create a presumption which will result in a denial of indemnification.

  4. In suits brought by or for the corporation, the same rule stated in 3 applies in general except that no indemnification shall be permitted where the director or other person has been adjudged to be liable for negligence or misconduct in the performance of his duty to the corporation. However, there is an exception that permits indemnification if the court in which the action or suit was brought determines that despite the adjudication of liability the director or other person is fairly and reasonably entitled to indemnification under the circumstances.

VI. Officers

A. Distinguished from directors:

  1. Officers are individual agents of the corporation.

  2. Each officer may bind the corporation by his individual acts within the actual or apparent scope of his authority, whereas an individual director, by virtue of his office alone, cannot legally bind the corporation.

  3. Officers and directors may be the same persons.

B. Selection and tenure:

  1. Elected by directors at such time and in such manner as prescribed in the bylaws.

  2. Officers are removable by the board of directors whenever in its judgment the best interests of the corporation are served. Persons so removed may have an action for breach of contract.

C. President:

  1. Presides at shareholders' and directors' meetings.

  2. Signs certificates of stock and major commitments on behalf of the corporation.

  3. Usually must be a director.

  4. Has authority in transactions that are part of usual and regular course of business.

D. Compensation: fixed by resolution of the board of directors; if none is so fixed, the law will imply that officer, who is not a director, is to be paid a reasonable remuneration for his services.

E. Officers' liability to the corporation is governed by the general rules of agency (see Agency, p. 46, IV.B).

F. Indemnification: Officers, employees, and agents have the same rights of indemnification as directors discussed above.

VII. Financial Structure, Capital, and Dividends

A. Capital: that portion of the value of property actually received by corporation for stock it issues, based upon the par value or the arbitrarily stated value of no-par stock.

B. Shares of capital stock:

  1. Represent the interest the holder has in the corporation; give the holder no right to particular corporate property.

  2. Issued in the form of stock certificates (shares).

  3. The Model Act denies the preemptive right, unless the corporate charter expressly grants this right.

  4. "Blue sky" laws: a popular name for state acts that provide for the regulation and supervision of the sale of stock and that aim at the protection of the investing public (e.g., protect the investor from investing in fraudulent corporations).

  5. Types of stock:

  a. Par value stock: stock given a fixed arbitrary value, such as $1 per share, which is allocated to the capital account; excess of purchase price over par value is allocated to capital surplus. Stock must not be issued at a price lower than par value (discount). If stock is issued in excess of par value, excess is known as paid-in capital or premium. The total amount received on a sale is known as contributed capital. The Model Act uses **stated capital** instead of legal capital.

b. No-par stock: stock that has no fixed par value given to it; state statutes require that part of the price received for no-par stock be allocated to capital stock account. That amount is known as stated value.

c. Authorized stock: maximum amount of stock that a corporation is authorized by its charter to issue.

d. Issued stock: part of authorized stock for which certificates are made out and delivered to shareholders.

e. Outstanding stock: issued stock in the hands of stockholders, i.e., excluding treasure shares.

f. Unissued stock: stock that is authorized but as yet not issued.

g. Treasury stock: stock that is authorized but not outstanding.
  (1) Issued stock returned to or reacquired by the corporation.
  (2) A corporation can only purchase its own stock out of surplus as permitted by state law to be used for this purpose (e.g., earned surplus, capital, or paid-in surplus); sale or purchase by a corporation of its own stock usually does not result in a taxable gain or deductible loss.
  (3) Corporation cannot vote its treasury stock.
  (4) Corporation may resell treasury stock without regard to par value or preemptive rights.
  (5) Does not participate in dividends or distributions.

h. Canceled stock: Shares reacquired by the issuing corporation and then canceled (retired), i.e., no longer issued and not subject to reissuance unlike treasury stock. Stated capital is reduced as a result.

C. Classes of stock:

  1. Common: Stockholder has the right to vote on the basis of one vote per share, unless common stock is designated nonvoting, but has no right to dividends unless directors, in their discretion, declare them. Shareholder has the right to share in the general distribution of assets.

  2. Generally, preferred stock has a number of characteristics that differentiate it from common stock. Often it is held by corporate rather than individual investors because corporations pay no tax on most dividend income. Preferred stock is often used in corporate mergers and reorganizations as a means of payment or raising capital without giving up control of the corporation.

  a. Often, preferred stock has no voting rights, or voting rights only if there has been no preferred dividend for a set period.

  b. Preferred stock often has a fixed dividend, payable even if there is no dividend on common stock.
    (1) Cumulative preferred: If the amount of a fixed dividend is not paid, the obligation to pay it continues and accumulates; common stock cannot receive a dividend until all accumulated preferred dividends have been paid.

        (2) Noncumulative preferred: If a dividend is not declared in any given year, the obligation to pay it ceases even though it is earned (provided there is a valid business reason for retention of the earnings.)

        (3) Participating preferred: participates in earnings over and above the amount necessary to pay dividends on the preferred; the remainder may be distributed to both preferred and common, usually on a percentage basis.

        (4) Often, even if there is no mandatory or cumulative preferred dividend, it is agreed that preferred dividends must be paid before any dividend may be paid on common stock.

  3. Redeemable (callable): subject to redemption (recall by the corporation) at a fixed price, which is usually above the issue price paid to the corporation by the stockholder. Call price is generally fixed in the articles of incorporation, but may also be subject to an agreement among the shareholders themselves. No redemption or purchase of redeemable shares shall be made when:

    a. The corporation is insolvent

    b. The purchase would render it insolvent, or

    c. The purchase would reduce the net assets in a way that would adversely affect the rights of other shareholders upon dissolution.

  4. Convertible: Preferred stockholders are given an option to convert into common stock at a fixed exchange rate.

D. Stock subscriptions:

  1. Definition: contract to take and pay for a certain number of shares of capital stock of a corporation already organized or to be organized.

  2. Legal effect:

    a. *The Model Act provides that a subscription is irrevocable for a period of 6 months.*

    b. Not binding on the subscriber until accepted by the corporation (i.e., the corporation is in existence and the subscription is approved).

    c. Upon acceptance, subscriber becomes liable, not merely on his subscription, but as a stockholder.

E. Contract to purchase stock:

  1. Executory agreement to purchase stock in the future; it is not a subscription.

  2. Purchaser becomes liable as a stockholder only when certificate is tendered and price is paid. However, he is liable on the contract.

  3. If party fails to perform, he is liable for breach of contract.

F. Corporate bonds:

  1. Definition: a certificate or evidence of debt of the corporation, with a stated interest payable at some fixed time or intervals and principal payable at face value at maturity. (See Investment Securities, p. 302.)

  2. Owners of bonds are creditors of the corporation.

  3. Types:

    a. Bearer: not registered in any name; bond has interest coupons attached.

    b. Convertible: owner may exchange for determined number of common shares of stock.

    c. Debenture: unsecured promise to pay by obligor corporation.

    d. Mortgage bond: has lien on specified property as security in addition to obligor's general promise to pay.

    e. Income: interest is payable only if, and to the extent, it is earned.

    f. Registered: obligor records bond in specific name of owner. Interest is mailed to owner. Contrast with bearer bond above.

G. Dividends. Broadly, dividends are payments made by the corporation to its shareholders as a means of transferring corporate earnings to the shareholders.

    1. Dividend policy is governed by many factors, among them:

        a. Taxation.

            (1) Dividends received by individual shareholders are generally taxable at the higher ordinary income rate.

            (2) 85% of the dividends received by corporate shareholders are free from income taxation.

            (3) If income were retained by the corporation, presumably that fact would be reflected in the market price of the stock. In that case, a shareholder could sell off a small portion of his stock to reap the benefit of corporate income, and also get the preferential capital gains tax rate.

        b. Despite the tax advantage to individuals of the retention of income by the corporation so that the shareholder may get capital gains treatment, many shareholders prefer the stream of cash provided by regular, high-tax dividends.

VIII. Mergers and Consolidations

A. Mergers and consolidations take many forms, and use a variety of mechanisms. Some involve two friendly parties, others a hostile acquiror and resisting target.

B. Asset purchase: The union of two or more corporations by the transfer of the assets and liabilities of one or more corporations to another (the surviving corporation) that continues in existence, the other or others being dissolved and merged therein.

    1. All the property, rights, privileges, and franchises of the merged corporation shall vest in, and be enjoyed by, the possessor corporation but subject to all the liabilities of the merged corporation and the rights of its creditors.

    2. Stockholder approval must be obtained; usually a majority (but in some states at least two-thirds) of the stockholders of the target must agree to the merger (or consolidation) with dissenting stockholders having a right to have their shares purchased by the corporation at fair market value (see p. 98, IV.C.11).

C. Stock purchase: Acquisition by one corporation of all or controlling interest of another corporation's stock.

    1. Target corporation becomes subsidiary of acquiring corporation.

    2. The rights of creditors of the target corporation are in no way impaired by the acquisition, and the target corporation retains all debts and liabilities existing against it.

3. Does not require shareholder approval. Acquiring corporation may simply purchase shares of the target corporation on the market.

4. Bypasses the management of the target corporation by going directly to the shareholders, and is therefore useful in hostile takeovers.

D. Mergers and consolidations are strictly governed by state statute as to the formalities to be complied with; local state law must be consulted. Moreover, mergers and consolidations must always be considered in the light of existing antitrust and tax laws. The Internal Revenue Code treats such types of statutory mergers and consolidations as one type of reorganization, which is typically tax-free.

IX. Dissolution

A. Definition: the termination of corporation's existence by surrender, forfeiture, cancellation, or other extinguishment of its charter so that not only are the corporation's affairs wound up and its assets distributed among creditors and stockholders, but corporation also ceases to exist as a legal entity.

B. Dissolution does not result from:
1. Sale of corporation's entire assets, or
2. Appointment of a receiver, or
3. Assignment for benefit of creditors.

C. Voluntary dissolution: brought about by corporation itself.
1. Expiration of duration for corporate existence is specified in the charter.
2. Merger or consolidation.
3. Filing of certificate to bring about surrender of the charter, without a judicial proceeding, may be done by:
   a. Incorporators prior to commencement of business or issuance of shares, or
   b. Written consent of all outstanding stockholders, or
   c. Resolution at a stockholders' meeting. The Model Act provides for a majority vote at a duly called meeting.
4. Judicial proceedings on petition of stockholders. Petition must show that a dissolution is desirable in the interests of the corporation (e.g., when corporation is hopelessly deadlocked).
5. Unless a receiver is appointed by the court, the directors at the time of dissolution acts as trustees for the creditors and stockholders to wind up the corporate affairs.

D. Involuntary dissolution:
1. May be brought about by the state, acting through the attorney general, upon one of the following grounds:
   a. Nonuser. (E.g., corporation fails to organize, commence business, or undertake its duties within a given period or ceases to function over a long period.)
   b. Fraud, or fraudulent concealment, in procuring a charter.
   c. Corporation has failed to pay taxes for a specified period of time.
   d. The corporation has continued to exceed or abuse its authority.
   e. The corporation has failed for 30 days to maintain a registered agent in the state.

   2. May be brought by a stockholder because:
   - **a.** Directors are deadlocked in the management of the corporate affairs.
   - **b.** Acts of the directors are illegal or oppressive.
   - **c.** Shareholders deadlocked and failed for two consecutive annual meetings to elect directors.
   - **d.** Corporate assets are being wasted.
   3. May be brought by a creditor because:
   - **a.** Judgment debt unsatisfied and corporation is insolvent.
   - **b.** Corporation has admitted in writing that debt is due and corporation is insolvent.
   4. Must submit to the attorney general a verified statement of the facts warranting the commencement of dissolution proceedings, e.g., corporation.
   5. If the attorney general fails to commence an action within a certain time after submission of the verified statement, the stockholders or creditors may apply to a court of competent jurisdiction for leave to proceed by themselves.

X. Federal Income Taxation of Corporations

A. The corporate tax entity: The corporation is taxed as a separate legal entity and files a federal corporate tax return, usually a state income tax return, and may possibly be taxed on its income by the governmental subdivisions, e.g., income earned in a foreign state. The payment of salaries and interest by a corporation constitutes a tax deduction against income, but these constitute taxable income to the recipient, even though a shareholder. Dividends are not a tax deduction to the declaring corporation and are income to the recipients, subject to limitations in item F below.

B. Normal tax rates: The corporation had previously been taxed at 22% on the first $25,000 of ordinary taxable income and at 48% on ordinary income in excess of $25,000. To help smaller corporations during the business slow-down of the midseventies, Congress lowered the rates as follows, effective January 1, 1983:

Up to $25,000	15%
$25,001–$50,000	18%
$50,001–$75,000	30%
$75,001–$100,000	40%
Over $100,000	46%

C. Net long-term capital gains (i.e., excess of net long-term capital gains in excess of short-term capital loss): may be included with the corporation's ordinary income and taxed accordingly. The corporation is not entitled to the 60% long-term capital gain deduction and must include the net long-term capital gain in full under this election. Or, it may elect the alternate capital tax gains rate of 28% on the full net long-term capital gain, in which case the net capital gain will constitute a tax preference item. Capital losses both short- and long-term normally may be carried back three years and forward five years from the tax year in which incurred. There is no deduction of capital loss against ordinary income as there is in the case of an individual.

D. Net operating loss deduction: is carried back 3 years and forward 15 years. This sequence is mandatory and if the loss cannot be used in that period of time, it is lost.

E. Charitable contribution: for any one year limited to 10% of taxable income computed before the charitable contribution deduction, before any net operating loss or capital loss carry back, and before the dividends-received deduction.

F. Dividends-received deduction: A corporation may exclude 85% of the amount of dividends from a domestic corporation and 100% of the amount of dividends received from a corporation that is a member of a "controlled group" with the recipient corporation. An individual taxpayer has a limit of $100 dividend exclusion.

G. Allowed a subchapter S election: A corporation that meets certain specified requirements (e.g., one class of stock, 35 or fewer shareholders) may elect *not* to be taxed as a corporation for federal income tax purposes. The treatment is very roughly analogous to that of a partnership; however, there are major differences between the taxation of an electing subchapter S corporation and a partnership.

H. Accumulated earnings tax: A regular corporation is subject to an additional tax for earnings retained in excess of $250,000 if such retention is unreasonable in relation to the corporation's business needs.

I. Salary payments to owner-director-officers must be reasonable under the circumstances. This requirement is imposed in order to prevent the siphoning off of the corporation's profits by using unreasonable salary payments which are deductible.

J. The Code permits the tax-free reorganization of corporations. If the reorganization is one defined by the Code (e.g., a statutory merger or consolidation), the corporations involved and shareholders of the acquired corporation are not subject to tax.

K. Beneficial tax aspects of the corporation: The problem is often exceptionally complex and depends upon, among other things, the corporate rates applicable as well as the individual rates, and the amount of dividends distributed or retained.

L. Caveat: A new tax act may bring many corporate tax changes.

Selected Problems from CPA Examinations on Corporations

Subjective Questions and Answers

Q. 1. The Decimile Corporation is a well established, conservatively managed, major company. It has consistently maintained a $3 or more per share dividend since 1940 on its only class of stock, which has a $1 par value. Decimile's board of directors is determined to maintain a $3 per share annual dividend distribution to maintain the corporation's image in the financial community, to reassure its shareholders, and to prevent a decline in the price of the corporation's shares which would occur if there were a reduction in the dividend rate. Decimile's current financial position is not encouraging although the corporation is legally solvent. Its cash flow position is not good and the current year's earnings are only $0.87 per share. Retained earnings amount to $17 per share. Decimile owns a substantial block of Integrated Electronic Services stock which it purchased at $1 per share in

1950 and which has a current value of $6.50 per share. Decimile has paid dividends of $1 per share so far this year and contemplates distributing a sufficient number of shares of Integrated to provide an additional $2 per share.

Required

Answer the following, setting forth reasons for any conclusions stated.

1. May Decimile legally pay the $2 per share dividend in the stock of Intergrated?
2. As an alternative, could Decimile pay the $2 dividend in its own authorized but unissued shares of stock? What would be the *legal* effect of this action upon the corporation?
3. What are the federal income tax consequences to the noncorporate shareholders—
   (a) If Decimile distributes the shares of Integrated?
   (b) If Decimile distributes its own authorized but unissued stock?

A. 1. Yes. The Model Business Corporation Act authorizes the declaration and payment of dividends in cash, property, or the shares of the corporation as long as the corporation is not insolvent and would not be rendered insolvent by the dividend payment. The act limits the payment of dividends in cash or property to the unreserved and unrestricted earned surplus of the corporation. Decimile meets this requirement since it has retained earnings of $17 per share. Thus, payment of the dividend in the shares of Integrated is permitted.

2. Yes. The Model Business Corporation Act permits dividends to be declared and paid in the shares of the corporation. However, where the dividend is paid in its authorized but unissued shares, the payment must be out of unreserved and unrestricted surplus. Furthermore, when the shares paid as a dividend have a par value, they must be issued at not less than par value. Concurrent with the dividend payment, an amount of surplus equal to the aggregate par value of the shares issued as a dividend must be transferred to stated capital.

3. (a) If the shares of Integrated stock are paid as a dividend to the noncorporate shareholders, the shareholders must include the fair market value of the Integrated shares as dividend income received. Such income is ordinary income subject to a $100 dividend exclusion. The recipient taxpayer will have as a tax basis for the Integrated shares an amount equal to the fair market value of the stock received.

   (b) If the shares of Decimile stock are paid as a dividend, the recipient taxpayer is not subject to tax upon receipt of the shares. Internal Revenue Code Section 305 provides that such stock dividends are not taxable. However, the recipient must allocate his basis (typically his cost) for the shares he originally owned to the total number he owned after the distribution.

5/79

Q. 2. Grace Dawson was actively engaged in the promotion of a new corporation to be known as Multifashion Frocks, Inc. On January 3, 1978, she obtained written commitments for the purchase of shares totaling $600,000 from a group of 15 potential investors. She was also assured orally that she would be engaged as the president of the corporation upon the commencement of business. Helen Banks was the principal investor, having subscribed to $300,000 of the shares of Multifashion. Dawson immediately began work on the incorporation of Multifashion, made several contracts for and on its behalf, and made cash expenditures of $1,000 in accomplishing these goals. On February 15, 1978, Banks died and her estate has declined to honor the commitment to purchase the Multifashion shares. At the first shareholders' meeting on April 5, 1978, the day the corporation came into existence, the shareholders elected a board of directors. With shareholder approval, the board took the following actions:

1. Adopted some but not all of the contracts made by Dawson.
2. Authorized legal action, if necessary, against the Estate of Banks to enforce Banks' $300,000 commitment.
3. Declined to engage Dawson in any capacity (Banks had been her main supporter).
4. Agreed to pay Dawson $750 for those cash outlays which were deemed to be directly beneficial to the corporation and rejected the balance.

Required

Answer the following, setting forth reasons for any conclusions stated.

Discuss the legal implications of each of the above actions taken by the board of directors of Multifashion.

A.   In general, preincorporation contracts are not binding upon a newly created corporation prior to their adoption by its board of directors. Overall, one would conclude that the board acted properly and legally with respect to the actions taken. Each item is discussed separately below.

1.   The board's action was proper and within its discretion. Care, however, should be taken to avoid an implied adoption by having the corporation avail itself of some or all of the benefits of a contract while purporting to reject the contract. The corporation is not legally bound prior to adoption, because it was not in existence at the time the contract was made. Dawson, on the other hand, has liability on the contracts she made prior to incorporation. Moreover, with respect to the contracts adopted by the corporation, she assumes the status of a surety unless a novation was entered into, releasing Dawson of all liability. The nonexistent principal rule would apply to Dawson unless the contract she made was contingent upon the corporation's adopting it after coming into existence.

2.   An exception is made to the general rule of preincorporation actions insofar as stock subscriptions are concerned. Due to necessity and practical considerations, the parties who agree to provide the capital vital to the corporation's creation are not permitted to withdraw their commitments for six months. The Model Business Corporation Act provides that "a subscription for shares of a corporation to be organized shall be irrevocable for a period of six months, unless provided by the terms of the subscription agreement or unless all of the subscribers consent to the revocation of such subscriptions." Hence, the subscription by Banks is valid and is a *bona fide* claim against the Estate of Banks.

3.   The board of a newly created corporation is, at its inception, free to either adopt or reject preincorporation contracts made on behalf of the corporation. This general rule also applies to the employment contract of a promoter such as Dawson. The rationale for the rule is founded upon the belief that the corporation should not be shackled by commitments that it did not have an opportunity to adequately consider. In addition, promoters as a class have often abused their power and made what have proved to be self-serving contracts. Thus, the board acted properly, and it need not engage Dawson.

4.   The only problem that arises is that Dawson was not paid in full. She might be entitled to the full $1,000 under two possible theories. The first is a contract implied in fact (an implied adoption) by the board accepting all the benefits of the $1,000 expenditure. The other theory would be a contract implied in law based upon unjust enrichment. Under this theory, if Dawson can prove that the corporation did receive benefits which were worth $1,000, she can recover the additional $250.

5/78

Q. 3.   Franklin Corporation was incorporated in 1970. At that time 150,000 shares of common stock with a par value of $10 per share were sold. Three of the original subscribers who were also the promoters and first directors of the corporation purchased 50,000 shares at $5 per share. The offering price to the public was $15 per share. The three promoters in question sold their shares for $8 per share after they were defeated for re-election as directors three years later. The corporation is now in bankruptcy. All other creditors with the exception of Mabry, Franklin's major creditor, have settled their claims. Mabry had loaned the corporation $500,000. At the time of the loan, Mabry insisted upon audited financial statements before he would extend credit. This was done and the audited financial statements clearly indicated that par value had not been paid by the promoters upon their purchase of the 50,000 shares.

Required

Answer the following, setting forth reasons for any conclusions stated.

1. What rights does Mabry have against the three promoters?

2. What rights does Mabry have against the purchasers who bought from the promoters?

A. **1.** Each of the three promoters in question is liable to Mabry for the amount of the difference between stated par value ($10) and what they actually paid ($5). The Model Business Corporation Act provides that par must be paid without qualification, and Mabry's knowledge of the fact that less than par was paid does not prevent recovery.

   2. Under the Model Business Corporation Act, Mabry has no right of recovery against the purchasers who bought from the promoters, assuming the purchases were not fraudulent (i.e., were made in good faith).

11/76

Q. **4.** Towne is a prominent financier, the owner of 1% of the shares of Toy, Inc., and one of its directors. He is also the chairman of the board of Unlimited Holdings, Inc., an investment company in which he owns 80% of the stock. Toy needs land upon which to build additional warehouse facilities. Toy's president, Arthur, surveyed the land sites feasible for such a purpose. The best location in Arthur's opinion from all standpoints, including location, availability, access to transportation, and price, is an 8 acre tract of land owned by Unlimited. Neither Arthur nor Towne wish to create any legal problems in connection with the possible purchase of the land.

Required

Answer the following, setting forth reasons for any conclusions stated.

1. What are the legal parameters within which this transaction may be safely consummated?

2. What are the legal ramifications if there were to be a $50,000 payment "on the side" to Towne in order that he use his efforts to "smooth the way" for the proposed acquisition?

A. **1.** The Model Business Corporation Act allows such transactions between a corporation and one or more of its directors or another corporation in which the director has a financial interest. The transaction is neither void nor voidable even though the director is present at the board meeting which authorized the transaction or because his vote is counted for such purpose if:

   - The fact of such relationship or interest is disclosed or known to the board of directors or committee that authorizes, approves, or ratifies the contract or transaction by a vote or consent sufficient for the purpose without counting the votes or consents of such interested directors; or
   - The fact of such relationship or interest is disclosed or known to the shareholders entitled to vote and they authorize, approve, or ratify such contract or transaction by vote or written consent; or
   - The contract or transaction is fair and reasonable to the corporation. Common or interested directors may be counted in determining the presence of a quorum at a meeting of the board of directors or a committee thereof that authorizes, approves, or ratifies such contract or transaction.

   2. A $50,000 payment to Towne would be a violation of his fiduciary duty to the corporation. In addition, it might be illegal depending upon the criminal law of the jurisdiction. In any case he would be obligated to return the amount to the corporation. Furthermore, the payment would constitute grounds for permitting Toy to treat the transaction as voidable.

5/79

Q. **5.** Duval is the chairman of the board and president of Monolith Industries, Inc. He is also the largest individual shareholder, owning 40 percent of the shares outstanding. The corporation is publicly held, and there is a dissenting minority. In addition to his position with Monolith, Duval owns 85% of Variance Enterprises, a corporation created under the laws of the Bahamas. During 1977 Carlton, the president of Apex Industries, Inc., approached Duval and suggested that a tax-free merger of Monolith and Apex made good sense to him and that he was prepared to recommend such a course of action to the Apex board and to the shareholders. Duval studied the proposal and decided that Apex was a most desirable candidate for acquisition. Duval informed the president of Variance about the overture, told him it was a real bargain, and suggested that Variance pick it up for cash and notes. Not hearing from Duval or Monolith, Carlton accepted an offer from Variance and the business was sold to Variance. Several dissenting shareholders of Monolith learned the facts surrounding the Variance acquisition and have engaged counsel to represent them. The Variance acquisition of Apex proved to be highly profitable.

Required

Answer the following, setting forth reasons for any conclusions stated.

Discuss the rights of the dissenting Monolith shareholders and the probable outcome of a legal action by them.

A.   Directors and officers of a corporation are fiduciaries in their relationship to the corporation they serve. As such, they can neither directly nor indirectly benefit in their dealings with or for the corporation. They cannot engage in transactions that are in violation of their fiduciary duty to protect and further the best interests of their principal. Making a secret profit or acquiring a personal advantage out of their office is an act which the corporation may seek to have set aside as voidable.

Based upon this general statement of directors' and officers' fiduciary duty, it appears that the dissenting shareholders could sue derivatively on behalf of Monolith. That is, they could institute legal action on behalf of and in the name of Monolith to set aside the Variance-Apex transaction and have the business transferred to Monolith along with the profits earned during the interim. As an alternative, they could seek to recover directly from Duval damages that would be payable to Monolith.

The result seems clear in light of the facts. First, the opportunity came to Duval in his capacity as the chairman of the board and president of Monolith. Next, he did not pursue the matter but instead informed Variance's president of the opportunity to purchase Apex. Duval's conduct appears to be a case of self-dealing, duplicity, secrecy, and perhaps deceit. Taking the law and all the circumstances surrounding the purchase of Apex assets by Variance, Monolith's dissenting shareholders would probably be successful in a derivative shareholder action.

5/78

Q. 6. Rex Corporation, one of your clients, has engaged you to examine its financial statements in connection with a prospective merger or a consolidation with King Corporation. Both methods of acquisition are being considered under applicable corporate statutory law. Rex is the larger of the two corporations and is in reality acquiring King Corporation.

Required

Answer the following, setting forth reasons for any conclusions stated.

1. Discuss the meaning of the terms merger and consolidation as used in corporate law with particular emphasis on the legal difference between the two.

2. What are the major legal procedures which must be met in order to accomplish either a merger or consolidation?

A. 1. The major legal difference between a merger and a consolidation relates to the continued existence of the corporations involved. In the case of a merger of two corporations, one corporation, the acquiring corporation, survives. The acquired corporation, on the other hand, transfers all its assets to the acquiring corporation. Consequently, it is absorbed by the survivor and dissolves. The surviving corporation takes all the assets and assumes all the liabilities of the acquired corporation. When two corporations consolidate, however, both corporate parties to the consolidation transfer their assets to a new corporation and then both dissolve. Liabilities of each of the two consolidating corporations are valid against the new consolidated corporation.

2. The major legal procedures that must be followed in order to accomplish a merger or consolidation under applicable corporate statutory law are essentially these:

(a) Approval of the plan of merger or consolidation must be given by the boards of directors of the two corporations who are parties to the merger or consolidation.

(b) Timely written notice must be given to all shareholders of record. A copy or summary of the plan must accompany the notice to shareholders.

(c) Approval must be given by a majority of the shareholders of each corporation who are entitled to vote on the proposed plan of merger or consolidation. Some states require a higher percentage for approval.

(d) The articles of merger or consolidation must be properly filed by an appropriate officer of each corporation.

11/76

Q. 7. Clayborn is the president and a director of Marigold Corporation. He currently owns 1,000 shares of Marigold which he purchased several years ago upon joining the company and assuming the presidency. At that time, he received a stock option for 10,000 shares of Marigold at $10 per share. The option is about to expire but Clayborn does not have the money to exercise his option. Credit is very tight at present and most of his assets have already been used to obtain loans. Clayborn spoke to the chairman of Marigold's board about his plight and told the chairman that he is going to borrow $100,000 from Marigold in order to exercise his option. The chairman was responsible for Clayborn's being hired as the president of Marigold and is a close personal friend of Clayborn. Fearing that Clayborn will leave unless he is able to obtain a greater financial interest in Marigold, the chairman told Clayborn: "It is okay with me and you have a green light." Clayborn authorized the issuance of a $100,000 check payable to his order. He then negotiated the check to Marigold in payment for the shares of stock.

Required

Answer the following, setting forth reasons for any conclusions stated.

What are the legal implications, problems, and issues raised by the above circumstances?

A. The Model Business Corporation Act specifically deals with loans to employees and directors. If the loan is not for the benefit of the corporation, then such a loan must be authorized by the shareholders. However, the board of directors may authorize loans to employees when and if the board decides that such loan or assistance may benefit the corporation. It would appear that the loan was made for the benefit of the corporation so the latter rule applies. However, the chairman's individual authorization clearly does not meet these statutory requirements and could subject him to personal liability. Therefore, a meeting of the board should be called to consider the ratification or recall of the loan.

5/79

Practice Questions

Q. 1. The XYZ Corporation was to be formed by Peter, a promoter. In order to operate the Corporation after incorporation, it was necessary for Peter to obtain stock subscriptions, lease certain facilities, and, of course, carry out the mechanics of incorporating. Peter accomplished all these things in short order including the execution of two separate leases in the corporate name, one covering office space and the other factory space, without revealing to the lessor that the Corporation had not yet been organized. The Corporation subsequently came into existence, directors were duly elected, and the board met and took the following actions:

a. Accepted all the subscriptions that Peter had obtained.

b. Declined to accept the lease of office space that Peter had executed in the corporate name.

c. Voted to move, and subsequently did move all the Corporation's machinery into the factory that Peter had leased. However, at no time did they vote to accept this lease.

d. Issued $50 par value stock to all subscribers; some of the subscribers paid $25 per share for the stock, which was marked fully paid. These shares were subsequently sold at $30 per share to other people who were unaware of the original price paid for the stock.

Required

1. According to the prevailing rule, what is the legal status of a preincorporation stock subscription? When does it become binding upon the subscriber? Explain.
2. Can the Corporation validly decline the lease of office space that Peter made in its name? Explain.
3. Does Peter have any liability on any of the leases he made? Explain.
4. Has the Corporation accepted the contract Peter made to lease factory space? Explain.
5. If it be assumed that the Corporation had formally accepted all the above leases, is Peter free from liability? Explain.
6. What rights do creditors of the Corporation have against shareholders who took the newly issued stock for less than par? Explain.
7. Do the creditors have any rights against the subsequent purchasers of the stock that was issued for less than par? Explain.

Q. 2. During the course of your year-end audit for a new client, Otis Corporation, you discover the following facts. Otis was incorporated in 1974 and is owned 94% by James T. Parker, president; 1% by his wife; and 5% by Wilbur Chumley. These three individuals were incorporators and are officers and directors of the corporation.

Otis manufactures and sells telephonic equipment. In 1974 it sold approximately $350,000 of its various products almost exclusively in the state of its incorporation. In 1975 it began to branch out and sold $550,000 of its products throughout that state and $50,000 of its products in a neighboring state. Otis expanded rapidly, and 1976 was a banner year with sales of $1,250,000 and profits of $175,000. Otis constructed a small office building on a tract of land it had purchased for expansion purposes in the neighboring state and used the top floor to establish a regional sales office and rented the balance of the building.

During the course of your audit for the year 1976, you discover that Parker commingles his personal funds with those of the corporation, keeps very few records of board and shareholder meetings, and at his convenience disregards corporate law regarding separateness of personal and corporate affairs. The corporation had 1976 sales in excess of $300,000 in the neighboring state. The corporation has not filed any papers with the Secretary of State of that state in connection with these operations.

In light of the above discoveries, it was deemed prudent to examine the original incorporation papers which were filed by Parker in 1974. The following irregularities were discovered. The powers and purposes clause states that the geographical territory in which the newly created corporation was to do business was solely the state of incorporation. Next, a certified copy of the corporate charter was not obtained and filed in the county in which the corporation's principal place of business is located, as required by state law. Additionally, Mr. Chumley and Mrs. Parker did not sign the articles of incorporation, and prior to the effective date of incorporation, a lease was taken out and a car purchased in the corporate name.

Required

Answer the following, setting forth reasons for any conclusions stated.

Discuss the legal problems which Otis may face as a result of the above facts. Do not consider any tax implications.

Q. 3. Maximum Corporation is a medium-sized manufacturing company whose shares are publicly traded. Maximum's capital structure consists of 500,000 shares of common stock and 200,000 shares of 8% noncumulative preferred. During each of the past five years, Maximum has earned an amount well in excess of the $16,000 which the preferred shareholders would be entitled to if any dividends were declared. The board has stated that it has refrained from declaring any dividends because of the need to expand its operations by construction of new facilities or the acquisition of another corporation. In fact, the real motivation behind the board's dividend policy is to depress the market value of the preferred shares which the board members have been quietly accumulating over the past two years. As a consequence of the foregoing the accumulated earnings and profits of Maximum are now $130,000.

Required

Answer the following, setting forth reasons for any conclusions stated.

What are the legal implications of the above facts?

Q. 4. While examining the financial statements of a corporation, questions may arise regarding the right of a stockholder to share in the earnings of the corporation and the related role, duties, and obligations of the board of directors in declaring and paying dividends.

Required

1. When does a dividend vest in a stockholder? Discuss.
2. How large a dividend may a corporation legally declare? Discuss.
3. What is a director's liability in the event of an illegal dividend? Discuss.

Q. 5. The Kramer Corporation, a closely held company, has 1,000,000 shares of common stock outstanding. The balance of retained earnings and cash accounts are presently $3,000,000 and $4,000,000, respectively. These amounts appear to be in excess of Kramer's historic business needs, having been accumulated during an unusually profitable period which is unlikely to recur. The Kramer Board of Directors recently decided to retain all of the Corporation's earnings for investment in projects which do not appear destined to increase, or even maintain, the Corporation's rate of return on capital. The board of directors indicated that it intended to withhold the payment of dividends indefinitely to finance the planned expansion. The board of directors has approved the payment of higher salaries and additional bonuses to several officers (who are also directors) as an incentive to administer the expansion program. The prices of Kramer's products are also to be reduced in an effort to expand sales.

A minority stockholder of Kramer, Mr. Moffat, is dissatisfied with the new dividend policy and suspects that the planned expansion program will not be in the best interests of the Corporation. Moffat and Kramer's management have a record of open hostility. You have been retained by Moffat as his accountant to aid his attorney in the determination of the relevant facts for a possible suit.

Required

1. Can Moffat accompanied by his attorney and accountant inspect the books and records of Kramer in this connection? State "yes" or "no" and explain. What are the corporation's rights in this connection?
2. Can Moffat compel the payment of a cash dividend by Kramer? State "yes" or "no" and explain.
3. Discuss the legal means by which Moffat may proceed to redress his grievances.

Practice Objective Questions

Instructions 1–15

Select the *best* answer for each of the following items. Mark only one answer for *each* item. Answer all items. Your grade will be based on your total correct answers.

Items 1 and 2 are based on the following information:

Dexter, Inc., was incorporated in its home state. It expanded substantially and now does 20% of its business in a neighboring state in which it maintains a permanent facility. It has *not* filed any papers in the neighboring state.

1. Which of the following statements is correct?
   a. Since Dexter is a duly incorporated domestic corporation in its own state, it can transact business anywhere in the United States without further authority as long as its corporate charter so provides.

b. As long as Dexter's business activities in the neighboring state do *not* exceed 25%, it need *not* obtain permission to do business in the neighboring state.

c. Dexter must create a subsidiary corporation in the neighboring state to continue to do business in that state.

d. Dexter is a foreign corporation in the neighboring state and as such must obtain a certificate of authority or it will *not* be permitted to maintain any action or suit in the state with respect to its intrastate business.

2. Which of the following statements is *incorrect?*

    a. Dexter has automatically appointed the secretary of state of the neighboring state as its agent for the purpose of service of legal process if it failed to appoint or maintain a registered agent in that state.

    b. Dexter will be able to maintain an action or suit in the neighboring state if it subsequently obtains a certificate of authority.

    c. Dexter *cannot* defend against a suit brought against it in the neighboring state's courts.

    d. The attorney general of the neighboring state can recover all back fees and franchise taxes which would have been imposed plus all penalties for failure to pay same.

3. Derek Corporation decided to acquire certain assets belonging to the Mongol Corporation. As consideration for the assets acquired, Derek issued 20,000 shares of its no-par common stock with a stated value of $10 per share, The value of the assets acquired subsequently turned out to be much less than the $200,000 in stock issued. Under the circumstances, which of the following is correct?

    a. It is improper for the board of directors to acquire assets other than cash with no-par stock.

    b. Only the shareholders can have the right to fix the value of the shares of no-par stock exchanged for assets.

    c. In the absence of fraud in the transaction, the judgment of the board of directors as to the value of the consideration received for the shares shall be conclusive.

    d. Unless the board obtained an independent appraisal of the acquired assets' value, it is liable to the extent of the overvaluation.

4. Which of the following *cannot* properly be received as the consideration for the issuance of shares?

    a. Promissory notes.

    b. Services actually performed for the corporation.

    c. Shares of stock of another corporation.

    d. Intangible property rights.

5. Watson entered into an agreement to purchase 1,000 shares of the Marvel Corporation, a corporation to be organized in the near future. Watson has since had second thoughts about investing in Marvel. Under the circumstances, which of the following is correct?

    a. A written notice of withdrawal of his agreement to purchase the shares will be valid as long as it is received prior to incorporation.

    b. A simple transfer of the agreement to another party will entirely eliminate his liability to purchase the shares of stock.

    c. Watson may *not* revoke the agreement for a period of six months in the absence of special circumstances.

    d. Watson may avoid liability on his agreement if he can obtain the consent of the majority of other individuals committed to purchase shares to release him.

6. Mr. Parker has been issued 100 shares of common stock of Capital, Inc., having a par value of $30 per share. What aggregate consideration must Mr. Parker pay for the shares of stock if he is to escape any contingent liability in connection with these shares in the future?

    a. At least $30.

    b. At least $3,000.

    c. Less than $3,000.

    d. Between $30 and $3,000.

7. Caskill Corporation issued 100 shares of its $10 par value common stock to Mr. Jason, its vice president, for a price of $1,000. In consideration he paid $200 cash, gave a note for $400, canceled $300 salary owed him for services rendered to the Corporation, and promised to render $100 worth of future services. His shares are:

    a. Paid in full.

    b. 50% paid for.

    c. 90% paid for.

    d. 20% paid for.

8. Miller Corporation declared a common stock dividend of 1 common share for every 10 common shares outstanding. The owner's equity accounts of the Corporation immediately prior to the declaration of the common stock dividend were as follows:

Stated capital (10,000 shares of common stock issued and outstanding, $1 par value per share)	$10,000
Earned surplus (retained earnings)	4,000

    No other transactions are relevant. Immediately after the issuance of the common stock dividend, stated capital will amount to:

    a. $11,000.

    b. $10,000.

    c. $9,000.

    d. $1,000.

9. Laser Corporation lent $5,000 to Mr. Jackson, a member of its board of directors. Mr. Jackson was also vice president of operations. The board of directors, but *not* the stockholders, of Laser authorized the loan on the basis that the loan would benefit the Corporation. The loan made to Mr. Jackson is:

    a. Proper.

    b. Improper because Mr. Jackson is an employee.

    c. Improper because Mr. Jackson is a director.

    d. Improper because Mr. Jackson is both a director and an employee.

10. Walter Thomas, as the promoter of Basic Corporation, made a contract for and on behalf of Basic with Fair Realty Corporation for the purchase of an office building. Thomas did *not* disclose that the corporation had *not* been created. Thomas will *not* have any liability on the contract:

    a. Because he made it in the name of the Corporation.

    b. If the Corporation subsequently adopts the contract.

    c. If the Corporation and Fair Realty enter into a novation regarding the contract.

    d. If the Corporation comes into existence and rejects the contract.

11. Donald Walker is a dissident stockholder of the Meaker Corporation, which is listed on a national stock exchange. Walker is seeking to oust the existing board of directors and has notified the directors that he intends to sue them for negligence. Under the circumstances, Walker:

    a. Can be validly denied access to the corporate financial records.

    b. Can be legally prohibited from obtaining a copy of the stockholder list because his purpose is *not bona fide*.

    c. Must show personal gain on the part of the directors if he is to win his lawsuit.

    d. Can insist that the Corporation mail out his proxy materials as long as he pays the cost.

12. The board of directors of Anchor Corporation and of Bridge, Inc., two corporations whose shares are listed on a major stock exchange, have discussed the possibility of merging the companies. Considering such a merger:

    a. Unanimous approval by both boards of directors of the merger would permit the merger without approval of shareholders of the corporations.

    b. Approval by at least a two-thirds majority of the board of directors of each corporation would permit merger without shareholder approval.

    c. If the merger were validly accomplished by an exchange of Anchor stock for Bridge stock with Bridge surviving, creditors of Anchor could look to Bridge for payment of their claims.

    d. The new board of directors immediately after the merger of Anchor into Bridge automatically consists of the previous boards of the two corporations.

13. Randolph Corporation would like to pay cash dividends on its common shares outstanding. Under corporate law, Randolph may *not* pay these dividends if it is insolvent or would be rendered so by the payment. For this purpose, an insolvent corporation is one which

    a. Is unable to pay its debts as they become due in the usual course of its business.

    b. Has an excess of liabilities over assets.

    c. Has an excess of current liabilities over current assets.

    d. Has a deficit in earned surplus.

14. A corporation may *not* redeem its own shares when it

    a. Is currently solvent but has been insolvent within the past five years.

    b. Is insolvent or would be rendered insolvent if the redemption were made.

    c. Has convertible debt that is publicly traded.

    d. Has mortgages and other secured obligations equal to 50% of its stated capital.

15. The consideration for the issuance of shares by a corporation may *not* be paid in

    a. Services actually performed for the corporation.

    b. Services to be performed for the corporation.

    c. Tangible property.

    d. Intangible property.

5

Estates and Trusts

AICPA Content Specification Outline

Formation and Purposes
Allocation Between Principal and Income
Fiduciary Responsibilities
Distributions and Termination

Contents

I. Estates

A. Creation of an estate. An estate comes into existence upon a person's death. It is the legal entity that succeeds to the title to the property of the decedent and also is liable for ("inherits") his debts. A party is said to die testate if he has executed a valid will that is in existence at his death, and intestate if he dies without a will (see p. 120, I.D and E).

    1. A will is the legal declaration of a person's intent as to the disposition of his property after his death, and normally names the person (the executor) whom he wishes to accomplish his intent; it may also include provisions for the guardianship of his children, the administration of his estate, and the elimination of the necessity of posting a surety bond.

    2. Intestate succession and administration. Where one dies without a will, the state intestate succession laws determine who is to inherit her property. Naturally, the spouse and children are considered first. The court, upon a proper petition, appoints an administrator for the estate, and a surety bond guaranteeing faithful performance by the administrator must be obtained. In the case where there is a will, but no executor is named in the will, the court also appoints an administrator with the will attached.

B. Nature of the interest created in the beneficiary:

    1. A will only becomes effective upon the death of the maker; transfers during lifetime are termed intervivos gifts.

    2. A will is ambulatory, i.e., the testator has the power to alter or revoke the will during his lifetime.

    3. A will is capable of passing property not owned by the maker at the time the will was made.

    4. A will does not affect the rights of joint tenants to succeed to the deceased's interest in jointly owned property, which has as its principal feature the right of survivorship. Thus, real property, stocks, bonds, and savings accounts held in joint tenancy pass to the survivor according to the terms of the joint ownership and not by will. Similarly, insurance benefits and other types of contractual arrangements, such as death benefits payable to a designated beneficiary pursuant to a pension plan, pass in accordance with the terms of the policy and not according to the will unless the estate is named as the beneficiary. The executor or administrator is not entitled to a commission for administering such property, although it is included in the gross estate of the deceased for estate tax purposes.

C. Legacy: a disposition of personalty under a will:

1. A *general* legacy is a gift of personal property payable out of the general assets of the testator (e.g., a bequest of $1,000).

2. A *specific* legacy is a bequest of personal property particularly specified (e.g., grandfather's gold watch).

3. The importance of the distinction is that a specific legacy adeems (is extinguished) unless it exists unchanged in substance at the death of the of the testator, i.e., if the specific property is destroyed prior to the testator's death, the gift would adeem (be extinguished). A general legacy does not adeem.

4. Even where there is a will, the surviving spouse may elect to receive what is known as a statutory share of the decedent spouse's estate, despite the fact that the decedent has cut the survivor out of the will or specified only a nominal amount. The size of the share is determined in accordance with the state's intestate succession laws. The spouse's share depends upon who else survives the decedent, particularly whether children survive the deceased's spouse.

D. Inheritance: in its restricted sense, something obtained through the laws of descent and distribution from an intestate (one who died without a will). In its popular sense, it includes property obtained by devise (will) or descent.

E. Rules of intestate succession, i.e., how the property is to be disposed of if the deceased died without a will (the rules vary from state to state).

1. Surviving spouse: States have enacted statutes permitting the surviving spouse to receive a given portion of the estate.

2. Partial order of distribution after spouse has received a share (prevailing law):

   a. To descendants (e.g., children, grandchildren of deceased), and if none survive:

   b. To ascendants (e.g., parents, grandparents of deceased), and if none survive:

   c. *Per stirpes:* a method of dividing an intestate share or a share stipulated in a will. A class or group of distributees takes the share that their deceased ancestor would have been entitled to. The representatives of the ancestor divide his share among themselves rather than taking it as individuals. For example, X, a widower, died intestate or provided in his will that his estate is to be divided among his surviving descendants in equal shares *per stirpes*. At his death, his son and two children of a deceased daughter survive him. The son gets one half and the two grandchildren divide the other half.

II. Estate Administration

A. Purposes:

1. To carry out decedent's wishes as expressed in a will.

2. To discover and collect the assets of the decedent.

3. To pay all claims and taxes against the estate.

   a. In order to pay the debts of the estate, the personal representative (executor or administrator) may sell the assets of the estate.

       b. He must sell the personalty first, and if this does not meet the claims, he may, with court authorization, sell the realty.

       c. Testator (the deceased) can, by will, empower the executor to sell realty for any and all purposes.

       d. Generally, a creditor who might have asserted a claim against the administrator or executor has no remedy against heirs, devisees, legatees, or distributees after the completion of the administration of the estate.

    4. Distribute the estate to those entitled to it.

B. Executors and administrators:

    1. Definitions:

       a. Executor: the person named in the will and then empowered by the court to act for the estate and to carry out its terms.

       b. Administrator: the person appointed by the probate court to administer an estate when the decedent dies intestate.

    2. General duties of executors and administrators:

       a. Required to use reasonable diligence and act in entire good faith in that this is a fiduciary relationship, i.e., a position of highest trust. He must not self-deal with the trust and make a profit at the trust's expense. Such transactions are voidable.

       b. May contract on behalf of the estate, subject to probate court approval under certain circumstances.

       c. May engage necessary legal, accounting, and other services.

       d. Must use reasonable care to promptly collect and preserve the assets of the estate; failure to exercise due care will impose tort liability on the negligent party. (E.g., he is liable for any shrinkage of assets due to negligence or violation of his duty.)

       e. Must not commingle the estate funds with his own.

          (1) Commingling is a misdemeanor in some states.

          (2) He is liable for shrinkage in assets if funds have been commingled.

       f. Represent the estate in suits brought against it.

       g. Must keep adequate accounting records to show disposition of the assets of the estate.

       h. At conclusion of his duties toward the estate, an accounting is generally rendered and a judicial settlement is secured in the probate court, thereby closing the estate. The financial accounting rendered should contain:

          (1) An inventory of all assets of the estate.

          (2) A statement of all debts of the estate.

          (3) The disposition of the assets and income according to the will or according to law.

          (4) Expenses, costs, and commission of the executor or administrator.

       i. In all matters relating to settlement of the estate, in addition to those above, the executor or administrator is subject to probate court control and the beneficiary or other interested persons may object.

C. Income versus principal:

    1. This area of law is governed by a uniform act, the Uniform Principal and Income Act. It was originally approved in 1924 and substantially revised in 1962. It has been adopted with some variations in more than two-thirds of the states. Therefore, it represents the majority rule.

2. Most of the disputes arising over the question of the proper distribution of the estate as between the income beneficiary and the ultimate taker arise in connection with the administration of an estate wherein the will created a life estate in one party and the remainder in another or where the will created a trust (see below).

3. Insofar as *receipts* are concerned, the Uniform Act treats estates and trusts alike in most respects. An appendix contains a simplified version of the most common rules applicable to both estate and trust distribution of receipts, where the will does not provide for allocation, see p. 127. The allocations are for state law purposes and not the same as those that apply to federal taxation.

4. In most instances the will provides the answer as to *charges* against the estate. The usual practice is to provide that charges incurred in administration are to diminish the residuary takers' share. If there is no provision as to allocation of expenses, the Uniform Act applies.

III. Trusts

A. Formation and purposes of a trust:

1. Definition: a fiduciary relationship in which one person holds legal title to property subject to an equitable obligation to keep or use it for the benefit of another.

2. Elements:

   a. Settlor or grantor: one who creates a trust.

      (1) A single individual may be settlor and trustee, or settlor and beneficiary, but not all three. See III.A.2.b(2) below.

      (2) May revoke a trust only if the trust instrument so provides.

      (3) Must have legal capacity to make an *inter vivos* transfer of property.

   b. Trustee: Generally, any person capable of taking title to property is competent. If a named trustee declines to serve by refusing to accept the trust property and the responsibility of serving as a trustee, the settlor cannot force him to do so.

      (1) Trustee has the legal, but not the beneficial, interest in the trust property.

      (2) Sole beneficiary cannot be the sole trustee of the trust; merger of the equitable and legal interests occurs, and hence there is no trust.

   c. Trust property: may consist of any interest in property that may be the subject of a present transfer. An attempt to create a trust in future property is not a present trust, but a contract to create a trust in the property when it is acquired.

   d. Beneficiary: has an equitable title or interest; it may be any ascertained or ascertainable person or group of persons, natural or artificial, including the settlor.

3. Purposes: spelled out in trust document

4. Creation: Settlor must manifest an intention usually in writing, or by conduct, to create a trust; however, knowledge and acceptance of the trust by the trustee or beneficiary are not required; it may be created by:

    a. *Inter vivos* transfer to the trustee; if personalty is the subject of the trust, there need not be a writing. This may provide for the ultimate disposition of the property in trust upon the death of the settlor without the necessity of submitting the trust instrument for probate. This is so since the property has been transferred to the trustee and no longer is a part of the settlor's estate upon death.

    b. Testamentary transfer to the trustee (i.e., a trust to take effect on the death of the settlor); must comply with the requirements for a valid will (i.e., be in writing and subscribed by at least two witnesses).

    c. Settlor declaring himself the trustee of property without any transfer.

5. Creation of a trust of real property or where performance is in excess of one year from the date of the making must be evidenced by a writing signed by the settlor in order to satisfy the Statute of Frauds (see Contracts, p. 148, III.E).

    a. Writing need be signed by the donor.

    b. Must sufficiently designate the property, beneficiary, and the purpose of trust.

    c. Oral trust is valid if the trust has been fully or partly executed.

6. No consideration is necessary for the present creation of any trust; however, a contract to create a trust in the future requires the same consideration as any other contract.

7. Restrictions.

    a. Trust must be "active," i.e., the trustee must actually have some duties to perform. (E.g., trustee has possession of property and has power to manage it.)

    b. Trusts of personal property may be created for any lawful purpose. The law of the domicile of the settlor governs the validity of trusts of personal property.

    c. In some states, trusts of real property are limited to a few purposes. (E.g., a trust to receive the rents and profits of real property and apply them to the use of the beneficiaries. This type of trust is known as a spendthrift trust in that it is often used to protect improvident persons; the equitable interest of the beneficiary is nontransferable (inalienable). The law of the situs (place) of the realty governs the validity of trusts of realty.)

    d. Duration is limited by the rule against perpetuities. The rule states that a trust cannot have a greater duration than lives in being plus 21 years. The measuring lives must be in being at the creation of the trust, the ultimate beneficiaries need not. This rule exists because, when a trust is created, the absolute power of alienation (transfer) of the property held in trust is suspended. The law wishes to prevent the tying up of title to property for an unreasonable length of time; it prefers to measure the period it will allow this suspension to continue in terms of human lives rather than fixed years. (E.g., a trust for 30 years with X as the trustee for the benefit of Y would fail.)

B. Business or Massachusetts trusts:

    a. Trust device used to carry on a business. Title of assets is given by investors to trustee.

      b. Business trusts have many characteristics of corporations.

        (1) Centralized management by trustee.

        (2) Usually limited liability.

        (3) Perpetual existence.

        (4) Investor's share can be sold like corporate stock.

        (5) Some business trusts are taxed as corporations. Many, however, e.g. real estate investment trusts (REITS) and oil royalty trusts are not taxed as corporations, but are able to avoid this by distributing the requisite amount of profits to the trust owners.

C. Administration of trusts:

    1. Duties of trustee:

      a. Those imposed by terms of the trust; however, deviation from those duties may be permitted in emergencies but normally with court approval.

      b. Those imposed by law.

        (1) Take possession of the trust property.

        (2) Defend the trust against attack by settlor or third parties if there are reasonable grounds for such a defense.

        (3) Reasonably protect trust property from loss or destruction and make the trust property productive.

        (4) Must not commingle trust funds with his personal funds; if a loss occurs, trustee will be liable, even if he is acting innocently and in good faith.

      c. Trustee, in absence of provision to the contrary, may:

        (1) Sell trust property if necessary to carry out the trust purpose.

        (2) Lease real estate even if the trust instrument prohibits its sale.

        (3) Compromise claims in connection with the trust estate.

      d. If more than one trustee is named for a trust, all must agree before any action may be validly taken.

    2. Liabilities of trustee:

      a. In contrast: as a general rule, personally liable on contracts made on behalf of the trust (unless the contract provides otherwise), but may reimburse himself from trust income.

      b. In tort: personally liable for torts committed by himself or his agents, but may reimburse himself if he was not personally at fault (e.g., in cases of liability without fault).

    3. Income versus principal *(corpus)*.

      a. Proceeds received from use of the trust property are treated as income for the income beneficiary. They include among others, the following:

        (1) Interest on notes and bonds owned by the trust.

        (2) Net rents (gross rents less cost of collection, insurance, and repairs).

        (3) Royalties from property that is subject to depletion.

      b. Ordinary expenses are chargeable to the trust income and include the following:

        (1) Cost of insurance on the trust property.

        (2) Interest on mortgage on the trust property.

        (3) Repair of the buildings on the trust property.

    c. Changes in form of the trust *res* (property) are treated as principal *(corpus)* for the remainderman's benefit and include the following:

        (1) Stock dividends in the form of the corporation's own stock. Dividends in the form of stock in another corporation are treated as income. Stock splits are, of course, principal.

        (2) Proceeds from the sale of a stock subscription right by the trustee.

        (3) Sums received in settlement of claims arising out of damage to the principal (e.g., insurance proceeds from the destruction of a house owned by the trust estate). However, any payment based on loss of the trust income is treated as income.

    d. Extraordinary expenses are chargeable to trust principal and include the following:

        (1) Cost incurred in sale or purchase of trust property.

        (2) Cost of improvements made by the trustee where the improvement will last longer than the income beneficiary's interest; the value of the income beneficiary's yearly interest in the improvement is calculated by dividing the cost of the improvement by the number of years of its expected duration. This amount is reserved annually by the trustee and added to the principal.

    e. For a more detailed presentation of the income versus principal problem, see the Appendix, beginning on p. 127.

  4. Accounting: periodic or final submission of accounts of trust property for court approval; it may be voluntary or by court order.

  5. Settlement: Account is settled when the court approves the trustee's handling of trust property as set forth in his account.

D. Distributions and termination:

  1. Natural termination at end of the designated trust period.

    a. Death of settlor or trustee during the trust period does not ordinarily terminate the trust unless he is the measuring life.

    b. Refusal of named trustee to serve will not ordinarily prevent the creation of the trust or terminate it. The court will appoint a substitute.

  2. Achievement of the trust purposes before natural termination of the trust period.

    a. If the settlor and all the beneficiaries agree to a termination, it may be granted by the court, although the trust purposes have not been accomplished.

    b. If only the beneficiaries consent to the termination without consent of the settlor, and if any of the trust purposes have not been accomplished, the termination will not be granted.

  3. Merger: The legal and equitable estates are vested in the same person (e.g., the sole trustee is the sole beneficiary).

  4. Failure of the trust purpose: If a private trust becomes impossible to perform or illegal, it terminates.

  5. Upon termination of the trust, the trustee has the duty to transfer with reasonable dispatch the trust property to those entitled to it. His legal interest is terminated when this has been accomplished.

    6. Resignation of a trustee:

        a. Generally, a trustee may resign only with the permission of the court or consent of all beneficiaries, or if the trust instrument permits it.

        b. May resign as a matter of personal convenience if serving without compensation, or without agreement as to duration.

E. Income taxation of trusts and estates:

    1. Both are taxable entities, but may not be subject to tax. An estate is allowed an exemption of $600 *per annum* and a simple trust $300. They are taxable upon the income received and retained, and are subject to the tax rules applicable to an individual.

    2. The gross income of the trust or estate is reduced by the ordinary and necessary expenses incurred (e.g., attorney's and accounting fees, trustee's commissions) and the distributions of income it makes to beneficiaries.

F. Federal estate and gift tax:

    1. Unification of estate and gift tax rates: The 1976 Tax Reform Act unified the tax rates for estates and gifts and applies a single rate schedule to the cumulative transfers during life and at death. Under the Economic Recovery Act of 1981 a donor may exclude $10,000 annually per donee from the value of the total gifts subject to tax. This exclusion amount becomes $20,000 where the spouse consents and joins in the gift. In addition, the amount paid on behalf of an individual as school tuition or as medical expenses will not be treated as a gift.

        The 1981 Act significantly reduced the rate on transfers over $2,500,000 during a four-year transitional period beginning in 1982. The 1985 maximum rate will drop from 55% to 50% in 1988.

    2. There is a unified credit against the gift and estate tax. In 1986 the credit is $55,800 which equals a $500,000 exemption. In 1987 the credit will reach its maximum of $192,800 which will give an exemption of $600,000.

    3. Marital deduction: The 1981 Act provides an unlimited estate marital deduction for descendents dying after January 1, 1982 and a 100% gift tax marital deduction for gifts to spouses after said date. Thus, where the first to die spouse leaves his or her entire estate to the surviving spouse, no estate tax will be due no matter how large the estate is. Likewise spouses may transfer property between themselves without tax liability.

    4. The 1981 Act reverses prior policy as to gifts in contemplation of death. In general, gifts made within three years of death are not considered in the computation of the taxable estate; an exception is life insurance.

    5. The gross estate: The deceased's gross estate will include all property owned at time of death—real, personal, whether tangible or intangible, and wherever situated.

    6. The net estate: Debts owed by decedent at time of death, funeral, and administrative expenses are deducted from the gross estate to arrive at the net estate. Charitable gifts are also a deduction.

Table I Receipts (Trusts and Estates)*

	Principal	Income	Apportion
1. Annuities			X
2. Bonds			
Call premium	X		
Interest		X	
Proceeds of sale	X		
3. Business (sole proprietor or partnership)			
Profit		X	
Loss	X		
4. Change in form of principal	X		
5. Condemnation proceedings	X		
6. Corporate distributions			
Call for shares	X		
Cash dividend (regular and extraordinary)		X	
In lieu of ordinary cash dividend		X	
Liquidation (total or partial)	X		
Merger, consolidation, reorganization	X		
Proceeds of rights of property distribution		X	
Rights to subscribe to share or securities of another corporation		X	
Rights to subscribe to shares or securities of distributing corporation	X		
Sale of rights of distributing corporation	X		
Stock dividend	X		
Stock in another corporation		X	
Stock split	X		
7. Depletion allowance	X		
8. Depreciation allowance	X		
9. Discount on Treasury bills and certificates		X	
10. Farming operation			
Profit		X	
Loss	X		
11. Insurance proceeds			
Life insurance	X		
On principal asset	X		
12. Interest			
E Bond increment, savings account, savings and loan deposits			
Periodically paid		X	
Prepaid		X	
13. Loan repayment	X		
14. Mutual fund — ordinary income distribution		X	
Other distributions (e.g., capital gain)	X		
15. Partnership interest			
Profit		X	
Loss	X		
16. Prepayment penalties (except bond call premium)		X	
17. Profit from change in form of principal	X		
18. Real estate investment trust—ordinary income		X	
All other distributions	X		
19. Refund of principal	X		
20. Regulated investment company			
Ordinary income distribution		X	
Other distributions (e.g., capital gain)	X		
21. Rental income (real and personal property)		X	
Arrears		X	
Prepaid or advance		X	
22. Sale or transfer of principal	X		

*This chart is a simplified version of the generally prevailing rules applicable to common allocation problems. It is based primarily on the Uniform Principal and Income Act. It applies when the trust does not contain its own provisions for allocation. It is used for state law purposes and does not represent the federal tax treatment of the trust.

Table II Charges (Trusts Only)

	Principal	Income	Apportion
1. Bond premium	X		
2. Capital improvements—an allowance for depreciation may be taken	X		
3. Depreciation allowance		X	
4. Expenses:			
Current management of principal and application of income			
Incurred in connection with principal	X		
Investing and reinvesting principal	X		
Ordinary, in the administration, management, or preservation of trust property		X	
Preparation of property for sale or rental	X		
5. Extraordinary repairs—an allowance for depreciation may be established	X		
6. Indebtedness—principal payments	X		
7. Judicial proceedings (including court costs, attorney, and other fees)			
Accountings (periodic)	½*	½*	
Construe trust	X*		
Primarily concerning income interest		X*	
Primarily concerning principal	X		
Protect trust or property	X*		
Title of trust property	X*		
8. Mortgage—principal payments	X		
9. Repairs (ordinary)		X	
10. Taxes			
Estate or inheritancee apportioned to trust on receipts defined as income	X	X	
11. Trustees fees (regular)	½	½	

*Unless the court directs otherwise.

Selected Problems from CPA Examinations on Estates and Trusts

Subjective Questions and Answers

Q. 1. You have been the CPA for Arnold Smith, who has died. Mr. Smith, a widower, left surviving his mother, age 86, and a son, Donald, age 26. Arnold Smith's daughter, Rita, died one year before he did, and is survived by her husband Bob and two children, Alice and Marie. At the time of Mr. Smith's death, Bob was still a widower and Alice and Marie were minors. Mr. Smith's will, which was duly probated, provides, in part:

> All the property which I shall own at the time of my death or which shall be subject to disposition under my will is hereinafter referred to as my Residuary Estate.
>
> If any descendant of mine shall survive me, my Residuary Estate shall be divided and set apart for my descendants who shall survive me, in equal shares *per stirpes*. The shares so set apart shall be dealt with as hereinafter provided in this Article, and I bequeath and devise them accordingly.
>
> (1) In the case of each share set apart for a descendant of mine who shall be under age twenty-five (25) years and who shall have been in being at the time of my death, my trustee shall hold such share as the principal of a separate trust for the primary benefit of such descendant, shall invest and reinvest such principal, and shall pay the net income therefrom to such descendant. Such trust shall continue until such descendant shall attain

the age of twenty-five (25) years or shall sooner die. Thereupon my trustee shall distribute the entire principal of such trust to such descendant, or if he shall not be living, shall distribute or otherwise deal with such principal as such descendant, by his last will duly admitted to probate and not otherwise shall direct (except that the power so granted to such descendant shall not be exercisable, to any extent, in favor of such descendant, his estate, his creditors or the creditors of his estate), and to the extent, if any, that such principal shall not be disposed of effectively through the exercise by such descendant of the power granted to him, my trustee shall distribute such principal to the XYZ charity, a home for foster children.

(2) In the case of each share set apart for any other descendant of mine, such share shall be distributed to such descendant.

If no descendant of mine shall survive me, I bequeath and devise my Residuary Estate to the XYZ charity.

Mr. Smith's Residuary Estate equals $100,000. The executor and the attorney for the estate have asked you to assist in preparing financial reports for the estate.

Required
1. Under the above terms of the will, who are the beneficiaries and what is the amount and nature of each of their legacies? Explain.
2. Assume that a beneficiary's share has been placed in trust under the terms of the will:
   a. If the trustee believes that the beneficiary is not in need of income currently, under the above terms of the will may he accumulate income for the beneficiary so that it can be paid to the beneficiary at a later time when he is in need? Explain.
   b. Describe the power that a beneficiary of a trust is given over the disposition of the principal of his trust.

A. 1. Mr. Smith's Residuary Estate is to be set apart for his surviving descendants, in equal shares *per stirpes*. Donald, Alice and Marie are all surviving descendants of Mr. Smith. The words *"per stirpes"* indicate that Alice and Marie are to share the amount which would have been received by their mother, Rita, if she had survived. Therefore, Donald is entitled to have a share in the amount of $50,000 set apart for him, and Alice and Marie are each entitled to have a share in the amount of $25,000 set apart for them. Since Donald is over the age of 25, he is entitled to have his share distributed to him outright. Since Alice and Marie are both under that age, their shares are to be placed in separate trusts for their primary benefit and they are to receive the net income from their respective trusts until they reach the age of 25, or sooner die. If they reach the age of 25, they receive the principal of the trust fund outright. If a beneficiary dies before reaching that age, the trust fund is payable in accordance with the terms of her will, or, if she does not effectively exercise the power given to her, it is payable to XYZ charity.

2. a. No. The trustee is given no power to accumulate income under the terms of the trusts. In absence of such an express power, the trustee is not authorized to accumulate income and must at reasonable intervals pay all of the net income from the trusts to the respective income beneficiaries pursuant to the terms of the trusts.

b. A beneficiary of a trust is given a "testamentary," "limited" power of appointment over the principal of this trust. The power is "testamentary" because it may only be effectively exercised on the death of the beneficiary, if he dies prior to reaching the age of 25 leaving a will which is duly admitted to probate and under which he has effectively exercised the power. The power is limited because it may only be exercised in favor of persons other than the beneficiary, his estate, his creditors or the creditors of his estate. The power is so limited in order to avoid the inclusion of the trust principal in the beneficiary's estate for estate tax purposes, if the beneficiary dies during the time the trust remains in effect.

11/66

Q. 2. You have been assigned by a CPA firm to work with the trustees of a large trust in the preparation of the first annual accounting to the court. The income beneficiaries and the remaindermen are in dispute as to the proper allocation of the following items on which the trust indenture is silent:
   (1) Costs incurred in expanding the garage facilities of an apartment house owned by the trust and held for rental income.

(2) Real estate taxes on the apartment house.

(3) Cost of casualty insurance premiums on the apartment house.

(4) A 2/1 stock split of common stock held by the trust for investment.

(5) Insurance proceeds received as the result of a partial destruction of an office building which the trust owned and held for rental income.

(6) Costs incurred by the trust in the sale of a tract of land.

(7) Costs incurred to defend title to real property held by the trust.

Required

1. Explain briefly the nature of a trust, the underlying concepts in the allocation between principal and income, and the importance of such allocations.

2. Indicate the allocations between principal and income to be made for each of the above items.

A. **1.** A trust generally involves a transfer of income-producing property (principal) by will, deed, or indenture to a trustee who takes legal title to the property subject to a fiduciary obligation to manage and conserve the property for the benefit of others who are described as beneficiaries. A trust generally provides that the trustee shall invest the trust principal and pay the income therefrom to the income beneficiary and at the termination of the trust transfer the trust principal to the remainderman. The property that composes the principal of the trust may change from time to time as the trustee sells and reinvests the proceeds.

The will or trust agreement can provide the rules for allocation of items between principal and income. In the absence of specific trust provisions, the law of the jurisdiction in which the trust is located will govern. For this purpose, most jurisdictions have adopted the Uniform Principal and Income Act or some variation thereof. Income produced by the investment and management of the trust principal is kept separate for distribution to the income beneficiary. However, ordinary operating expenses incurred by the trust in generating earnings are charged against income. Similarly, expenses incurred in acquiring or protecting the trustee's title to principal are charged against principal. Thus, the allocation between principal and income of a trust is of great importance because it affects the respective benefits derived from the trust by the income beneficiary and the remainderman.

2. (1) Principal

(2) Income

(3) Income

(4) Principal

(5) Principal

(6) Principal

(7) Principal

5/76

Q. **3.** Frugal, for whom you perform accounting services, told you, his CPA, that he plans to create his own *inter vivos* trust (living trust) and that he plans to name you the trustee.

Frugal showed you the following provision in a draft of the disposition he plans for the trust principal at his death.

> On my death the then principal of the trust shall be distributed to my then living descendants, in equal shares *per stirpes*.

Required

1. Would such a trust instrument have to be probated as a will at Frugal's death, since the trust instrument provides for disposition of the property at death? Explain.

2. If you do not wish to serve as trustee is there any way of your avoiding the responsibility even if Frugal insists that he will name you as trustee over your objection? Explain.

3. State the percentage of trust principal that each party would receive at Frugal's death if during his life Frugal had only two children, Rita and Selma, and was survived by (a) his brother John, (b) his sister Susan, (c) his daughter Rita, (d) his grandchildren Thomas and Mary, whose mother is Rita, and (e) his grandchild Albert (whose mother, Selma, predeceased Frugal).

A.   **1.** No. If the trust is to be effective at its creation, the property comprising the principal of the trust must be conveyed by Frugal to the trustee of the trust who is to hold the property in accordance with the terms of the trust for the benefit of the beneficiaries of the trust: The trust property, therefore, no longer belongs to Frugal, the settlor of the trust: So long as the trust is not revoked prior to Frugal's death, the property will not be a part of Frugal's probate estate at his death.

      2. Yes. If the named trustee refuses to serve as trustee and refuses to accept delivery of the trust property and assume the responsibility of serving as trustee, the settlor cannot force him to do so.

      3. Rita and Albert would each receive 50% of the Trust principal at Frugal's death. John, Frugal's brother, and Susan, Frugal's sister, would not be entitled to any share since they are collateral relatives rather than descendants of Frugal. Rita, Frugal's child, is a descendant and would be entitled to 50% of the trust principal. Rita's children, Thomas and Mary, are descendants but are not entitled to share since their mother, Rita, is living. Albert, Selma's child, is a descendant and is entitled to 50% of the trust principal, receiving in place of his deceased mother, Selma, pursuant to the *per stirpes* distribution, the share which she would have received had she survived.

5/68

Q.   **4.** Thomas has transferred his transistor manufacturing business to the X Trust Company in trust for the benefit of his son Peter for life, with the remainder to go to Peter's son, James. The X Trust Company insured the business with the Y Insurance Company by taking out two policies. The first policy was a standard fire insurance policy covering the building, equipment, etc. The other policy was secured to cover the loss of income during any period that the business was inoperable as a result of tornado, earthquake, or fire. The buildings and equipment were subsequently destroyed by fire, and the Y Insurance Company paid the proceeds to the X Trust Company. Both Peter and James claim the entire proceeds of the insurance policies.

Required

What disposition should the X Trust Company make of the entire proceeds under the terms of the trust? Explain.

A.   The insurance proceeds on the building and equipment must be retained as a part of the corpus and the insurance proceeds representing lost income should be held for the benefit of, or paid to, the life beneficiary.

      As a general rule, sums received on an insurance policy in settlement of claims arising out of damage to the corpus are treated as corpus. Such sums will be used to repair or replace the damaged or destroyed property. However, payments received on a policy specifically taken out to cover lost income will be treated as income and the life beneficiary will be entitled to receive same.

11/61

Practice Questions

Q.   **1.** Wellington purchased several thousand dollars worth of corporate securities in the joint names of "Wellington and Potter or the survivor."

      Later, Wellington decided that Potter should not receive the corporate securities at Wellington's death because Potter had become wealthy. Wellington, therefore, went to his attorney and executed a codicil to his Last Will and Testament naming his brother as the party to receive the securities upon his death.

      Wellington is now dead.

Required

Who is entitled to the securities in question? Explain.

Q. 2. X, as trustee for the benefit of Y, the life beneficiary, received the $1,000 annual cash dividends on the stock that made up the corpus of the trust. Y was abroad at the time of receipt, and X in good faith and with complete honesty deposited the money in his own (X's) bank account. Before Y returned, X's bank failed and the dividend in bankruptcy will only amount to 50 cents on the dollar. Y claims that X must make up the difference.

Required

Is X liable? Explain.

Q. 3. In December 1958 Howard transferred 1,000 shares of Z Company stock to the X Trust Company in trust for the benefit of his wife for life, with the remainder to go to his son. The Z Company declared a noncash dividend in 1960 of 10 shares of stock of the M Company for each 100 shares of Z Company stock. The M Company stock had been bought by Z Company as an investment. The son claims that this dividend should be added to the principal, whereas the wife claims that she is entitled to the dividend.

Required

How should the Trust Company treat the dividend? Explain.

Q. 4. All the facts are the same as in the preceding question except that in 1960 the Z Company split up its stock 2-for-1. Subsequently, the trustee sold half of the 2,000 shares of the Z Company stock at a profit, and the son and wife both claim the proceeds.

Required

How should the trust company treat the stock split-up and the proceeds from the sale? Explain.

Practice Objective Questions

Instructions 1–12

Select the *best* answer for each of the following items. Make only one answer for *each* item. Answer all items. Your grade will be based on your total correct answers.

1. The intestate succession distribution rules.
   a. Do *not* apply to property held in joint tenancy.
   b. Do *not* apply to real property.
   c. Effectively prevent a decedent from totally disinheriting his wife and children.
   d. Apply to situations where the decedent failed to name an executor.
2. Which of the following receipts should be allocated by a trustee exclusively to income?
   a. A stock dividend.
   b. An extraordinary year-end cash dividend.
   c. A liquidating dividend whether in complete or partial liquidation.
   d. A stock split.
3. The Unity Trust Company is the trustee of a trust which has large real estate investments. Which of the following receipts or charges should be allocated by the trustee to income?
   a. Paving assessment for a new street.
   b. Prepaid rent received from tenants.
   c. A loss on the sale of one of the rental properties.
   d. The proceeds from an eminent domain proceeding.

4. An executor named in a decedent's will
    a. *Cannot* be the principal beneficiary of the will.
    b. Must serve without compensation unless the will provides otherwise.
    c. Need *not* serve if he does *not* wish to do so.
    d. Must consent to serve, have read the will, and be present at the execution of the will.

5. Which of the following receipts or disbursements by a trustee should be credited to or charged against income?
    a. Amortization payment on real property subject to a mortgage.
    b. Capital gain distributions received from a mutual fund.
    c. Stock rights received from the distributing corporation.
    d. The discount portion received on redemption of treasury bills.

6. Harris is the trustee named in Filmore's trust. The trust named Filmore as the life beneficiary, remainder to his children at age 21. The trust consists of stocks, bonds, and three pieces of rental income property. Which of the following statements *best* describes the trustee's legal relationships or duties?
    a. The trustee has legal and equitable title to the rental property.
    b. The trustee must automatically reinvest the proceeds from the sale of one of the rental properties in like property.
    c. The trustee is a fiduciary with respect to the trust and the beneficiaries.
    d. The trustee must divide among all the beneficiaries any insurance proceeds received in the event the real property is destroyed.

7. Kilgore created an irrevocable 15-year trust for the benefit of his minor children. At the end of the 15 years, the principal (corpus) reverts to Kilgore. Kilgore named the Reliable Trust Company as trustee and provided that Reliable would serve without the necessity of posting a bond. In understanding the trust and rules applicable to it, which of the following is correct?
    a. The trust is *not* a separate legal entity for federal tax purposes.
    b. The facts indicate that the trust is a separate legal entity for both tax and nontax purposes.
    c. Kilgore may revoke the trust after eleven years, since he created it, and the principal reverts to him at the expiration of the fifteen years.
    d. If Kilgore dies ten years after creation of the trust, it is automatically revoked and the property is distributed to the beneficiaries of his trust upon their attaining age 21.

8. Fifteen years ago Madison executed a valid will. He named his son, Walker, as the executor of his will and left two-thirds of his estate to his wife and the balance equally to his children. Madison is now dead and the approximate size of his estate is one million dollars. Which of the following statements is correct?
    a. The will is invalid because it was executed at a time which is beyond the general statute of limitations.
    b. The estate is *not* recognized as a taxable entity for tax purposes.
    c. All the property bequeathed to his wife will be excluded from the decedent's estate for federal estate tax purposes.
    d. Walker must, in addition to being named in the will, be appointed or approved by the appropriate state court to serve as the executor.

9. Hacker is considering the creation of either a lifetime *(inter vivos)* or testamentary (by his will) trust. In deciding what to do, which of the following statements is correct?
    a. An *inter vivos* trust must meet the same legal requirements as one created by a will.
    b. Property transferred to a testamentary trust upon the grantor's (creator's) death is *not* included in the decedent's gross estate for federal tax purposes.
    c. Hacker can retain the power to revoke an *inter vivos* trust.
    d. If the trust is an *inter vivos* trust, the trustee must file papers in the appropriate state office roughly similar to those required to be filed by a corporation.

10. If a CPA firm is engaged by a law firm to aid it in the administration of a decedent's estate, its duties will invariably *not* include
    a. Preparation of the federal estate tax return.
    b. Preparation of the estate's fiduciary income tax returns.

    c. Presentation of the necessary schedules and summations to be used in rendering an accounting to interested parties.

    d. Consideration of the validity of the surviving spouse's right to take against the will.

11. Parker died 10 years after executing a valid will. He named his son, Walker, as the executor of his will. He left two-thirds of his estate to his wife and the balance equally to his children. Which of the following is a right or duty of Walker as executor?

    a. Walker must post a surety bond even if a provision in the will attempts to exempt him from this responsibility.

    b. Walker has an affirmative duty to discover, collect, and distribute all the decedent's assets.

    c. If the will is silent on the point, Walker has complete discretion insofar as investing the estate's assets during the term of his administration.

    d. Walker can sell real property without a court order, even though he has *not* been expressly authorized to do so.

12. When Wayne died in 1976 his will created a testamentary trust out of the residue of his estate for the benefit of his wife during her lifetime and the remainder to his son, Eric, upon Mrs. Wayne's death. The residue of the estate included rental property subject to a $45,000 first mortgage. Probate of the estate has been completed, and the property deeded to the trustee to hold pursuant to the terms of the will. Carlton, Wayne's attorney and advisor, was named as executor and the Jefferson Trust Company was named as the sole trustee. Which of the following parties does *not* have an interest in the trust property sufficient to obtain fire insurance on said property?

    a. The son, Eric

    b. Wayne's wife.

    c. The first mortgagee.

    d. Eric's wife.

3

CONTRACTS (15%)

Chapter 6. Contracts

6

Contracts

AICPA Content Specification Outline

Offer and Acceptance
Consideration
Capacity, Legality, and Public Policy
Statute of Frauds
Statute of Limitations
Fraud, Duress, and Undue Influence
Mistake and Misrepresentation
Parol Evidence Rule
Third Party Rights
Assignments
Discharge, Breach, and Remedies

Contents

I. Definition
II. Types of Contracts
    A. Express contract
    B. Implied contract
    C. Bilateral contract

D. Unilateral contract

E. Executory and executed contracts

III. Elements Necessary for an Enforceable Agreement

    A. Offer and acceptance

    B. Consideration

    C. Valid subject matter

    D. Legal capacity of the parties

    E. The Statute of Frauds requirement

IV. Reality of Assent

    A. Mutual assent

    B. Mistake

    C. Innocent misrepresentation

    D. Fraud

    E. Duress

    F. Undue influence

    G. Unconscionable contracts

V. Interpretation of Contract—Parol Evidence Rule

    A. Agreements reduced to writing bind the parties

    B. Exceptions

VI. Assignment of Rights, Delegation of Duties, and Third-Party Beneficiary Contracts

    A. Assignment of rights

    B. Delegation of duties

    C. Third-party beneficiaries

VII. Discharge of the Contract

    A. By agreement

    B. By performance

    C. By operation of law

    D. Statute of Limitations

    E. Breach of contract

    F. Remedies

Selected Problems from CPA Examinations on Contracts

Subjective Questions and Answers

Practice Questions

Practice Objective Questions

I. Definition: For Any Agreement between Two or More Parties to Be Enforceable in Law—That Is, a Contract—There Must Be:

A. An offer (statement of intent) to be bound to do or refrain from doing something which has been accepted,

B. Sufficient legal consideration,

C. A valid subject matter,

D. Legal capacity of parties, and

E. For those contracts to which the Statute of Fraud applies, its requirements must be met.

II. Types of Contracts

A. Express contract: an actual agreement of the parties, the terms of which are openly stated or declared at the time of making it, in distinct and explicit language, either orally or in writing.

B. Implied contract:

   1. Implied in fact: one whose existence is inferred from the acts of conduct of the parties; the circumstances surrounding the transaction making it a reasonable or even a necessary assumption that a contract existed between them by tacit understanding.

   2. Quasi contract: implied in law; not actually a contract since it is not necessarily pursuant to the intention of a party and is possibly against his will. Quasi contract is based on the broad principle that a person who has been unjustly enriched at the expense of another will be required to make restitution.

C. Bilateral contract: a promise given in exchange for a promise, i.e., mutual promises. (E.g., I promise you $10 if you promise to cut my hedge.)

D. Unilateral contract: a promise on one side only, the consideration for the promise being an act by the other party. (E.g., I promise to give you $10 for your act of cutting my hedge.)

E. Executory contract: one that has not yet been performed; only promises have been given.

   1. Wholly executory: no performance by either party.

   2. Partially executory: only part of the contract has been performed, e.g., one party has performed.

   3. When parties have all performed and no obligation remains, the contract is executed.

III. Elements Necessary for an Enforceable Agreement

A. Offer and acceptance: manifesting mutual assent to be bound. There must be **an objective meeting of the minds** on the terms of the contract.

   1. Offer.

      a. Offer may be either written or oral.

      b. There must be clear intention to contract.

         (1) If offeree (person to whom offer is made) knows or has reason to know that there is no intention on the part of the offeror to express an offer, there is no offer (e.g., offers made in jest). The test is an objective one; would a reasonable person believe that the offer was made with the requisite intent?

         (2) Invitations to trade (such as price lists, ads, quotes, and bids) and mere proposals to negotiate are usually not found to constitute offers—the test being whether from the words and conduct of the parties a reasonable person would believe an offer had been made.

    (3) Promises made in jest or excitement and statements of opinion are not offers.

  c. Offer must be definite and certain as to what is agreed upon.

    (1) The essential terms are parties, price, time for performance, and subject matter.

    (2) A court cannot enforce an agreement where the things to be done are indefinite or uncertain, i.e., the court cannot determine what was agreed upon.

    (3) Offers originally need not be certain if certainty can be determined at a later date. Indefinite offers will create valid contracts where they may become definite by subsequent words or agreement. (E.g., X promises to sell Y a house, to be chosen by Y from a number of houses that X owns, and Y promises to pay a specified price for it. Since X must give up a house that Y will choose and Y must pay for it, there is a valid offer, although at the outset it is not clear which house will be sold.)

UCC RULE   [2-204]:   Even though one or more terms of a contract for the sale of goods is left open, the contract will not fail for indefiniteness if the parties intended to make a contract and there is reasonably certain basis for giving an appropriate remedy. The UCC thus liberalizes contract law in respect to the definiteness and certainty requirement, and fosters the formation of a greater number of sales contracts than would be the case at common law.

Note   The Uniform Commercial Code (hereinafter UCC) has made substantial inroads in the common law of contracts, which is the basis for this topic. Such changes are of major significance and are included throughout the contracts topic in distinctive type in order to highlight their importance and to provide meaningful contrast. However, it should be clearly recognized that *the UCC changes in contract law apply almost exclusively to contracts for the sale of goods.* The older common law rules still apply to all other contracts, such as contracts for the sale of real property, employment contracts, insurance contracts, etc. However, the UCC is often applied by anology to areas not specifically within its coverage.

  d. Offers must be communicated to the offeree by the offeror or his agent.

    (1) Offeree must learn of the offer by the medium intended by the offerer.

    (2) Offeree may learn of a public offer (e.g., a reward) in any way.

  e. **Option:** an irrevocable offer that is **actually a contract if it is supported by an independent consideration** (see p. 145, III.B) sufficient to make the offer irrevocable. Some states, however, do not require any consideration for an irrevocable offer if it is in writing, signed by the person to be charged and states its irrevocability. Rules as to mistakes in making the offer are the same as in ordinary contracts.

UCC RULE   [2-205]:   An *option* or "firm offer," which states that it will not be withdrawn, needs no consideration to be valid if it is made in a signed writing by a merchant. However, an option without consideration may not last more than three months. These provisions apply only to option contracts for the purchase or sale of goods. Note that if the offeree-merchant supplies the form on which the option appears, the form must be separately signed by the offeror-merchant. If the offer is supported by consideration, it may be for any period, and bind a nonmerchant.

The rules described above, i.e., the signed writing requirement and the three-month limitation, do not apply if consideration is given for the option. Nor is it necessary that the grantor be a merchant. In such a case, general contract rules apply (e.g., X grants Y an oral six-month option to buy his car for $150 in exchange for $1).

2. Acceptance.
a. Acceptance may be either oral or written.
   (1) Oral asset may form a contract even where the parties intend to write down their agreement later. However, oral assent may, if so intended, be merely a preliminary expression that is only to become final with the adoption of a writing.

   (2) In an auction "with reserve," offer is by bid, acceptance is by fall of the hammer.

   (3) In reward cases, acceptance is by doing the act requested—a classic unilateral contract.

b. Offer may call for an acceptance in the form of a promise (bilateral contract—see p. 139, II.C) or an act (unilateral contract—see p. 139, II.D).

c. Acceptance must be made with knowledge of the offer. (E.g., B, returning A's lost watch without knowledge of A's offer of $100 reward, would not be entitled to the reward.) Cross offers do not constitute a contract since the acceptance requirement is not satisfied.

d. Acceptance must conform to all terms of the offer and be unequivocal and unconditional.

   (1) A reply to an offer that adds qualifications or conditions is not an acceptance but a rejection and a counteroffer; mere inquiry is not a counteroffer.

   (2) Acceptance that "requests" a change or addition of terms is valid if the acceptance is not made to depend upon assent to the proposed change. (E.g., A offers to sell B 50 boxes of oranges at $10 a box. B accepts but adds his wish that, if possible, delivery should be made in installments. A and B have a contract, but A is not bound to make delivery in installments.)

   (3) Where a type of acceptance is specified (i.e., a promise or act), the offeree must conform to the specification; however, an offer is interpreted when possible to permit acceptance by either an act or a promise to perform it.

   (4) Where an offer describes the time or manner of acceptance, it must be complied with; however, if the offer merely *suggests* a time or manner, another method of acceptance is not precluded.

When an offer calls for a promise, acceptance must be communicated to the offeror; when an offer calls for an act, notification of completion of the act is not necessary unless the offer has no means of knowing that the act has been completed.

UCC RULE   [2-207]:   A literal and unequivocal acceptance is not required under the code. An acceptance that contains additional terms is a valid acceptance. The additional terms are treated as
proposals for *additions to the contract.* As between *merchants,* these additional terms
become a part of the contract unless the offer precludes such an occurrence; or the new terms
materially alter the offer; or the original offeror gives notification of objection to such changes
within a reasonable time after he receives notice of them.

An order or other offer to buy goods for prompt or current shipment shall be construed as
inviting acceptance, either by a prompt promise to ship (thereby forming a bilateral contract)
or by the prompt or current shipment of the goods (thereby forming a unilateral contract).

These are major conceptual changes from the above common law rules. Again they
foster formation of the sales contract.

    f. Silence rarely constitutes acceptance, except in special circumstances:
        (1) The offeree, instead of rejecting, uses services that reasonably appear to
be offered only if payment will be made. (E.g., X gives tennis lessons to
Y, intending to charge Y. Y, although not requesting these lessons,
remains silent knowing they are being given with the expectation of
payment from Y. Y is bound to pay for these lessons.) Or
        (2) The offeror indicated that silence would constitute an acceptance, and
the offeree intended his silence as an acceptance. Or
        (3) Previous dealings and consequent reliance create the understanding that
silence is acceptance.
    g. Offer can only be accepted by or for the benefit of the person to whom it is
made. Offers are *not* assignable, but option contracts are.
3. Objective theory.
    a. Validity of offer and acceptance is determined in court by an objective
standard of apparent intent.
        (1) Only the overt acts and words of the parties are considered in a de-
termination of mutual assent.
        (2) Subjective feeling (secret intent) is immaterial.
4. Transmission of acceptance and time when it takes effect.
    a. Offeror may signify the manner in which he desires the acceptance transmit-
ted and any time limit thereon.
    b. Unless otherwise indicated, either by facts or in the offer, an acceptance may
be sent by the means used by offeror, or any reasonable means offeree wishes
to use.
    c. If acceptance is transmitted by the means authorized by offeror, or by the
same means used to transmit the offer if no means was specifically authorized, **the acceptance is effective as soon as it is put out of the offeree's
possession** and into the possession of an independent agency for transmission. (E.g., X received via the mails an offer that did not specify the means of
acceptance; therefore, a letter of acceptance forms a contract upon its being
posted.) The acceptance must be correctly addressed and the fee or postage
properly paid.
        (1) Whether the acceptance ever reaches its destination is immaterial unless
offeror provides otherwise; the theory being that the offeror has implicitly designated the independent agency as his agent for acceptance.

    (2) Acceptance sent from a distance will only operate upon dispatch, provided it is sent with precautions ordinarily taken to ensure safe transmission (e.g., adequate postage, proper address).

d. If acceptance is not by authorized means, it is not operative upon dispatch, but it will take effect upon receipt, if received within the time in which an authorized acceptance would have arrived. (E.g., acceptance by public messenger is valid when received, if promptly delivered by acceptor's own messenger.)

UCC RULE   [2-206]   Unless otherwise *unambiguously* indicated, an offer for the sale or purchase of goods shall be construed as inviting acceptance in *any* manner and by *any* medium reasonable in the circumstance. The Code therefore does not require the use of the same means as the offer to make acceptance effective on dispatch as does the common law.

5. Termination of offer.
  a. Rejection by the offeree.
    (1) Communication declining acceptance is rejection; it must be communicated to the offeror.
    (2) Counteroffer is a rejection unless an intent of reserving original offer for further consideration is manifested (E.g., I am interested in your offer to sell for $60, but I am willing to buy at once if you will accept $55.) For the UCC rule, see p. 142.
    (3) Rejection does not terminate possibility of acceptance until it is received, but it limits the power of a later acceptance to create a contract upon dispatch. A later acceptance must arrive before an earlier rejection to be valid. (E.g., X mails Y an offer, which Y rejects by mail; however, within the time allowed for acceptance and before the rejection is received by X, Y's telegram of acceptance reaches X. A contract arises upon the receipt of the acceptance.)
    (4) Where a rejection is received by the offeror before a later acceptance, the acceptance, not creating a contract upon its dispatch—see (3)—can only be considered a counteroffer, since an offeror who received a late or otherwise defective acceptance cannot at his election regard it as valid.
  b. Lapse of time.
    (1) Termination occurs upon the lapse of the time specified in the offer of acceptance. If the time has elapsed, the offer is dead.
    (2) If no time is specified in the offer, termination occurs upon lapse of a reasonable time, which is a question of fact. However, where an offer is sent by mail, acceptance sent on the day of receipt of the offer is sent within a reasonable time.
    (3) Time for acceptance is not extended by a delay in communication (regardless of fault of the offeror) if the offeree knew of the delay. However, if the offeree had no knowledge of the time taken by the delay, that amount of time is added to offeree's time for acceptance. (E.g., X sent Y an offer which is delayed in the mail. The markings upon the envelope make it apparent that there has been a 3-day delay. If X has given Y 10 days in which to accept, Y now must accept within 7 days.

However, if it was not apparent from the markings and Y had no knowledge of the delay, the delay would not affect the amount of time allowed for acceptance.)

(4) Offeror may also specify that the offer lapses upon the happening of an event; offeree need not be informed of the event's occurrence.

c. Revocation by the offeror.

(1) A communication stating or implying a revocation is effective if received before the offeree's power of acceptance is exercised.

(2) Where an offer is for the sale of goods, it is revoked upon the offeree's learning of the sale of the goods by the offeror if that sale has actually been made. (E.g., X makes Y an offer to sell his car, acceptance to be in 1 week. Within a week, Y is told by Z that X has sold his car to another; however, Y proceeds to accept. If X has sold his car, there is no contract. If Z's information was incorrect, there is a contract.) This rule applies generally to all offers (e.g., an offer to sell goods).

(3) An offer publicized to a group of unknown persons is revoked by an equivalent publicizing of a revocation by the offeror.

(4) An offeror may revoke the remaining unaccepted offers that were part of a series of proposed contracts although some binding contracts have already been created through acceptance. However, if the original offer was for formation of a single contract, rather than a series of contracts calling for a series of acceptances, the offeror can no longer revoke. (E.g., X offers to sell 50 pounds of coal to Y every week for one year and does so for two months. X then revokes the offer and stops delivery. If the parties intended a new contract to be formed each time there was a delivery, the revocation of X prevents the formation of new contracts. If they originally intended the formation of a single contract to run for one year, Y's acceptance of X's original offer prevents X from effectively revoking.)

(5) Where there has been part performance in response to an offer of a unilateral contract, the majority rule is that the offeror has no power of revocation, unless full performance is not completed within the time allowed, or, if no time for performance is stated, within a reasonable time. The minority rule permits revocation but reimburses the offeree by allowing recovery for part performance in quasi contract (see p. 139, II.B.2). (E.g., X tells Y that if Y will carry his bag to the station X will promise to pay him. Y carries the bag halfway and X revokes. Under the majority rule X's revocation is ineffective, and if X does not allow Y to finish this job, he will be liable for damages.)

UCC RULE   [2-206]:   The code adopts the majority view but in addition requires that notice of acceptance be given to the offeror within a reasonable time after the offeree begins performance.

(6) Option contracts (see p. 140, III.A.1.e) may not be revoked until after the time given for acceptance has elapsed, or if no time is stipulated, after a reasonable time.

     d. Offeror's death or insanity before acceptance: Offer is terminated upon death or insanity of offeror; however, death or insanity does not affect rights under an option contract since a contract is already binding upon the parties.

     e. Illegality or impossibility: If after making an offer, but before acceptance, the proposed contract becomes illegal or impossible to perform, the offer is terminated.

B. Consideration:

    1. Definition: an act or forbearance, or the promise thereof, which is offered by one party to an agreement, and accepted by the other as an inducement to that other's act or promise.

    2. Legal consideration: some value given or promise of same or detriment sustained or promised (forbearance of some legal right that otherwise could be exercised, e.g., giving up smoking) that is recognized by the law as capable of supporting a contract. Examples of promises that will *not* fulfill this requirement are:

      a. Promises based only on a moral rather than legal obligation (e.g., parents' love for a child).

      b. Promises to fulfill a duty already in existence, i.e., a preexisting legal duty (e.g., a promise to continue one's employment under an already existing contract in exchange for a promise by the employer to pay an additional amount, or a promise not to commit a tort or crime).

      c. Promises that are merely illusory and, therefore, do not give rise to any mutuality of obligation, i.e., a promise that, in effect, means no more than that the promisor can perform if he wishes, but that does not bind him to perform.

    3. Consideration need not have a pecuniary value or a value equal to the value of the act for which it is exchanged, i.e., courts will not inquire into the adequacy of consideration, except when unequal amounts of fungible goods or money are exchanged (e.g., I promise to give you $10 for your $5).

      a. Consideration must be bargained for; parties must intend to suffer legal detriment (i.e., the giving up of a legal right).

      b. Forbearance to sue on a claim is good consideration; the claim need not be valid if it was made in good faith.

      c. Past consideration is insufficient for a new contract (not bargained for).

    4. The seal formerly served this purpose. It has been abolished. For certain contracts (e.g., options) a signed writing is sufficient despite the lack of consideration. The UCC, of course, does this, but some states validate such options and other contracts if there is a signed writing.

UCC RULE The UCC has abolished the legal effect of the seal insofar as contracts for the sale of goods are concerned.

      b. Moral obligation: generally not consideration, except:

        (1) Void usurious agreements—see p. 161, VII.B.1.e(5). At common law usurious agreements were void, but if the usurious elements are eliminated and the debtor subsequently promises to repay the original loan, some courts hold a moral consideration and enforce the promise.

    (2) Promise to perform a previously voidable duty. A ratification or promise to perform an antecedent voidable legal duty, not previously avoided, if made after the privilege of avoidance has terminated, is binding and enforceable (e.g., ratification by infant upon reaching majority).

c. Promise to pay a debt barred by some positive rule of law if such promise is evidenced by a writing and signed by the party to be charged thereunder.

    (1) Bankruptcy: A promise to pay all or part of a debt discharged in bankruptcy may be binding.

    (2) A new promise to pay a debt barred by the statute of limitations—see p. 162, VII.D.(4)—is virtually always enforced.

d. Waiver: Some courts hold that a new promise to fulfill a duty originally conditional upon the performance of a condition by another is binding, in spite of the nonperformance of the condition by the other, if the promise was made with full knowledge of the fact that the condition would not be performed and the condition was not a substantial part of what was to have been given as consideration (e.g., X waives the requirement of a $10 deposit, originally required as a condition for his starting performance). (See p. 158, VII.A.1.)

e. Option contracts or irrevocable offers (see p. 140, III.A.1.e).

f. Written agreement to change, modify, or discharge an obligation (see p. 140, VII.A.1.b).

g. Promissory estoppel: To prevent injustice, recovery is based on one party's justifiable reliance on the promises of a second party even though no contract exists. It is called promissory estoppel because by inducing reliance, the second party is estopped from denying the existence of a contract. This is a minority rule.

    (1) In some states, in varying degrees, a promise lacking consideration will be enforced where:

        (A) A promissor makes a definite promise that he expects will induce action or forbearance of a substantial nature on the part of the promisee, and

        (B) The promise in fact induces such action or forbearance of a substantial character, and

        (C) Injustice can be avoided *only* by enforcing the promise or by compensating the aggrieved party for his expenses.

    (2) Promissory estoppel is distinguished from ordinary estoppel, which occurs when there is a misrepresentation of existing facts. (E.g., A knew or should reasonably have known that he would mislead B, who was misled and damaged. The court would estop A from denying the truth of his own statement.)

UCC RULE   The code has made several major inroads into the rigid consideration requirement in respect to waivers, modifications, and options. They should be studied with great care (see pp. 163, 158, 140).

C. Valid subject matter: An agreement is unenforceable if its object is illegal or violates public policy.

1. Violation of positive laws.
   a. Rules of common law: commission of crime or tort, i.e., a civil wrong (e.g., defrauding others, breach of public or fiduciary duty).
   b. Statutory rules: Legislature in exercising police power may regulate the making of contracts (e.g., services rendered without the regulatory license, crimes, usury, and wagers.)
   c. Timing.
      (1) If subject matter becomes illegal after the offer but before acceptance, offer terminates.
      (2) If it becomes illegal after acceptance, the contract is discharged because of impossibility of performance.

2. Agreements contrary to public policy.
   a. Contracts may be illegal and void even though the acts contemplated are not expressly prohibited by common law or statute (e.g., agreements of immoral tendency, agreements obstructing justice or affecting the freedom or security of marriage, insurance contracts where there is no insurable interest).
   b. Agreements restraining trade and competition (antitrust) and promises not to compete are against public policy and unenforceable if the restraints are unreasonable (e.g., time limitations and geographical restrictions not reasonably necessary to protect the interests of the contracting party).
   c. Agreements that relieve a party from liability resulting from his negligence toward the other party are not favored; however, most courts will enforce such agreements between private parties in relatively equal bargaining positions. Where activities of the party affect the public interest, such agreements will not always be enforced (e.g., by a public utility).

3. Enforcement of illegal agreements.
   a. Void agreements will not be enforced; however, a court may enforce agreements that are illegal, but not so offensive as to be found void. (E.g., X subdivides lots and sells homes but forgets to obtain a license to do so. Y, a buyer, refuses to pay for a home. The court may allow X to recover, regardless of the fact that it was illegal to sell without a license).
   b. If the agreement is illegal only in part, that part that is legal may be enforced if it can be separated from the rest of the agreement, but not otherwise.
   c. Agreement may be void regardless of the knowledge of the parties, since, in general, ignorance of the law is no excuse.

4. Recovery of money.
   a. There is no action to enforce an illegal agreement, but the court may allow recovery of the consideration (e.g., money) in an action to disaffirm (repudiate) the contract where:
      (1) The party seeking recovery is less guilty, or
      (2) Recovery is sought by a person the statute meant to protect (e.g., a borrower suing on usurious contract), or
      (3) The transaction has not been consummated and the party repents.
   b. There is no recovery in quasi contract (see p. 139, II.B.2).

D. **Legal capacity of the parties:** An agreement between parties in which one or both lack the capacity to contract is, void or voidable.

1. Infants
   a. Contracts are voidable only by him: An infant can disaffirm his contracts without being liable on them, unless they are contracts made for necessaries.
      (1) He can disaffirm at any time during his minority and within a reasonable time after attaining his majority. Majority age is set by statute at 18 years in almost all states.
      (2) Necessaries include whatever is reasonably needed for his subsistence, health, comfort, or education, considering age and his customary economic status; the infant is liable only for the reasonable value of necessaries furnished him.
      (3) A fraudulent misrepresentation by the minor of his age will preclude his disaffirmance in many states or give rise to a counterclaim for fraud.
   b. Upon attaining majority, the infant can ratify any contract that could have been disaffirmed.
2. Married women: generally no disabilities in contracting (elimination by statute of common law disabilities.)
3. Insane persons
   a. Contract is void from inception if made after adjudication of insanity.
   b. Contract is voidable if made prior to adjudication of insanity.
      (1) Contract is valid if there was no knowledge of the insanity by the other party who has contracted in good faith and performed up to this time so that disaffirmance would cause him loss, i.e., the insane person can only avoid liability under the contract if he can restore the consideration he has received.
      (2) Quasi contracts—see p. 139, II.B.2—are valid.
4. Drunkards: Contracts are enforceable unless the drunkard was so intoxicated at the time of contracting that he lacked capacity to make an intelligent offer or acceptance. If he lacked such capacity, the contract is voidable by the drunkard.
   a. Quasi contracts are valid.
5. Corporations
   a. Can only contract through the authority of an agent.
   b. Power to contract is limited by charter in respect to the subject matter of contracts. Agreement must reasonably accomplish some object for which the corporation was created (see Corporations, p. 93, III.D.2).

E. **The Statute of Frauds requirement:**

1. Contracts *within* the provisions of the Statute of Frauds must be in writing and signed by the party to be charged thereunder in order to be enforceable. Many contracts are not subject to the Statute of Frauds requirements (e.g., contracts for the sale of goods for less than $500). In addition, even though the contract is within the Statute of Frauds, the Statute may be satisfied in a way other than a writing in the case of contracts for the sale of goods or contracts for the sale of real property (see p. 149, III.E.2).

    a. A contract may be contained in a signed memo, but the memo must contain all the material terms of the agreement.

    b. Several writings (e.g., letters) may be pieced together to fulfill the requirement of a memo.

    c. Writing need not be delivered unless it is a deed to land.

    d. Writing must contain:

        (1) The subject matter.

        (2) The names of the parties.

        (3) The consideration.

        (4) The terms of contract.

        (5) The signature of party to be charged, i.e., the party seeking to avoid the contract.

    e. Writing need not come into existence at time of the agreement—it need only be the evidence of an agreement.

UCC RULE   [2-201]:   The UCC contains a Statute of Frauds section in its treatment of sales (Article 2). It applies exclusively to the sale of goods having a value of $500 or more (see pp. 150-151). All that is required to satisfy the UCC Statute of Frauds section is some writing sufficient to indicate that a contract for the sale of goods has been made between the parties and signed by the party against whom it is sought to be enforced or by his authorized agent. A writing is not insufficient because it omits or incorrectly states a term of the contract albeit material, but it must at least state the quantity of goods sold. This represents a major liberalization of the writing requirement in respect to the sale of goods.

    2. Contracts *within* the Statute include contracts that:

    a. By their terms are not to be performed within one year from the making thereof. (E.g., X makes a contract for a year's duration beginning one week from the date of the agreement; the contract is unenforceable if not in writing. However, a contract made today for a year's duration with work beginning tomorrow is not within the Statute, and hence enforceable without a writing.)

        (1) If performance is contingent on something that could take place in less than one year, an oral agreement is enforceable.

        (2) If terms call for more than one year, it must be in writing, even though performance may be completed in less than one year.

    b. Are for sale of real property. Part performance of a substantial nature will also satisfy the Statute of Frauds (e.g., a purchaser under an oral land contract takes possession and makes either partial payment or valuable improvements).

    c. Promise to answer for the debt, default, or miscarriage of another where such a promise is collateral rather than an original promise. (E.g., X says to Y, "If you will sell Z goods worth $30, I will guarantee Z's account." Such a promise comes under the Statute; however, where X says, "Sell Z goods worth $30, and I will pay the bill," the promise is not under the Statute, for it is an original promise.)

     d. Are promises by an executor or administrator to pay with his own funds obligations of the estate.

     e. Are contracts intended to create a nonpossessory security interest (see p. 341).

     f. Are for the sale of goods for the price of $500 or more.

     g. Are contracts for the sale of "securities" as defined in Article 8 (Investment Securities), which, in general, means an instrument commonly dealt in upon securities exchanges or markets or commonly recognized in any area in which it is issued or dealt in as a medium of investment (e.g., corporate stocks, corporate bonds, municipal bonds, transferable warrants, etc.).

UCC RULE [8-318]: Provides that a contract for the sale of **securities** is not enforceable by way of action or defense unless:

(1) There is some writing signed by the party against whom enforcement is sought or by his agent or broker sufficient to indicate that a contract has been made for sale of a stated quantity of described securities at a defined or stated price; or

(2) Delivery of the security has been accepted or payment has been made, but the contract is enforceable under this provision only to the extent of such delivery or payment; or

(3) Within a reasonable time a writing in confirmation of the sale or purchase and sufficient against the sender under paragraph (4) has been received by the party against whom enforcement is sought and he has failed to send written objection to its contents within 10 days after its receipt; or

(4) The party against whom enforcement is sought admits in his pleading, testimony, or otherwise in court that a contract was made for sale of a stated quantity of described securities at a defined or stated price.

     h. Are contracts which create a nonpossessory "security interest" in the creditor (see Secured Transactions, p. 338, for the UCC definition of "security interest").

     i. Are contracts for the sale of intangible personal property (choses in action), such as patent rights or copyrights, not covered by f, g, or h above and having a value in excess of $5,000 (e.g., the sale by a party of his rights under a bilateral contract or rights to royalties having a value in excess of $5,000).

  3. Some typical contracts *not* within the Statute:

     a. Sale of goods under $500.

     b. Guarantee of a *del credere* agent (where a sales agent, as a condition of the agency, guarantees the accounts of the customers to his principal).

     c. Promise of indemnity regardless of fault (e.g., insurance).

     d. Assignor's promise to assignee, guaranteeing performance of the *obligor*.

     e. Oral joint debts.

     f. Surety's promise which is principally or primarily for the surety's benefit.

     g. Specially manufactured goods unfit for sale in ordinary marketplace, if seller had made a substantial start in their manufacture.

UCC RULE [2-201]: A contract for **the sale of goods for the price of $500** or more is generally not enforceable without some writing signed by the party to be charged sufficient to indicate that the contract had been made (see above). However, UCC provides the following additional ways of fulfilling its requirements:

(1) Written confirmations: A written confirmation of the contract of sale of goods between merchants will satisfy the Statute as long as the confirmation binds the sender and as long as the recipient has knowledge of or reason to know its contents and does not object to the confirmation within 10 days.

(2) Specially manufactured goods: Where a seller has made a substantial beginning toward the manufacture of goods not suitable for sale to other than the buyer (e.g., custom-built golf clubs), the Statute will be satisfied without a signed writing if the contract is valid in other respects.

(3) Admissions by a party: If the party against whom enforcement is sought admits in his pleading, testimony, or otherwise in court that a contract for sale was made, the contract will be enforceable without a signed writing to the extent of the quantity of goods admitted.

(4) Part performance: With respect to those goods for which payment has been made or that have been received or accepted, the contract will be enforceable without a signed writing, but only to the extent of those goods received or paid for.

IV. Reality of Assent

A. Mutual assent being essential to every contract, agreements may be void or voidable because of one of the following:

B. Mistake: a belief not in accordance with the actual facts. Failure to read a contract before signing is generally no excuse.

    1. Mutual mistake (both parties are mistaken) may relate to:

        a. The terms of the contract, or

        b. Identity of the parties, or

        c. The existence, nature, quantity, or identity of the subject matter, or

        d. Other material facts assumed by the parties as the basis on which they entered into the transaction.

            (1) Mutual mistake in regard to a material provision of the contract makes the contract *voidable* by the party whose obligations under the contract will be materially increased if the mistake is enforced, unless:

                (A) The welfare of innocent third parties will be unfairly affected, or

                (B) The party seeking to avoid the transaction can obtain reformation, performance of the contract according to its original intent, or compensation from any loss he may sustain because of the mistake.

            (2) Where, because of the nature of the mutual mistake, there was in effect no contract made by the parties, the mistake makes the contract *void*.

    2. Mistake does not make the contract voidable where:

        a. There is a **unilateral mistake** (where only one party to the contract is mistaken) unless there is:

            (1) Fraud (see IV.D.1), or

            (2) Knowledge by the other party of the existence of the misapprehension or reason to know of same.

        b. The acceptor is bound in contract, though he is actually ignorant of the terms of a written offer or of their proper interpretation. Failure to read the terms of a contract will not excuse a party from performance. The acceptor binds himself to any terms included in the writing he assents to unless:

            (1) It is required by statute to be conspicuous and it is not, or

(2) It is part of a standardized agreement submitted by the other party with reason to believe that the term(s) would not be agreed to, and the acceptor did not notice it.

c. One party knows of an ambiguity unknown to another, and that person does nothing to clarify the ambiguity, i.e., knowing the other party may attach an alternative meaning to the contract, that person binds himself or herself in accordance with the other party's interpretation of the ambiguity.

C. **Innocent or unintentional misrepresentations:** An innocent misstatement (i.e., one made with an honest and justifiable belief) if material, is treated as a mutual mistake, giving the other party an action for rescission of the contract. Each party must return any benefits received.

D. **Fraud: known or reckless misrepresentation** of a material fact with the intention that the misrepresentation shall be acted upon by the other party, and which is acted upon by him to his injury.

1. For actual fraud to exist there must be:
   a. A false representation and not mere nondisclosure. However, nondisclosure or concealment is enough where:
      (1) There are active steps taken to prevent discovery of the truth, or
      (2) There is suppression of the facts by revealing only part truths, or
      (3) Under the circumstances, failing to disclose defects implies that they do not exist.
   b. A misrepresentation of a past or existing material fact. Therefore, there is no fraud where:
      (1) There is an expression of opinion, belief, or expectation, or
      (2) There is a mere expression of intention. However, the representation that a certain intention presently exists when it does not is a false representation of existing fact.
   c. A representation known to be false. Such representation is fraudulent if:
      (1) It is actually known to be false, or.
      (2) It is made in reckless disregard of whether true or not, or
      (3) The party represents it as his or her personal knowledge, knowing that the statement is false and will be relied upon.
   d. Justified reliance upon a representation that was made with an intent to be relied upon. Thus, no fraud exists where:
      (1) There are only opinions of value, especially where parties are equally incapable of giving opinions (e.g., neither party is an expert), or
      (2) There are available means of checking the accuracy of the statement, but they are not used.
      (3) Representation need not be made directly to the other party if it is intended to be communicated to him and acted upon by him.
   e. The representation must deceive, induce, and cause injury (i.e., be relied upon to one's detriment or damage).

2. Constructive fraud: a doctrine equivalent to unconscionability, where unfairness, inequality of bargaining power, overreaching, deceptive nondisclosure, etc., are present, but not rising to the level of actual fraud or duress.

3. Fraud may occur:
  a. In the inducement: antecedent fraud.
    (1) Occurs during the negotiation that preceeds the making of the contract.
    (2) The contract is valid, but *voidable* at the option of defrauded party.
  b. In the execution.
    (1) Exists when a person by trickery is made to sign an instrument other than the one intended, so that there is no meeting of the minds.
    (2) Contract is then *void*.
4. Remedies for fraud.
  a. If contract is voidable:
    (1) Defrauded party may:
      (A) Affirm and sue for damages for deceit, or if sued on the contract, set up the fraud in reduction of the damages, or
      (B) Bring an action at law for rescission (a return to the state at which the parties began, each returning any consideration received), thereby waiving damages for deceit, or
      (C) Sue in equity for both avoidance of the contract and equitable relief.
    (2) Defrauded party cannot rescind after affirming the contract (e.g., accepting benefits, or suing on it).
      (A) Delay in rescinding after discovery may amount to an affirmance or bar action on the grounds of laches (delay in enforcing claim, making enforcement inequitable.)
      (B) Right to rescission may be defeated where there are third persons who have acquired an interest under the contract for value, without notice of the fraud.
    (3) The transaction cannot be avoided in part, i.e., it must be entirely avoided or not avoided at all.
  b. If the contract is void, defrauded party may sue for fraud (action for deceit) and recover damages.
  c. Punitive damages may be available.

E. Duress:
  1. Duress is the actual or threatened causing of an action or inaction, which, contrary to a party's free will and judgment, forces him to enter into a contract. The contract can be avoided because of invalid consent.
    a. The duress must have been against the contracting party, or his wife, husband, parent, child, or close relative under such circumstances as to deprive the contracting party of freedom to contract.
    b. The duress must have been initiated by the other party to the contract, or by one acting with his knowledge or on his behalf.
    c. The duress must have induced the party to enter into the contract.
      (1) Threat of criminal prosecution, regardless of guilt or innocence, constitutes duress; however, threat of civil suit normally does not.
      (2) Unlawful detention of another's goods under oppressive circumstances or their threatened destruction may constitute duress.
  2. Effect of duress: Contract is voidable at option of the victim.

      3. Economic duress: If one party places the other in desperate economic condition, contract may be voidable.

  F. Undue influence:

      1. Brought about where unfair advantage is taken of:

         a. The relationship of the parties (e.g., though the abuse of a close relationship or position of trust), or

         b. Weakness of mind.

      2. Effect: renders contract voidable at option of injured party.

  G. Unconscionable contracts: an offensive contract whereby one party takes severe, unfair advantage of the other because of the former's superior bargaining power, e.g., education, political, or economic power. A court may void the contract or reform any unconscionable terms. A court will not use this remedy merely because a bad deal has been made. Unusual, harsh, or unfair advantage must have been used to force the contract.

UCC RULE   [2-302]: If the court as a matter of law (i.e., a judge, not a jury, decides) finds that a contract or any clause of the contract to have been unconscionable *at the time it was made,* the court may refuse to enforce the contract, or it may enforce the remainder of the contract without the unconscionable clause, or it may so limit the application of any unconscionable clause so as to avoid any unconscionable result. This provision is not intended to remedy deals that looked good and then went bad, only those that were unconscionable from the beginning. Although this section is limited explicitly to transactions involving goods, it has been very influential, and has been applied by analogy in other settings.

V. Interpretation of Contract—Parol Evidence Rule

  A. Agreements reduced to writing bind the parties, and they may not offer any proof of oral agreements, contradicting the terms of the writing. Applies to all written contracts, regardless of the applicability of the Statute of Frauds.

  B. Exceptions: Parties may present oral proof:

      1. Of the invalidity of the contract: the proof, rather than contradicting, goes to the entire existence of a written contract and destroys it (e.g., oral proof of fraud, or lack of consideration, mistake, illegality, or duress), or

      2. Of a condition precedent—see p. 160, VII.B.1.b(2)(B)(i): proof that parties agreed to a condition that had to be fulfilled before agreement was effective, thereby showing no contract exists, or

      3. To explain an ambiguity or omission: proof cannot contradict terms in the contract but can explain them, or

      4. Of a subsequent modification: a later oral agreement must be supported by consideration and not subject to the Statute of Frauds, or

      5. Of an agreement such as might naturally be made as a separate agreement by parties situated as were the parties to the written contract.

UCC RULE [2-202]: Under the UCC, written terms may be supplemented or explained by course of dealing, usage of trade, or course of performance. Thus, a specialized meaning attached to the terms by the parties will be recognized. This section also honors a statement of the writing's exclusivity, by refusing to admit additional terms when such a clause appears.

VI. Assignment of Rights, Delegation of Duties, and Third-Party Beneficiary Contracts

A. Assignment of rights: in general, rights arising under a contract are assignable, and duties delegable.

1. Parties;
   a. Obligee: the party entitled under the contract to receive the benefit of a contract.
   b. Obligor: the party required by the contract to perform a benefit for the obligee.
   c. Assignor: The party who assigns the right to receive a benefit under a contract. Usually the same person as the obligee.
   d. Assignee: the party who acquires by assignment the right to receive the benefit of the contract.

2. Under some circumstances, a person not a party to a contract may obtain the rights of one of the parties; an assignment may result from:
   a. A voluntary act of the party to whom the right is owed.
      (1) Contract rights may be assigned unless:
         (A) The contract involves exclusively personal services, personal credit, trust, or confidence.
         (B) The assignment would materially vary the duty or the risk agreed to by the obligor (person obligated to perform).
         (C) Provisions of the contract prohibit assignment.
            (i) Some jurisdictions interpret the clause as making an attempted assignment void.
            (ii) In other jurisdictions, despite a clause purportedly prohibiting assignment, the courts will allow the assignment to stand, but require the assignor to pay damages to the obligor, if any.
         (D) Assignment is forbidden by statute (e.g., nonassignment of a claim against the United States).

UCC RULE [2-210]: The UCC favors assignments. The most important change in the prior law of assignments made by the UCC is to negate attempted contractual agreements prohibiting the assignment of *nonexecutory* rights. Thus, the UCC provides, "A right to damages for breach of *the whole contract* or a right arising out of the assignor's due performance of *his entire obligation* can be assigned despite agreement otherwise." [emphasis ours]. E.g., X, a seller, has fully performed his contractual undertaking. Despite the fact that the contract provides that the rights arising under the contract are nonassignable, X may nevertheless assign his rights to another party. The prohibition is invalid since X's rights are no longer executory.

(2) **Effect of an assignment**

(A) A debtor without notice of the assignment may assert against the assignee all defenses and counterclaims good against the assignor, including payment.

(B) Where the debtor has been given notice, the assignee takes subject to all defenses good against the assignor. With regard to counterclaims, however, the debtor may assert only those based on facts existing prior to his receipt of notice.

UCC RULE   [9-318]:   A debtor who has received notice may assert all defenses and all counterclaims that arise from the contract sued upon. He may also assert all other counterclaims that accrued prior to the receipt of notice. In nonconsumer contracts, the UCC permits the debtor to expressly waive all defenses and counterclaims as against the assignee [9-206].

(3) Validity of an assignment

(A) An assignment may be oral or written.

(B) Assent to assignment by assignee is necessary.

(i) Presumption of assent exists, but

(ii) Assignee has the privilege of disclaimer within a reasonable time after he acquires knowledge of assignment.

(C) As between the assignor and assignee, the assignment is valid without notice to the debtor, but the debtor would be discharged if, without notice of the assignment, he paid the assignor.

(D) Assignment of future rights or earnings under:

(i) An existing contract is valid.

(ii) A nonexistent contract is invalid (e.g., assignment of wages from a job to be obtained).

UCC RULE   [9-204]:   All future interests are assignable under the UCC, whether based on existing or nonexisting contracts. This is a highly significant liberalization of the common law rule.

(E) An option contract is assignable. Offers are not.

(4) Gratuitous assignments: Assignments given without consideration are valid although subject (unlike assignments for a consideration) to revocation upon:

(A) Assignor's death, or

(B) Subsequent assignment for value by assignor, or

(C) Notice of assignor's revocation actually received either by assignee or by obligor, unless:

(i) Assignee reduced the debt to possession, e.g., by collection or obtaining judgment, or

(ii) Assignment was embodied in a writing or tangible token whose surrender is required to be made to the debtor by the original agreement (e.g., an IOU, savings passbook), or

(iii) Assignee received payment in good faith, or

(iv) Assignee received a new contract right against obligor by novation (see p. 159, VII.A.2).

(5) Priority between assignees: Where an assignee wrongfully makes several assignments of the same right, one of the following rules will be used to determine the rights of the successive assignees who have given consideration for the assignment. The UCC Rule below applies in most cases.

(A) English rule: First assignee who gave notice of the assignment to the debtor or person liable prevails.

(B) New York rule: Assignee who obtained the first assignment from the assignor prevails. The New York rule is the majority rule.

UCC RULE   [9-302]:   An assignee must file a financing statement to "perfect" his or her interest in the assigned rights. Between assignees of the same right, the first to file will prevail.

b. Operation of law: Rules of law operate to transfer rights and liabilities (e.g., a transfer of an interest in land includes an assignment of covenants running with the land).

B. **Delegation of duties:**

1. Performance or unconditional offer of performance by delegatee has same legal effect as performance by the party who was originally bound, and who still remains liable for any default, except that the party bound cannot delegate, nor is obligee legally bound to accept performance of delegatee where:

a. Materially different performance would result, or where contract calls for skill or is founded on personal confidence.

b. Delegation is forbidden by:

(1) Statute, or

(2) Policy of equity or common law, or

(3) Provision of contract.

C. **Third-party beneficiaries:** those persons who are intended to receive benefits from agreements made between promisors and promisees although they are not parties to the agreement and have given no consideration (see the diagram on p. 11).

1. A third party is permitted by a majority of states to enforce a promise if he or she is a:

a. Creditor beneficiary: a third party to whom a debt is owed and which debt his or her debtor intends to discharge by contracting with another for a performance to be rendered to the third party. (E.g., X lent Y $1,000 on Y's promise to repay it to Z, a creditor of X's to whom X owes $1,000. On Y's failure to repay, Z may sue Y as a creditor beneficiary. Of course, Z retains all rights he or she formerly had against X.) Or

b. Donee beneficiary: a third party to whom the promisee intends to confer a gift by contracting with a promisor for a performance to be rendered to the third party (e.g., X lent Y $1,000 on Y's promise to repay the sum to Z, on whom

X intended to confer a gift. On Y's failure to repay, Z may sue as a donee beneficiary.) The donee beneficiary normally must be either a close relative or the public.

2. Incidental beneficiary: a third party whom the contract was not intended to benefit, but who nevertheless may derive an incidental benefit. Such a party has no enforceable rights.

3. Under the English and Massachusetts rules, the third-party beneficiary doctrine is not recognized.

4. A beneficiary's rights are subject to the defenses that the promisor had against the promisee.

5. A creditor beneficiary can maintain an action against either of the contracting parties for nonperformance.

6. A donee beneficiary must proceed solely against the promisor.

VII. Discharge of the Contract

A. By agreement:

1. Release, waiver, mutual rescission, or cancellation.

a. Mutual release: an express agreement that the contract shall no longer bind either party.

(1) Waiver is a relinquishment of a condition—see UCC Rule, p. 163, VII.B.1.b(2)—under a contract; release is an abandonment of a right (e.g., discharging a party from his obligation under the contract).

(2) Mutual rescission is a complete undoing of the contract and contemplates restoration of the parties to their original position, i.e., as if the contract had never been made.

   (A) Normally, only divisible contracts may be rescinded in part where this is essential to a just result.

(3) Cancellation signifies defacing of a written contract with intent to destroy its legal effect.

b. Statutes in many states provide that an agreement to change, modify, or discharge an obligation shall not be invalid because of the absence of consideration, provided that the agreement or release is in writing and signed by the party to be bound. Otherwise, consideration is necessary to support such an agreement.

UCC RULE   [2-209]:   An agreement modifying or rescinding a contract for the sale or purchase of goods needs no consideration to be binding. Thus, the UCC permits the parties readily to modify or rescind certain of their contractual undertakings that would fail at common law because of lack of consideration. Furthermore, this may be done *orally* unless the contract *as modified* is within the Statute of Frauds or there is a signed writing that precludes modification or rescission except in writing. However, even if a signed writing is required, the writing need not be supported by consideration to be valid. For example, X contracts to sell Y 200 widgets at $4 per 100. The price of widgets drops drastically, and X orally agrees to reduce the price to $2 per 100. The contract has been effectively modified, and Y need only pay $2 per 100 widgets unless there is a signed agreement precluding such oral modifications. The Statute of Frauds would not apply, due to the dollar amount as modified. In any event, even if a writing were required, the modification would not fail for want of consideration as would be the case under the common law preexisting legal-duty rule. (see p. 145, III.B.2.b).

2. **Novation:** a substituted contract.
   a. A new contract duty is expressly substituted for the old.
   b. The old contract is entirely terminated.
   c. a new contract with at least one new party is substituted for the old one, i.e., one of the original parties is released by the other party to the contract and a new party substituted in his place.
   d. A novation discharges the contractual obligation of the old promisor; there is no standby obligation when the delegation is accomplished via novation.
   e. Novation is distinguished from a merger. In a merger the new contract is nothing more than another form of old contract merged into the new.
3. Provisions for discharge contained in the contract.
   a. **Condition subsequent.** Contract contains an express or implied provision for its termination under certain circumstances, or the happening of a future event. It will be discharged upon:
      (1) The nonfulfillment of a specified term, or
      (2) Occurrence of a stipulated event, or
      (3) Exercise of right of discharge provided for in the contract or exercised by right of custom, which forms a part of the contract.

B. By performance:

1. Where promises have been performed (bilateral) or a promise has been performed and an act given (unilateral):
   a. Time of performance.
      (1) Where no time is specified for performance, it must be performed within a reasonable time.
         (A) What constitutes a reasonable time depends upon the circumstances.
      (2) If the contract specifies a time for performance, it must be performed within that time; if not, the other party may offset, against payment, any damage caused by the delay, or if time is "of the essence," he or she may reject performance entirely.
         (A) Time is of the essence when:
            (i) The parties so stipulate, or
            (ii) Nonperformance within the time fixed will defeat the purpose of the contract.
   b. **Satisfactory performance.**
      (1) In absence of specific provisions, performance is satisfactory if it should satisfy a reasonable person.
      (2) Satisfactory performance must comply with conditions of the contract.

(A) Conditional contracts: an executory contract, the performance of which depends upon a condition.

(B) Classification of conditions:

(i) Precedent: one that is to be performed or happen before a particular duty of performance arises.

(ii) Subsequent: a future even which will extinguish an obligation.

(iii) Concurrent: mutually dependent events to be performed at the same time. Unless otherwise provided, conditions are presumed to be concurrent.

(C) Satisfaction guaranteed: where one party guarantees satisfaction, the contract will be held to require satisfaction of a reasonable person and not personal satisfaction of the individual, unless personal taste or fancy is involved and the contract contemplated personal satisfaction.

(i) Parties may agree that performance shall be to the satisfaction of some third person and, if so, there is no liability until said person is satisfied, unless fraud or collusion can be shown.

c. **Substantial performance:** Under common law an express contract had to be completed to the last detail (the perfect tender doctrine), but under the doctrine of substantial performance, performance is satisfied if:

(1) There was a substantial performance of the contract, and

(2) There was a *bona fide* effort to comply fully, and

(3) There was no willful or deliberate departure from the terms, and

(4) The deviations were minor, and

(5) The damage sustained from the defects was deducted from the price.

UCC RULE   [2-601]:   The UCC nominally adopts the perfect tender rule, but a number of related sections lessen the effect of that provision. A buyer who has accepted goods is subject to the substantial performance rule if he wishes to revoke acceptance [2-608], and the seller of goods rejected under the perfect tender rule has a right to "cure," to try to correct the problem [2-508].

d. Payment: consists of the performance of a contract by:

(1) Delivery of money, or

(2) Delivery of a negotiable instrument that is taken in absolute discharge of payee's right, or (as presumed in most jurisdictions) conditionally, in that if it is not paid when due, payee will revert to his original rights.

(3) If at or before the time of payment debtor specified the application that is to be made of the payment, this direction must be followed (e.g., apply to principal rather than interest). Where there is no direction, some courts require payment to be applied first for interest due; others allow the creditor the choice in allocating payment to principal or interest; but if she or he does not exercise this choice, payment will go toward interest.

    e. Interest.

        (1) Interest is allowed on matured debts of specific amounts. Parties, subject to (5) below, may fix the applicable interest rate. Where no interest rate is stated but interest is to be paid, the law provides a specific rate called the legal rate of interest.

        (2) Interest is not allowed on running accounts that are unliquidated until they are settled and become liquidated, unless permitted by statute or trade usage, and parties agree to it.

        (3) Interest on a debt payable on demand accrues and starts from time of demand or, where there is no specific demand, at commencement of suit.

        (4) Where there is an undated instrument providing for interest, but not specifying the date it is to run from, interest runs from date of issue.

        (5) Usury is taking a greater sum for use of money than law permits; it voids the contract. The maximum lawful rate of interest (contract rate) is a limit set by law, which limit the parties cannot exceed. This maximum rate is normally higher than the legal rate discussed above.

    f. Tender: an offer or attempt to perform:

        (1) Where there is an offer to pay something promised, refusal by promisee to accept payment does not discharge the debt, which can be collected later, but prevents the running of interest.

        (2) Where there is an offer to do something promised, refusal to accept by promisee discharges the promisor from the contract and allows him to sue for breach (see p. 162, VII.E.3).

        (3) Late tender may subject defaulting party to action for damages incurred.

C. By operation of law:

    1. Impossibility of performance: excuses performance that:

        a. Has become objectively impossible, as opposed to subjectively impossible (e.g., through personal lack of funds), which will never excuse performance. Objective impossibility is created where:

        (1) Legislation makes the purpose unlawful.

        (2) Subject matter, which is essential to performance, is destroyed without fault of the promisor.

        (3) Personal service is required and incapacity prevents discharging these services (e.g., death, illness).

        b. If the risk of impossibility was bargained for, then excuse by reason of the doctrine of impossibility is not applicable.

    2. Impracticality of performance: Unexpected difficulty and expense encountered by the promisor generally do not excuse his duty. However, in extreme cases a few courts accept this as an excuse.

    3. Frustration of purpose (doctrine is now well recognized in the United States).

        a. Where the value of the performance bargained for is destroyed by supervening events, promisor's duty is discharged. (E.g., a lease on property to be used only as a saloon is discharged when prohibition law prevents this.)

(1) Performance may still be possible.

(2) Theory is based on failure of consideration.

   (A) Value of performance must be totally or almost totally destroyed, and

   (B) Frustrating events must not have been anticipated at the time contract was made.

4. Alteration of a written instrument: A deed or contract in writing altered by an addition or erasure is discharged if the alteration is made:

   a. In a material part, so that it changes the legal effect of the instrument, even if not prejudicial to the other party.

   b. By a party to the contract, or a stranger with his consent.

   c. Intentionally.

   d. Without consent of the other party.

D. **Statute of limitations** bars actions at law on contracts unless they are brought within prescribed periods of time. Statute does not effect a discharge, but constitutes a bar to enforcement, which may be pleaded as a defense by a defending party.

   1. Statute is "tolled" (suspended) by:

      (A) Disability of a plaintiff to sue (e.g., infancy, insanity), or

      (B) Absence of a defendant from jurisdiction so as not to be subject to legal process.

   2. Full time allowed under the statute will begin to run anew when there is:

      (A) Clear acknowledgment of the debt, or

      (B) Part payment on account.

   3. Statute begins to run from the date the cause of action accrues:

      (A) On open book accounts, from the date of entry of the last item in the account.

      (B) On a bill or note payable, from date of maturity. In case of a demand note, statute runs from the date of execution unless there are circumstances showing that the intention of the parties is that the statute shall not run until making of the demand (e.g., note payable three days after demand).

   4. A written promise to pay money due is binding if the antecedent debt was once enforceable and still would be except for the effect of the statute of limitations— see p. 146, III.B.4.c(2). But if the promise is conditional, performance becomes due only upon happening of the condition.

E. Breach of contract:

   1. Renunciation of contract.

      a. **Anticipatory breach,** i.e., renunciation before the time of performance, discharges the other party if he so chooses, and entitles him to sue at once for the breach. (Accepted in a majority of states, and under the UCC).

      b. Renunciation of contract in course of performance discharges other party from a continuing performance and entitles him to sue at once for breach.

   2. Impossibility created by one party (either before or in course of performance), making performance by the other party impossible, discharges the other party, who may sue at once for breach.

3. Violation of terms of contract.

    a. Failure of performance may discharge the obligation of the other party or merely give him a right of action for breach, depending upon whether the promises are:

        (1) Conditional upon each other: There is a discharge.

        (2) Independent of each other: Normally there is no discharge, for there is an absolute promise wholly unconditional upon performance of other party. The intention of the parties must clearly have been to have independent promises; if this is found, performance must be completed by one party, regardless of the nonperformance of the other.

    b. Tortious interference with a contract, i.e., inducing a party to violate terms of the contract, makes the inducer liable in damages to the injured party.

4. Discharge of right of action arising from breach.

    a. By agreement of the parties:

        (1) Release and convenant not to sue: a formal writing supported by consideration that recites a present relinquishment of rights therein described; effect is to immediately relieve one of the parties of some or all of his duties.

UCC RULE [1-107]: The code does not require consideration for the waiver or renunciation of any claims arising out of an alleged breach if the waiver or renunciation is in writing signed and delivered by the aggrieved party. This rule applies to all types of claims and rights under the UCC; it is not limited to contracts for the sale of goods. E.g., X breaches his security agreement on the purchase of an automobile for failing to make his installment payment on the due date. Y in a signed writing agrees to waive his right to sue for breach of contract. This waiver is valid without consideration. This is another major shift from the common law rules regarding consideration (see p. 146, III.d.4).

        (2) Accord and satisfaction: agreement between parties to a dispute to accept new arrangement in place of the *disputed* one (e.g., agreeing upon a given sum as due, in place of conflicting claims on the amount due).

           (A) Where accord is carried out, it is said to be "satisfied," and there is an accord and satisfaction that is binding although there is no new consideration for this agreement.

           (B) Where an accord is executory, i.e., not yet followed by a satisfaction, any party is free to press his original claim. The minority rule states that the parties to a valid accord must be given a reasonable time in which to perform the satisfaction.

           (C) For an accord there must be:

               (i) Genuine dispute, and

               (ii) A disputed amount of damage, (an unliquidated claim), as contrasted with liquidated damages, where the amount of damages in case of breach of the contract is set in the contract.

(D) Assent by the creditor.
 (i) There is no accord unless there is an offer by the debtor for substituted performance, and acceptance thereof by the creditor.
 (ii) Retention or cashing of a check offered as settlement is almost always held to operate as full satisfaction if at the time no word of dissent is sent to the debtor; if the creditor promptly informs the debtor that he will not accept this as full performance, but only apply it to the balance, a few jurisdictions will hold that no accord or satisfaction occurs, whereas most jurisdictions hold that an accord and satisfaction has occurred.

b. Discharge by arbitration:
 (1) Definition: the voluntary submission of legal disputes to resolution outside the courts. It is estimated that over 70% of private legal disputes, excluding personal injury cases, are resolved in this manner.
 (2) Characteristics: Relative to court proceedings, arbitration is generally speedy, informal, convenient, inexpensive, private, and conclusive.
 (3) Agreements to arbitrate existing disputes are generally enforceable. Agreements in contracts to submit *potential* disputes to arbitration are also enforced by many states.
 (4) Benefits: The extensive use of arbitration to resolve legal disputes is beneficial to the judicial process since it diverts a large workload from heavily burdened courts. In addition, legislatures have been stimulated to encourage through reform of procedural statutes, a more speedy, efficient, and simplified administration of justice.

c. Discharge by judgment: Right to sue for breach is terminated upon final judgment of a court of competent jurisdiction, whether in favor of or against a party.
 (1) Where a party wins a suit, the cause of action merges in the judgment.
 (2) Where a party loses, the judgment estops him.

d. Bankruptcy effects a statutory release from debts and liabilities that are provable and dischargeable under the Bankruptcy Act when the bankrupt has obtained a discharge from the court.

e. Lapse of time:
 (1) May affect the remedy of the parties to a contract (e.g., laches-neglect or delay in enforcing a right, making it inequitable to permit the party to enforce it). The statute of limitations usually controls.

F. Remedies:

1. Where contract is breached, there is:
 a. Right of action on contract: suit for damages. Recovery is generally designed to place party suing in same position as if the contract had been performed, allowing him recompense for his loss, which directly and naturally resulted from the breach.
 (1) Damages must have been within contemplation of both parties at the time of contracting as the natural result of a breach. Unless special damages were provided for, i.e., damages arising from special circumstances beyond the normal course of events, they are not recoverable.

> (2) Liquidated damages: Parties may assess damages themselves by provision in the contract, but cannot provide for amounts that are so high as to be considered a penalty. (I.e., recovery should only attempt to place a party in the position he or she would be in if there had been performance as determined at the time of contracting, *not* at the time of breach.)

UCC RULE   [2-718]:   Under the UCC, the amount of the liquidated damages at the time need only be reasonable at the time of making the contract in light of the anticipated or actual harm caused by the breach.

> **b. Specific performance:** a suit in equity to enforce performance where no adequate remedy at law exists, i.e., where money damages will not suffice. (E.g., a court will enforce a contract to convey a unique object, as in the conveyance of land.)
>
> **c.** *Quantum meruit:* a suit for reasonable value of services, i.e., recovery for anything the party suing may have done on the contract. The action is based upon **quasi contract,** rather than arising under the terms of the original contract.

UCC RULE   For a discussion of the rights and remedies of the parties upon breach of a sales contract, see pp. 321–325.

Selected Problems from CPA Examinations on Contracts

Subjective Questions and Answers

Q. 1. Clauson Enterprises, Inc., was considering adding a new product line to its existing lines. The decision was contingent upon its being assured of a supply of an electronic component for the product at a certain price and a positive market study which clearly justified the investment in the venture.

Clauson's president approached Migrane Electronics and explained the situation to Migrane's president. After much negotiation, Migrane agreed to grant Clauson an option to purchase 12,000 of the necessary electronic components at $1.75 each or at the prevailing market price, whichever was lower. Clauson prepared the option below incorporating their understanding.

> Option Agreement
> Clauson Enterprises/Migrane Electronics
>
> Migrane Electronics hereby offers to sell Clauson Enterprises 12,000 miniature solid state electronic breakers at $1.75 each or at the existing market price at the time of delivery, whichever is lower, delivery to be made in 12 equal monthly installments beginning one month after the exercise of this option. This option is irrevocable for six months from January 1, 1978.
>
> Clauson Enterprises agrees to deliver to Migrane its market survey for the product line in which the component would be used if it elects not to exercise the option.

Both parties signed the option agreement and Migrane's president signed Migrane's corporate name alongside the last sentence of the first paragraph. On May 1, 1978, Migrane notified Clauson that it was revoking its offer. The market price for the component had increased to $1.85. On May 15, 1978, Clauson notified Migrane that it accepted the offer and that if Migrane did not perform, it would be sued and held liable for damages. Migrane replied that the offer was not binding and was revoked before Clauson accepted. Furthermore, even if it were binding, it was good for only three months as a matter of law.

Upon receipt of Migrane's reply, Clauson instituted suit for damages.

Required

Answer the following, setting forth reasons for any conclusions stated.

   Who will prevail? Discuss all the issues and arguments raised by the fact situation.

A.   Clauson Enterprises will prevail. The option in question is supported by consideration and consequently is a binding contract. The offer is definite and certain despite the fact that the pricing terms are not presently determinable. The Uniform Commercial Code is extremely liberal regarding satisfaction of the pricing terms.

Except for the presence of consideration in the form of the promise by Clauson to deliver the market survey to Migrane, the option would not have been binding beyond three months and Migrane would have prevailed. Section 2-205 of the Uniform Commercial Code provides as follows:

> An offer by a merchant to buy or sell goods in a signed writing which by its terms gives assurance that it will be held open is not revocable, for lack of consideration, during the time stated or if no time is stated for a reasonable time, but in no event may such period of irrevocability exceed three months; but any such term of assurance on a form supplied by the offeree must be separately signed by the offeror.

It is apparent from the wording of this section that the option was valid without consideration, but only for three months. It was an offer by a merchant contained in a signed writing and clearly stated its irrevocability. Furthermore, the separately signed requirement where the form is supplied by the offeree was satisfied. But the section is inapplicable to the facts of this case since bargained-for consideration was present. The Uniform Commerical Code's three-month limitation does not apply to options where consideration is present. Hence, Clauson's acceptance was valid, and if Migrane refuses to perform, Clauson will be entitled to damages.

11/78

Q. 2. Novack, an industrial designer, accepted an offer from Superior Design Corporation to become one of its designers. The contract was for three years and expressly provided that it was irrevocable by either party except for cause during that period of time. The contract was in writing and signed by both parties. After a year, Novack became dissatisfied with the agreed compensation which he was receiving. He had done a brilliant job and several larger corporations were attempting to lure him away.

Novack, therefore, demanded a substantial raise, and Superior agreed in writing to pay him an additional amount as a bonus at the end of the third year. Novack remained with Superior and performed the same duties he had agreed to perform at the time he initially accepted the position. At the end of the three years, Novack sought to collect the additional amount of money promised. Superior denied liability beyond the amount agreed to in the original contract.

Required

Answer the following, setting forth reasons for any conclusions stated.

   Can Novack recover the additional compensation from Superior?

A.   No. The preexisting legal duty rule applies. Novack has not given any consideration for Superior's promise of additional compensation. The common law rules apply to contracts for services, and modifications of such contracts must be supported by consideration. In essence, Novack was already bound by a valid contract to perform exactly what he did perform under the modified contract. Hence, he did nothing more than he was legally obligated to do. As a result, there is no consideration to support Superior's promise to pay the bonus.

Section 2-209 of the Uniform Commercial Code, which provides that an agreement modifying a contract needs no consideration to be binding, is not applicable to an employment contract because Section 2-209 covers only the sale of goods.

11/78

Q. 3. The basic facts are the same as stated in *the previous question* except that one of Superior's competitors, Dixon Corporation, successfully lured Novack away from Superior by offering a substantially higher salary. Dixon did this with full knowledge of the terms of the original three-year contract between Novack and Superior.

Required

Answer the following, setting forth reasons for any conclusions stated.

1. Does Superior have any legal redress against Dixon?
2. Would Superior be successful if it seeks the equitable relief of specific performance (an order by the court compelling Novack to perform his contractual undertaking) for the remaining two years of the contract?

A. 1. Yes. A cause of action based upon Dixon's intentional interference with a contractual relationship would be available. All the requirements necessary to state such a cause of action are present, particularly the knowledge of the existing contractual relationship between Novack and Superior. The law treats Dixon's conduct as tortious and allows a recovery for damages against Dixon.
2. No. A court exercising its equity powers will not force a person to fulfill a contract for personal services. To do so smacks of involuntary servitude.

11/77

Q. 4. Granville Motors, Inc., wished to acquire a 4-acre tract of land owned by Bonanza Realty Developers in an industrial city. Granville did not want to waste time and money considering the suitability of the property unless assured that the plant site would be available if studies indicated that the proposed purchase would be desirable. Granville did not discuss this concern with Bonanza but proposed to Bonanza that an option be drafted granting Granville 30 days in which to purchase the plant site for $62,950. Bonanza agreed and mailed to Granville the following written option:

> For ONE DOLLAR ($1.00) and other valuable consideration, Bonanza Realty Developers hereby grants to Granville Motors, Inc., the exclusive option to purchase for SIXTY-TWO THOUSAND NINE HUNDRED FIFTY DOLLARS ($62,950) the 4-acre tract of land known as the N.E. corner site . . . *(assume legal description included)* for THIRTY (30) days. This option is exclusive and irrevocable and will automatically expire on September 15, 1977.
>
> > *Joseph T. Verona*
> > Joseph T. Verona, President
> > Bonanza Realty Developers

The letter containing the option was mailed on August 14, but due to a delay in the mails, did not reach Granville until August 18. Upon receipt Granville promptly engaged an expert to do a feasibility study with respect to the location and began to solicit bids on the construction of the proposed plant. Bonanza had no knowledge of these facts. Granville had no further correspondence with Bonanza after the receipt of the option, and Granville neither paid the $1.00 nor gave any other bargained for consideration.

On September 15, Jordon, Granville's president, telephoned Verona intending to accept the offer for Granville. However, before Jordon could accept, Verona stated that the property had already been sold at a higher price. The purchaser had no actual knowledge of the above facts. Jordon nevertheless accepted on Granville's behalf. The next day Jordon sent a written confirmation which stated that Granville expected performance by Bonanza, and that if Bonanza failed to perform, Granville would be forced to sue to protect its interests. Jordon also reminded Verona that the offer was irrevocable and that substantial time, money, and effort had been expended in a feasibility study. In addition Jordon noted the adverse effect which a refusal would have on Granville's future profits in that plans had been finalized calling for the plant to be on line by April 1978 to supply the increased demand of its customers.

Required
Answer the following, setting forth reasons for any conclusions stated.

1. Is the option legally binding on Bonanza?
2. Assuming Granville will prevail, is specific performance available to Granville?
3. Assuming Granville will prevail, what would Granville be entitled to recover if it seeks damages as a form of relief?

A. 1. The option is not legally binding on Bonanza. The issue is whether the option fails for want of legal consideration. The option involved here must meet the necessary common law requirements to establish a legally enforceable contract. Since land is the subject matter of the option, it is tested under the common law rules as contrasted with the more liberal Uniform Commercial Code rule on options. The main pitfall is the lack of consideration. Despite the facts that the promise was written and was signed by the offeror, and that it recited consideration, and manifested a clear intent that it be irrevocable for 30 days, it is not legally binding. It is not supported by actual consideration and, therefore, fails to meet the requirements necessary to establish a valid contract under common law principles.

   Neither the signed written offer, nor the expenditures made by Granville constitute consideration. With respect to the feasibility study, the parties did not bargain for the performance of such acts and expenditures by Granville in exchange for the promise contained in the option. The facts indicate that Bonanza had no knowledge that Granville was incurring the expense of a feasibility study prior to reaching a decision whether to exercise the option.

   Although the courts generally are receptive to a formal satisfaction of the consideration requirement by the actual payment of $1.00 or some other bargained for token consideration, they do not accept fictional statements of receipt of consideration. If the option were valid, the acceptance would of course be timely even if made orally on September 15, provided the fact of acceptance could be established. One need not use the same means of communication in order to have a valid acceptance, provided it is received prior to the termination of the offer.

2. No. Although specific performance generally is not available as a remedy for breach of contract, there is a notable exception with respect to contracts for the sale of real property. Real property is deemed to be unique, and therefore, specific performance usually is available. However, when there has been a subsequent sale to a good faith third-party purchaser, the courts will let the title rest where they find it. Thus, Granville would fail unless the third party had actual or constructive notice of the option granted by Bonanza to Granville. If this option agreement had been recorded, the third party would be deemed to have constructive notice.

3. Granville would be limited to recovery of the typical contract measures of damages, that is, the difference between the fair market value and the contract price at the date the contract was to be performed. The sale at the higher price to the third party will have strong evidentiary value as to the fair market value. Recovery for the expenditures made is possible but not probable unless these facts were known to the seller and thus was within the contemplation of the parties at the time the contract was made. Such does not appear to be the case. This would also apply to the lost future profits. In addition, the lost future profits are at best speculative and would appear to be unattainable as damages.

Q. 5. El Greco Artists United is a very prominent group of established portrait painters. Nelson is the founder and dominant force behind Nelsonics, a maker of mini computer components. Nelson decided that it would be appropriate to celebrate the corporation's silver anniversary with a suitable oil painting depicting himself chairing the July 1977 annual Board of Directors meeting with a large existing portrait of the original board 25 years ago as a conspicuous part of the background. This then could be photographed and used on the cover page of the twenty-fifth anniversary annual report. Accordingly, Nelson engaged El Greco to paint the picture of the current board with Nelson in the chair and the portrait of the original board prominently displayed in the background. Under the terms of the contract between El Greco and Nelson, the portrait was to be completed prior to the month of April immediately preceding the annual board meeting in July and was subject to the personal approval and satisfaction of Nelson.

Difficulty arose in connection with the painting. Whitlow, the artist doing the likeness of Nelson, clashed repeatedly with Nelson on the artistic details and in particular the expression which the face of Nelson's likeness should bear. Nelson also wanted some minor alterations insofar as his features and coloring were concerned in order to appear more youthful and robust. After much acrimony, the picture was submitted to Nelson on April 1, 1977. Nelson rejected it, claiming that it lacked artistic merit.

Required

Answer the following, setting forth reasons for any conclusions stated.

What are the legal issues involved in the above facts and what is the probable result?

A. The legal issue posed by the facts primarily involves the personal approval or satisfaction rule as it relates to satisfactory performance of a contractual undertaking. The usual answer to such a question is that unless the satisfaction requirement has been met there is no enforceable contract. This is the case in that the test is strictly construed as a subjective test when personal taste or predilection is involved as long as the party rejecting the tendered performance is acting in good faith. If the case were litigated, El Greco would contend that the rejection by Nelson was made in bad faith. From the facts stated, it would be difficult to prove that Nelson acted in bad faith. That the portrait was not submitted until April 1, 1977, would not be justification for rejection by Nelson unless the contract provided that time was of the essence.

11/76

Q. 6. Your client, Super Fashion Frocks, Inc., agreed in writing to purchase $520 worth of coat hangers from Display Distributors, Inc., with payment terms of net/30 after delivery. Delivery was to be made within five days from the signing of the contract. Two days prior to the due date for delivery, Display Distributors called and offered a flat $25 discount if payment were made upon delivery instead of the original net/30 terms. Super Fashion Frocks agreed and tendered its check for $495 upon delivery. Display Distributors cashed the check and now seeks to enforce the original contract calling for payment of $520 (i.e., seeks to recover $25 from Super Fashion). It bases its claim upon the following arguments:

1. The Statute of Frauds applies to the contract modification.
2. The Parol Evidence Rule prohibits the introduction of oral evidence modifying the terms of a written agreement.
3. There was no consideration given for Display's promise to take a lesser amount.

Required

Discuss the validity of each argument.

A. 1. The Statute of Frauds is not applicable because the dollar amount is less than $500 after the modification. Since the contract as modified is not included under the Statute of Frauds, the statute has no impact upon the contractual adjustment made by the parties. The Uniform Commercial Code provides that if a modification is agreed upon, it need not be in writing as long as the contract is not within the Statute of Frauds.

2. The Parol Evidence Rule has no application to the facts stated. It prohibits the contradiction of the written terms of a contract by any prior oral agreement or a contemporaneous oral agreement. It is not applicable to a subsequent oral modification of a written contract.

3. Under the Uniform Commercial Code an agreement to modify a contract for the sale of goods requires no consideration. But, even if consideration were necessary, Super Fashion provided consideration by paying earlier than required by the terms of the original agreement. Thus, Super Fashion prevails under either rule.

Q. 7. Mark Candy Wholesalers, Inc., entered into a contract with Brown & Sons, a family partnership, which owned three small candy stores. Mark agreed to supply Brown & Sons with "its entire requirements of candy for its stores for one year" at fixed prices. Brown agreed to purchase its requirements exclusively from Mark. The price of sugar increased drastically shortly after the first month of performance. Mark breached the contract because the prices at which it was required to deliver imposed a severe financial hardship which would be ruinous. Mark asserts the following legal justifications for its actions:

    1. The contract is unenforceable for want of consideration in that Brown & Sons did not agree to take any candy at all. That is, Brown & Sons was not specifically required to purchase candy if it did not require any.

    2. The contract is too indefinite and uncertain as to the quantity which might be ordered and hence is unenforceable.

    3. Performance is excused on the ground of legal impossibility because of the severe financial hardship imposed upon Mark as a result of the drastic rise in the price of sugar. This unforeseen event falls within the rule of implied conditions and makes the contract voidable.

Required

Discuss the validity of each of the legal justifications asserted by Mark.

A. **1.** This asserted legal justification is invalid. First, Brown & Sons did give consideration in that they promised to purchase their candy needs exclusively from Mark. Second, the courts have sustained the validity of such requirement contracts based upon a logical interpretation of the agreement on the buyer's part to act in good faith and to take his usual or normal amount of the product involved.

    2. This asserted legal justification is also invalid. Although some limited indefiniteness and uncertainty is present, this will not invalidate the agreement. The Uniform Commercial Code provides that a contract of sale does not fail for indefiniteness even though one or more terms are left open if the parties have intended to make a contract and there is a reasonably certain basis for giving an appropriate remedy. Furthermore, the code provides that when a contract measures the quantity in terms of output of the seller or requirements of the buyer, it means such actual output or requirements as may occur in good faith. Mark's good faith is presumed, and prior requirements may be used to ascertain the quantities.

    3. The asserted legal justification based upon a drastic change in price is invalid. The courts will not recognize a subsequent implied condition of this nature to permit a party to avoid his obligation under a contract. Moreover, while the modern trend of the courts may be somewhat more lenient in finding the existence of impossibility, they will not excuse performance unless the performance is rendered physically and objectively impossible.

        The development of an additional financial burden or hardship upon a party to a contract is not sufficient to provide a legal excuse for his nonperformance. To excuse performance in these circumstances would seriously hamper the conduct of business transactions and impair the validity of many contracts.

5/76

Q. 8. On June 1, 1975, Markum Realty, Inc., offered to sell 1 acre of land in an industrial park it owned to Johnson Enterprises, Inc. The offer was by mail and, in addition to the other usual terms, stated: "This offer will expire on July 2, 1975, unless acceptance is received by the offeror on or before said date."

    Johnson decided to purchase the tract of land, and on July 1 telegraphed its acceptance to Markum. The acceptance telegram was delayed due to the negligence of the telegraph company, which had admitted that delivery was not made to Markum until July 3. Markum decided not to sell to Johnson because it had received a better offer, but it remained silent and did not notify Johnson of its decision.

When Johnson did not hear from Markum by July 11, its president called the president of Markum and inquired when Johnson might expect to receive the formalized copy of the contract the two companies had entered into. Markum's president responded that there was no contract.

Required

1. Did a contract result from the dealings between Markum and Johnson? Discuss the legal implications of *each* communication between the parties in your explanation.
2. Assuming a contract did not arise, does Johnson have any legal recourse against the telegraph company? Explain?

A. **1.** No. Markum's offer to Johnson dated June 1, 1975, specifically stipulated that the acceptance must be received by Markum on or before July 2, 1975. Even though Johnson dispatched its acceptance by telegram on July 1, 1975, the offer had expired or terminated on July 2, 1975, because the acceptance had not been received by Markum on that date. The delay by the telegraph company is irrelevant to the relations between Markum and Johnson. Even if Johnson had used the same means of communication (the mails), its acceptance would have had to reach Markum on July 2, 1975, to be a valid acceptance because this was a specific stipulation in the offer.

Under the circumstances, Markum's silence does not constitute an acceptance of Johnson's telegram. The telegram must be considered a counteroffer because it arrived after the expiration date of Markum's original offer. Markum had no obligation to reply, and its actions were legally correct. Hence, because the terms of the offer were not met, no contract resulted from the dealings between Markum and Johnson.

2. Yes. A legal action by Johnson against the telegraph company will be successful in that the telegraph company was negligent in delivering the telegram. As a result of its negligence, the telegraph company prevented Johnson from completing formation of the contract in question. It seems apparent that Johnson suffered damages as a result of the telegraph company's negligence. Hence, a recovery based upon the tort of negligence or breach of contract would be appropriate.

11/75

Q. **9.** On July 1, 1974, Franklin Novelties, Inc., offered to sell Major Toy Marketing Corporation 12,000 velocipedes at $6.25 each, delivery f.o.b. Franklin's warehouse not later than December 15, 1974.

Major Toy wired Franklin as follows:

> We accept your offer of July 1, 1974. However, due to the proximity of the Christmas season, we must insist that delivery be made not later than November 1, 1974. This acceptance is expressly made conditional on your assent to the different delivery date.
>
> *Major Toy*

Franklin decided to stick with its original terms and, consequently, sold the 12,000 velocipedes to Fremont Toys. It, therefore, ceased entirely its dealings with Major Toy.

Major Toy subsequently learned of the sale to its competitor, Fremont Toys, and promptly dispatched to Franklin the following telegram:

> We hold you liable on your offer of July 1, 1974, re: the sale of 12,000 velocipedes. Our modification of the terms was a mere proposal, which we herewith waive. In any event, *your silence constitutes acceptance of our modified terms*. We expect delivery not later than December 15, 1974.
>
> *Major Toy*

Required

What are the legal implications to Franklin Novelties as a result of the above facts? Explain.

A.   Franklin Novelties is not liable to Major Toy. Although Franklin made a valid offer to sell velocipedes to Major Toy, Major Toy's acceptance varied the terms of the offer and was made expressly conditional upon Franklin's making delivery not later than November 1, 1974. Such a purported acceptance is no acceptance. Instead, it constitutes a rejection and a counter offer by Major Toy. In other words, the original offer is terminated and a new offer has been made by the original offeree, Major Toy. The counter offer must in turn be accepted in order to create a contractual obligation. Since Franklin never responded and since silence would not here constitute acceptance, there is no contract. Furthermore, once an offer is rejected, it can no longer be revived by the party who rejected it. Major Toy's attempt to revive the original offer has no legal merit.

11/74

Q. 10. Albert Gideon, Jr., doing business as Albert's Boutique, ordered $480 of miniskirts from Abaco Fashions. Abaco refused to make delivery, having had previous collection problems with Gideon. Albert's father, Slade Gideon, a prominent manufacturer, called Abaco and said, "Ship the goods my son needs, and I will pay for them." Abaco delivered the miniskirts, and they were received by Albert's Boutique. Albert's Boutique is in bankruptcy, and Slade Gideon refuses to pay. You are the accountant for Abaco Fashions.

Required

What are Abaco's rights against Slade Gideon? Explain.

A.   Abaco can proceed successfully against Slade Gideon to collect the debt. Slade Gideon created a direct obligation to Abaco (a third-party beneficiary contract) by his statement, "Ship the goods my son needs, and I will pay for them." The Statute of Frauds is not at issue because the debt is less than $500. Were the Statute of Frauds at issue, it would have been satisfied by the shipment of the merchandise by Abaco and its receipt by Albert's Boutique.

11/73

Q. 11. A $26,000 positive account-receivable confirmation request was returned by Thompson Bike Company with the comment that the balance due Kell was overstated by $5,000.

Investigation revealed the following information regarding the $5,000 in question. Kell received a written order from Thompson for immediate shipment of 2,000 size #2 bike chains at $2.50 each. The order specified that the chains were to be shipped by rail, f.o.b. Kell's shipping dock. Kell promptly packed the chains and shipped them according to Thompson's requirements.

The day following shipment, Kell sent Thompson an acknowledgment of the order. The acknowledgement was received by Thompson two days later.

Unfortunately, the goods were delayed several days in transit, due to flooding that destroyed a bridge along the delivery route. As a result of the delay, Thompson ordered identical bike chains from a competing manufacturer and wired Kell to cancel the order.

Kell contends that Thompson is liable for the purchase price of the chains. Thompson claims that there was no contract since acceptance by Kell by prompt delivery or notice had not been received within a reasonable time.

Required

Is Thompson liable to Kell for the bike chains ordered? Explain.

A.   Yes. The Uniform Commercial Code provides that "an order or other offer to buy goods for prompt or current shipment shall be construed as inviting acceptance either by a prompt promise to ship or by prompt shipment . . . of the goods." Since Kell promptly shipped the goods, a unilateral contract was formed. Once the contract was formed, any attempt by Thompson to cancel his order would be ineffective and any subsequent loss of the goods would fall upon him, thus obligating him to pay.

11/72

Q. 12. You are the in-charge accountant on the examination of the financial statements of the Kell Manufacturing Corporation. After gathering information concerning account-receivable and payable confirmation exceptions, your assistant seeks your guidance in clearing the follow exception:

A $6,000 positive account-receivable confirmation request was returned by Beck Company, stating that no balance is due to Kell.

Investigation has revealed the following background information.

Kell received a telephone order from Beck, offering to purchase 1,000 bike sprockets at $6 per sprocket. The sprockets were an odd size, were to be manufactured specifically for Beck, and could not be sold to other customers in the ordinary course of business. Kell changed its production molds to accomodate the odd size and started production. Kell then received a phone call from Beck canceling the order because the order that Beck had received requiring the special sprockets had fallen through.

Kell, insisting that the contract was valid and that Beck was obligated to take and pay for the odd-sized sprockets, sent Beck an invoice for the purchase price of the 1,000 sprockets. Beck's purchasing agent returned the sales invoice with a note that the contract of sale was oral and that Beck has no obligation to pay.

Required

Is Beck liable on the oral contract? Explain.

A.   Yes. Although the contract of sale equals or exceeds $500 and hence is within the Statute of Frauds, it is enforceable without a writing if otherwise valid. The Uniform Commercial Code provides an exception to the Statute of Frauds where goods are "specially manufactured for the buyer and not suitable for sale to others in the seller's business and the seller before notice of repudiation is received . . . has made a substantial beginning of their manufacture." Under the facts of the case, it would appear that the exception clearly applies and that Beck is liable under the oral contract.

11/72

Practice Questions

Q. 1. In the course of an examination of the financial statements of Harrison and Company you find that a claim has been made against the Company by Roth Corporation. Your examination of the purchase order file reveals copies of the following letters and telegrams.

Roth in New York and Harrison in California are dealers in equipment used in garment factories. On October 1 Harrison sent and Roth received the following telegram:

> Enter my order for 10 Model 104 sewing machines at $110; two weeks delivery; 30 days net cash.
>
> */s/Harrison*

On the same day, without replying, Roth shipped Harrison the 10 machines which arrived at Harrison's place of business on October 13. But on October 3, Harrison had changed his mind and telegraphed Roth "Cancel my order of October 1. */s/Harrison.*"

When Roth received Harrison's telegram, he immediately wrote Harrison a letter explaining that the goods had been shipped. Harrison refused to accept the machines, claiming he had no contract with Roth.

Required

1. What legal problems are suggested by these facts? Discuss.
2. How should this transaction be reflected in the financial statements of Harrison? Discuss.

Q. 2. On April 1, 1971, Howard, a dealer in mining stocks, sold Hayley 10,000 shares of Alaska Uranium Ltd. at $1 per share, knowingly misrepresenting that the Corporation had proven uranium deposits in its Alaska tract. Hayley paid for the stock on April 1, 1971, and on April 15, 1971, on the advice of friends, he had the Corporation investigated and found that it never had any prospects of uranium but that it had just discovered a copper vein on the tract and was putting it into production. On February 1, 1972, Hayley received a check from the Corporation for its 1 cent share dividend and deposited it. One month later Hayley regretted his purchase and commenced legal action against Howard and Alaska Uranium Ltd.

Required

What legal problems are suggested by these facts? Discuss.

Q. 3. Cobb and Claire, an accounting firm operating nationally over a long period of years with branch offices in all major cities and coverage of all major industrial areas in the United States, acquired the entire practice and goodwill of Wingfield and Lavender, another accounting firm operating nationally and with branch offices in all major cities. The price was to be paid in 10 annual installments. The agreement provided that the five major partners of Wingfield and Lavender, both individually and as members of the accounting firm, were not to engage in practice anywhere in the United States for three years.

Required

What legal problems are suggested by these facts? Discuss.

Q. 4. On July 9, 1971, Benjamin Wade, president of American Philatelic Corporation, with the approval of the board of directors, engaged Nikal, a certified public accountant, to conduct a special interim review of the Corporation's financial statements for the nine months ended September 30, 1971, and to render his report on November 30, 1971, for inclusion in the prospectus to be issued in conjunction with an issuance of common stock. No definite sum for the engagement was agreed upon. Nikal proceeded at reasonable speed, but on November 10 he complained to Wade that the Corporation's staff was so inefficient and uncooperative that it might be impossible to meet the deadline. Wade said, "Don't worry. I'll fix that." Nikal went on with his work, but the staff of the Corporation showed no improvement. Despite Nikal's reasonable efforts, the report was not ready until December 12. Wade, acting on behalf of the Corporation, refused to accept the report or pay for the accounting services since delivery of the report by November 30 was a condition of the contract and now it did not serve its intended purpose.

Required

1. What legal problems are suggested by these facts? Discuss.
2. How should this transaction be reflected in the financial statements of American Philatelic Corporation at December 31, 1971?

Q. 5. General Drug Corporation was interested in the promotion in the state legislature of a certain bill designed to prohibit misrepresentations describing brand-name drugs as superior to those described generically where the chemical composition and quality are identical. It agreed to pay Jennings Duval, an attorney, $7,500 for his services in drawing the proposed legislation, procuring its introduction in the legislature, and making an argument for its passage before the legislative committee to which it would be referred. Duval rendered these services and submitted his bill for payment, which was unpaid at the end of the accounting period.

Required
1. What legal problems are suggested by these facts? Discuss.
2. How should this transaction be reflected in the financial statements of General Drug Corporation?

Q. 6. In the course of an examination of the financial statements of the Lilliputian Shop, a retailer, it was learned that a lawsuit was being brought against the Company by Jack and Jill Creations, Inc. Further investigation disclosed the following:

Jack and Jill Creations, Inc., a children's clothing manufacturer, entered into a written contract that was complete in all its terms for the sale of 1,000 boy and girl sailor suits to the Lilliputian Shop at $10 each. Five days later they orally agreed that the written agreement be changed to double the quantity to 2,000 suits and to reduce the price to $9 each. When the time for delivery came, Jack and Jill had been unable to manufacture the extra 1,000 suits and offered to deliver 1,000 suits at $10 each. Lilliputian refused to accept delivery.

Required
What legal problems are suggested by these facts? Discuss.

Practice Objective Questions

Instructions 1–21
Select the *best* answer for each of the following items. Mark only one answer for *each* item. Answer all items. Your grade will be based on your total correct answers.

1. Arthur sold his house to Michael. Michael agreed to pay the existing mortgage on the house. The Safety Bank, which held the mortgage, released Arthur from liability on the debt. The above declared transaction (relating to the mortgage debt) is
   a. A delegation.
   b. A novation.
   c. Invalid in that bank did *not* receive any additional consideration from Arthur.
   d. *Not* a release of Arthur if Michael defaults, and the proceeds from the sale of the mortgaged house are insufficient to satisfy the debt.
2. Williams purchased a heating system from Radiant Heating, Inc., for his factory. Williams insisted that a clause be included in the contract calling for service on the heating system to begin *not* later than the next business day after Williams informed Radiant of a problem. This service was to be rendered free of charge during the first year of the contract and for a flat fee of $200 per year for the next two years thereafter. During the winter of the second year, the heating system broke down and Williams promptly notified Radiant of the situation. Due to other commitments, Radiant did *not* send a man over the next day. Williams phoned Radiant and was told that the $200 per year service charge was uneconomical and they could *not* get a man over there for several days. Williams in desperation promised to pay an additional $100 if Radiant would send a man over that day. Radiant did so and sent a bill for $100 to Williams. Is Williams legally required to pay this bill and why?
   a. No, because the preexisting legal duty rule applies to this situation.
   b. No, because the Statute of Frauds will defeat Radiant's claim.
   c. Yes, because Williams made the offer to pay the additional amount.
   d. Yes, because the fact that it was uneconomical for Radiant to perform constitutes economic duress which freed Radiant from its obligation to provide the agreed-upon service.
3. Austin is attempting to introduce oral evidence in court to explain or modify a written contract he made with Wade. Wade has pleaded the parol evidence rule. In which of the following circumstances will Austin *not* be able to introduce the oral evidence?

    a. The contract contains an obvious ambiguity on the point at issue.

    b. There was a mutual mistake of fact by the parties regarding the subject matter of the contract.

    c. The modification asserted was made several days after the written contract had been executed.

    d. The contract indicates that it was intended as the "entire contract" between the parties and the point is covered in detail.

4. Montbanks' son, Charles, was seeking an account executive position with Dobbs, Smith, and Fogarty, Inc., the largest brokerage firm in the United States. Charles was very independent and wished *no* interference by his father. The firm, after several weeks deliberation, decided to hire Charles. They made him an offer on April 12, 1979, and Charles readily accepted. Montbanks feared that his son would *not* be hired. Being unaware of the fact that his son had been hired, Montbanks mailed a letter to Dobbs on April 13 in which he promised to give the brokerage firm $50,000 in commission business if the firm would hire his son. The letter was duly received by Dobbs and they wish to enforce it against Montbanks. Which of the following statements is correct?

    a. Past consideration is *no* consideration, hence there is *no* contract.

    b. The preexisting legal duty rule applies and makes the promise unenforceable.

    c. Dobbs will prevail since the promise is contained in a signed writing.

    d. Dobbs will prevail based upon promissory estoppel.

5. Philpot purchased the King Pharmacy from Golden. The contract contained a promise by Golden that he would *not* engage in the practice of pharmacy for one year from the date of the sale within 1 mile of the location of King Pharmacy. Six months later Golden opened the Queen Pharmacy within less than a mile of King Pharmacy. Which of the following is a correct statement?

    a. Golden has *not* breached the above covenant since he did *not* use his own name or the name King in connection with the new pharmacy.

    b. The covenant is reasonable and enforceable.

    c. The contract is an illegal restraint of trade and illegal under federal antitrust laws.

    d. The covenant is contrary to public policy and is illegal and void.

6. Keats Publishing Company shipped textbooks and other books for sale at retail to Campus Bookstore. An honest dispute arose over Campus's right to return certain books. Keats maintained that the books in question could *not* be returned and demanded payment of the full amount. Campus relied upon trade custom which indicated that many publishers accepted the return of such books. Campus returned the books in question and paid for the balance with a check marked "Account Paid in Full to Date." Keats cashed the check. Which of the following is a correct statement?

    a. Keats is entitled to recover damages.

    b. Keats' cashing of the check constituted an accord and satisfaction.

    c. The preexisting legal duty rule applies and Keats is entitled to full payment for all the books.

    d. The custom of the industry argument would have *no* merit in a court of law.

7. Abacus Corporation sent Frame Company an offer by a telegram to buy its patent on a calculator. The Abacus telegram indicated that the offer would expire in 10 days. The telegram was sent on February 1, 1979, and received on February 2, 1979, by Frame. On February 8, 1979, Abacus telephoned Frame and indicated they were withdrawing the offer. Frame telegraphed an acceptance on the 11th of February. Which of the following is correct?

    a. The offer was an irrevocable offer, but Frame's acceptance was too late.

    b. Abacus' withdrawal of the offer was ineffective because it was *not* in writing.

    c. Since Frame used the same means of communication, acceptance was both timely and effective.

    d. *No* contract arose since Abacus effectively revoked the offer on February 8, 1979.

8. Strattford Theaters made a contract with Avon, Inc., for the purchase of $450 worth of theater supplies. Delivery was to take place in one month. One week after accepting the order, the price of materials and labor increased sharply. In fact, to break even on the contract, Avon would have to charge an additional $600. Avon phoned Strattford and informed them of the situation. Strattford was sympathetic and said they were sorry to hear about the situation but that the best they would be willing to do was split the rise in price with Avon. Avon accepted the modification on Strattford's terms. As a result of the above modification, which of the following is correct?

    a. Avon's continuing to perform the contract after informing Strattford of the price difficulty constitutes consideration for the modification of the price.

b. The oral modification is *not* effective since there was *no* consideration.

c. The Statute of Frauds applies to the contract as modified.

d. The contract contained an implied promise that it was subject to price rises.

9. Mara Oil, Inc., had a contract with Gotham Apartments to supply it with its fuel oil needs for the year, approximately 10,000 gallons. The price was fixed at 10 cents above the price per gallon that Mara paid for its oil. Due to an exceptionally cold winter, Mara found that its capacity to fulfill this contract was doubtful. Therefore, it contacted Sands Oil Company and offered to assign the contract to it for $100. Sands agreed. Which of the following is correct as a result of the above assignment?

a. The contract with Gotham was neither assignable nor delegable.

b. Mara is now released from any further obligation to perform the Gotham contract.

c. Mara has effectively assigned to Sands its rights and delegated its duties under the terms of the contract with Gotham.

d. In the event Sands breaches the contract with Gotham, Mara has *no* liability.

10. Almovar Electronics was closing out several lines of electronic parts which were becoming outdated. It sent a letter on March 8 to Conduit Sales & Service Company, one of its largest retail customers, offering the entire lot at a substantial reduction in price. The offer indicated that it was for "immediate acceptance." The terms were "cash, pick up by your carrier at our loading dock and *not* later than March 15." It also indicated that the terms of the offer were *not* subject to variance. The letter did *not* arrive until March 10 and Conduit's letter accepting the offer was *not* mailed until March 12. The letter of acceptance indicated that Conduit would take the entire lot, would pay in accordance with the usual terms (2/10, net/30), and would pick up the goods on March 16. Which of the following *best* describes the legal relationship of the parties.

a. The acceptance was *not* timely, hence *no* contract.

b. The different terms of the acceptance are to be construed as proposals for changes in the contract.

c. The different terms of the acceptance constituted a rejection of the offer.

d. Since both parties were merchants and the changes in the acceptance were *not* material, there is a valid contract.

11. Major Steel Manufacturing, Inc., signed a contract on October 2, 1978, with the Hard Coal & Coke Company for its annual supply of coal for three years commencing on June 1, 1979, at a price to be determined by taking the average monthly retail price per ton, less a 10 cent per ton quantity discount. On March 15, 1979, Major discovered that it had made a bad bargain and that it could readily fulfill its requirements elsewhere at a much greater discount. Major is seeking to avoid its obligation. Which of the following is correct?

a. The pricing term is too indefinite and uncertain hence there is *no* contract.

b. Since the amount of coal required is unknown at the time of the making of the contract, the contract is too indefinite and uncertain to be valid.

c. Major is obligated to take its normal annual coal requirements from Hard or respond in damages.

d. There is *no* contract since Major could conceivably require *no* coal during the years in question.

12. Martin Stores, Inc., decided to sell a portion of its 8-acre property. Consequently, the president of Martin wrote several prospective buyers the following letter:

> Dear Sir: We are sending this notice to several prospective buyers because we are interested in selling 4 acres of our property located in downtown Metropolis. If you are interested, please communicate with me at the above address. Don't bother to reply unless you are thinking in terms of at least $100,000.
>
> *James Martin*, President

Under the circumstances, which of the following is correct?

a. The Statute of Frauds does *not* apply because the real property being sold is the division of an existing tract which had been properly recorded.

b. Markus, a prospective buyer, who telegraphed Martin that he would buy at $100,000 and forwarded a $100,000 surety bond to guarantee his performance, has validly accepted.

c. Martin must sell to the highest bidder.

d. Martin's communication did *not* constitute an offer to sell.

13. Fashion Swimming Pools, Inc., mailed a letter to Direct Distributors offering a three-year franchise dealership. The offer stated the terms in detail and at the bottom stated that "the offer would *not* be withdrawn prior to October 1, 1978." Under the circumstances, which of the following is correct?

    a. The offer is an irrevocable option which can *not* be withdrawn prior to October 1, 1978.

    b. A letter of acceptance from Direct to Fashion sent on October 1, 1978, but *not* received until October 2, 1978, would *not* create a valid contract.

    c. The Statute of Frauds would *not* apply to the proposed contract.

    d. The offer *cannot* be assigned to another party if Direct chooses *not* to accept.

14. Mayer wrote Jackson and offered to sell Jackson a building for $50,000. The offer stated it would expire 30 days from July 1, 1978. Mayer changed his mind and does *not* wish to be bound by his offer. If a legal dispute arises between the parties regarding whether there has been a valid acceptance of the offer, which of the following is correct?

    a. The offer *cannot* be legally withdrawn for the stated period of time.

    b. The offer will *not* expire prior to the 30 days even if Mayer sells the property to a third person and notifies Jackson.

    c. If Jackson phoned Mayer on August 1 and unequivocally accepted the offer, it would create a contract, provided he had *no* notice of withdrawal of the offer.

    d. If Jackson categorically rejects the offer on July 10, Jackson *cannot* validly accept within the remaining stated period of time.

15. Exeter Industries, Inc., orally engaged Werglow as one of its district sales managers for an 18-month period commencing April 1, 1978. Werglow commenced work on that date and performed his duties in a highly competent manner for several months. On October 1, 1978, the company gave Werglow a notice of termination as of November 1, 1978, citing a downturn in the market for its products. Werglow sues seeking either specific performance or damages for breach of contract. Exeter pleads the Statute of Frauds and/or a justified dismissal due to the economic situation. What is the probable outcome of the lawsuit?

    a. Werglow will prevail because the Statute of Frauds does *not* apply to contracts such as his.

    b. Werglow will prevail because he was partially performed under the terms of the contract.

    c. Werglow will lose because the reason for his termination was caused by economic factors beyond Exeter's control.

    d. Werglow will lose because such a contract must be in writing and signed by a proper agent of Exeter.

16. Ames and Bates have agreed that Bates will sell a parcel of land to Ames for $10,000 if the land is rezoned from residential to industrial use within six months of the agreement. Bates agreed to use his best efforts to obtain the rezoning, and Ames agreed to make a $2,000 good-faith deposit with Bates two weeks after the date of the agreement. What is the status of this agreement?

    a. *No* contract results because the event is contingent.

    b. The agreement is probably unenforceable because Bates would be required to attempt to influence governmental action.

    c. The parties have entered into a bilateral contract subject to a condition.

    d. Ames is *not* obligated to make the deposit at the agreed time even though Bates has by then made an effort to procure a rezoning.

17. The Johnson Corporation sent its only pump to the manufacturer to be repaired. It engaged Travis, a local trucking company, both to deliver the equipment to the manufacturer and to redeliver it to Johnson promptly upon completion of the repair. Johnson's entire plant was inoperative without this pump, but the trucking company did not know this. The trucking company delayed several days in its delivery of the repaired pump to Johnson. During the time it expected to be without the pump, Johnson incurred $5,000 in lost profits. At the end of that time Johnson rented a replacement pump at a cost of $200 per day. As a result of these facts, what is Johnson entitled to recover from Travis?

    a. The $200 a day cost incurred in renting the pump.

    b. The $200 a day cost incurred in renting the pump plus the lost profits.

    c. Actual damages plus punitive damages.

    d. Nothing because Travis is *not* liable for damages.

18. Milbank undertook to stage a production of a well-known play. He wired Lucia, a famous actress, offering her the lead in the play at $2,000 per week for six weeks from the specified opening night plus $1,000 for a week of rehearsal prior to opening. The telegram also said. "Offer ends in three days." Lucia wired an acceptance the same day she received it. The telegram acceptance was temporarily misplaced by the telegraph company and did not arrive until five days after its dispatch. Milbank, not hearing from Lucia, assumed she had declined and abandoned the production. Which of the following is correct if Lucia sues Milbank?

    a. The contract was automatically terminated when Milbank decided *not* to proceed.

    b. Lucia has entered into a valid contract and is entitled to recover damages if Milbank fails to honor it.

    c. Lucia may *not* take any other engagement for the period involved if she wishes to recover.

    d. Milbank is excused from any liability since his action was reasonable under the circumstances.

19. Higgins orally contracted to pay $3,500 to Clark for $4,000 of 30-day accounts receivable that arose in the course of Clark's office equipment leasing business. Higgins subsequently paid the $3,500. What is the legal status of this contract?

    a. The contract is unenforceable by Higgins since the Statute of Frauds requirement has *not* been satisfied.

    b. If Higgins failed to notify the debtors whose accounts were purchased, they will, upon payment in good faith to Clark, have *no* liability to Higgins.

    c. The contract in question is illegal because it violates the usury laws.

    d. Higgins will be able to collect against the debtors free of the usual defenses which would be assertable against Clark.

20. Franklin engaged in extensive negotiations with Harlow in connection with the proposed purchase of Harlow's factory building. Which of the following must Franklin satisfy to establish a binding contract for the purchase of the property in question?

    a. Franklin must obtain an agreement signed by *both* parties.

    b. Franklin must obtain a formal, detailed, all-inclusive document.

    c. Franklin must pay some earnest money at the time of final agreement.

    d. Franklin must have a writing signed by Harlow which states the essential terms of the understanding.

21. Haworth Discount Stores mailed its order to Eagle Recordings, Inc., for 100 eight-track cassette recordings of "Swan Songs" by the Paginations at $5.50 per cassette. Eagle promptly wired its acceptance, delivery to take place within two weeks from date of Haworth's order and terms of net 30 days. Before delivery was made by Eagle, the retail price of this recording by the Paginations fell to $4.95. Haworth informed Eagle of this and pleaded with Eagle, "because we have been good customers, give us a break by either reducing the price of $4.95 so we can break even or by allowing us to cancel the order." Eagle's sales manager called Haworth the next day and informed them that the price would be $4.95 per cassette, *not* the price that appeared on the original invoice. Which of the following is correct insofar as the modification of the initial Haworth-Eagle contract?

    a. The modification is invalid due to lack of consideration.

    b. The modification is voidable by Eagle at any time prior to shipment of the 100 cassettes.

    c. The modification must be written and signed by the parties to be valid if there is *no* consideration given for the reduced price.

    d. The modification need *not* satisfy the Statute of Frauds.

4

DEBTOR-CREDITOR RELATIONSHIPS (10%)

7

Suretyship

AICPA Content Specification Outline

Liabilities and Defenses
Release of Parties
Remedies of Parties

Contents

I. Characteristics

A. Definition: a promise by a person who binds himself to perform upon the default of another (i.e., he agrees with the creditor to satisfy the obligation if the debtor does not)

    1. A tripartite relationship:

        a. The principal debtor: the primary obligor of the debt owed to the creditor; he or she should perform and bears the ultimate burden of performing.

        b. The creditor: the obligee of the debt owed by the principal debtor; the party to whom the surety is bound to satisfy upon default.

        c. Surety or guarantor: promises he will perform upon default of the principal debtor.

        d. Suretyship problems can be simplified by referring to the diagram below and identifying the contract (K) relevant to the particular dispute. A simple suretyship arrangement involves three distinct contracts. Confusion in studying and handling suretyship problems often arises because of a failure to distinguish the various contracts which attend the suretyship transaction. In the simplest situation there are three different contracts (Ks): (1) The contract on which the principal debtor (PD) is liable to the creditor, C − K-1; (2) the contract on which the surety S is liable to the creditor K-2; and (3) the contract on which the principal debtor is liable to the surety − (K-3). In diagramatic form, the suretyship contract looks like this:

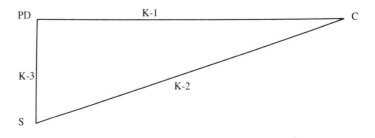

B. Capacity to act as a surety or guarantor:

1. Individuals: The rules applicable to general capacity to contract apply. See Contracts, p. 148, III. D.
2. Partners: An individual partner's authority to bind the partnership is strictly limited. See Partnerships, p. 61, I.F.1.b.
3. Partnerships: ordinarily may enter into contracts of suretyship or guaranty unless the partnership agreement expressly prohibits it.
4. Corporations: Very little remains of prior restrictions on corporations entering into a surety relationship as a result of the Model Business Corporations Act. See Corporations, p. 92, III.C.5.

C. Suretyship and guaranty:

1. As used in the law generally, guaranty is treated as a synonym for suretyship. It is so treated in this chapter.
2. Types of guaranty.
   a. **Unconditional or absolute guaranty of payment:** Since the guarantor unconditionally promises to pay, the guarantor is liable when the debt is due and the principal debtor does not pay (i.e., further action by the creditor versus the principal debtor is not necessary). **This is the typical surety relationship.**
   b. **Conditional guaranty**: Some condition must be met before guarantor will pay (e.g., guaranty of collection); a type of guaranty that requires the creditor to give notice and to exhaust his remedies against the principal debtor first (i.e., have a judgment returned unsatisfied).
   c. Single guaranty: limited to one transaction.
   d. Continuing graranty: covers a succession of liabilities for which, as and when they accrue, the guarantor becomes liable.
3. As used in this outline, surety will include guaranty, except the conditional guaranty, which is distinct and which will be specifically labeled where referred to hereinafter.

D. Common situations in which a *suretyship relationship exists:*

1. By express contract (e.g., where the surety promises to pay the debts of the principal debtor if credit is extended to said principal debtor).
2. Where one other than a qualified indorser indorses a negotiable instrument; the indorser, by engaging to pay if the instrument is not paid after presentment and notice, is, in effect, a surety.
3. An accommodation indorser is treated the same as any other indorser. He is the surety for the person accommodated. An accommodation maker or acceptor is liable without notice and presentment. He has rights against the party accommodated.
4. Where a party sells mortgaged property and the purchaser expressly assumes the obligation (commonly called the assuming assignee), i.e., the purchaser or assignee personally promises to pay the mortgage debt. The seller is a surety and the purchaser is the principal debtor (see Mortgages, p. 388, IV).
5. One of the most commonplace and important surety undertakings arises in connection with the closely held corporation. When the credit of the corporation is insufficient to justify the loan in the creditor's mind, he or she will typically

insist that the owners guarantee the corporation's loan. Thus, the owners become noncompensated sureties for their corporation's loan.

6. Surety bond: by definition an acknowledgment of an obligation to make good the performance by another of some act or duty. It is:

a. A bond with a condition, e.g., faithful performance. The performance of the condition by the principal debtor discharges the obligation.

b. Issued by a surety company engaged in business of assuming risks for compensation.

c. Types

(1) Fidelity bonds guarantee faithful performance of duties on the part of an employee. The employee's duties may not be significantly varied without the surety company's consent; to do so without consent releases the surety.

(2) Performance bonds guarantee faithful performance of a contract. They most frequently concern construction, supply, and government contracts.

E. Statute of Frauds:

1. Contracts of suretyship and guaranty are "promises to answer for the debt, default, or miscarriage of another," within the meaning of the Statute of Frauds and must be in a writing signed by the party to be charged—the surety. In general, see Contracts, p. 149, III.E.2.c).

2. Transactions resembling suretyship but not within the Statute.

a. Third-party beneficiary contract. "Ship goods to my corporation and I will pay for them." There is no promise to answer for the debt of another. Instead, it is a direct and sole promise to pay for the goods regardless of the actions of another. Only one party is bound to pay.

b. Warranty: As used, for example, in the sale of personal property or in contracts of sale, warranty signifies a representation or promise as to title, quality, or fitness made by the seller to the buyer: a two-party transaction. Some confusion arises from the fact that the term "guaranty" is used as a synonym for warranty.

c. Novation: Where it involves a tripartite transaction, in which one obligor is substituted for another, no suretyship relationship exists, in that there is always only one obligor liable at any one instant of time.

d. Indemnity: The promisor agrees to hold a person harmless from loss, irrespective of liability of a third person (e.g., insurance).

(i) Indemnity is a two-party transaction, whereas a surety relationship is tripartite.

(ii) The indemnitor (e.g., an insurance company) pays because it has assumed the risk of loss, not because of any default by principal debtor as in suretyship.

3. Exceptions to the statute.

a. Promises made to the debtor to pay the debtor's debts are not within the Statute of Frauds.

b. *Del credere* agent: See Agency, p. 44, IV.A.3.f.

c. The "main purpose" rule. This rule is invoked when the main object of the second promisor is to subserve some pecuniary interest of her own. This is the reason for her participating in the principal contract and making its obligation her own. E.g., D owes C $10,000, C is about to levy an attachment against D's business. S is also a creditor and customer of D's. S, fearing that attachment will ruin his chance of collecting and will destroy a valuable customer, persuades C to delay legal proceedings. S orally promises C that if C will refrain from proceeding with the attachment, he will pay D's debt if D does not. S's oral promise is enforceable.

II. Defenses, Rights, and Remedies of the Surety

A. Bases for the surety's defense:

1. Consideration. A surety undertaking is invariably created by contract. The consideration requirement is usually satisfied by the extension of the loan in exchange in part for the surety's promise. An independent consideration is not necessary, although it is always present in the form of a premium if the surety is compensated.

2. The suretyship contract itself is void. (E.g., S guarantees P's promise to make an illegal campaign payment or guarantees a usurious loan.)

3. Fraud or duress.
   a. If the creditor obtains *the surety's promise,* either by fraud or duress, the contract is voidable at the surety's option. (E.g., C, by threats upon S's life, obtains S's signature as a surety.)
   b. Fraud or duress by the principal debtor on the surety will not permit the surety to avoid liability to the creditor if the creditor has extended credit in good faith, relying on the security of the surety's promise. (E.g., P, by fraud, induces S to become a surety; P then obtains credit from C, who relies on S's promise and who has no knowledge of the fraud used by P to obtain S's signature. S may not avoid liability to C.)
   c. *If the creditor obtains the principal debtor's promise* by fraud or duress, the surety is not liable to the creditor unless the surety had knowledge of the fraud or duress. (E.g., C fraudulently induces P to contract with him; S without knowledge of the fraud becomes a surety for P's performance. S has a good defense and may avoid liability.)

4. Impossibility of performance by the principal debtor. (E.g., S is surety for performance of a contract that becomes impossible to perform as a result of a change in federal law.)

5. Mere tender of performance by the principal debtor or surety:
   a. Discharges the surety.
   b. May not discharge the principal debtor (e.g., the principal debtor must still perform his obligation to pay money owed—see Contracts, p. 161, VII. B.1.f). However, tender will stop the running of interest against the debtor.

6. Proper performance by the principal debtor discharges the surety.

7. Release of the principal debtor by the creditor, without the consent of the surety, discharges the surety unless:

   a. The creditor expressly reserves his rights against the surety in the release. The creditor's reservation shows that he has no intention of releasing the surety; it is merely a convenant not to sue the principal debtor and does not change the surety's rights of subrogation or reimbursement if he performs (see p. 190, II.C.2.a,b). This type of release is not typical and is illogical since, despite the release of the debtor, the creditor may nevertheless recover from the surety who may then proceed against the debtor.

   b. The release was obtained by fraud or duress. The surety is only discharged to the extent that he has been prejudiced. (E.g., S is surety on a debt owed by P to C. P fraudulently obtains a release, and on the strength of this release, S returns collateral of P's, which he was holding. C rescinds the release, but not before P has absconded with the collateral. S's liability is reduced to the extent of the value of the collateral security.)

  8. Material failure by the creditor to give the consideration agreed upon for the principal's obligation: if not due to the fault of the principal, the surety is not liable to the creditor.

  9. For the effect of release of collateral held by the creditor, see p. 192, III.C.5.

 10. The surety's right of set-off: The surety may normally set off any claims that he has against the creditor even though they did not arise out of the surety obligation. The creditor may apply payment to whichever debts of the debtor he wishes and is not obligated to apply the payment against the debt that has a surety unless the debtor so specifies.

 11. Nondisclosure of facts by the creditor that materially increase the surety's risk: If the creditor knows or subsequently learns of facts of such a nature that the surety would not have assumed the obligation had he been aware of these facts, and if the creditor, having had a reasonable opportunity, failed to notify the surety, the surety may assert this as a defense to avoid liability (e.g., failure to report to the surety the fact that an employee had previously stolen money from the company).

 12. Statute of limitations: Generally, measured from the date of default by the principal debtor, and will bar a cause of action against the surety after lapse of the appropriate period of time (e.g., six years from date of default by the principal debtor).

 13. **Varying the surety's risk by modifying the principal debtor's duty:**

   a. It is sometimes stated in the law of suretyship that a special standard or principle is applicable to the obligation of the surety. The modern, prevailing view is that the general rules of interpretation applicable to contracts apply.

    (1) This special standard requires that the surety's obligation be limited to the letter of the law; any variance, no matter how minor, will be interpreted as increasing the obligation of the surety, thereby permitting the surety to be discharged.

    (2) This standard or principle is referred to as *strictissimi juris.*

    (3) No matter which standard is applied, the surety is not released if the creditor modifies the principal's duty and such modification can only be beneficial to the surety (e.g., a creditor reduces the interest rate from 18 to 15%).

    b. Some of the more common variations that have been held to release the surety are:

       (1) A change in the identity of the principal debtor or debtors. (E.g., the creditor permits the principal debtor to substitute another for performance of his debt or duty; or in the case of a partnership, one of the partners withdraws or retires or an additional partner is admitted to the firm and the creditor grants further credit on a continuing guaranty.)

       (2) A legally enforceable variance in the amount, place, time, or manner of the principal debtor's payments (such variance *must be binding* on the creditor).

       (3) A change in the duties of the principal. (Eg., a surety company bonds the performance of a principal as assistant cashier of X Bank, and he is subsequently promoted to head cashier.)

       (4) The creditor's surrender or impairment of security held by him for the performance by the principal debtor. (E.g., the creditor returns to principal debtor bonds held as part security; the surety is released *pro tanto*—see p. 192, III.C.5.)

    c. In order to release the surety, there must be an actual variation in the terms rather than an option or election that the principal debtor can exercise under the express terms of the agreement that the surety has guaranteed. (E.g., P elects to continue his lease for two years, exercising an option that was a part of the original contract between P and C and upon which S assumed the obligation as a surety.)

    d. Regarding all variations, if the creditor obtains the consent of the surety to make the variance, the surety is not discharged.

    e. The *Restatement of Security* makes a further distinction or limitation on the discharge of the surety:

       (1) If the surety is a *compensated surety* (a commercial surety that is in the business of acting as a surety for a premium), the surety is generally discharged only if the modification materially increases the risk. Release of funds held to insure performance of a building contract would be an example of such a material modification.

       (2) If the modification does not increase the risk materially, the obligation is reduced only by the extent of loss due to the modification. This rule applies to all extensions of time (i.e., the compensated surety is only entitled to have the obligation reduced by the extent of loss due to the extension of time).

B. Defenses not available to the surety:

    1. Death or insolvency (including discharge in bankruptcy) of the principal does not release the surety.

    2. Lack of capacity of the principal debtor is not a defense available to the surety. (E.g., surety for an infant principal cannot use this as a defense to avoid liability.)

    3. The surety, except in the case of a conditional guaranty (see p. 185, I.C.2.b), is not discharged because the creditor takes no action to enforce his claim against the principal debtor.

4. The creditor's failure to give notice of default is not a defense available to the surety, unless the rules of Article 3 of the Uniform Commercial Code (Commercial Paper) apply, or unless the surety's obligation is conditional on notice, being given, e.g., a guarantor of collection.

5. Failure of the creditor to resort to the collateral security that he holds.

    a. The surety is not discharged so long as the creditor does not surrender it; however, if the creditor does not make timely resort to the collateral, he may be accountable to the surety for any depreciation in its value.

    b. The surety may not compel the creditor to first proceed against the collateral security unless he can show undue hardship or that there has been a conditional guaranty.

C. Rights and remedies available to the surety:

1. If the surety cannot avoid liability, he may, nevertheless, attempt to shift the ultimate burden in whole or in part.

2. In this connection, the following are the most common rights or remedies available to the surety:

    a. Reimbursement or indemnity: The duty of the principal to repay or reimburse the surety where the surety, upon default of the principal, performed the obligation owed by the principal debtor to the creditor:

        (1) Where the surety was obtained by or with the consent of the principal, the surety is entitled to his reasonable outlay.

            (A) The surety may only recover for the amount that he paid the creditor in satisfaction of the debt— e.g., if the surety settles with the creditor for less than the full amount of the debt, the surety can only recover the lesser amount. He cannot profit.

            (B) The statute of limitations begins to run (in favor of the principal debtor) against this right of the surety from the date the surety satisfies the creditor, not from the date of default by the principal debtor.

        (2) Where the surety is obtained without the consent of the principal (e.g., the creditor on his own initiative obtains a surety), the surety is entitled to a reimbursement to the extent that he, the debtor, has been unjustly enriched.

        (3) A surety who is a mere volunteer is not entitled to reimbursement.

    b. Subrogation: Where the surety pursuant to his contractual undertaking fully satisfies the obligation of the creditor, the surety, to the extent he has contributed to the satisfaction, has the same rights as the creditor (i.e., succeeds to the creditor's rights):

        (1) In security held for the principal's performance. (E.g., P owes C $500 secured by five $100 bonds held by C as collateral security. P defaults and S, upon payment of the $500, which he is contractually obligated to pay, is entitled to the bonds or their equivalent.)

        (2) Against the principal debtor. E.g., S was legally bound as the surety on P's bond for payment of employees' wages. P defaulted and became a bankrupt. S paid the wage earners' claims. As a result, S would be subrogated to the wage earners' rights to a priority in bankruptcy.)

    c. Exoneration: The surety seeks equitable relief, after maturity of the debt, to compel the principal debtor to pay the creditor. Normally, not available if the creditor demands prompt performance upon default.

    d. Contribution: arises only where there is a co-surety relationship (see p. 192, IV.B).

III. The Creditor's and Surety's Rights in Collateral Pledged by the Principal Debtor

A. In addition to the surety's obligation, collateral to secure performance of the principal debtor's duty is often pledged with either the surety or creditor.

B. Collateral pledged with the surety:

    1. The creditor's rights in the collateral *prior to default:*

        a. Collateral pledged with the surety for the creditor's protection.

            (1) The surety must retain the collateral as trustee for the benefit of the creditor.

            (2) Equitable relief may be obtained by the creditor to prevent the surety from releasing or otherwise impairing the collateral.

        b. Collateral pledged with the intent that it only benefit the surety.

            (1) Even if both the surety and the principal debtor are solvent, the creditor has an interest in the collateral pledged.

            (2) Equitable relief may be obtained to prevent the surety from releasing or otherwise impairing the collateral pledged as security.

    2. The creditor's rights in the collateral *after* the principal debtor's default:

        a. Unless the debt owed to the creditor is fully satisfied, the security must be utilized to satisfy the principal debtor's duty to the creditor.

        b. However, creditor may choose to disregard the collateral held by the surety and go immediately against the surety on his promise.

    3. Surety's rights in the collateral:

        a. In general, the surety holds any collateral as trustee for the creditor's benefit, and as such he is a custodian subject to equitable duties to retain and preserve the collateral. Any income from the collateral belongs to the principal debtor, subject only to the surety's right of reimbursement if retained by him.

        b. The surety has the right of reimbursement (see p. 190, II.C.2.a), but only upon satisfaction of the creditor. (E.g., S holds $1,000 in bonds as collateral to secure P's $1,000 debt to C; P defaults and S satisfies P fully by paying him $1,000. S has a right of reimbursement and may resort to the collateral he holds.)

C. Collateral pledged with the creditor:

    1. The creditor must return the collateral upon payment by the principal debtor prior to default.

    2. The creditor need not resort to the collateral pledged even though it is in excess of the amount due; instead, he may, immediately upon default, proceed against the surety on his promise. The creditor thus avoids the inconvenience and delay that resort to the collateral may entail, e.g., foreclosure of a mortgage.

    3. Upon default, the creditor may resort to collateral he holds if he so desires.

         a. Excess, if any, must be returned to the principal debtor.

         b. If the collateral is insufficient to satisfy the debt, the creditor retains his rights to the balance as against the surety and the principal debtor.

         c. In general, if both the principal and the surety provide collateral and the creditor elects to resort to the collateral, he must first exhaust the principal debtor's collateral before resorting to the surety's collateral.

     4. The surety, upon satisfaction of the principal debtor's obligation to the creditor, is subrogated (see p. 190, II.C.2.b) to the creditor's rights to the collateral.

     5. Surrender, or willful or intentional destruction, of the collateral held by the creditor reduces the surety's obligation by that amount.

IV. Co-Suretyship

  A. Characteristics:

     1. Co-suretyship is defined as the relation between two or more sureties who are bound to answer for the same duty of the principal, and who, as between themselves, should share the loss caused by the default of the principal.

     2. Elements:

         a. Each surety is bound to answer for *the same duty*, and *shares in the burden* upon default of the principal.

         b. Co-sureties need not know of each other's existence at the time of undertaking their obligations.

         c. Both are usually bound for the same amount, but they still may be co-sureties even if they are bound for different amounts, so long as they share the same burden.

         d. Generally co-sureties are jointly and severally liable; creditor may sue them jointly or proceed against each individually to the extent he has assumed liability.

         e. Right of contribution among co-sureties: see below, B.

         f. Rights and duties are normally fixed by contract among the co-sureties; in absence of such a contract, the rules of equity apply.

         g. Judicial preference is to find a co-surety relationship where there are two or more sureties and no express agreement to the contrary.

     3. Co-suretyship distinguished from subsuretyship: In subsuretyship, the subsurety is entitled to have the principal surety bear the entire burden, i.e., the subsurety is in effect a surety for the principal surety. (E.g., X owes Y $1,000. S is the surety on this obligation. He secures SS to act as surety for him, i.e., to perform the surety obligation in the event he cannot perform. S is the principal surety and SS the subsurety.)

  B. **The right of contribution among co-sureties:** a right that arises when a co-surety, in performance of his obligation, pays more than his proportionate share, and that entitles the co-surety to compel the other co-sureties to compensate him for the excess amount paid. (E.g., X and Y are equal co-sureties on a $10,000 obligation, i.e., each guarantees the $10,000 debt. The principal debtor defaults; X pays the entire $10,000 and has a right of contribution against Y for $5,000. Had Y guaranteed only $5,000 of the debt while X guaranteed $10,000, X upon paying the full amount would have a right of contribution against Y for $3,333.33.)

1. Statute of limitations: begins to run against the co-surety's right of contribution as of the time the payment is made by the co-surety to the creditor, provided payment is after maturity of the debt.
2. Collateral and its effect on co-sureties:
   a. Collateral held by the creditor does not prevent the creditor from proceeding immediately against one or all of the co-sureties.
   b. Collateral pledged with a co-surety does not affect the right of contribution.
   c. However, in the final settlement of their liability to each other, each co-surety is entitled to share in any collateral in proportion to his liability for the principal debtor's debt. (E.g., X and Y are co-sureties on a $20,000 debt and they hold collateral of $15,000. X is surety for $20,000 and Y is surety for only $10,000. Upon default of the principal debtor and payment of the debt by the sureties, X has a right to $10,000 of the collateral and Y to $5,000.)

C. Release of co-surety by creditor:

1. Unless there is a reservation of rights against the co-sureties, release of one co-surety reduces the other's obligation to the extent the released co-surety could have been compelled to make a contribution. (E.g., X, Y, and Z are co-sureties, each guaranteeing fully a $12,000 debt owed by P to C. If C releases X, C can collect only $8,000 from the remaining sureties, since either Y or Z could have compelled X to contribute $4,000.)

Selected Problems from CPA Examinations on Suretyship

Subjective Questions and Answers

Q. 1. Your client, Donaldson Manufacturing, Inc., a family-owned corporation, approached the Faber Corporation to purchase raw materials on a credit basis of 2/10, net/60. Faber Corporation insisted that John Donaldson, Donaldson Manufacturing's president and principal stockholder, guarantee payment of the corporation's debt. John Donaldson did so. After eight months of prompt payments within the 60 days, Donaldson Manufacturing was unable to make payment within 60 days. Consequently, Faber refused to make further deliveries, demanded immediate payment plus interest, and threatened to sue Donaldson Manufacturing and John Donaldson on the debt. Shortly thereafter, Donaldson Manufacturing tendered full payment in cash to Faber. Faber refused to accept the cash because it was after banking hours.

Required

1. What are legal implications resulting from Faber's actions in respect to John Donaldson's personal liability? Explain.
2. What are the legal implications to Donaldson Manufacturing as a result of Faber's refusal to accept the tender of payment? Explain.

A. 1. A valid tender of performance by the principal debtor, Donaldson Manufacturing, releases the surety from his obligation. Hence, John Donaldson has no personal liability even if Donaldson Manufacturing cannot subsequently make payment on its obligation.
   2. Faber's refusal to accept the tender of performance (payment of the balance due plus interest) does not release Donaldson Manufacturing from the debt owed. However, the tender stops the running of interest from the date of tender.

11/75

Q. 2. Fox Construction Corporation obtained a $20 million contract from the United States government to construct a federal office building. The contract required Fox to obtain a surety (or sureties) guaranteeing performance of the contract. After contacting several surety companies, Fox learned that no one company would write a bond for that amount. However, Fox was able to obtain a $10 million bond from Ace Surety Company and a $5 million bond each from Empire Surety and the Excelsior Surety Company. Fox breached the contract and, as a result, the United States government suffered a $2 million loss.

11/75

Required
1. What are the rights of the United States against the three surety companies? Explain.
2. When finally settled, for what amount will each surety company be liable? Explain.

A. 1. The United States could proceed against one or more of the co-sureties to collect the $2 million damages resulting from Fox's having breached the construction contract. The three surety companies are co-sureties on the Fox Construction Corporation obligation. As such, they are jointly and severally liable. Assuming Ace pays the entire amount ($2 million), it will have a right of contribution from the other sureties as discussed below.
   2. Ace will be liable to $1 million, Empire for $500,000, and Excelsior for $500,000. In the event that a co-surety pays more than its proportionate share of the surety obligation, it has a right of contribution from its fellow sureties in proportion to the several undertakings. Thus, if Ace were to pay the $2 million liability, it would have the right to receive $500,000 each from Empire and Excelsior.

11/80

Q. 3. The King Surety Company, Inc., wrote a performance bond for Allie Stores, Inc., covering the construction of a department store. Rapid Construction Company, the department store contractor, is a general contractor and is simultaneously working on several buildings. Until the entire building is completed, the bond contained a provision that obligated Allie to withhold 20% of the progress payments to be made to Rapid at various stages of completion. After approximately two-thirds of the project had been satisfactorily completed, Rapid pleaded with Allie to release the 20% withheld to date. Rapid indicated that he was having a cash flow problem and unless funds were released to satisfy the demands of suppliers, workmen, and other creditors, there would be a significant delay in the completion date of the department store. Rapid claimed that if the 20% withheld were released, the project could be completed on schedule. Allie released the amounts withheld. Two weeks later Rapid abandoned the project, citing as its reason rising cost which made the contract unprofitable. Allie has notified King of the facts and demands that either King complete the project or respond in damages. King denies liability on the surety bond.

Required
Answer the following, setting forth reasons for any conclusions stated.
   Who will prevail?
A.   King Surety Company will prevail. The creditor (Allie), without King's consent, has modified the surety contract. Under these circumstances, a noncompensated surety would be discharged without question: however, a compensated surety is not discharged completely unless the modification materially increases the risk. If the risk is not materially increased, the obligation is decreased to the extent of the loss. In this case, there was a material increase in the risk. First, there is nothing to indicate that the monies released by Allie were committed by Rapid to the particular project (Allie's department store) because Rapid had several simultaneous projects. Moreover, it is clear that the monies withheld provided a strong inducement for a builder such as Rapid to

complete the undertaking since the expected final payment would have been large in relation to the final outlays to complete construction. Finally, the withheld payments reduced the exposure of the surety to the extent of 20%.

11/79

Q. 4. Barclay Surety, Inc., is the surety on a construction contract that the Gilmore Construction Company made with Shadow Realty, Inc. By the terms of the surety obligation, Barclay is not only bound to Shadow, but also is bound to satisfy materialmen and laborers in connection with the contract. Gilmore defaulted, and Barclay elected to complete the project and pay all claims and obligations in connection with the contract, including all unpaid materialmen and laborers' claims against Gilmore. The total cost to complete exceeded the construction contract payments Barclay received from Shadow. Some of the materialmen who were satisfied had either liens or security interests against Gilmore. Gilmore has filed a voluntary bankruptcy petition.

Required
Answer the following, setting forth reasons for any conclusions stated.
   What rights does Barclay have as a result of the above facts?
A.   Barclay is, of course, entitled to reimbursement from Gilmore. However, since Gilmore is bankrupt, Barclay will receive the same percentage on the dollar as will all other general creditors of Gilmore's estate. However, Barclay is subrogated to the rights of the materialmen and laborers it has satisfied. Specifically, it would have the right to assert the liens and security interests of the materialmen. Furthermore, wage earners are entitled to a limited priority in a bankruptcy proceeding, which Barclay could assert.

11/79

Q. 5. Hardaway Lending, Inc., had a four-year $800,000 callable loan to Superior Metals, Inc., outstanding. The loan was callable at the end of each year upon Hardaway's giving 60 days written notice. Two and one-half years remained of the four years. Hardaway reviewed the loan and decided that Superior Metals was no longer a prime lending risk and it therefore decided to call the loan. The required written notice was sent to and received by Superior 60 days prior to the expiration of the second year. Merriweather, Superior's chief executive officer and principal shareholder, requested Hardaway to continue the loan at least for another year. Hardaway agreed, provided that an acceptable commercial surety would guarantee $400,000 of the loan and Merriweather would personally guarantee repayment in full. These conditions were satisfied and the loan was permitted to continue.

   The following year the loan was called and Superior defaulted. Hardaway released the commercial surety but retained its rights against Merriweather and demanded that Merriweather pay the full amount of the loan. Merriweather refused, asserting the following:
* There was no consideration for his promise. The loan was already outstanding and he personally received nothing.
* Hardaway must first proceed against Superior before it can collect from Merriweather.
* Hardaway had released the commercial surety, thereby releasing Merriweather.

Required
Answer the following, setting forth reasons for any conclusions as stated.
   Discuss the validity of each of Merriweather's assertions.
A.   The first two defenses asserted by Merriweather are invalid. The third defense is partially valid.
   Consideration on Hardaway's part consisted of foregoing the right to call the Superior Metals loan. The fact that the loan was already outstanding is irrelevant. By permitting the loan to remain outstanding for an additional year instead of calling it, Hardaway relinquished a legal right, which is adequate consideration for Merriweather's surety promise. Consideration need not pass to the surety; in fact, it usually primarily benefits the principal debtor.

There is no requirement that the creditor first proceed against the debtor before it can proceed against the surety, unless the surety undertaking expressly provides such a condition. Basic to the usual surety undertaking is the right of the creditor to proceed immediately against the surety. Essentially, that is the reason for the surety.

Hardaway's release of the commercial surety from its $400,000 surety undertaking partially released Merriweather. The release had the legal effect of impairing Merriweather's right of contribution against its cosurety (the commercial surety). Thus, Merriweather is released to the extent of one-third ($400,000 (commercial surety's guarantee)/$1,200,000 (the aggregate of the cosuretie's guarantees) of the principal amount ($800,000)), or $266,667.

11/80

Practice Questions

Q. 1. The Friendly Finance Company is engaged in the personal loan business. Some loans made by the company are secured by a pledge of collateral such as diamonds, rare coins, works of art, etc. The Company has a surety bond with Safety Surety Company covering its employees.

Charles Johnson was employed by Friendly Finance as a collection agent and was covered in this capacity by Safety's surety bond. Subsequently Johnson was promoted to the position of assistant cashier. In this position he received payments on loans and also had access to the vault in which the collateral was kept. Surety was not advised of Johnson's promotion. Several months after this promotion Johnson began substituting imitations for the pledged diamonds and rare coins. His thefts have been detected and the loss amounts to $15,000. Friendly Finance seeks recovery from Safety Surety Company. In your audit of Friendly Finance you find that the Company has recorded an account receivable of $15,000 from Safety in anticipation of collection of its claim.

Required
Is Friendly justified in recording the account receivable? Explain.

Q. 2. James Harper borrowed $20,000 from Franklin Jackson. William Samson & Company, a customer of Harper's, was the surety on the loan. Harper became insolvent and defaulted on several debts owed to his creditors. Jackson joined with several other creditors in petitioning for an involuntary bankruptcy proceeding against Harper. Harper was duly adjudicated a bankrupt and his assets distributed to creditors. Jackson seeks to hold Samson & Company on the surety undertaking to the extent he was not satisfied on the loan. Samson & Company wants to be reimbursed by Harper to the extent it is liable to Jackson. You are the accountant for Samson & Company and are concerned with the effect of the above facts upon Samson & Company's balance sheet.

Required
1. How should Jackson's rights against Samson & Company be treated? Explain.
2. What effect will Harper's discharge in bankruptcy have against any claim to reimbursement that Samson & Company may have? Explain.

Q. 3. During the course of your examination of the financial statements for the year ended March 31, 1971, for Finest Fashions, Inc., a company with a dozen retail stores specializing in the sale of exclusive maxi coats and dresses, you learned of a claim of $50,000 asserted against the Corporation by Fancy Fabrics. Upon investigation you learned that the Corporation purchased most of its merchandise from Terry Knitting Mills, a large manufacturer. Several months ago when Terry was in financial difficulty and could no longer purchase raw materials from Fancy Fabrics on credit, Terry asked the Corporation and Grand Gowns, Inc., to sign as co-sureties its purchase order to Fancy Fabrics for raw materials costing $50,000. Both companies did so on the same day that Terry signed the purchase order. When Terry did not pay on the due date, Fancy Fabrics did not notify either surety. However, 15 days later the Corporation received a demand for payment of the entire purchase price of $50,000 from Fancy Fabrics. The Corporation has refused to pay, contending that its contract as surety was unenforceable because (a) it did not receive any consideration, (b) it received no notice of default, and (c) its maximum liability, if any, is $25,000.

Required
1. Discuss the validity of each defense asserted by your client, Finest Fashions, Inc.
2. If Finest Fashions pays $50,000 to Fancy Fabrics, what would be its rights against Grand Gowns? Explain.
3. If Finest Fashions pays $50,000 to Fancy Fabrics, what would be its rights against Terry? Explain.
4. If Fancy Fabrics extended Terry's time for payment for another six months without Finest Fashions' consent, what would be the legal effect on the Corporation's obligation? Explain.

Q. 4. During your examination of the financial statements of H. R. Dacy, Inc., a letter from Dacy's attorney revealed the following facts:

Dacy's principal supplier of children's clothing, Watkins, Inc., was unable to obtain fabric for manufacturing its fall line from Bowdin. Watkins had been slow in making payments to Bowdin, and in recent months a number of its checks to Bowdin were returned for insufficient funds. Bowdin refused to grant further credit to Watkins.

To protect its source of supply, Dacy's president wrote Bowdin stating, "We will pay for any fabrics supplied to Watkins, Inc., for the fall season in the event that Watkins does not pay."

In reliance upon this letter, Bowdin supplied Watkins with fabric. Watkins is substantially in arrears in payment of invoices for these goods. Bowdin has notified Dacy of its responsibility for the debt.

Required
1. What are the rights and obligations of H. R. Dacy, Inc.? Explain.
2. What are the financial-reporting implications for H. R. Dacy, Inc., arising out of these circumstances? Explain.

Q. 5. Superior Construction Company, Inc., submitted the successful bid for the construction of your client's new factory. As a part of the contract, Superior was required to obtain a performance bond from an acceptable surety company. Ace Surety, Inc., wrote the surety bond for the proposed building.

After the project was about one-third completed, Superior suggested several major changes in the contract. These included the expansion of the floor space by 10% and construction of an additional loading platform.

Required
1. What problem does your client face if it agrees to the proposed changes? Explain.
2. What advice would you suggest in order to avoid this problem?

Practice Objective Questions

Instructions 1–12
Select the *best* answer for each of the following items. Mark only one answer for *each* item. Answer all items. Your grade will be based on your total correct answers.

1. Clark is a surety on a $100,000 obligation owed by Thompson to Owens. The debt is also secured by a $50,000 mortgage to Owens on Thompson's factory. Thompson is in bankruptcy. Clark has satisfied the debt. Clark is

    a. Only entitled to the standing of a general creditor in bankruptcy.

    b. A secured creditor to the extent of the $50,000 mortgage and a general creditor for the balance.

    c. Entitled to nothing in bankruptcy since this was a risk he assumed.

    d. Not entitled to a priority in bankruptcy, even though Owens could validly claim it.

2. Which of the following defenses by a surety will be effective to avoid liability?

    a. Lack of consideration to support the surety undertaking.

    b. Insolvency in the bankruptcy sense by the debtor.

    c. Incompetency of the debtor to make the contract in question.

    d. Fraudulent statements by the principal-debtor which induced the surety to assume the obligation and which were unknown to the creditor.

3. Dinsmore & Company was a compensated surety on the construction contract between Victor (the owner) and Gilmore Construction. Gilmore has defaulted and Victor has released Dinsmore for a partial payment and other consideration. The legal effect of the release of Dinsmore is

    a. To release Gilmore as well.

    b. Contingent on recovery from Gilmore.

    c. Binding upon Victor.

    d. To partially release Gilmore to the extent that Dinsmore's right of subrogation has been diminished.

4. In relation to the principal debtor, the creditor and a fellow co-surety, the co-surety is *not* entitled to

    a. Exoneration against the debtor under any circumstances.

    b. A pro rata contribution by his fellow surety or sureties if he pays the full amount.

    c. Be subrogated to the rights of the creditor upon satisfaction of the debt.

    d. Avoid performance because his co-surety refuses to perform.

5. Dustin is a very cautious lender. When approached by Lanier regarding a $2,000 loan, he not only demanded an acceptable surety but also collateral equal to 50% of the loan. Lanier obtained King Surety Company as his surety and pledged rare coins worth $1,000 with Dustin. Dustin was assured by Lanier one week before the due date of the loan that he would have difficulty in making payment. He persuaded Dustin to return the coins since they had increased in value and he had a prospective buyer. What is the legal effect of the release of the collateral upon King Surety?

    a. It totally releases King Surety.

    b. It does *not* release King Surety if the collateral was obtained after its promise.

    c. It releases King Surety to the extent of the value of the security.

    d. It does *not* release King Surety unless the collateral was given to Dustin with the express understanding that it was for the benefit of King Surety as well as Dustin.

6. When the debtor has defaulted on its obligation, the creditor is entitled to recover from the surety, unless which of the following is present?

    a. The surety is in the process of exercising its right of exoneration against the debtor.

    b. The debtor has died or become insolvent.

    c. The creditor could collect the entire debt from the debtor's collateral in his possession.

    d. The surety is a guarantor of collection and the creditor failed to exercise due diligence in enforcing his remedies against the debtor.

7. Dependable Surety Company, Inc., issued a surety bond for value received which guaranteed: (1) completion of a construction contract Mason had made with Lund and (2) payment by Mason of his workmen. Mason defaulted and did not complete the contract. The workers were not paid for their last week's work. Mason had in fact become insolvent, and a petition in bankruptcy was filed two months after the issuance of the bond. What is the effect upon Dependable as a result of the above events?

    a. If Dependable pays damages to Lund as a result of the default on the contract, Dependable is entitled to recover in the bankruptcy proceedings the entire amount it paid prior to the payment of the general creditors of Mason.

    b. If Dependable pays the workers in full, it is entitled to the same priority in the bankruptcy proceedings that the workers would have had.

    c. If Dependable has another separate claim against Lund, Dependable may *not* set it off against any rights Lund may have under this contract.

    d. As a compensated surety, Dependable would be discharged from its surety obligation by Mason's bankruptcy.

8. Marbury Surety, Inc., agreed to act as a guarantor of collection of Madison's trade accounts for one year beginning on April 30, 1980, and was compensated for the same. Madison's trade debtors are in default in payment of $3,853, as of May 1, 1981. As a result

    a. Marbury is liable to Madison without any action on Madison's part to collect the amounts due.

    b. Madison can enforce the guarantee even if it is *not* in writing since Marbury is a *del credere* agent.

    c. The relationship between the parties must be filed in the appropriate county office since it is a continuing security transaction.

    d. Marbury is liable for those debts for which a judgment is obtained and returned unsatisfied.

9. Hargrove borrowed $40,000 as additional working capital for her business from the Old Town Bank. Old Town required that the loan be collateralized to the extent of 60%, and an acceptable surety for the entire amount be obtained. Prudent Surety Company agreed to act as surety on the loan and Hargrove pledged $24,000 of bearer negotiable bonds, which belonged to her husband, with Old Town. Hargrove has defaulted. Which of the following is correct?

    a. As a result of the default, Prudent and Hargrove's husband are co-sureties.

    b. Old Town must first proceed against Hargrove and obtain a judgment for payment before it can proceed against the collateral.

    c. Old Town must first liquidate the collateral before it can proceed against Prudent.

    d. Prudent is liable in full immediately upon default by Hargrove, but will upon satisfaction of the debt be entitled to the collateral.

10. Allen was the surety for the payment of rent by Lear under a lease from Rosenthal Rentals. The lease was for two years. A clause in the lease stated that at the expiration of the lease, the lessee had the privilege to renew upon 30 days' prior written notice or, if the lessee remained in possession after its expiration, it was agreed that the lease was to continue for two years more. There was a default in the payment of rent during the extended term of the lease and Rosenthal is suing Allen for the rent due based upon the guarantee. Allen contends that he is liable only for the initial term of the lease and not for the extended term. Allen is

    a. Not liable since it does *not* appear that a judgment against Lear has been returned unsatisfied.

    b. Not liable because there has been a material alteration of the surety undertaking.

    c. Not liable because there was a binding extention of time.

    d. Liable on the surety undertaking which would include the additional two years.

11. Doral is the surety on a loan made by Nelson to Gordon. Which statement describes Doral's legal relationship or status among the respective parties?

    a. As between Gordon and Doral, Doral has the ultimate liability.

    b. Upon default by Gordon and payment by Doral, Doral is entitled to subrogation to the rights of Nelson or to obtain reimbursement from Gordon.

    c. Doral is a fiduciary insofar as Nelson is concerned.

    d. Doral is *not* liable immediately upon default by Gordon, unless the agreement so provides.

12. Don loaned $10,000 to Jon, and Robert agreed to act as surety. Robert's agreement to act as surety was induced by (1) fraudulent misrepresentations made by Don concerning Jon's financial status and (2) a bogus unaudited financial statement of which Don had no knowledge, and which was independently submitted by Jon to Robert. Which of the following is correct?

    a. Don's fraudulent misrepresentations will *not* provide Robert with a valid defense unless they were contained in a signed writing.

    b. Robert will be liable on his surety undertaking despite the facts since the defenses are personal defenses.

    c. Robert's reliance upon Jon's financial statements makes Robert's surety undertaking voidable.

    d. Don's fraudulent misrepresentations provide Robert with a defense which will prevent Don from enforcing the surety undertaking.

CHAPTER

8

Bankruptcy

AICPA Content Specification Outline

Voluntary and Involuntary Bankruptcy
Effects of Bankruptcy on Debtor and Creditors
Reorganizations

Contents

I. Introduction to the Bankruptcy Reform Act of 1978 and the Bankruptcy Amendments and Federal Judgeship Act of 1984

A. Background:

1. The 1978 Bankruptcy Act was the first major revision of federal bankruptcy law in 40 years. It represents a substantially revised set of rules dealing with many critical aspects of bankruptcy; prior law has been repealed. The Act represents a major departure from prior law in many instances; its changes are both far-reaching and dramatic. However, the new bankruptcy law has benefited from, and is based upon, prior law and experience to a large extent. The effective date of the new Act is October 1, 1979.

2. The Bankruptcy Amendments and Federal Judgeship Act of 1984 makes a number of amendments to the 1978 Bankruptcy Act to curb abusive misuse of bankruptcy and to promote fully informed proceedings. The 1984 amendments are applicable to cases filed after October 7, 1984.

B. Purposes of the Bankruptcy Reform Act:

1. The Act continues the basic purposes of its predecessors:
   a. To provide a national uniform bankruptcy law pursuant to the Constitution.
   b. To provide a means whereby an honest but insolvent debtor may secure relief from his debts. This is popularly referred to as a "fresh start."
   c. To give all creditors an equal chance to share in the debtor's assets in proportion to their claims.

2. The specific purposes of the 1978 Act are to:
   a. Reflect the changes in secured financing that have occurred as a result of Article 9 (Secured Transactions) of the Uniform Commercial Code.
   b. Take into account the current debtor-creditor relationships that the credit card and other "soft" lending policies have created.

C. Overview: The Act contains three generally applicable chapters: 1, General Provisions; 3, Case Administration; and 5, Creditors, the Debtor, and the Estate. The only exception to the general application of these chapters is Chapter 9, which deals with municipalities and which is self-contained. Chapter 1 consists largely of definitions. Several of these key definitions contain a substantial amount of substantive law and must be mastered. Chapters 3 and 5 are the nuts and bolts parts of a bankruptcy case. They apply to liquidations, reorganizations, and adjustments of debts of an individual, three of the four operative chapters of the Act.

The Act contains four operative chapters. Our primary concern is their application to debtors who are in liquidation (Chapter 7). These are the chapters under which a party takes action to commence bankruptcy proceedings. They may be resorted to by the debtor or the creditors depending upon the circumstances in a liquidation or reorganization in the event of insolvency. Each of the operative chapters will be briefly described below. The chapters are as follows:

Chapter 1   General Provisions
Chapter 3   Case Administration
Chapter 5   Creditors, the Debtor, and the Estate
Chapter 7   Liquidation
Chapter 9   Adjustment of Debts of a Municipality
Chapter 11   Reorganization
Chapter 13   Adjustment of Debts of an Individual with Regular Income

1. **Liquidation.** This form of relief, as the term implies, embodies *finality* insofar as the bankrupt's estate and the bankrupt are concerned. All eligible assets are distributed in the process of liquidation and the debtor is discharged from his obligations thereby obtaining for the debtor a "fresh start," unfettered by prior debts. All other forms of relief lack this requisite of finality as their underlying purpose. However, with the exception of municipalities, a debtor seeking relief under the reorganization chapter (e.g., see the W. T. Grant bankruptcy) or an individual with regular income resorting to Chapter 13 may find itself in straight bankruptcy.

2. **Adjustment of debt of a municipality:** Chapter 9 attempts to provide a better method for resolving the pressing financial problems of our cities. This area of bankruptcy has never been considered to be a part of business law and is beyond the scope of the business law exam.

3. **Reorganization:** In general, any "person" who is eligible to use the liquidation chapter is eligible to use the reorganization chapter. However, although stockholders and commodity brokers must use the liquidation chapter, they are precluded from resort to the reorganization provisions. Conversely, railroads are not included within the liquidation provisions but are eligible for a reorganization. The Act consolidated the four types of reorganization available under prior law. It thereby avoids costly legal battles waged to determine which kind of reorganization was appropriate.

In recent years publicly held corporations frequently have been forced to resort to the reorganizations provisions. The reorganization provisions are resorted to in lieu of a liquidation. The reorganization provisions are designed to provide an effective method to salvage large and small businesses from financial distress. The importance of major corporations to the economy in terms of jobs provided to employees and its purchases and sales dictates their continued existence and viability, if possible. Thus, where it appears that the financial distress is temporary and can ultimately be corrected, logic compels that they be resurrected from their financial plight instead of being liquidated. Thus, the purpose of Chapter 11 (Reorganization) is to restore financially distressed businesses to a state whereby they may continue to operate and, hopefully, attain financial stability. The chapter is designed to permit a viable option to liquidation.

4. Individual with regular income: The Act provides an alternative for an individual, other than a stockbroker or commodity broker, whose income is sufficiently stable and regular to enable such individual to make payments under a plan that qualifies under Chapter 13. Once again, the attempt is to provide an alternative to liquidation without the disruption and stigma that a straight bankruptcy proceeding carries with it.

   An individual with regular income, or an individual with regular income and his or her spouse, may proceed under Chapter 13, subject to dollar amount restrictions. The debtor must have unsecured debts that aggregate less than $100,000 and secured debts that aggregate less than $350,000. These requirements will permit some small sole proprietors (for whom a Chapter 11 reorganization is too cumbersome a procedure) to use Chapter 13. The chapter is still primarily designed to handle salaried employees, professionals, and other "wage earners," but it is not as limited as its predecessor. The prior Act's provisions were limited to "wage earners."

D. The Bankruptcy Amendments Act of 1984:

Under the 1984 amendments, prior to the commencement of the case, consumer debtors must be given notice by the clerk of the court indicating that the debtor may proceed under either Chapter 13 or Chapter 7.

   A consumer debtor who chooses to proceed under the liquidation provisions of Chapter 7 rather than the reorganization provisions of Chapter 13 must state in her or his bankruptcy petition that she or he is aware of and understands each form of relief available.

E. Definitions: The Act contains 40 definitions. Several definitions are central to an understanding of the materials that follow.

   1. **Custodian:**
      a. A receiver or trustee of any of the property of the debtor, appointed in a case or proceeding not under this Act;
      b. An assignee under a general assignment for the benefit of the debtor's creditors; or
      c. A trustee, receiver, or agent under applicable law, or under a contract, that is appointed or authorized to take charge of property of the debtor for the purpose of enforcing a lien against such property, or for the purpose of general administration of such property for the benefit of the debtor's creditors.

      (The importance of this definition is that it provides an objective basis for creditors to involuntarily petition a debtor into bankruptcy. See p. 207.)
   2. Entity: a person, estate, trust, or governmental unit.

3. Individual with regular income: an individual whose income is sufficiently stable and regular to enable such individual to make payments under a plan under Chapter 13 of this title, other than a stockbroker or a commodity broker.

4. **Insider:**
   a. If the debtor is an individual:
      (1) Relative of the debtor or of a general partner of the debtor;
      (2) Partnership in which the debtor is a general partner;
      (3) General partner of the debtor; or
      (4) Corporation of which the debtor is a director, officer, or person in control.
   b. If the debtor is a corporation:
      (1) Director of the debtor;
      (2) Officer of the debtor;
      (3) Person in control of the debtor;
      (4) Partnership in which the debtor is a general partner;
      (5) General partner of the debtor; or
      (6) Relative of a general partner, director, officer, or person in control of the debtor.
   c. If the debtor is a partnership:
      (1) General partner in the debtor;
      (2) Relative of a general partner in, general partner of, or person in control of the debtor;
      (3) Partnership in which the debtor is a general partner;
      (4) General partner of the debtor; or
      (5) Person in control of the debtor.

   (This definition is of major importance in the preference area since if an insider is the preferential transferee, the trustee has one year to set it aside.)

5. **Insolvent:**
   a. With reference to an entity other than a partnership, financial condition such that the sum of such entity's debts is greater than all of such entity's property, at a fair valuation, exclusive of:
      (1) Property transferred, concealed, or removed with intent to hinder, delay, or defraud such entity's creditors;
      (2) Exempt property.
   b. With reference to a partnership, financial condition such that the sum of such partnership's debts is greater than the aggregate of, at a fair valuation:
      (1) All of such partnership's property, exclusive of property of the kind specified above in 5.a(1).
      (2) The sum of the excess of the value of each general partner's separate property, exclusive of exempt property, over such partner's separate debts.

   (This definition is the traditional "insolvency in the bankruptcy sense" test of insolvency. It is essentially a balance sheet approach. This test is generally used throughout the Act with the vital exception of involuntary proceedings under Chapter 7 liquidation. There, a simpler, modified version of "insolvency in the equity sense" is used. Insolvency in the equity sense has been defined traditionally as the inability of the debtor to meet its debts as they mature, e.g., checks are being returned marked "insufficient funds.")

6. **Order for relief:** entry of an order for relief. (This language replaces the prior term "Adjudication of Bankruptcy.") In a voluntary proceeding, the order for relief is entered upon the filing of the petition. If the proceeding is involuntary and is controverted, the order for relief will be entered after a hearing to determine whether the debtor is generally not paying its debts as they mature or a custodian has been appointed or took possession during 120-day perior prior to the filing of the petition.

7. Person: includes an individual, partnership, and corporation.

II. Chapter 7 Liquidations (Straight Bankruptcy)

A. General description of liquidations: Chapter 7 represents the classic type of relief that bankruptcy has afforded financially troubled debtors and their creditors. The Act calls this type of bankruptcy a "liquidation." It is also popularly known as "straight bankruptcy." These terms are used interchangeably in the text as descriptive of a Chapter 7 liquidation, which means that a debtor or its creditors are proceeding under Chapter 7 in order to obtain relief. The debtor may proceed voluntarily, that is, the debtor initiates the proceedings by filing a petition seeking relief in the form of a discharge. Similarly, creditors have the authority to commence involuntary proceedings by the filing of a petition seeking relief. Their relief takes the form, in general, of a pro rata distribution of the debtor's nonexempt, unsecured property. This distribution is called a "dividend," and it is paid from the bankrupt's "estate." In order to accomplish this, the Act provides that the commencement of a bankruptcy case creates the estate of the bankrupt and all eligible property of the debtor automatically becomes a part of the estate. Certain property of the debtor is exempt from inclusion in the estate. An interim trustee is appointed by the court until the election of the continuing trustee by the creditors.

The trustee is the key figure in the administration of the bankrupt's estate under Chapter 7. He has far-reaching powers and duties aimed at ensuring that all eligible property is included in the estate and that only valid claims are paid. In this connection, the trustee will seek to avoid fraudulent conveyances and preferential transfers and examine proofs of claims and object to any improper claims. (The administration of the estate naturally involves much more than is discussed in this oversimplified presentation. However, if you can obtain a feel for the overall process, the individual parts will fit in with much greater ease.)

Upon completion of the various phases of administration and the distribution of the estate's funds to the creditors pro rata, subject to any priorities, the case is ready to go to the bankruptcy court for the granting of a discharge. Only individuals are granted discharges and, in general, they must be "honest" debtors, that is, debtors who have not engaged in fraudulent acts, made false oaths, or otherwise attempted to subvert the proper administration of the estate. Despite the fact that the individual debtor is honest and is granted a discharge, certain debts are nondischargeable. The most notable debt that is not discharged is taxes. However, with the exception of the nondischargeable debts, the debtor walks away from the case with the opportunity for a "fresh start" in life or business. On the other hand, the creditors will have received a pro rata distribution of the debtor's eligible property. Thus, Chapter 7 is characterized by finality; this characteristic is not found in the other operative chapters.

B. Voluntary and involuntary bankruptcy proceedings:

1. **Voluntary bankruptcy proceedings:**

   a. In general, any person who resides or has a domicile, a place of business, or property in the United States is eligible to be a debtor under the Act. Railroads, banks, insurance companies, and savings and loan institutions may not file for voluntary liquidation under Chapter 7, since there are other special provisions for them. However, municipalities may file under Chapter 7.

   b. The voluntary petitioner need not be insolvent to file for an order for relief. However, in the overwhelming preponderance of cases, the debtor is insolvent. Only to the extent that the debtor is being harrassed by his creditors (or perhaps out of spite) would a solvent debtor file for relief.

   c. The debtor instigates the action by filing a petition seeking an order of relief.

   d. The debtor will normally file in situations where he is hopelessly insolvent in the bankruptcy and equity senses in order to start afresh. Remember, however, that the "cleansing bath of bankruptcy" can only be taken once in six years.

   e. The bankruptcy exemptions should be considered here (see p. 208).

   f. No individual may be a debtor if he has been a debtor in a case pending under the act at any time in the preceeding 180 days if:

      (1) the case was dismissed by the court for willful failure of the debtor to appear before or abide by orders of the court; or

      (2) the debtor obtained voluntary dismissal of the case by filing a request for relief from the automatic stay provisions.

   g. Under new authority granted by the 1984 amendments, after notice and a hearing, the court, on its own motion and not at the request or suggestion of any party in interest, may dismiss a case filed by an individual debtor under Chapter 7 whose debts are primarily consumer debts if the court finds that the granting of relief would be a substantial abuse of the provisions of Chapter 7. This provision will be a powerful tool for judges who believe that granting relief under Chapter 7 to a consumer debtor would be unfair use of the Code by a debtor who would be able to pay off his debt under Chapter 13.

2. **Involuntary petitions:**

   a. The 1978 Act changes. Radical changes have been made in this important aspect of bankruptcy law. Acts of bankruptcy and the requirement of establishing insolvency in the bankruptcy sense (see p. 207) have been eliminated in favor of a straightforward, simpler set of requirements for petitioning a debtor into bankruptcy. The ability of a creditor or creditors to proceed against an involuntary bankrupt has been made immeasurably easier by the adoption of a modified version of the "bankruptcy in the equity sense" test of insolvency. This is discussed more fully below.

   b. Creditors may proceed against any debtor with the exception of:

      (1) Those listed above who cannot voluntarily file.

    (**2**) Farmers who as individuals derive more than 80% gross income from a farm.

    (**3**) Charitable organizations.

c. An involuntary case under the liquidation chapter is commenced by the filing with the bankruptcy court of a petition:

    (**1**) By three or more creditors, each of which is either a holder of a claim against the debtor that is not contingent as to liability nor the subject of a *bona fide* dispute, or by an indenture trustee representing such a holder, if such claims aggregate at least $5,000 more than the value of any lien on property of the debtor securing such claims held by the holders of such claims.

    (**2**) By one or more creditors, if there are fewer than 12 such holders (excluding employees, insiders, and certain transferees whose transfers are voidable), provided the creditor or creditors hold in the aggregate at least $5,000 of such claims.

    (**3**) If such person is a partnership, by fewer than all of the general partners in such partnership, or by the trustee of a general partner if all are bankrupt or a holder of a claim against the partnership.

d. The answer. The debtor (or a general partner of a partnership debtor) may file an answer to the involuntarily filed petition. A bond may be required of the petitioners to indemnify the debtor.

e. The order for relief. If the petition is not timely controverted, the court shall order relief (an adjudication of bankrupt status) against the debtor. If an answer is timely filed by the debtor and the issue of insolvency is raised, then the court shall grant the order for relief only if the debtor:

    (**1**) Is generally not paying such debtor's debts as they become due, or

    (**2**) Has had a custodian of the debtor's property appointed within 120 days before the filing of the petition.

    (**3**) Note well, the above changes are of *major* importance from both a conceptual and practical standpoint. Despite the apparent continued use of the traditional insolvency test of bankruptcy by the Act in its definitions section, this has been rejected insofar as involuntary petitions in bankruptcy are concerned. Instead, the less demanding, simpler, and provable equity test is used. The bankruptcy definition of insolvency remains intact for the rest of the Act; however, as far as involuntary petitions are concerned, the test is a modified version of "insolvency in the equity sense." Thus, it will be easier for creditors to successfully petition a debtor into bankruptcy.

    (**4**) If the petition is rejected by the court, the debtor may recover costs, attorney's fees, and limited damages. If the petition was filed in bad faith, general damages plus punitive damages may be recovered.

C. Administration of the bankrupt's estate: A bankruptcy proceeding may in many respects be equated with a comedy of errors. There have been many errors, and many things have gone wrong for both the debtor and the creditors. Unlike most of the areas of law included in the text (e.g., contracts, where typically two parties are involved), bankruptcy involves a multiplicity of actors or participants, and a bankruptcy case is not truly an adversary proceeding. Furthermore, the area is categorized by an overabundance of procedural technicalities as contrasted with conceptual niceties, which are prevalent in other areas. The administrative sections of the Act are both numerous and detailed; no one expects you to know all of them. Certainly, much of the procedural aspects of bankruptcy practice are not germane to the accountant's function, nor are they within the scope of the business law part of the exam. In order to further aid you in grasping the administrative aspects of a bankruptcy case, it will be helpful if you know the actors or participants and their functions. They are:

1. The debtor: a person (individual, partnership, or corporation) concerning which a bankruptcy case has been commenced.
2. The bankruptcy court judge: a federal judge having special jurisdiction over bankruptcy cases. The judge sits as an adjunct to the federal district court and passes on bankruptcy issues and disputes that arise in the course of the case as it proceeds through administration. The bankruptcy judge may have little contact with the case other than reviewing the trustee's final report and accounting and then granting the discharge.
3. The trustee: the duly elected or designated person who acts for, and on behalf of, the estate and whose goal is to ensure that all eligible property is included in the estate and that an equitable distribution is made to creditors.
4. Secured creditors: those creditors who have a secured interest in the property of the debtor and who will have their claims satisfied out of said property.
5. General creditors: an unsecured entity (including individuals) that has a claim against the debtor that arose on or before the order for relief.
6. The creditor's committee: the creditors may elect a committee of not fewer than 3 nor more than 11 to consult with the trustee in connection with the administration of the estate, make recommendations respecting the trustee's performance, and submit to the court any questions affecting the administration of the estate. A committee would normally not be elected unless the estate and the number of creditors was large.
7. The supporting cast: includes lawyers and accountants for the various parties.

D. The debtor's duties and benefits:

1. Debtor's duties: The debtor shall:
   a. File a list of creditors, a schedule of assets and liabilities, a schedule of current income and current expenditures, and a statement of financial affairs.
   b. Cooperate with the trustee to enable the trustee to perform properly.
   c. Surrender to the trustee all property of the estate and any recorded information (books, documents, etc.) relating to the property of the estate.
   d. Appear at the hearing to determine whether to grant a discharge.
2. **The exemption benefit:** Debtors are entitled under bankruptcy law to exempt certain property from the bankruptcy estate and hence insulate the property from the claims of creditors. There is now a semblance of uniformity regarding the amount and type of property that is exempt from inclusion in a bankrupt's estate. The Act contains federal rules governing exemptions. Prior federal law had left the exemption area to be determined by state law. However, the Act did not

preempt state law in this area of bankruptcy. Instead, the debtor is permitted to resort to existing state exemption laws if they are more favorable or to choose federal law. Furthermore, the Act permits the states to provide that the federal exemptions are not available. Under the 1984 amendments, a husband and wife are required to elect together to use state or federal exemption law. If the parties cannot agree on the alternative to be elected, they shall be decreed to elect the federal exemptions.

As previously indicated (see p. 206) exemptions play an important part in the strategy of creditors since it is not profitable to force a debtor into bankruptcy if the bulk of the assets are exempt. Undoubtedly, the federal exemption laws represent the "uniform law" for exam purposes. The federal exemptions are:

a. A homestead exemption, not to exceed $7,500, in real or personal property or in a cooperative apartment that the debtor or a dependent uses as a residence.

b. A motor vehicle valued at $1,200 or less.

c. A maximum of $200 per item in value of household goods, furnishings, and clothing used by the debtor or family for personal use, not to exceed an aggregate of $4,000.

d. Jewelry with a maximum value of $500 held primarily for personal or family use.

e. An interest in any kind of property not to exceed $400 plus up to $3,750 of any unused portion of the above homestead exemption.

f. A debtor's interest in implements, professional books, or tools of the debtor's trade not to exceed $750.

g. A life insurance contract, other than credit insurance.

h. A maximum of $4,000 in dividend, interest, or loan value of a life insurance policy.

i. Professionally prescribed health aids.

j. Certain future earnings benefits. These include social security, unemployment benefits, veterans benefits, alimony, support, or separate maintenance. These are exempted only to the extent reasonably necessary for the support of the debtor and his dependents.

k. Certain rights to compensation for losses. These include crime victim's reparations awards, wrongful death benefits, life insurance proceeds, compensation for bodily injury ($7,500 limit), and future earnings payments.

E. The trustee: the representative of the estate, who has the capacity to sue and to be sued.

1. Interim trustee: Promptly after the order for relief has been entered, the court appoints a disinterested person from a panel of trustees to serve as interim trustee. The interim trustee serves until a trustee is elected or designated.

2. Election of a trustee: At the first meeting of creditors, the creditors holding at least 20% in amount of claims may request an election for a trustee.

a. Eligibility of a creditor to vote: All creditors holding an allowable, undisputed, fixed, liquidated, unsecured claim entitled to distribution are allowed to vote, unless the creditor:

(1) Has an interest materially adverse to the above creditors entitled to a distribution.

(2) Is an insider.

b. The election: The trustee is elected if:

(1) Creditors with at least 20% in amount of the claims indicated above (2.a) actually vote.

(2) The proposed trustee receives the votes of creditors holding a majority in amount of the claims specified above (2.a) that are held by creditors that vote for the trustee.

3. Duties of a trustee: The trustee shall:

a. Collect and reduce to money the property of the estate and close up such estate as expeditiously as is compatible with the best interests of parties in interest.

b. Be accountable for all property received.

c. Investigate the financial affairs of the debtor.

d. If a purpose would be served, examine proofs of claims and object to the allowance of any improper claim.

e. If advisable, oppose the discharge of the debtor.

f. Unless the court orders otherwise, furnish such information concerning the estate and the estate's administration as is requested by a party in interest.

g. If the business of the debtor is authorized to be operated, file with the court and with any governmental unit charged with responsibility for collection or determination of any tax arising out of such operation, periodic reports, and summaries of the operation of such business, including a statement of receipts and disbursements, and such other information as the court requires.

h. Make a final report and file a final account of the administration of the estate with the court.

F. **Preferences:** This is the most important American contribution to Anglo-American bankruptcy jurisprudence; it is an essential part of our bankruptcy law. Its goal simply is to set aside preferential transfers to creditors that are made on the "eve" (generally within 90 days) of bankruptcy. Unless such transfers are avoided, the "favored" creditor usually is fully satisfied from the property transferred or it is used to secure an unsecured debt, thereby diminishing the amount available to satisfy the other general creditors. In order to avoid this inequitable situation, the trustee is charged with determining and setting aside any preferential transfer. This doctrine has been a favorite topic of prior business law examinations. It has been substantially changed by the 1978 Bankruptcy Act and these changes have been stressed below. The five requirements that must be met in order for the trustee to set aside a transfer, as preferential are:

1. The transfer must be made to or for a creditor's benefit.

2. The transfer must be on account of an antecedent debt owed by the debtor prior to the transfer. In essence, the creditor is seeking to obtain payment or to change his general creditor status to that of a secured creditor at the expense of his fellow creditors.

3. The transfer must be made while the debtor is insolvent. Under prior law, the trustee had the burden of proving this often difficult requirement. Insolvency as

used here is insolvency in the "bankruptcy sense"—see p. 204. Despite the requirement that the debtor be insolvent, the Act provides a presumption of insolvency during the 90 days prior to the date the petition was filed. Thus, the trustee need not prove insolvency on the debtor's part if the transfer is within that period if the preferential transferee does not offer some evidence rebutting the presumption. As a practical matter, the debtor is invariably insolvent and it is virtually impossible to prove the debtor was solvent or insolvent in any event due to the lack of adequate records or information.

4. As to transfers in general, they must have been made *within 90 days prior to the commencement of the bankruptcy proceedings* unless the transfer was to an "insider," see above, p. 204. Regarding insiders, the trustee may avoid transfers made within 90 days of the filing of the petition and for an additional period of time, which, when combined with the 90 days, equals one year.

5. The transfer is such that it enables the creditor to obtain a preference, i.e., it prefers him or her over other creditors.

6. Exemptions: In addition to defining and explaining the preference doctrine, the Code specifically exempts certain transfers from its application. Major exemptions include:

   a. Cash sales, including those which unavoidably involve brief extensions of credit. A simultaneous exchange of goods for cash is not by definition preferential, since there is no antecedent debt. However, the term cash sale has been broadened to include "substantially contemporaneous exchanges."

   b. Certain payments of debts incurred in the ordinary course of business. In order to qualify for this exemption, a transfer must be:

      (1) In payment of a debt incurred in the ordinary course of business or financial affairs of the debtor and the transferee,

      (2) Made not later than 45 days after such debt was incurred,

      (3) Made in the ordinary course of business or financial affairs of the debtor and the transferee, and

      (4) Made according to ordinary business terms.

   c. Enabling loans. This type of loan occurs where new value is provided to the debtor to enable him or her to subsequently obtain the collateral in question. As long as the new value is used for this purpose and the security interest is perfected within 10 days after the debtor receives possession of such property, it is not preferential. This conforms to the Uniform Commercial Code. (See Secured Transactions, p. 347).

7. Summary and conclusions: The current preference section represents a major departure from prior law.

   a. First, insolvency for the 90-day period prior to filing is presumed.

   b. Second, the trustee need not prove that the preferential transferee had knowledge or reason to know that the debtor was insolvent in the bankruptcy sense, if the transfer was made within the 90 days of the filing. These two changes immeasurably simplify the trustee's ability to establish and set aside transfers within the 90-day period as preferences.

   c. The provisions relating to insiders extend the period of time that transfers may be set aside to one year.

G. Fraudulent conveyances: Transfers that are made by a debtor (typically to a related "person") with a deliberately illegal intent to avoid his or her just debts are naturally treated harshly under the Act. Although there may be some overlap with the preference area, the distinguishing characteristic of the fraudulent conveyance is that it is made either for insufficient or for no consideration. The trustee is charged with setting aside such transfers or obligations incurred that are made within one year from the filing of the petition in bankruptcy. The situation is readily recognizable. The potential bankrupt sees bankruptcy looming on the horizon, panics, and begins to transfer assets in its name to relatives or to an entity (e.g., a corporation) that it controls. An alternative approach is to incur inflated obligations to relatives or controlled entities thereby decreasing the amounts payable to *bona fide* creditors in bankruptcy. For example, relatives may be added to the payroll, or some token property may be purchased at a grossly inflated price. Such conduct cannot be tolerated and the Act contains provisions that prevent such abuses.

   1. The trustee may avoid any transfer of an interest of the debtor in property, or any obligation incurred by the debtor, that was made or incurred on or within one year before the date of the filing of the petition, if the debtor either:
      a. Made such transfer or incurred such obligation with actual intent to hinder, delay, or defraud any creditor to which the debtor was, or became, indebted. The transfer or obligation incurred is fraudulent without regard to the debtor's solvency. Or
      b. Received less than a reasonably equivalent value in exchange for such transfer or obligation with the result that the debtor:
         (1) Was insolvent or became insolvent on the date that such transfer was made or such obligation was incurred.
         (2) Was engaged in business, or was about to engage in business or a transaction, for which any property remaining with the debtor was an unreasonably small capital, i.e., the transfer resulted in a serious undercapitalization.
         (3) Intended or believed it would incur debts beyond its ability to pay them as they matured.
   2. Additionally, the trustee of a partnership debtor may avoid any transfer of an interest of the debtor in property, or any obligation incurred by the debtor, that was made or incurred on or within one year before the date of the filing of the petition, to a general partner of the debtor, if the debtor was insolvent on the date such transfer was made or such obligation was incurred, or became insolvent as a result of such transfer or obligation.
   3. Unless otherwise voidable, the transferee or obligee of a transfer or obligation that was taken for value and in good faith has a lien on any interest transferred, to the extent that such transferee or obligee gave value to the debtor in exchange for such transfer or obligation.

H. Claims against the debtor's estate:

   1. Filing of proofs of claims: A creditor may file with the court a timely proof of claim or it will be barred. The Rules of Bankruptcy Procedure will set the time limits, the form, and procedure for filing that will determine whether claims are

timely or tardily filed (a six-month bar period currently applies). If the creditor does not timely file, the Act permits a surety, the debtor, or the trustee to file such a claim on the creditor's behalf.

2. **Allowance of claims arising prior to bankruptcy proceeding:** A claim and the proof thereof that is filed is deemed allowed unless a party in interest (e.g., another creditor) objects. Thus, a timely filed claim is afforded *prima facie* validity and, if there is no objection, it is approved.

3. **Disallowance of claims:** The following claims are disallowed:
   a. Claims that are unenforceable against the debtor or his property, e.g., the usual defenses to a contract, such as lack of consideration, fraud, or the statute of limitations apply.
   b. Claims for unmatured interest.
   c. Claims that may be offset against a debt owing to the debtor.
   d. A claim for tax assessed against property of the estate, if such claim exceeds the value of the estate's interest.
   e. Claims for services by insiders or the attorney of the debtor to the extent the claim exceeds the reasonable value of the services, i.e., the court must pass on the reasonableness of such claims.
   f. Claims for unmatured debts, i.e., those arising after the date of the filing of the petition and that are excepted from discharge.
   g. Claims by lessors for damages resulting from the termination of a lease on real property above certain specified amounts.
   h. Claims by employees for damages resulting from the termination of an employment contract exceeding one year's salary plus any unpaid compensation due as of the date of the filing of the petition or the date of the termination of the employee, whichever was earlier.

I. The general **order of distribution** of the debtor's estate:

1. **First to secured creditors:** Technically, property that is subject to a valid security interest is not a part of the debtor's estate for distribution purposes. Consequently, such property, to the extent of the security interest, "belongs" to the secured creditor, rather than being a distribution to him. This, of course, is subject to the voidable preference doctrine discussed above. If the secured creditor's security interest is valid, he has a right to the property or its cash equivalent. In the event the property is insufficient to satisfy the claim, he or she becomes a general creditor for the balance. As to any excess realized upon disposition of the property securing the debt, it belongs to the estate.

2. As a matter of policy, the Act assigns a priority of payment to the claims of certain creditors. All priority claims to the extent allowable and in order of their priority will be paid in full or receive a substantial percentage payment of their claims.

3. Only after satisfaction of secured creditors and priority claimants do the general creditors share in what is now frequently a substantially diminished or totally depleted debtor's estate.

J. **Priorities:** The following expenses and unsecured claims have priority in the following order:

1. Administrative expenses.
2. Claims arising in the ordinary course of the debtor's business after the filing of the petition but before appointment of the trustee.
3. Claims to the extent of $2,000 for wages, salaries, or commissions, including vacation, severance, and sick leave pay earned by an individual within 90 days before the date of the filing of the petition, or the date of cessation of the debtor's business, whichever occurs first.
4. Claims for contributions to employee benefit plans arising from services rendered within 180 days before the date of the filing of the petition or the date of the cessation of the debtor's business, whichever occurs first. The amount of this priority is determined by taking the maximum allowable wage priority ($2,000) times the number of employees covered by the plan less the total distribution paid in the third category (3, above).
5. Claims of individuals, to the extent of $900 per individual, arising from the deposit, before the commencement of the case, of money in connection with the purchase, lease, or rental of property, or the purchase of services, for the personal, family, or household use of such individuals, that were not delivered or provided by the debtor.
6. Certain tax claims of governmental units.

K. **Discharge of a bankrupt.** The bankruptcy court will grant a discharge to an *individual* from his or her dischargeable debts **unless** the debtor:

1. Intentionally hindered, delayed, or defrauded a creditor with an intent to transfer, remove, destroy, or conceal property within one year before the filing of the petition.
2. Destroyed, falsified, concealed, or failed to keep books of account or records from which his financial condition and business transactions can be ascertained, unless justified, under the circumstances.
3. Knowingly and fraudulently in connection with the case:
   a. Made a false oath or account.
   b. Presented or used a false claim.
   c. Engaged in bribery.
   d. Withheld information from a proper officer of the estate.
4. Failed to explain satisfactorily any loss of assets or deficiency of assets to meet the debtor's liabilities.
5. Refused to obey lawful court orders or answer valid material questions.
6. Committed any of the acts described above within one year of the filing of the petition in connection with another case involving an insider.
7. Has been granted a discharge in bankruptcy within six years before the date of filing of the petition.
8. Has filed pursuant to Chapter 13 (Adjustment of Debts of an Individual) and has been granted a discharge but failed to make the requisite payments.
9. Has executed a written waiver of discharge, which the court approved, and which was executed after the order for relief.

L. **Nondischargeable debts:** Despite the fact that most of a debtor's debts will be discharged in bankruptcy, certain debts are not discharged despite the fact that the debtor is eligible for, and obtains, a discharge. The debts that remain after a debtor has been granted a discharge are:

1. Taxes.
2. Debts that have been incurred by use of a false financial statement. The Act makes it clear that only the particular debt is denied discharge and that the conduct does not result in a complete denial of discharge. There must be reliance by the creditor and such reliance must have been reasonable. The provision also encompasses renewal of credit by false pretenses, false representations, and actual fraud in obtaining credit.

    There is a presumption that consumer debts owed to a single creditor and aggregating more than $500 for luxury goods or services incurred within 40 days before the order for relief, or cash advances aggregating more than $1,000 that are extentions of consumer credit under an open-end credit plan incurred within 20 days before the order for relief are nondischargeable.
3. Unscheduled debts.
4. Debts that arose from fraud, embezzlement, or larceny.
5. Alimony maintenance or support.
6. Debts in connection with willful or malicious injury.
7. Fines or penalties.
8. Educational loans, unless the loan became due more than five years prior to the filing of the bankruptcy petition, or if denial of discharge of the debt would impose an undue hardship on the debtor or his or her dependents.
9. Debts that arose from a judgment or consent decree against the debtor for liability incurred as a result of operating a motor vehicle while intoxicated.
10. Debts that were, or could have been, listed or scheduled in a prior bankruptcy in which the debtor waived discharge or was denied one.

III. Reorganization

A. Overview (see *supra*, p. 202).

B. *The Bankruptcy Amendments of 1984*. The Act contains a new section which deals with *rejection of collective bargaining agreements by a bankrupt company*.

1. The U.S. Supreme Court's decision in two cases were a major consideration by Congress in enacting a procedure for rejection of a collective bargaining contract.

    a. In the first case, the Supreme Court (9–0) held that a court should permit rejection of a labor bargaining agreement if the bankruptcy company can show that the labor contract burdens the bankrupt's estate and that after due consideration, the equities favor rejection of the contract.

    b. In the second case, the court, in a 5–4 decision, held that a bankrupt company is not guilty of an unfair labor practice even if it unilaterally changes the terms of the collective bargaining agreement after filing its petition in bankruptcy, but before authorization by the court.
2. *The statutory standards*. The collective bargaining agreement can be rejected in an attempt by the debtor company to reorganize under the reorganization provisions of the Bankruptcy Code (Chapter 11) if:

     a. The company has proposed "necessary" changes in the agreement to the
        union.
     b. The union has rejected the proposals "without just cause."
     c. On balancing the equities involved, it is determined that the equities "clearly
        favor" rejection.

Selected Problems from CPA Examinations on Bankruptcy

Subjective Questions and Answers

Q. **1.** A small business client, John Barry, doing business as John Barry Fashions, is worried about an involuntary bankruptcy proceeding being filed by his creditors. His net worth using a balance sheet approach is $8,000 ($108,000 assets − $100,000 liabilities). However, his cash flow is negative and he has been hard pressed to meet current obligations as they mature. He is, in fact, some $12,500 in arrears in payments to his creditors on bills submitted during the past two months.

Required
Answer the following, setting forth reasons for any conclusions stated.

1. What are the current requirements for a creditor or creditors filing an involuntary petition in bankruptcy and could they be satisfied in this situation?
2. Will the fact that Barry is solvent in the bankruptcy sense result in the court's dismissing the creditors' petition if Barry contests the propriety of the filing of a petition?

A. **1.** Under the Bankruptcy Reform Act of 1978, an involuntary petition may be filed by three or more creditors having claims aggregating $5,000 more than the value of any liens securing the claims. In the event there are fewer than 12 creditors, one or more creditors with claims of $5,000 or more can file. The facts indicate that Barry has $12,500 in overdue debts. It would appear likely that these requirements could be met and an involuntary petition could be validly filed. The act permits the involuntary debtor to file an answer to the petition.
    2. No. Under the 1978 act, the principal defense available to an involuntary debtor would still be solvency. However, the defense of solvency in the bankruptcy sense (essentially a balance sheet approach) has been rejected when an involuntary liquidation is sought. Instead, the act has adopted a modified or expanded version of insolvency in the equity sense. A debtor is insolvent if he or she is generally not paying debts as they become due. In addition, a debtor is insolvent if within 120 days before the date of the filing of the petition a custodian was appointed or took possession of the debtor's property. Barry, of course, appears to be squarely within the scope of the first part of this test. Realistically, he could not hope to have the petition dismissed on grounds of solvency.

11/81

Q. **2.** In connection with the audit of One-Up, Inc., a question has arisen regarding the validity of a $10,000 purchase money security interest in certain machinery sold to Essex Company on March 2. Essex was petitioned into bankruptcy on May 1 by its creditors. The trustee is seeking to avoid One-Up's security interest on the grounds that it is a preferential transfer, hence voidable. The machinery in question was sold to Essex on the following terms: $1,000 down and the balance plus interest at 9% (nine percent) to be paid over a three-year period. One-Up obtained a signed security agreement which created a security interest in the property on March 2, the date of the sale. A financing statement was filed on March 10.

Required
Answer the following, setting forth reasons for any conclusions stated.

1. Would One-Up's security interest in the machinery be a voidable preference?
2. In general, what are the requirements necessary to permit the trustee to successfully assert a preferential transfer and thereby set aside a creditor's security interest?

A. **1.** No. The Bankruptcy Reform Act of 1978 has not only modified the requirements for establishing a voidable preference, it has also specified transactions that do not constitute preferences. One such transaction is the creditor's taking a security interest in property acquired by the debtor as a contemporaneous exchange for new value given to the debtor to enable him to acquire such property (a purchase money security interest). The security interest must be perfected (filed) within 10 days after attachment. The act is in harmony with the secured transactions provisions of the Uniform Commercial Code. Thus, One-Up has a valid security interest in the machinery it sold to Essex.

2. The Bankruptcy Reform Act of 1978 does not require that the creditor have knowledge or reasonable cause to believe the debtor is insolvent in the bankruptcy sense. Instead, under the act, where such insolvency exists on or within ninety days before the filing of the petition, knowledge of insolvency by the transferee need not be established. The act also assumes that the debtor's insolvency is presumed if the transfer alleged to be preferential is made within 90 days. Finally, the time period in which transfers may be set aside is 90 days unless the transferee is an "insider." If the transfer is to an insider, the trustee may avoid transfers made within one year prior to the filing of the petition. Thus, the trustee may avoid as preferential any transfer of property of the debtor that is

* To or for the benefit of a creditor.
* For or on account of an antecedent debt owed by the debtor before such transfer was made.
* Made while the debtor was insolvent in the bankruptcy sense (however, if the transfer is made within 90 days, the debtor's insolvency is presumed).
* Made on or within 90 days of the filing of the petition (or if made after the 90 days but within one year prior to the date of the filing of the petition and the transfer was to an "insider," it may be set aside if the transferee had reasonable cause to believe the debtor was insolvent at the time of the transfer).
* Such that it enables the creditor to receive more than he would if it were a straight liquidation proceeding.
The bankruptcy act contains a lengthy definition of the term "insider" that includes common relationships that the transferee has to the debtor, which, in case of an individual debtor, could be certain relatives, a partnership in which he is a general partner, his fellow general partners, or a corporation controlled by him.

11/80

Q. **3.** Disco Records, Inc., was in dire financial condition which was widely known in the relevant business community. Disco's liabilities exceeded its assets by approximately $200,000. Jolly Plastics, Inc., one of Disco's creditors, was pressing Disco to pay $30,000 of overdue accounts. Disco decided to mortgage or sell its warehouse to improve its cash position, provide funds to forestall creditors, and permit it to work out its financial difficulties.

Disco first approached several banks and attempted to mortgage the property. However, the banks would only loan an amount equal to 50% of the value of the property. The maximum funds that Disco could obtain from a bank was $30,000 which was not enough to forestall bankruptcy. Disco abandoned this approach.

Disco then placed the property on the market. The property was listed with several brokers on a nonexclusive basis and was advertised in the local papers. Jolly learned of the proposed sale and, because of unique advantages of the property to Jolly, offered $62,500. This was $2,500 more than any other prospective purchaser had offered. The purchase price consisted of cancellation of the $30,000 overdue debt and $32,500 in cash.

The sale was consummated on July 1, 1980. On October 14, 1980, a petition in bankruptcy against Disco was duly filed by a group of its aggrieved creditors. The trustee in bankruptcy has attacked the sale of the land as a preferential transfer.

Required

Answer the following, setting forth reasons for any conclusions stated.

Will the trustee prevail?

A.   No. The transaction as described is not a preference. Under the Bankruptcy Act of 1978, a transfer must be made within 90 days prior to the filing of the petition in order to be preferential. Hence, under current law, it is outside the requisite time period. A four-month time period was used under prior law so the answer has changed from "yes" to "no." But, assuming the transfer was within the 90-day period, the new Act requires that in order to constitute a preference under the Bankruptcy Act, there must be a transfer of property of a debtor, while insolvent, to a creditor for, or on behalf of, an antecedent debt. It must also prefer the creditor over the debtor's other creditors. Here, the sale of the real property in question was partially for the cancellation of an antecedent debt and partially for new and contemporaneous value. Since the transfer was in part for the cancellation of an antecedent debt, it constitutes a preference in part. Thus, the preference would be voidable and could be set aside. The $32,500 in cash would be refunded and the property reconveyed to the trustee in bankruptcy. Jolly would then stand in the position of a general creditor to the extent of $30,000.

11/79

Practice Questions

Q.   1.   The MIB Corporation has been petitioned into bankruptcy. The petition was filed February 1, 1980. Among its creditors are the following:

A. Viscount Machine Manufacturing, Inc.

Viscount sold MIB two tractor trailers in August 1979 and filed and recorded its financing statement on December 15, 1979, after it learned that MIB was in severe financial difficulty. The outstanding balance due Viscount is $9,000 which is the current fair market value of the two tractor trailers. Viscount is attempting to repossess the tractor trailers in order to recover its outstanding balance.

B. Second National County Bank

Second National holds a first mortgage on the real estate where MIB has its principal plant, office, and warehouse. The mortgage is for $280,750 representing the unpaid balance due on the original $350,000 mortgage. The property was sold for $290,000, its fair market value as established by bids received by the trustee. The mortgage was taken out two years ago and duly filed and recorded at that time.

C. Marvel Supply Company

Marvel, a major supplier of parts, delivered $10,000 worth of parts to MIB on January 17, 1979. Upon delivery Marvel received 50% cash and insisted on the balance by the end of the month. When the balance was not paid, Marvel obtained from MIB a duly executed financing statement which Marvel filed on February 2, 1980.

D. Sixty-five wage earners

This class of employee is mainly composed of the machine operators and others employed in MIB's plant and warehouse. They were not paid for the final month. All were paid at the minimum wage level and each has a claim for $400 which equals $26,000 in total.

E. Federal, state, and local taxing authorities

MIB owes $6,800 in back taxes.

F. Administration costs

These total $12,000.

G. Various general creditors

Excluding items A through F stated above, general creditors have provable claims of $1,614,900. The bankrupt's total estate consists of $850,000 of assets in addition to the real estate described in B.

Required
Answer the following, setting forth reasons for any conclusions stated.

1. Discuss the legal implications and the resulting rights of each of the persons or entities described above in A through G as a result of the facts given and the application of bankruptcy law to them.
2. What is the bankruptcy dividend (percentage on the dollar) that each general creditor will receive? Show calculations in good form.

Practice Objective Questions

Instructions 1–15
Select the *best* answer for each of the following items. Mark only one answer for *each* item. Answer all items. Your grade will be based on your total correct answers.

1. Skipper was for several years the principal stockholder, director, and chief executive officer of the Canarsie Grocery Corporation. Canarsie had financial difficulties and an order of relief was filed against it, and subsequently discharged. Several creditors are seeking to hold Skipper personally liable as a result of his stock ownership and as a result of his being an officer-director. Skipper in turn filed with the bankruptcy judge a claim for $1,400 salary due him. Which of the following is correct?
    a. Skipper's salary claim will be allowed and he will be entitled to a priority.
    b. Skipper has *no* personal liability to the creditors as long as Canarsie is recognized as a separate legal entity.
    c. Skipper *cannot* personally file a petition in bankruptcy for seven years.
    d. Skipper is personally liable to the creditors for Canarsie's losses.
2. Mac, doing business as Mac's Restaurant, has an involuntary petition in bankruptcy filed against him. Which of the following is a correct legal statement regarding such a filing?
    a. Mac has the right to controvert the validity of the petition and if Mac is successful, the petition will be dismissed and Mac may recover his costs including a reasonable attorney's fee.
    b. The filing of the petition by a majority of the creditors creates a binding presumption that Mac is insolvent.
    c. A single creditor may file the petition regardless of the number of creditors if its provable claim exceeds $7,500.
    d. A trustee is appointed upon the filing of the petition and is vested by operation of law with the bankrupt's title as of the date of the filing.
3. An audit client is in serious financial trouble. On November 1, 1981, several creditors filed an involuntary petition in bankruptcy. Which of the following is correct?
    a. As long as the client generally can meet current debts as they mature, the court will deny relief against the client in a bankruptcy proceeding.
    b. If the client creates a new corporation and transfers most of its assets to the newly created corporation, it can avoid bankruptcy.
    c. As long as the client's assets, at fair value, exceed its liabilities, the creditors' petition will be denied.
    d. Unless the client commits an act of bankruptcy, the creditors *cannot* force the client into bankruptcy.
4. The Bankruptcy Reform Act of 1978 provides that certain allowed expenses and claims are entitled to a priority. Which of the following is *not* entitled to such a priority?
    a. Claims of governmental units for taxes.
    b. Wage claims, but to a limited extent.
    c. Rents payable within the four months preceding bankruptcy, but to a limited extent.
    d. Unsecured claims for contributions to employee benefit plans, but to a limited extent.
5. Which of the following was a significant reform made in the reorganization provisions of the Bankruptcy Reform Act of 1978?
    a. Separate treatment of publicly held corporations under its provisions.
    b. Elimination of the separate and competing procedures contained in the various chapters of the prior Bankruptcy Act.

    c. Elimination of participation in bankruptcy reorganizations by the Securities and Exchange Commission.

    d. The exclusion from its jurisdiction of partnerships and other noncorporate entities.

  6. A client has joined other creditors of the Martin Construction Company in a composition agreement seeking to avoid the necessity of a bankruptcy proceeding against Martin. Which statement describes the composition agreement?

    a. It provides a temporary delay, *not* to exceed six months, insofar as the debtor's obligation to repay the debts included in the composition.

    b. It does *not* discharge any of the debts included until performance by the debtor has taken place.

    c. It provides for the appointment of a receiver to take over and operate the debtor's business.

    d. It must be approved by all creditors.

  7. In a bankruptcy proceeding, the trustee

    a. Must be an attorney admitted to practice in the federal district in which the bankrupt is located.

    b. Will receive a fee based upon the time and fair value of the services rendered, regardless of the size of the estate.

    c. May *not* have had any dealings with the bankrupt within the past year.

    d. Is the representative of the bankrupt's estate and as such has the capacity to sue and be sued on its behalf.

  8. Haplow engaged Turnbow as his attorney when threatened by several creditors with a bankruptcy proceeding. Haplow's assets consisted of $85,000 and his debts were $125,000. A petition was subsequently filed and was uncontested. Several of the creditors are concerned that the suspected large legal fees charged by Turnbow will diminish the size of the distributable estate. What are the rules or limitations which apply to such fees?

    a. None, since it is within the attorney-client privileged relationship.

    b. The fee is presumptively valid as long as arrived at in an arm's-length negotiation.

    c. Turnbow must file with the court a statement of compensation paid or agreed to for review as to its reasonableness.

    d. The trustee must approve the fee.

  9. If a secured party's claim exceeds the value of the collateral of a bankrupt, he will be paid the total amount realized from the sale of the security and will

    a. Not have any claim for the balance.

    b. Become a general creditor for the balance.

    c. Retain a secured creditor status for the balance.

    d. Be paid the balance only after all general creditors are paid.

  10. In order to establish a preference under the federal bankruptcy act, which of the following is the trustee required to show where the preferred party is *not* an insider?

    a. That the preferred party had reasonable cause to believe that the debtor was insolvent.

    b. That the debtor committed an act of bankruptcy.

    c. That the transfer was for an antecedent debt.

    d. That the transfer was made within 60 days of the filing of the petition.

  11. The federal bankruptcy act contains several important terms. One such term is "insider." The term is used in connection with preferences and preferential transfers. Which among the following is *not* an "insider?"

    a. A secured creditor having a security interest in at least 25% or more of the debtor's property.

    b. A partnership in which the debtor is a general partner.

    c. A corporation of which the debtor is a director.

    d. A close blood relative of the debtor.

  12. Bunker Industries, Inc., ceased doing business and is in bankruptcy. Among the claimants are employees seeking unpaid wages. The following statements describe the possible status of such claims in a bankruptcy proceeding or legal limitations placed upon them. Which one is an *incorrect* statement?

    a. They are entitled to a priority.

    b. If a priority is afforded such claims, it *cannot* exceed $2,000 per wage earner.

    c. Such claims *cannot* include vacation, severance, or sick-leave pay.

    d. The amounts of excess wages *not* entitled to a priority are mere unsecured claims.

  13. Merchant is in serious financial difficulty and is unable to meet current unsecured obligations of $25,000 to some 15 creditors who are demanding immediate payment. Merchant owes Flintheart $5,000 and Flintheart has decided to file an involuntary petition against Merchant. Which of the following is necessary in order for Flintheart to validly file?

a. Flintheart must be joined by at least two other creditors.

b. Merchant must have committed an act of bankruptcy within 120 days of the filing.

c. Flintheart must allege and subsequently establish that Merchant's liabilities exceed Merchant's assets upon fair valuation.

d. Flintheart must be a secured creditor.

14. Hapless is a bankrupt. In connection with a debt owed to the Suburban Finance Company, he used a false financial statement to induce it to loan him $500. Hapless is seeking a discharge in bankruptcy. Which of the following is a correct statement?

a. Hapless will be denied a discharge of any of his debts.

b. Even if it can be proved that Suburban did *not* rely upon the financial statement, Hapless will be denied a discharge either in whole or part.

c. Hapless will be denied a discharge of the Suburban debt.

d. Hapless will be totally discharged despite the false financial statement.

15. Markson is a general creditor of Black. Black filed a voluntary petition in bankruptcy. Markson is irate and wishes to have the bankruptcy court either deny Black a general discharge or at least *not* have his debt discharged. The discharge will be granted and it will include Markson's debt even if

a. It is unscheduled.

b. Markson lied under oath in a bankruptcy proceeding.

c. Markson was a secured creditor who was *not* fully satisfied from the proceeds obtained upon disposition of the collateral.

d. Black had received a previous discharge in bankruptcy within six years.

5

GOVERNMENT REGULATION OF BUSINESS (10%)

Chapter 9. Regulation of Employment
Chapter 10. Federal Securities Acts

Regulation of Employment

AICPA Content Specification Outline

Federal Insurance Contributions Act
Federal Unemployment Tax Act
Worker's Compensation Acts

Contents

    C. Insurance requirements

    D. Administration of claims

    E. Lawsuits for damages

    F. Types of benefits

Selected Problems from CPA Examinations on Regulation of Employer-Employee
    Relationship

Subjective Questions and Answers

Practice Question

Practice Objective Questions

I. Federal Insurance Contributions Act (Social Security)

A. Basic statute is the Federal Social Security Act. This Act is popularly known as the Social Security Act and it covers three basic programs:

    1. Social insurance.

    2. Public assistance to the needy.

    3. Children's services.

B. The social insurance provisions are those that bear upon the employer-employee relationship. They consist of:

    1. Old-age, survivor's, and disability insurance.

    2. Hospital insurance (Medicare).

    3. Unemployment insurance.

C. Financing social insurance:

    1. Old-age, survivor's disability, and hospital insurance are financed out of taxes paid by employers, employees, and self-employed under provisions of the Federal Insurance Contributions Act and the Self-Employment Contributions Act.

    2. Unemployment Insurance. Taxes paid by employees are:

        a. Taxes imposed under state unemployment insurance laws.

        b. Taxes imposed under federal unemployment insurance laws.

D. Employment taxes (withholding):

    1. Rates.

        a. Taxes under Federal Insurance Contributions Act are the same rate for both employer and employee, except as indicated.

Year	Base Income	Tax Rate, %	
1984	$37,800	6.70	(employees)
		7.00	(employers)
1985	39,600	7.05	
1986	41,700*	7.15	
1987	44,100*	7.15	
1988	46,800*	7.51	
1989	49,800*	7.51	
1990		7.65	

*Projected estimates.

      b. Employee must pay tax (withheld from salary by employer) on earnings up to base amount. The employee is entitled to refund if tax paid on amount is in excess of base amount, e.g., if employee works for two or more employers. The employee may not itemize this tax as a deduction on the income tax return. Employer takes deduction for its portion.

      c. Every employer is liable for the payment of the tax.

  2. Employment taxes

      a. Employer must withhold employee tax by deducting amount of tax from employee's wage as and when paid.

      b. Employer must furnish each employee with a written statement as to wages paid during calendar year.

  3. Self-employment tax:

Year	Base Income	Tax Rate, %
1983	$35,700	9.35
1984	37,800	11.30
1985	39,600	11.80

E. Unemployment Insurance Tax Act:

  1. Employer must pay a federal unemployment tax if he employs even one person in employment covered by the Federal Unemployment Act. Only 3.5% on the first $7,000 of wages is taxable for 1984. After January 1, 1985, the tax rate will rise to 6.7%.

  2. Employers are entitled to credit against federal unemployment tax for contributions paid under state unemployment compensation laws up to a maximum of 2.7%.

  3. Experience rating: Employer's contribution payments under state laws may be adjusted based on the employer's employment experience. An additional credit is allowed against federal unemployment tax if the state payments are reduced.

F. What are wages?

  1. Not limited to money; includes other forms of compensation.

  2. Do not include employee benefits (e.g., hospitalization, insurance premiums from a qualified plan).

  3. Basic pay of military personnel is subject to tax.

  4. Special rules for farm workers, domestic workers, and casual workers.

  5. Payments on account of sickness, medical, or hospitalization expenses are not considered wages and are not taxable for old-age, survivor's, and disability insurance.

      a. Employer's plan must make such provision for all employees.

      b. Exemption also runs to payments by an employer for insurance or into a fund.

  6. Payments to an employee or a plan on account of employee's retirement is also not taxable. The same conditions apply to health benefits.

  7. Bonuses and commissions paid as compensation are considered wages.

  8. Travel expenses are not wages.

  9. Supplemental unemployment benefit plan payments are:

   a. Considered wages if the individual employee has a beneficial interest in the fund.

   b. Not wages if no interest is established until the employee is eligible to receive benefits from the fund.

10. Vacation and dismissal allowances constitute wages.

11. Tips paid in cash if greater than $20 in any calendar month are wages.

G. Coverage:

1. To pay tax and receive benefits:

   a. One must be an "employee."

   b. Services rendered must be "employment."

   c. Compensation received must be wages.

2. Definition of employee:

   a. This relationship exists when a person for whom services are performed has the right to control not only the result to be accomplished but also how that result is to be accomplished (otherwise, one is an independent contractor—see Agency, p. 40, II.A.3.a).

   b. Partners, self-employed persons, and independent contractors are not covered by unemployment provisions. They are covered as self-employed persons for old-age, survivor's, and disability insurance purposes.

   c. Officers and directors of corporations are "employees" within the meaning of the definition if they perform services and receive remuneration for them from the corporation, as are part-time employees.

3. Definition of employer:

   a. Old-age, survivor's, and disability insurance provisions contain no explicit definition of employer. Employer can be an individual, corporation, partnership, trust, or other unincorporated group or entity.

   b. For Federal Unemployment Tax Act: one who employs one employee for a total of at least 20 calendar days during a year, each such day being in a different week. State definitions may differ.

4. Definition of employment:

   a. Any service performed by an employee for a person employing him irrespective of citizenship or residence of either (problems only arise when service is outside United States for an employer not sufficiently connected with the United States).

   b. Only services not covered by the social security system are those specifically exempted.

   c. Special rules and tests as to coverage for agricultural labor, casual labor, domestic workers, and government employees.

   d. Work must be continuing or recurring.

H. Election of coverage:

1. The Federal Unemployment Tax Act makes no provision for coverage of services that are exempt from statutory coverage.

2. Old-age, survivor's, and disability insurance coverage may be extended to certain classes of services otherwise excluded, e.g., state and local government employees.

I. Benefits:

1. Various kinds of benefits are payable under the social security system, depending upon the average monthly earnings and the relationship of the beneficiary to the retired, deceased, or disabled worker. The individual upon whose earnings record the benefits are based must have attained a certain "insured status" by acquiring "quarters of coverage."

2. Quarters of coverage for wages: An individual must be paid $50 or more during a quarter to be credited with a quarter of coverage. The quarters of coverage are used in determining whether the worker is fully insured.

3. Fully insured workers:
   a. When a worker has 40 quarters of coverage, he is fully insured for life, regardless of **b,** below.
   b. To be fully insured, a worker needs one quarter of coverage for each year after 1950 (or after the year in which he attained age 21 if that was later than 1950) and before the year in which he died or the year he attained retirement age.
   c. Retirement age for full benefits if 65; however, retirement benefits are increased if retirement is postponed beyond age 65.

4. An individual is insured for disability insurance benefits if he or she meets a statutory insured status test based upon quarters of coverage.

5. Currently insured: To be currently insured, a worker must have not less than six quarters of coverage during the 13-quarter period ending with the quarter in which she dies, become entitled to old-age benefits, or most recently became entitled to disability benefits.

6. If a worker is both fully insured and currently insured, then the following benefits are available:
   a. Benefits for dependents of retired or disabled workers.
   b. Survivor's benefits for dependents.
   c. Lump-sum death payment.

7. Benefits are subject to an earning test such that benefits are reduced with increased earnings of the beneficiary.

8. Taxability of social security benefits: Prior to 1984 not subject to income tax. Under the 1984 Tax Act benefits are taxable up to 50% maximum of gross benefit for taxpayers over designated threshold income brackets.

9. Medical care for the aged, i.e., for persons 65 and over, requires:
   a. A hospital insurance plan.
   b. A voluntary medical insurance plan.
   c. Both plans are financed from individual premium payments. The medical insurance premiums are matched dollar for dollar by government contributions.

II. Workers' Compensation Acts

A. Compulsory and elective acts. The states are split; some have:

1. A compulsory law that requires all employers within its scope to insure in order to provide those benefits specified. This is the law in the majority of states.

2. An elective system whereby the employer may accept or reject the act; if he rejects it, he loses the three common law defenses against an employee's suit for damages: assumption of risk, negligence of fellow employees, and contributory negligence (see p. 231, II.E.1).

B. Scope of workers' compensation legislation:

1. Every state has a workers' compensation law. In addition, there are federal workers' compensation laws such as the Workmen's Compensation Law of the District of Columbia and the Federal Employee's Compensation Act.
   a. Purpose is to accord employees certainty of benefits with little difficulty and no expense for job-related injuries or disease.
   b. No fault need be shown: payment is thus automatic if requirements are satisfied.
2. In no jurisdiction does the law apply to all forms of employment. Generally, those not covered include: agricultural workers, domestic workers, enterprises with fewer than fixed number of employees, public employees, and casual workers.
3. To constitute employment, the following rights must be found to be retained by the employer:
   a. The exercise of control over the details of work.
   b. The payment of compensation; not required to be in money.
   c. The power to hire and fire.
4. Numerical exceptions: Generally, employers are exempt if they employ less than a certain number of people. Most acts permit voluntary acceptance.
5. Charitable institutions generally are excluded by compensation acts unless the acts are voluntarily accepted.
6. Contractors and subcontractors are usually excluded and should cover the risk by insurance.
7. Occupational diseases: The trend is to include this danger within the scope of the compensation acts.
8. Second injuries: Since it is unfair to impose the total cost of compensation on the latest employer, second injury funds have been created by almost all states. Consequently, the employer pays only for compensation resulting from the second injury, while the employee receives total compensation.
9. Actions against third parties: Acceptance of the workers' compensation act by the employee is in lieu of an action for damages against the employer and bars such suit.
   a. There is no prohibition against an action for damages against a third party whose negligence has caused an injury.
   b. If an employee accepts workmen's compensation benefits and sues the third party, she must reimburse the employer for the employee's compensation cost.
10. Coverage of minors under the workers' compensation laws: most acts cover minors and many provide double compensation or additional penalities if the minor is illegally employed.

11. Public employees: Many states provide a compensation for public employees or at least certain classes of them.

C. Insurance requirements for workers' compensation:

1. Nearly all states require the employer to obtain adaquate insurance or to submit proof of financial ability to carry its own risk, i.e., to "self-insure."

2. Several states have state funds, which the employer must insure with; others have state funds, but the employer may use a private insurance company in lieu thereof if he wishes.

D. Administration of claims:

1. There are two general methods.
   a. By the state judicial system (used in only a few states).
   b. By a compensation board or commission created by state law to specifically administer the workers' compensation laws.

2. The employer is required under penalty of law to report all injuries. In many jurisdictions the insurance companies take the burden off the employer after he has submitted the preliminary report to them.

3. The employee is required to give prompt notice of injury to the employer (not the insurance company), usually within 30 days.

4. The employee is also required to file his claim with the board or other appropriate authority within a period from 60 days to 2 years, depending upon the jurisdiction.
   a. Failure to file a timely claim may bar recovery unless the board waives the requirement.
   b. In other states the employee who fails to file a timely notice will be barred only if the failure to file is prejudicial to the employer.

5. Time at which the period begins to run in respect to 2, 3, and 4, above, is subject to a split of authority. Most commonly, the time the accident is first noticed is used instead of the time it occurred.

6. Claim must arise out of, and in course of, employment.
   a. Injuries arising while traveling to and from work are not covered.
   b. Out-of-state work is often covered.

E. Lawsuits for damages:

1. Employers who are required or accept coverage of the workers' compensation laws are generally exempt from damage suits by employees. This does not apply where employer's coverage is inadequate. Those who reject workers' compensation laws in elective jurisdictions are not obliged to pay compensation but are subject to suits for damages. In such cases the three common law defenses are not available to the employer. These are:
   a. Contributory negligence, i.e., the worker's own negligence caused the accident in whole or in part.
   b. The fellow servant (employee) doctrine, i.e., a fellow worker caused the injury.
   c. Assumption of the risk, i.e., by taking a hazardous job, the employee assumed the risk of being hurt.

2. Covers "on the job" injuries, i.e., those injuries to workers connected with, and arising out of, their work. Negligence, even if gross, is not a bar to recovery. However, intentionally self-inflicted injuries are not covered nor are injuries due to self-intoxication. The liability of the employer is a form of strict liability, i.e., the employer is liable even if the employer was not at fault.

3. Employees are not covered by workers' compensation while in transit to or from the employer's place of business. However, once the employee has arrived upon the employer's property, he is usually covered.

4. In the event the employee rejects workers' compensation coverage and the employer is required to provide it or has accepted it, the law generally allows the employer to resort to the above three common law defenses.

5. In about two-thirds of the states, the employee may sue for damages if the employer has failed to provide an adaquate self-insured compensation plan or has not paid for insurance coverage. The above defenses are not available.

6. Employer shares employee's right of action against third party after employee is compensated by workers' compensation to extent of benefits provided or as recovery is equitably apportioned by the court.

F. Types of benefits:

1. Disability benefits: Employee receives a percentage of his weekly wage. The benefits are:
   a. Subject to maximum and minimum weekly amounts.
   b. Payable for a stated maximum number of weeks unless there is a permanent total disability; in such a case, a few states provide for payment for life.

2. Death benefits: Schedules are usually provided containing a maximum and minimum benefit; in some states, payment is provided to a surviving spouse for life or until remarriage and to children until a specified age, normally 18.

3. Medical benefits: Necessary medical aid and care are required to be furnished to an injured employee. This is in addition to compensation or other benefits. Many states require this to be furnished without limit as to time or amount so long as the board finds it to be necessary.

4. Rehabilitation: If the employee is unable to engage in her previous occupation after the accident and recovery period, some states provide that she shall receive training, paid for by the state, to prepare her for another occupation.

5. Specified injuries: A schedule of compensation that covers the loss of certain members of the body is normally provided. This benefit is based solely upon the loss of the member and is not dependent upon the loss of earning power.

6. Waiting period: Most workers' compensation laws provide for a specified waiting period after injury before disability benefits are paid.
   a. This waiting period has no application to medical benefits, to which the employee is immediately entitled.
   b. If disability continues for a certain number of weeks, most states provide that weekly disability benefits are to be computed retroactively to the date of the injury.

Selected Problems from CPA Examinations on Regulation of the Employer-Employee Relationship

Subjective Questions and Answers

Q. 1. Eureka Enterprises, Inc., started doing business in July 1977. It manufactures electronic components and currently employs 35 individuals. In anticipation of future financing needs, Eureka has engaged a CPA firm to audit its financial statements. During the course of the examination, the CPA firm discovers that Eureka has no workmen's compensation insurance, which is in violation of state law, and so informs the president of Eureka.

Required
Answer the following, setting forth reasons for any conclusions stated.

1. What is the purpose of a state workmen's compensation law?
2. What are the legal implications of not having workmen's compensation insurance?

A. 1. Workmen's compensation laws provide a system of compensation for employees who are injured, disabled, or killed as a result of accidents or occupational diseases in the course of their employment. Benefits also extend to survivors or dependents of these employees.

2. In all but a distinct minority of jurisdictions, workmen's compensation coverage is mandatory. In those few jurisdictions that have elective workmen's compensation, employers who reject workmen's compensation coverage are subject to common law actions by injured employees and are precluded from asserting the defenses of fellow-servant, assumption of risk, and contributory negligence. The number of such jurisdictions having elective compensation coverage has been constantly diminishing. The penalty in those jurisdictions is the loss of the foregoing defenses.

The more common problem occurs in connection with the failure of an employer to secure compensation coverage even though he is obligated to do so in the majority of jurisdictions. The one uniform effect of such unwise conduct on the part of the employer is to deny him the use of the common law defenses mentioned above.

In addition to the foregoing, an increasing number of states have provided for the payment of workmen's compensation by the state to the injured employee of the uninsured employer. The state in turn proceeds against the employer to recover the compensation cost and to impose penalties that include fines and imprisonment. Other jurisdictions provide for a penalty in the form of additional compensation payments over and above the basic amounts, or they require an immediate lump-sum payment.

11/78

Q. 2. Henry was engaged by the Acme Corporation as a lathe operator. One day during regular working hours, he sustained a serious injury while trying to adjust a faulty mechanism on his lathe. Henry claims benefits under the Workmen's Compensation Law of the state in which he works.

Required
1. The Acme Corporation contests the claim on the grounds that Henry is an independent contractor and therefore not subject to the benefits available under the Workmen's Compensation Law. Henry contends that he is an employee of Acme Corporation. Discuss fully those factors that would be relevant in establishing that Henry is an employee rather than an independent contractor.

2. Assume that Henry is an employee. Acme Corporation, as employer, contests the claim on the grounds that Henry was grossly negligent in attempting to fix the faulty mechanism while the motor of the lathe was running. Will Henry recover? Explain.

A.   **1.** Basic to the distinction between the employer-employee relationship and that of the independent contractor is the degree of right to control retained over the physical conduct of the person performing the service. An employee is subject to control by his employer concerning the method of his performance; an independent contractor is a person who contracts to do a certain job according to his own judgment and methods. The independent contractor has the right to employ his own workmen and direct and control their actions independently of the other party to the contract. Thus, the independent contractor is free from any superior authority in the other party to the contract to say how the agreed upon work shall be done; as a primary contracting party he need only answer as to the result of his work.

2. Yes, Henry will recover. State laws governing workmen's compensation afford a method of compensating employees or their estates for accidental injuries or death due to and arising in the course of their employment. This right to recover is not barred by the employee's negligent conduct, even though such conduct consists of gross negligence. It is the fact that the injury occurred during the course of the employment (which the given facts describe) that gives the employee the right to recovery under the Workmen's Compensation Act.

11/64

Practice Question

Q. **1.** Yeats Manufacturing is engaged in the manufacture and sale of convertible furniture in interstate commerce. Yeats' manufacturing facilities are located in a jurisdiction which has a compulsory workmen's compensation act. Hardwood, Yeat's president, decided that the company should, in light of its safety record, choose to ignore the requirement of providing workmen's compensation insurance. Instead, Hardwood indicated that a special account should be created to provide for such contingencies. Basset was severely injured as a result of his negligent operation of a lathe which accelerated and cut off his right arm.

Required
Discuss Yeats' potential liability as a result of the accident and Yeats' failure to obtain Workers' Compensation insurance.

Practice Objective Questions

Instructions 1–15
Select the *best* answer for each of the following items. Mark only one answer for *each* item. Answer all items. Your grade will be based on your total correct answers.

1. During the 1976 examination of the financial statements of Viscount Manufacturing Corporation, the CPAs noted that although Viscount had 860 full-time and part-time employees, it had completely overlooked its responsibilities under the Federal Insurance Contributions Act (FICA). Under these circumstances, which of the following is true?

a. *No* liability under the act will attach if the employees voluntarily relinquish their rights under the act in exchange for a cash equivalent paid directly to them.

b. If the union which represents the employees has a vested pension plan covering the employees which is equal to or exceeds the benefits available under the act, Viscount has *no* liability.

c. Since employers and employees owe FICA taxes at the same rate and since the employer must withhold the employees' tax from their wages as paid, Viscount must remit to the government a tax double the amount assessed directly against the employer.

d. The act does *not* apply to the part-time employees.

2. The social security tax does *not* apply to which of the following?
   a. Payments on account of sickness including medical and hospital expenses paid by the employer.
   b. Compensation paid in forms other than cash.
   c. Self-employment income of $1,000.
   d. Bonuses and vacation time pay.

3. The theatrical agency of Power & Tyrone employs two people full time. Which of the following is true with regard to federal unemployment insurance?
   a. In terms of industry and number of employees, Power & Tyrone is within the class of employers covered by the federal unemployment tax.
   b. Service agencies are exempt.
   c. Since the number of employees is small, an exemption can be obtained from coverage if a request is filed with the appropriate federal agency.
   d. If the employees all reside in one state and do *not* travel interstate on company business, Power & Tyrone is exempt from compliance with the act.

4. The Social Security Act provides for the imposition of taxes and the disbursement of benefits. Which of the following is a correct statement regarding these taxes and disbursements?
   a. Only those who have contributed to Social Security are eligible for benefits.
   b. As between an employer and its employee, the tax rates are the same.
   c. A deduction for federal income tax purposes is allowed the employee for Social Security taxes paid.
   d. Social Security payments are includable in gross income for federal income tax purposes unless they are paid for disability.

5. Musgrove Manufacturing Enterprises is subject to compulsory worker's compensation laws in the state in which it does business. It has complied with the state's worker's compensation provisions. State law provides that where there has been compliance, worker's compensation is normally an exclusive remedy. However, the remedy will *not* be exclusive if
   a. The employee has been intentionally injured by the employer personally.
   b. The employer dies as a result of his injuries.
   c. The accident was entirely the fault of a fellow servant of the employee.
   d. The employer was only slightly negligent and the employee's conduct was grossly negligent.

6. Ichi Ban Mopeds, Inc., is a Japanese manufacturer which has a manufacturing facility in the United States. United States business comprises ten percent (10%) of the sales of Ichi Ban of which four percent (4%) is manufactured at its United States facility. Under these circumstances
   a. Ichi Ban is exempt from state workmen's compensation laws.
   b. Ichi Ban is exempt from the Fair Labor Standards Act provided it is governed by comparable Japanese law.
   c. Ichi Ban is subject to generally prevailing federal and state laws applicable to American employees with respect to its employees at the United States facility.
   d. Ichi Ban could legally institute a policy which limited promotions to Japanese-Americans.

7. Harris was engaged as a crane operator by the Wilcox Manufacturing Corporation, a company complying with state worker's compensation laws. Harris suffered injuries during regular working hours as a result of carelessly climbing out on the arm of the crane to make an adjustment. While doing so, he lost his balance, fell off the arm of the crane and fractured his leg. Wilcox's safety manual for the operation of the crane strictly forbids such conduct by an operator. Wilcox denies any liability, based upon Harris' gross negligence, his disobedience and a waiver of all liability signed by Harris shortly after the accident. Wilcox further asserts that Harris is *not* entitled to worker's compensation because he is a skilled worker and is on a guaranteed biweekly salary. Which of the following is a correct statement insofar as Harris' rights are concerned?
   a. If he elects to sue under common law for negligence, his own negligence will result in a denial of recovery.
   b. Harris is *not* entitled to worker's compensation because he is *not* an "employee."
   c. Harris is *not* entitled to recovery because his conduct was a clear violation of the safety manual.
   d. Harris waived his rights by signing a waiver of liability.

8. Which of the following is a correct statement regarding the federal income tax treatment of social security tax payments and retirement benefits?

   a. The employer's social security tax payments are *not* deductible from gross income.

   b. Social security retirement benefits are fully includable in the gross income of the retiree if he earns an amount in excess of certain established ceilings.

   c. Social security retirement benefits are excludable from the retiree's gross income even if the retiree has recouped all he has contributed.

   d. The employee's social security tax payments are deductible from the employee's gross income.

9. Which of the following provisions is a part of the Social Security law?

   a. Social Security benefits must be fully funded and payments, current and future, must constitutionally come only from Social Security taxes.

   b. Upon the death of an employee prior to his retirement, his estate is entitled to receive the amount attributable to his contributions as a death benefit.

   c. A self-employed person must contribute an annual amount which is less than the combined contributions of an employee and his or her employer.

   d. Social Security benefits are taxable as income when they exceed the individual's total contributions.

10. At age 66, Jonstone retired as a general partner of Gordon & Co. He no longer participates in the affairs of the partnership but does receive a distributive share of the partnership profits as a result of becoming a limited partner upon retirement. Jonstone has accepted a part-time consulting position with a corporation near his retirement home. Which of the following is correct regarding Jonstone's Social Security situation?

   a. Jonstone's limited partner distributive share will be considered self-employment income for Social Security purposes up to a maximum of $10,000.

   b. There is *no* limitation on the amount Jonstone may earn in the first year of retirement.

   c. Jonstone will lose $1 of Social Security benefits for each $1 of earnings in excess of a statutorily permitted amount.

   d. Jonstone will be subject to an annual earnings limitation until he attains a stated age which, if exceeded, will reduce the amount of Social Security benefits.

11. If an employer carried workmen's compensation coverage on his employees, an injured employee would:

   a. Probably be covered even if the injury was caused by a co-worker.

   b. *Not* be covered if the injury was caused by grossly negligent maintenance by the employer.

   c. Probably *not* be covered if the injury was due to a violation of plant rules in operating the machine.

   d. Be covered if the employee was driving to work from his home.

12. An employee was injured while working on a machine in his employer's plant. The employer carried workmen's compensation with Ace Casualty as the carrier. In this circumstance:

   a. If the injury was the fault of a third person covered by insurance, contribution is the usual method of apportioning the effect of the injury.

   b. The existence of workmen's compensation covering the injury precludes an action against the machine manufacturer if faulty design caused the injury.

   c. If the injury was covered, the employee normally has *no* cause of action for damages against the employer.

   d. Payment by the carrier usually subrogates the carrier to the injured worker's rights against a negligent employer.

13. The Federal Social Security Act applies in general to both employers and employees. Hexter Manufacturing is a small business as defined by the Small Business Administration. Regarding Hexter's relationship to the requirements of the Social Security Act, which of the following is correct?

   a. Since Hexter is a small business, it is exempt from the Social Security Act.

   b. Social Security payments made by Hexter's employees are tax deductible for federal income tax purposes.

   c. Hexter has the option to be covered or excluded from the provisions of the Social Security Act.

   d. The Social Security Act applies to both Hexter and its employees.

14. Wilton was grossly negligent in the operation of a drill press. As a result he suffered permanent disability. His claim for workmen's compensation will be

   a. Reduced by the percentage share attributable to his own fault.

   b. Limited to medical benefits.

   c. Denied.

   d. Paid in full.

15. Jones has filed a claim with the appropriate Workmen's Compensation Board against the Atlas Metal & Magnet Company. Atlas denies liability under the State Workmen's Compensation Act. In which of the following situations will Jones recover from Atlas or its insurer?

   a. Jones intentionally caused an injury to himself.

   b. Jones is an independent contractor.

   c. Jones is basing the claim upon a disease unrelated to the employment.

   d. Jones and another employee of Atlas were grossly negligent in connection with their employment, resulting in injury to Jones.

10

Federal Securities Acts

AICPA Content Specification Outline

Securities Registration
Reporting Requirements
Exempt Securities and Transactions

Contents

I. Registration under the Securities Act of 1933

A. Purpose:

1. The underlying purposes of the Act are to provide the investing public with the facts needed to evaluate the merit of the security being offered and to protect the investor from fraudulent or misleading statements by those seeking to sell the security.

2. The Act is popularly known as "the truth in securities law." It requires complete and honest disclosure to the public in marketing securities.

3. The SEC in no way passes on the merit or value of the securities being sold, nor on the wisdom of investing in them. Instead, the SEC seeks to ensure that the requisite information is available to investors so that they can make their own determination of whether or not to invest in the securities being marketed.

B. The Act's basic prohibition:

1. The Act forbids a public sale without a registration statement being duly and properly filed with the SEC and which has become effective prior to an offer to sell, and prior to sale, distribution, or solicitation to sell securities in interstate commerce.

2. In order to provide the investing public with the pertinent information contained in the registration statement, investors must be furnished a prospectus to enable them to make informed investment decisions.

3. The Act contains an antifraud provision that prohibits misrepresentation, deceit, and other fraud in the offer or sale of securities generally (whether or not registration is required). Note that the antifraud provision applies to offers or sales which are exempt from registration.

4. Where securities are marketed without complying with the registration and prospectus requirements of the Act, civil liability, administrative proceedings (i.e., stop orders), and criminal sanctions are provided. The parties responsible include, among others, the issuer, signers of the registration statement, directors, controlling persons, underwriters, and *accountants,* engineers, and other experts (see Accountant's Legal Responsibility, p. 11, III). Issuers are insurers, i.e., they are liable without fault, for any misrepresentations. The other parties also have a liability for misrepresentation that borders on that of an insurer. (See below.)

    5. Summary of the elements that determine whether there must be a registration:

      a. Is interstate commerce involved (e.g., use of the mails, telephone, stock exchange)?

      b. Are securities offered to the "public"?

      c. Is an issuer, controlling person, underwriter, or dealer involved? (See below).

      d. Is there an exemption available? (See below.)

C. Definitions:

    1. General: Much of the law in this area is either contained in, or depends upon, the definitions that follow.

    2. Security: The Act states a broad listing of known types of securities (e.g., stocks, bonds, etc.) or in general any interest commonly known as a "security" (e.g., a limited partnership interest) or any certificate of interest or participation in, temporary or interim certificate for, receipt for, guaranty of, or any warrant or right to subscribe to or purchase any of the foregoing.

    3. Person: again, broadly defined to include corporations, partnerships, trusts, and other entities within the term.

    4. Sale: includes a sale, offer to sell, and offer for sale. This term contains one major exclusion; preliminary negotiations or dealings between an issuer and underwriter. (The SEC has issued a rule that categorizes the typical merger or consolidation as a sale.)

    5. Interstate commerce: trade or commerce in securities or any transportation (e.g., use of the mails) or communication relating thereto, among the several states or territories of the United States (including Puerto Rico, the Virgin Islands, and the Canal Zone).

    6. Prospectus: any prospectus, notice, circular, advertisement, or letter of communication, in writing or by radio or television, that offers any security for sale or confirms the sale of any security. The prospectus is a liability document and consequently is couched in terms of hedges, limitations, and caveats. For special rules applicable to the so-called "red herring" prospectus, see p. 241, III.D.3. Liability may result from the issuance of a false or misleading prospectus even though the registration statement itself is correct.

    7. Issuer: any person who issues or proposes to issue any security. This includes foreign as well as domestic issuers and foreign governments and their instrumentalities. A "controlling person" (see 9, below) is included within this term and is deemed to be an issuer for registration purposes. The major impact of this functional categorization of controlling persons as issuers is the inclusion of secondary offerings by those who directly or indirectly control the corporation that actually issued the securities. The term is much broader than the conventional financial meaning of the term. In summation, it includes corporations or other entities and those who control them.

    8. Underwriter: any person who has purchased from an issuer *with a view to* the distribution of a security, or who offers to, or sells for, an issuer. Thus, a broker may be deemed to be an underwriter if he sells securities owned by a controlling person who in turn is deemed to be an issuer.

9. Controlling person: not defined in the Act, but is used in connection with the terms issuer and underwriter above. These three definitions must be read in conjunction with each other in order to grasp their full meaning and importance. The factors to be considered are:

a. Stock ownership is looked to first; majority ownership naturally constitutes control.

b. Actual or practical control, however, is the test. A 5% owner (or even less) may be a controlling person if he is on the board.

c. In general, a controlling person has the power to influence the management and policies of the issuer.

d. The power to exercise control is sufficient even if not exercised.

e. Whether the person or group in question could procure the signing of a registration statement.

f. If an officer and/or director is on the executive committee, a low percentage of stock would suffice.

g. Under Rule 405(f) the term "control" (including the terms "controlling," "controlled by," and "under common control with") means the possession, direct or indirect, of the power to direct or cause the direction of the management and policies of a person, whether through the ownership of voting securities, by contract, or otherwise. This is a question of fact.

10. Dealer: any person who engages either full- or part-time directly or indirectly as an agent, broker, or principal in the business of offering, buying or selling, or otherwise dealing or trading in securities issued by another person.

D. The registration process:

1. Preparation of the registration statement generally proceeds as follows:

a. Determine the proper form to be used, see III.D.6., below.

b. Follow Regulation S-K, augmented by industry guides, disclosure instructions.

c. Regulation S-X, together with Accounting Series Releases, set forth the form and content requirements for financial statements required to be filed.

d. Regulation C is then looked to in preparing and filing the particular registration statement.

2. Information generally required to be disclosed:

a. A description of the registrant's properties and business.

b. A description of the significant provisions of the security to be offered for sale and the relationship to the registrant's other capital securities.

c. Information about the management (directors and principal officers).

d. Financial statements (see the Accountant and the Law, p. 12, III.A.3).

3. Upon the filing of the registration statement and prospectus with the SEC, they become public information. However, it is unlawful to offer to sell prior to the effective date. However, the SEC permits the making of limited announcements of a proposed public offering pursuant to the future compliance with the registration process. In addition, a preliminary or "red herring" prospectus may be distributed between the time of the first filing with the SEC and the effective date.
date.

a. This time interval is commonly referred to as the "waiting period."

b. A legend in red is printed on this preliminary prospectus indicating that a registration statement has been filed but has not become effective.

c. Sales and offers to buy may not be made or accepted prior to the effective date.

4. Registration statements become effective on the 20th day after filing, or the 20th day after filing the last amendment. The SEC has the discretionary power to advance the effective date if it deems such action to be appropriate. Despite this short, 20-day period, significant delays may be encountered as a result of SEC requests for additional information or an amendment (deficiency letter).

5. Registration statements are examined in detail by the SEC's Division of Corporate Finance to ensure compliance with the disclosure requirements.

a. In the event the statement appears to be materially incomplete or inaccurate, the registrant is notified by letter and normally afforded an opportunity to amend.

b. The SEC has the power to refuse or suspend the effectiveness of any registration statement if it finds, after a hearing, that the registration statement is materially misleading, inaccurate, or incomplete. If the registration contains deliberate concealments or misrepresentations, a stop order will normally be issued suspending the effectiveness of the registration statement. The resultant delay will normally kill the offering.

6. The Integrated Disclosure System: Under the Securities Exchange Act of 1934, certain issuers are required to continue to report information about themselves after registration and distribution of an offering pursuant to the Securities Act of 1933. (See pp. 249–250.) In certain cases this registrant-oriented information may be incorporated by reference in a subsequent registration of a new offering by a prior issuer. Although there are several other forms for tailored situations (i.e., S-8 for employee benefit plans or S-18 for small businesses), there are three registration forms which constitute the basic framework for registration statements under the Securities Act:

a. Form S-1 requires complete disclosure and permits no incorporation by reference. It may be used by any registrants who choose to do so or for whom no other form is available.

b. Form S-2 combines reliance on incorporating Exchange Act reports by reference with delivery to purchasers of streamlined information. In general, if a registrant has been in the Exchange Act reporting system for the last three years it may:

   (1) Deliver a copy of its annual report along with the transaction-specific information in the prospectus; or

   (2) Present registrant-oriented information comparable to that of the annual report in the prospectus along with the description of the offering.

In either case, the more complete information about the registrant in the reports described in III.D.2 is incorporated by reference.

c. Form S-3 allows maximum use of incorporation by reference and requires the least disclosure to be presented in the prospectus. To be eligible to use Form

S-3 a registrant must meet the criterion of Form S-2 plus come under one of the following transactions:

(1) Offering by a registrant having at least $150 million of voting stock held by the public or, alternatively, $100 million or more and annual trading volume of such voting stock of 3 million shares or more;

(2) Nonconvertible debt and preferred securities that are of "investment grade," which is typically one of the four highest categories assigned by a nationally recognized statistical rating organization;

(3) Secondary offerings of securities listed on an exchange or quoted by the National Association of Securities Dealers. If the other requirements for use of Form S-3 are met, this eases the registration burden of a controlling person or a statutory underwriter. (See I.D.7, 8, and 9.)

(4) Certain specific other types of offerings, including dividend or interest reinvestment plans.

The S-3 prospectus is not required to present any information concerning the registrant unless there has been a material change which has not been filed in an Exchange Act report.

7. Shelf registration permits the registration of an amount of security that may reasonably be expected to be sold on a delayed or continuous basis over a two-year period. On matters such as changes in interest rates, redemption, maturities, and prices, the issuer can make the prospectus current by simply affixing a sticker. A posteffective amendment to the registration statement (printing a new prospectus) is only necessary if there is a material change in the contemplated manner of distribution. In addition, a posteffective amendment must be filed if the registration statement is not on Form S-3 (see I.D.6.c above) or on Form S-8 (employee benefit plans) of an issuer reporting under the Exchange Act (see III.D.2 below) if:

a. The information in the original registration statement is more than 16 months old after the first 9 months of registration; or

b. There is a "fundamental" change in the information in the registration statement.

8. State regulation of securities offerings. In addition to meeting federal registration requirements, the securities must be registered or cleared ("blue skied") in those states in which the securities are to be sold.

E. The antifraud provisions:

1. Broader in scope than the registration provisions, they apply to *all persons using interstate commerce,* means of communication (the telephone), or the mails to offer to sell, or to sell securities (the exemptions in III.A and B do not apply) if such persons, directly or indirectly:

a. Employ any device, scheme, or artifice to defraud.

b. Obtain money or other property by means of any untrue statement of a material fact or by the omission of a material fact deemed necessary to make the statements not misleading.

c. Engage in any transaction, practice, or course of business that operates as a fraud or deceit upon the purchaser.

   2. The 1933 Act's scienter requirement. In June 1980 the Supreme Court held that
   scienter was not required in a civil action by the SEC seeking injunctive relief
   under the 1933 Act's antifraud provisions indicated above in E.1.b. and c.
   Negligent conduct is sufficient. The scienter requirement for such SEC actions remains insofar as H.1.a. and Section 10(b) of the 1934 Act are concerned. This negligence standard only applies to SEC actions.

F. Criminal penalties:

   1. The Act contains criminal penalties of fine and imprisonment or both (maximum
   of $10,000 and five years—a felony) for any person who willfully:

   a. Violates the Act or the SEC's rules and regulations.

   b. Makes an untrue statement of any material fact in the registration statement
   or prospectus or fails to state any material fact deemed necessary to make the
   statement not misleading.

   c. Fails to register.

G. Civil liabilities:

   1. If the registration statement becomes effective and contains a false statement or
   omission of a material fact required to avoid misleading any person, then such
   person who is unaware of the false statement or omission of a material fact may
   sue in federal court. He may proceed against:

   a. The issuer or one deemed to be an issuer;

   b. Any person who signed the registration statement;

   c. Any director of the issuer or a person who consents to being named in the
   registration statement as about to become one;

   d. Any accountant, attorney, engineer, appraiser, or other expert for any
   authorized statement made by him in the prospectus or for any certification or
   valuation used in the registration statement;

   e. Every underwriter of the security.

   f. The SEC has no power to award or to recover damages.

   2. The basis for the suit is an alleged false statement or omission of a material fact in
   the registration statement.

   a. Such a claim by the party suing (the plaintiff) establishes a *prima facie* case,
   i.e., one that will suffice unless contradicted by other evidence.

   b. Thus, the plaintiff does not have the usual burden of proving that the
   defendants (issuers, directors, and other parties) were negligent or fraudulent.

   c. Plaintiff need not prove reliance upon the financial statement or that the loss
   suffered was the proximate result of the false statement or misleading
   omission, but he must not have taken with actual knowledge.

   d. In effect, much of the burden of proof typically required of a plaintiff has
   been shifted to the defendant. Insofar as an issuer is concerned, the fact that
   negligence is not present is irrelevant.

   3. The "due diligence" defense: No person, *other than the issuer,* shall be liable if
   he can sustain the following burden of proof:

   a. Issuers have no defenses with the exception of showing the plaintiff knew of
   the falsity or omission. Normally this defense either does not exist or is not
   provable.

    b. Those who sign the statement, directors, and underwriters, to the extent of their underwriting commitment, can assert the "due diligence" defense and if they can prove they exercised "due diligence" can avoid liability.

      (1) Regarding parts of the registration statement not purporting to be made by an expert, he had, *after reasonable investigation, reasonable ground to believe and did believe* the registration statements to be true and not to contain any omission of material fact.

      (2) Regarding parts of the registration statement purporting to be made on the authority of an expert (other than himself), he had no reasonable ground to believe and did not believe that the expert's statements were untrue or contained any omission of material fact.

    c. Experts: Regarding authorized statements, reports, valuations or certifications by an expert in the registration statement, he will not be liable if he had, after reasonable investigation, reasonable grounds to believe and did believe that the statements he made were true and did not contain any omission of material fact. For further discussion of the liability of an expert, see Accountant's Legal Responsibility, p. 14, III.A.9.

4. The standard of reasonableness is that required of a prudent man in the management of his own property. Judicial elaboration on this general test is contained in the *Bar Chris* case.

5. Generally, recovery, where a registration containing a false statement or omission has been filed and becomes effective, is based upon the difference between the amount paid for the security (not exceeding the price at which the security was offered to the public) and

    a. The value at the time of suit, or

    b. The value at the time the security was disposed of prior to suit, and

    c. In no event may recovery exceed the price at which the security was offered to the public.

6. In addition to the above liability, the Act provides:

    a. That any person who offers or sells a security in violation of the Act's registration requirement by failing to file a required registration statement; (see p. 14, III.A.10) shall be liable to the person suing for:

      (1) The amount paid, plus interest, less the amount of income received upon tender of the security (rescission).

      (2) Damages if the party no longer owns the security.

    b. The same liability indicated above in 6.a (rescission) applies to offers or sales of securities (whether or not exempted) in interstate commerce or by use of the mails, by the means of a prospectus or oral communication that contains an untrue statement or omission of a material fact.

7. The Act contains a two-part statute of limitations, which bars actions under its provisions.

    a. First, any action must be brought within one year after discovery of the untrue statement or omission, or after such discovery should have been made by the exercise of reasonable diligence. In cases where there is a failure to register, within one year after the violation upon which the suit is based.

    b. Second, in no event can an action be brought more than three years after the security was offered in good faith to the public.

II. The 1933 Act's Exempt Securities and Transactions

A. **Exempt securities:** The 1933 Act provides a number of types of securities that are exempted for various policy reasons. The chief reasons for exemption are that the issuer is regulated by another government agency, the issuer is such that the normal protection is not deemed necessary, or in the case of commercial paper, common sense, convenience, and necessity. Despite the presence of a valid exemption, the securities exempted are subject to the Act's *antifraud* provisions. The following securities are exempt from registration:

1. Securities sold prior to July 17, 1933.
2. Securities of federal, territorial, state, and local governments and their public instrumentalities, banks, carriers, building and loan associations, and farm cooperatives.
3. Commercial paper, i.e., checks, notes, and similar paper arising out of a current transaction and that have a maturity not exceeding nine months.
4. Securities issued by charitable, religious, educational and other similar organizations.
5. Insurance and conventional annuity contracts; however, variable annuities have twice been held to be "securities" by the Supreme Court.
6. Any security exchanged by the issuer with its existing holders exclusively where no commission or remuneration is paid or given directly or indirectly for soliciting such exchanges (e.g., a stock split or other common type of recapitalization).
7. Securities issued in reorganizations that are subject to court control (e.g., a Chapter 11 reorganization pursuant to the Bankruptcy Act).
8. Intrastate issues of securities: where the issuing corporation and all persons to whom the issue is offered reside in one state or territory and the entire distribution is completed therein. As a warning, it must be pointed out that the intrastate exemption is both complex and difficult to attain. Furthermore, if the offer or sale of any of the securities in question does not qualify for the intrastate exemption, the exemption is lost for the entire issue. The SEC further requires that no resales be made within nine months of the distribution to nonresidents.
9. The SEC may, pursuant to its own regulations, exempt a transaction if it is deemed to be unnecessary for public protection and such issue does not exceed $1.5 million. In order to obtain such an exemption, the issuer must meet the requirements contained in Regulation A, issued pursuant to the 1933 Act. Although the requirements in Regulation A are not as onerous or as costly as a full registration, the investor is amply protected and liability is the same as that provided for violation in connection with a full registration. Sales must be made via the use of an offering circular, which is a substitute for the prospectus. Accompanying financials usually need not be audited. (Securities of SBIC'S may be exempted.)
10. Regulation D is a series of six rules, designated 501–506, establishing three exemptions. Rules 501–503 set forth definitions, terms, and conditions that apply generally throughout the regulation. Rules 504 and 505 provide "safe

harbors" for the small offering exemption and Rule 506 sets forth standards for transactions exempted as private placements.

a. Rule 504 exempts up to $500,000 of securities sold in a 12-month period to any number of investors. No general solicitation is allowed, and the securities are restricted as to resale unless the offering is conducted exclusively in states where it is registered under "blue sky" laws requiring delivery of a disclosure document. No specific disclosure is required by Rule 504.

b. Rule 505 exempts up to $5,000,000 in a 12-month period and Rule 506 allows private placement of an unlimited amount. Both rules permit sales to 35 purchasers that are not accredited investors and to an unlimited number of accredited investors. Rule 506 additionally requires that each purchaser who is not an accredited investor either alone or with his purchaser representative have such knowledge and experience in financial and business matters that he is capable of evaluating the merits and risks of the investment. Accredited investors are:

(1) Institutional investors such as banks and insurance companies or pension funds with assets over $5,000,000.

(2) Private business development companies such as venture capital funds.

(3) Tax exempt organizations such as endowment funds with assets over $5,000,000.

(4) Directors, executive officers, or general partners of an issuer.

(5) A purchaser of at least $150,000 of the securities if the price does not exceed 20% of the investor's net worth.

(6) An individual whose net worth is at least $1,000,000.

(7) An individual who had an income in excess of $200,000 in each of the last two years and expects over $200,000 the current year.

Under both Rule 505 and Rule 506 no general solicitation is permitted and the security is restricted as to resale. If the security is purchased solely by accredited investors, the rules require no specific disclosure; however, if a nonaccredited investor purchases, audited statements and information similar to Form S-18 must be supplied. All Regulation D offerings require filing Form D with the SEC as a condition of exemption. Regulation D offerings lose their exemption if there is a prompt reoffering to the public. The purchaser would be characterized as an underwriter.

The practice is to obtain from the offerees a so-called investment letter which manifests an intent to take for investment and not for resale. The securities themselves usually bear a legend stating they have not been registered and referring to restrictions on transferability ("letter stock"). Such statements are not conclusive. The securities generally must be held for at least two years. The investment letter is important, but not nearly as important as what the purchaser actually does with the security. To avoid becoming a "statutory underwriter" the regulation D purchaser should conform to Rule 144, discussed below.

B. Exempt transactions:

1. Transactions by any person other than an issuer, underwriter, or dealer: If a person is not within one of the above-proscribed classes of people, he may sell his securities with impunity, i.e., he need not file a registration statement, nor is he required to sell via a prospectus. This broad exemption covers the overwhelming preponderance of sales by investors. It does not cover "a controlling person" of the issuer if he is categorized as an underwriter or sells through someone who would be deemed an underwriter. Transactions involving a "controlling person" represent the most controversial and legally significant part of this otherwise broad exemption. Reread the definitions of issuer, underwriter, and controlling person (see above, pp. 240–241).

   a. A "controlling person" holds "restricted stock," i.e., stock that normally cannot be disposed of without registration (e.g., a secondary offering by a majority owner). This is the case whether the stock was bought from the issuer or in the open market, or whether held for many years or previously registered.

   b. A controlling person may be categorized as an underwriter if he sells significant amounts of his restricted stock to the public. Thus, the exemption will be unavailable.

   c. Similarly, if the controlling person sells restricted stock in the open market through his broker, the exemption will again be lost, since the broker may be categorized as an underwriter and the controlling person becomes an issuer. In order to permit limited sales by controlling persons, the SEC issued Rule 144, which is discussed next.

2. Brokers' transactions involving "controlling persons" who hold restricted securities: The SEC pursuant to its rule-making function promulgated Rule 144 relating to a "controlling person's" sale of limited amounts of stock in the open market through a broker. The Act, as previously indicated, had exempted an individual's broker transactions where an issuer, including a "controlling person," underwriter or dealer was not involved. However, no provision in the Act exempted sales by "controlling persons" without a registration statement being filed unless it constituted a private placement as discussed above. Rule 144 permits limited sales by "controlling persons" through a broker if the following requirements are met:

   a. The broker performs only the usual functions, i.e., executes the order on an agency basis as the seller's broker and receives only the "usual or customary" broker's commission. He does not act as a principal and does not solicit people to purchase the securities.

   b. The controlling person pays the usual commission and does not, at least as far as is known to the broker, pay any additional amount to anyone else.

   c. The securities must be owned or beneficially owned for a period of at least 2 years by the person for whose account they are sold.

   d. The amount shall not exceed 1% of the class outstanding, or if traded on an exchange, the lesser of that amount or the average weekly volume on all such exchanges during the four weeks preceding the sale.

   e. Finally, adequate information about the issuer (corporation) must be available to the public and notice of sale must be filed with the SEC concurrently with the sale.

f. In effect, by meeting all of the above requirements, *the broker is exempt,* i.e., he is not deemed to be an underwriter, and this exemption inures to the benefit of the "controlling person," thereby permitting sales of limited amounts of stock by those who are in control of the issuer (corporation).

3. Certain postregistration transactions by a dealer (including an underwriter no longer so acting). These include transactions that:

a. Occur at least 40 days after the first date the security was *bona fide* (i.e., in compliance with the Act) offered to the public by the issuer or through an underwriter.

b. Occur at least 40 days after a registration statement has become effective in respect to the security, unless securities of the issuer have not been previously sold pursuant to an earlier effective registration statement (i.e., this is the issuer's first public offering). In such cases, i.e., an initial public offering, the applicable period is 90 days.

c. Unsolicited broker or dealer transactions at any time. This exemption applies only to the broker's or dealer's part in the transaction. The selling customer must still establish he or she is not an issuer, underwriter, or dealer.

III. The Securities Exchange Act of 1934

A. General: The 1934 Act, in addition to creating the SEC, is concerned with:

1. The integrity of the markets for outstanding securities including the national stock exchanges and over-the-counter markets.

2. The integrity of the proxy and tender offer machinery inherent in the operation of a growing corporate democracy.

3. The dealing by insiders in the stocks of their companies.

4. The regulation of broker-dealers, including the hypothecation (pledge) of customers' securities, the regulation of short selling, and the financial responsibility of broker-dealers.

5. The engaging in foreign corrupt practices by American corporations doing business abroad.

B. Applicability: The Act's original scope has been substantially increased as a result of amendments. Some of the Act's provisions apply to any person using interstate commerce. Other provisions apply exclusively to those required to register or who have their securities registered with the SEC.

C. The registration requirement:

1. National securities exchanges (e.g., the New York Stock Exchange) must register. This makes the Act applicable to members, brokers, and dealers of these exchanges.

2. Brokers and dealers engaged in interstate commerce must register.

3. Securities traded on any national securities exchange must be registered.

4. Securities of any issuer having in excess of $3 million in assets and a class of equity securities held by more than 500 persons. Corporations not required to register are not subject to many of the Act's requirements, e.g., reporting insider trading, the accurate records requirements of the Foreign Corrupt Practices Act, and the rules on proxies. However, the antifraud provisions still apply.

D. Reporting requirements:

1. Companies required to register their securities (indicated in C.3 and C.4, above) must file a registration application with the exchange on which the securities are traded and with the SEC or if they are not traded on an exchange, with the SEC.

    a. The SEC's rules prescribe the nature and content of these registration statements, including audited financials.

    b. The required data is generally comparable to, but less extensive than, the disclosure requirements required in the 1933 Securities Act registration.

2. Periodical and other reports.

    a. Annual reports. Every issuer whose securities are registered must file an annual report Form 10-K for each fiscal year after the last full fiscal year for which financial statements were filed in the registration statement. Normally, the report must be filed within 120 days after the close of the fiscal year, and the financial statements must be certified by independent certified public accountants. Annual reports to shareholders must include these financials.

    b. Quarterly reports. Financial statements (balance sheets, earning and profits, and other financial matters) must be filed. These need not be certified.

    c. Current reports. A current report of certain specified corporate and financial events must be filed within 10 days after the close of the month in which they occur.

3. The Act also requires that reports be filed for three years after a registration statement by issuers who have 300 or more equity shareholders.

E. The antifraud provisions:

1. Section 10b of the Act in conjunction with Rule 10b-5 represents the most controversial, dynamic, and ill-defined area of the Act. Without a doubt, the antifraud provisions have caused a virtual revolution in respect to corporate directors', officers', and others' responsibilities to the shareholders of the corporation.

2. The Act provides: "It shall be unlawful for any person . . . by the use . . . of interstate commerce or the mails, or any facility of any national securities exchange, to use or employ [in respect to any security] any manipulative or deceptive device or contrivance in contravention of such rules and regulations as the SEC may prescribe as necessary and appropriate in the public interest or for the protection of investors."

3. Obviously, Section 10b of the Act leaves much to be desired in the way of guidance and clarity. Therefore, pursuant to the SEC's rule-making authority, it promulgated the following rule involving the employment of manipulative and deceptive devices. Rule 10b-5 makes it unlawful for any person to:

    a. Employ any device, scheme, or artifice to defraud;

    b. Make any untrue statement of a material fact or omit to state a material fact necessary in order to make the statements made, in light of the circumstances under which they were made, not misleading; or

      c. Engage in any act, practice, or course of business which operates or would operate as fraud or deceit on any person in connection with the *purchase or sale* of any security.

4. Purpose: These provisions seek to curb misrepresentations and deceit, market manipulation, and other fraudulent acts and practices, and to establish and maintain just and equitable principles of trade conducive to the maintenance of open, fair, and orderly markets. Pursuant to this end, the SEC's rules and regulations seek to:

      a. Afford a remedy to a defrauded *seller* or buyer; the 1933 Act's provisions protected the buyer; this provision closed the previously existing loophole in respect to sellers.

      b. Define acts or practices that constitute a "manipulative or deceptive device or contrivance" prohibited by the Act.

5. Scope: The 1934 Act's antifraud provisions apply to all transactions involving interstate commerce, the mails, or transactions on any national exchange involving the purchase *or* sale of securities. Thus, the securities need not be registered for the Act's prohibitions to apply and it covers *any person,* not just insiders, as defined in the short-swing profit provisions.

6. In order to prevail under the antifraud provisions, the plaintiff:

      a. Need not establish all the elements of common law fraud (see Contracts, p. 152, IV.D). Some need not be proved at all and others have been substantially watered down. For example, a specific intent to injure the plaintiff need not be proved. However, scienter must be established.

      b. Must show that a purchase or sale was made based upon materially false, misleading, or undisclosed information. In effect, if there is a materially false statement or omission, all that is required of the plaintiff is that he did not know it.

      c. May seek recourse from any person who has made unfair use of material information that is undisclosed or about which a false or misleading statement has been issued. In general, virtually anyone (e.g., an employee such as a geologist who has discovered a significant find and is in possession of material information obtained in the course of his employment) is an insider within the meaning of the antifraud provisions. It also applies to undisclosed, false, or misleading bad news.

      d. Is not obligated to show that the insider's purchase or sale was made on a face-to-face basis. Typically, the transaction would be made on a national securities exchange or through a brokerage house in an over-the-counter market. No direct communication or lack thereof to the plaintiff is required. An intent to injure the plaintiff is not required.

      e. Scienter must be established. This can be done by showing that the defendant had actual knowledge of falsity or that the false statement was made with a reckless disregard of the truth.

7. Materiality: The determination of what is material inside information is crucial. Unfortunately, the Act does not define the term. In the leading case under Section 10b (*Texas Gulf Sulphur*) the Second Circuit Court defined the meaning of materiality in the following terms:

    a. "The basic test of materiality . . . is whether a reasonable man would attach importance . . . in determining his choice of action in the transaction in question. . . . This, of course encompasses any fact . . . which in reasonable and objective contemplation might affect the value of the corporation's stock or securities. . . . Thus, material facts include not only information disclosing the earnings and distribution of a company, but also those facts which affect the probable future of the company and those which may affect the desire of investors to buy, sell, or hold the company's securities."

    b. The court also indicated: ". . . whether facts are material within Rule 10b-5 when the facts relate to a particular event and are undisclosed by those persons who are knowledgeable thereof will depend at any given time upon a balancing of both the indicated probability that the event will occur and its impact in the light of the totality of the company activity. . . ."

    c. However, in a recent Supreme Court case *(TSC Industries v. Nordway)* the court defined the term material in relation to proxy statements as follows: "An omitted fact is material if there is a *substantial likelihood* that a reasonable shareholder would consider it important in deciding how to vote." It is believed that this stricter standard will apply to Section 10b.

    d. Court cases: Examples of the type of undisclosed information that has been deemed material include:

        (1) A significant ore strike, categorized as one of the most important in modern times.

        (2) The fact that there was a corporate contract for the sale of its assets to a third party at a higher price per share.

        (3) A dividend cut.

        (4) The fact that a merger was in the offing.

    e. The New York Stock Exchange and the American Exchange have listed types of information that must be reported by the companies listed on these exchanges.

8. Nondisclosure: At present there is no specific statutory duty on the part of the corporation, directors, and other insiders (with the exceptions indicated below) to affirmatively disclose material information. However, the law is in a state of flux; conceivably, such a duty might be imposed by the courts. An SEC release strongly urged disclosure of material information even if all parties forgo trading.

    a. Assuming that the facts are material and that they are not disclosed, all corporate insiders (any persons connected with the corporation and having such inside information) must forgo any trading in the stock of the corporation.

    b. These would obviously include directors, officers, shareholders, other corporate employees, lawyers, accountants, geologists, and engineers who are aware of the material information.

    c. The prohibition would also preclude tipping by such persons; although the insider does not trade personally, relatives and friends may be informed and trade with knowledge of the undisclosed material information. Furthermore, the tippees who received the information from the insider must forgo trading in the security or face potential liability under the Act.

    d. As discussed above, the stock exchanges have reporting requirements that apply to their listed corporations. It has been suggested that the New York Stock Exchange reporting requirements will be used by the courts in all cases involving nondisclosure under Rule 10b-5, thereby making them generally applicable to all corporations whether listed or not. Although the law is still being clarified at present, it seems clear that nondisclosure, even when the information is not used for trading by the corporate insiders and others, poses a serious legal problem and a potential liability. Furthermore, the 1934 Act, although it may not specifically require immediate disclosure of significant events as they occur, does require:

      (1) The annual filing of Form 10-K, which calls for full financial statements, but only limited disclosures in other areas.

      (2) Monthly (8K) and quarterly (10Q) reporting, but of a very limited nature.

      (3) A fairly limited disclosure pursuant to the proxy rules.

   9. False or misleading press releases and disclosures: Obviously, if insiders must forgo trading in the stock of the corporation to which they have material inside information and fail to disclose it, it is even more apparent that the issuance of false or misleading information will result in liability to those profiting by it.

Selected Problems from CPA Examinations on Federal Securities Regulation

Subjective Questions and Answers

Q. 1. Various Enterprises Corporation is a medium sized conglomerate listed on the American Stock Exchange. It is constantly in the process of acquiring smaller corporations and is invariably in need of additional money. Among its diversified holdings is a citrus grove which it purchased eight years ago as an investment. The grove's current fair market value is in excess of $2 million. Various also owns 800,000 shares of Resistance Corporation which it acquired in the open market over a period of years. These shares represent a 17% minority interest in Resistance and are worth approximately $2½ million. Various does its short-term financing with a consortium of banking institutions. Several of these loans are maturing; in addition to renewing these loans, it wishes to increase its short-term debt from $3 to $4 million.

    In light of the above, Various is considering resorting to one or all of the following alternatives in order to raise additional working capital.

- An offering of 500 citrus grove units at $5,000 per unit. Each unit would give the purchaser a 0.2% ownership interest in the citrus grove development. Various would furnish management and operation services for a fee under a management contract and net proceeds would be paid to the unit purchasers. The offering would be confined almost exclusively to the state in which the groves are located or in the adjacent state in which Various is incorporated.

- An increase in the short-term borrowing by $1 million from the banking institution which currently provides short-term funds. The existing debt would be consolidated, extended, and increased to $4 million and would mature over a nine-month period. This would be evidenced by a short-term note.

- Sale of the 17% minority interest in Resistance Corporation in the open market through its brokers over a period of time and in such a way so as to minimize decreasing the value of the stock. The stock is to be sold in an orderly manner in the ordinary course of the broker's business.

Required

Answer the following, setting forth reasons for any conclusions stated.

In separate paragraphs discuss the impact of the registration requirements of the Securities Act of 1933 on each of the above proposed alternatives.

A.   The impact of the registration requirements of the Securities Act of 1933 on each of the proposals is as follows:
- The offering of the participation units in the citrus groves, although ostensibly the sale of an interest in land, constitutes an offer to sell, or the sale of, securities within the meaning of Section 2 of the Securities Act of 1933. Although land itself is not a security, the offering of the land in conjunction with a management contract has been held to constitute the offering of a security. Since interstate commerce and communications are to be used and since there is no apparent transactional exemption available, a registration under the 1933 Act is required. Whatever hope there was of an intrastate offering exclusion is dashed by the fact that the units will be offered and sold in two states.
- The short-term borrowings evidenced by the promissory notes of Various Enterprises are exempt from registration. This exemption from categorization as a security for purposes of registration under the act applies to commercial paper such as notes, drafts, checks, and similar paper arising out of a current transaction that have a maturity not exceeding nine months. In addition, the private placement exemption is applicable.
- If Various is deemed to be a controlling person insofar as Resistance is concerned, it must register the securities in question before it can legally sell them. The Securities Act of 1933 provides in connection with its definition of the term "underwriter," that, "the term 'issuer' shall include, in addition to an issuer, any person directly or indirectly controlling or controlled by the issuer, or any person under direct or indirect common control with the issuer."

     Securities Act rule 405(f) further defines the term "control." It states that "the term 'control' . . . means the possession, direct or indirect, of the power to direct or cause the direction of the policies of a person, whether through the ownership of voting securities, by contract, or otherwise." It is obvious that "control" as defined is a question of fact. In general, a controlling person has the power to influence the management and policies of the issuer. If an individual is an officer, director, or member of the executive committee, a low percentage of stock would suffice. Actual or practical control is sufficient and the power to exercise control will also be sufficient even if it is not exercised. Stock ownership is looked to and majority ownership naturally constitutes control. Although ownership of 17% of the stock is certainly not conclusive, it is a substantial block of stock and, if any of the above factors is also present, it would be most likely that Various would be a controlling person. Thus, although not the issuer of the stock, it would need to register the securities. This resembles a secondary offering of a large block by the owners of the corporation. This sale through the brokers will in no way insulate the transaction from registration.

5/82

Q. **2.** Marigold Corporation is incorporated in one of the states of the United States and does substantially all of its business within that state. It is considering reliance upon the intrastate exemption to the Securities Act of 1933 in order to offer and sell its securities without registering them under the 1933 Act. Its proposed offering will consist of $800,000 of common stock and $1 million of debentures. Most of the people it has talked to about the feasibility of such an offering are very wary of such a course of action and warn of significant limitations and dangers inherent in such action.

Required

Answer the following, setting forth reasons for any conclusions stated.

1. What are the requirements, limitations, and problems that are typically encountered in an intrastate offering?
2. Even if the Securities Act's requirements for the exemption can be satisfied, what must be done from the standpoint of state law?

A. **1.** The Securities Act of 1933 exempts from registration "any security which is part of an issue offered and sold only to persons resident within a single state . . . where the issuer of such security is a corporation incorporated by and doing business within such state." If an offering otherwise qualifies for this exemption, the use of the facilities of interstate commerce is permitted. According to the facts, Marigold could qualify for the intrastate exemption.

However, very strict requirements apply to the offerees and purchasers: They must all be "residents" of the single state in question. Consequently, an offer to one nonresident can nullify the entire exemption. Meticulous care must be taken to ensure that no offers or sales are made to nonresidents, which, from a practical standpoint, may be extremely difficult to ascertain. A further limitation applies to issuers. Since the underlying rationale of the exemption as articulated by the SEC is "to provide for local financing for local industries carried out through local investment," the judicial and administrative interpretations of "doing business" have been strict. Essentially, the SEC has ruled that an issuer is doing business within the state if it derives 80% of its revenues from the state, has 80% of its assets within the state, and intends to use 80% of the proceeds from the offering within the state, and has its principal office within the state.

Were the above requirements and limitations not enough, an added requirement regarding resale of the distributed securities must be satisfied. In effect, there must not be a resale of the securities to nonresidents for a period of nine months.

2. Even if an exemption to federal registration is available, state law must be complied with. State securities laws popularly known as "blue sky" laws are not entirely uniform; however, at least a minimum filing generally will be required as well as a clearance to offer and sell the securities within the state.

5/81

Q. **3.** The directors of Clarion Corporation, their accountants, and their attorneys met to discuss the desirability of this highly successful corporation going public. In this connection, the discussion turned to the potential liability of the corporation and the parties involved in the preparation and signing of the registration statement under the Securities Act of 1933. Craft, Watkins, and Glenn are the largest shareholders. Craft is the Chairman of the Board; Watkins is the Vice Chairman; and Glenn is the Chief Executive Officer. It has been decided that they will sign the registration statement. There are two other directors who are also executives and shareholders of the corporation. All of the board members are going to have a percentage of their shares included in the offering. The firm of Witherspoon & Friendly, CPAs, will issue an opinion as to the financial statements of the corporation which will accompany the filing of the registration statement, and Blackstone & Abernathy, Attorneys-at-Law, will render legal services and provide any necessary opinion letters.

Required
Answer the following, setting forth reasons for any conclusions stated.
Discuss the types of potential liability and defenses pursuant to the Securities Act of 1933 that each of the above parties or classes of parties may be subject to as a result of going public.

A. The Securities Act of 1933 permits an aggrieved party to sue various parties connected with the registration statement for an untrue statement of a material fact in the registration statement or the omission of a material fact required to be stated therein or necessary to make the statements therein not misleading. Those having potential liability include issuers of the security, those who signed the registration statement, every director, underwriter, and expert.

Any acquirer of the security may sue unless it is proved that at the time of such acquisition he knew of such untruth or omission.

Since all the directors and signers are also issuers along with the corporation, they may be sued in that capacity, since with the one exception mentioned above, issuers may not avoid liability for untrue statements or omissions. They are insurers of the truth contained in the registration statement; that is, they are liable without fault.

Contrast their liability with that of the accountants and lawyers who are both experts. As such, they are not liable for parts of the registration statement on which they did not render an expert opinion. Moreover, as experts, they have the benefit of the "due diligence" defense. That is, liability can be avoided if it can be shown by the expert that he had, after reasonable investigation, reasonable ground to believe and did believe at the time such part of the registration statement became effective that the parts for which he gave expert opinion were true and that there was no omission to state a material fact required to be stated.

The Act also provides certain defenses based on the amount of damages and their relationship to the misstatements or omissions.

5/80

Q. 4. Glover Corporation is a small, rapidly-expanding manufacturing company. In 1977 Glover made a public offering of its shares for $400,000 in accordance with Regulation A, issued by the Securities and Exchange Commission pursuant to the Securities Act of 1933. The shares are not listed on any exchange, but are sometimes bought and sold in interstate commerce. At the end of 1977 Glover had total assets of $900,000, 429 shareholders, and sales of $650,000 for the year.

Required
Answer the following, setting forth reasons for any conclusions stated.

1. What is a Regulation A offering and what are the general requirements which must be met in order to qualify for making such an offering?
2. What difference is there in the potential liability of the parties making an offering under Regulation A as contrasted with a full registration?
3. What are the time limitations in which an aggrieved party may commence an action for failure to comply with the Securities Act of 1933?
4. What are the major provisions of the Securities Exchange Act of 1934 which do *not* apply to Glover and its officers, directors, and principal shareholders after the public offering and which major provisions do apply?

A. 1. The Securities Act of 1933 gives the Securities and Exchange Commission authority to exempt certain small public offerings from full registration. The dollar amount of the offering may not exceed $1.5 million (until recently increased, this amount was $500,000). In order to obtain an exemption, the issuer must meet the filing requirements contained in Regulation A. These requirements are not as onerous as a full registration, although considerable documentation is required. The financial statements generally need not be audited, and supplemental disclosures are not as extensive. Sales must be made only by an offering circular, which is similar to a prospectus, and it must be supplied to each purchaser.

2. None. The same liability for a false statement or a material omission that applies to a full registration applies to a Regulation A offering.

3. The act contains a two-part statute of limitations. First, any action must be brought within one year after discovery of the untrue statement or omission or after such discovery should have been made by the exercise of reasonable diligence. Second, in no event can an action be brought more than three years after the security was bought in good faith.

4. Because of its size [less than $1 (now $3 million) million assets and less than 500 shareholders] and the fact that it is not listed on a national stock exchange, Glover is not required to register under the Securities Exchange Act of 1934. Consequently, it is not subject to the act's corporate reporting requirements, proxy rules, insider trading provisions, or tender rules. However the antifraud provisions of the act apply.

11/78

Practice Questions

Q. 1. Otis Corporation has grown steadily and Mr. Parker, its chairman and president, is seeking additional capital of $800,000 for further expansion. To achieve this goal, he rejected other forms of financing and decided to issue new preferred stock. In this connection, he raises the following questions:

1. In light of the high expenses incidental to an SEC registration of a first public offering of securities, are there any viable alternatives to this method of selling the preferred stock?
2. From the standpoint of both the issuers and the purchasers, what are the federal income tax consequences of issuing preferred stock instead of debt assuming that the purchasers of the stock will include other corporations as well as individuals?

Required
Answer the following, setting forth reasons for any conclusions stated.
     What response should be given to Mr. Parker's questions?

Q. 2. Darius Corporation has 1,000,000 shares of common stock outstanding of which 450,000 shares are publicly traded over the counter and 550,000 are owned by Lynn, its president. The market price of the stock has ranged from $3 to $4 per share over the past year. Lynn obtained his Darius shares on August 10, 1976, when Darius acquired a company wholly owned by Lynn pursuant to an exchange of 550,000 Darius shares for all of the shares of Lynn's company. The Darius shares received by Lynn were unregistered and contained a legend which restricted transfer except on the opinion of counsel that the shares were transferable. The number of Darius shares held by the public was 450,000 both before and after the August 10 exchange.

On September 22, 1976, Archer & Co., Lynn's broker, purchased from Lynn, for its own account and in ten separate transactions, a total of 10,000 shares of Darius at $4.50 per share. The next day Archer purchased from Lynn in eight separate transactions an additional 8,000 shares in total at $5.50 per share, again for its own account. These were the only transactions on September 22 and 23, and trading in Darius shares over the counter had otherwise been light in recent months. On September 24, 1976, Archer circulated a story that there was an active demand for Darius shares. Within a few days, Darius stock was quoted over the counter at $9 per share.

On September 30, 1976, Archer sold, as agent for Lynn, 50,000 of Lynn's Darius shares for $9 a share to buyers in several states which Archer had solicited in the open market. Archer also sold for $9 per share the 18,000 Darius shares purchased the prior week for its own account. Soon thereafter, trading activity in Darius stock subsided to its normally light volume which was reflected in the market price retreat to $3 per share.

Required
Answer the following, setting forth reasons for any conclusions stated.

1. What is the general statutory rule requiring registration under the Securities Act of 1933, and would the Darius shares sold by Archer be exempt as so-called "transactions by any person other than an issue underwriter or dealer" or as a so-called "brokers' transaction"?
2. Is Lynn liable to Darius under the Securities Exchange Act of 1934 because he sold 68,000 shares of Darius?

Practice Objective Questions

Instructions 1–12
Select the *best* answer for each of the following items. Mark only one answer for *each* item. Answer all items. Your grade will be based on your total correct answers.
1. Tweed Manufacturing, Inc., plans to issue $5 million of common stock to the public in interstate commerce after its registration statement with the SEC becomes effective. What, if anything, must Tweed do in respect to those states in which the securities are to be sold?
   a. Nothing, since approval by the SEC automatically constitutes satisfaction of any state requirements.
   b. Make a filing in those states which have laws governing such offerings and obtain their approval.
   c. Simultaneously apply to the SEC for permission to market the securities in the various states without further clearance.

    d. File in the appropriate state office of the state in which it maintains its principal office of business, obtain clearance, and forward a certified copy of that state's clearance to all other states.

2. Harvey Wilson is a senior vice president, 15% shareholder and a member of the Board of Directors of Winslow, Inc. Wilson has decided to sell 10% of his stock in the company. Which of the following methods of disposition would subject him to SEC registration requirements?

    a. A redemption of the stock by the corporation.

    b. The sale by several brokerage houses of the stock in the ordinary course of business.

    c. The sale of the stock to an insurance company which will hold the stock for long-term investment purposes.

    d. The sale to a corporate officer who currently owns 5% of the stock of Winslow and who will hold the purchased stock for long-term investment.

3. Mr. Jackson owns approximately 40% of the shares of common stock of Triad Corporation. The rest of the shares are widely distributed among 2,000 shareholders. Jackson needs funds for other business ventures and would like to raise about $2,000,000 through the sale of some of his Triad shares. He accordingly approached Underwood & Sons, an investment banking house in which he knew one of the principals, to purchase his Triad shares and distribute the shares to the public at a reasonable price through its offices in the United States. Any profit on the sales could be retained by Underwood pursuant to an agreement reached between Jackson and Underwood. In this situation

    a. The securities to be sold probably do *not* need to be registered with the Securities and Exchange Commission.

    b. Underwood & Sons probably is *not* an underwriter as defined in the federal securities law.

    c. Jackson probably is considered an issuer under federal securities law.

    d. Under federal securities law, *no* prospectus is required to be filed in connection with this contemplated transaction.

4. Under the Securities Act of 1933, which of the following is the most important criterion to determine whether a private placement to a limited number of persons or a public offering has been made?

    a. The size of the issuing corporation.

    b. The type of security being offered.

    c. The prompt resale of the securities by the purchasers.

    d. The participating purchasers have signed an investment letter.

5. The Securities and Exchange Commission is *not* empowered to

    a. Obtain an injunction which will suspend trading in a given security.

    b. Sue for damages.

    c. Institute criminal proceedings against accountants.

    d. Suspend a broker-dealer.

6. One of the major purposes of federal security regulation is to

    a. Establish the qualifications for accountants who are members of the profession.

    b. Eliminate incompetent attorneys and accountants who participate in the registration of securities to be offered to the public.

    c. Provide a set of uniform standards and tests for accountants, attorneys and others who practice before the Securities and Exchange Commission.

    d. Provide sufficient information to the investing public who purchases securities in the marketplace.

7. Under the Securities Act of 1933, subject to some exceptions and limitations, it is unlawful to use the mail or instruments of interstate commerce to sell or offer to sell a security to the public *unless*

    a. A surety bond sufficient to cover potential liability to investors is obtained and filed with the Securities and Exchange Commission.

    b. The offer is made through underwriters qualified to offer the securities on a nationwide basis.

    c. A registration statement has been properly filed with the Securities and Exchange Commission, has been found to be acceptable, and is in effect.

    d. The Securities and Exchange Commission approves of the financial merit of the offering.

8. Under which of the following circumstances is a public offering of securities exempt from the registration requirements of the Securities Act of 1933?

    a. There was a prior registration within one year.

  b. The corporation is a public utility subject to regulation by the Federal Power Commission.

  c. The corporation was closely held prior to the offering.

  d. The issuing corporation and all prospective security owners are located within one state, and the entire offering, sale, and distribution is made within that state.

9. Bonanza Real Estate Ventures is a limited partnership created pursuant to the law of a state which has adopted the Uniform Limited Partnership Act. It has three general partners and 1,100 limited partners living in various states. The limited-partnership interests were offered to the general public at $5,000 per partnership interest. Under these circumstances which of the following statements is true?

  a. The general partners must contribute capital of at least $5,000 each.

  b. The general partners have unlimited liability; thus, they *cannot* purchase a limited-partnership interest also.

  c. The limited-partnership interests are "securities" within the meaning of the Securities Act of 1933.

  d. The limited-partnership interest *cannot* be sold in any state which has *not* adopted the Uniform Limited Partnership Act.

10. The Securities Act of 1933 specifically exempts from registration securities offered by any person

  a. Other than an issuer, underwriter, or dealer.

  b. Who is an issuer of a public offering.

  c. If the securities in question have previously been registered.

  d. In a small company.

11. Of the following securities transactions, which is exempt from federal securities regulation?

  a. An offering of $800,000 of corporate bonds.

  b. The sale of $1 million of limited partnership interests.

  c. A secondary offering of stock that had been previously registered.

  d. The sale of $500,000 of common stock to a single sophisticated purchaser for investment purposes.

12. The Securities Act of 1933 applies to the:

  a. Sale in interstate commerce of insurance and regular annuity contracts.

  b. Sale by a dealer of securities issued by a bank.

  c. Sale through a broker of a controlling person's investment in a public corporation.

  d. Sale in interstate commerce of bonds issued by a charitable foundation.

6

UNIFORM COMMERCIAL CODE (25%)

CHAPTER

11

Commercial Paper

AICPA Content Specification Outline

Types of Negotiable Instruments
Requisites for Negotiability
Transfer and Negotiation
Holders and Holders in Due Course
Liabilities, Defenses, and Rights
Discharge

Contents

I. Types
  A. Introduction
  B. The four types of negotiable instruments
  C. Negotiability under other articles
II. The Concept of Negotiability
  A. Importance of the concept
  B. Characteristics
III. Requisites of Negotiability
  A. In writing and signed by maker or drawer
  B. Unconditional promise or order to pay a sum certain in money

I. Types*

    A. Introduction: The law of negotiable instruments has undergone its most recent codification in Article 3 (Commercial Paper) of the Uniform Commercial Code. The outline reorganizes the provisions of UCC Article 3 and Article 4, Part 4 (in the

---

*Commercial paper is an aggregate term for four types of negotiable instruments (draft, check, certificate of deposit, and note). Investment securities, documents of title, and money are negotiable instruments but are not included in the term "commercial paper." This chapter outlines the law of commercial paper, these additional types of negotiable instruments are treated in the next chapter.

section on checks), and paraphrases their contents to provide a logical presentation and to facilitate the student's comprehension.

B. The UCC describes four types of negotiable instruments included within the scope of Article 3. Each must satisfy the requirements for negotiability and, if it does, it is one of the following:

1. **Draft:** a written order addressed by one person* called the drawer, to another called the drawee, directing the drawee to pay a sum certain in money to the order of another, called the payee, or to bearer of the draft.

   a. Domestic draft: one which on its face is both drawn and payable within the United States.

   b. Foreign draft: one which on its face is either drawn or payable outside the United States. Upon dishonor, a formal protest is required.

   c. Sight draft: draft payable upon delivery and presentment to the drawer.

   d. Documentary sight draft: sight draft accompanied by a shipping document, e.g., a bill of lading.

   e. Time draft: payable at some future, determinable time, usually acceptance by the drawee.

   f. Money order: instrument with name of its purchaser and the payee on its face, and drawn on a bank or a post office.

   g. Banker's acceptance: draft drawn on and accepted by a bank.

   h. Trade acceptance: draft drawn by seller of goods on the buyer and accepted by the buyer. Consider the following example:

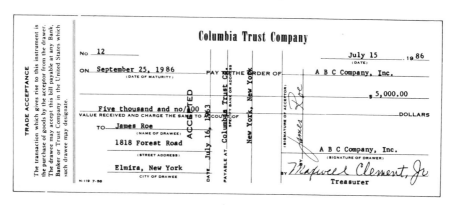

TRADE ACCEPTANCE

2. **Check:** a draft drawn on a bank and payable on demand.

   a. Bank draft: a check drawn by one bank against funds deposited in its account in another bank.

   b. Cashier's check: a check drawn by a bank on itself payable to its customer's order.

---

*"Person" as applied to parties to negotiable instruments is not restricted to people or legal entities. (E.g., an unincorporated association may be the payee of a negotiable instrument.) A person need only be identified with reasonable certainty by the instrument.

3. **Certificate of deposit:** an acknowledgment by a bank of receipt of money with an engagement to repay it. Some certificates do not meet the requisites of negotiability and therefore are not commercial paper.

4. **Note:** a written promise (other than a certificate of deposit) by a person called the maker to pay a sum certain in money to the order of another called the payee. Conceptually, the note is the simplest of the four types.

C. Although an instrument is not negotiable within the meaning and scope of Article 3, it may be negotiable under another article, e.g., an investment security as per Article 8—discussed in the next chapter.

II. The Concept of Negotiability

A. Importance of the concept:

1. **The concept of negotiability** is the leading principle of the law of negotiable commercial paper. This paper is used to supplement the money supply, and in order to foster its ready acceptance in commerce, it is given many distinct benefits not afforded to ordinary contract rights (see below). The key to this area of law is the ability or legal power of a transferor, under certain circumstances, to transfer better rights than he has.

2. In order to obtain the distinct benefits of negotiability, the party holding the instrument must attain the status of a *holder in due course*. At the outset, it will be helpful briefly to summarize in logical sequence the steps that must be followed to obtain these benefits:

   a. The instrument must be *negotiable* (see III).

   b. The person asserting the rights must be a *holder*, that is, he must take by *negotiation* (see IV).

   c. The holder must satisfy the requirements for *holding in due* course (see V.A.)

   d. The defense asserted must be a *personal defense* as contrasted with a *real defense* (see V.B.)

3. It may be helpful to think of these four steps as rungs in a ladder; you must satisfy each one of them to reach the top. Study them with great care in the succeeding parts of the text. Your mastery of them is *essential* to an understanding of this rather technical area of law. They are the foundation upon which the balance of this chapter is built.

4. Another useful aid in analyzing problems in this area is the use of a diagram. Not only is the law complicated by so many rules, but so too are the facts complicated, due to the multiplicity of parties involved. A diagram of the transaction clearly indicating who each party is in relation to the instrument is strongly recommended.

B. Characteristics: differences between negotiable instruments and ordinary contracts

1. Negotiable instruments must pass freely from hand to hand. (This is not true of ordinary contract rights, which, in some cases, cannot be transferred at all.)

2. Negotiable instruments are transferred by indorsement and delivery or sometimes by delivery alone. Contract rights in some cases may be assigned orally.

3. In all but a very few cases, the rights of the assignee of a contract right are the same as those of his assignor. In the case of a negotiable instrument, a holder in

due course (see p. 273, V) acquires greater rights because he takes free of most defenses. (I.e., The major advantage of a negotiable instrument is that it circulates, unburdened by claims of ownership or personal defenses of the maker, drawer, or subsequent transferees.)

4. Every negotiable instrument is deemed *prima facie* to have been issued for a consideration. The defendant may rebut this presumption.

    a. The words "value received" need not be in the instrument, as the presumption of consideration exists without them.

    b. The necessary consideration for the issue of a negotiable instrument is any consideration that would support a simple contract. An antecedent indebtedness is also value, although it may not constitute consideration.

    c. In the hands of a holder in due course, consideration is conclusively presumed.

III. Requisites of Negotiability

A. Instrument **must be in writing and signed** by the maker or drawer.

    1. If the instrument is signed by an authorized agent, the agent must disclose his principal's name and his own representative capacity, or he will be personally liable upon the instrument. A proper indorsement by an agent would read: "X Company by Y, President of X Company," or other agency designation.

    2. The signer may use his own name, an assumed name, his initials, a symbol, or a rubber stamp, as long as what he uses is intended by him as a signature.

B. **Must contain an unconditional promise or order to pay a sum certain in money.**

    1. Promise: an engagement to pay that is more than an acknowledgment of an obligation (e.g., an IOU is a mere acknowledgment, hence nonnegotiable).

    2. Order: a direction to pay that is more than an authorization or request addressed to one or more persons (drawees) identifiable with reasonable certainty. The word "pay" contained in your check is an order or command to your bank.

    3. Promise or order must be unconditional.

        a. A promise or order is not rendered conditional although the instrument:

            (1) States its consideration, or

            (2) Refers to the transaction out of which it arose or any other separate agreement, or

            (3) States that it is secured by a mortgage or other security device, or

            (4) Indicates a particular account, fund, or source from which payment may be drawn, or

            (5) If issued by a government or a governmental agency, states that it is to be paid only out of a particular fund or source, or

            (6) Is payable only out of the entire assets of a partnership, unincorporated association, estate, or trust.

        b. A promise or order is conditional if the instrument:

            (1) States that it is "subject to" or "governed by" another agreement, or

            (2) States that it is to be paid "only" out of a particular fund or source except as mentioned in III.B.3a(5) and (6).

    4. Sum certain: the sum payable is certain although it is to be paid:

      a. With stated interest, including different rates of interest before and after default, or

      b. By stated installments, or

      c. With a stated discount or addition for early or late payment, or

      d. With exchange added or deducted, whether a fixed or current rate, or

      e. With costs of collection or attorney's fees or both upon default.

5. Money: defined as a medium of exchange authorized or adopted by a domestic or foreign government as part of its currency.

      a. If the sum payable is stated in a foreign currency, it may be paid in that number of dollars that said sum would purchase on the day of payment unless the instrument specifies the foreign currency as the medium of payment.

6. Instrument that contains an order or promise to do any act in addition to the payment of money is nonnegotiable; however, the negotiable character of an instrument is not affected by a provision that:

      a. States that collateral has been given and authorizes its sale upon default, or

      b. Requires maintenance or protection of collateral or the giving of additional collateral, or

      c. Authorizes a confession of judgment upon default, or

      d. Waives the benefit of any law intended for the advantage of the obligor, or

      e. States that by indorsing or cashing a draft, the payee acknowledges full satisfaction of drawer's obligation.

C. Instrument must be **payable on demand or at a definite time.**

    1. Instrument is payable on demand if:

      a. It so states, or

      b. It is payable at sight or on presentation, or

      c. No time for payment is stated, or

      d. It is issued when payment is overdue.

    2. Instrument is payable at a definite time when by its terms it is payable:

      a. On or before a stated date or at a fixed period after a stated date, or

      b. At a fixed period after sight, or

      c. At a definite time subject to any acceleration. An acceleration clause is a term allowing the payee or his successor to demand full payment immediately. Such acceleration is allowed only if provided for in the instrument, or

      d. At a definite time subject to extension either at the option of the holder or of the maker or acceptor, or automatically upon the occurrence of a specified act or event.

    3. Instrument which is payable *only* upon the occurrence of an act or event uncertain as to time of occurrence (e.g., a promise to pay C $500 upon B's death or upon the sale of Blackacre is not payable at a definite time and therefore not negotiable).

D. Instrument must be **payable to order or to bearer (the "magic words" of negotiability).**

    1. Instrument is payable to order when it is payable to the order of any person that it specifies with reasonable certainty, or to his or her order or to a specified person or his or her assigns.

    a. Instrument may be payable to the order of:

      (1) Maker or drawer, or

      (2) Drawee, or

      (3) Payee other than maker, drawer, or drawee, or

      (4) Two or more payees together or in the alternative (if payable to payees in the alternative, it is payable to any one of them, and any one of them with possession of the instrument may negotiate, discharge, or enforce it. If payable to payees jointly, it is payable to all of them and may be negotiated, discharged, or enforced only by all of them), or

      (5) An estate, trust, or fund (in such case it is payable to the order of the representative of the estate, trust, or fund), or

      (6) An officer or an officer by his title alone, or

      (7) A partnership or unincorporated association.

      (8) An instrument payable to a specified person or his or her assigns is an order paper despite the omission of the words "order of."

    b. Instrument is payable to bearer if it states it is payable to:

      (1) Bearer or the order of bearer, or

      (2) A specified person or bearer, or

      (3) "Cash" or to the order of "cash," or any other indication in which a specific payee is not designated.

  2. These words are the most frequently omitted of the requisites for AICPA exam purposes. If an instrument is presented for analysis be sure to look for these "magic words."

E. Amplification and rules of construction:

  1. A nonnegotiable instrument is nevertheless enforceable as a contract. However, the transferee is a mere assignee and subject to both real and personal defenses.

  2. An instrument may still be negotiable even though it is antedated or postdated (providing this was not done for illegal purposes).

    a. The person who receives such an instrument acquires title thereto as of the date of delivery.

    b. An instrument need not be dated at all in order to be negotiable.

  3. An instrument is not rendered nonnegotiable because place for payment is not specified. But remember, the drawee must be clearly designated.

  4. An instrument expressly payable at a bank or other special place is referred to as a "domiciled" instrument.

  5. An instrument that is signed but is incomplete in some necessary respect (e.g., failure to state amount payable) cannot be enforced until it is completed.

    a. It may be completed by any one given the authority to do so, and when it is completed in accordance with authority given, it is effective as completed.

    b. An unauthorized completion of such instrument is a material alteration (see p. 275, V.B.2.f), but it will not defeat a holder in due course.

    c. The party who asserts that completion was unauthorized has the burden of proving that fact.

  6. Ambiguities: rules of construction.

    a. Written words control over sums denoted by figures unless words are ambiguous or uncertain.

    b. An undated instrument is considered dated as of the time of issue.

    c. Written provisions prevail over printed provisions.

    d. Interest runs from the date of the instrument if there is no specification to the contrary, and, if there is no date, it runs from the date of issue.

    e. Where a signature is so placed that it is not clear in what capacity a person signed, he or she is deemed an indorser.

    f. Where an instrument containing the words "I promise to pay" is signed by two persons, those persons are deemed jointly and severally liable.

    g. Where there is doubt whether the instrument is a draft or a note, the holder may treat it as either at his election.

    h. The drawer and drawee of a draft may be the same; if so, the holder may treat it as a note.

F. Summary illustrative example and analysis:

    The defendant, Safety First Insurance Company, admitted liability for $603.50 on an automobile collision policy. It issued the draft below for this amount. What kind or type of instrument is it? Is it negotiable?

January 12, 1986

This payment as evidenced by the proper indorsement is in full settlement and final satisfaction and discharge of all claims for loss by collision on February 28, 1984 under our Automobile policy 24506/13/501 issued at Norwalk, Conn.

    Pay to the order of   William Jackson $603.50

Six hundred and three ⁵⁰/₁₀₀ _____ *dollars*

                             Safety First Insurance Co.
                             by John C. Thorpe
                             Chief Claims Adjuster

Yale Trust Company   *(signed)* _____
New Haven, Connecticut

---

    a. The instrument in question is a check which in turn is one type of draft. It is drawn on a bank (Yale Trust Company) and is payable on demand. Thus, it meets the requirement for qualification as a check.

    b. The instrument is negotiable, it satisfies the five requisites of negotiability and it is initially order paper. The introductory language in italics does not render the instrument subject to or conditioned upon another agreement. Thus, it is unconditional and the language is a mere recitation of the transaction out of which it arose.

IV. Issue and Negotiation

A. Issue: the first delivery (voluntary transfer of possession) of an instrument to a holder (normally to the person to whom the instrument is payable, i.e., the payee).

B. Negotiation: subsequent transfer of the instrument in such a way that the transferee is a "holder."

    1. Bearer paper is negotiated *by delivery alone*. (However, the holder may be required to indorse or may indorse if he wishes.)

2. **Order paper** is negotiated *by an indorsement* by the person whose order the instrument is payable, *and delivery*.

    a. Indorsement: signing one's name, with or without other words, on the instrument.

        (1) May be typewritten or rubber stamped if intended as an indorsement. Is this the customary way the party signs?

        (2) May be by an agent on behalf of the holder.

        (3) Indorsements are also made for purposes other than the transfer of the instrument. (E.g., X, not a party to the instrument, writes his name on the back of Y's note as an accommodation indorser—see p. 280, VI.F.1 and 2—so that Y may obtain a loan.)

C. Types of indorsement:

    1. **Blank:** transferor's signature alone. Converts order paper to bearer paper.

    2. **Special:** made to a specified person called an indorsee (e.g., "Pay X," signed Y). Bearer paper so indorsed becomes order paper. Further negotiation requires the indorsee's signature.

    3. **Restrictive:** An indorsement is restrictive if it is:

        a. Conditional (E.g., "Pay X if but only if . . .," signed Y.)

        b. An indorsement containing the words "For deposit," "For collection," "Pay any bank or banker," or like terms. [These indorsements and conditional indorsements require the immediate (first) transferee and all subsequent transferees (with the exception of intermediary and payor banks* in the instrument collection process that may disregard the restrictions) to comply with the restrictions in paying value for the instrument. To the extent that said transferees do so, they are holders and are not prevented from being holders in the due course if they fulfill the other requirements for that status (see p. 273, V.A.).]

        c. An indorsement purporting to prohibit further transfer (e.g., "Pay X only," signed Y). Neither such an indorsement nor any other restrictive indorsement prevents further transfer or negotiation.

        d. An indorsement that indicates it is for the use or benefit of the indorser or another person (e.g., "Pay X in trust for Z," signed Y). "Trust" indorsement requires only the immediate transferee to comply with the restriction. Any subsequent transferee may disregard the restriction, and his holder in due course status (see p. 273, V.A.) is not affected thereby unless he knows that the first transferee did not comply with the restriction.

    4. **Qualified** (e.g., "Without recourse," signed Y): Transferor disclaims contract liability on the instrument, i.e., he does not promise to pay upon dishonor (see p. 279, VI.E.2). Does not prevent transferee from being a holder in due course.

    5. **Illustrations.** The foregoing indorsements may be illustrated as follows (assuming William Smith as payee):

        a. Blank

            (1) *William Smith*

---

*A "payor bank" is a bank at which an instrument is payable as drawn or as accepted. A drawee bank is a payor bank.

     b. Special
       (1) Pay to John Jones or order
          William Smith
       (2) Pay to John Jones
          William Smith
     c. Restrictive
       (1) Pay to John Jones only
          William Smith
       (2) For collection and deposit to my account
          William Smith
       (3) Pay to John Jones for my use
          William Smith
       (4) Pay to John Jones in trust for his son
          William Smith
       (5) Pay to John Jones on completion of Lincoln Square Project
          William Smith
     d. Qualified
       (1) Without recourse
          William Smith
     e. Conditional (the UCC treats this as one type of restrictive indorsement)
        It is possible to combine several types of indorsements. For example, "Pay to the order of the X bank, for deposit only, without recourse to me, signed William Smith." This indorsement combines the special, restrictive, and qualified types of indorsement.

D. Amplification and explanation:

  1. Above types of indorsement can be used in combination as long as the combination is not by definition inconsistent (e.g., "Pay X Bank, for deposit" is both special and restrictive).

  2. Transfer for value of order paper without an indorsement operates as an assignment, and title to the instrument vests in the transferee. Such a transferee has the right to require the transferor to indorse the paper subsequent to the transfer. However, the transferee becomes a holder as of the date of the indorsement. It is at this later time that he must meet the requirements for holding in due course. (E.g., X takes a negotiable instrument payable to Y's order by mere delivery. He will not become a holder until he obtains Y's indorsement. If at any time prior to his obtaining Y's indorsement he learns of a defense to the instrument, he will not qualify as a holder in due course.) However, he may be able to assert the rights of a prior holder in due course.

  3. A payee or indorsee whose name is incorrectly spelled on the instrument should so indorse the instrument. The transferee may require his proper signature in addition.

  4. Negotiation involving one of the following is effective to transfer the instrument but is subject to rescission unless the rescission is asserted against a subsequent holder in due course.
    a. Where transferor is an infant or any other person without capacity, or
    b. Where obtained by fraud, duress, or mistake of any kind, or
    c. Where part of an illegal transaction, or made in breach of duty.

5. Only the entire amount of the instrument can be negotiated; an attempted transfer of part of the face value of a negotiable instrument will be treated as a partial assignment, not a negotiation.

V. Holders and Holder in Due Course

A. Requisites:

1. The person **must be a holder** (i.e., the payee or a transferee who takes via negotiation) of a negotiable instrument.

2. Holder must take the instrument **for value.** A holder gives value in the following ways:

   a. By performing the agreed consideration. Any consideration sufficient to support a simple contract may be value, but only to the extent that it has been performed. When part of the agreed consideration is executory (un-performed) at the time of notice of an infirmity or defect in an instrument, the holder will qualify as a holder in due course only to the extent that he has performed. (E.g., X bought notes from Y aggregating $1,000. X paid $250 and promised to pay $500 at a later date. Before X had paid any additional money, he learned that Y had obtained the notes from the maker by duress. X may recover only the $250 from the maker.)

   b. By acquiring a security interest in or a lien on the instrument otherwise than by legal process. (E.g., X, in order to borrow money from the bank, pledges bearer negotiable instruments with the bank. The bank will have given value to the extent of the loan.)

   c. By taking the instrument in payment of, or as security for, an antecedent claim (e.g., debt, contract right) against any person. As in the case above where the instrument is taken as security for a loan, the holder qualifies as a holder in due course only to the extent of the amount owed.

   d. By giving one's own negotiable instrument in exchange (despite the fact that in the case of a check, for example, the party could stop payment after learning of a defense).

   e. In the case of a bank, by the depositor withdrawing the value of the instrument from the bank account. (E.g., X deposits a $500 check in B Bank. B Bank credits X's account with that amount. Later X withdraws the $500 from the account.) The bank has given value. In determining when a depositor has withdrawn the amount of the item in question, the FIFO (first-in–first-out) rule prevails.

   f. Even though a negotiable instrument sells at a substantial discount, the value requirement is nevertheless fulfilled and the holder will qualify as a holder in due course for the face value (full amount of the instrument) provided the holder took it in good faith. (E.g., X, in good faith, pays $75 for a $100 promissory note.)

3. Holder must take the instrument in **good faith** (honestly) and **without notice** that it is overdue or has been dishonored or that any person has a defense against or claim to it. This requirement as interpreted and applied is almost exclusively a subjective test (i.e., did *the particular person* asserting holder in due course status take in good faith or have knowledge?). The test is not whether he or she was negligent or whether a reasonable person (an objective test) would or should

have known. This subjective approach is sometimes described as "the pure in heart but empty-headed" test.

a. Holder has notice of a claim or defense when he or she knows or has reason to know of it. Clearly, the without-notice requirement is a specific treatment of one aspect of good faith. There is overlap here, since one having notice of a defense clearly cannot take in good faith.

b. The instrument itself puts the holder on notice of a defense if it is so incomplete as to suggest forgery or alteration or is otherwise so irregular as to call into question its validity, terms, or ownership.

c. A domestic check is presumed to be overdue 30 days after issue. Other demand instruments are overdue after a reasonable time has elapsed.

d. Knowledge that an incomplete instrument has been completed does not put the holder on notice of a defense unless the holder knows or has reason to know of any improper completion.

e. Notice that one or more but less than all of the prior parties have been discharged does not put the holder on notice of a defense as far as the remaining parties to the instrument are concerned. However, those discharges of which the holder *does* have notice will be effective against such a holder although he or she may be a holder in due course as to the other parties.

B. Rights of a holder in due course:

1. Any holder of a negotiable instrument has the right to transfer or negotiate it, to discharge it or enforce payment in the holder's own name, and to strike out any indorsements not necessary to provide proper title.

2. A *holder in due course*, in addition, takes the instrument free from all title claims to it by any person, and free from all defenses of any party with whom he or she has not dealt, except the following:

   a. Infancy. To the extent that the law of the jurisdiction makes this a defense to a simple contract, it is effective against a holder in due course (see Contracts, p. 148, III.D.1).

   b. *Void* instruments. To varying extents in different jurisdictions the following may render an instrument void:

      (1) Incapacity other than infancy (typically insanity—see Contracts, p. 148, III.D.2–5).

      (2) Duress in the execution, e.g., an instrument executed with a gun to your head.

      (3) Illegality of the transaction, e.g., usury, bribery, etc.

   c. Fraud as to the nature and essential terms of the instrument, fraud in the execution. (See Contracts, p. 153, IV.D.3.b.) The UCC speaks of "such misrepresentation as had induced the party to sign the instrument with neither knowledge nor reasonable opportunity to obtain knowledge of its character or its essential terms." For example, X is asked to sign a "receipt" for the delivery of goods. The "receipt" is in fact a negotiable instrument. This type of fraud is rare. The typical fraud is fraud in the inducement and it is a common personal defense.

   d. Unauthorized signatures: mainly the forged signature of a maker or drawer and forged indorsements.

        (1) Such signatures are wholly inoperative unless ratified. They are real defenses.

        (2) Negligence inviting forgery or otherwise unauthorized signing prevents a party from raising the defense (an estoppel), e.g., where the check imprinting machine that signs the instrument is left lying around carelessly.

  e. Imposters, fictitious payees and wrongdoing agents.

        (1) The **imposter rule** applies to situations where an imposter by use of the mails or otherwise (e.g., face-to-face) has induced the maker or drawer to issue the instrument to the imposter or his confederate in the name of the payee (the person impersonated). E.g., X impersonates Y in obtaining a loan. The check is made out to Y and is delivered to X, who indorses Y's name. Despite the forged endorsement of Y's signature, it is effective against the drawer in the hands of a holder in due course. Otherwise, it would be a real defense.

        (2) The **fictitious payee rule** applies to situations where the person signing as or on behalf of the maker on drawer intends the payee to have no interest in the instrument. E.g., X having the authority to sign checks makes several payable to fictitious companies, which checks he endorses in their names. Once again, if the instrument is in the hands of a holder in due course, he will obtain good title as a result of the indorsement. The real defense of a forged indorsement is thus overcome.

        (3) **Wrongdoing agents or employees** who supply the maker or drawer with the name of the payee intending the latter to have no interest in it, have the power to indorse the instrument in the payee's name. Here, as above, no interest is intended in the party named although that party may exist in fact. Thus, the real defense of a forged indorsement is ineffective against a holder in due course. This is a common type of defalcation scheme. E.g., X, a payroll clerk, draws checks payable to fictitious parties, has the company's treasurer sign them, steals them, and indorses the name of the payee in the process of cashing them. His indorsement is good insofar as the party cashing it is concerned.

  f. Material alteration.

        (1) Anything that alters the contract of the party to the instrument in any respect is a material alteration. Raising the amount or changing the payee's name are the most common types of such alterations.

        (2) If the instrument is materially altered, the maker or drawer and/or prior indorser remain liable on the instrument to a holder in due course, according to its original tenor (terms). A wrongful or unauthorized filling in or completion is treated as a material alteration. However, if the wrongful filling in or completion is done without knowledge of its invalidity on the part of the holder in due course, he takes free of this defense.

        (3) Negligence inviting alteration prevents a party from raising this defense (estoppel). This normally represents your only and last chance to prevail.

  g. Discharge in insolvency proceedings, i.e., bankruptcy.

3. The defenses listed above are termed **"real" defenses.** All defenses other than those listed above are termed **"personal" defenses** and are not available against the holder in due course (e.g., simple contract defenses, fraud in the inducement, breach of warranty, payment, and lack of delivery).

4. One can acquire the rights of a holder in due course, without being one, by taking title through a holder in due course. [E.g., X, a holder in due course of a note originally procured through fraud, gives it to Y, who knows of the fraud. Y, although not a holder in due course (no value given and with knowledge) acquires X's right as a holder in due course and can collect the proceeds if she did not take part in the fraud.] The exception to this rule is that a holder of an instrument who does not qualify as a holder in due course cannot better her rights by transferring the instrument to a holder in due course and then reacquiring it. One who was a party to the fraud cannot, of course, benefit from the rule.

VI. Contractual Liability of the Parties

A. Conditions percedent to holding certain parties liable:

1. Introduction: Drawers of drafts and checks and indorsers of drafts, checks, and notes do not assume primary liability for payment of the instrument. Instead, it is contemplated that a person other than those persons will pay. In the case of drafts and checks, the drawee is the party who should make payment and, in the case of notes, the maker should pay. Thus, drawers and indorsers are said to be *secondarily liable*. This means that unless excused or waived, the party seeking payment from drawers and indorsers must fulfill certain conditions precedent (presentment, notice of dishonor, and, in certain cases, protest) in order to charge these people with liability on the instrument. The importance of this distinction is that failure to comply with these conditions precedent completely discharges indorsers from secondary liability and discharges the drawer at least to the extent that he has been injured by failure to fulfill the conditions precedent. Each of these conditions is discussed in detail below.

2. **Presentment for acceptance:** The drawer's act of drawing a draft does not make the drawee liable on the instrument. Oddly enough, no one has primary liability on a draft at the time of its issue. Drafts payable at a stated date may be required to be presented, or may be voluntarily presented, for acceptance. If the drawee then promises to pay the draft when due, he is said to have accepted or "honored" the draft and thereby becomes *primarily liable*. Presentment for acceptance applies mainly to time drafts.

   a. Presentment for acceptance is only required to hold the drawer and indorsers when:
      (1) Draft so provides, or
      (2) Draft is payable elsewhere than at drawee's residence or place of business, or
      (3) Date of payment depends on such presentment (e.g., draft payable 30 days after the presentment or sight).

   b. The failure to make valid presentment for acceptance, *where required*, discharges indorsers entirely and discharges drawers to the extent of the injury (i.e., to the extent that the drawer has been harmed by the failure to meet the requirement the drawer, a bank, fails).

c. Otherwise, time drafts may be voluntarily presented for acceptance or may simply be presented for payment on the due date, without prior presentment for acceptance.

d. Acceptance is made only by the drawee's writing his signature, with or without other words, on the face of the draft.

e. General acceptance: Drawee accepts draft exactly as presented.

f. Acceptance varying draft (e.g., acceptance varying time or amount of payment or designating exclusive place for payment).
   (1) Holder may refuse such acceptance and treat draft as dishonored.
   (2) Assent by the holder to such acceptance discharges any drawer or indorser who does not also affirmatively assent.

g. If drawee refuses to accept the draft or fails to accept it before the close of the next business day following presentment, the draft is dishonored.

h. Time of presentment: Where necessary, presentment must be made on or before date payable. For drafts payable after sight, presentment must be made within reasonable time after issue or date of draft, whichever is later.

i. Excuse of delay in presentment for acceptance (see p. 279, VI.A.6).

j. How presentment may be made (see below, VI.A.3.g).

3. Presentment for payment.

a. Relates to any commercial paper.

b. Made to maker of note, drawee or acceptor of draft, drawee of a check, or other payor.

c. If the party to pay refuses to pay or fails to do so before the close of business on the day of presentment, the instrument is dishonored.

d. Due presentment for payment necessary to fully hold maker of bank-domiciled note (see p. 279, VI.C), acceptor of bank-domiciled draft, any drawer, or any indorser.
   (1) Failure to make a valid presentment for payment completely discharges all indorsers, and
   (2) Discharges others mentioned above in 3.d to the extent they have been injured.

e. Time of presentment unless otherwise excused:
   (1) Demand note must be presented within a reasonable time after issue.
   (2) Demand draft (excluding checks), to hold a drawer or indorser, must be presented within a reasonable time after the party sought to be held becomes liable on it.
   (3) Check must be presented 30 days after date or issue, whichever is later, to hold the drawer, and 7 days after a person's indorsement to hold said indorser. The drawer will be discharged only to the extent he suffers a loss, e.g., if the bank fails.
   (4) Where an instrument is accelerated (p. 268, III.C.2.c), presentment must be made within a reasonable time after the acceleration.
   (5) Instrument that states date on which it is payable must be presented on that date. If said date is not a full business day, presentment must be made on the next full business day.

    f. Excuse of delay in presentment for payment (see p. 279, VI.A.6).

    g. Presentment for payment or acceptance usually made:

        (1) By mail, with receipt of the mail effecting presentment, or through a clearing house (a group of banks or other payors that meets so that each member may present instruments to the other members for payment and acceptance).

        (2) The person to whom presentment is made may require exhibition of the instrument, identification of person making presentment and evidence of his authority to do so, and a signed receipt on the instrument upon full or partial payment with surrender of the instrument upon full payment.

    h. Instrument payable at a bank (bank-domiciled) is treated in some jurisdictions as equivalent to a draft drawn on the bank designated. In other jurisdictions such an instrument is deemed merely to designate a place of payment, giving no order or authority to the bank to pay it.

4. Notice of dishonor.

    a. Dishonor is nonacceptance of a time draft or nonpayment of a draft or note. However, return of an instrument because of lack of a proper indorsement is not a dishonor.

    b. Due notice of dishonor is necessary to fully hold maker of bank-domiciled note, acceptor of bank-domiciled draft, any drawer, or any indorser. Indorsers are completely discharged; the others mentioned above are discharged to the extent that they were harmed by failure to meet the notice requirement.

    c. May be given orally or in writing.

    d. Must identify the instrument and state that it has been dishonored.

    e. Return of the instrument bearing a stamp, ticket, or other writing to the effect that it has been dishonored, or notice of debit of the account is sufficient notice of dishonor.

    f. Time for giving notice of dishonor.

        (1) By banks: by midnight of the next banking day.

        (2) By other parties: by midnight of the third business day after knowledge of dishonor.

    g. Excuse of delay in giving notice (see below, VI.A.6).

    h. Any party who may be compelled to pay the instrument may notify any party who may be liable on it. (I.e., the person notified need not be liable to the person giving notice for said notice to be effective.)

    i. Notice operates for the benefit of all parties who have rights on the instrument against the party notified.

    j. Notice to joint parties who are not partners must be given to each individually unless one has authority to receive such notice for the others.

    k. Notice to a party dead or incompetent may be sent to his last known address or given to his personal representative.

5. Protest: formal attestation of dishonor.

    a. Only necessary on drafts drawn or payable on their face outside the United States ("foreign" drafts), including checks.

    b. Must be made and sealed by United States consular officer, or notary public, or other person authorized to make protest by the law of the jurisdiction where dishonor occurs.

        c. Any necessary protest is due at the time notice of dishonor is due.

        d. Failure to comply with the protest requirement completely discharges all indorsers and drawers.

    6. Excuse of delay in presentment, notice of dishonor, or protest.

        a. Excused when the party is without notice that it is due (e.g., when note accelerated without his knowledge), or

        b. When caused by circumstances beyond his control; when cause of delay ceases to operate, he must act with reasonable diligence.

    7. Presentment or notice of dishonor or protest not required:

        a. As to party who dishonored the instrument, and

        b. As to any party who waives it before or after it is due, and

        c. When the maker, acceptor, or drawee of any instrument is dead or an insolvency proceeding has been instituted after issuance of the instrument.

B. **Contract liability** (liability on instrument) of a **maker** of a note and **acceptor** of a draft:

    1. Each engages to pay it according to its terms at the time of making or acceptance respectively, or as later completed, when completed as authorized.

    2. Each admits the existence of the payee and his capacity to indorse.

    3. Acceptor of draft is liable to holder in due course even though draft bears a forged drawer's signature.

    4. None of the conditions of presentment, notice of dishonor, and protest is necessary to hold these parties, as they are **primarily liable.**

C. The Code makes a distinction regarding the contract liability of maker of bank-domiciled ("payable at a bank") note and acceptor of bank-domiciled draft.

    1. In these uncommon situations, each engages to pay as stated in VI.B.1 above, *provided that* due presentment of the respective instrument for payment at the bank designated (domiciliary bank) is made and that any necessary notice of dishonor or protest is given.

D. **Contract liability of any drawer:**

    1. Engages that upon dishonor of the draft and notice of dishonor or protest, if necessary, he will pay the amount of the draft to the holder or to any indorser who assumes responsibility on it.

    2. Effect of delay in fulfilling or failure to fulfill these conditions is to discharge the drawer to the extent he suffers a loss, e.g., the bank fails.

    3. Admits the existence of the payee and his capacity to indorse.

    4. Drawer may disclaim his liability by drawing without recourse.

E. **Contract liability of indorsers:**

    1. Every indorser *other than a qualified indorser* engages that upon dishonor and any necessary notice of dishonor or protest he will pay the instrument according to its terms at the time of his indorsement to the holder or to any subsequent indorser who assumes responsibility on it.

    2. A qualified indorser disclaims this liability by writing a disclaimer (e.g., "without recourse") on the instrument. He eliminates contract liability.

    3. Delay in fulfilling or failure to fulfill the conditions precedent (i.e., presentment, notice of dishonor, or protest) *completely* discharges any indorser.

    4. Indorsers are liable to one another in the order of indorsement unless they agree otherwise.

F. **Liability of accommodation party:**

    1. Accommodation party is in effect a surety in that he signs the instrument and thus assumes possible liability on it in order to accommodate another party to it. This is done to facilitate a loan or transfer the instrument. As between the accommodation party and the party accommodated, the latter should perform and bears the ultimate liability. E.g., X wishes to borrow $1,000 from Y and offers to give his promissory note for the loan. Y is unwilling to lend the money unless X obtains another party (a surety) against whom Y can seek recovery if X defaults. Z, in order to accommodate his friend X, signs the negotiable promissory note either as a comaker or indorser. As such, Z is an accommodation party.

    2. Accommodation party is liable in the capacity in which he signs (e.g., maker, acceptor, indorser, etc.), even though the taker knows of the accommodation as long as the instrument has been taken for value before it is due.

    3. Accommodation party is not liable to the party accommodated and can proceed against the party accommodated if he has to pay the instrument.

VII. **Warranty Liability of the Parties**

  A. Introduction: In addition to the contractual liability discussed in VI above, certain implied warranties attach to the sale of commercial paper.

  B. **Warranties to persons accepting or paying:**

    1. A person other than a holder in due course making presentment for acceptance or payment and any prior transferor of the instrument warrants to the person accepting or paying that:

      a. He has good title (i.e., all indorsements are genuine and authorized) or is an authorized representative of a person with good title, and

      b. He has no knowledge that the signature of the maker or drawer is unauthorized, and

      c. The instrument has not been materially altered.

    2. A holder in due course making presentment:

      a. Warrants that he has a good title.

      b. Does not make warranty 1.b (above) if he is acting in good faith to a maker or drawer with respect to their respective signatures, or to an acceptor to whom he is making presentment for payment.

      c. Does not make warranty 1.c (above) to a maker or drawer, to an acceptor with respect to an alteration made prior to acceptance if the holder in due course took the draft after acceptance, or to an acceptor with respect to an alteration made after acceptance.

  C. **Warranties to transferees and subsequent holders:**

    1. Any person who transfers by indorsement and for consideration warrants to his transferee and to any subsequent holder that:

      a. He has good title or is an authorized representative of a person with good title, and

     b. All signatures are genuine or authorized, and

     c. The instrument has not been materially altered, and

     d. No defense of any party is good against him, and

     e. To his knowledge no insolvency proceedings have been instituted with respect to the maker or acceptor or the drawer of an unaccepted instrument.

  2. An indorser who transfers "without recourse" (qualified indorser) makes the same warranties listed above in VII.C.1.a–e, with the exception that with respect to 3.d he warrants only that, to his knowledge, no defense of any party is good against him. Thus, although a "without recourse" indorser is able to completely negate his contractual liability, he does not entirely eliminate possible warranty liability.

  3. A person who transfers for consideration but without indorsement (e.g., transfer of a bearer instrument) makes the same warranties listed in VII.C.1.a–e, but he makes them only to his immediate transferee and not to subsequent holders. Since he did not sign the instrument, he has no contractual liability.

  4. The official draft of the UCC eliminates warranty liability for the accommodation party who does not receive consideration, but some adopting states (e.g., New York) have added a provision making him liable on warranties a, b, c, and e of VII.C.1 above.

VIII. Checks

  A. Definition: a draft, drawn on a bank, payable on demand. Note that we have already considered many of the rules applicable to the parties to a check in prior parts of the text, i.e., the contractual liability of the parties and especially the warranty liability of the parties. When a check is received in payment of a debt, the underlying obligation for which the check is given is not extinguished, except in rare instances where the check is taken in absolute payment. Consider the following diagram in analyzing the right duties and relationships of the various parties.

Diagramatic Sketch:

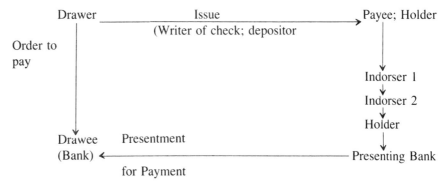

     We shall consider first the relationship between the writer of a check and his bank.

  B. Relationship of bank and depositor:

    1. Ordinary deposit or checking account: A debtor and creditor relationship exists, and the bank is the depositor's agent for payment.

      a. A check does not operate as an assignment in the absence of special facts.

      b. Bank may set off debts owed it by its depositor.

   2. Special deposit for a specific purpose: A bailee and bailor relationship exists, and depositor has title to the deposits.

C. Right to compel payment:

   1. Payee has no right to compel payment as against drawee bank, even though depositor has funds on deposit.

   2. Payee can compel payment by drawer, if drawee bank refuses to pay and the proper procedural steps (see p. 279, VI.D) have been taken in respect to dishonor.

   3. Payee can compel payment by drawee bank only after certification of check (see below VIII.D). Bank has "accepted" by certification and is primarily liable.

   4. Only the drawer has a right of action against the bank for a wrongful dishonor (e.g., slander of credit).

      a. When dishonor occurs through mistake, liability is limited to actual damages proved.

      b. A bank is under no obligation to pay a check more than 6 months old, other than a certified check; hence, dishonor is not wrongful. However, payment of such a check is not improper. Bank practice is not to pay.

D. **Certification:** bank's recognition of a depositor's check and acceptance of it as a valid appropriation of the amount specified. The bank warrants that sufficient funds are on deposit and have been set aside.

   1. Major advantage: Drawee bank becomes primarily liable to the holder of the instrument.

   2. If the holder procures certification:

      a. Bank becomes primarily liable.

      b. Drawer and indorsers are discharged.

   3. If the drawer procures certification:

      a. Bank is primarily liable.

      b. Drawer remains secondarily liable.

   4. Bank's refusal to certify is not dishonor; only refusal to pay is dishonor.

   5. Certification of overdraft.

      a. Holder may collect full amount of check from drawee bank.

      b. Drawer is liable to drawee for the difference.

      c. If certification of the overdraft was knowingly made by bank official, he is liable to bank.

      d. It may be a crime for a bank to wrongfully certify.

E. Drawer's right to **stop payment:**

   1. Stop-payment order must reach bank in time for bank to avoid certifying the check or making final payment on it.

   2. Oral stop-payment order is valid but lapses after 14 days. It may be confirmed in writing within that period and is effective for 6 months unless further renewed in writing.

3. Bank is liable to drawer if it pays after effective stop-payment order.

    a. This liability may be varied by agreement; however, no agreement can disclaim or limit a bank's liability for damages caused by its own lack of good faith or its negligence.

4. The drawer has the burden of proving that the failure to obey his stop-payment order caused the loss. I.e., if the drawer would have to pay in any event, the bank's failure to stop payment is meaningless (e.g., the check is in the hands of a holder in due course and the defense is a personal defense).

5. If drawer stops payment, he is liable to the holder of the check unless he has a valid, assertable defense.

F. Drawer's responsibility with respect to **unauthorized signatures or alterations:**

1. If drawer's negligence has substantially contributed to the unauthorized signatures or alterations, he bears the loss resulting from a good faith payment by the bank.

2. Drawer who knowingly or unknowingly makes a check payable to an imposter or to a fictitious payee bears the loss.

3. Drawer who receives a bank statement with paid checks enclosed may not recover from the bank any amount paid on a forged or altered check if he is negligent in informing the bank promptly after receipt of the paid check and the bank can prove it has been harmed by said failure to give prompt notice. In addition, a negligent failure to notify the bank of the forgery or alteration within 14 days causes the drawer to bear the loss on additional checks, forged or altered by the same wrongdoer, thereafter paid in good faith by the bank.

4. If the drawer can prove that the bank was also negligent in paying a forged or altered check, then his negligence in notification of the bank does not preclude his recovery against the bank.

5. Regardless of negligence on the part of the drawer or the bank, a drawer who fails to report his unauthorized signature or any alteration within one year after receiving his bank statement or fails to report any unauthorized indorsement within three years bears the loss.

6. Where bank bears loss resulting from payment of a forged or altered check, it may look to the warranties of the party making presentment and prior transferors of the check for recovery. As to whether the bank will prevail, see p. 280, VII.B and C. In addition, the forger is liable to the bank independently of these warranties.

7. Example: F forges D's signature on a blank check and negotiates it to I, a holder in due course. I presents the check for payment to the B Bank, which honors it. D promptly notifies the bank upon return of the canceled check. Who will bear the loss? The bank will lose. It must credit the depositor's account (D's) since the order was not proper and D gave prompt notice. B Bank cannot recover against I, since it is absolutely bound to know its depositors' signatures. I did not warrant to the B Bank that the signature of the drawer was genuine.

8. Example: F forges the signature of P, the payee of a check, which had been lost. F negotiates to I, a holder in due course. I presents the check for payment at the B Bank, which pays it. D, B Bank's depositor, promptly notifies the bank when the check is returned and he learns that the bank did not pay P. Among the parties involved, who will bear the loss? I, the holder in due course will. D has a right to have his account credited since the bank did not follow his order to pay P. P was never paid, hence he has the right to the check or another in its place. The bank is not absolutely liable to know the genuineness of indorsers' signatures and, therefore, may recover the payment from I based upon the breach of a warranty he has given.

Selected Problems from CPA Examinations on Commercial Paper

Subjective Questions and Answers

Q. **1.** Your CPA firm was engaged to audit the Meglo Corporation. During the audit you examined the following instrument:

April 2, 1977

Charles Noreen
21 West 21st Street
St. Louis, Missouri

I, Charles Noreen, do hereby promise to pay to Roger Smith, Two Thousand Dollars ($2,000) one year from date, with 8% interest upon due presentment.

FOR: Payment for used IBM typewriters.

Charles Noreen

Meglo purchased the instrument from Smith on April 10, 1977, for $1,700. Meglo received the instrument with Smith's signature and the words "Pay to the order of Meglo Corporation" on the back. Upon maturity, Meglo presented the instrument to Noreen, who refused to pay. Noreen alleged that the typewriters were defective and did not satisfy certain warranties given in connection with the purchase of the used IBM typewriters which were guaranteed for one year. Noreen had promptly notified Smith of this fact and had told him he would not pay the full amount due.

Required
Answer the following, setting forth reasons for any conclusions stated.

1. Is the instrument in question negotiable commercial paper?
2. Assuming that the instrument is negotiable, does Meglo qualify as a holder in due course entitled to collect the full $2,000?
3. Assuming that the instrument is negotiable, is Noreen's defense valid against a holder in due course?
4. Assuming that the instrument is nonnegotiable, what is the legal effect of the transfer by Smith to Meglo?

A. **1.** No. Although it meets all of the other requisites of negotiability pursuant to the Uniform Commercial Code, it lacks the specific terminology of negotiability. That is, it is neither payable to Smith's "order" nor payable to "bearer." Consequently, it is a nonnegotiable promissory note. This defect is not cured by Smith's indorsement despite the fact he used the words "pay to the order of." The indication of the nature of the transaction is legally insignificant.

2. Yes. The note is not overdue, and Meglo took it for value and without notice or knowledge of any defect in it. The only possible assertion that could be made by Noreen to defeat Meglo's status as a holder in due course is that the size of the discount was so large as to indicate a lack of good faith. In the absence of any further information, a $300 discount on a one-year note such as this is not of such amount as to suggest a lack of good faith. Under these circumstances, Meglo would collect the full $2,000.

3. No. It is a mere personal defense and as such would not prevail against a subsequent holder in due course.

4. Since the instrument is not negotiable it cannot be "negotiated" to another person so as to enable him to qualify as a holder in due course. However, the transferor does assign all his rights to collect on the promise. Therefore, even if the typewriters were defective, Meglo would be entitled to sue on the promise and collect the amount due, decreased by damages for breach of warranty.

5/78

Q. 2. On July 1, 1974, Martin Hayes signed a promissory note that was made payable to the order of Jones Fabricating, Inc., for $10,000 plus 8% interest, payable 90 days from date. On the front of the note above his signature Hayes wrote: "Subject to satisfactory delivery of goods purchased this date. Delivery to be made no later than July 31, 1974."

Jones' president indorsed the note on behalf of the corporation and transferred it to Acme Bank in consideration of the bank's crediting $9,800 against a $20,000 debt owed to the bank by Jones Fabricating.

When the due date arrived, the bank asked Hayes to pay, but Hayes refused, saying that Jones had not delivered the goods he had bargained for in giving the note. The next day Acme Bank gave notice of dishonor to Jones.

Required

1. Is the note negotiable commercial paper? Explain.

2. Assuming the note is nonnegotiable paper, can Acme Bank collect the amount due from Hayes if Hayes can prove that the goods he bargained for were not delivered? Explain.

3. Assuming the note is negotiable, can Acme Bank successfully collect from Hayes? Explain.

4. Assuming the note is negotiable and that Acme Bank is a holder in due course, can Acme successfully sue Jones Fabricating to collect the proceeds of the note? Explain.

A. 1. No. To be valid commercial paper, the note must meet the requirements of negotiability. While the information given indicates it met some of these elements payable at a particular time, signed, in writing, payable to the order of a particular person, and a sum certain, it does not conform to the element requiring the paper to be unconditional. Since it was made "subject to satisfactory delivery of goods purchased," it has a condition which would excuse payment under the circumstances.

2. No. If the note is not negotiable, any contract defense can be used to refuse payment. Lack of performance by the other party is a good contract defense.

3. Yes. But for the note to be negotiable, it must be presumed that the condition placed on the note by the maker is nonexistent. Under these circumstances, if Acme Bank is a holder in due course it could collect, because a contract or personal defense such as nondelivery of goods is not available against a holder in due course. The bank seems to meet the elements of a holder in due course because it gave value ($9,800 debt credited), it was a holder of properly indorsed paper, and as far as can be determined from the facts, it acted in good faith, without knowledge of defenses or others' claims at the time it took the note when it appeared to be a normal acquisition of a note that was not overdue.

4. Yes. A holder in due course can sue the maker of the note, Hayes, or an unqualified indorser of the note such as Jones Fabricating, Inc., which has been given proper notice of dishonor. Since Jones had received notice of dishonor from the bank by the close of the business day following dishonor, it has been properly notified and is legally liable to pay the note.

11/74

Q. 3. Marvin Farber cashed a check for Harold Kern which was made to the order of Charles Walker by Marglow Investments & Securities. The check had the following indorsements on the back:

  1. *Charles Walker*
  2. Without recourse
     Doris Williamson
  3. Pay to the order of Harold Kern
     Jack Dixon
  4. Pay to the order of Marvin Farber

Kern neglected to sign his indorsement when he gave the check to Farber, and Farber did not notice this until the following day. Before Farber could locate Kern and obtain his signature, Farber learned that Walker had fraudulently obtained the check from Marglow (the drawer). Farber finally located Kern and obtained his signature. Farber promptly indorsed the check in blank and cashed it at National Bank. National Bank presented the check for payment through normal banking channels, but it was dishonored by Marglow's bank pursuant to a valid stop order. National Bank contacted Farber and informed him of the situation. Farber repaid the amount and the check was returned to him with National Bank's blank indorsement on the back.

Required
Answer the following, setting forth reasons for any conclusions stated.

1. Identify the type of indorsement and indicate the liability for each indorsement numbered 1, 2, and 3 above.
2. Will Farber prevail in a legal action seeking payment of the check by Marglow?

A. 1. Walker (indorsement 1) is a blank indorser. A blank indorsement specifies no particular indorsee and may consist of a mere signature. Williamson (indorsement 2) is a "without recourse" or qualified indorser. As such, she does not guarantee payment. Furthermore, the warranty that no defense of any party is good against the indorser, which is given by other indorsers, is limited by a without-recourse indorsement to a warranty that *the indorser has no knowledge of such defense*.

Dixon (indorsement 3) is a special indorser. A special indorsement specifies the person to whom or to whose order it makes the instrument payable. Any instrument specially indorsed becomes payable to the order of the special indorsee and may be further negotiated only by indorsement.

Indorsers in general have contract liability and also give certain warranties upon transfer. The Uniform Commerical Code provides that, unless otherwise agreed, indorsers are liable to one another in the order in which they indorse. This is presumed to be the order in which their signatures appear on the instrument. Both blank and special indorsers state that upon dishonor and notice, they will pay the instrument according to its tenor at the time of their indorsement to the holder or any subsequent indorser. The obligation is, in effect, a contractual undertaking to act as a guarantor. Walker and Dixon are subject to this liability; Williamson is not.

2. Yes. Although Farber cannot personally qualify as a holder in due course because he had notice of the defense (fraud) asserted by Marglow prior to the completion of the negotiation, he can assert the standing of his transferor (Kern). Thus Farber will prevail.

Farber could not assert a subsequent indorser-transferor's standing as a holder in due course (his bank's) in that the Uniform Commercial Code provides that a prior holder who had notice of a defense or claim against him cannot improve his position by taking it from a later holder in due course.

5/78

Q. 4. Barton Fashion, Inc., was in poor financial condition and desperate for cash. Wilcox, its major owner and president, contacted Marvel Department Stores, Inc., and offered to sell them 2,000 genuine alligator handbags at a bargain price. Wilcox showed several of the bags to Marvel's chief purchasing officer. These were duly examined and found to be of first quality in every respect. Marvel's chief purchasing officer placed an order with Barton for the 2,000 handbags. Payment was to be made upon delivery and inspection by Marvel. In fact, Barton had about 100 real alligator bags, the rest were clever imitations. Wilcox had the cartons packed in such a way that the genuine alligator bags were on the top of each carton. The shipment was made, and Marvel's initial inspection revealed that everything was apparently in order. Marvel delivered a check to Barton's agent who turned it over to Wilcox. Wilcox as president of Barton promptly negotiated the check to Walker, one of Barton's creditors who was threatening to file bankruptcy proceedings against Barton. Barton received $3,000 in cash and full credit against its debt to Walker for the balance of the check. Upon discovery of the fraud, Marvel promptly notified its bank, First Commerce, to stop payment on the check. When the check was presented for payment the next day, payment was refused.

Required

Answer the following, setting forth reasons for any conclusions stated.

1. What are the rights of Walker against First Commerce?
2. What are the rights of Walker against Marvel?
3. What are the rights of Marvel against Wilcox?
4. What are the rights of Marvel against Barton?

A. 1. Walker has no rights against First Commerce. First Commerce validly obeyed its customer's stop order. Hence, under the circumstances it had no potential liability to Walker.

2. Walker, as a holder in due course, has a valid claim against Marvel. The defense in question is a mere personal defense and as such is not available against a holder in due course. Furthermore, Walker may collect in full; both the cash and antecedent indebtedness constitute "value" under the Uniform Commercial Code.

3. Marvel has the right to recover any damages for loss from Wilcox because Wilcox acted in a fraudulent manner by misrepresentation followed by concealment of goods that did not conform to the contract. The fact that Wilcox was acting in an agency capacity will not relieve him from liability to Marvel.

4. Barton is liable to Marvel for the actions taken by its agent, Wilcox, who acted in a fraudulent manner. The basic rule establishing the principal's liability for his agent's tort is applicable. Furthermore, Barton received the benefit of the $3,000 cash paid on the check and credit for the balance on its indebtedness owing to Walker.

11/76

Q. 5. Davidson was one of Fenner Corporation's chief stock clerks. His net weekly salary was $125. Unfortunately, he lost a substantial sum of money betting on sports events, and he owed $2,000 to the loan sharks. Under these circumstances; he decided to raise the amount of his paychecks to $725 per week. His strategem was to wait until the assistant treasurer, in whose office the paymaster's check imprinting machine was located, was away from his desk. He would then go into the office and artfully strike the number 7 over the number 1 and raise the paycheck amount from $125 to $725. The checks were promptly negotiated to Smith, a holder in due course, who cashed them at his own bank, and the checks were subsequently paid by Fenner's bank, Beacon National. The fraudulent scheme was discovered within a week after Beacon returned Fenner's canceled checks for the month. By that time five weekly paychecks had been raised by Davidson and cashed by Smith. Fenner promptly notified Beacon of the fraud.

Required

Answer the following, setting forth reasons for any conclusions stated.

1. To whom is Davidson liable?
2. What are the rights and liabilities of Fenner?

3. What are the rights and liabilities of Beacon?

4. What are the rights and liabilities of Smith?

A. **1.** The embezzler, Davidson, is liable to whichever party bears the ultimate loss.

   2. Fenner Corporation would normally be able to recover $600 per check from Beacon National because it has a real defense (material alteration), which is valid even against a holder in due course. However, Beacon National has a possible defense of contributory negligence by Fenner on the basis that Fenner did not exercise proper safeguards to prevent improper use of the check-imprinting machine. The Uniform Commercial Code provides that any person who by his negligence substantially contributes to a material alteration of the instrument is precluded from asserting the alteration against a holder in due course or against a drawee or other payor who pays the instrument in good faith and in accordance with the reasonable commercial standards of the drawee's or payor's business. In any event, Fenner is still liable to the extent of the original amount of $125 per check.

   3. Normally, Beacon National must credit Fenner's account for the overpayments. It in turn has an action against the parties endorsing the instruments based upon a breach of their warranty that there were no material alterations. However, as discussed above, the possible defense of contributory negligence would be equally applicable here.

   4. Smith, as a holder in due course, has the same rights and liabilities as Beacon National as they are given above.

11/74

Q. 6. Herman Watts sold a used printing press to Marshall Offset, Inc., for $2,000. Watts requested that Marshall make the check payable to the order of the Foremost Finance Company because Watts was in arrears on a loan it owed to Foremost. That same day Watts delivered the check to Foremost, which, in turn, presented the check and received payment from Marshall's bank.

Marshall subsequently discovered serious defects in the printing press purchased from Watts. The defects unquestionably represented a breach of the express warranties given by Watts in the contract of sale. Immediately upon discovery of the defect, Marshall notified his bank to stop payment, but this was several days after the bank had processed the check.

Watts is hopelessly insolvent. Marshall seeks to rescind the transaction and recover the payment on the check from Foremost or its own bank.

Required

What legal remedies are available to Marshall in the situation described? Explain.

A.   Marshall has no rights against Foremost or its own bank. Both qualify as holders in due course and will prevail against the personal defense of breach of warranty. The fact that the check was initially made payable to the order of Foremost does not prevent Foremost from qualifying as a holder in due course if it gave value and took the check in good faith. An antecedent debt constitutes value, and there is no indication of any facts which would establish a lack of good faith on Foremost's part. The bank also qualifies as a holder in due course. The stop order is ineffective because it was initiated too late. Thus, Marshall's only recourse is to proceed against Watts.

11/74

Q. 7. For several years Dillon & Dodd, CPAs, has been retained to examine the financial statements of Marc Corporation. Shortly before beginning the examination for the year ended December 31, 1974. Mr. Dodd received a telephone call from Marc's president indicating that he believed something unusual was going on and that it probably involved some sort of embezzlement. The president further indicated that his suspicions were first aroused about three months earlier when he noted that the cash position was significantly lower than in prior years. The president then requested that Dillon & Dodd immediately undertake a special investigation to determine the amount of embezzlement if any.

After a month of investigation, Dillon & Dodd uncovered an embezzlement scheme involving the collusion of the head timekeeper and the treasurer's secretary. The scheme worked as follows:

- The treasurer's secretary processed all paperwork in conjunction with cash disbursements, including payroll, and typed all checks for the treasurer's signature.
- The treasurer relied on his secretary and routinely signed checks without reviewing the underlying documentation. The treasurer returned the signed checks to his secretary for mailing or distribution.
- The timekeeper supplied the treasurer's secretary with punched time cards for fictitious employees and invoices, receiving reports, and purchase orders for fictitious suppliers.
- The treasurer's secretary would prepare checks for the fictitious employees and suppliers, and after the checks were signed, she would extract the "bogus" checks. Then, either she or the timekeeper would indorse the checks and cash them or deposit them in various banks where they maintained accounts in the names of the fictitious payees.

The investigation revealed that the embezzlement scheme had been operating for 10 months and that more than $18,000 had been embezzled by the time the scheme was exposed. Most of the money had already been dissipated.

On the basis of the facts revealed by the investigation, Marc seeks to hold either the banks that cashed the checks or its own bank responsible for the loss.

Required

Will Marc prevail? Explain.

A.   No. Although a forged indorsement provides a defense against one's own bank for not following the order to pay the proper party, the Uniform Commercial Code provides that "an indorsement by any person in the name of a named payee is effective if . . . an agent or employee in the name of the maker or drawer has supplied him with the name of the payee intending the latter to have no such interest."

The rule, commonly known as "the fictitious payee rule," is clearly applicable here. The secretary and timekeeper were the employees of the corporation and submitted the checks for the treasurer's signature without intending the named payees to have any interest therein; they were fictitious. Their wrongful indorsement of the named payees is valid insofar as Marc is concerned. The only hope Marc might have for recovery against the banks would be to establish some gross negligence on the part of the banks which could be deemed sufficient to have put them on notice of the embezzlement. This is most unlikely, however.

5/75

Q. 8. (The facts of the prior question are continued.) Payday at Marc Corporation occurred five days before the embezzlement scheme was exposed by Dillon & Dodd. Having become suspicious of the questions the auditors were asking and the additional information they were seeking and obtaining, the timekeeper and the secretary decided to work their embezzlement one more time and then flee the state. They submitted 12 bogus checks totaling $1,380 and absconded with them on payday. They immediately deposited the checks in the various bank accounts that they had set up to facilitate their fraudulent scheme. Most of the banks permitted the embezzlers to withdraw the entire balance of the account prior to clearance of the final deposit. Others insisted that the embezzlers wait until the checks cleared.

When Marc's treasurer was informed of the embezzlement scheme, he immediately called the corporation's bank and told the bank manager to stop payment on the bogus checks. This was confirmed in writing two days later. It was subsequently learned that Marc's bank (the drawee bank) had processed the 12 bogus checks as follows:

- Prior to receiving the oral stop-payment order, six checks totaling $850 were processed and paid.
- At the time of receiving the oral stop-payment order, three checks totaling $250 were being processed and were, in fact, paid after Marc's bank received the oral stop-payment order.
- The other three checks totaling $280 were processed one week after receipt of Marc's stop-payment order. Of these checks, one for $100 was paid by Marc's bank. The remaining two checks, one for $110 and one for $70, were caught by the bank's employees, payment was stopped, and the checks were returned to the appropriate banks. Only the bank where the $110 check was returned had not let the embezzlers withdraw the funds; thus, the $110 amount was charged against the embezzlers' account balance.

Required

What, if anything, can Marc recover from the banks in question? Discuss all items.

A.   Probably only $110. The $850 representing checks which had already been paid is not recoverable from the banks which had the money withdrawn from the accounts. The Uniform Commercial Code provides that a bank gives value when a check is paid or the amount is withdrawn. Under the circumstances, these banks would qualify as holders in due course of the checks even if they had not been paid. Here, having paid in good faith, they are free from liability. In addition, Marc's bank has no liability for the $850 because the stop-payment order was too late; that is, it had already paid the other banks in question.

            Under prior law there might be a real defense based upon a forged indorsement or unauthorized signature of the payee, which could be asserted against the banks involved. However, the Uniform Commercial Code has laid this problem to rest by providing that "an indorsement by any person in the name of a named payee is effective if . . . an agent or employee of the maker or drawer has supplied him with the name of the payee intending the latter to have no such interest."

            Obviously, from the facts of the situation presented, this rule is clearly applicable. Hence, there is no real defense available to Marc.

            Without more facts it is impossible to determine whether Marc can recover on the $250 of checks paid after receipt of the oral stop-payment order. The oral stop-payment order is valid for 14 days; however, Marc's bank must be afforded a reasonable opportunity to act on the stop-payment order prior to taking any action (e.g., paying) on the checks. If in fact the bank was not afforded, such reasonable opportunity to stop payment, it is not liable even though the stop-payment order was antecedent to payment. The information is not given regarding this question of fact.

            The balance of $280 is not recoverable with the exception of the $110. Payment of this $110 item was effectively stopped and the instrument dishonored. Furthermore, the depository bank has not, and certainly will not, pay it. Therefore, the $110 will not be collectible against Marc.

            The $100 check poses a different problem. Although a stop-payment order must be honored by the customer's bank, wrongful payment will not result in liability to the payee bank unless the customer establishes the fact and amount of loss from wrongful payment. This problem lies with the fact that even if the bank had stopped payment, it was just too late to be of any benefit to Marc. That is, the depository bank had already paid the item and consequently would have the standing of a holder in due course vis-à-vis Marc. Hence, no loss was caused by the wrongful action by Marc's bank. The same concept is applicable to the remaining check for $70, even though it was not wrongfully paid.

                                                                                                                                    5/75

Q.   9.   During your examination of the financial statements of Arista Corporation, you encounter a check payable to Arista for $5,000 that has just been returned by the drawee bank marked "Insufficient Funds." The check was drawn by Seymore Enterprises, Inc., in payment for a printing press purchased from Arista.

            Before accepting the check, Arista insisted upon the accommodation indorsements of Charles Morgan, Seymore's chairman of the board, and Frank Johnston, its president. Both signed in blank. The check had been promptly deposited and processed by the United States banks involved. Investigation reveals that Seymore has filed a voluntary petition in bankruptcy.

Required

1. What steps should Arista take to protect its rights on the check? Explain.
2. What rights if any, does Arista have against Seymore Enterprises, the drawee bank, Charles Morgan, and Frank Johnston? Explain.

A.   1.   The procedures required for Arista to protect its rights on the check are presentment and notice of dishonor. Protest is not required because the check was not drawn on a foreign bank or payable outside the United States.

Presentment was accomplished by the prompt deposit and processing of the check by Arista and the banks. Notice of dishonor must be made by Arista to Seymore, Morgan, and Johnston. Accommodation indorsers are treated the same as any other indorser and must be given notice of dishonor to hold them liable.

Notice of dishonor may be given orally, but a written notice is the better practice. This may be accomplished by a simple statement that after valid and timely presentment, the check was dishonored by the drawer.

2. Arista has the following rights against the various parties to the check.

Seymore Enterprises. Assuming proper notice of dishonor, Seymore bears the ultimate liability on the check. However, since Seymore is in financial difficulty, collection is, at best, questionable.

The drawee bank. Arista has no rights against the drawee bank. A drawee bank has no liability to the party presenting a check for payment, including a holder in due course. In this case where sufficient funds were not available to pay the check, the bank properly dishonored it. Even if there were sufficient funds available to pay the check, the bank would have liability only to its depositor, Seymore, for wrongful dishonor.

Charles Morgan and Frank Johnson. Both are, in effect, sureties, having guaranteed the performance or debt of Seymore. Assuming a proper notice of dishonor, either or both must pay the amount due on the check.

11/73

Q. 10. John Ford signed a check for $1,000 on January 25, 1975, payable to the order of Charles Benson Manufacturing, a sole proprietorship. The check was dated February 1, 1975. Benson indorsed the check to Francis Factoring, Inc., by writing on the back of the check: "Pay only to Francis Factoring, Inc., Charles Benson." After Benson delivered the check to Francis Factoring, Francis Factoring immediately took the check to First National Bank, the drawee, and had the check certified. Francis Factoring then indorsed the check in blank to Hills Brokerage Corporation in payment of materials purchased.

Required

1. Did the indorsement, "Pay only to Francis Factoring, Inc.," stop the negotiability of the check and legally require the drawee bank to pay the proceeds of the check to Francis Factoring only? Explain.
2. Can Hills Brokerage qualify as a valid holder of the check with all the rights of a holder in due course? Explain.
3. Assuming Hills Brokerage qualifies as a holder in due course, can it successfully sue First National Bank if the bank refuses to honor the check on February 1? Explain.
4. Assuming Hills Brokerage qualifies as a holder in due course, can it successfully sue Ford for the proceeds of the check if the bank refuses to honor it on February 1? Explain.
5. Assuming Hills Brokerage qualifies as a holder in due course, can it successfully sue Benson for the proceeds of the check if the bank refuses to honor it on February 1? Explain.
6. Assuming Hills Brokerage qualifies as a holder in due course, can it successfully sue Francis Factoring for the proceeds of the check if the bank refuses to honor it on February 1? Explain.

A. 1. No. Once a check is negotiable, no indorser can stop its negotiability. In legal effect, the restrictive indorsement "Pay only to Francis Factoring, Inc." will be charged to "Pay to the order of Francis Factoring, Inc." Thus, Francis can negotiate the check further by indorsement.
2. Yes. The elements of a holder in due course will not be affected by the restrictive indorsement, by the fact that the check was certified, or by the fact that the check was postdated. Hills gave value, took it in good faith, had no knowledge of defenses, and the check had been properly indorsed by Benson and Francis.
3. Yes. In certifying the check the bank promises to honor the check when presented within a reasonable time after the date payable, February 1, 1975.
4. No. While a drawer of a check is normally liable to pay the amount of the check if it is dishonored by the drawee-bank, this secondary liability of the drawer, Ford, was terminated when the check was certified at the request of a holder of the check, Francis Factoring.
5. No. Benson would also be released from the secondary liability he had as an unqualified indorser by the later certification of the check by Francis Factoring.

6. Yes. Certification of a check releases all parties who signed or become secondarily liable on the check before the certification, but all indorsers after the certification remain liable to pay on the check if the bank does not pay it.

5/75

Practice Questions

Q. 1. On September 30, 1975, Dayton Blasting Company purchased 25 cases of blasting caps from Whitten Blasting Cap Company. In this connection, it gave Whitten the following instrument:

```
                                                        September 30, 1975


    Dayton Blasting Company hereby promises to pay Whitten Blasting Cap Company Six
    Hundred Fifty Dollars ($650.00) on December 1, 1975, plus interest at 6% per annum
    from date.
                                             Dayton Blasting Company


                                       By    Malcolm Smalley
                                             MALCOLM SMALLEY, President
```

Whitten promptly transferred the above instrument to Vincent Luck for $600. James Whitten, president of Whitten, indorsed the instrument on the back as follows: "Pay to the order of Vincent Luck" signed Whitten Blasting Cap Company per James Whitten, President.

Approximately half of the blasting caps were defective and Dayton refused to pay on the instrument. Dayton returned the defective cases and used the balance.

Required

What are Vincent Luck's rights on the instrument in question? Explain.

Q. 2. Joseph Martin persuaded his employer, Robert Franklin, to issue a check payable to the order of Milton Small in the amount of $1,000. Martin represented to Franklin that Small was entitled to a refund of $1,000 for merchandise returned that day by Small. Franklin delivered the check to Martin and instructed him to mail it to Small.

Martin's statement was false. He did not know any person called Milton Small. When Martin received the check intended for Small, he indorsed the check in the name of Milton Small and delivered it to Arthur Smith, a holder in due course. Martin absconded, and when Franklin discovered what had happened, he stopped payment on the check. Smith sues Franklin.

Required

1. Was the check bearer paper or order paper at the time of issue? Explain.
2. Was Martin's indorsement effective to negotiate the check? Explain.
3. May Smith recover from Franklin? Explain.

Q. 3. During your initial examination of the payroll procedures and transactions of Fox Burglar Alarm, Inc., you discover the following facts. Martin Goodson is employed as a payroll officer. Some time ago he became addicted to narcotics, and in order to support his drug habit, he bagan preparing payroll checks made out to fictitious parties. Fox's treasurer, unaware of the fraud, signed the checks in the ordinary course of his duties.

After signature, Goodson would pick up the checks to distribute to the employees. In the process, Goodson removed the checks payable to the fictitious parties. He would then cash the checks at various check-cashing agencies, forging the names of the payees appearing on each check.

Required

What rights, if any, does Fox Burglar Alarm have against its own bank, which paid the checks, the check-cashing agencies, and Goodson? Explain.

Q. 4. Lawrence executed and delivered a check for $1,000 payable to the order of Evans. Lawrence used due care in preparing the check. However, Evans (by methods best known to forgers) raised the amount to $10,000 and negotiated the check for value to Mark, who took the check in good faith without notice of the alteration. When Mark presented the check for payment, it was returned marked "Insufficient Funds." Mark then sued Lawrence. In connection with his examination of Lawrence's financial statements, a CPA is attempting to determine the liability and related loss on this item, if any.

Required

1. Can Mark recover? Explain.
2. If so, how much? Explain.

Q. 5. Robert Little mailed his $180 check drawn upon the Last National Bank to Wilfred, his creditor. An employee of Wilfred stole the check from Wilfred's office, indorsed Wilfred's name on it, and delivered it to Sam's Grocery Store for $30 in groceries and $150 in cash. Sam indorsed the check "for deposit" and deposited it in his account with Valley National Bank, which collected it from Last National Bank and credited the $180 to Sam's account. Last National Bank charged Little's account.

Required

Assume that yesterday Wilfred complained to Little that he had not received the check and that Wilfred and Little then discovered what had happened to it. Discuss separately the rights and liabilities of each of the following with respect to the check:

1. Little.
2. Last National Bank.
3. Valley National Bank.
4. Sam.
5. Wilfred.

Q. 6. Arthur purchased securities from William, giving William his check payable to William's order and drawn on Produce Bank in payment. At William's insistence, the check was indorsed by Arthur's friend Gregory before it was delivered. William then indorsed the check to the order of Robert, "without recourse," and it was accepted by Robert in payment of a debt owed him by William. Robert indorsed the check in blank and delivered it to his son Charles as a birthday gift. Arthur has discovered that the securities sold him by William are worthless and has directed Produce Bank to stop payment.

Required

1. Identify the status of all parties to the described above at each step in its negotiation, explaining such identifications.
2. When Produce Bank refuses to pay Charles on the check and Charles sues Arthur, may Arthur assert the defense of failure of consideration against Charles? Explain.

3. Assuming Charles knew Gregory signed the check as an accommodation to William and received no value for his accommodation, may Charles nevertheless recover from Gregory on the Bank's failure to honor the check? Explain.

4. Assume Arthur has no defense on the check and is insolvent, that Charles took the check from Robert for value, and that the Bank refused to pay the check for lack of funds in Arthur's account. Discuss the rights and liabilities of Charles, Robert, William, and Gregory.

Q. 7. On July 9, 1971, Donnell, hard pressed for cash, borrowed $2,000 from Munro in exchange for his promissory note for $2,000 plus 12% interest payable on January 9, 1972, to the order of Munro. The statutory legal rate of interest for this transaction was 8%. In August 1971 Munro indorsed the note in blank and sold and delivered it to Gaylord for $2,000 cash. On January 3, 1972, Gaylord sold and delivered the note without indorsement to Tucker for $2,100 in cash. Tucker failed to present the note for payment on January 9, 1972 and on March 1, 1972, he indorsed the note in blank "without recourse" and sold and delivered it to Dunfee for $1,950 cash. Neither Gaylord, Tucker, nor Dunfee had any knowledge of the transaction in which the note originated.

Required

1. Was Tucker a holder in due course? State "yes" or "no" and discuss.
2. Is Dunfee entitled to the rights of a holder in due course? State "yes" or "no" and discuss.
3. Is Donnell liable to Dunfee? State "yes" or "no" and discuss.
4. Is Gaylord liable to Dunfee? State "yes" or "no" and discuss.
5. Is Tucker liable to Dunfee? State "yes" or "no" and discuss.

Practice Objective Questions

Instructions 1–20

Select the *best* answer for each of the following items. Mark only one answer for *each* item. Answer all items. Your grade will be based on your total correct answers.

1. There are several legally significant differences between a negotiable instrument and a contract right and the transfer of each. Which of the following statements is correct?
   a. A negotiable instrument is deemed *prima facie* to have been issued for consideration whereas a contract is *not* deemed *prima facie* to be supported by consideration.
   b. Generally, the transferee of a negotiable instrument and the assignee of a contract right take free of most defenses.
   c. Neither can be transferred without a signed writing or by a delivery.
   d. The Statute of Frauds rules apply to both.

2. An instrument reads as follows:

$5,000.00	Boise, Idaho	October 1, 1978

Thirty Days after date I promise to pay to the order of _____ *cash* _____
at *120 BROADWAY, New York City*
   Value received with interest at the rate of eight percent per annum.
This instrument arises out of a separate agreement.

No. *20 Due October 31, 1978*   *H. G. Loeb*

Which of the following statements about this instrument is correct?

a. The instrument is negotiable.

b. The instrument is order paper.

c. The instrument is a time draft.

d. Failure to make a timely presentment will excuse Loeb from liability.

3. Your client, Robert Rose, has the following instrument in his possession.

March 1, 1976

One month from date, I, Charles Wallace, do hereby promise to pay Edward Carlson seven hundred and fifty dollars ($750.00).

Charles Wallace

Edward Carlson wrote "pay to the order of Robert Rose" on the back and delivered it to Rose.

a. Robert Rose is a holder in due course.

b. The instrument is a negotiable promissory note.

c. Edward Carlson is a holder in due course.

d. All defenses, real and personal, are assertible by Wallace against Rose.

4. Maxwell is a holder in due course of a check which was originally payable to the order of Clark and has the following indorsements on its back:

Clark

Pay to the order of White

Smithers

Without Recourse

White

Dobbins

Which of the following statements about this check is correct?

a. If the bank refuses to pay, Maxwell's only recourse is to sue Dobbins.

b. The instrument was bearer paper in Dobbins' hands.

c. Clark's signature was *not* necessary to negotiate the instrument.

d. White has *no* warranty liability to Maxwell on the instrument.

5. Which of the following is a characteristic of the "without recourse" indorsement?

a. It can only be used where the instrument is a draft.

b. It puts the person acquiring it on notice of some defect or defense which could be asserted against the transferee of the instrument.

c. It modifies but does *not* completely eliminate the indorser's warranty liability to subsequent holders.

d. It will *not* limit the indorser's liability to an immediate transferee.

6. An otherwise valid negotiable instrument is nonnegotiable if it is

a. Postdated.

    b. Undated.

    c. Payable 30 days after a stated date but with the right of the holder to demand immediate payment at his option.

    d. Payable only upon the happening of an event which is uncertain as to the time of occurrence.

7. Price has in his possession an otherwise negotiable instrument which reads:

        "I, Waldo, hereby promise to pay to the order of Mark or bearer. . . ."

    Which of the following is true with respect to the above instrument?

    a. Mark's signature is required to negotiate the instrument.

    b. The instrument is nonnegotiable.

    c. If Mark indorses the instrument, Mark assumes potentially greater liability to subsequent transferees than if Mark transfers it by mere delivery.

    d. Since the instrument is payable to Mark's order, it is a draft.

8. Your client, Commercial Factors, Inc., discounted a $2,000 promissory note, payable in two years, for $1,500. It paid $500 initially and promised to pay the balance ($1,000) within 30 days. Commercial paid the balance within the 30 days, but before doing so learned that the note had been obtained originally by fraudulent misrepresentations in connection with the sale of land which induced the maker to issue the note. For what amount will Commercial qualify as a holder in due course?

    a. None because the 25% discount is presumptive or *prima face* evidence that Commercial is *not* a holder in due course.

    b. $500.

    c. $1,500.

    d. $2,000.

9. Johnson lost a check that he had received for professional services rendered. The instrument on its face was payable to Johnson's order. He had indorsed it on the back by signing his name and printing "for deposit only" above his name. Assuming the check is found by Alcatraz, a dishonest person who attempts to cash it, which of the following is correct?

    a. Any transferee of the instrument must pay or apply any value given by him for the instrument consistent with the indorsement.

    b. The indorsement is a blank indorsement and a holder in due course who cashed it for Alcatraz would prevail.

    c. The indorsement prevents further transfer or negotiation by anyone.

    d. If Alcatraz simply signs his name beneath Johnson's indorsement, he can convert it into bearer paper and a holder in due course would take free of the restriction.

10. Archer has in his possession a bearer negotiable instrument. He took it by negotiation from Perth who had stolen it from Cox's office along with cash and other property. The robbery of Cox's office had received appropriate coverage in the local papers in the area in which both Archer and Cox reside. Archer did *not* know that Perth had stolen the instrument when he purchased it at a 20% discount. Cox refuses to pay and Archer has commenced legal action asserting that he is a holder in due course. Which of the following statements is correct?

    a. Even if all other requisites are satisfied, Archer's title is defective in that there was *no* delivery by Cox of the instrument.

    b. Archer is a holder in due course and will prevail.

    c. Archer is prevented from qualifying as a holder in due course because there had been general notice published in the community about the robbery.

    d. The discount in and of itself prevents Archer from qualifying as a holder in due course or at least prevents him from so qualifying as to the 20%.

11. Path stole a check made out to the order of Marks. Path forged the name of Marks on the back and made the instrument payable to himself. He then negotiated the check to Harrison for cash by signing his own name on the back of the instrument in Harrison's presence. Harrison was unaware of any of the facts surrounding the theft or forged indorsement and presented the check for payment. Central County Bank, the drawee bank, paid it. Disregarding Path, which of the following will bear the loss?

    a. The drawer of the check payable to Marks.

    b. Central County Bank.

    c. Marks.

    d. Harrison.

12. Troy fraudulently induced Casper to make a negotiable instrument payable to the order of Troy in exchange for goods he never intended to deliver. Troy negotiated it to Gorden, who took with notice of the fraud. Gorden in turn negotiated it to Wagner, a holder in due course. Wagner presented it for payment to Casper, who refused to honor it. Wagner contacted Gorden who agreed to reacquire the instrument by negotiation from Wagner. Which of the following statements is correct?

    a. Casper would have been liable if Wagner had pursued his rights on the negotiable instrument.

    b. Gorden was initially a holder in due course as a result of the negotiation to him from Troy.

    c. Casper is liable to all parties except Troy in that it was his fault that the instrument was issued to Troy.

    d. Gorden can assert the rights of his prior holder in due course, Wagner, as a result of the repurchase.

13. Franco & Sons, Inc., was engaged in the furniture manufacturing business. One of its biweekly paychecks was payable to Stein, who negotiated it to White in payment of a gambling debt. White proceeded to raise the amount of the check from $300 to $800 and negotiated it to Carson, a holder in due course, for cash. Upon presentment by Carson at the drawee bank, the teller detected the raising of the amount and contacted Franco who stopped payment on the check. Franco refuses to pay Carson. Carson is seeking to recover the $800. Under the circumstances, which of the following is a correct statement?

    a. Franco is liable, but only for $300.

    b. Franco is liable for the $800.

    c. Stein is liable for the $800.

    d. Franco has *no* liability to Carson.

14. Martindale Retail Fish Stores, Inc., purchased a large quantity of fish from the Seashore Fish Wholesalers. The exact amount was *not* ascertainable at the moment, and Martindale, rather than waiting for the exact amount, gave Seashore a check which was blank as to the amount. Seashore promised *not* to fill in any amount until it had talked to Martindale's purchasing agent and had the amount approved. Seashore disregarded this agreement and filled in an amount that was $300 in excess of the correct price. The instrument was promptly negotiated to Clambake & Company, one of Seashore's persistent creditors, in payment of an account due. Martindale promptly stopped payment. For what amount will Martindale be liable to Clambake? Why?

    a. Nothing because Martindale can assert the real defense of material alteration.

    b. Nothing because Clambake did not give value and the stop order is effective against it.

    c. Only the correct amount because the wrongful filling in of the check for the $300 excess amount was illegal.

    d. The full amount because the check is in the hands of a holder in due course.

15. Filbert Corporation has in its possession an instrument which Groves, the maker, assured Filbert was negotiable. The instrument contains several clauses which are *not* typically contained in such an instrument and Filbert is *not* familiar with their legal effect. Which of the following will adversely affect the negotiability of the instrument?

    a. A promise to maintain collateral and to provide additional collateral if the value of existing collateral decreases.

    b. A term authorizing the confession of judgment on the instrument if *not* paid when due.

    c. A statement to the effect that the instrument arises out of the November 1, 1978, sale of goods by Filbert to Groves.

    d. A statement that it is payable only out of the proceeds from the resale of the goods sold by Filbert to Groves on November 1, 1978.

16. A negotiable instrument is examined during an audit engagement. If the instrument contains *no* agreement about a delayed presentment, then which of the following is the proper time for presentment?

    a. On the same date all other negotiable instruments are presented.

    b. Ten days after the due date if it is a promisory note.

    c. Within 30 days after issue for the usual uncertified check.

    d. A reasonable time after issuance of the instrument regardless of its type.

17. Wilson drew a sight draft on Foxx, a customer who owed Wilson money on an open account, payable to the order of Burton, one of Wilson's creditors. Burton presented it to Foxx. After examining the draft as to its authenticity and after checking the amount against outstanding debts to Wilson, Foxx wrote on its face "Accepted—payable in 10 days" and signed it. When Burton returned at the end of the 10 days, Foxx told him he could *not* pay and was hard pressed for cash. Burton did *not* notify Wilson of these facts. Two days later when Burton again presented the instrument for payment, Burton was told that Foxx's creditors had filed a petition in bankruptcy that morning. Which of the following statements is correct?

a. The instrument in question is a type of demand promissory note.

b. Wilson had primary liability on the draft at its inception.

c. Foxx was secondarily liable on the instrument prior to acceptance.

d. Foxx assumed primary liability at the time of acceptance.

18. Davidson bore a remarkable physical resemblance to Ford, one of the town's most prominent citizens. He presented himself one day at the Friendly Finance Company, represented himself as Ford, and requested a loan of $500. The manager mistakenly, but honestly, believed that Davidson was Ford. Accordingly, being anxious to please so prominent a citizen, the manager required *no* collateral and promptly delivered to Davidson a $500 check payable to the order of Ford. Davidson took the check and signed Ford's name to it on the back and negotiated it to Robbins, who took in the ordinary course of business (in good faith and for value). Upon learning the real facts, Friendly stopped payment on the check. Robbins now seeks recovery against Friendly. Under these circumstances, which of the following statements is correct?

a. Friendly could *not* validly stop payment on the check.

b. Davidson's signature of Ford's name on the check constitutes a forgery and is a real defense which is valid against Robbins.

c. Since both Friendly and Robbins were mistaken as to Davidson's real identity, they will share the loss equally.

d. Davidson's signature of Ford's name on the check is effective and Robbins will prevail against Friendly.

19. Certification of a check by the drawee bank

a. Is obligatory if demanded by a holder in due course.

b. Is the drawee's signed engagement to honor it when presented.

c. Where procured by a holder discharges all prior indorsements, but does *not* affect the drawer's liability.

d. Is ineffective regarding any indorsement made after certification and creates *no* liability for the subsequent indorser.

20. Gardner Owen purchased some bearer bonds from P & L Securities, Inc., and gave them a promissory note. P & L Securities negotiated the instrument, for value, to Barbara Stapp by a blank indorsement. Stapp had no knowledge of the securities transaction. Stapp presented the instrument to Owen for payment on the due date. Owen refused to pay the note alleging a failure of consideration and that the securities were absolutely worthless. Stapp sued Owen on the note. What is the probable outcome of the lawsuit?

a. Stapp will prevail because Owen's defense is a personal defense which is *not* assertible against Stapp.

b. Owen will prevail because his defense is a real defense which is assertible against Stapp.

c. Stapp will be required to institute suit against P & L Securities.

d. Owen will be required to give the bearer bonds to Stapp.

CHAPTER 12

Documents of Title and Investment Securities

AICPA Content Specification Outline

Warehouse Receipts
Bills of Lading
Issuance, Transfer, and Registration of Securities

Contents

III. Investment Securities
  A. Definition
  B. Form
  C. Issuer
  D. Rights acquired by a purchaser
  E. *Bona Fide* purchaser
  F. Warranties of a transferer
Practice Question
Practice Objective Questions

I. Introduction: Article 3 (Commercial Paper) excludes instruments not defined by its terms; investment securities are specifically excluded. Documents of title and most investment securities (stock certificates) are excluded because the instruments are not payable in money. Corporate bonds are payable in money but large numbers of them are conditional and would therefore be excluded. But even if they were not conditional, they are excluded from qualification as commercial paper as a matter of policy. Both documents of title and investment securities are nevertheless negotiable if in proper form. The importance of each in the areas of sales, finance, and secured transactions is immense.

  A. Although excluded from the scope of commercial paper, the law that applies to them (Articles 7 and 8) bears a marked similarity to Article 3. Conceptually, if you have grasped the commercial paper area, you will be able to quickly assimilate this part of the text.

  B. The key feature of both is that if either the document of title or investment security is in the hands of a party who closely resembles our friend, the holder in due course, then that party is not subject to most defenses.

II. Documents of Title: We are dealing here almost exclusively with negotiable bills of lading issued by a carrier, or negotiable warehouse receipts issued by a bailee-warehouseman. They are intangible personal property, but they represent very tangible personal property—the goods shipped or stored.

  A. Definitions:
   1. Bailee: the person who by a warehouse receipt, bill of lading, or other document of title acknowledges possession of goods and contracts to deliver them.
   2. Bill of lading: a document evidencing the receipt of goods for shipment issued by a person engaged in the business of transporting or forwarding goods; it includes an airbill.
   3. Document of title: includes bills of lading, warehouse receipts, and any other document that in the regular course of business or financing is treated as adequately evidencing that the person in possession of it is entitled to receive, hold, and dispose of the document and the goods it covers.
   4. Holder: a person who is in possession of a document of title or an instrument or

an investment security drawn, issued, or indorsed to him or to his order, or in blank or to bearer.

5. Issuer: a bailee who issues a document.

6. Warehouse receipt: a receipt issued by a person engaged in the business of storing goods for hire.

B. Form of a negotiable document of title. A warehouse receipt, bill of lading, or other document of title is negotiable:

    a. If by its terms the goods are to be delivered to bearer or to the order of a named person, or

    b. Where recognized in overseas trade, if it runs to "a named person or assigns."

    c. Any other document is nonnegotiable. Indorsement of a nonnegotiable bill neither makes it negotiable nor adds to the transferee's rights.

C. Negotiation: A negotiable document of title running to the order of a named person is negotiated by his indorsement and delivery. After indorsement in blank or to bearer, any person can negotiate it by delivery alone. A negotiable document of title is also negotiated by delivery alone when by its original terms it runs to bearer.

    a. When a document running to the order of a named person is delivered to him, the effect is the same as if the document had been negotiated.

    b. Negotiation of a negotiable document of title after it has been indorsed to a specified person requires indorsement by the special indorsee as well as delivery.

D. **Due negotiation:** This concept is comparable to that of acquiring *holder in due course* status. A negotiable document of title is "duly negotiated" when it is negotiated to a holder who purchases it in good faith without notice of any defense against or claim to it on the part of any person and for value, unless it is established that the negotiation is:

    a. Not in the regular course of business or financing, or

    b. Involves receiving the document in settlement or payment of a money obligation. The big difference here is that if the document is received for an antecedent debt, it will *not* constitute value.

E. Rights acquired by due negotiation (subject to limited exceptions):

    a. A holder to whom a negotiable document of title has been duly negotiated acquires thereby:

        (1) Title to the document,

        (2) Title to the goods,

        (3) All rights accruing under the law of agency or estoppel, including rights to goods delivered to the bailee after the document was issued, and

        (4) The direct obligation of the issuer to hold or deliver the goods according to the terms of the document free of any defense or claim by him except those arising under the terms of the document or under Article 7 in general.

        (5) In the case of a delivery order the bailee's obligation accrues only upon acceptance, and the obligation acquired by the holder is that the issuer and any indorser will procure the acceptance of the bailee.

    b. Title and rights so acquired are not defeated by any stoppage of the goods represented by the document or by surrender of such goods by the bailee, and are not impaired even though the negotiation or any prior negotiation constituted a breach of duty; or even though any person has been deprived of possession of the document by misrepresentation, fraud, accident, mistake, duress, loss, theft, or conversion; or even though a previous sale or other transfer of the goods or document has been made to a third person.

    c. *One exception* contained in the Article **involves goods that are stolen** or otherwise misappropriated, *then* placed in a warehouse or shipped, and for which a negotiable document of title is obtained. The defense is valid against a holder to whom the document of title has been duly negotiated.

III. Investment Securities

A. Definition: Securities governed by Article 8 (Investment Securities) are **negotiable instruments.** A security is an instrument that:

    1. Is issued in bearer or registered form; and

    2. Is of a type commonly dealt in upon securities exchanges or markets or commonly recognized in any area in which it is issued or dealt in as a medium for investment, and

    3. Is either one of a class or series or by its terms is divisible into a class or series of instruments, and

    4. Evidences a share, participation, or other interest in property or in an enterprise or evidences an obligation of the issuer.

    5. A writing that is a security is governed by this Article and not by Article 3 of the Uniform Commercial Code (Commercial Paper) even though it also meets the requirements of that Article.

B. Form: A security is in:

    1. *Registered form: when it specifies a person* entitled to the security or to the rights it evidences and when its transfer may be registered upon books maintained for that purpose by or on behalf of an issuer or the security so states.

    2. *Bearer form; when it runs to bearer* according to its terms and not by reason of any indorsement.

C. Issuer: With respect to obligations on, or defenses to, a security, issuer includes a person who places or authorizes the placing of his name on a security (otherwise than as authenticating trustee, registrar, transfer agent or the like) to evidence that it represents a share, participation, or other interest in his property or in an enterprise; or to evidence his duty to perform an obligation evidenced by the security.

D. Rights acquired by a purchaser: Upon delivery of a security, the purchaser acquires the rights in the security that his transferor had or had actual authority to convey, except that a purchaser who has himself been a party to any fraud or illegality affecting the security or who, as a prior holder, had notice of an adverse claim cannot improve his position by taking from a later *bona fide* purchaser.

    1. Adverse claim: includes a claim that a transfer was, or would be, wrongful or that a particular adverse person is the owner of, or has an interest in, the security.

2. A *bona fide* purchaser, in addition to acquiring the rights of a purchaser, also acquires the security free of any adverse claim.

E. *Bona fide* purchaser: **A bona fide purchaser is a purchaser for value in good faith and without notice of any adverse claim who takes delivery of a security in bearer form or of one in registered form issued to him or indorsed to him or in blank.** E.g., If stock certificates in blank are endorsed, subsequently stolen and transferred to a *bona fide* purchaser, the purchaser will be able to take free of the prior party's claim of title.

F. Warranties of a transferee: A person by transferring a security to a purchaser for value warrants only that:

1. His transfer is effective and rightful; and
2. The security is genuine and has not been materially altered; and
3. He knows no fact that might impair the validity of the security.

Practice Question*

Dwight Corporation purchased the following instrument in good faith from John Q. Billings:

No. 7200 • • • REGISTERED • • • $10,000
Magnum Cum Laude Corporation

Ten year 14% Debenture, Due May 15, 1990

Magnum Cum Laude Corporation, a Delaware Corporation, for value received, hereby promises to pay the sum of TEN THOUSAND DOLLARS ($10,000) to JOHN Q. BILLINGS, or registered assigns, at the principal office or agency of the Corporation in Wilmington, Delaware.

On the reverse side of the instrument, the following appeared:

"For value received, the undersigned sells, assigns, and transfers unto DWIGHT CORPORATION, (signed) JOHN Q. BILLINGS." Billings' signature was guaranteed by Capital Trust Company.

Magnum's 14% debentures are listed on the Pacific Coast Exchange.

Required
Answer the following, setting forth reasons for any conclusions stated.

1. What type of instrument is the above? Is it negotiable?
2. Has Dwight Corporation taken via a due negotiation so as to qualify as a *bona fide* purchaser?
3. If, or assuming that, the instrument is negotiable and Dwight is a *bona fide* purchaser, what are the benefits it derives as a result of such status?

*During the period of time that this topic, Documents of Title and Investment Securities (Chapter 12), has been included in the AICPA examination coverage, there has never been subjective testing of the topic. The above question is based upon a recent objective question.

Practice Objective Questions

Instructions

Select the *best* answer for each of the following items. Mark only one answer for *each* item. Answer all items. Your grade will be based on your total correct answers.

1. The Uniform Commercial Code deals differently with negotiable documents of title than with commercial paper. Which of the following will prevent a due negotiation of a negotiable document of title?
    a. The transfer by delivery alone of a title document which has been endorsed in blank.
    b. The receipt of the instrument in payment of an antecedent money obligation.
    c. The taking of a bearer document of title from one who lacks title thereto.
    d. The fact that the document of title is more than one month old.

2. Under the Uniform Commercial Code's rule, a warehouseman
    a. Is liable as an insurer.
    b. Will *not* be liable for the nonreceipt or misdescription of the goods stored even to a good faith purchaser for value of a warehouse receipt.
    c. *Cannot* limit its liability in respect to loss or damage to goods while in its possession.
    d. Is liable for damages which could have been avoided through the exercise of due care.

3. A negotiable bill of lading
    a. Is one type of commercial paper as defined by the Uniform Commercial Code.
    b. Can give certain good faith purchasers greater rights to the bill of lading or the goods than the transferor had.
    c. *Cannot* result in a loss to the owner if lost or stolen, provided prompt notice is given to the carrier in possession of the goods.
    d. Does *not* give the rightful possessor the ownership of the goods.

4. While auditing the common stock ledger of Sims Corporation a CPA uncovers the following situation. An investor has purchased a certificate representing 500 shares of common stock of the Sims Corporation from a former clerk of the corporation. It was the duty of the clerk to prepare stock certificates from a supply of blanks for signature of the corporate secretary. The clerk forged the corporate secretary's signature on a bearer certificate and delivered the certificate for value to the investor who did not have notice of the forgery and who now demands a reissued certificate in the investor's name from the corporation. The corporation asserts that it has no liability to reissue a certificate in the name of the investor and that the investor's bearer certificate is null and void. Which of the following is correct?
    a. The certificate is valid and the investor is entitled to a reissued certificate.
    b. The certificate issued is invalid and the corporation has *no* liability to reissue.
    c. An appropriate recourse of the investor is to sue the corporation and clerk for dollar damages and to sue the clerk for the crime of forgery.
    d. The corporation is required to reissue a certificate only if appropriately compensated by the investor.

5. Wilberforce & Company has in its possession certain securities which it took in good faith and for value from Dunlop. An adverse claim or defense has been asserted against the securities. Which of the following warranties may Wilberforce validly assert against Dunlop, its prior transferor?
    a. There is *no* defect in the prior chain of title.
    b. The securities are genuine and have *not* been materially altered.
    c. There is *no* defect which might impair the validity of the securities.
    d. Dunlop will defend the purchasers' title from adverse claim or defects which would impair the validity of the securities.

6. Hargrove lost some stock certificates of the Apex Corporation which were registered in his name, but which he had indorsed in blank. Flagg found the securities and sold them through a brokerage house to Waldorf. Apex, unaware of Hargrove's problem, transferred them to Waldorf. Hargrove is seeking to recover the securities or damages for their value. Which of the following is correct?
    a. The stock in question is transferable but Waldorf takes subject to Hargrove's claim of title.
    b. Waldorf is a holder in due course of a negotiable instrument and therefore will prevail.
    c. Apex is liable for wrongfully transferring Hargrove's stock to Waldorf.
    d. Waldorf qualifies as a bona fide purchaser and acquires the stock free of Hargrove's adverse claim.

13

Sales

AICPA Content Specification Outline

Contracts Covering Goods
Warranties
Product Liability
Risk of Loss
Performance and Obligations
Remedies and Defenses

Contents

I. Characteristics and Contracts Covering Goods

A. Introductory note: This section is based exclusively on the rules contained in Article 2 (Sales) of the UCC with the exception of the common law developments included in II.E., Products Liability and the Magnuson-Moss Federal Warranty Act.

B. Modifications of common law contract principles. During your consideration of contract law, you encountered several provisions of Article 2, Sales, which deviated in important respects from traditional contract rules. The more important of these provisions are summarized below. Reference back to the appropriate pages should help you remember them:

   1. *Determination of price.* The parties possess the power to stipulate in their contract either the actual price or the manner in which the price is to be determined. Should they fail to exercise their power, the Code provides that the price shall be a reasonable one determined as of the time and place of delivery. For related discussion see p. 140.

2. *Offer and acceptance.* Where an acceptance includes additional terms, the terms are to be regarded as proposed additions to the contract. Where merchants are involved, the proposed additions will be deemed accepted unless they materially alter the contract, or the original offeror objects to the modifications within a reasonable time.

3. *Options (firm offers).* When the offeror is a merchant and the offer is contained in a signed writing, the offer will be irrevocable for a reasonable time not exceeding three months, even though no consideration is given.

4. *Statute of frauds.* Contracts for the sale of goods priced at $500 or more must be in writing. The only absolutely essential term of the signed writing is a statement of the quantity involved. A merchant who receives a letter of confirmation will be bound by its provisions unless he notifies the other party within ten days, and in writing, of his objections. Partial performance does not remove the entire contract from the signed writing requirement; only the part of the contract which has been performed will be enforceable.

5. *Parol evidence rule.* It is permissible and proper to consider evidence of the pattern of prior dealing between the parties, the meaning given to certain contract language within the trade, and the ordinary course of dealing within the trade. See p. 155.

6. *Implied conditions.* A seller is excused from delivering goods when his performance has become commercially impracticable due to unforeseen supervening circumstances not contemplated when the contract was created. One is not excused from a contract because of increased cost or inconvenience, nor when a greater than normal burden was knowingly assumed. See p. 161.

7. *Output, requirement, and exclusive dealing contracts.* Such contracts are enforceable where the parties have acted in good faith and the quantity offered or demanded is not unreasonably disproportionate to any stated estimate or previous normal requirements or output. See p. 140.

C. Definitions:

1. Sale: consists of the passing of title from the seller to the buyer for a price.
2. Contract for sale: includes both a present sale of goods and an agreement to sell goods at a future time.
3. Present sale: a sale that is accomplished by the making of the contract.
4. Goods:
   a. All things (including specially manufactured goods) that are movable at the time of identification to the contract for sale other than:
      (1) The money in which the price is to be paid.
      (2) Investment securities.
      (3) Things in action (intangible personal property such as accounts receivable).
   b. Includes the unborn young of animals and growing crops and other identified things attached to reality.
   c. Fungible goods means goods of which any unit is, by nature or usage of trade, the equivalent of any other like unit.

5. Merchant: a person who deals in goods of the kind involved or who otherwise by his occupation holds himself out as having knowledge or skill peculiar to the practices of the trade or goods involved in the transaction.

6. C.O.D.: shipments: collection on delivery.

7. F.O.B.: free on board; freight charges are paid by the seller, who also bears the risk of loss to the destination of the goods shipped.

   a. Destination contract: seller pays for freight because place of destination is named (F.O.B. destination city).

   b. Shipping contract: buyer pays for freight as place of shipment is named (F.O.B. shipping city).

8. C.I.F.: cost, insurance, and freight included in price. Buyer has risk of loss after seller puts goods in hands of carrier and obtains insurance in buyer's name.

9. F.A.S. vessel: free alongside the vessel named; seller delivers goods alongside the named vessel at his own risk and expense.

10. No arrival, no sale: neither party is liable unless buyer receives the goods.

11. Sale or return: goods may be returned without the commission of breach of contract. Although title is in seller, the buyer has risk of loss.

12. Sale on approval: conforming goods may nevertheless be returned; seller retains risk and title until buyer's acceptance.

D. Other commercial transactions distinguished from sales:

1. Bailment:

   a. Definition: a delivery of personal property by one person to another for a particular purpose, upon condition that the property be subsequently returned, kept until reclaimed, or disposed of pursuant to agreement.

      (1) Bailor: delivers the property, has title but not possession.

      (2) Bailee: accepts it, has possession but not title.

      (3) Both have an insurable interest in the property.

   b. Elements.

      (1) Personal property.

         (A) No bailment of real property.

         (B) Valid chattel: No rights can arise from illegal goods. (E.g., bailor cannot reclaim narcotics stored in warehouse.)

      (2) Transfer of possession and control either by actual delivery of the property itself, or constructive delivery (e.g., where a key to the place where the goods are stored is delivered to the bailee or he is given documents of title representing the actual goods).

      (3) Bailments are normally contractual (express contract), but they may also be constructive (implied contract, e.g., a finder of lost goods).

      (4) Acceptance of possession: Acceptance is normally pursuant to a contract or agreement by the parties; however, acceptance may be implied as in the case of a finder of lost goods.

      (5) Title remains in the transferor (bailor). Appointment of a receiver over bailee's property would not affect bailor's title.

      (6) In a mutual benefit bailment, the bailee has the duty of exercising reasonable care of the bailed property. He is not an insurer, i.e., he will not be liable unless negligent or otherwise at fault.

    2. Consignment: a special type of bailment or an agency for sale.

        a. Transfer of possession, but not title, for shipment or sale.

        b. Consignee normally the agent of consignor for purpose of selling the property involved (see Secured Transactions, p. 345).

    3. Bulk transfers. Article 6 of the UCC (Bulk Transfers) applies to all those whose principal business is the sale of merchandise from stock, including those who manufacture what they sell (e.g., a toy manufacturer who produces toys in one part of his shop and sells them in another). A bulk transfer is any transfer in bulk that is not made in the ordinary course of business, but that consists of a major part of the materials, inventory, or equipment of a business. A bulk transfer to provide security for performance or settlement of a security interest is exempted.

E. Elements of a sale:

    1. Parties must have capacity to contract (see Contracts, p. 148, III.D).

    2. Price.

        a. The parties, if they so intend, can conclude a contract for sale even though the price is not settled. In such a case the price is a reasonable price at the time for delivery if:

            (1) Nothing is said as to price, or

            (2) The price is left to be agreed upon by the parties and they fail to agree, or

            (3) The price is to be fixed in terms of some agreed market or other standard as set or recorded by a third person or agency and it is not so set or recorded.

        b. A price to be fixed by the seller or by the buyer means a price for him to fix honestly and (in the case of a merchant) according to commercially reasonable standards.

    3. Subject matter: goods that have:

        a. Validity (see Contracts, p. 147, III.C.).

        b. Actual existence and identity.

            (1) Goods must be both existing and identified to the contract before any interest in them can pass.

            (2) Goods that are not both existing and identified are "future goods." A purported present sale of future goods or of any interest therein operates as a contract to sell, not a present sale.

        c. Where goods whose continued existence is presupposed by the agreement are destroyed without fault of either party before the risk of loss has passed to the buyer:

            (1) If the loss is total, the contract is avoided.

            (2) If the loss is partial, the buyer may avoid the contract or take the surviving goods with a price adjustment.

F. Merchants and the UCC:

    1. Special rules apply to transactions among merchants (see, e.g., p. 311, II.C.3.c). In general, the UCC fosters the creation of legal rights more easily when the agreement is solely between merchants rather than between a consumer and a merchant, since the concern for protecting the inexperienced and untutored consumer is not present.

2. Article 2 sets special standards for merchants in many special areas. These include: firm offer by a merchant; Statute of Frauds; conflicting offers and acceptances; modification of existing contracts; warranty of merchantable quality; duty to follow instructions; retention of possession; power of sale of goods entrusted to merchants; and risk of loss and goods rejected by a merchant buyer.

II. Warranties

A. Introduction: the UCC's treatment of warranties represents a significant shift toward greater consumer protection. Article 2 has made express warranties of certain warranties that were implied under prior law, and the UCC defines the ambiguous term "merchantability." Also, in the area of disclaimers the Code's provisions are aimed at greater consumer protection. The UCC does, however, take an equivocal position on the question of privity (see p. 312, II.F.1), leaving this decision to a local law.

B. Express warranties:

1. Express warranties by the seller are created as follows:
   a. Any affirmation of fact or promise made by the seller to the buyer that relates to the goods and becomes part of the basis of the bargain creates an express warranty that the goods shall conform to the affirmation or promise.
   b. Any description of the goods that is made part of the basis of the bargain creates an express warranty that the goods shall conform to the description.
   c. Any sample or model that is made part of the basis of the bargain creates an express warranty that the whole of the goods shall conform to the sample or model.
2. It is not necessary to the creation of an express warranty that the seller use formal words such as "warrant" or "guarantee" or that he have a specific intention to make a warranty. However, an affirmation merely of the value of the goods or a statement purporting to be merely the seller's opinion or commendation of the goods does not create a warranty. The borderline between "affirmations of fact" or "promises" and expressions of "value" or "opinion" remains imprecise.
3. No warranty is created when the seller is merely "puffing" his goods; that is, where the promise or affirmation is a value judgment or opinion of the goods (e.g., the clothes will "wear like iron"). However, the Code's tightening of the rules of disclaimer (see D below) should make the "puffing" salesman more guarded in his statements and thus add to consumer protection.
4. UCC Section 2–209 has eliminated the contract requirement of consideration for agreements modifying a sales contract (see Contracts, p. 145, III.B.2.b). Elimination of this requirement has validated most postcontractual promises made by the seller and has significantly expanded the consumer's express warranty protection.

C. Warranty of title and against infringement:

1. There is in a contract for sale a warranty by seller that:
   a. The title conveyed shall be good and its transfer rightful.
   b. The goods shall be delivered free from any security interest or other lien or encumbrance of which the buyer at the time of contracting has no knowledge.

2. A warranty under 3.a. above will be excluded or modified only by specific language or by circumstances that give the buyer reason to know that the person selling does not claim title in himself or that he is purporting to sell only such right or title as he or a third person may have. (E.g., "I do not claim to have clear title to the goods in question and any defects in title must be assumed by you, the buyer.")

3. Unless otherwise agreed, a seller who is a merchant regularly dealing in goods of the kind sold warrants that the goods shall be delivered free of the rightful claim of any third person by way of patent or trademark infringement or the like, but a buyer who furnished specifications (e.g., plans or drawings for manufacture) to the seller must hold the seller harmless against any such third-party claim that arises out of compliance with the specifications.

4. Although it is not mentioned specifically in the UCC provision, the official comment to that provision states that the disturbance of the buyer's quiet possession of the goods is one way of establishing a breach of the title warranty.

5. For any breach of the warranty of title, the buyer must seasonably (i.e., within a reasonable time) notify seller.

6. The UCC is silent on whether this warranty is express or implied.

D. Implied warranties of quality:

1. Merchantability

  a. Unless excluded or modified, a warranty that the goods shall be merchantable is implied in a contract for their sale if the seller is a merchant with respect to goods of that kind. The serving for value of food or drink to be consumed either on the premises or elsewhere is a sale of goods.

  b. Goods to be merchantable must be at least such goods as:

  (1) Pass without objection in the trade under the contract description, and

  (2) In the case of fungible goods (i.e., movable goods such as grain, which may be sold on the basis of weight, measure, or number) are of fair average quality within the description, and

  (3) Are fit for the ordinary purposes for which such goods are used, and

  (4) Run, within the variations permitted by the agreement, of even kind, quality, and quantity within each unit and among all units involved, and

  (5) Are adequately contained, packaged, and labeled as the agreement may require, and

  (6) Conform to the promises or affirmations of fact made on the container or label if any.

  (7) Goods sold by a brand name must have average quality of that brand.

  c. Unless excluded or modified, other implied warranties may arise from course of dealing or usage of trade.

2. Creation of the **warranty of fitness** for a particular purpose.

  a. Seller must have actual or constructive knowledge of the particular purpose for which the buyer needs the goods (e.g., knowledge that shoes would be used for mountain climbing).

  b. Seller must furnish or select the goods.

  c. Buyer must rely on the seller's skill or judgment. Insistence by the buyer on a particular brand (e.g., Ajax) would ordinarily indicate that the buyer is not relying on the seller's skill and judgment: hence, no warranty. However, the mere fact that the article purchased has a particular trade name is not sufficient to indicate nonreliance if the article has been recommended by the seller as adequate for the buyer's purpose (e.g., "Ajax will take tobacco stains off your woodwork").

d. This warranty applies equally to merchants and nonmerchants.

E. Cumulation and conflict of express or implied warranties:

1. Warranties, whether express or implied, shall be construed as consistent with each other and as cumulative, but if such construction is unreasonable, the intention of the parties shall determine which warranty is dominant. In ascertaining that intention, the following rules apply:

a. Exact or technical specifications displace an inconsistent sample or model or general language of description.

b. A sample from an existing bulk displaces inconsistent general language of description.

c. Express warranties displace inconsistent implied warranties other than an implied warranty of fitness for a particular purpose.

2. The rules set forth above are not absolute but are mere guides that may be changed by evidence showing that the parties had some other intention.

F. **Limitations on warranty protection:**

1. Requirement of **privity.**

a. Early common law restricted the scope of warranty protection to the party or parties directly contracting with the seller. (E.g., if a woman buys defective food for her family from a grocery, only she has an action of warranty against the grocer, even if other members of the family were injured by it. Furthermore, there would be no warranty action available against the manufacturer or intermediate distributor of the food because there is no privity between either of them and our housewife, the ultimate consumer.)

b. The UCC originally extended the warranty protection only to the buyer's family, household, and guests if it is reasonable to expect that they would use, consume, or be affected by the goods. A seller may not exclude or limit the operation of this warranty.

c. Most states have broken down the privity requirement between manufacturers and distributors and the ultimate consumer. Recent landmark cases in several former citadels of privity indicate a clear trend away from this antiquated rule. This is particularly so in the case of food and drugs. The UCC set forth three alternate provisions, two of which are antiprivity. Thus, a majority of states currently reject a requirement of privity.

2. Exclusion or modification of warranties (**disclaimers**).

a. The UCC seeks to protect a buyer from unexpected and unbargained-for language of disclaimer by:

(1) Denying effect to such language when inconsistent with language of express warranty.

(2) Permitting the exclusion of implied warranties only by clear and conspicuous language or other circumstances that protect the buyer from surprise.

b. To disclaim the warranty of merchantability, the seller must normally use the word "merchantable" in the disclaimer (e.g., "no warranty exists as to the merchantability"); and if the disclaimer is written, it must be a conspicuous writing.

c. To exclude the implied warranty of fitness for a particular purpose, the disclaimer must be in writing and conspicuous.

d. All warranties of quality may be excluded by:

(1) Language such as "with all faults" or "as is" or other similar language that in common understanding clearly calls the buyer's attention to the exclusion of warranties and makes plain there is no implied warranty.

(2) An unrestricted examination of the goods by the buyer or a refusal to examine will negate all implied warranty protection as to the defects that an examination ought, in the circumstances, to have revealed to him.

(3) A course of dealing or usage of trade (e.g., where an end-of-season sale of remaining stock to a person dealing in such property is deemed to be final and without warranty protection).

e. As with the seller's and buyer's remedies (see p. 323, VI.E), the parties are free to bargain for their own warranties and remedies for breach of warranty. (For the buyer's remedies for improper delivery, including breach of warranty, see p. 323, VI.E.2.)

3. The parol evidence rule: Where the contract is in writing and governed by the parol evidence rule (see Contracts, p. 154) the buyer will not be able to rely upon evidence of earlier conflicting oral express warranties relating to the goods. However, the implied warranties of merchantability and fitness are not affected except by use of a written express disclaimer, which would be sufficient to preclude them (see b and c above).

G. Statute of limitations: The UCC contains a four-year statute of limitations for the sale of goods. The parties may reduce the period to one year, but they may not lengthen it. Time of breach of warranty:

1. Breach occurs when tender of delivery is made.

2. When the warranty explicitly extends to future goods, the cause of action accrues when the breach is, or should have been, discovered.

H. Magnuson-Moss Federal Warranty Act:

1. Purpose: The Magnuson-Moss Act became effective in 1975. While the Act does not require manufacturers or sellers of consumer products to issue written warranties, it does state the disclosure requirements when a manufacturer or seller chooses to issue a warranty. The FTC is charged with the task of issuing rules delineating how a "consumer products firm" must comply with the Act.

2. Definition.

a. Consumer buyer of any consumer product, a transferee of the buyer, or any other person who is entitled under the terms of the warranty or by state law to enforce the terms of the warranty.

b. Consumer product: "tangible personal property which is distributed in commerce and which is normally used for personal, family or household purposes."

    c. Supplier: any person engaged in the business of making a consumer product directly or indirectly available to consumers.

    d. Warrantor: any supplier or other person who gives or offers to give a written warranty or who is or may be obligated under an implied warranty.

    e. Written warranty:

        (1) Any written affirmation of fact or written promise made in connection with the sale of a consumer product which relates to the nature of the material or workmanship over a specified period of time.

        (2) Any written undertaking a supplier makes in connection with a consumer sale to refund, repair, replace, or take other remedial action in the event that the product fails to meet the specifications set forth in the undertaking.

3. Scope.

    a. The Act is generally limited to consumer buyers of consumer products.

    b. The Act applies to all express warranties if the product sells for more than $15.00.

    c. A service contract to maintain and/or repair a product which substitutes for a written warranty is regulated by the Act.

4. Disclosure requirements: The Act is primarily a disclosure statute and the maker of a written warranty must comply with the following provisions:

    a. On all products selling for more than $10.00 the written warranty must be designated as "full" or "limited." A product may have both warranties if they are clearly and conspicuously differentiated.

    b. A full warranty means that:

        (1) A defective product must be repaired or replaced without charge and within a reasonable period of time.

        (2) Anyone owning the product during the warranty period, even if not the original purchaser, may enforce the warranty.

        (3) "Anti-lemon" provision: if a product cannot be repaired after repeated attempts, the consumer is entitled to either a replacement or a refund at the consumer's option.

        (4) A warrantor may give a registration card but can not make the return of the card a requirement for a warranty. It must be clear to the consumer that the return of the warranty card is voluntary.

        (5) A fully warranty designation does not imply that the entire product is covered by the terms of the warranty or that it is covered for any specified period.

    c. Limited warranty: if a warranty fails to meet the federal minimum standards for a full warranty it must be "clearly and conspicuously designated as Limited."

    d. Service contracts must disclose their terms and conditions "fully, clearly and conspicuously."

5. Implied warranties can not be disclaimed or modified if:

    a. A written warranty has been made to the contrary.

    b. A service contract was entered into between the supplier and consumer at the time of the sale or 90 days thereafter.

6. Presale availability of warranties: the seller must make the terms of the warranty available to the consumer through one of the following means:
   a. Display the warranty text in close proximity to the product.
   b. Display notice disclosing the warranty text.
   c. Display the product on which the written warranty is clearly visible.
   d. Maintain a book containing warranties in such a location that the consumer has ready access to the information.
7. Remedies.
   a. Informal settlement of disputes are encouraged by Congress under the Act. The warrantor may establish such informal dispute settlement procedures if:
      (1) A warrantor establishes the procedure,
      (2) FTC rules governing the procedure are met, and
      (3) The written warranty incorporates a requirement that the consumer must resort to the informal settlement procedure before initiating any legal action to recover under the warranty.
   b. Civil action: after pursuing the informal settlement procedure, if one has been established by the warrantor, the consumer may sue as an individual or in a class action suit in federal court for damages and other legal or equitable relief if:
      (1) The individual claim is at least $25.00.
      (2) The amount in controversy is at least $50,000.00 ("computed on the basis of all claims to be determined in the suit") exclusive of costs and interest.
      (3) If a class action is brought there must be at least 100 plaintiffs.

III. Product Liability

A. Generally:
   1. Definition: The liability of manufacturers, distributors, retailers, and others for damage caused by defects or dangers in their products, whether the damage be suffered by those with whom they deal or by others.
      a. Underlying policy is to afford the consumer a legally enforceable right against the manufacturer to proceed on the assumption that the product will serve in normal use without causing injury.
      b. Doctrine of products liability is not considered applicable to losses of a solely economic nature, where a product does not perform as expected or intended, which losses are actionable under sales warranty.
      c. Neither a manufacturer, seller, distributor, retailer, or supplier is an insurer of the safety of his product, or an insurer against accidental injury arising out of the use of such product; a manufacturer is not under an obligation to make a product accidentproof or foolproof.
   2. Possible **causes of action** are not mutually exclusive:
      a. Causes of action include:
         (1) **Breach of warranty:** may be express or implied.
         (2) Common law **negligence:** seller's duty of ordinary care.

            (3) **Strict liability** in tort: it is a civil wrong to place dangerous and defective items on the market. Defective includes design defects.

        b. The purchaser of a defective product may sue based on breach of warranty, strict liability, or negligence; the right to sue on strict liability in tort is available to users and consumers of a product even though they are not its purchasers.

B. Warranties (see Sales, p. 310, II.C):

    1. Implied warranty (UCC Sections 2-314 and 2-315)

        a. Merchantability.

        b. Fitness for particular purpose.

        c. Usage of trade.

    2. Express warranty (UCC Section 2-313).

C. Common law negligence:

    1. Duty on the manufacturer to exercise ordinary care.

        a. Industry standards are generally controlling; if manufacturer's conduct in manufacturing, inspecting, or testing the product falls below industry standards, he is negligent.

        b. Negligence per se: an unexcused violation of an applicable federal or state statute (designed to protect the class of people of whom the injured party is a member from the risk of harm, which the manufacturer's violation caused) is negligence without further evidence, regardless of industry standards.

        c. *Res Ipsa Loquitur:* There is a rebuttable presumption of negligence where the accident is of a type that is generally a result of negligence, the manufacturer has exclusive control of all injury-causing factors, and the injured party is free from negligence.

    2. The injured party must prove:

        a. An injury and damages.

        b. A defective product was involved (by industry standard).

        c. The defect was the proximate cause of his injury.

    3. Defenses:

        a. Contributory negligence or comparative negligence.

        b. Assumption of risk.

        c. Consent.

D. **Strict liability** in tort: liability is imposed, without regard to the exercise of reasonable care, on one who sells a product in a defective condition unreasonably dangerous to the user or consumer, if the seller is engaged in the business of selling such product, and the product is expected to and does reach the user or consumer without substantial change in the condition in which it is sold.

    1. Purpose: to insure that the costs of injuries resulting from defective products are borne, as a cost of doing business, by the persons who put the products into the channels of commerce, rather than by the injured persons who are ordinarily powerless to protect themselves, without imposing on such persons the problems inherent in pursuing negligence remedies.

    2. Liability is placed on the party primarily responsible, since such party is in the best position to most effectively reduce the hazards to life and health from its products, and to secure an adequate remedy for the injured party.

3. Strict liability was adopted under the guise of, or evolved from, the theory of implied warranty; it is essentially the liability of implied warranty divested of its accompanying contract doctrines.

4. Degree of care used by the seller is not an issue in strict liability as it is in common law negligence; contributory negligence of the user is not a defense.

5. Defenses of lack of notice of breach, disclaimer, and lack of privity are unavailable for strict liability although they are available in implied warranty.

IV. Title, Risk of Loss, and Third-Party Rights

A. The limited importance of title: Under prior law, many critical legal consequences were determined by location of title to the goods. Now it serves a relatively minor residual purpose.

   1. Where passage of title retains vitality:

      a. Parties may agree as to when title passes once the goods are identified to contract. Otherwise, title passes when seller completes his performance regarding physical delivery of the goods.

      b. If the seller has no duty to move the goods in any manner, passage of title occurs when the documents of title are delivered, providing the goods are identified or fungible. If there is no existing document of title, passage occurs at time and place of contracting, as long as goods are identifiable.

   2. Under the UCC, however, specific provisions govern the legal consequences of various situations irrespective of title. These include provisions regarding risk of loss (see B below), the seller's right of action for the price, insurable interest, and other situations.

B. Risk of loss:

   1. In the event of a breach:

      a. In general, the UCC quite properly places the risk of loss on the party who has breached the contract. It also takes into account the fact that the goods sold are normally insured.

      b. Where a tender or delivery of goods so fails to conform to the contract as to give a right of rejection, the risk of their loss remains on the seller until cure (see p. 320, V.C) or acceptance.

      c. Where the buyer rightfully revokes acceptance, he may, to the extent of any deficiency in his effective insurance coverage, treat the risk of loss as having rested on the seller from the beginning.

      d. Where the buyer as to conforming goods already identified to the contract for sale repudiates or is otherwise in breach before risk of their loss has passed to him, the seller may, to the extent of any deficiency in his effective insurance coverage, treat the risk of loss as resting on the buyer for a commercially reasonable time.

   2. In the absence of breach:

      a. Where the contract requires or authorizes the seller to ship the goods by carrier:

    (1) If it does not require him to deliver them at a particular destination, the risk of loss passes to the buyer when the goods are duly delivered to the carrier.

    (2) If it does require him to deliver them at a particular destination and the goods are there duly tendered while in the possession of the carrier, the risk of loss passes to the buyer when the goods are so tendered as to enable the buyer to take delivery.

    (3) The UCC presumes that the seller is not obligated to deliver at a named destination and bear the concurrent risk of loss until arrival, unless he has specifically agreed to make delivery or the commercial understanding of the terms used by the parties contemplates such delivery.

    (4) The UCC has made certain widely used shipping terms an integral part of its rules regarding when delivery is required, thereby determining who has the risk of loss, e.g., F.O.B. (see I.C.6–12.)

  b. Where the goods are held by a bailee to be delivered without being moved, the risk of loss passes to the buyer:

    (1) On his receipt of a negotiable document of title covering the goods, or

    (2) On acknowledgment by the bailee of the buyer's right to possession of the goods, or

    (3) After his receipt of a nonnegotiable document of title or other written direction to deliver.

  c. In any case not within the above subsections a and b, the risk of loss passes to the buyer on his receipt of the goods if the seller is a merchant; otherwise the risk passes to the buyer on tender of delivery.

  d. The application of the above subsections (a, b, and c) is subject to the following limitations:

    (1) The contrary agreement of the parties: The UCC rules apply only where the parties have not allocated risk of loss in their contract. Clearly, the parties to the sale should expressly cover this point in their contract.

    (2) In "sales on approval" the risk of loss does not pass to the buyer until acceptance, and in "sale or return" transactions the risk of loss is on the buyer until the goods are returned.

    (3) As previously indicated, where there has been a breach of contract, the rules contained in B.1 (p. 317) apply.

3. As a matter of policy, Article 2 has made an attempt to correlate possession and risk of loss in some situations. Thus, where the goods are not to be shipped, the risk of loss passes to the buyer on his receipt of the goods if the seller is a merchant; otherwise the risk passes to the buyer on tender of delivery. In any event, risk of loss may be covered by insurance. When either party can suffer loss, that party acquires an insurable interest.

C. Wrongful sales to third parties:

1. Power to transfer title to good faith purchaser of goods. A purchaser of goods acquires all title that his transferor had or had power to transfer except that a purchaser of a limited interest acquires rights only to the extent of the interest purchased. A person with voidable title has power to transfer a good title to a good faith purchaser for value. When goods have been delivered under a transaction of purchase, the purchaser has such power even though:

a. The transferor was deceived as to the identity of the purchaser, or

b. The delivery was in exchange for a check, that is later dishonored, or

c. It was agreed that the transaction was to be a "cash sale," or

d. The delivery was procured through fraud punishable as larcenous under the criminal law.

2. Entrusting.

    a. Any entrusting of possession of goods to a merchant who deals in goods of that kind gives him power to transfer all rights of the entruster to a buyer in ordinary course of business.

    b. "Entrusting" includes any delivery and any acquiescence in retention of possession regardless of any condition expressed between the parties to the delivery or acquiescence and regardless of whether the procurement of the entrusting or the possessor's disposition of the goods have been such as to be larcenous under the criminal law.

    c. The rights of other purchasers of goods and of lien creditors are governed by the Articles on Secured Transactions (Article 9), Bulk Transfers (Article 6), and Documents of Title (Article 7).

3. Stolen goods. Where goods are stolen, the thief's title is void, i.e., the thief has no title. Thus a *bona fide* purchaser obtains no title and the owner can regain the property or seek damages for conversion (tort). This rule does not apply to a holder in due course of a negotiable instrument.

V. Performance and Obligations

A. Seller's rights upon buyer's insolvency:

1. Where the seller discovers the buyer to be insolvent, he may refuse delivery except for cash, including payment for all goods previously delivered under the contract, and stop delivery in transit as discussed in B, below.

2. Where the seller discovers that the buyer has received goods on credit while insolvent, he may reclaim the goods upon demand made within 10 days after receipt, but if a written misrepresentation of solvency has been made to the seller within three months before delivery, this 10-day limitation does not apply.

    (1) Reclamation is subject to the rights of buyers in the ordinary course of business and other good faith purchasers.

    (2) Successful reclamation of goods excludes all other remedies in respect to them.

B. Stoppage in transit: The seller may stop delivery of goods in the possession of a carrier or other bailee (e.g., a warehouseman) irrespective of the size of shipment when he discovers the buyer to be insolvent. He may also stop delivery of carload, truckload, planeload, or larger shipments of express or freight when the buyer repudiates or fails to make a payment due before delivery. Stoppage can be made at any time until:

1. Receipt of the goods by the buyer.

2. Acknowledgment to the buyer by any bailee of the goods, except a carrier, that the bailee holds the goods for the buyer.

3. Such an acknowledgment by a carrier by reshipping the goods for the buyer or such acknowledgment being made to the buyer where the goods are being held by the carrier in the capacity of a warehouseman.

4. Transfer to the buyer of any negotiable document of title (e.g., a negotiable bill of lading or negotiable warehouse receipt).

C. Cure. Where the buyer rejects a nonconforming tender:

1. If the time for performance has not expired, the seller may "cure" or correct the deficiency by seasonably notifying the buyer of his intention and may then within the contract time make a conforming delivery.

2. If the seller had reasonable grounds to believe the goods would be acceptable with or without money allowance, the seller may, if he seasonably notifies the buyer, have a further reasonable time to substitute a conforming tender. Buyer must particularize the defect.

    a. The purpose of this provision is to prevent "surprise rejections," which were frequently used under prior law in situations where the buyer was seeking to avoid his contractual obligations.

    b. "Reasonable grounds" can lie in prior course of dealing, course of performance, or usage of trade, as well as in the particular circumstances surrounding the making of the contract.

D. Insurable interest and identification of goods. This subject matter is discussed fully in the insurance chapter, p. 397.

VI. Remedies and Defenses

A. Introduction: Many of the remedies discussed in this part of the text have been considered as they relate to contracts in general (see Contracts, p. 137). However, the UCC has made many significant additions to, and modifications and refinements of, the traditional remedies available to parties to contracts for the sale of goods. In general, the UCC gives the parties wide discretion to determine their own remedies by specifying them in their contract. Unless construction of the contractual language precludes such an interpretation, the remedies specified are to be deemed additions to those that the UCC provides (see below). This discretion to determine the remedies is subject to the following limitations in connection with:

1. Liquidated damages: Although specifically permitted, the liquidation is enforceable only at an amount that is reasonable in light of the anticipated or actual harm caused by the breach, the difficulties of proof of loss, and the inconvenience or nonfeasibility of otherwise obtaining an adequate remedy. Excessive liquidated damages are void as a penalty.

2. Unconscionable modifications and limitations: In general, unconscionable clauses are invalid. Specifically, limitations of consequential damages—see p. 325, VI.C.4.c(2)—for injury to the person in the case of consumer goods is *prima facie* unconscionable, but limitation where the loss is commercial is not.

B. Right to assurances: When reasonable grounds for insecurity arise with respect to the performance of either party, the other may demand in writing adequate assurance of due performance. The aggrieved party may also:

1. Suspend his own performance pending the outcome of the demand, if it is commercially reasonable to do so.
2. Treat the contract as broken if his reasonable grounds for insecurity are not cleared up within a reasonable time.

C. Anticipatory repudiation by either party:

1. Occurs when one party demonstrates a clear intention, with respect to a performance obligation *not yet due,* not to perform or else acts in a way that renders performance impossible.
2. When the repudiation will substantially impair the value of the contract to the aggrieved party, that party (seller or buyer) may:
   a. For a commercially reasonable time, await performance by the repudiating party, or
   b. Resort to any remedy for breach, even though he has notified the repudiating party that he would await the latter's performance and has urged retraction, and
   c. In either case suspend his own performance or proceed in accordance with provisions on the seller's right to identify goods to the contract, notwithstanding breach, or complete unfinished goods.

D. Seller's remedies:

1. Before buyer's receipt or acceptance of goods: Where the buyer *wrongfully* rejects or revokes acceptance of goods or fails to make a payment due on or before delivery or repudiates either wholly or in part, then with respect to any goods directly affected (and if the breach is of the whole or entire contract then also in respect of the whole undelivered balance), the *aggrieved seller* may:
   a. Withhold delivery of such goods.
   b. Stop delivery in transit (see above).
   c. Identify goods to the contract (see below).
   d. Complete unfinished goods (see below).
   e. Resell and recover damages (see below).
   f. Recover damages for nonacceptance (see below).
   g. Recover the price in proper case (see below).
   h. Cancel.
2. Identification of the goods to the contract: An aggrieved seller may:
   a. Identify to the contract conforming goods in his possession or control where not already identified to the contract at the time he learned of the breach.
   b. Treat goods that have demonstrably been intended for the particular contract, even though unfinished, as the subject of resale.
3. Complete unfinished goods: Where the goods are unfinished, an aggrieved seller (as described in 1 above) may *in the exercise of reasonable commercial judgment* for the purpose of avoiding loss and of effective realization (e.g., by resale)

either finish the goods and identify them to the contract, or cease manufacture and resell for scrap or salvage value, or proceed in any other reasonable manner.

4. Resale.

   a. An aggrieved seller (see 2 above) may sell the goods concerned or the undelivered balance thereof.

   b. Where the seller elects to resell and the resale is made in good faith and in a commercially reasonable manner, the seller:

   (1) Is not accountable for any profit made on any resale.

   (2) May recover the difference between the resale price (this in effect determines the fair market value for the purpose of computing recovery) and the contract price together with any incidental damages, but less expenses saved in consequence of buyer's breach (e.g., shipping charges saved by not having to deliver to the breaching buyer).

   c. The resale may be public (subject to certain requirements) or private (if private, seller must give buyer reasonable notice of intention to resell), and said resale must be reasonably identified as referring to the broken contract.

   d. Good faith purchasers at resale take free of any rights of the original buyer even though the seller fails to comply with the stated requirements (e.g., seller fails to give notice to original buyer of intent to resell).

5. **Damages** for nonacceptance or repudiation.

   a. If the aggrieved seller does not elect to proceed under the resale provisions, as discussed above, he is entitled to an amount equal to the standard measure of damages for breach of contract. That is, the difference between the market price at the time and place for tender and the unpaid contract price, plus incidental damages but less expenses saved.

   b. If the measure of damages provided above is inadequate to put the seller in as good a position as performance would have done, then the measure of damages is the profit (including reasonable overhead) that the seller would have made from full performance by the buyer, plus incidental damages, with due allowances for costs, and due credit for payments or proceeds of resale. E.g., if a dealer with a large supply of refrigerators finds a buyer who at first agrees to purchase one refrigerator for the standard price of $200 and then breaks his agreement, the buyer's breach injures the seller even if the seller is able to resell the refrigerator at the identical price. This is so since the seller made only one sale rather than two. This rule allows the seller to seek his lost profit as the measure of damages. This rule will also be resorted to in situations where there is no fair market value upon which to base damages.

6. **Action for the price.**

   a. When the buyer fails to pay the price as it becomes due, the seller may recover the price, plus any incidental damages, in three limited cases:

   (1) The buyer has accepted the goods.

   (2) The goods have been lost or destroyed after the risk of loss has passed to the buyer.

   (3) The seller is unable, after a reasonable effort, to effect a resale of goods identified to the contract.

  b. Goods that have been identified to the contract and are still in the seller's control must be held for the buyer unless resale becomes possible.

  c. A seller who is not entitled to recover the price is nevertheless entitled to damages.

7. Incidental damages: include any commercially reasonable charges, expenses, or commissions incurred in stopping delivery, in transportation, care, and custody of goods after the buyer's breach, in connection with return or resale of the goods, or otherwise resulting from the breach.

E. Buyer's remedies:

1. In general:

  a. Where the seller fails to make delivery or repudiates or the buyer rightfully rejects or justifiably revokes acceptance, then with respect to any goods involved, and with respect to the whole if the breach goes to the whole contract, the buyer may cancel and, whether or not he has done so, may in addition to recovering so much of the price as has been paid;

   (1) "**Cover**" and obtain damages (see p. 324, VI.C.4.b) for the goods affected, whether or not they have been identified to the contract, or

   (2) Recover damages for nondelivery.

  b. Where the seller fails to deliver or repudiates, the buyer may also:

   (1) Recover goods identified to the contract and paid for where seller becomes insolvent (see p. 325, VI.C.6).

   (2) In a proper case, obtain specific performance or replevy the goods (see p. 325, VI.C.5).

  c. On rightful rejection or justifiable revocation of acceptance, a buyer has a security interest in the goods in his possession or control for any payments made on their price and any expenses reasonably incurred in their inspection, receipt, transportation, care, and custody and may hold such goods and resell them in like manner as an aggrieved seller. However, if a profit results, it must be turned over to the seller.

2. Improper delivery (e.g., breach of warranty): If the goods or the tender of delivery fails in any respect to conform to the contract (e.g., as when fruit delivered under a contract is undersized), the buyer may:

  a. Reject all of the goods. If the buyer elects to reject, he must:

   (1) Do so within a reasonable time.

   (2) Seasonably notify the seller of his election (said election does not preclude recovery of damages).

   (3) Take reasonable care of the goods until the seller retrieves them.

   (4) Not exercise ownership of them (e.g., he may not resell them for his own account.

   (5) Particularize reasonably discoverable defects. If the buyer fails to particularize (e.g., neglects to state that the fruit was undersized), he may not later use this fact to justify his rejection of the goods. The seller may have a right to cure the defects (see p. 320, V.C).

  b. If he has at first accepted defective goods, the buyer may later revoke his acceptance:

(1) If the defects were hidden (e.g., if there were worms inside the fruit) or if the seller had assured him that the defects would be cured and they were not, and

(2) If he notifies the seller of the breach within a reasonable time after discovery.

(3) If he returns the goods and cancels the contract. This alternative would not preclude the buyer's right to damages for breach of contract.

c. Accept any commercial unit or units, and reject the rest and recover damages.

d. Accept all of the goods. Acceptance does not preclude the buyer from recovering damages as long as he has notified the seller of the breach. Again, the old election-of-remedies rule has been clearly overturned.

3. Disposition of rejected goods:

a. A merchant buyer must follow any reasonable instructions that the seller gives him for the disposition of the goods. If the goods are perishable or of a type that will immediately decline in value, the merchant buyer who has received no instructions must make a reasonable effort to sell the goods (i.e., he must not allow a rejected shipment of peaches to rot if there is a ready market for them).

b. A nonmerchant buyer who receives no instructions from the seller may:

(1) Store the goods.

(2) Send the goods back to the seller.

(3) Resell the goods for the seller. If the goods are resold, the seller must reimburse the buyer for any expenses incurred in the sale.

4. **Buyer's damages.**

a. Measure of damages: the difference between the contract price and the market price of comparable goods *at the time the buyer learns of the breach,* plus any incidental and consequential damages.

(1) Where the market price in the buyer's area is difficult to determine:

(A) Figures in trade journals, official publications, newspapers, and periodicals of general circulation may be used as evidence of established commodity market prices.

(B) The buyer may use the price prevailing within any reasonable time before or after the time described or at any other place that in commercial judgment or under usage of trade would serve as a reasonable substitute.

(2) Where the buyer has accepted the goods but has notified the seller of the breach, his damages are measured by the loss resulting in the ordinary course of events from the seller's breach as determined in any reasonable manner.

b. **Cover.**

(1) Permits a buyer to procure substitute goods in the open market when the seller has repudiated or failed to deliver. His primary damages become the difference between the actual cost of replacement and the contract price.

(2) The buyer is under no duty to "cover" or take the least expensive course of action, as long as his choice of conduct is reasonable and in good faith.

(3) If the buyer chooses not to cover, he may receive damages for nondelivery (see above, 4.a).

   c. Incidental and consequential damages.

      (1) Incidental damages are expenses reasonably incurred as a result of the delay or breach, including:

         (A) Inspection, receipt, transportation, and care and custody of goods rightfully rejected.

         (B) Any commercially reasonable charges, expenses, or commissions in connection with effecting cover.

      (2) Consequential damages include:

         (A) Any damage resulting from the buyer's needs of which the seller at the time of the contracting had reason to know, and that could not reasonably be prevented by cover or otherwise, and

         (B) Injury to person or property proximately resulting from any breach of warranty.

5. Specific performance, replevin, and recoupment.

   a. To obtain specific performance:

      (1) The goods must be unique (e.g., a famous painting), or

      (2) Other proper circumstances must exist (e.g., inability to cover).

   b. Generally, replevin (i.e., recovering possession of the goods) is given only where cover is not reasonably available.

   c. Upon notification of breach to the seller, the buyer is permitted to deduct from the price still due (recoup) all or any part of the damages resulting from the seller's breach.

6. Buyer's rights on seller's insolvency. Goods whether delivered or undelivered may be recovered by the buyer if:

   a. The buyer has paid all or a part of the purchase price and keeps open an offer to pay the rest, and

   b. The buyer has a special property interest in the goods. To create such an interest, the goods must be identified to the contract (i.e., the buyer must prove that the particular goods are the ones he contracted to buy), and

   c. The seller becomes insolvent within 10 days after receipt of the first installment on the price of the goods.

Selected Problems from CPA Examinations on Sales

Subjective Questions and Answers

Q. 1. On May 30, 1978, Hargrove ordered 1,000 spools of nylon yarn from Flowers, Inc., of Norfolk, Virginia. The shipping terms were "F.O.B., Norfolk & Western RR at Norfolk." The transaction was to be a cash sale with payment to be simultaneously exchanged for the negotiable bill of lading covering the goods. Title to the goods was expressly reserved in Flowers. The yarn ordered by Hargrove was delivered to the railroad and loaded in a boxcar on June 1, 1978. Flowers obtained a negotiable bill of lading made out to its own order. The boxcar was destroyed the next day while the goods were in transit. Hargrove refused to pay for the yarn and Flowers sued Hargrove for the purchase price.

Required

Answer the following, setting forth reasons for any conclusions stated.

Who will prevail?

A.   Flowers will prevail because Hargrove has the risk of loss. The shipping terms determine who had the risk of loss. Section 2-509(1) of the Uniform Commercial Code provides that "Where the contract requires or authorizes the seller to ship the goods by carrier, (*a*) if it does not require him to deliver at a particular destination, the risk of loss passes to the buyer when the goods are duly delivered to the carrier, even though the shipment is under reservation. . . ."

The fact that title was reserved by Flowers and that Flowers retained the negotiable bill of lading do not affect the determination of who is to bear the risk of loss. The code makes it clear that title is irrelevant in determining the risk of loss.

11/78

Q.   2.   Max Motors, Inc., sold a 1973 used station wagon to Sarah Constance for $3,350. Constance has corresponded with Max Motors on several occasions and has alleged that Fogarty, an experienced salesman for Max Motors, made several express oral warranties in connection with her purchase of the car. Constance alleges that there has been a breach of warranty and as a result she has suffered damages to the extent of $1,025 for expenses incurred to repair the car. Constance also indicated that in the event she does not receive a refund of $1,025, she will take appropriate legal action to obtain satisfaction.

In various letters, Constance stated that she went to Max Motors and contacted Fogarty. Before she finally made a deal for the car, she asked many questions about the car. Fogarty assured her that the car was in good condition and that he had driven the car several times. In addition, Fogarty stated that "This is a car I can recommend and it is in A-1 shape."

Constance informed Fogarty that her husband had been transferred to another state, that her child was only two years old, and that she needed the car so she could join her husband. She stated that Fogarty assured her that he knew the car and knew the person who traded it in and it was "mechanically perfect." He also told her that, "it would get her any place she wanted to go and not to worry." Constance indicated she knew nothing about cars but would like to drive it. Fogarty replied this was not possible because he was the only man on duty at the lot that day and he could not leave to accompany her as required by company policy.

Constance stated she purchased the car in reliance on the statements made by Fogarty. Unfortunately, these statements proved to be incorrect. The car began knocking and finally broke down after being driven about 300 miles. The car was repaired by Master Mechanics and a copy of a receipted bill for $1,025 accompanied one of her letters to Max Motors.

Fogarty indicated that he believed what he stated was true, as far as he knew the car wasn't in bad condition, and he knew of no important defects in the car. He also indicated he told Constance that he could not warrant the car because it was over two years old and had an excess of 50,000 miles.

Required

Answer the following, setting forth reasons for any conclusions stated.

1. Is it likely that Constance will prevail in a legal action against Max Motors? Discuss all relevant issues.
2. Identify, but do not discuss, other warranties that Constance might rely upon in addition to the oral express warranties.

A.   1.   Yes. The main issue is whether Fogarty's statements constitute an affirmation of fact as contrasted with mere opinion.

This issue has been resolved in many cases in favor of purchasers, such as Constance. It often is difficult to draw the line between an affirmation of fact, which when relied upon constitutes a warranty, and mere sales talk, which is a statement of the seller's opinion. However, the combination of the various statements made by Fogarty and perhaps the language "mechanically perfect" constituted a warranty under the circumstances.

Furthermore, the relative expertise of the parties is validly taken into account under such circumstances. Fogarty was a used car salesman with long experience and was familiar with the mechanical aspects of automobiles. It would be only natural for Constance to take his statements as being something more than idle chatter. Her total lack of knowledge of automobiles and their engines would lead her to rely on Fogarty's representations.

In addition, all the other elements necessary to establish an oral express warranty are present. Fogarty's good faith or honest belief in the truth of his statements is irrelevant. Knowledge of falsity has nothing to do with warranty. The Uniform Commercial Code reads as follows: "Any affirmation of fact or promise made by the seller to the buyer which relates to the goods and becomes part of the basis of the bargain creates an express warranty that the goods shall conform to the affirmation or promise." Additionally, the code states, "It is not necessary to the creation of an express warranty that the seller use familiar words, such as warrants or guarantees or that . . . a specific intention to make a warranty be present."

The facts clearly indicate that the affirmation or promise was a basis of the bargain; that is, that the language was intended to be relied upon by the buyer and it was. Finally, the buyer relied upon it to her detriment and suffered damages as a result. Although the Uniform Commercial Code includes cautionary language that an affirmation merely of the value of the goods or a statement purporting to be merely the seller's opinion or commendation of the goods does not create a warranty, it appears that the facts clearly establish an oral express warranty.

Another issue is the legal effect of Fogarty's statement that he could not give a warranty on the auto sold. Does this validly disclaim the oral express warranty protection? There is a general hostility manifested by the Uniform Commercial Code and the courts to allowing broad uninformative disclaimers to legally negate warranty protection. Warranties are not to be disclaimed without due notice and fairness shown to the purchaser under the circumstances. Where there are words tending to negate an oral express warranty, the purported disclaimer shall be constructed wherever reasonable as consistent with the warranty. Hence, a purported negation or limitation is inoperative to the extent that such a construction is unreasonable. Thus, it appears that the warranty has not been disclaimed.

2. Constance might rely upon the implied warranties of merchantability and fitness for a particular purpose.

11/77

Q. 3. A claim has been asserted against Ajax Motors for $7,000 arising out of the sale of a used 1975 automobile. Knox purchased the automobile in February 1977 and subsequently learned that it was a stolen car. The serial numbers had been changed, but it has been conclusively determined that the car belongs to Watts who has duly repossessed it. The contract contained a disclaimer which read as follows: "Ajax Motors hereby disclaims any and all warranties, express or implied, which are not contained in the contract." Knox has brought a legal action against Ajax Motors alleging breach of warranty.

Required

Answer the following, setting forth reasons for any conclusions stated.

What is the probable outcome of such a legal action? Discuss fully the legal basis upon which Knox is relying and any defense that Ajax Motors may assert.

A. The case should be decided in favor of Knox. The basis for recovery would be the title warranties provided under the Uniform Commercial Code which states that the title conveyed should be good and its transfer rightful, but here Watts was the rightful owner and entitled to repossess the car. The code does not indicate whether such a warranty is to be construed as an express or implied warranty. However, it can only be excluded by specific language or circumstances that give the buyer reason to know that the person selling does not claim title in himself. From this it would appear that a seller would have to clearly indicate that he does not purport to own the item in question and that the buyer is assuming the risk that the title is defective. Such was not the case. However, Ajax Motors will undoubtedly claim that the disclaimer is legally operative.

11/77

Q. 4. Fashion Footwear Company received an order on June 15, 1977, from Footloose Shoes, Inc., for 300 pairs of shoes at a price of $6.85 per pair. Footloose is the predecessor corporation to Nemo Exclusives, Inc., which acquired Footloose by statutory merger on October 12, 1977. Fashion is seeking to recover the contract price from Nemo.

    The evidence shows that Footloose placed a written order with Fashion for 300 pairs of shoes at $6.85 per pair to be delivered September 1, 1977. Fashion's acceptance was dated June 17, 1977. The order incorporated a form letter which contained a stipulation that it would not be possible to consider cancellations after shoes had been cut. On June 30, 1977, all the shoes ordered by Footloose had been cut. On that same day Footloose advised Fashion to cancel the entire order. On July 1, 1977, Fashion wrote Footloose the following letter: "In accordance with our previous correspondence, we proceeded with your order for fall shoes. We are unable to cancel your order since cutting is completed."

    On September 1, 1977, Footloose refused to accept delivery of the shoes, whereupon Fashion then made several unsuccessful attempts to resell the shoes elsewhere at a reasonable price.

    Nemo states it was not a party to the above transaction and that in any event, Fashion can only recover its damages and not the full price for the shoes delivered and refused.

Required

Answer the following, setting forth reasons for any conclusions stated.

    Who will prevail? Discuss all issues and problems raised by the above facts.

A.   Fashion will prevail against Nemo. The fact that Fashion's contract was with Footloose is no defense because the surviving corporation in a statutory merger assumes the contract obligations of the absorbed corporation.

    An action to recover the price of the finished shoes is clearly recognized by the Uniform Commercial Code. Although as a general proposition a seller must stop work when ordered to do so by the buyer to mitigate damages and prevent economic waste, the proposition is clearly inapplicable here. The code provides in the section dealing with the seller's remedies that where the goods are unfinished an aggrieved seller may in the exercise of reasonable commercial judgment for the purpose of avoiding loss and of effective realization either complete the manufacture and wholly identify the goods to the contract or cease manufacture and resell for scrap or salvage value or proceed in any other reasonable manner. An action to recover the price of the shoes will be successful if the goods are those identified in the contract and if the seller is unable, after reasonable effort, to resell them at a reasonable price or the circumstances reasonably indicate that such an effort will be unavailing. The situation between Fashion and Nemo (Footloose) is clearly within these rules.

11/77

Q. 5. During your examination of the financial statements of Wyatt Associates, Inc., for the fiscal year ended June 30, 1974, you discovered the following facts relating to a transaction with Flinko Corporation. The transaction occurred during April 1974.

    Flinko, one of Wyatt's major competitors, was insolvent in the equity sense, i.e., it could not meet the claims of its current creditors. Wyatt offered to purchase all of Flinko's assets, including furniture, fixtures, equipment, materials, supplies, inventory, and any and all other assets owned by Flinko. Wyatt's offering price equaled 105% of the total of all outstanding claims of Flinko's creditors. Flinko agreed to satisfy all creditors' claims out of the proceeds of sale and to hold Wyatt harmless from any claims of creditors. Meglo, Flinko's president and sole stockholder, accepted the offer. However, Meglo notified no one of the sale, absconded with the entire proceeds, and has not been heard from since.

Required

Discuss the legal and the financial-reporting implications of the above transaction to Wyatt. Ignore antitrust considerations.

A.   Wyatt will have to pay the claims of the creditors of Flinko or hold all the assets it purchased from Flinko for the benefit of its creditors.

The transaction in question is a bulk transfer (often referred to as a bulk sale) and is ineffective against any creditor of the seller (transferor) unless the buyer (transferee) requires the seller (transferor) to furnish a list of his existing creditors. Furthermore, the buyer (transferee) is required to give notice to any known creditors of the seller (transferor) ten days prior to taking possession of the goods or when it pays for them, whichever happens first.

Obviously, Wyatt has not fulfilled these requirements. Wyatt neither requested, much less obtained, a list nor did it give notice to Flinko's creditors. Therefore, it must suffer the consequences. Wyatt's only recourse is to attempt to recover against the missing Meglo.

As recovery from Meglo is highly improbable, Wyatt has incurred a loss in the amount of the claims of Flinko's creditors which must be recorded in the fiscal year ended June 30, 1974, creating a related liability of the same amount. The June 30, 1974, balance sheet should include any unpaid claims at that date. The loss should be reported in the income statement, probably as an extraordinary item.

11/74

Q. 6.   Your annual examination of the financial statements of Mars Distribution Corporation revealed that Colossal Computer Company sold Mars 1,000 desk computers. The contract stated in bold type:

> The buyer hereby purchases these computers with all faults, and all warranties are hereby expressly excluded.

After Mars had sold approximately 200 of the computers, three significant problems arose.
- First, Major Computer Components sued Mars for conversion in that one of the major components in Colossal's computers had been stolen from Major's warehouse.
- Second, B.M.I. Computers has indicated that the computers in question infringe on its existing patents.
- Third, 90% of the computers sold have proven to be defective.

Mars' customers have claimed that the computers are nonmerchantable. Colossal, when informed of the various problems encountered by Mars, said, "That's your tough luck, we rely on the disclaimer in the contract."

Required

What are the rights of Mars against Colossal? Explain.

A.   Mars has no right against Colossal for the quality of the goods because of the bold disclaimer in the contract, i.e., that Mars accepted the "computers with all faults." However, Mars may have a right against Colossal on the warranty of title and warranty against patent or other trade infringements implicit in any transaction between merchants. In spite of the general disclaimer, Colossal warranted that it had good title and that the transfer was proper. It also warranted against title impairment resulting from patent and other trade infringements. These warranties may be excluded only by specific wording including knowledge by the customer that the seller is not representing that he has title or by agreement that title may be impaired by patent or other trade infringements.

11/73

Q. 7.   During the course of your examination of the financial statements of Grand Fashions, Inc., a retail dress merchant, you learned of the following transactions with wholesale dress merchants:

Transaction 1
The Corporation telephoned Stevens Company and ordered from Stevens' catalog 50 Junior Model dresses in assorted sizes for a total price of $300. The next day the Corporation received a written confirmation of the order from Stevens with a request that it sign and return the duplicate of the confirmation, which it did not do. A month later the Corporation sought to avoid the contract claiming that it was not liable since it did not sign the confirmation order.

Transaction 2
The Corporation placed a telephone order with Scott Company for 10 dozen dresses for $1,000. The next day the Corporation received, inspected and accepted 5 dozen of the dresses. The Corporation refused to accept the balance when tendered and sought to return the other 5 dozen dresses claiming that it was not obligated.

Transaction 3
The Corporation purchased 25 dozen all-silk dresses from Lawrence Company after examining a sample all-silk dress that Lawrence Company submitted. The written confirmation received by the Corporation contained the words "as per sample submitted to the company." Upon delivery, inspection and testing the Corporation determined that the dresses were 65% silk and 35% dacron and immediately informed Lawrence Company that it wanted to return the dresses for full credit. Lawrence Company insisted that the Corporation take the dresses less a 25% discount, but the corporation refused to do so.

Transaction 4
The Corporation executed a written contract with Roberts Company to purchase a miscellaneous collection of dresses for $5,000. A week before the agreed shipment date, Roberts called the Corporation and said "We cannot deliver at $5,000; unless you agree to pay $6,000, we will cancel the order." After considerable discussion the Corporation agreed to pay $6,000 if Roberts would ship as agreed in the contract. After the goods had been delivered and accepted by the Corporation, it refused to pay $6,000 insisting that it is legally obligated to pay only $5,000.

Required
Discuss separately the validity of the contentions made by Grand Fashions, Inc. with respect to each of the four transactions.

A.
Transaction 1
The Corporation is liable. An oral contract for the sale of goods for a price of less than $500 is enforceable because the contract is not subject to the Statute of Frauds.

Transaction 2
The Corporation is liable for payment of the purchase price of 5 dozen dresses. Although a contract for the sale of goods for the price of $500 or more is not enforceable unless there is sufficient writing to indicate that a contract for sale has been made between the parties and signed by the party against whom enforcement is sought, the oral contract here is enforceable for the goods which have been received and accepted. However, the oral contract is not enforceable for the remaining 5 dozen dresses which the Corporation has neither received, accepted, nor paid for.

Transaction 3
The Corporation may reject the goods. Any sample or model which is made a part of the basis of the bargain creates an express warranty that the whole of the goods shall conform to the sample or model. Moreover, any description of the goods which is made a part of the basis of the bargain creates an express warranty that the goods shall conform to the description. If the goods fail in any respect to conform to the contract, the company may reject the whole, accept the whole, or accept any commercial unit or units and reject the rest. Here the Corporation lawfully may reject the goods because of breach of express warranty and timely rejection.

Transaction 4

The Corporation is liable for $6,000. The agreement which modified the original written contract needs no consideration to be binding. However, the Statute of Frauds must be complied with if the contract as modified is to be within its provisions. Although the oral modification agreement related to a contract for the sale of goods for the price of $500 or more, the oral contract satisfied the Statute of Frauds because the company received and accepted the goods, and thus the oral contract is enforceable with respect to such goods.

5/71

Practice Questions

Q. 1. You are the in-charge accountant on the examination of the financial statements of the Kell Manufacturing Corporation. After gathering information concerning the accounts-receivable and payable confirmation exceptions, your assistant seeks your guidance in clearing the following exception:

An account-payable confirmation request received from one of Kell's major vendors, Rosser, Corp., reflects an invoice which Kell has not recorded. Your assistant has discovered that Kell sent Rosser an order for 3,000 gears to be shipped by rail, F.O.B. Rosser's place of business. The goods were received by Kell, but inspection revealed that the gears were badly pitted and did not conform to Kell's specifications. Kell promptly notified Rosser that it refused to accept the shipment and that it was holding the gears for Rosser's disposal. The day after Rosser received notification of the refusal, a fire in Kell's warehouse further damaged the gears. Rosser notified Kell that it must pay the agreed contract price for the gears; or, at least pay for the damage caused by the fire. Neither party had insurance on the gears destroyed by the fire.

Required

Does Kell have any liability to Rosser? Explain.

Q. 2. X Company, a manufacturer of clothing, received a brochure from Y Company, extolling the virtues and describing in detail the specifications and results of laboratory tests regarding the strength, flexibility, resistance to strain, workability, and other attributes of various types of its plastic materials. Relying upon data contained in the brochure, X ordered a large quantity of one certain type of plastic material that was made into raincoats. To X's dismay, the material was wholly unsatisfactory for this purpose, as it had a definite tendency to tear under ordinary use. X seeks to recover damages from Y for breach of warranty.

Required

Does X have a valid claim against Y?

Q. 3. Franks contracted to sell to Acme Construction Corporation 1,000 cases of first-quality blue roofing shingles that were to be exactly ½ inch thick. The contract required that delivery be made by November 1, 1969. Franks made delivery on October 15, 1969, and was notified on October 20, 1969, that 100 cases contained shingles that were less than ¼ inch thick and 50 additional cases contained shingles that were off-color. These cases had inadvertently been included in the shipment as the result of a new employee's selecting some cases from an area that contained seconds.

Franks immediately notified Acme that he would ship 150 replacement cases. The cases were delivered on October 30, 1969, but Acme refused to accept them. Acme insisted that the contract had been breached and that Acme was no longer obligated to perform. Acme also indicated all cases would be returned to Franks.

Required

Assuming Acme returns all the cases of shingles, would it have any liability as a result of its action? Explain.

Q. 4. Typewriter Supply Company contracted to sell to Harper Corporation 75 Wonder model typewriters. The terms were $600 per typewriter, delivery and payment to be made one month from the date of the execution of the contract. Two weeks after the contract was executed, Typewriter Supply notified Harper Corporation that the obligation would not be fulfilled because prior commitments had entirely depleted the supply of Wonder typewriters. Harper immediately purchased 75 Wonder typewriters elsewhere at the prevailing market price of $625 per typewriter.

Prior to the expiration of the one-month delivery date contained in the original contract between Typewriter Supply and Harper, Star Typewriter Manufacturing introduced a new model. This depressed the market price for Wonder typewriters to $550, which was the prevailing market price at the scheduled delivery date to Harper.

Required

1. What was the legal effect of Typewriter Supply's notification that delivery of the Wonder typewriters would not be made? Explain.
2. What rights and remedies were available to Harper as a result of receipt of the notification that Typewriter Supply would not perform? Explain.
3. What, if any, is the amount of damages to which Harper is entitled? Explain.

Q. 5. Ozgood purchased a used automobile from Superior Auto Sales Corporation. Unfortunately the car was defective. In order to put the car in adequate running condition, Ozgood had to replace the clutch and have a complete overhaul of the motor. The car was only one year old and appeared to be in good condition at the time of purchase. The salesman orally assured Ozgood that the car was an excellent buy and in "good shape." Ozgood offered to have the car examined by his mechanic, but the salesman assured him this would not be necessary. Ozgood demanded that Superior Auto Sales Corporation repair the auto, but they refused. He, therefore, took it to several authorized dealers and, after several bids on the repair job, selected the low bid. This amounted to $625. He now seeks to recover that amount based upon breach of warranty. Superior Auto Sales relies upon the following disclaimer clause: "All warranties express and implied are hereby disclaimed." This appeared on the back of the form along with a large number of standardized provisions that were all in very small type.

Required

1. What warranties are created as a result of the above fact situation?
2. Will the disclaimer clause effectively preclude Ozgood from recovery of the $625? Discuss.

Q. 6. Fan Motor Company purchased a motor from the Excello Motor Manufacturing Company. The contract contained several written express warranties followed by a written description of the motor purchased and a disclaimer clause. It stated in the description that the motor had a kilowatt capacity of 650. This kilowatt capacity was very important to Fan Motor. It turned out that the motor had a kilowatt capacity of less than 600, which rendered the motor worthless for Fan Motor's use. Fan Motor seeks to rescind the transaction. Excello refuses, stating that the motor meets all the requirements contained in the express warranties, which is true. Excello admits that the motor did not meet the 650-kilowatt capacity but asserts that this was merely a part of the description and not an express warranty. Furthermore, the disclaimer clause admittedly effectively precludes any reliance upon implied warranty protection.

Required

As between Fan Motor and Excello, who will prevail? Explain.

Q. 7. Martha purchased a can of Pure Best Quality Company's beef stew from the corner grocer. This was served to her maid at the luncheon meal. One hour later the maid developed an acute case of ptomaine poisoning. The maid is seeking to recover damages against the corner grocer, who asserts that he has no liability to her in that she was not the purchaser of the contaminated stew.

Required

Can the maid sue and recover from the corner grocer? Discuss.

Practice Objective Questions

Instructions 1–15

Select the *best* answer for each of the following items. Mark only one answer for *each* item. Answer all items. Your grade will be based on your total correct answers.

1. Donaldson sold Randal six bundles of mink skins. The contract contained *no* specific provision regarding title warranties. It did, however, contain a provision which indicated that the skins were sold "with all faults and defects." Two of the bundles of skins sold to Randal had been stolen and were reclaimed by the rightful owner. Which of the following is a correct statement?

   a. Since there was *no* express title warranty, Randal assumed the risk.

   b. The disclaimer "with all faults and defects" effectively negates any and all warranties.

   c. The contract automatically contained a warranty that the title conveyed is good and can only be excluded by specific language.

   d. The implied warranty of title is eliminated by the parol evidence rule.

2. Marco Auto Inc., made many untrue statements in the course of inducing Rockford to purchase a used auto for $3,500. The car in question turned out to have some serious faults. Which of the following untrue statements made by Marco should Rockford use in seeking recovery from Marco for breach of warranty?

   a. "I refused a $3,800 offer for this very same auto from another buyer last week."

   b. "This auto is one of the best autos we have for sale."

   c. "At this price the auto is a real steal."

   d. "I can guarantee that you will never regret this purchase."

3. If a seller repudiates his contract with a buyer for the sale of 100 radios, what recourse does the buyer have?

   a. He can "cover," i.e., procure the goods elsewhere and recover the difference.

   b. He must await the seller's performance for a commercially reasonable time after repudiation.

   c. He can obtain specific performance by the seller.

   d. He can recover punitive damages.

4. Duval Liquor Wholesales, Inc., stored its inventory of goods in the Reliable Warehouse Company. Duval's shipments would arrive by truck and be deposited with Reliable who would in turn issue negotiable warehouse receipts to Duval. Duval would resell the liquor by transferring the negotiable warehouse receipts to the buyer who was responsible for transporting it to his place of business. In one of the sales of liquor to a retailer, the liquor was badly damaged and a question has arisen as to who has the risk of loss, Duval or the retailer. If the contract is silent on this point, when did the risk of loss pass to the retailer?

   a. When the goods have been placed on the warehouseman's delivery dock awaiting pick up by the retailer.

   b. When the goods have been identified to the contract.

   c. On his receipt of the negotiable warehouse receipts covering the goods.

   d. When the goods have been properly loaded upon the retailer's carrier.

5. Franklin purchased 100 sets of bed frames from Tully Manufacturing, Inc. Franklin made substantial prepayments on the purchase price. Tully is insolvent and the goods have *not* been delivered as promised. Franklin wants the bed frames. Under the circumstances, which of the following will prevent Franklin from obtaining the bed frames?

   a. The fact that he can obtain a judgment for damages.

   b. The fact that he was *not* aware of Tully's insolvency at the time he purchased the bed frames.

   c. The fact that the goods have *not* been identified to his contract.

   d. The fact that he did *not* pay the full price at the time of the purchase even though he has made a tender of the balance and holds it available to Tully upon delivery.

6. Gordon purchased 100 automatic sprinklers from Thompson, a jobber. Conrad was the rightful owner of the sprinklers which had been stolen from his warehouse. He had the sheriff repossess them and has asserted his ownership of them. Gordon's bill of sale specifically indicated that it made *no* implied warranties. The bill of sale did *not* contain any warranties of title. Which of the following is correct based on the above facts?

    a. The title warranties have been effectively negated.

    b. It is *not* possible to disclaim the title warranties.

    c. Gordon's best course of action is to assert his superior title to the sprinklers since he is a good faith purchaser for value.

    d. Thompson is liable in that he warranted that the title conveyed was good and his transfer rightful.

7. Parks furnished specifications and ordered 1,000 specially constructed folding tables from Metal Manufacturing Company, Inc. The tables were unique in design and had *not* appeared in the local market. Metal completed the job and delivered the order to Parks. Parks sold about 600 of the tables when Unusual Tables, Inc., sued both Parks and Metal for patent infringement. If Unusual wins, what is the status of Parks and Metal?

    a. Metal is liable to Parks for breach of the warranty against infringement.

    b. Parks is liable to Metal for breach of the warranty against infringement.

    c. The warranty against infringement is *not* available to either Parks or Metal.

    d. Parks and Metal are jointly and severally liable and, as such, must pay the judgment in equal amounts.

8. Devold Manufacturing, Inc., entered into a contract for the sale to Hillary Company of 2,000 solid-state CB radios at $27.50 each, terms *2/10, N/30*, F.O.B. Hillary's loading platform. After delivery of the first 500 radios, a minor defect was discovered. Although the defect was minor, Hillary incurred costs to correct the defect. Hillary sent Devold a signed memorandum indicating that it would relinquish its right to recover the costs to correct the defect, provided that the balance of the radios were in conformity with the terms of the contract and the delivery dates were strictly adhered to. Devold met these conditions. Shortly before the last shipment of radios arrived, a dispute between the parties arose over an unrelated matter. Hillary notified that it was *not* bound by the prior generous agreement and would sue Devold for damages unless Devold promptly reimbursed Hillary. In the event of litigation, what would be the result and the basis upon which the litigation would be decided?

    a. Devold will lose in that Hillary's relinquishment of its rights was *not* supported by a consideration.

    b. Devold will win in that the defect was minor and the substantial performance doctrine applies.

    c. Hillary will lose in that the communication constituted a waiver of Hillary's rights.

    d. Hillary will win in that there was a failure to perform the contract, and Hillary suffered damages as a result.

9. Badger Corporation sold goods to Watson. Watson has arbitrarily refused to pay the purchase price. Under what circumstances will Badger *not* be able to recover the price if it seeks this remedy instead of other possible remedies?

    a. If Watson refused to accept delivery and the goods were resold in the ordinary course of business.

    b. If Watson accepted the goods but seeks to return them.

    c. If the goods sold were destroyed shortly after the risk of loss passed to the buyer.

    d. If the goods were identified to the contract and Badger made a reasonable effort to resell them at a reasonable price but was unable to do so.

10. Viscount Appliances sold Conway a refrigerator. Viscount wishes to disclaim the implied warranty of fitness for a particular purpose. Which of the following will effectively disclaim this warranty?

    a. The fact that the refrigerator is widely advertised and was sold under its brand name.

    b. A conspicuous written statement which states that "any and all warranty protection is hereby disclaimed."

    c. A conspicuous written statement indicating that "there are *no* warranties which extend beyond the description contained in the contract of sale."

    d. An inconspicuous written statement which specifically negates the warranty.

11. Vega Manufacturing, Inc., manufactures and sells hi-fi systems and components to the trade and at retail. Repossession is frequently made from customers who are in default. Which of the following statements is correct concerning the rights of the defaulting debtors who have had property repossessed by Vega?

    a. Vega has the right to retain all the goods repossessed as long as it gives notice and cancels the debt.

    b. It is unimportant whether the goods repossessed are defined as consumer goods, inventory, or something else in respect to the debtor's rights upon repossession.

    c. If the defaulting debtor voluntarily signs a statement renouncing his rights in the collateral, the creditor must nevertheless resell them for the debtor's benefit.

    d. If a debtor has paid 60% or more of the purchase price of consumer goods in satisfaction of a purchase money security interest, the debtor has the right to have the creditor dispose of the goods.

12. Wilcox Manufacturing repudiated its contract to sell 100 radios to Ready Stores, Inc. What recourse does Ready Stores have?

    a. It can obtain specific performance by the seller.

    b. It can recover punitive damages.

    c. It can "cover," that is, procure the goods elsewhere and recover any damages.

    d. It must await the seller's performance for a commercially reasonable time after repudiation if it wishes to recover anything.

13. In connection with a contract for the sale of goods, in which the following ways can the implied warranty of merchantability be excluded by the seller?

    a. By an oral statement which mentions merchantability.

    b. By a written statement without mentioning merchantability.

    c. By an oral statement which does *not* mention merchantability.

    d. By an inconspicuous written statement which mentions merchantability.

14. In connection with risk and expense associated with the delivery of goods to a carrier for shipment under a sales contract, the term "F.O.B. the place of shipment" means that

    a. The seller bears the risk but *not* the expense.

    b. The buyer bears the risk but *not* the expense.

    c. The seller bears the risk and expense.

    d. The buyer bears the risk and expense.

15. In connection with risk and expense associated with the delivery of goods to a destination under a sales contract, the term "F.O.B. place of destination" means that

    a. The seller bears the risk and expense.

    b. The buyer bears the risk and expense.

    c. The seller bears the risk but *not* the expense.

    d. The buyer bears the risk but *not* the expense.

Secured Transactions

AICPA Content Specification Outline

Attachment of Security Agreements (Interests)
Perfection of Security Interests
Priorities
Rights of Debtors, Creditors, and Third Parties

Contents

I. Introduction

A. Transactions covered and excluded:

    1. The Article applies to any transaction that is intended to create a security interest in personal property or fixtures including goods, documents, instruments, general intangibles, chattel paper, and accounts. **It also includes the outright sale of accounts or chattel paper.**

    2. The following transactions are excluded:
      a. Real property mortgages and liens.
      b. Landlords' liens.
      c. The sale of accounts or chattel paper as a part of the sale of a business from which they arose.

      d. The sale of general corporate debentures by a corporation.

      e. Mechanics' liens, except as to priority.

      f. Transfers of claims for wages, salary, or other compensation.

      g. Judgments, other than those taken as a right to payment that was collateral.

      h. Transfers of tort claims.

B. Goals of Article 9:

    1. To provide basic uniformity throughout the United States in the secured transactions area of commercial law. Prior legislation covering such traditional security devices as conditional sales, chattel mortgages, trust receipts, and others was repealed in favor of one, all-encompassing device, the "secured interest." However, the older, more descriptive, terminology is still in use.

    2. To eliminate the previous dependence upon title as the means to determine the rights, obligations, and remedies of the parties to a secured transaction.

    3. To simplify, clarify, and modernize the law of secured transactions and to promote the validity and effectiveness of secured interests.

C. Definitions:

    1. Security interest: an interest in personal property or fixtures that secures payment or performances of an obligation. Such a security interest is either possessory or nonpossessory. This definition is an all-encompassing term that includes all types of security devices involving personal property.

    2. Secured party: a lender, seller, or other person in whose favor there is a security interest, including a person to whom accounts or chattel paper has been sold.

    3. Purchase-money security interest: A security interest is a "purchase-money security interest" to the extent that it is taken or retained by the seller of the collateral to secure payment of all or part of the purchase price, or taken by a person who gives value to the debtor to enable him to acquire the collateral. As you will see, this is a most important definition, since the purchase-money lender is favored in several respects under the Code.

    4. Proceeds: Includes whatever is received upon the sale, exchange, or other disposition of collateral or proceeds. Insurance payable by reason of damage to the collateral, payable to a person who is a party to the security agreement, is proceeds.

    5. Fixture: Goods are fixtures when they become so related to particular real estate that an interest in them arises under real estate law (see Property, p. 363).

    6. Securities: Instruments commonly dealt in upon security exchanges or markets for investment purposes. For a more complete description, see Investment Securities, p. 302.

D. Classification of collateral:

    1. Tangible collateral: The Code divides tangible property into four different classes of goods. This classification of tangible collateral should be thoroughly mastered. Many of the rules that follow depend upon the type of property involved. *You must master these definitions.*

      a. Consumer goods: goods used or bought primarily for personal, family, or household purposes.

    b. Equipment: goods used or bought primarily for use (including farming or a profession) or by a debtor who is a nonprofit corporation or governmental subdivision or agency, or goods not included in the definitions of inventory, farm products, or consumer goods.

    c. Farm products: crops or livestock or supplies used or produced in a farming operation, or products of crops or livestock in their unmanufactured state, if they are in possession of a debtor engaged in raising, fattening, grazing, or other farming operations.

    d. Inventory: goods that a person holds for sale or lease, or to be furnished under contracts of service; or, if he has so furnished them, or if they are raw materials, work in progress, or materials used or consumed in a business. A person's inventory is not classified as his equipment.

    e. The categorization is determined not necessarily by the physical characteristics of the property but by the use to which the goods are put or held by the owner-buyer or the owner-borrower. For example, a television set in the hands of a manufacturer or retailer would be inventory. However, in the buyer-borrower's hands, it is a consumer good. **It is this last person's use or holding that will determine the type of goods involved.**

    f. Where collateral has varying uses (e.g., an automobile used by a salesman for both professional and personal needs), the Code permits only one definition in a particular circumstance and the primary use governs (the one established either by declaration of the debtor-owner at the time of acquisition of the collateral, or by the physical facts existing at that time).

2. Intangible collateral: The Code establishes two classifications for intangible property.

    a. Account: any right to payment for goods sold or leased or for services rendered that is not evidenced by an instrument or chattel paper, whether or not it has been earned by performance. An account receivable is the classic example. **The Code applies to the outright sale of accounts.**

    b. General intangibles: any personal property (including things in action) other than goods, accounts, chattel paper, documents, instruments, and money. This is a residual definition intended to cover any collateral not within the above categories. Examples include assignments of royalties under patents or copyrights, and rights to payments under performance or exhibition contracts. The Code does not cover the sale of general intangibles; it only applies where they are used to secure a loan.

3. Documentary collateral: The Code defines three kinds of documentary collateral.

    a. Instrument: a negotiable instrument as defined in the Commercial Paper Article or a security.

    b. Documents: includes documents of title (such as a bill of lading, dock warrant, dock receipt, warehouse receipt, or order for delivery of goods) and any other document of title issued or addressed to a bailee (a keeper of goods) and giving instructions concerning goods in the bailee's possession. For a more complete description, see Documents of Title, p. 300, II.

    c. Chattel paper: a writing or writings that evidence both a promise to pay and a security interest in, or a lease of, specific goods (e.g., X purchases an auto, signs a promissory note and a security agreement. Collectively, the writings constitute chattel paper).

II. The Problem

A. In order to understand this complex area of law, it is helpful to place yourself mentally in the shoes of a secured creditor. As such, you have to be concerned with the competing interests and claims of several people or classes of people. Your aim is to be able to resort to the property if necessary to satisfy your loan; you must worry about the following people:

B. **The debtor:** essentially, a secured creditor's rights vis-à-vis his debtor are determined by the contract (security agreement) once the security interest attaches (see p. 341, III). Formalities are minimal in relation to this party.

C. **Lien and attaching creditors:**

1. These competing creditors of the debtor are creditors who as a last resort have employed judicial process against the debtor in order to recover a debt.
2. A formal act known as levy is usually required to render service of process effective. This consists of finding property of the debtor and seizing it or fastening a notice to it.
3. A faulty security interest (one not complying with the Code's rules of secured transactions) will normally be defeated by a lien creditor's levy.
4. The lien creditor:
    a. Attaches property of a debtor prior to suit in order to secure his claim.
    b. Becomes a judgment creditor when he wins a suit and obtains judgment against the debtor.
    c. Executes his judgment by selling the debtor's property either attached before judgment or levied upon after judgment.

D. **The trustee in bankruptcy** (see Bankruptcy, pp. 209–210):

1. A most worthy adversary, he represents the interests of the general creditors of the debtor in question.
2. His aim is to defeat any and all secured claims in order to maximize the dividend payable to the general creditors.
3. Has the power to, and is charged with, setting aside preferences. The taking of a security interest may be a preference. (See Bankruptcy, p. 210).

E. **The good faith** *(bona fide)* purchaser. There are two types:

1. Generally, **one who buys, i.e., pays value, for his personal use and buys in good faith, i.e.** is unaware either actually or constructively (by a filing), of the existence of any security interest in the property. Such persons will normally defeat the rights of a secured party. For example, X purchases a television set from a neighbor. X was unaware of the fact that Y owed $200 to the seller who had sold it on credit. The seller had not filed a financing statement. X will prevail. See also VI, pp. 347–349.

2. Buyers in the ordinary course of business from one (the debtor) who regularly deals in goods of the kind involved. The seller-creditor intends that the goods be resold. Such buyers will invariably defeat the rights of a secured creditor even if his security interest is perfected, and even if the purchaser was aware of it. Only in the event that the buyer is aware that the sale is in violation of the security agreement will he take subject to it. For example, S Appliance Company buys its inventory on credit from M Manufacturing. Under the terms of the security agreement, S is authorized to sell the inventory. C, a consumer, buys one of the M appliances. Even though M files a financing statement covering the inventory and C somehow knows this, C will prevail. See also VI, p. 341.

III. Attachment of a Security Interest

A. A security interest must attach to be enforceable.

B. The Code distinguishes between the attachment of an interest and its perfection.

1. *Attachment* is used to describe the rights of the secured party in the collateral upon creation of the security interest. Satisfaction of the attachment requirements creates the security interest.

2. *Perfection* relates to some additional act that may be required to make the security interest effective against third parties (e.g., filing). The one very important exception to this otherwise clear cut distinction between attachment and perfection occurs in the case of a purchase-money security interest in consumer goods. Perfection occurs upon attachment (see p. 343).

C. Mechanics of attachment:

1. A security interest attaches when three elements are present:
   a. The collateral is in the possession of the secured party pursuant to agreement or the debtor has signed a security agreement that contains a description of the collateral. The agreement:
      (1) Must contain a description reasonably identifying the collateral, e.g., all the inventory, work in process, and raw materials at the X Factory.
      (2) Must be in a writing signed by the debtor. *This in effect is a Statute of Frauds requirement.*
      (3) If growing crops or timber are the collateral, the land must also be described.
   b. Value has been given by the creditor.
   c. The debtor has rights in the collateral.

2. A security interest cannot attach in the absence of any of these three elements, and it comes into existence at the very moment all three coexist, unless an explicit agreement postpones the attachment to a later date. The absence of an element is not fatal to the agreement, but merely means that the security interest does not attach until the missing element comes into existence.

D. Future goods and after-acquired property as collateral:

1. The parties to the transaction may agree that goods not yet in existence or not yet owned by the debtor shall be subject to the secured party's interest. The security interest cannot exist until there has been an attachment.

2. A security agreement may provide that collateral, whenever acquired (i.e., after-acquired property), shall secure all obligations covered by the agreement.

3. No security interest attaches to an after-acquired property clause in consumer goods when given as additional security unless the debtor acquires rights in them within 10 days after the secured party gives value. This provision prevents the seller-creditor from taking a secured interest in all after-acquired property of the purchaser unless the creditor advanced additional value for the purchase of the after-acquired property.

4. The powers of the parties mentioned above, coupled with the recognition of the debtor's right to use or dispose of the collateral, in effect legalize a floating lien on a shifting stock of goods, thereby overcoming pre-Code law hostile to such a device.

E. Priority of an unperfected security interest that has attached:

1. As between the secured party and debtor:
    a. Is effective even if not perfected.
    b. If a special security interest is lost, the creditor at least qualifies as a general creditor of the debtor.
    c. The relationship is contractual and the contract is good as between the debtor and creditor.

2. As between third parties and the creditor:
    a. In general, an unperfected security interest is subordinate to interests of third parties (e.g., a lien creditor) even if the third person has knowledge of the unperfected security interest.
    b. An unperfected security interest is subordinate to the rights of:
        (1) Persons entitled to priority under the Code (see p. 347).
        (2) A person who becomes a lien creditor before the security interest is perfected.
        (3) In the case of goods, instruments, documents, and chattel paper, an unsecured person who is a transferee in bulk or other buyer not in ordinary course of business, or is a buyer of farm products in ordinary course of business, to the extent that he gives value and receives delivery of the collateral without knowledge of the security interest and before it is perfected.
        (4) In the case of accounts and general intangibles, a person who is not a secured party and who is a transferee to the extent that he gives value without knowledge of the security interest and before it is perfected.
    c. If the secured party files with respect to a purchase-money security interest before or within 10 days after the debtor receives possession of the collateral, he takes priority over the rights of a transferee in bulk or of a lien creditor that arise between the time the security interest attaches and the time of filing. This provides the purchase-money lender a 10-day grace period in which to file and not have its secured interest subordinated.

IV. Perfection of a Security Interest

A. *Perfection is required to have a security interest that will be good against third parties,* attaching creditors, and a trustee in bankruptcy. *The normal or usual* *method of perfection is the filing of a financing statement.* Structurally, the Code requires a filing unless there is an exception (e.g., where there is possession).

B. Mechanics of perfection:

  1. Perfection depends on:
    a. The nature of the collateral involved.
    b. The use of the collateral.
    c. The relationship between the debtor and the secured party.
  2. Perfection may occur in three ways: by attachment of the security interest; by possession of the collateral; or by the filing of a financing statement. Any one of the three will usually suffice.

C. *Perfection by attachment*:

  1. Neither possession nor filing is required for perfection when the creditor obtains a purchase-money security interest (see p. 338) in consumer goods so long as the collateral is neither a fixture nor a motor vehicle (special laws apply).
  2. Before the Code, the seller or other party financing the buyer (e.g., a bank) could obtain a perfected security interest only by retaining possession (layaway plan) or by filing the conditional sales contract or chattel mortgage. This is one of several major innovations introduced by the Code. The security interest is perfected upon attachment without further formalities.
  3. Perfection by attachment is good against the purchaser of consumer goods, the creditors of the purchaser and the trustee in bankruptcy. It is not good against a *bona fide* purchaser from the debtor. To protect against a wrongful sale by the debtor, a filing would be necessary.
  4. Example: ABC Appliance Store sells C a hi-fi system, a consumer good, for $750. ABC's security interest *attached* at the time of sale. It is also *perfected* at that time since ABC was a purchase-money lender. Thus, without filing or possession, it has a perfected security interest in the hi-fi set, which is good against C's creditors. However, it is not perfected as against a *bona fide* purchaser (e.g., a neighbor) who buys it.

D. *Perfection by possession* of the collateral:

  1. Article 9 substantially preserves the common law possessory interest (as typified by the pledge) by requiring little or no formality to perfect a possessory security interest in property other than possession. The security agreement can be oral, and notice to third parties is given by possession.
  2. The Code provides that a security interest in goods, instruments, negotiable documents, chattel paper, and letters of credit, may be perfected by possession. Where the collateral is in the possession of a bailee and it is not goods covered by a negotiable document, possession by the secured party is deemed to take place at the time the bailee receives notification of the secured party's interest (e.g., notice would have to be given where the bailee had possession and issued a nonnegotiable bill of lading or warehouse receipt).
  3. In general, perfection occurs at the time of possession, there is no relation back, and it continues only as long as possession is retained subject to the 21-day temporary relinquishment rule (see below).

4. Field warehousing: This pre-Code device was developed to overcome the vulnerability of financing arrangements where the inventory securing the loan was constantly shifting or after-acquired property or both. In addition, such inventory frequently was temporarily released in order to make minor changes or alterations or to handle packaging or labeling. The courts questioned the validity of perfection of such security interests by a general filing covering such inventory. Resort to the use of an outside warehouse that would in turn issue a negotiable warehouse receipt proved both inconvenient and expensive. In response to the above quandary, "field warehousing" was developed. As previously indicated, the Code has validated this type of inventory financing, which involves shifting and after-acquired inventory and the proceeds therefrom, by a general filing. The result has diminished the importance of field warehousing. This novel financing arrangement is characterized by the following:

   a. Depends on perfection by possession; hence similar to the pledge.

   b. Although legally simple, it is sometimes realistically awkward where there is in actuality no physical transfer out of the reach of the debtor.

   c. Formalities below must be carefully adhered to since the actual arrangement may be challenged on the basis of inadequate or ineffective possession by the "warehouseman," i.e., unfettered dominion over the property by the debtor will invalidate the secured party's interest in the property.

   d. The debtor subleases a portion of his premises to the creditor or perhaps an independent warehouseman engaged to facilitate the on-premises warehousing.

   e. A separate area is fenced off if not already so separated or a separate room or facility is used.

   f. Locks on all access gates and doors are installed or changed and the warehouseman is given *sole dominion* and *control* of the keys. Dominion and control are critical.

   g. Signs are conspicuously posted showing possession by the creditor.

   h. The warehouseman may be an employee of the debtor temporarily on detached duty to the creditor, an employee of the creditor, or an independent warehouseman. If the first instance, he is bonded and his wages are paid by the creditor and in turn charged to the debtor.

   i. Temporary and limited relinquishment similar to that discussed below in respect to documents of title is permitted.

5. Instruments: Security interest in instruments (negotiable instruments and securities) can *only* be perfected by possession with relatively minor exceptions:

   a. Where the creditor gives new value under a written security agreement, he has a perfected security interest without filing or taking possession for 21 days after attachment.

   b. The Code also permits a temporary relinquishment. If the instrument is relinquished for sale, exchange collection, etc., the creditors' security interest remains perfected for 21 days.

   c. However, in both situations the holder in due course or a *bona fide* purchaser of the security will defeat the creditors' security interest.

6. Negotiable documents: From a practical standpoint, possession is the only way to perfect a security interest in negotiable bills of lading or negotiable warehouse receipts, although the Code does permit filing. Such a filing is worthless, however, since the document represents the goods, and a holder (good faith purchaser) to whom the instrument has been duly negotiated will defeat the secured creditors' interest since filing is not notice to the holder.

    a. The same type of automatic perfection prior to possession for 21 days from the time of attachment discussed above (5) applies here.

    b. Temporary relinquishment of documents. Where the goods are to be sold or processed, the Code provides for a 21-day continuation of perfection.

    c. Even though the Code authorizes the secured creditor to give up possession and retain his perfected security interest for 21 days, a holder (*bona fide* purchaser) to whom the instrument was duly negotiated will prevail.

7. Chattel paper: Possession is not required by the Code, but it certainly is the safest way of perfecting an interest in such collateral. If the debtor has possession and sells it to a third person who takes possession in the ordinary course of business without knowledge of the secured interest, he will take free of it. Furthermore, if the security interest in the chattel paper which is claimed applies to proceeds of inventory subject to a security interest, the purchaser in the ordinary course will have priority even if he knows.

E. Perfection by filing: Unless the creditor has possession of the collateral or unless the security interest is perfected by attachment in the case of a purchase-money security interest in consumer goods, a filing is necessary. The filing gives public notice to third parties of the creditor's security interest in the collateral.

    1. Unless otherwise perfected, a financing statement must be filed to perfect a nonpossessory security interest in accounts, general intangibles, inventory, goods on consignment, equipment, chattel paper, and documents of title. Filing is also required for the outright sale of accounts or chattel paper.

    2. The Code provides that a financing statement is legally sufficient if it:

        a. Gives the names of the debtor and creditor and is signed by the debtor,

        b. Gives an address of the secured party from which information concerning the security interest may be obtained,

        c. Gives the mailing address of the debtor, and

        d. Contains a statement indicating the types or describing the items of collateral.

    3. A financing statement filed in accordance with state law meets the filing requirements unless a federal statute requires a special method of filing (such as applies to a copyright or patent) to perfect a particular type of security interest.

    4. Depending on the collateral involved and particular local preferences and variations in filing and recording techniques, the UCC prescribes a series of alternative rules that may be considered by each state. A filing is good for five years.

    5. *Consignments:* The Code was amended in 1972 to make it clear that so-called "true" consignments, those that were not used for the purpose of obtaining a security interest, are subject to the Code's filing requirements and that actual notice must be given to certain creditors to perfect the security interest.

        a. A consignment is essentially a sales arrangement. If it is a "true consignment, the consignee is the agent of the consignor (manufacturer-seller) who receives a commission for goods sold. The argument was that since the consignee is merely the sales agent of the consignor and ownership of the property is retained by the consignor, there is no debtor-creditor relationship and no security interest involved; hence it is not covered by the secured transactions provisions of the Code. The 1972 amendments rejected this approach. A true consignment has the following characteristics:

(1) Title retention by the consignor.

(2) No obligation on the consignor's part to buy the goods.

(3) All proceeds belong to the consignor.

b. Having established that there is a consignment, "true" or otherwise, the sales article of the Code provides that the consignor in order to perfect his interest must do one of the following:

(1) Comply with local law providing for posting as a method of disclosing the consignor's interest, or

(2) Establish that the consignee is generally known as engaged in selling the goods of others, or

(3) File under Article 9 (Secured Transactions).

(4) Since (1) and (2) are impractical in most instances, filing is the only sensible way to proceed.

c. To perfect, the consignor must file and give notice in writing to the holders of competing security interests who have filed financing statements covering the same type of goods, prior to the consignor's filing.

F. Perfection and proceeds:

1. The creditor's ability to assert rights against the "proceeds" received by the debtor upon disposition of the collateral is vital, particularly in inventory financing. If the goods are constantly being turned over in the ordinary course of business, access to the proceeds upon default by the debtor must be an integral part of the financing arrangement.

2. Proceeds include whatever is received upon sale, exchange, or other disposition of collateral or proceeds. Insurance proceeds for loss or destruction of the collateral are proceeds if payable to a party to the security agreement. Money, checks, deposit accounts, and the like are cash proceeds. All other proceeds are noncash proceeds.

3. A security interest continues in the *collateral,* notwithstanding sale or other disposition, unless the disposition was authorized by the secured party in the security agreement or otherwise; it also continues in identified proceeds, including collections received by the debtor.

4. Rights in proceeds. The right to proceeds even beyond an initial 10-day period is automatic without any additional filing or formality for all intents and purposes. The Code first provides that a security interest in proceeds is a continuously perfected security interest if the interest in the original collateral was perfected, but it ceases to be a perfected security interest and becomes unperfected 10 days after receipt of the proceeds by the debtor unless:

a. A filed financing statement covers the original collateral and the proceeds are identifiable cash proceeds; or

     b. A filed financing statement covers the original collateral and the proceeds are collateral in which a security interest may be perfected by filing in the office where the financing statement has been filed; and, if the proceeds are acquired with cash proceeds, the description of collateral in the financing statement indicates the types of property constituting the proceeds; or

     c. The security interest in the proceeds is perfected by filing or possession before the expiration of the 10-day period.

V. Priorities of Several Conflicting Security Interests in the Same Security

A. Generally speaking, the priority of conflicting security interests in the same collateral is determined as follows:

    1. If the conflicting interests are each perfected by filing, priority is determined by the order of filing regardless of which security interest first attached and whether it attached before or after filing;

     a. An exception to this general rule of "first to file" exists in the case of a purchase-money security interest that is perfected at the time the debtor receives the collateral, or within 10 days thereafter. In that case, the purchase-money security interest, if filed within 10 days of receipt of the collateral, would defeat any non-purchase-money security interest filed earlier during the 10-day period. This 10-day relation back rule does *not* apply to inventory.

    2. In the order of perfection, unless both are perfected by filing as above, regardless of which security interest attached first and in the case of a filed security interest, whether it attached before or after filing; and,

    3. If none of the conflicting security interests is perfected, priority is determined by the order of attachment.

B. Knowledge of competing security interests. Security interests, perfected or unperfected, will normally have a priority over a third party who may have a perfected security interest or a lien upon the collateral by levy, attachment, or the like:

    1. Which is subsequent in time and was obtained with knowledge of the existence of the prior security interest.

    2. Essentially, the party taking with notice has not taken in good faith and is thereby precluded from obtaining a priority.

C. Where a negotiable document of title is involved, conflicting claims will be resolved in favor of the party who holds the document.

D. Possession of other documents: Priority is granted to a secured party in possession of chattel paper or negotiable or nonnegotiable instruments, or securities as against the claim of a secured party with a nonpossessory security interest in the same collateral.

VI. Rights of Third-Party Purchasers

A. Introductory note: Before proceeding to debtors' and creditors' rights upon default below, let us review and summarize the rights of purchasers vis-à-vis creditors who hold a perfected security interest in the property purchased. It is clear that the equities have shifted and the rights of the "good faith" purchaser are usually paramount. (There is some duplication here of prior parts of the text. However, this is intentional in light of the importance that prior examinations have placed on the subject.)

B. The first situation is commonplace. You buy an appliance in a discount store, where the inventory is almost sure to be financed by either the manufacturer or a lending institution. The creditor has filed a financing statement, and let us assume that somehow, you actually know that the appliance dealer has borrowed to finance his inventory. Are you subject to a perfected security interest in the appliance? The answer is a resounding no, unless you were also aware that the appliance dealer is selling in violation of the financing agreement. But you would never know this; and if you did, and still bought the appliance, you would deserve to lose. Thus, the law favors you, *the purchaser, in the ordinary course of business* in virtually all cases. The reason for this rule is simple. The intent of the manufacturer-creditor or lending institution was to permit resale by the retailer. Once resale is authorized by agreement (express, implied, or otherwise), filing is of no avail against the buyer in the ordinary course of business (see p. 341). The secured party must look to the proceeds.

C. In following the same appliance into the hands of the ultimate consumer, we may encounter another buyer who will be afforded protection against the creditor holding a perfected security interest in the consumer good. This rule applies to consumer goods exclusively. As you will recall, the retailer obtains a perfected purchase-money security interest in the appliance without filing upon the sale of the appliance, assuming he financed the purchase. This perfection occurs upon attachment and is good against the buyer's creditors and the trustee in bankruptcy. However, the perfected security interest is not valid against a subsequent *bona fide* purchaser from the consumer, e.g., if the purchaser resells to a neighbor. In order to qualify under the "good faith" rule, the purchaser must purchase for personal or family use and not have actual knowledge of the appliance store's interest, nor can he have constructive notice of this fact by a filing. Thus, if the retailer does not file a financing statement covering the consumer-purchaser's acquisition of the appliance, he is vulnerable in respect to *bona fide* purchasers, despite a perfected security interest. But why wouldn't the retailer file? The risk may not be great, or the cost of filing as compared with buying insurance covering this eventuality may be uneconomical.

D. Where perfection is by possession, the goods are relinquished and there is no filing, buyers who purchase without knowledge of the security interest will prevail. The protection against such buyers is only good as long as possession is maintained. In the case of instruments (commercial paper and securities), perfection by possession is the only method of perfection available. If there is a transfer to a holder in due course or a *bona fide* purchaser in the case of securities, the secured party loses. Despite the 21-day acquisition and relinquishment rules (see p. 344), they are ineffective against buyers qualifying as holders in due course or *bona fide* purchasers. It is possible to file as an alternative to possession in the case of negotiable documents of title and the same type of 21-day rules apply. However, the negotiable document represents the goods, and if the negotiable document is negotiated to a holder (one who purchases in good faith and for value), that person will prevail despite a filing and the 21-day rules. The subsequent buyer who purchases chattel paper in the ordinary course of business and takes possession of the collateral, will take free of a security interest perfected by filing if he has no actual knowledge of it.

VII. Debtors' and Creditors' Rights on Default

A. Unless otherwise agreed, if the secured transaction is not at the outset a possessory one, a secured party has the right to take possession of the collateral after default.

B. When the collateral is accounts receivable, contract rights, general intangibles, chattel paper, or instruments, the secured party is entitled to notify the obligor to make payment directly to him (the secured party) where the assignor-debtor was previously making collections.

C. A secured party may dispose of collateral by sale or lease or in any other manner calculated to produce the greatest benefit for all parties concerned.

D. The debtor has a right to require the secured creditor to dispose of the goods:
  1. If the debtor has paid 60% of the cash price in the case of a purchase-money security interest in consumer goods or 60% of the loan in the case of another security interest in consumer goods.
  2. After satisfying disposition costs and repaying the balance of the debt, the debtor is entitled to the residuary, if any.
  3. The purpose of this clause is to protect consumers against unfairness by secured creditors.

E. If it can be established that a secured creditor is not proceeding in accordance with the provisions of the Code or in good faith, an interested party may apply to the court for relief.

F. In addition to the above, the parties may agree to other remedies for the secured party, so long as they are not prohibited by the Code.

Selected Problems from CPA Examinations on Secured Transactions

Subjective Questions and Answers

Q. 1. After much study and deliberation, the marketing division of Majestic Enterprise, Inc., has recommended to the board of directors that the corporation market its products almost exclusively via consignment arrangements instead of other alternate merchandising-security arrangements. The board moved favorably upon this proposal.

Required

Answer the following, setting forth reasons for any conclusions stated.

   What are the key legal characteristics of a consignment?

A.   A consignment is a selling arrangement between the owner, called the *consignor,* and the party who is to sell the goods, called the *consignee.* The consignee is appointed the agent to sell the owner's merchandise. The following are the key characteristics.

   1. Title to the goods remains at all times with the consignor.
   2. The consignee is at no time obligated to buy or pay for the goods.
   3. The consignee receives a commission for the goods sold.
   4. The proceeds belong to the consignor.

5/80

Q.   2. Norwood Furniture, Inc., found that its credit rating was such that it was unable to obtain a line of unsecured credit. National Bank indicated that it would be willing to supply funds based upon a "pledge" of Norwood's furniture inventory which was located in two warehouses. The bank would receive notes and bearer negotiable warehouse receipts covering the merchandise securing the loans. An independent warehouseman was to have complete control over the areas in the warehouse set aside as field warehousing facilities. The Hastings Field Warehousing Corporation was selected to serve as the independent warehouseman. It was to retain keys to the posted area in which the inventory was contained. Negotiable bearer warehouse receipts were issued to Norwood when it delivered the merchandise to Hastings. The receipts were then delivered by Norwood to National to secure the loans which were made at 80% of the market value of the furniture indicated on the receipts. Upon occasion, Norwood would take temporary possession of the furniture for the purpose of packaging it, surrendering the warehouse receipt for this limited purpose. As orders were filled out of the field warehouse inventory, the requisite receipt would be relinquished by National, the merchandise obtained by Norwood, and other items substituted with a new receipt issued.

Required

Answer the following, setting forth reasons for any conclusions stated.

1. Based upon the facts given, is the field warehousing arrangement valid?
2. When does a security interest in the negotiable warehouse receipts attach?
3. What, if anything, is necessary to perfect a security interest in goods covered by negotiable warehouse receipts?
4. What are the dangers, if any, that National faces by relinquishing the warehouse receipts to Norwood?

A.   1. Yes. Independent dominion and control by the field warehouseman is the essential test that must be met in order to create a valid security interest in the field warehoused goods. If the debtor (Norwood) were allowed to retain dominion and control of the goods placed in the field warehouse on its premises, the validity of the field warehousing arrangement would be questionable. But where the warehouseman is an independent warehousing company and where the formalities are adhered to (that is, posting, and the keys are in the warehouseman's exclusive control), the arrangement will withstand an attack upon its validity.

   2. The Uniform Commercial Code provides that a security interest attaches when
       a. The collateral is in possession of the secured party pursuant to agreement or the debtor has signed a security agreement that contains a description of the collateral
       b. Value has been given.
       c. The debtor has rights to the collateral.
       (Typically the security interests in such situations arise upon delivery of the warehouse receipts to the creditor.)

3. Nothing. A security interest in goods covered by negotiable documents may be perfected by taking possession of the documents. When possession is obtained, no filing is necessary.

4. The danger inherent in relinquishing the negotiable document of title to Norwood is that he may "duly negotiate" it to a holder. The code provides that "such holders take priority over an earlier security interest even though perfected. Filing . . . does not constitute notice of the security interest to such holders. . . ."

    Negotiation of a negotiable bearer document of title is by delivery alone. The instrument is "duly negotiated" when negotiated "to a holder who purchases it in good faith without notice of any defense against or claim to it on the part of any person and for value, unless it is established that the negotiation is not in the regular course of business or financing or involved receiving the document in settlement or payment of a money obligation."

Q. 3. National Finance Company engages in a wide variety of secured transactions which may be broken down into three categories.

    I. Consumer loans in connection with the purchase of automobiles, appliances, and furniture. National makes these loans in two ways. First, it makes direct loans to the consumer-borrower who then makes the purchase with the proceeds. Second, it is contacted by the seller and provides the financing for the purchase by the customer. In either case National takes a security interest in the property purchased.

    II. Collateralized loans to borrowers who deliver possession of property, such as diamonds, to National to secure repayment of their loans.

    III. Loans to merchants to finance their inventory purchases. National takes a security interest in the inventory and proceeds.

    Except for category III, National does not file a financing statement.

Required

Answer the following, setting forth reasons for any conclusions stated.

1. When does National's security interest in the various types of property attach?

2. As a secured creditor, against what parties must National protect itself?

3. Does National have a perfected security interest in any of the above property? If so, against whom?

4. If the facts indicate that National does not have a perfected security interest against all parties, what should it do?

5. Can National fully protect itself against all subsequent parties who might claim superior rights to the property involved?

A. 1. The Uniform Commercial Code provides that a security interest attaches in property when three events occur. First, collateral is in possession of the secured party pursuant to agreement, or the debtor has signed a security agreement that contains a description of the collateral. Second, value has been given by the creditor. Third, the debtor has rights in the collateral.

    Insofar as National is concerned, a security interest in all three categories of secured transactions has attached. In categories I and III, there must be a security agreement signed by the debtor. Regarding the collateralized property in category II, possession pursuant to agreement without a signed writing is sufficient. In all instances, value has been given and the debtor has rights in the collateral.

2. There are four potential parties against whom National must protect itself. These are the debtor, the debtor's creditors, the trustee in bankruptcy, and subsequent purchasers for value from the debtor.

3. National's rights against the debtor are contained in the security agreement and the Uniform Commercial Code provisions relating to the agreement and the relationship between the parties. It is not necessary to file a financing statement in order to obtain these rights against the debtor; the agreement itself is sufficient.

    To perfect a security interest against other parties, the creditor must either take possession (as in category II) or file a statement except where the creditor has taken "a purchase-money security interest in consumer goods." In the latter case, perfection occurs at the time the security interest attaches, but it is only valid against the debtor's creditors and a trustee in bankruptcy and not against a *bona fide* purchaser unless a financing statement has been filed. Whether National uses either method described in category I to finance the purchase of the consumer goods, it will have a purchase-money security interest if it gave value to enable the debtor to acquire rights in or the use of collateral if such value is in fact so used.

Where a creditor provides financing for a debtor to enable him to obtain and resell inventory items, the security interest is perfected by filing. However, since resale is clearly contemplated, purchasers for value take free of the perfected security interest.

4. The only practical suggestion would be to file a financing statement in respect to the loans described in category I, which would then provide protection against subsequent purchasers from the debtor. National already is protected against the other parties in category I upon attachment of the security interest.

5. No. As indicated above, where the goods are inventory in the hands of the debtor, a purchaser for value in the ordinary course of business takes free of the creditor's perfected security interest. In such cases, it is not possible for the lender to completely protect itself against all parties without obtaining possession.

11/78

Q. 4. You have been assigned by the CPA firm of Stanford, Cox, & Walsh to audit the accounts of Super Appliances, Inc., a retail discount chain. Super sells almost exclusively to retail customers in the ordinary course of business. It typically requires 25% as a down payment and takes a promissory note and a signed security agreement for the balance. However, if the purchase price of the appliance or appliances purchased by the customer exceeds $500, it arranges with a local financing company, Friendly Finance, to have credit extended to the customer. In such cases, Friendly supplies the 75% financing and takes a promissory note and a signed security agreement. A financing statement is neither obtained nor recorded by Super or Friendly.

Required
Answer the following, setting forth reasons for any conclusions stated.

1. Does Super or Friendly have a "purchase-money security interest" in respect to the appliances sold to Super's customers?
2. What is the legal importance of the distinction between a "purchase-money security interest" and the usual nonpossessory security interest?

A. 1. Yes. Both Super, the seller, and Friendly, who financed many of the purchases by Super's customers, qualify as "purchase-money security" lenders. The Uniform Commercial Code provides that a security interest is a "purchase-money security interest" to the extent that it is—
   (a) taken or retained by the seller of the collateral to secure all or part of its price; or
   (b) taken by a person who, by making advances or incurring an obligation, gives value to enable the debtor to acquire rights in or the use of collateral if such value is in fact so used.
   Those items financed by Super meet the requirements of (a) and those items financed by Friendly meet the requirements of (b).

2. A nonpossessory security interest is one in which the lender or seller does not have possession of the property subject to the security interest. In such situations, the lender or seller perfects the security interest against third parties by filing a financing statement. An exception is made for the purchase-money security interest relating to consumer goods (for example, installment sales to the consumer) wherein the lender or seller is protected against other creditors of the debtor (but not *bona fide* consumer purchasers for value from the debtor) without the necessity of filing a financing statement. Hence, bothersome and costly paperwork is eliminated unless the secured party wishes to protect itself from a fraudulent sale by the consumer to a *bona fide* consumer purchaser for value. The risk is relatively unimportant in relation to the cost of filing, consequently many sellers and commercial lenders assume this risk themselves.

5/77

Q. 5. Anderson Corporation is in the business of selling goods. It commonly sells on credit terms requiring payment within 30 days from the end of the month in which the goods are delivered. A few years ago Anderson borrowed $10,000 from Searles for which Anderson signed a promissory note payable in full on April 30, 1976. Anderson also signed a security agreement under which Searles was granted collateral described as "all of Anderson's current and thereafter acquired accounts receivable." The security agreement was silent on whether the secured party was entitled to notify Anderson's accounts-receivable debtors to make payments directly to Searles. Searles filed a financing statement in this connection on the day that it lent the $10,000 to Anderson. Pursuant to the security agreement, Anderson from time to time had notified Searles of the amounts and identities of its outstanding accounts-receivable debtors. Searles' files indicate that as of April 23, 1976, Anderson had accounts receivable of $50,000 in total. The largest three accounts each amounted to $5,000 arising out of deliveries in April. On April 30, 1976, Anderson notified Searles that it would be unable to repay the $10,000 in the near future.

Required

Discuss the rights of Searles against the accounts-receivable debtors of Anderson under this loan transaction both prior to and subsequent to April 30, 1976.

A. The Uniform Commercial Code provides that when the debtor agrees, or on default, a secured party is entitled to notify accounts-receivable debtors to make payment directly to him even though the debtor had been making collection on the account. Because the security agreement is silent on giving notice, Searles has no right to notify and collect directly from Anderson's accounts-receivable debtors prior to default by Anderson.

Here, however, Anderson is in default by not having repaid the $10,000 when due on April 30, 1976. After that date, Searles may notify Anderson's present accounts-receivable debtors to make payment directly to Searles until $10,000 has been received by Searles. Searles may notify the present accounts-receivable debtors because it is a secured party with respect to Anderson's accounts receivable that existed as of the date of the security agreement plus those that were acquired by Anderson after the date of the security agreement. Searles attained this secured status because the Uniform Commercial Code permits the obligations covered by a security agreement to be secured by such after-acquired collateral.

If requested by an accounts-receivable debtor, Searles must furnish reasonable proof that the assignment of a security interest in the accounts has been made. Unless Searles gives such proof, the accounts-receivable debtor may pay Anderson.

Upon default, Searles also may commence an action on the debt and reduce his claim to judgment. This alternative involves the judicial process whereas collection from the accounts-receivable debtors does not.

5/76

Practice Questions

Q. 1. On January 14, 1985, Thelma Corporation sold and delivered to Dey Corporation inventory goods priced at $5,000 on terms which required payment within 30 days after delivery. Because of business reverses, Dey found that it was unable to pay the amount due Thelma. On February 9, 1985, Thelma's credit manager validly filed a properly signed financing statement. On February 18, 1985, he met with Dey's officers to effect a plan of repayment. At this meeting, Thelma obtained a $5,000 promissory note and security agreement signed by Dey and secured by Dey's presently existing and thereafter acquired inventory.

Required

Does Thelma have a perfected security interest? Explain.

Q. 2. Sill Corporation operates a retail appliance store. About a year ago, Sill borrowed $3,000 from Castle to supplement its working capital. At that time it granted to Castle a security interest in its present and future inventory pursuant to a written security agreement signed by both parties. Castle duly filed a properly executed financing statement a few days later. In the ordinary course of business, a customer purchased a $500 television set from Sill. The customer knew of the existence of Castle's security interest.

Required

What rights does Castle have against Sill's customer? Explain.

Q. 3. Wonder Television Manufacturing, Inc., manufactures television sets under its brand name, Wonder TV, and sells the sets directly to retail stores. To increase sales, Wonder incorporated WOMAC financial Corporation to provide credit to customers who purchase Wonder TV sets from the retail stores. Wonder's arrangement with the retailers stipulates that WOMAC will provide the financing for the purchase of Wonder TV sets to any customer who meets WOMAC's financial requirements. These financial requirements are based on standard credit practices. The financing is put in motion by the retailers telling their customers that financing is available through WOMAC if they wish to purchase a set on time.

After a recent analysis of its experience, WOMAC has found that it would be cheaper not to file a financing statement covering each individual set purchased by the retailers' customers. As a result, WOMAC is considering an alternative plan whereby WOMAC will take a negotiable promissory note and a security agreement signed by the borrower-purchaser. These papers will be retained by WOMAC, and monthly collections will be made on the notes. The retailers will receive immediate payment on a discounted basis for each sale financed.

Required

Assuming WOMAC implements its alternate plan, discuss its rights against each of the following:

1. A retailer upon the default by one of its customers who purchased a Wonder TV financed by WOMAC.
2. The creditors or the trustee in bankruptcy of a purchaser of a Wonder TV financed by WOMAC in the event of default by the purchaser.
3. A subsequent *bona fide* purchaser who bought a used set from an original retail customer who had financed his original purchase through WOMAC.

Q. 4. Monolith Industries, Inc., manufactures appliances and has been the major supplier of appliances to Wilber Force Corporation, a chain of retail appliance stores. The financing arrangement between Monolith and Wilber Force calls for the sale by Monolith to Wilber Force of appliances to be resold to the public through Wilber Force's chain of appliance stores. Title to the merchandise has been retained by Monolith until receipt of payment. Monthly accountings and payments have been rendered by Wilber Force to Monolith.

Monolith filed a financing statement with the appropriate jurisdictions involved pursuant to the Uniform Commercial Code. The financing statement clearly revealed the debtor-creditor relationship between the parties, described the goods in general terms, and set forth Monolith's security interest in the various appliances sold to Wilber Force. It also contained a provision asserting Monolith's rights against any and all proceeds arising from the sale of said appliances by Wilber Force.

Wilber Force is in financial difficulty. Monolith is asserting rights to certain chattel paper (i.e., installment-sales contracts and nonnegotiable notes) received by Wilber Force arising from the sale of Monolith appliances to its retail customers. Double Discount Corporation purchased the chattel paper in question from Wilber Force in the ordinary course of its business and took possession of all the paper at the time it was purchased. Double Discount was aware of Monolith's security interest in the inventory. Both Monolith and Double Discount claim ownership of the paper.

Required

1. Does Monolith have a perfected security interest? Explain.
2. Assuming Monolith has a perfected security interest, does it include proceeds? Explain.
3. Does Monolith have any rights against Double Discount regarding the chattel paper? Explain.

Q. 5. While examining accounts receivable during the current audit of Dodson Corporation, you encountered the following situation involving Excelsior Sales Distributors, Inc., one of Dodson's customers.

In the past, Dodson had sold Excelsior various hi-fi components for sale to its retail customers in the ordinary course of business. The credit arrangement between the parties provided for payment by Excelsior on a 2/10, net/30 basis. Excelsior fell behind on payments for merchandise it had purchased, and Dodson demanded a security interest in the merchandise for which payment had not been received. Negotiations between the parties resulted in the following plan, which has been executed.

- Excelsior returned to Dodson all of the unsold merchandise in its possession that had been delivered by Dodson. (This was insufficient to cover the outstanding obligation to Dodson because merchandise that previously had been delivered had been sold by Excelsior and was not available for repossession.) Dodson placed the merchandise in a bonded warehouse, retaining a negotiable warehouse receipt for the items repossessed from Excelsior. The merchandise was segregated in the warehouse for identification.
- Excelsior agreed to pay all storage and delivery costs on the repossessed merchandise.
- Dodson agreed to release the repossessed merchandise to Excelsior upon payment in cash for each delivery.
- Dodson agreed not to file a financing statement on the repossessed merchandise.
- All future sales were to be made on a cash basis, but only after Excelsior satisfied all outstanding debts to Dodson.

Subsequently, under a separate agreement, Excelsior's owners, who were also its directors and officers, guaranteed all outstanding obligations of Excelsior to Dodson including any deficiency that may arise on disposition of the repossessed merchandise.

Six months later, Excelsior filed a voluntary petition in bankruptcy. Dodson is asserting rights to the merchandise it sold and repossessed. Dodson also seeks to collect from Excelsior's owners on their guarantee for the deficiency resulting from merchandise previously delivered less the proceeds from the sale of merchandise repossessed.

Required

1. Does Dodson have a perfected security interest in the repossessed merchandise? Explain.
2. Assuming Dodson is a secured creditor of Excelsior, can the duly appointed trustee in bankruptcy set aside Dodson's security interest in the repossessed merchandise? Explain.
3. Can Dodson recover against Excelsior's owners upon their guarantee for any remaining deficiency after a valid auction sale of the repossessed merchandise? Explain.

Practice Objective Questions

Instructions 1–15

Select the *best* answer for each of the following items. Mark only one answer for *each* item. Answer all items. Your grade will be based on your total correct answers.

1. Migrane Financial does a wide variety of lending. It provides funds to manufacturers, middlemen, retailers, consumers, and home owners. In all instances it intends to create a security interest in the loan transactions it enters into. To which of the following will Article 9 (Secured Transactions) of the Uniform Commercial Code *not* apply?
   a. A second mortgage on the borrower's home.
   b. An equipment lease.
   c. The sale of accounts.
   d. Field warehousing.
2. Bigelow manufactures mopeds and sells them through franchised dealers who are authorized to resell them to the ultimate consumer or return them. Bigelow delivers the mopeds on consignment to these retailers. The consignment agreement clearly states that the agreement is intended to create a security interest for Bigelow in the mopeds delivered on consignment. Bigelow wishes to protect itself against the other creditors of and purchasers from the retailers who might assert rights against the mopeds. Under the circumstances, Bigelow

    a. Must file a financing statement and give notice to certain creditors in order to perfect his security interest.

    b. Will have rights against purchasers in the ordinary course of business who were aware of the fact that Bigelow had filed.

    c. Need take *no* further action to protect himself, since the cosignment is a sale of return and title is reserved in Bigelow.

    d. Will have a perfected security interest in the mopeds upon attachment.

3. Johnson loaned money to Visual, Inc., a struggling growth company, and sought to obtain a security interest in negotiable stock certificates which are traded on a local exchange. To perfect his interest against Visual's other creditors, Johnson

    a. Need do nothing further in that his security interest was perfected upon attachment.

    b. May file or take possession of the stock certificates.

    c. Must take possession of the stock certificates.

    d. Must file and give the other creditors notice of his contemplated security interest.

4. Gladstone Warehousing, Inc., is an independent bonded warehouse company. It issued a warehouse receipt for 10,000 bales of cotton belonging to Travis. The word "NEGOTIABLE" was conspicuously printed on the warehouse receipt it issued to Travis. The warehouse receipt also contained a statement in large, clear print that the cotton would only be surrendered upon return of the receipt and payment of all storage fees. Travis was a prominent plantation owner engaged in the cotton growing business. Travis pledged the warehouse receipt with Southern National Bank in exchange for a $50,000 personal loan. A financing statement was *not* filed. Under the circumstances, which of the following is correct?

    a. Travis' business creditors *cannot* obtain the warehouse receipt from Southern National unless they repay Travis' outstanding loan.

    b. The bank does *not* have a perfected security interest in the cotton since it did *not* file a financing statement.

    c. Travis' personal creditors have first claim, superior to all other parties, to the cotton in question because the loan was a personal loan and constituted a fraud upon the personal creditors.

    d. The fact that the word "NEGOTIABLE" and the statement regarding the return of the receipt were conspicuously printed upon the receipt is *not* binding upon anyone except Travis.

5. Andrew asked Judy about the possibility of borrowing $10,000. Judy replied that she would be happy to make the loan if Andrew would provide collateral to secure payment. Andrew gave Judy his promissory note for $10,000, bearing interest at 7%, and delivered to Judy convertible bearer bonds with coupons attached. The bonds had a current market value of $12,000. During the period in which the loan was outstanding the bonds increased in market value to $18,000. In addition, one of the interest coupons became due. There is no express agreement between the parties as to their respective rights in the interest or profits. Under the circumstances, which of the following is correct?

    a. Judy owns the coupon representing matured interest due.

    b. Judy may elect to sell the bonds and retain the proceeds in excess of $12,000.

    c. If Judy sold the bonds to an innocent third party, the third party would obtain valid title.

    d. Such a financing arrangement must be filed in the appropriate recordation office in order to be valid.

6. As a secured creditor under the Uniform Commercial Code, Dawson has invariably perfected a security interest in goods which provide the underlying security for various loans. Under the circumstances, which of the following is correct?

    a. Dawson is assured that the debts will be repaid.

    b. Dawson's security interest *cannot* be perfected by possession.

    c. Dawson is entitled to "resort to" or obtain the property even as against a trustee in bankruptcy.

    d. Dawson has a priority in bankruptcy and therefore is entitled to defeat the claims of all creditors which are asserted against the goods.

7. Field warehousing is a well-established means of securing a loan. As such, it resembles a pledge in many legal respects. Which of the following is correct?

    a. The field warehouseman must maintain physical control of and dominion over the property.

    b. A filing is required in order to perfect such a financing arrangement.

    c. Temporary relinquishment of control for any purpose will suspend the validity of the arrangement insofar as other creditors are concerned.

    d. The property in question must be physically moved to a new location although it may be a part of the borrower's facilities.

8. Weatherall seeks to create a valid perfected security interest in goods under the provisions of the Uniform Commercial Code. Which of the following acts or actions will establish this?

    a. Weatherall obtains a written agreement under which Weatherall takes possession of the security.

    b. Weatherall obtains an unsigned written security agreement.

    c. Weatherall obtains a security agreement signed only by the debtor.

    d. Weatherall files a financing statement which is *not* in itself a security agreement.

9. Article 9 (Secured Transactions) of the Uniform Commercial Code:

    a. Does *not* apply if the secured transaction involves personal property that has a value of less than $500.

    b. Has been adopted by the Congress of the United States and thus is the law of all the states.

    c. Only codified most of the majority rules existing at common law or contained in widely adopted state statutes applicable to secured transactions.

    d. Does *not* apply to purchase-money real estate mortgages.

10. Maxim Corporation, a wholesaler, was indebted to the Wilson Manufacturing Corporation in the amount of $50,000 arising out of the sale of goods delivered to Maxim on credit. Wilson and Maxim signed a security agreement creating a security interest in certain collateral of Maxim. The collateral was described in the security agreement as "the inventory of Maxim Corporation, presently existing and thereafter acquired." In general, this description of the collateral:

    a. Applies only to inventory sold by Wilson to Maxim.

    b. Is sufficient to cover all inventory.

    c. Is insufficient because it attempts to cover after-acquired inventory.

    d. Must be more specific for the security interest to be perfected against subsequent creditors.

11. In the case of consumer goods, a buyer from the original purchaser takes the goods free of a perfected security interest if:

    a. He buys without knowledge of the security interest, for value, for his own personal purposes, and the secured party has *not* filed a financing statement covering such goods.

    b. He buys without knowledge of the security interest, for value, for his own personal purposes, and price to the purchase the secured party has filed a financing statement covering such goods.

    c. He buys with knowledge of the security interest, and after the purchase the secured party files a financing statement covering such goods.

    d. He buys with knowledge of the security interest, and the secured party has *not* filed a financing statement covering such goods prior to delivery of the goods.

12. The scope of secured transactions in the Uniform Commercial Code does *not* include

    a. Pledges.

    b. Transactions where title has *not* passed.

    c. After-acquired collateral.

    d. Sale of corporate debentures.

13. On June 10, Central Corporation sold goods to Bowie Corporation for $5,000. Bowie signed a financing statement containing the names and addresses of the parties and describing the collateral. Central filed the financing statement on June 21, noting the same in its accounting books.

    a. Central need *not* sign the financing statement to perfect its security interest in the collateral.

    b. Central must file the financing statement prior to the sale if a security interest is to be perfected.

    c. Central must sign the financing statement in order to perfect its security interest.

    d. Central had a perfected security interest in the collateral even before the financing statement was filed.

14. Your client, Ace Audio Sales, sold a Magnificent Hi-Fi System to Marcus on the installment basis. Marcus signed an installment agreement for the balance due ($2,000) on the purchase price. Ace's policy was *not* to file a financing statement in the appropriate recordation office. Marcus subsequently sold the hi-fi to Franks without disclosing the debt owed to Ace. Franks purchased the hi-fi in good faith, knowing nothing about the debt owed by Marcus to Ace. Marcus is bankrupt. Wallace, a general creditor of Marcus, has asserted rights to the hi-fi in question. Under the circumstances:

    a. Marcus takes title free and clear of any claims because Ace did not file.

   b. Ace can defeat the claim of Franks in that Franks is a mere third-party beneficiary.

   c. Ace's rights against Marcus under the contract of sale are unimpaired despite the lack of filing.

   d. In the final analysis Wallace will prevail.

15. Kelmore Appliances, Inc., sells various brand name appliances at discount prices. Kelmore maintains a large inventory which it obtains from various manufacturers on credit. These manufacturer-creditors have all filed and taken secured interest in the appliances and proceeds therefrom which they have sold to Kelmore on credit. Kelmore in turn sells to hundreds of ultimate consumers; some pay cash but most buy on credit. Kelmore takes a security interest but does *not* file a financing statement for credit sales. Which of the following is correct?

   a. The appliances in Kelmore's hands are consumer goods.

   b. Since Kelmore takes a purchase-money security interest in the consumer goods sold, its security interest is perfected upon attachment.

   c. The appliance manufacturers can enforce their secured interests against the appliances in the hands of the purchasers who paid cash for them.

   d. A subsequent sale by one of Kelmore's customers to a *bona fide* purchaser will be subject to Kelmore's secured interest.

7

PROPERTY (10%)

15

Real and Personal Property

AICPA Content Specification Outline

Distinctions Between Realty and Personalty
Types of Ownership
Lessor-Lessee
Deeds, Recording, Title Defects, and Title Insurance

Contents

IV. Landlord and Tenant
   A. Characteristics
   B. Leases: rights, duties, and liabilities
   C. Termination of the tenancy
Selected Problems from CPA Examinations on Property
Subjective Questions and Answers
Practice Questions
Practice Objective Questions

I. Personal Property

A. Definition: everything that is the subject of ownership not coming under the denomination of real property (see Property, p. 363, II.A.2).

   1. Personal property is divisible into:
   a. Corporeal personal property (choses in possession): property of a personal, tangible, and movable nature (e.g., cattle, tools, furniture).
   b. Incorporeal personal property (choses in action): intangible personal rights not reduced to possession, but recoverable by a suit at law (e.g., corporate bonds or shares of stock, accounts receivable, tort claims, patents, copyrights).

B. Acquisition of property. Title to personal property may be acquired by:

   1. Inheritance.
   2. Purchase.
   3. Acquisition of unowned property. Intentional exercise of exclusive domain over an unowned object of personal property creates a property right in the object by appropriation (e.g., capture of wild animals or catching of fish).
   4. Creation of products by personal labor, physical or mental (e.g., manufacture, artistic productions).
   5. Accession: owner's right to additions to his property brought about naturally or artificially, e.g., natural increase in herd of animals. (Automobile sold on conditional sale contract gives seller rights that will embrace additions that the buyer adds if they may not be readily removed without damage.)
   6. Confusion (merger, blending, or intermingling): goods of a similar character belonging to two persons are so mingled that separation of the precise goods is impossible. The title of neither party is lost and the law recognizes a tenancy in common (in unequal shares if such be the facts) in the commingled whole, and either party may sue for severance.
   a. If in a severance case the plaintiff fraudulently, knowingly, and wrongfully caused the mingling, he will be held to have forfeited his title. This rule (forfeiture) does not apply if the plaintiff was merely negligent.
   7. Gift: a voluntary transfer of personal property without consideration.

    a. Gift *inter vivos:* a gift between two living people; irrevocable where there is:
      (1) Competency of parties.
      (2) Voluntary transaction with donative intent.
      (3) Transfer of possession: there must be delivery and acceptance.
        (A) A delivery may be actual (e.g., manual delivery of ring) or constructive (e.g., delivery of bill of sale, savings bankbook).
      (4) Intent to pass title.
    b. Gift *causa mortis:* gift in contemplation and fear of approaching death where elements of a gift *inter vivos* are present (see above, a), and
      (1) There is contemplation of impending death by donor, and
      (2) Donor died shortly after making the gift before recovering from illness that induced him to contemplate death, and
      (3) Donor has not revoked the gift prior to his death, and
      (4) Donee has not died before the donor.
        (A) If death does not occur, the condition of the gift fails and the donor recovers the gift.
    c. A promise to make a gift is unenforceable.

II. Real Property Characteristics

A. Definitions:

  1. Property: in the strict legal sense, an aggregate of rights relating to ownership and resultant control of things tangible and intangible, guaranteed and protected by the law.

  2. Real property (or realty): land, and, generally, whatever is erected or growing upon or affixed permanently to land.
    a. Realty includes the surface, air rights, and contents of land.
    b. Natural products of land are realty while attached to the land (e.g., growing trees), but personalty when severed from the land (e.g., timber).

  3. Chattel (or personalty): an article of personal property, a movable thing. A chattel real is any interest in real estate less than a freehold (see below, II.B.1.a).

  4. Fixture: something that was originally a chattel (i.e., personalty), but that was annexed to land so as to become "a part thereof."
    a. Requisites for conversion of a chattel (personalty) to a fixture (realty):
      (1) Actual annexation to the realty, or to something appurtenant (belonging) thereto, and
      (2) Use of the personal property for the purpose for which the real property is used (e.g., heavy machinery necessary for the operation of a factory may become part of the realty).
      (3) Intention (the key requisite) to make the article a permanent addition to the freehold, as gathered from the intention of the parties expressed in the agreement, the nature of articles affixed, the relation and situation of the person making annexation, the structure and mode of annexation, and the purpose or use for which it has been made.
    b. Trade "fixtures" remain personal property. They include readily detachable items such as refrigerators and removable equipment.

B. Estates in land (interests that persons have in land):

1. Estates are classified as to duration (freehold and nonfreehold).

   a. Freehold: estate for life or greater duration. The owner is seized of the land (i.e., he possesses a freehold interest in land).

   (1) Estate in fee simple: estate of potentially infinite duration.

   (A) Fee simple absolute: an estate in fee simple that is not subject to a restriction—see (B) below. (E.g., A conveys Blackacre "to B and his heirs.")

   (i) Ownership of the estate is undivided.

   (ii) It is the greatest estate with respect to ownership rights.

   (iii) It is now the estate preferred by law.

   (B) Fee simple defeasible: estate in fee simple subject to one or more restrictions that may bring an end to ownership for example:

   (i) Special limitation: causes the created interest *automatically* to expire upon the occurrence of a stated event. (E.g., A conveys Blackacre "to B and his heirs, so long as it is used for educational purposes.")

   (ii) Condition subsequent: causes the conveyor or his successor in interest to have the *power to terminate* the interest upon the occurrence of a stated event. (E.g., A conveys Blackacre "to B and his heirs, but if there is gambling on the premises, then A has the right to reenter and repossess.") Reversion is not automatic.

   (C) Transfer of fee simple:

   (i) *Inter vivos:* from one living person to another by deed.

   (ii) Intestate succession: where the owner dies without leaving a will.

   (iii) Devise: where the owner dies making provision for passage of property in his will.

   (2) Life estate. (A to B for life.) After the death of the life tenant, depending upon the grantor's wishes, the estate will revert to the grantor, or pass to a specified third person. See p. 365, II.B.2.b. below.

   (A) Not an inheritable estate (cannot be transferred by will in that the duration of the estate is invariably measured by life of testator, i.e., the person making the will).

   (B) Estate specifically described as to duration in terms of the life or lives of one or more human beings.

   (C) May not be terminable at any fixed or computable period of time. (E.g., A conveys Blackacre "to B for the term of his natural life.")

   (D) Life tenants may not misuse or allow the land to deteriorate during their tenancy and must keep it in repair.

   (E) Life tenants may alienate (transfer by sale or gift) or mortgage their interests in the land unless this has been prohibited. Note that this transfer lasts only as long as the life tenant lives.

   b. Nonfreehold estates (chattel real; no seisin, only possession).

   (1) Estates for years. Even if the estate is for 10,000 years, it is not considered a life estate—see above, II.B.2. (E.g., L leases Blackacre "to T for the period of two years.")

    (2) Estate at will: land held subject to the will of the transferor or transferee.

        (A) An estate that is terminable at will of the transferor or transferee, upon giving notice, and that has no other designated period of duration. (E.g., L leases Blackacre to T for "as long as L wishes.")

        (B) Estate from period to period: an estate at will that will continue for successive periods of a year, or successive periods of a fraction of a year, until it is terminated. Notice of termination only takes effect at the end of the current period. (E.g., L leases Blackacre to T for a two-year period from April 1, 1980 to April 1, 1982, at a rental of $50 per month, payable in advance, on or before the 10th day of the month. T holds possession beyond April 1, 1982, and on April 9, 1982, tenders $50 to L, which L accepts. Notice of termination could only take effect at the end of the month.)

    (3) Estates at sufferance: When a person who had a possessory interest in land by virtue of an effective conveyance wrongfully continues in the possession of the land after the termination of such interest, but without asserting a claim of superior title; actually there is no tenancy at all, merely a wrongful possession. This is neither an estate nor property. (E.g., L leases Blackacre to T for a period and T continues to occupy the land after that period without L's consent.)

    (4) Statutory tenancies: estates in land created by statute; these vary, depending upon state law (e.g., a tenancy created during the war as a result of emergency legislation to deal with housing shortages).

2. Estates classified as to time of possession.

    a. Present or possessory estate: an estate now existing, vested in a holder who has present use or possession of the property.

    b. Future estate: the right or use of possession by the owner is deferred to a future time.

        (1) Reversion: the balance of fee that reverts to the grantor after a lapse of a particular precedent estate granted by him. (E.g., A to B for life. When B dies, the property will revert to A.)

        (2) Remainder: the balance of a larger estate that passes to a third party other than the grantor after a particular precedent estate expires. (E.g., A to B for life, remainder to C. When B dies, the property will pass to C.)

3. Concurrent estates.

    a. *Joint tenancy:* estates acquired by two or more persons.

        (1) Every joint tenancy requires the four unities of:

            (A) Time: All tenants take their interests in the premises at the same instant of time.

            (B) Title: All tenants take their interests from the same source (the same deed or the same will).

            (C) Interest: Every tenant has the same identical interest in the property as every other tenant.

            (D) Possession: Every joint tenant owns the undivided whole of the property. He does not own a fractional interest; he is part and parcel of the group that owns the whole. (E.g., A conveys "to B and C absolutely in joint tenancy.")

(E) Note that the four unities required for a joint tenancy can be satisfied by a deed in the form "A to A and B."

(2) At common law, when the type of tenancy was unclear, a finding of the existence of a joint tenancy was preferred over the finding of a tenancy in common (see below, II.B.3.b). Today, by statute, a tenancy in common is preferred over a joint tenancy.

(3) Survivorship: Upon the death of one joint tenant, the survivor or survivors own the whole of the property and nothing passes to the heirs of the decedent either by will or intestacy.

(A) A severance of the joint tenancy can only be made by *inter vivos* conveyance, never by will, because survivorship is prior to, and defeats, the effect of the will.

(B) If all the tenants except one die without having severed their interests, the lone survivor owns the whole property.

b. *Tenancy by the entirety:* joint tenancy held by a husband and wife.

c. *Tenancy in common:*

(1) Owned concurrently by two or more persons.

(2) Each person owns an undivided interest in the whole.

(A) Each tenant can dispose of his undivided fractional part by deed or by will.

(B) No right of survivorship; upon death the interest passes by will or descends to heirs.

(C) May be destroyed by merger, when the entire title vests in one person. (E.g., X, a tenant in common with Y, purchases Y's undivided interest.)

d. Community property: In several states, property owned by each spouse before marriage remains his or her separate property; however, property acquired during the marriage, excepting that which is acquired by gift, descent, or devise, as the separate property of one, becomes joint property of the husband and wife.

e. Tenancy by severalty: an estate that a person owns by himself.

C. Intangible rights relating to land.

1. Easement.

a. Definition: right to use the land of another or to have the land of another used in a particular way. This is a common "title defect."

b. Classification by type:

(1) In gross: a mere personal right to use the land of another, existing for the convenience of, and not in connection with, any land owned by the holder of the easement. (E.g., X sells all his land to Y, reserving the right to hunt upon it.)

(2) Appurtenant: exists in conjunction with the land of the holder of the easement; it is held by virtue of ownership of an estate in land.

(A) Servient land: land subject to the easement.

(B) Dominant land: land served by the easement. E.g., X sells part of his land to Y, giving Y a right to hunt on all the land. Y has an appurtenant easement; the dominant estate is Y, the servient estate X.)

      (3) An easement appurtenant is preferred over an easement in gross: hence, if there is doubt as to whether an easement is appurtenant or in gross, it is construed as an easement appurtenant.

c. Classification by use:

      (1) Affirmative: entitles the easement owner to do affirmative acts on the land in the possession of another.

      (2) Negative: takes from the owner of the servient tenement the right to do some things on his land that he would have a right to do were it not for the easement.

d. Creation by:

      (1) Grant or reservation. (E.g., A conveys to B one-half of Blackacre, granting a right of way on A's remaining land, while reserving to his remaining land a right of way on B's land.)

      (2) Natural right: A landowner has the natural right to have his land supported by the adjoining landowner's land. (E.g., A may not excavate on his land at a point so close to B's land as to cause a cave-in upon B's property.)

      (3) Necessity. (E.g., A purchases land in the middle of a large tract with no right of way included in the deed; a right of way will be implied in this situation because of the necessity of entrance and exit.)

      (4) Prescription: arises when land is used for the period of the statute of limitations (which limits the owner's right to take action against the user after a specific period of time) if the use is:

         (A) Wrongful, without permission of owner.

         (B) Open and notorious.

         (C) Continuous and without interruption. An easement by prescription may be prevented by an action for trespass.

      (5) Custom: public use of land, meeting the requirements for an easement by prescription leading to the acquisition of a public easement by the general public.

e. Extinguishment, expiration, and regulation.

      (1) Extinguishment:

         (A) Release of rights by the holder of the easement.

         (B) Abandonment (express) amounting to more than mere nonuse.

         (C) Adverse obstruction of the easement by the owner of the servient land for a period longer than the statutory period—see above, d(4).

         (D) Union of dominant and servient estates (merger).

      (2) Expiration:

         (A) Of time; determined at the time of its creation.

         (B) By operation of statutes in some states.

      (3) Limitations: Servient tenant can enjoin the dominant tenant's excessive use of the easement.

f. Conveyance.

      (1) Easement contained in deed "runs" with the land; thus buyer of land gets easement, classified as appurtenant since it is attached to the land.

      (2) Easements in gross are not assignable (to anyone but the owner of the servient land, i.e., subject to the easement) unless it was within the expectations of the parties on formation. An easement in gross is not appurtenant to the land, but a personal right.

2. License: permission for a person to come onto land in the possession of another without being a trespasser (c.g., a movie ticket).
   a. Arises from consent given by the one in possession of land; consent being given, no prescriptive right can arise through a license.
   b. Distinguished from a lease in that a licensee can never have possession of land, whereas a lessee always has possession.
   c. Distinguished from an easement in that an easement is a substantial interest in land of another, whereas a license is not an interest in land and requires no formalities for its creation.

3. Profit *a prendre*.
   a. Definition: right to go upon the land of another and take part of the soil or produce (e.g., wood, minerals, game).
   b. Creation.
      (1) Express or implied grant.
      (2) Express reservation.
      (3) Prescription.

III. Conveyance of Title to Real Property

A. Marketable title:

1. Title free from:
   a. Encumbrance: a financial claim against property, e.g., a mortgage, lien, or unpaid taxes.
   b. Encroachments: right of another party to some use of the property, such as an easement.
   c. Restrictions, except zoning laws.
   d. Doubt as to validity.

2. Marketable title need not be perfect title. Even if subordinate rights as to temporary use and possession exist, it is marketable if a court of equity would grant specific performance of the contract of sale and compel the vendee to accept.

B. Conveyance of title:

1. Contract for sale of real property:
   a. Usually entered into before a deed is given in exchange for payment.
   b. Generally must be in writing and signed by the party to be charged in order to fulfill the requirements of the Statute of Frauds (see Contracts, p. 148, III.E).
   c. Contains an implied covenant that title will be marketable, unless otherwise stated.
      (1) Some contracts provide for insurable title; this means one that a title insurance company is willing to insure against defects, liens, and invalidity. See 2.b, below.
   d. Seller's remedies for breach of contract by the buyer.
      (1) May retain any part payment made by the buyer.
      (2) May take action for damages for breach of contract.

       (3) May take action at law for recovery of the balance of the purchase price.

    e. Buyer's remedies for breach of contract by the seller (if title is not marketable);

       (1) Rescission and recovery of any part payment made to the seller.

       (2) Action for damages for breach of contract.

       (3) Foreclosure of the buyer's lien, equal to the amount of any part payment made by the buyer.

       (4) Suit for specific performance.

2. Search of title:

    a. Abstract of title: a condensed history of the title of the land containing a summary of conveyance, mortgages, liens, and liabilities affecting the land.

    b. Title insurance: insurance against loss or damage caused by unknown defects, or failure of title to a particular parcel of realty.

       (1) A guaranty of title given by a title insurance company under which it agrees to make good to the buyer loss resulting from a defect or failure of the title, usually up to the purchase price of the property.

       (2) A certificate of title furnished by a title insurance company is merely the company's opinion on the status of title, and the company is liable only for want of care or skill on the part of its examiner and is subject to the statute of limitations for torts.

3. Closing of title: The purchaser makes payment and executes such instruments as are required in contract of sale, and the seller delivers a valid deed duly executed.

    a. Escrow: grantor delivers the deed to a third person (escrow agent) to be held by him until performance of a condition (e.g., payment in full).

4. Parts of a deed:

    a. Premises clause: includes the date, names of grantor and grantee, any recitals that may be employed to explain the purpose of the conveyance, and a statement of consideration.

    b. Granting clause: includes the words of conveyance, and frequently the limitation of the estate, and the description of the land conveyed.

    c. Habendum or "to have" clause: sets forth the estate transferred and the degree of ownership granted.

    d. Reddendum: contains any reservations or conditions attached.

    e. Covenants: contains the warranties of the grantor as to the title.

    f. Conclusion: contains the signature, seal, and attestation (signature of witnesses).

       (1) In many states today there is a simple statutory short form of deed.

5. Kinds of deed:

    a. Full covenant and warranty. Grantor warrants that:

       (1) He owns property and has right to convey it.

       (2) Purchaser will be protected against an eviction by the grantor or a person asserting a paramount right.

       (3) Premises are free from encumbrances, except those specified.

       (4) He will execute and procure any further documents or assurances necessary to perfect the title.

       (5) He will defend grantee's title against adverse claimants.

        b. Bargain and sale: conveyance of title without the above warranties; however, the grantor does warrant that he has done nothing during his term of ownership that would impair title.

        c. Quitclaim: seller does not purport to convey title, but rather releases any claim he has to the property.

    6. Execution of deed; it must be:

        a. Signed by the grantor.

           (1) In many states the deed must also be sealed; this is the common law rule.

           (2) An agent may sign for the grantor where the agency was created in writing and signed by the grantor.

           (3) Printed signatures are usually allowable but unwise, in that they might be attacked on the grounds of nonexecution.

        b. Witnessed or acknowledged.

           (1) Attestation: the signing by witnesses who attest to the grantor's execution of the deed.

           (2) Acknowledgment: the act of the grantor acknowledging his signature before a notary or other public official.

           (3) States require either (1) or (2) or both.

        c. Actually delivered: final and actual passing of possession of a deed in such a manner that it cannot be recalled.

           (1) Where there is a recitation of consideration within the deed, it is immaterial if this payment is actually made; delivery itself passes title.

           (2) May be delivered to anyone, representing the buyer.

    7. Recording:

        a. A deed when delivered is effective between immediate parties without recording.

        b. Statutes providing for recording of deeds (perfection).

           (1) Recording protects the holder of a recorded deed against third parties acquiring another deed to the same land by placing the whole world on notice that the holder of the recorded deed has a claim to the land. A third party is deemed to have notice of a recorded deed.

           (2) Unrecorded deeds are not good against innocent purchasers in that no notice has been given. One cannot qualify as an innocent purchaser if a stranger is openly occupying the land.

    8. Reformation: Where there is a misspelling in the deed or an obvious mistake made in the deed, the court will reform it upon petition of the holder.

IV. Landlord and Tenant

    A. Characteristics:

    1. Definition: the relationship that arises from a contract for the possession and control of real property, usually for a fixed duration.

        a. Landlord retains a reversionary interest, tenant has possessory interest.

        b. Contract is called a lease (it is a conveyance as well as a contract).

           (1) Landlord is the lessor.

           (2) Tenant is the lessee.

         c. Consideration for the contract is called rent.

    2. Elements of the landlord-tenant relationship.
        a. Contract: express or implied, that fulfills the following requirements:
            (1) Parties capable of making a contract (capacity).
            (2) Consideration. When consideration is not specified, the law will imply an obligation to pay a reasonable value for use and occupation.
            (3) Mutual consent.
            (4) Valid subject matter.
            (5) Writing: when the Statute of Frauds so requires (e.g., when the duration of the lease is greater than one year—see Contracts, p. 148, III.E). However, where there is actual possession and partial payment, the contract will be enforceable even without a writing.
        b. Exclusive possession by the tenant: The tenant has the right to exclusive possession and may maintain an action in ejectment to recover possession. He is distinguished from a mere licensee (person who has permission to use land, but does not have the right of exclusive possession, e.g., the owner of a coin-operated washing machine installed in the basement of an apartment building would be a licensee and not a tenant).
        c. Tenant's rights are subordinate to the landlord's title.
        d. Reversion in the landlord (i.e., land or space reverts to the landlord at the termination of the lease).
    3. Types of tenancies:
        a. Tenancy for a definite period of time, including tenancy for years; usually created by a lease.
        b. Tenancy from period to period: one that will continue for successive periods of a year or successive periods of a fraction of a year unless it is terminated and that is typically created by an express agreement.
        c. Tenancy at will: one that can be terminated at will by either party, usually on 30 days' notice.
        d. Tenancy by sufferance:
            (1) Exists when a tenant comes into possession rightfully, but holds over wrongfully.
            (2) Tenant can usually be evicted as a trespasser upon the landlord's giving due notice.
            (3) Landlord may instead elect to treat the tenant as having renewed the lease in accordance with the prior terms.
        e. Statutory tenancies: Emergency rent laws prevent the landlord from removing the tenant so long as he pays a reasonable rent.

B. Leases: rights, duties, and liabilities:

    1. Landlord implicitly covenants (compare with a deed where no covenants will be implied):
        a. To give the tenant the legal right to possession.
        b. To give the tenant the right to quiet enjoyment (see p. 273).
        c. That the tenant will not be evicted.
            (1) This covenant is only breached when there has been an eviction.
            (2) Eviction may be either actual or constructive.

(A) Actual: an intentional physical ouster of the tenant by the landlord from all or part of the premises granted.

(B) Constructive: an injurious interference with the tenant's beneficial use and enjoyment of the premises (e.g., failure to supply heat during the winter); tenant may elect to treat this as an eviction and surrender possession. Eviction need not be intentional.

2. Major provisions of the lease.

a. Term or duration of the lease.

b. Rent: payable in advance only when so specified in the lease.

c. Description of the premises.

d. Use of the premises.

e. Fitness for use. The tenant should require that the landlord covenant that the premises will be fit for a particular purpose, or the landlord will be under no obligation, unless he has made fraudulent statements concerning this matter.

f. Repairs. The common law duty to make repairs is on the tenant, except when:

(1) Landlord assumes the duty by lease.

(2) Duty is imposed on the landlord by statute.

(3) Landlord has exclusive possession of portions of the premises used in common (e.g., stairways).

(4) Repairs are of a structural nature.

g. Destruction or substantial injury to the premises. In most states tenants may surrender possession without further obligation to pay rent, unless:

(1) Damage or destruction is due to the tenant's fault, or

(2) The lease provides otherwise.

h. Removal of fixtures and improvements made by the lessee. There can be removal if items are personalty, but not if they are realty (see Property, p. 363, II.A.4).

i. Insurance and taxes. In absence of any provision in the lease, the tenant is under no duty to insure premises or to pay taxes.

j. Condemnation of leased premises. In absence of a provision in the lease, the amount taken under eminent domain must be apportioned between the landlord and tenant.

k. Assignment or subletting.

(1) Definitions depend on legal effect, and not on the labels attached by parties.

(A) Assignment is the transfer by the lessee of his entire interest without reserving *any* reversion therein in himself. Assignor will remain liable on the express terms of the lease despite the assignment. (I.e., if the assignee defaults in payment of the rent, the assignor will nevertheless be liable.)

(B) Subletting is the transfer of only part of the sublessor's interest, leaving a reversion in him as to the premises sublet. (E.g., L leases an apartment to T for one year and a day; T immediately sublets the apartment to S, but only for one year. L is a lessor, T is a tenant and sublessor, and S is a sublessee.)

(i) A new landlord-tenant relationship is created between the sublessor and his sublessee, and the sublessee will not be liable to the original lessor on any of the covenants contained in the original lease, and the landlord must enforce the lease provisions by acting against T, the tenant-sublessor, and not directly against S, the sublessee.

(ii) Sublessor will remain liable to the lessor for performance of all the terms of his original lease.

(2) Most leases contain a clause prohibiting assignments and subletting unless the landlord gives his consent in writing.

(A) **A provision in a lease prohibiting either one of these does not thereby prohibit the other. This is frequently on the exam.**

(B) Consent (in writing) by the landlord to one assignment is deemed to be a consent to all subsequent assignments, but the rule as to subletting is otherwise.

(C) There exists a division of authority on whether or not the landlord may arbitrarily withhold his consent.

l. Compliance by the tenant with laws and ordinances.

(1) Most leases require this compliance.

(2) Generally, this provision in a lease does not extend to the making of substantial improvements or building changes.

m. Quiet enjoyment.

(1) Landlord implicitly covenants that:

(A) He has paramount title to let the premises, and

(B) Neither he, nor any person claiming a paramount title, nor any condition subject to his control, shall disturb the tenant's right to absolute possession of premises.

(C) Generally, the doctrine of quiet enjoyment provides the basis for a suit by the tenant only where the conditions are so severe that the tenant must abandon all or part of the premises.

(2) An express covenant of quiet enjoyment by the landlord, and its limitations, will override this implied covenant.

n. Tenant's right to habitable premises.

(1) Generally, at common law, there is no warranty by the landlord of the habitability of the premises, so long as the landlord did not defraud the tenant. The doctrine of *caveat emptor* applied.

(2) Now, many jurisdictions find an implied warranty of habitability of the premises, measured by housing or building code minimums.

o. Tenant's remedies.

(1) Rescind the lease.

(2) Move to new quarters, and sue old land lord for higher cost of new premises.

(3) Sue landlord to obtain injunction requiring repairs, etc.

(4) Repair and offset: Tenant pays for repairs, and deducts from rent. Usually must be an emergency.

p. Landlord's remedies.

(1) Tenant doesn't pay rent, but remains in premises.

             (A) Right to reenter and remove tenant. May not be forcible.

             (B) Distraint (i.e., seizing tenant's goods). May be limited by state law; may require court proceedings.

             (C) Summary eviction or dispossess action (requires court proceedings).

          (2) Tenant vacates premises, doesn't pay rent.

             (A) Accept termination, rerent space, i.e., is a rescission.

             (B) Leave space empty, sue tenant for rent.

             (C) Rerent space, sue tenant for any deficiency.

             (D) Clearly, which of these remedies the landlord chooses depends upon whether a new tenant can be found, and whether at a price higher or lower than the original tenant was paying.

             (E) Some, but not all, jurisdictions require the landlord to minimize the burden on the tenant by rerenting the premises at the best price available.

    3. Liability to third parties.

      a. Tenant is liable to third parties for injuries due to dangerous conditions where he or she has exclusive possession of the premises.

      b. Tenant is not liable for injuries caused on the premises not under his exclusive possession.

      c. Landlord is liable when he leases the premises with a nuisance on them and injury results therefrom.

        (1) Tenant is also liable in such case if he or she discovers the nuisance and fails to report it.

        (2) Lease can contain a provision that the tenant will hold the landlord harmless. Thus, the tenant must pay the landlord if the latter has to pay an injured party in cases where both the landlord and tenant are liable.

    4. Alterations of the lease (see Contracts, p. 162, VII.C.4).

C. Termination of the tenancy:

    1. Expiration of the lease.

      a. If the tenant "holds over," the landlord may:

        (1) Treat the tenant as a trespasser.

        (2) Sue him for damages and remove him by legal proceedings, or

        (3) Treat him as obligated for additional rent, according to the terms of the prior lease, for the period of the holdover.

        (4) Neither (1) nor (2) above applies when the tenant "holds over" because of sickness or when emergency rent laws provide otherwise.

    2. Forfeiture of the tenant's right to possession of the premises.

      a. May result from:

        (1) Nonpayment of rent.

        (2) Using the premises for an unauthorized purpose.

        (3) Unauthorized assignment or subletting.

      b. Remedies for nonpayment of rent:

        (1) Suit for rent.

      (2) Summary proceedings to dispossess the tenant.

      (3) In some states both can be done in one proceeding.

3. Eviction: breach of landlord's covenant of quiet enjoyment.

  a. Actual eviction: an intentional physical ouster of the tenant by the landlord from all or part of the premises granted.

  b. Constructive eviction: The tenant is forced to quit the premises not by some direct act of the landlord, but because of an act or condition under the landlord's control, which he permits to exist.

      (1) Conditions not under the landlord's control cannot constitute constructive eviction.

      (2) Tenant must quit the premises promptly if he or she is to claim a constructive eviction.

  c. Eviction by paramount title: The tenant is ousted by someone who has title superior to the landlord's.

  d. There is no breach of the covenant of quiet enjoyment when the eviction is by government exercise of eminent domain.

4. Surrender:

  a. Tenant yields the remainder of his term to the landlord, and

  b. Landlord accepts and repossesses the premises. If the landlord does not "accept" the tenant's surrender, the tenant remains liable for damages.

5. Destruction or substantial injury to the premises (see p. 372, IV.B.2.g).

6. Termination by operation of law.

  a. Tenant:

      (1) Death of the tenant does not terminate a tenancy for years, unless the lease so provides.

      (2) Bankruptcy of the tenant may terminate the lease.

  b. Landlord:

      (1) Death of the landlord has no effect on tenancy for years or at will.

      (2) Bankruptcy of the landlord has no effect on tenancy.

Selected Problems from CPA Examinations on Property

Subjective Questions and Answers

Q. 1. Hammar Hardware Company, Inc., purchased all the assets and assumed all the liabilities of JoMar Hardware for $60,000. Among the assets and liabilities included in the sale was a lease of the building in which the business was located. The lessor-owner was Marathon Realty, Inc., and the remaining unexpired term of the lease was nine years. The lease did not contain a provision dealing with the assignment of the leasehold. Incidental to the purchase, Hammar expressly promised JoMar that it would pay the rental due Marathon over the life of the lease and would hold JoMar harmless from any future liability thereon.

    When Marathon learned of the proposed transaction, it strenuously objected to the assignment of the lease and to the occupancy by Hammar. Later, after this dispute was resolved and prior to expiration of the lease, Hammar abandoned the building and ceased doing business in that area. Marathon has demanded payment by JoMar of the rent as it matures over the balance of the term of the lease.

Required

Answer the following, setting forth reasons for any conclusions stated.

1. Was the consent of Marathon necessary in order to assign the lease?
2. Is JoMar liable on the lease?
3. If Marathon were to proceed against Hammar, would Hammar be liable under the lease?

A. 1. No. In the absence of a restriction on the right to assign specifically stated in the lease, a lessee may assign his leasehold interest to another. Only in unusual circumstances, where the lease involves special elements of personal trust and confidence as contrasted with mere payment for occupancy, will the courts limit the right to assign.
    2. Yes. Although JoMar may effectively assign the lease, which in effect is an assignment of the right to occupy the leasehold premises and a delegation of its duty to pay Marathon, it cannot shed its liability to Marathon for the rental payments. In the absence of a release, JoMar remains liable. The transaction described in the fact situation is in the nature of a surety relationship.
    3. Yes. Marathon is a third-party creditor beneficiary of Hammar's promise to JoMar. As such, Marathon can assert rights on the promise even though it was not a party to the contract. Marathon is not barred by lack of privity or the fact that it gave no consideration to Hammar for the promise.

5/79

Q. 2. The Merchants and Mechanics County Bank expanded its services and facilities as a result of the economic growth of the community it serves. In this connection, it provided safe deposit facilities for the first time. A large vault was constructed as a part of the renovation and expansion of the bank building. Merchants purchased a bank vault door from Foolproof Vault Doors, Inc., for $65,000 and installed it at the vault entrance. The state in which Merchants was located had a real property tax but did not have a personal property tax. When the tax assessor appraised the bank building after completion of the renovation and expansion, he included the bank vault door as a part of the real property. Merchants has filed an objection claiming the vault door was initially personal property and remains so after installation in the bank.

There are no specific statutes or regulations determinative of the issue. Therefore, the question will be decided according to common law principles of property law.

Required

Answer the following, setting forth reasons for any conclusions stated.

1. What is the likely outcome as to the classification of the bank vault door?
2. The above situation involves a dispute between a tax authority and the owner of property. In what other circumstances might a dispute arise with respect to the classification of property as either real or personal property?

A. 1. Based upon the facts of the problems and the legal criteria discussed below, the vault door will probably be classified as real property. The criteria applicable are these:
    • Annexation—the mode and degree to which the chattel is physically attached to the real property.
    • Adaptation—the extent to which the chattel is used in promoting the purpose for which the real property is used.
    • Intention—whether the chattel was intended as a permanent improvement of the real property.

    Applying these criteria to the facts demonstrates that the degree of annexation of a vault door is by necessity very high. Furthermore, the adaptation of the personal property (the vault door) to the use of the real property by the bank also argues for a finding in favor of real property classification. Finally, the last criterion, the intent of the bank to make a permanent improvement of the real property, appears to have been satisfied. Taking these criteria together, it would appear that the bank door has become real property.

2. In addition to tax collectors, disputes involving the categorization of property as real or personal have arisen in respect of:
   - Real property mortgagees versus creditors of the same debtor who have a security interest in personal property (chattel mortgagees).
   - Landlord versus tenant upon expiration of the lease and the question of what property may be removed.
   - Takers under a will versus the executor in cases where different takers will receive the property, based upon its classification.
   - The seller versus the purchaser of real property, where a dispute arises concerning the removal of certain property by the seller.
   - The mortgagor versus mortgagee, when the question arises regarding what property is included under the scope of the mortgage.

5/79

Q. 3. Reynolds leased a manufacturing building from Philip under a written lease for a period of five years at a specified rental and with a provision that the lessor would keep the structure in repair.

Reynolds subleased a portion of the lower floor to Signor, giving him access through a hallway from the main entrance. Philip subsequently mortgaged the building, and Central Savings, the mortgagee, ultimately foreclosed and acquired good title to the property. Reynolds was unable to get Central Savings to make certain minor repairs and had witheld rent in an amount equal to the repairs he was forced to make. Central Savings meanwhile notified both Reynolds and Signor that the lease was terminated and that both were to pay rent directly to it for one month and then vacate.

Required
1. Discuss Reynolds' right to withhold rent in the amount of repairs.
2. Absent a breach by the tenants, discuss Central Savings' right to:
   a. Evict the tenants.
   b. Require Signor to pay the rent directly to it.
A. **1.** Reynolds had no right to witold rent in the amount of repairs. Covenants by lessor and lessee are deemed independent unless it is clear that the parties intended the contrary. However, if the breach were sufficiently serious, it might furnish the basis for a claim of constructive eviction. This does not seem to be the case on the facts.
   2. **(a)** Central Savings has no right to evict the tenants. When the lease preceded the mortgage, the tenant's term is not affected by the later mortgage absent an agreement by the tenant to the contrary.
   (b) Signor is a sublessee and, as such, a tenant of Reynolds. Absent a provision in the lease prohibiting the sublease, Reynolds committed no breach by the subletting, and the sublessee, as a tenant of the sublessor, has no direct obligations to the lessor.

5/74

Q. 4. In the course of your examination of the financial statements of Lomax Manufacturing, Inc., you discovered the following facts relating to a real-estate transaction by the company during the current year.

Lomax purchased from Dunbar Corporation 4 acres of land in a proposed industrial-park site for $45,000. At the closing, Dunbar delivered to Lomax a bargain-and-sale deed with a covenant against the grantor's acts. Guaranty Indemnity Company wrote a title insurance policy for $45,000 covering the transaction.

Lomax disclosed to you that it recently learned of a defect in its title to the 4 acres of land due to a restriction placed on the land by John Jason, a former owner. Jason had included in his warranty deed a covenant ". . . that the land should be used exclusively for residential purposes." Jason's warranty deed was to an owner preceding

Dunbar and conveyed all of the land now included in the proposed industrial park as well as surrounding land which has been developed for residential purposes. As a result of this restriction the value of the land acquired by Lomax has decreased by $15,000 according to an independent appraisal. Guaranty Indemnity had failed to discover this restriction at the time Lomax acquired the property.

Required

Discuss the rights of Lomax against the following:

1. Dunbar Corporation.
2. Guaranty Indemnity Company.

A. 1. Lomax has no rights against Dunbar Corporation because its deed only contained a warranty which protected Lomax from claims resulting from the grantor's (Dunbar's) acts during its ownership. Since the problem involved a defect which arose prior to Dunbar's obtaining title and was in no way the result of its actions, Dunbar is not liable for the loss.

   2. Guaranty Indemnity Company is liable on its title insurance policy. It guaranteed the title of Lomax against any defects in title to which it did not take an exception. Clearly there was a defect present in the limitation on the use of the land. Therefore, Guaranty Indemnity must pay Lomax, who it insured, for the loss which resulted.

11/74

Q. 5. You are in the midst of your annual examination of the financial statements of Winkler Corporation, which is engaged in residential land development. Early in the engagement you learned that the company intended to subdivide a tract of land it had acquired for $150,000 several years ago and then undertake an active advertising and sales campaign to sell the home sites. The land has been recorded on the company's books and reported on its balance sheet at $150,000 since acquisition.

   While investigating the costs of subdividing the tract, you learn that the county where the tract is located has offered $100,000 for the land to convert it into a community park. You also learn that if Winkler refuses this offer, the county has indicated in writing that it will institute legal proceedings to condemn the property at $100,000.

Required

Discuss the legal implications of the above facts and how they should affect the financial statements of Winkler Corporation.

A.   Governments in general have the power to condemn property via eminent domain for public use. Objections can be raised to the validity of a given condemnation. However, if the use is a proper one and there is a showing of need, it is difficult to persuade a court to deny the government's right to obtain title via condemnation.

   Assuming the county can condemn the property, this does not mean that they can do so without paying just compensation for the property. The condemnation award should represent the fair market value of the property. The offer of $100,000 is not necessarily indicative of the actual worth of the property. In fact, the fair market value of the property may exceed the $150,000 at which it is recorded on Winkler's books. This is supported by the fact that the company was willing to pay $150,000 for the property several years ago and is now willing to invest additional money to subdivide, advertise, etc. Nevertheless, establishing the fair market value is a question of fact. Where there is a dispute, it can only be resolved at a condemnation proceeding after a consideration of all the facts by a trial board.

   The pending condemnation and related facts should, of course, be disclosed in Winkler's financial statements, including the opinion of Winkler's independent counsel as to the probable outcome of the condemnation proceedings. Whether the carrying value of the land should be adjusted (creating a corresponding loss) depends on an assessment of all the evidence regarding the pending condemnation and its probable outcome. There is insufficient evidence presented to reach a conclusion on this question.

11/74

Practice Questions

Q. 1. While vouching additions to the land and buildings accounts during your examination of the financial statements of Dandy Manufacturing, Inc., you learn that Dandy had purchased a factory building from Howard Luff for $247,500. Dandy had engaged the Bigelow Title Insurance Company, Inc., to do the title search and to issue a $247,500 title policy insuring Dandy's fee interest in the real property. Bigelow issued the title policy without exception. Howard Luff gave a typical bargain-and-sale-deed with a covenant against the grantor's acts; or, as it is sometimes referred to, a special warranty deed. It was subsequently discovered that the executor of Luff's father's estate had failed to pay the estate taxes due on the property.

Required
1. What are Dandy's rights against Luff on the deed? Explain.
2. What are Dandy's rights against Bigelow Title? Explain.

Q. 2. In your search for unrecorded liabilities during the annual audit of Roscoe Hand, Inc., you encountered an unrecorded tax liability assessed by Jackson County. Further investigation revealed that Hand had decided to renovate his factory loft and in the process installed a new heating, air-conditioning, and exhaust system. The system was permanently installed in the basement of the factory, and a new set of ducts was installed. Hand's factory is located in Jackson County, which taxes real property but does not tax personal property. The county real estate assessor has increased the value of the real property by the cost of the new system. Hand objects, claiming that the property is personalty and not realty.

Required
1. What are the criteria for determining whether property is real or personal?
2. How should the new heating, air-conditioning, and exhaust system be categorized?

Q. 3. Your client, Abe Starr, owns 100 acres of undeveloped land on the outskirts of New City. He bought the land several years ago to build an industrial park in the event New City grew and prospered. The land was formerly used for grazing and truck gardening. A subsequent inspection revealed that several adjacent landowners recently had been using a shortcut across his land in order to reach a newly constructed highway.

Required
What are the legal implications of the above facts? Explain.

Q. 4. Rollo owned certain land which he developed into a successful and valuable cranberry farm. The farm included an elaborate water and sprinkling system. Needing additional capital, Rollo borrowed $25,000 from the Mortgage Savings and Loan Bank. He executed a note for the $25,000 secured by a real estate mortgage on the farm. This mortgage was recorded the next day. After describing the land, the mortgage provided:

> Together with all and singular tenements, hereditaments thereunto belonging or in anywise appertaining and any and all fixtures upon said premises at the time of execution or at any time during the term of this mortgage.

Subsequently Rollo borrowed $5,000 from the Cranberry Credit Association, giving a note for $5,000 secured by certain chattel mortgages covering the watering and sprinkling system. Rollo defaulted on the debt owed to

Mortgage Savings and Loan and they foreclosed the real estate mortgage. The Cranberry Credit Association intervened and claimed a lien superior to that of the Mortgage Savings and Loan Bank insofar as the water and sprinkling system, was concerned. The property in dispute, i.e., the water and sprinkling system, included pipe lines consisting of trunk lines and lateral pipe lines, sprinkler heads, pumps, motors, frames, power poles, wiring, and transformers. The above property constituted an integrated system installed with the intent of making a permanent improvement, actually annexed to the realty, and designed and constructed to make the particular land a commercial cranberry farm.

(1) Define the term *fixture* as used in real property.

(2) List *and* explain the rules or tests followed in deciding whether personal property attached to land has become real property.

Q.   5. In your audit of the financial statemenst of Kirby Real Estate Company you must evaluate an account receivable for rent due on a three-year lease for office space executed one year before by John Lane. The lease provides for a rental of $200 per month and Lane posted three months' rent as security pursuant to the terms of the lease. Three months ago Lane died.

Your examination of the lease reveals that it gives the tenant the right to sublet the space but makes no provision for what is to happen if the tenant should die. Since Lane's death, the Company has attempted to relet the premises and placed a "For Rent" sign on the door in an attempt to lessen the damages. Lane's executor contacted the Company and indicated that he does not believe the estate is liable on the lease and stated that he intends to remove all of the decedent's furniture from the office. The executor contends:

a. In absence of a contrary provision in the lease, leases automatically terminate on the death of the tenant.

b. Kirby Real Estate Company's action in attempting to relet the premises and placing a "For Rent" sign on the office door constituted an acceptance of a surrender of the lease by operation of law.

c. The most to which Kirby Real Estate Company is entitled is the amount of the security posted when the lease was signed.

Required

1. Discuss and evaluate each of the executor's arguments that the estate should not be responsible on the lease.

2. Under what common law remedy would a landlord be able to assert a right to retain control over the decedent's furniture until his claim for rent is satisfied?

3. Assume the executor is able to sublet the office to a desirable tenant who is willing to pay $250 per month rent for the remainder of the lease and informs the landlord that he intends to be bound by the lease and to sublet. Summarize the rights and duties of the executor and the subletting tenant. As a part of your answer distinguish between a sublease and an assignment of a lease.

Practice Objective Questions

Instructions 1–15

Select the *best* answer for each of the following items. Mark only one answer for *each* item. Answer all items. Your grade will be based on your total correct answers.

1. Winslow conveyed a 20-acre tract of land to his two children, George and Martha, "equally as tenants in common." What is the legal effect of this form of conveyance?

   a. George and Martha are joint owners with a right of survivorship.

   b. Each must first offer the other the right to purchase the property before he or she can sell to a third party.

   c. Neither may convey his or her interest in the property unless both join in the conveyance.

   d. Each owns an undivided interest in the whole, which he or she may dispose of by deed or by will.

2. Charles is a commercial tenant of Luxor Buildings, Inc. The term of the lease is five years and two years have elapsed. The lease prohibits subletting, but does *not* contain any provision relating to assignment. Charles approached Luxor and asked whether Luxor could release him from the balance of the term of the lease for $500. Luxor refused unless Charles would agree to pay $2,000. Charles located Whitney who was interested in renting in Luxor's building and transferred the entire balance of the lease to Whitney in consideration of his promise to pay Luxor the monthly rental and otherwise perform Charles' obligations under the lease. Luxor objects. Which of the following statements is correct?
   a. The assignment is invalid without Luxor's consent.
   b. The assignment does *not* extinguish Charles' obligation to pay the rent if Whitney defaults.

3. Harrison purchased Bigacre from Whitmore. The deed described the real property conveyed and the granting clause read: "Seller hereby releases, surrenders, and relinquishes to buyer any right, title, or interest that he may have in Bigacre." The deed contained no covenants. What is Harrison's legal status concerning title to Bigacre?
   a. Harrison has obtained a quitclaim deed.
   b. If an adverse claimant ousts Harrison from Bigacre, Harrison will have recourse against Whitmore.
   c. The only warranty contained in the deed is an implied warranty of marketability of title.
   d. Harrison's deed is neither insurable nor recordable.

4. In connection with the audit of Fiske & Company, you found it necessary to examine a deed to certain property owned by the client. In this connection, which of the following statements is correct?
   a. A deed purporting to convey real property, but which omits the day of the month, is invalid.
   b. A deed which lacks the signature of the grantor is valid.
   c. A quitclaim deed which purports to transfer to the grantee "whatever title the grantor has" is invalid.
   d. A deed which purports to convey real property and recites a consideration of $1 and other valuable consideration is valid.

5. Olson conveyed real property to his sons, Sampson and David, but the deed was ambiguous as to the type of estate created and the interest each son had in relation to the other. David died intestate shortly after Olson. David's widow and children were contending that they have rights in the property. Which of the following would be the widow's and children's *best* argument to claim valid rights in the real property?
   a. The conveyance by Olson created a life estate in Sampson with a contingent remainder interest in David.
   b. The conveyance by Olson created a joint tenancy with a right of survivorship.
   c. The conveyance by Olson created a tenancy in common.
   d. The widow is entitled to her statutory share.

6. Which of the following is true with respect to an easement created by an express grant?
   a. The easement will be extinguished upon the death of the grantee.
   b. The easement *cannot* be sold or transferred by the owner of the easement.
   c. The easement gives the owner of the easement the right to the physical possession of the property subject to the easement.
   d. The easement must be in writing to be valid.

7. Under certain circumstances personal property may be converted into and become a part of real property. Which of the following is *least* relevant in ascertaining whether this has occurred?
   a. The mode and degree of annexation.
   b. The use and purpose the property serves in relation to the real property.
   c. The legal formalities which the parties satisfied in relation to the property in question, such as a signed, sealed, and witnessed document.
   d. The actual intent of the parties.

8. A joint tenant's interest in real property
   a. Can only be created by deed.
   b. Need *not* be created at the same time *nor* pursuant to the same instrument.
   c. Will *not* pass under the laws of intestate succession.
   d. *Cannot* be sold or severed during the life of the joint tenancy.

9. The failure to record a deed will
   a. *Not* affect the rights between the parties to the deed.
   b. Constitute a fraud upon the creditors of the seller.

   c. Defeat the rights of the buyer if the seller subsequently conveys the property to a third party who has actual knowledge of the prior conveyance.

   d. Be disregarded in respect to the rights of subsequent third parties if the deed is a mere quitclaim.

10. Vance obtained a 25-year leasehold interest in an office building from the owner, Stanfield.

   a. Vance's interest is nonassignable.

   b. The conveyance of the ownership of the building by Stanfield to Wax will terminate Vance's leasehold interest.

   c. Stanfield's death will *not* terminate Vance's leasehold interest.

   d. Vance's death will terminate the leasehold interest.

11. Your client, Albert Fall, purchased a prominent industrial park from Josh Barton. At the closing, Barton offered a quitclaim deed. The contract of sale called for a warranty deed with full covenants.

   a. Fall should accept the quitclaim deed since there is *no* important difference between a quitclaim deed and a warranty deed.

   b. An undisclosed mortgage that was subsequently discovered would violate one of the covenants of a warranty deed.

   c. Fall *cannot* validly refuse to accept Barton's quitclaim deed.

   d. The only difference between a warranty deed with full covenants and a quitclaim deed is that the grantor of a quitclaim does *not* warrant against defects post his assumption of title.

12. In 1960, Octane, Inc., a Delaware corporation, purchased certain land in Montana from the Dillingers but neglected to record the deed. In 1970, the Dillingers sold the same property to Bently, a domiciliary of Montana, who purchased in good faith and recorded his deed. In a suit by Octane against Bently to resolve the title question, Octane will lose because

   a. Octane had no reasonable excuse for its failure to record the deed.

   b. Most recording acts provide a statutory preference for individuals over corporations.

   c. Most recording acts provide a statutory preference for domiciliaries over nondomiciliaries.

   d. A good faith purchaser from the record owner has paramount title over an unrecorded claim of which he has no knowledge.

13. An individual who has obtained title to land by adverse possession

   a. Can convey good title to a subsequent purchaser.

   b. Must record his interest in the property in order to perfect his interest against the holder of record.

   c. Must have occupied the property initially with the permission of the owner of record.

   d. Need *not* have occupied the land for an uninterrupted period of time as long as the sum total of years he has occupied the land is equal to or greater than the prescribed period.

14. Waldo Carpets, Inc., decided to sell a portion of its 2-acre property and the president of Waldo wrote several prospective buyers the following letter:

Dear Sir:

We are sending this solicitation to several prospective buyers because we are interested in selling one acre of our property located in downtown Metropolis. If you are interested, please communicate with me at the above address. Under no circumstances will we consider a price of less than $90,000.

                                                            Cordially,
                                                            James Waldo
                                                            James Waldo, President
                                                            Waldo Carpets, Inc.

   In this situation

   a. The Statute of Frauds does *not* apply because the real property being sold is the division of an existing tract which had been properly recorded.

    b. Markus, a prospective buyer who telegraphed Waldo that he would buy at $90,000 and forwarded a $90,000 surety bond to guarantee his performance, has validly accepted the offer.

    c. Waldo must sell to the highest bidder.

    d. Waldo's communication did *not* constitute an offer to sell.

15. A joint tenancy

    a. *Cannot* be created by deed.

    b. Will be found to exist by judicial preference if it is unclear as to whether a joint tenancy or tenancy in common was intended by the grantor.

    c. *Cannot* be created in respect to personal property.

    d. Provides a right of survivorship in the surviving joint tenant.

Mortgages

AICPA Content Specification Outline

Characteristics
Recording Requirements
Priorities
Foreclosure

Contents

      C. Marshalling of assets
      D. Defenses to the mortgage obligation
  IV. Sale of the Mortgaged Property
      A. Sale of mortgaged property
      B. Taking subject to
      C. Assumption of the mortgage
      D. Releases, variance, and suretyship rules
  V. Foreclosure and Termination
      A. Foreclosure
      B. Termination of the mortgage lien
Selected Problems from CPA Examinations on Mortgages
Subjective Questions and Answers
Practice Questions
Practice Objective Questions

I. Characteristics

A. A mortgage is a "pledge" or security of particular property for the payment of a debt. The mortgagor-debtor grants rights to the mortgagee to assert a lien against the real property securing the loan in the event of default by the mortgagor.

    1. In most states ("lien theory") the transfer creates a mere lien and title remains with the mortgagor. The above definition is based upon this theory.

    2. Under common law ("title theory") the transfer, while giving no right of possession to the mortgagee, did transfer conditional title and create an estate.

B. Purchase-money mortgage: a special type of real estate mortgage given concurrently with a sale of land by the vendee (buyer) to the vendor (seller) to secure the unpaid balance of the purchase price; it creates a nonpossessory lien that attaches to the land purchased. In effect, the seller lends money to the buyer so that the buyer can purchase the property.

C. A real estate mortgage differs from:

    1. A chattel mortgage in that a chattel mortgage has as the subject matter of the lien personal property.

    2. A trust deed on real estate, which is a mortgage on property executed by the mortgagor to a third person who acts for the benefit of several mortgagees. A "trustee" is usually used only where there are multiple mortgagees or creditors of the same mortgagor. It is a species of mortgage, but should be distinguished from the usual mortgage relationship between a debtor and a single creditor.

    3. A conditional sale, which is a *sale* of personal property (typically the sale of consumer goods), wherein the transfer of title is made to depend upon the performance of a condition, usually the payment of the price.

D. Elements of a mortgage:

1. Parties:
   a. Mortgagor: the one who pledges his or her property as security for the obligation; the debtor.
   b. Mortgagee: the one to whom the mortgage is executed and delivered to secure the obligation due him or her; the lender.
2. The property: any transferable interest in land may be mortgaged.
3. The obligation secured: any obligation capable of reduction to a monetary equivalent may be secured by a mortgage.
4. Personal liability of the mortgagor:
   a. The mortgagor personally assumes the mortgage debt either by promising to pay, as a part of the provisions of the mortgage agreement, or by executing a collateral promise, called a bond.
   b. Where there is a mortgage on the property and a promise within the mortgage or a bond is executed:
      (1) The real property is the primary security for the mortgage debt.
      (2) However, if the mortgagor defaults, and the sale of the land is not sufficient to pay off the mortgage in full, the mortgagor is personally liable for the deficiency.

E. Contents of a mortgage. A mortgage usually contains at least the following items:

1. Names of the parties (mortgagor and mortgagee).
2. The principal amount of indebtedness secured, the due date, and the rate of interest payable thereon.
3. A complete description of the property mortgaged.
4. The mortgagor usually covenants that:
   a. He or she will pay the indebtedness.
   b. He or she will insure the property for the mutual benefit of the mortgagor and mortgagee.
   c. He or she will not remove, demolish, or otherwise destroy the buildings without the mortgagee's consent.
   d. The entire indebtedness will become payable forthwith upon default for a certain period of time (the acceleration clause).
   e. The mortgagee shall not be required to accept prepayment of the mortgage obligation unless there is a prepayment clause or the mortgagee so desires.
   f. The mortgagee may appoint a receiver to collect rent in the event of default and foreclosure proceedings.
5. The possession of the property mortgaged shall remain or vest in the mortgagor.

F. Formalities in the execution of a mortgage:

1. A mortgage is considered "an interest in real property" within the meaning of the Statute of Frauds and therefore must be in writing and signed by the mortgagor (see Contracts, p. 149, III.E).
2. Generally speaking, a mortgage must conform to the same formalities as are necessary for the execution of a deed.

II. Rights of the Mortgagor and Mortgagee

A. Mortgagor:

1. Retains possession of the land.
2. In a majority of states retains legal title to the land mortgaged (lien theory, see p. 385, I.A.1, V.A.2).
3. May lease the land, and is entitled to the rents and profits thereon.
4. In case of default by the mortgagor, the mortgagor has an equity of redemption, which is defined as the right of the mortgagor to redeem the property after default, usually by paying the whole amount of the debt, interest, and costs.
    (1) It cannot be waived or bargained away at the inception of the mortgage.
    (2) It exists until cut off by foreclosure.
    (3) It rests upon equity principles.
5. Has a *right* of redemption after the foreclosure sale.
    (1) Commences when the equity of redemption ends.
    (2) It is strictly statutory and varies from state to state.

B. Mortgagee:

1. Usually has a lien on the land; however, under the title theory (see p. 385, I.A.2), the mortgagee gets title subject to defeasance (i.e., a title is actually conveyed to the mortgagee, which is defeated or extinguished upon payment of the debt due).
2. May assign the mortgage to a third party who succeeds to the rights of the mortgagee.
3. Obtains a lien against the land that is superior to subsequent purchasers, lessors, or mortgagors of the land, unless there is a failure to record the mortgage and a sale (or mortgage) to an innocent purchaser by the mortgagor. However, foreclosure of the lien will cut off all subsequently created interests.
4. Should record the mortgage so that all persons who subsequently acquire an interest in the mortgaged property will take subject to the recorded mortgage.
5. If the mortgage is not recorded, the mortgage will not be effective against subsequent good faith purchaser or lender who had no knowledge of the mortgage.

III. Recordation and Priorities

A. Conflicting mortgage claims. If there are mortgages on the same property, properly executed and duly recorded, the first in time will have priority over subsequent ones. But for a subsequent mortgagee to have priority, there must be no knowledge of a prior, unrecorded mortgage. (See p. 370, III.B.7.)

B. Foreclosure and satisfaction of claims. Upon foreclosure the first mortgage, in order of priority, will be fully satisfied before any payment is allocated to subsequent mortgages.

C. Marshalling of assets. The doctrine of marshaling of assets may help the second mortgagee obtain a share (i.e., if the first mortgagor holds a mortgage on property other than that to which the second mortgagee's lien attaches, the second mortgagee may compel the first mortgagee to first foreclose the other property available as security.)

D. Defenses to the mortgage obligation: To the extent that the secured obligation is invalid, or subject to a defense, so also is the mortgage securing it (e.g., usurious interest rates, gambling debts).

IV. Sale of the Mortgaged Property

A. The grantee (buyer) may take the land subject to the mortgage or may personally assume the mortgage, depending upon his bargain with the mortgagor-grantor. This presupposes that the mortgage is assignable or the mortgagee consents. Current lending practice by the banks is to require full payment in the event the mortgaged property is sold, thereby avoiding having their money outstanding at low interest rates. Older mortgages were assignable.

B. Grantee taking subject to the mortgage (nonassuming grantee) or a grantee who takes in ignorance of a duly recorded mortgage:

 1. Grantee is not personally liable for the mortgage debt.
 2. Mortgaged property is a "surety" for the mortgage debt, i.e., it may be foreclosed and sold to satisfy the debt.
 3. If the property does not satisfy the debt upon foreclosure, the grantee is not personally liable; however, the original mortgagor will be liable on his promise to pay the debt.

C. Grantee who assumes the mortgage (assuming grantee) is personally liable, as the principal debtor, for the mortgage debt and the mortgagor-grantor is the surety for the mortgage debt. (I.e., mortgagee may hold either the grantee or grantor for the full amount of the mortgage debt, but the grantee will be liable to the grantor if he pays, since the grantee has assumed the debt.)

D. Suretyship rules control the mortgagor's release upon the grantee's securing a change in the mortgage terms, e.g., an extension of time—see Suretyship, p. 188, II.A.13.

V. Foreclosure and Termination

A. Can foreclose the mortgage upon default in payment of the debt due:

 1. Suit to foreclose is a proceeding in equity.
 2. Successful foreclosure results in a judgment that directs that the property be sold at a foreclosure sale.
 3. Surplus, after expenses, goes to the mortgagor; similarly, mortgagor is liable for any resulting deficit.
 4. Even after the mortgagor defaults, the mortgagee is still subject to the mortgagor's right and equity of redemption until foreclosure is final.

B. Termination of the mortgage lien:

 1. Merger occurs when the mortgagor and the mortgagee are in effect one and the same and therefore the mortgage interest is merged into the greater estate.

2. Payment: Upon due payment of the debt, the mortgagor is entitled to a satisfaction piece and surrender of the bond or note and the mortgage.

3. Tender: If the mortgagor, on or after maturity of the debt, tenders the amount due and the mortgagee refuses the tender, the mortgage will be terminated, i.e., the lien ends, but the debt is not extinguished.

4. By operation of the statute of limitations: If there are no payments made after maturity for the prescribed period as set forth in the state statutes, then the mortgage lien and debt will be unenforceable where the statute is pleaded as a defense.

Selected Problems from CPA Examinations on Mortgages

Subjective Questions and Answers

Q. 1. Vance Manufacturing, Inc., needed an additional plant location. The executive committee of Vance made a survey to determine what property was available and to select the most desirable location. After much deliberation, Vance decided to purchase a 4-acre tract of land belonging to Dave Lauer. Lauer was in financial difficulty and desperately needed to raise money. Vance felt that the asking price of $70,000 was too high and that Lauer would come down to $60,000 in light of his financial difficulties. After much negotiation, Lauer agreed to sell for $61,000. Vance's attorney promptly examined Lauer's title to the property and found that a $40,000 mortgage had recently been filed by Second Bank & Trust Company. Lauer had mentioned this and indicated that the mortgage would be satisfied out of the $61,000 sale price. The title search, completed on February 2, 1981, revealed that Lauer's title was otherwise clear. Closing was scheduled for March 1.

Meanwhile, desperate for additional financing, Lauer had been negotiating a second mortgage with Adventure Mortgage Company. Lauer did not reveal to Adventure that he was in the process of selling the property to Vance, nor did he tell Vance about the second mortgage. Adventure loaned Lauer $10,000 on February 20 and took a second mortgage on the property. This mortgage was filed by Adventure on February 22. Vance's attorney made a cursory final examination of the title on February 20, and the parties proceeded to close on March 1 as scheduled. Lauer promptly cashed his check for $21,000 and disappeared. Adventure is demanding that it be paid by Vance and threatens foreclosure of its second mortgage.

Required
Answer the following, setting forth reasons for any conclusions stated.
Discuss the legal rights and liabilities of each of the parties involved in the above situation.

A. Adventure Mortgage Company is correct in its assertion. Adventure had not actual or constructive notice of the fraud. It has a valid second mortgage that was properly filed and recorded prior to the closing. Vance Manufacturing, Inc., had constructive notice of the mortgage as a result of the filing and took title to the property subject to the Adventure mortgage. Vance must either pay Adventure or be subject to a foreclosure action.

Although Vance stands to lose $10,000 with respect to Adventure's claim, it is likely that Vance can recover the loss from its attorney, based on an action for negligence. The attorney's final examination of the title prior to closing was clearly inadequate. It was made at a time that was too far in advance of the closing to provide the protection needed. Final examination of title is generally made immediately prior to closing.

Of course, Vance would have a cause of action against Lauer based on deceit (fraud), although recovery seems unlikely. Vance's attorney, assuming he is liable as a result of a finding that he was negligent, would be subrogated to the rights of his client and entitled to recover from Lauer for deceit.

Q. 2. In the course of your examination of the financial statements of your client, Lazy L Motels corporation, you discovered certain problems relating to the corporation's most recently acquired motel units. On November 15, 1973, Lazy L acquired title to a newly constructed 36-unit motel complex. In connection with the purchase, Lazy L obtained a real-property title search and title insurance from the Safety Title Insurance Company, Inc. The deed was promptly recorded.

Subsequently, the following facts were discovered:

1. There was an unrecorded first mortgage of $200,000 on the real property. Lazy L was unaware of this mortgage when the motel complex was purchased.
2. The furniture, appliances, trade fixtures, and all other personal property were subject to a $25,000 security interest per an agreement with the Ace Loan Corporation. The agreement had been properly recorded by Ace. Lazy L was unaware of this security interest when the motel complex was purchased.

Required

In separately numbered paragraphs, discuss the legal implications to Lazy L of each of the above discoveries.

A. 1. Lazy L's rights are superior to those of the unrecorded first mortgagee. Lazy L purchased the property without constructive knowledge (via recordation) or actual knowledge of the adverse mortgagee's interest; hence, Lazy L takes the property free of the mortgage.

2. Depending on the type of deed received by Lazy L, its best recourse is to proceed against the seller. Ace has a paramount interest in the personal property subject to its security agreement. Having duly filed the agreement, the Uniform Commercial Code protects Ace against sales to third parties such as Lazy L. Furthermore, Lazy L does not have any claim against the title company because a special search of personal-property defects was not requested. Notwithstanding, Lazy L would have rights against the seller in that it failed to disclose the personal-property security interest of Ace.

Q. 3. Hammar Hardware Company, Inc., purchased all the assets and assumed all the liabilities of JoMar Hardware for $60,000. Among the assets and liabilities included in the sale was a lease of the building in which the business was located. The lessor-owner was Marathon Realty, Inc., and the remaining unexpired term of the lease was nine years. The lease did not contain a provision dealing with the assignment of the leasehold. Incidental to the purchase, Hammar expressly promised JoMar that it would pay the rental due Marathon over the life of the lease and would hold JoMar harmless from any future liability thereon.

When Marathon learned of the proposed transaction, it strenuously objected to the assignment of the lease and to the occupancy by Hammar. Later, after this dispute was resolved and prior to expiration of the lease, Hammar abandoned the building and ceased doing business in that area. Marathon has demanded payment by JoMar of the rent as it matures over the balance of the term of the lease.

5/74

Required

Answer the following, setting forth reasons for any conclusions stated.

1. Was the consent of Marathon necessary in order to assign the lease?
2. Is JoMar liable on the lease?
3. If Marathon were to proceed against Hammar, would Hammar be liable under the lease?

A. 1. No. In the absence of a restriction on the right to assign specifically stated in the lease, a lessee may assign his leasehold interest to another. Only in unusual circumstances, where the lease involves special elements of personal trust and confidence as contrasted with mere payment for occupancy, will the courts limit the right to assign.

2. Yes. Although JoMar may effectively assign the lease, which in effect is an assignment of the right to occupy the leasehold premises and a delegation of its duty to pay Marathon, it cannot shed its liability to Marathon for the rental payments. In the absence of a release, JoMar remains liable. The transaction described in the fact situation is in the nature of a surety relationship.

3. Yes. Marathon is a third-party creditor beneficiary of Hammar's promise to JoMar. As such, Marathon can assert rights on the promise even though it was not a party to the contract. Marathon is not barred by lack of privity or the fact that it gave no consideration to Hammar for the promise.

Q. 4. An examination of the financial statements of Bardlow, Inc., disclosed that Bardlow had purchased a plant site from Charles Swinton for cash. Because he was in serious financial difficulty, Swinton sold the property for $69,500, about $5,000 less than its fair market value. A cursory check by Bardlow's attorneys of Swinton's title did not disclose that Security State Bank held a duly recorded $25,000 first mortgage on the property. Swinton did not mention the mortgage at any time during the negotiations. At the closing, Bardlow received a warranty deed with full covenants.

Swinton intended to continue to make the mortgage payments, but additional financial setbacks made this impossible. Swinton later fled the jurisdiction. The mortgage payments are three months in arrears.

5/79

Required

1. How should the transaction be handled on Bardlow's balance sheet? Explain.
2. What rights and/or liabilities does Bardlow have as to (a) Security State Bank, (b) Swinton, and (c) Bardlow's attorneys?

A. 1. The balance sheet should include the mortgage as a liability, thereby decreasing Bardlow's net worth. Although unaware of the mortgage prior to the purchase of the plant site, Bardlow is deemed as a matter of law to have had constructive notice of it via recordation. In effect, Bardlow took the property subject to the mortgage. While an offsetting account receivable from Swinton should also be legally recognized in conjunction with this liability, the fact that Swinton has fled the jurisdiction would indicate the probable uncollectibility of the account and thereby require the recordation of a provision against this loss.

2. (a) *Security State Bank*. Even though Bardlow had no knowledge of the mortgage, it acquired the property subject to the mortgage. It incurred no personal liability on the mortgage; however, it risks the loss of the acquired property if the mortgage is not satisfied. Bardlow has the right to protect this interest. If the mortgage contains a prepayment clause, Bardlow can protect its interest by paying the entire amount outstanding plus interest. If the mortgage does not contain a prepayment clause, Bardlow can pay the arrearage and the balance over the stated time. It might also be possible that the mortgage contained an acceleration clause whereby on default for a specified period of time or upon conveyance of the property the bank could demand a complete satisfaction of the mortgage. Under these circumstances, Bardlow can pay the entire amount to protect its interest in the property. The bank cannot refuse Bardlow's payments under any of these alternatives.

(b) *Swinton*. Bardlow has the right to sue on the covenants contained in the warranty deed or to proceed against him on the basis of misrepresentation or fraud. Since Swinton is probably insolvent and has fled the jurisdiction, assertion of these rights seems impractical.

(c) *Bardlow's attorneys*. Bardlow has the right to sue for negligence in that the attorneys failed to discover the existence of the duly recorded first mortgage.

11/72

Practice Questions

Q. 1. Mark mortgaged his farm, Blackacre, worth $5,000, to Eazy to secure a debt of $3,000 payable in installments. Eazy sued for a defaulted installment, got judgment, and levied execution upon Blackacre. Clark, learning of the entire transaction and desiring to bid at the execution sale, wants to know what interest, if any, he would get, and how much he should bid. What advice should Clark be given?

Q. 2. Mann mortgaged Blackacre to Hall to secure a debt. Mann later gave a second mortgage to Jones. Both mortgages were recorded. Hall later took a conveyance from Mann. Hall then conveyed the property by warranty deed to Able. All this was without any actual knowledge of the second mortgage. The property is now not worth the combined total of the two mortgage debts. Jones brings an action to foreclose and claims to be paid ahead of any possible claim based on the mortgage to Hall. Should Jones prevail?

Q. 3. Mills, a mortgagor, sold his interest in the mortgaged property to Ard "subject to the mortgage." When the debt came due Edgars, the mortgagee, although he knew the terms on which Ard bought, by a binding agreement with Ard extended for one year the time for the payment of the mortgage debt. At the end of that time, the mortgage being unpaid, Edgars sued Mills. Has Mills a defense to the action?

Practice Objective Questions

Instructions 1–10

Select the *best* answer for each of the following items. Mark only one answer for *each* item. Answer all items. Your grade will be based on your total correct answers.

1. A real estate mortgage
   a. Need *not* be in writing.
   b. Creates an intangible personal property right for the mortgagee.
   c. If properly recorded, gives constructive notice to subsequent purchasers and mortgagees of the recording mortgagee's interest.
   d. Is *not* assignable by the mortgagee.

2. Amos purchased a building from Thoms. He paid a small amount of cash and took the building subject to a mortgage given by Thoms to National Bank. Under these circumstances:
   a. Sale of the building to Amos would normally give National Bank an immediate right of action against Thoms.
   b. Amos became primarily liable on the debt to National Bank.
   c. Amos incurred *no* personal liability on the debt.
   d. Payment of the mortgage debt by Amos would give Amos a right of subrogation against Thoms.

3. Paxton owned Blackacre, and he obtained a $10,000 loan from a bank secured by a real property mortgage on Blackacre. The mortgage was properly recorded. Paxton subsequently sold Blackacre to Rogers, expressly warranting that there were *no* mortgages on the property. Rogers was unaware of the bank's interest in the property. Paxton has disappeared, and the bank has demanded payment from Rogers. Rogers has refused, and the bank is seeking to foreclose its mortgage. Which of the following statements is correct?
   a. Rogers is personally liable on the mortgage loan.
   b. As a *bona fide* purchaser for value, Rogers will prevail and retain the property free of the mortgage.
   c. The bank will prevail in its foreclosure action.
   d. The bank must obtain a judgment against Paxton before it can foreclose the mortgage.

4. Lutz sold his moving and warehouse business, including all the personal and real property used therein, to Arlen Van Lines, Inc. The real property was encumbered by a duly recorded $300,000 first mortgage upon which Lutz was personally liable. Arlen acquired the property subject to the mortgage but did not assume the mortgage. Two years later, when the outstanding mortgage was $260,000, Arlen decided to abandon the business location because it had become unprofitable and the value of the real property was less than the outstanding mortgage. Arlen moved to another location and refused to pay the installments due on the mortgage. What is the legal status of the parties in regard to the mortgage?
   a. Lutz must satisfy the mortgage debt in the event that foreclosure yields an amount less than the unpaid balance.
   b. If Lutz pays off the mortgage, he will be able to successfully sue Arlen because Lutz is subrogated to the mortgagee's rights against Arlen.
   c. Arlen took the real property free of the mortgage.
   d. Arlen breached its contract with Lutz when it abandoned the location and defaulted on the mortgage.

5. Donaldson, Inc., loaned Watson Enterprises $50,000 secured by a real estate mortgage which included the land, buildings, and "all other property which is added to the real property or which is considered as real property as a matter of law." Star Company also loaned Watson $25,000 and obtained a security interest in all of Watson's "inventory, accounts receivable, fixtures, and other tangible personal property." There is insufficient property to satisfy the two creditors. Consequently, Donaldson is attempting to include all property possible under the terms and scope of its real property mortgage. If Donaldson is successful in this regard, then Star will receive a lesser amount in satisfaction of its claim. What is the probable outcome of Donaldson's action?

   a. Donaldson will *not* prevail if the property in question is detachable trade fixtures.
   b. Donaldson will prevail if Star failed to file a financing statement.
   c. Donaldson will prevail if it was the first lender and duly filed its real property mortgage.
   d. The problem will be decided by taking all of Watson's property (real and personal) subject to the two secured creditors' claims and dividing it in proportion to the respective debts.

6. Miltown borrowed $60,000 from Strauss upon the security of a first mortgage on a business building owned by Miltown. The mortgage has been amortized down to $50,000. Sanchez is buying the building from Miltown for $80,000. Sanchez is paying only the $30,000 excess over and above the mortgage. Sanchez may buy it either "subject to" the mortgage, or he may "assume" the mortgage. Which is a correct statement under these circumstances?

   a. The financing agreement ultimately decided upon must be recorded in order to be binding upon the parties.
   b. The financing arrangement is covered by the Uniform Commercial Code if Sanchez takes "subject to" the existing first mortgage.
   c. Sanchez will acquire *no* interest in the property if he takes "subject to" instead of "assuming" the mortgage.
   d. Sanchez would be better advised to take "subject to" the mortgage rather than to "assume" the mortgage.

7. The facts are the same as those stated above in number 8, but the property purchased by Sanchez has declined in value and the mortgage is in default. It has now been amortized to $43,000. The property is sold under foreclosure proceedings and $39,000; net of costs, is received. Which is a correct legal conclusion if Sanchez acquired the property "subject to" the mortgage?

   a. Sanchez has *no* further liability after foreclosure.
   b. Miltown *cannot* be held personally liable by Strauss for the $4,000 deficiency.
   c. Sanchez is *not* liable to Strauss, but is personally liable to Miltown if Miltown pays the deficiency.
   d. Miltown and Sanchez will have to satisfy the deficiency equally, that is, each owes $2,000.

8. Jane Luft, doing business as Luft Enterprises, owned a tract of land upon which she had intended to build an additional retail outlet. There is an existing first mortgage of $70,000 on the property which is held by the First County National Bank. Luft decided *not* to expand, and a buyer, Johnson, offered $150,000 for the property. Luft accepted and received a certified check for $80,000 plus a signed statement by Johnson promising to pay the existing mortgage. What are the legal rights of the indicated parties?

   a. Luft remains liable to First County despite Johnson's promise to pay.
   b. First County must first proceed against Johnson on the mortgage before it has any rights against Luft.
   c. The delegation of the debt is invalid if Johnson does *not* have a credit rating roughly comparable to Luft's.
   d. The bank is the incidental beneficiary of Johnson's promise to pay the mortgage.

9. Lutz sold his moving and warehouse business, including all the personal and real property used therein, to Allen Van Lines, Inc. The real property was encumbered by a $300,000 first mortgage upon which Lutz was personally liable. Allen acquired the property subject to the mortgage. Two years later, when the mortgage outstanding was $260,000, Allen decided to abandon the business location because it had become unprofitable and the value of the real property was less than the outstanding mortgage. Allen moved to another location and refused to pay the installments due on the mortgage. What is the legal status of the parties in regard to the mortgage?

   a. Allen took the real property free of the mortgage.
   b. Allen breached its contract with Lutz when it abandoned the location and defaulted on the mortgage.
   c. Lutz must satisfy the mortgage debt in the event that foreclosure yields an amount less than the unpaid balance.
   d. If Lutz pays off the mortgage, he will be able to successfully sue Allen because Lutz is subrogated to the mortgagee's rights against Allen.

10. Carter wished to obtain additional working capital for his construction company. His bankers indicated that they would be willing to lend the company $50,000 if the bank could obtain a first mortgage on the real property belonging to the business. Carter reluctantly acquiesced and mortgaged all his real property to secure repayment of the loan. Unknown to the bank one portion of the real property was already mortgaged to Johnson for $30,000, but Johnson had neglected to record the mortgage. The bank promptly recorded its mortgage. Which of the following is correct regarding the rights of the parties?

   a. Johnson's failure to record makes the mortgage invalid against Carter.

   b. The bank's mortgage will have a priority over Johnson's mortgage.

   c. Both mortgagees would share the proceeds from any foreclosure on a pro rata basis.

   d. The bank will be deemed to have notice of Johnson's mortgage and will take subject to the mortgage.

CHAPTER

17

Fire and Casualty Insurance

AICPA Content Specification Outline

Coinsurance
Multiple Insurance Coverage
Insurable Interest

Contents

I. Characteristics

A. Definition: a contract whereby, for a stipulated consideration, one party (the insurer) undertakes to compensate the other (the insured) for loss on a specified subject by specified perils.

    1. Property insurance (e.g., fire, theft) is primarily an indemnity against risk of actual loss by distributing the loss over a group.

    2. Insurance normally does not protect against willful intentional destruction by the insured, but it does protect against negligence by the insured and its employees. It also covers intentional torts, including arson by its employees, where the employer is not a party to it.

    3. Note, for coverage of title insurance, see Property, p. 369, III.B.2.

B. Elements of the insurance contract:

    1. Mutual assent (see Contracts, p. 139, III.A).

      a. The application for insurance made by the prospective insured constitutes the offer.

      b. Acceptance is usually made by the company at its home office. The application will usually so provide.

    2. Consideration (see Contracts, p. 145, III.B).

      a. By the insured: payment, or promise of payment, of premium.

      b. By the insurer: promise to indemnify the policyholder for loss that may occur.

      c. By the beneficiary (the person to whom a policy of insurance is payable; is invariably also the insured). If the beneficiary is not the insured, he gives no consideration and is not a party to the contract, but rather a third-party beneficiary (see Contracts, p. 159, VI.C) and he recovers on this basis.

II. Insurable Interest in Property

A. Any legally recognized or any substantial economic interest in the safety or preservation of the property insured against loss, destruction, or other pecuniary damage.

    1. The objectives of this requirement are:
        a. Measurement of the insured's loss,
        b. Prevention of wagering, and
        c. Guarding against moral hazard (e.g., arson).

B. Must actually exist at the time the loss occurs.

C. The following persons have the requisite insurable interest:

    1. A mortgagor has an insurable interest to the extent of the full value of the property mortgaged; the mortgagee has an insurable interest to the extent of the unpaid debt.

    2. A tenant has an insurable interest in the property he leases.

    3. A stockholder has an insurable interest in the property owned by a corporation.

    4. A general creditor does not have an insurable interest in the property of his debtor while the debtor is alive; however, a secured creditor or judgment lienor does have an insurable interest in the specific property that secures the debt or against which the judgment attaches.

    5. A bailee has an insurable interest in the property held in his possession although he does not have legal title thereto.

    6. A person has an insurable interest in the property of another if the person has potential *liability* in the event of its destruction.

UCC RULE The UCC has made some important changes in respect to the buyer's insurable interest in goods that are the subject matter of a contract of sale. These rules are in addition to those discussed above, and are intended to foster an early creation of the buyer's insurable interest in the goods. They are in no way intended to impair any insurable interest recognized by any other statute or rule of law.

    (1) The buyer obtains a "special property and insurable interest" in goods by *identification* of existing goods as those to which the contract refers. The rule applies even though the goods identified are nonconforming and the buyer would have the option of returning them.

    (2) Identification can be made at any time and in any manner explicitly agreed to by the parties. In the absence of explicit agreement, identification occurs:
        (a) When the contract is made, if it is for the sale of goods already in existence and identified.
        (b) In the case of future goods (other than growing crops and the unborn young of animals), when the goods are shipped, marked, or otherwise designated by the seller as the goods to which the contract refers.

    (3) The seller retains an insurable interest in goods so long as title to, or any security interest in the goods remains in him or her.

D. Insurance against crimes: no "insurable interest" by the insured against crimes to be committed by him. But there is an "insurable interest" against crimes to be committed against him (e.g., can insure against theft by another, including his employees).

E. Rationale: Insurance is distinguishable from a wager in that insurance is, and must be, based on a valid insurable interest, which the insured seeks to protect against risk of loss; moreover, insurance is entered into in common with others resulting not only in an individual benefit, but also in a benefit to an entire group.

III. Fire Insurance (Property)

A. Nature and coverage:
   1. Indemnifies the insured against property destroyed or damaged by fire within a specified period.
   2. The person insuring must have an "insurable interest" at the time of the loss (see p. 397, II.B).
   3. Fire insurance, like most property insurance, is nontransferable in that the contract is a personal contract between the parties.
   4. Covers loss due directly to a hostile fire, and also loss accompanying or resulting from a hostile fire (e.g., damage caused by smoke, water, or chemicals).
   5. Does not normally include a loss caused by a friendly fire.
       a. Friendly fire: a fire burning in the place where it was intended to burn (e.g., an oil burner damaged by overheating would not be a loss covered by a standard fire policy).
       b. Hostile fire: one that breaks out from its confines, where it was intended to be contained, and becomes a hostile element.
   6. Smoke, water, and other damage caused by a friendly fire may be insured against by adding the "extended coverage indorsement."

B. Types of fire insurance policies:
   1. Blanket (compound) policy: a policy of fire insurance that contemplates that the risk is shifting or varying, and is applied to a class of property rather than to any particular article or thing.
   2. Specific policy: covers a particular piece of property or property at a specific location (e.g., the building and machinery located at the X factory).
   3. Floater policy: a policy intended to supplement specific insurance, the purpose of which is to provide indemnity for property that cannot, because of its frequent change in location and quantity, be covered by specific insurance.
   4. Valued policy: one in which a definite valuation is, by agreement of both parties, put on the subject matter of the insurance and written on the face of the policy; such value, in the absence of fraud or mistake, is conclusive in the event of a total loss.
   5. Open or unvalued policy: one in which the value of the property is not settled in the policy, merely a maximum for which the company will be liable; value recoverable will be determined at the time of the loss, based upon the fair market value of the loss at that date.
   6. Binder: usually a brief memorandum or oral agreement for insurance, intended to give temporary protection, pending investigation of the risk by the insurer in

order to determine whether or not to issue a formal policy; although most commonly used in auto or fire insurance, a binder may be used in any type of insurance.

C. Amount recoverable:

1. Under either a valued or an open policy, if there is partial destruction, only the actual loss sustained is recoverable.
2. In the event of a total loss:
   a. Under a valued policy, the insured will recover the amount stated in the policy without proof of actual value.
   b. Under an open policy, the insured will recover only the cash value of property destroyed as subsequently proved, i.e., to indemnify for the loss. (E.g., X insures with the I Insurance Company, taking out an open policy with a maximum of $25,000. The property is totally destroyed. X will receive the actual value of the property destroyed even though it is less than the $25,000 maximum.)

D. Coinsurance *(applies only to partial loss):*

1. Coinsurance provides that if the owner insures his property up to a given percentage (usually 80%) of its value, he will recover any loss in full up to the face amount of the policy, but if he insures for less than the fixed percentage he must himself bear proportionately any loss.
2. Assuming the facts indicated in the parentheses, the formula for determining the amount of recovery is as follows:
   a.

$$\frac{\text{Amount of insurance (\$16,000)}}{\text{Coinsurance \% (80\%)} \times \text{value of property (\$40,000)}} = 50\%$$

   b. 50% × Amount of loss ($12,000) = recovery ($6,000)
3. Note well, this clause is one of the most frequently tested parts of insurance law on the exam.

E. Multiple coverage or pro rata clause: Where the owner has insurance with several companies, and the aggregate exceeds the actual loss, she can collect from each company only that company's proportionate liability to the total amount of insurance. (E.g., X takes out two open-value fire insurance policies with two different insurance companies, each having a $10,000 maximum. In the event of total destruction of the property, which has a replacement value of $15,000, X can only collect $7,500 from each insurer.)

F. Other standard clauses:

1. An option to restore or rebuild is generally given to the insurance company.
   a. Protects the insurer against necessity of contesting inflated claims.
   b. Tends to discourage arson, which is generally motivated by a desire for a cash payment.
2. Occupancy of premises: Standard policy provides that if the premises become vacant or unoccupied for a given number of days (e.g., 10 days), then the entire policy shall be suspended until the premises are reoccupied unless otherwise provided.

3. Assignment of policy:

   a. Normally nonassignable, since the relationship between insurer and insured is a personal one; therefore, policy usually provides that it will be void if assigned (prior to loss) without the company's consent indorsed on the policy.

   b. After loss caused by a fire, the insured may assign his claim against the insurance company.

   c. Fire insurance on property that is transferred does not accompany the property transferred; instead, the policy is void upon the transfer of the property due to the personal nature of fire insurance and the loss of an insurable interest. However, the insurer may give its consent to the assignment.

4. Notice of loss within a specified period of time or immediate notice of loss:

   a. In the event of loss, the insured is required to give notice within a specified period of time, or the policy may require that notice of loss be "immediate"; failure to comply will permit the insurer to avoid liability.

   b. The word "immediate" has been universally construed by the courts to mean as soon as is reasonably possible under the circumstances, in accordance with due diligence.

5. Satisfactory proof of loss:

   a. The standard provision requires that "satisfactory" proof of loss (a verified written statement) be filed by the insured within a specified period of time (typically, 60 days).

   b. "Satisfactory" proof of loss has been construed by the courts to require that the insured do all in his power to furnish the information requested in the policy.

6. Cancellation of policy can be brought about by either the insured or insurer at will, usually on 5 days' notice.

G. Subrogation. For the definition of this term, see Suretyship, p. 190.

   1. As used in insurance law, the insurer is subrogated to the rights of, or is substituted in the place of the insured for the purpose of claiming indemnity from a third person whose conduct caused the loss covered by insurance.

   2. Right of Subrogation: The standard fire policy, covering only a mortgagee's interest, specifically provides that the insurance company shall be subrogated and succeed to all rights and remedies that the mortgagee has against the mortgagor. (E.g., X, a mortgagee, insures the property, securing the debt for his own exclusive benefit. As a result of a fire that destroys the premises, the insurance company is obligated to pay X the full amount of the debt plus interest due on the mortgage. Upon payment, the insurance company will be subrogated to mortgagee's rights against the mortgagor.)

   3. Under an accident, automobile (collison), or fire insurance policy, the insurer who pays the claim is subrogated to any rights that the insured may have against a third party. (E.g., X takes out an auto insurance policy—collision—with the Y Insurance Company; X's car is badly damaged as a result of T's negligent driving into X's parked car. Upon payment, the insurer is subrogated to X's rights against T.)

4. A general release of the third-party tort-feasor by the insured, without the consent of the insurer, will release the insurer from its obligation in that the insured has cut off the insurance company's right to subrogation (see Suretyship, p. 187, II.A.7).

H. Interest of those other than the name insured in the proceeds of fire insurance policies:

1. Mortgagor's (debtor's) and mortgagee's (creditor's) rights under a fire insurance policy:
   a. Each may take out a separate policy covering his own insurable interest—see p. 397, II.C.1.
      (1) Mortgagor's interest in the policy procured by the mortgagee:
         (A) If the mortgagee insures independently and for his own benefit, the mortgagee may recover the full amount of his loss (i.e., the balance due) up to the maximum amount of the policy free from any claim of the mortgagor.
         (B) The insurer will be subrogated to the mortgagee's claim against the mortgagor (see above).
      (2) Mortgagee's interest in policy procured by the mortgagor.
         (A) If the mortgage calls for the mortgagor to insure for the benefit of the mortgagee, the mortgagee shares in the proceeds to the extent of the unpaid balance on the mortgage.
         (B) If the mortgagor procures the policy for his own benefit, then, in absence of the above agreement to insure for the benefit of the mortgagee, the mortgagor takes the full amount of the insurance payment free of any specific claim by the mortgagee (i.e., the mortgagee has no greater rights than a general creditor to the proceeds. However, he retains his rights on the mortgage).
   b. A single policy may be jointly procured by the parties to protect their respective interests. This is the usual practice.
      (1) A standard or "union" clause may be included in the policy; in such a case there is a collateral independent agreement between the mortgagee and the insurer that protects the mortgagee's right to recover even though there be a default or breach on the part of the mortgagor. (E.g., where there is a standard or "union" clause, and the mortgagor deliberately sets fire to the property, the mortgagee can nevertheless collect as against the insurance company on his "independent contract.")
      (2) The policy may contain a loss payable clause (i.e., "loss is payable to the mortgagee as his interest may appear"). In such a case the mortgagee can collect to the extent of his loss, but he is a beneficiary and, therefore, his rights may be defeated by a default on the part of the mortgagor.

2. General creditor's rights under a fire insurance policy:
   a. Creditor has no rights prior to destruction of the property, nor may he force the debtor to surrender the policy in order to obtain a refund for the unused portion.
   b. After loss, the creditor may treat the proceeds as any other asset of the debtor;

a secured creditor having a lien on property, in the absence of any agreement, has a lien on the proceeds of the insured debtor's policy. The UCC so provides.

3. Life tenant and remainderman's rights under a fire insurance policy:

    a. If the policy is taken out for the benefit of both parties, the owner of the life estate is entitled to have:

        (1) The proceeds applied to rebuilding of the estate destroyed, or

        (2) The use of the proceeds during life, remainder to the remainderman.

    b. If the life tenant, in the absence of any agreement to insure for the benefit of the remainderman, takes out insurance for his own benefit, he is entitled, as against the remainderman, to the full proceeds of the policies in the event of loss.

    c. If the remainderman insures separately for his own benefit, the life tenant has no interest in the proceeds received by the remainderman.

4. Vendor's (seller's) and vendee's (buyer's) interest in a fire insurance policy:

    a. The vendee has a right to the insurance proceeds of a policy on real property procured by the vendor where the premises have been destroyed after making of the contract of sale but prior to delivery of the deed, provided that the vendee pays the money due the vendor on the contract.

        (1) Some states do not follow this rule because the common law rule, that the risk of loss is on the vendee during the period between the making of the contract of sale and transfer of the deed, has been changed by statute.

        (2) The vendor is not entitled to all or part of the proceeds of a policy procured independently by the vendee that is taken out after the making of the contract of sale.

IV. Automobile Insurance

A. Definition: insurance against loss or damage to a motor vehicle caused by fire, windstorm, theft, collision, or other insurable hazards, and also against legal liability for death or personal injuries or damage to property resulting from operation of the vehicle.

B. Types:

1. Fire and theft: insures against damage to the car and its usual equipment, but not personal belongings.

2. Collision: insures against damage to insured's car caused by collision; most policies contain a $50 or $100 deductible clause.

3. Liability and property damage: indemnifies against liability on account of death or injuries caused to another or his property.

    a. "Permissive user" clause: Policy covers anyone who drives the car with the owner's permission.

    b. "Drive any other car" clause: Insured is covered in any car in which he drives.

4. Comprehensive: a policy in which the scope of the insured event is stated to be any loss or damage to a subject matter insured (e.g., fire, theft, explosion), with the exception of collision or upset.

5. No fault: a form of strict liability, whereby the driver is liable for damages regardless of whether he or the injured party or both were at fault (negligent). It is a bold departure from prior law which was based upon the theory that liability should not be imposed unless the defendant was negligent and the plaintiff was not.

V. Insurer's Defenses: Warranties, Representations, and Concealments

A. Warranty: a term of the insurance contract that prescribes as a condition precedent of the insurer's liability the existence of a fact that tends to diminish, or the nonexistence of a fact that tends to increase, the risk of the occurrence of *any* loss, damage, or injury. It has the following characteristics:

1. A warranty is in the nature of a condition precedent.
2. The warranty *must* appear on the face of, be embodied in, or be attached to the policy itself; applications for insurance are so attached.
3. Theoretically, a warranty is susceptible to no construction other than that the parties mutually intended that the policy should not be enforceable unless such statement or term be literally true.
   a. The legal consequence of a breach of a warranty is that the policy is voidable at the option of the insurer.
   b. Thus, at common law, if the insured warrants that there will be a crew of 50 men on board his ship during a voyage and during a part thereof he has less than 50, the insurance company can avoid liability on the policy even though at the time of the loss the crew numbers 50 and the event causing the loss had no relation to that particular warranty. Statutory changes in the common law in respect to property insurance have been rare.

B. Warranties may be affirmative or continuing (promissory):

1. Affirmative: relates to the existence or nonexistence of fact at the time the contract is made (e.g., the factory is located within 1 mile of the fire station).
2. Continuing: relates to the existence or nonexistence of fact throughout the term of the contract (e.g., 25 working fire extinguishers shall be maintained at all times on the premises).

C. Representations and concealments:

1. Representations: statements as to past or present facts, either oral or in writing, by the applicant to the insurer preliminary to the making of the contract, and that are not inserted in the policy.
   a. Insured is said to be under a duty of utmost good faith and honesty in answering the insurer's questions, in that the facts are primarily within his knowledge. The same rule applies as to concealments.
   b. If there has been a representation that was *material* to acceptance of the risk, the insurer can avoid liability on the policy.
2. Concealments: failure of the applicant for insurance to communicate to the insurer his knowledge of a material fact that the insurer does not know is a concealment. In most types of insurance, including fire, it must be shown that the insured knew the concealment was material to the risk, in order to invalidate the policy.

      a. The test of materiality is whether or not the insurer would accept the risk knowing the fact in question.

      b. Knowledge of materiality by the insured is difficult to prove that unless the insurer can show actual knowledge of materiality on the insured's part, he must prove that the nondisclosure was palpably material, i.e., a reasonable person must have known that it was material.

    D. Mitigating doctrines: waiver, estoppel, and election

      1. Waiver: the intentional or voluntary relinquishment of a known right; it is generally used in the law of insurance to indicate any conduct by the insurer or his agents that has the legal effect of relinquishing a defense by the insurer based upon the insured's failure to comply with a condition of the insurance contract. (E.g., the insured's fails to give prompt notice of claim but, nevertheless, the insurer processes the claim without objecting to the delay.)

      2. Estoppel: representation of fact made by the insurer to the insured that is reasonably relied on by the insured in changing his position to such an extent that it would be inequitable to allow the insured to deny the truth of its representation. (E.g., the X Insurance Company requests that Y—the insured—turn over all evidence to its attorneys despite the fact the insured's notice was late. As a result he does not obtain his own lawyer.)

      3. Election: a voluntary act of choosing between two alternative rights or privileges. (E.g., the X Fire Insurance Company accepts and retains premiums after knowledge of a breach of a condition in the policy concerning storage of gasoline on the premises. In that the company would not be entitled to the premium unless the policy was valid, the insurer has made an election to excuse the breach and is bound despite the breach of the condition.)

Selected Problems from CPA Examinations on Insurance

Subjective Questions and Answers

Note: Recent examinations have not used the problem-type question in the insurance area. The most notable exception is contained in the November 1982 Examination (Number 5.a) which appears below.

Q. **1.** While auditing the financial statements of Jackson Corporation for the year ended December 31, 1981, Harvey Draper, CPA, desired to verify the balance in the insurance claims receivable account. Draper obtained the following information:

- On November 4, 1981, Jackson's Parksdale plant was damaged by fire. The fire caused $200,000 damage to the plant, which was purchased in 1970 for $600,000. When the plant was purchased, Jackson obtained a loan secured by a mortgage from Second National Bank of Parksdale. At the time of the fire the loan balance, including accrued interest, was $106,000. The plant was insured against fire with Eagle Insurance Company. The policy contained a "standard mortgagee" clause and an 80% continuance clause. The face value of the policy was $600,000 and the value of the plant was $1,000,000 at the time of the fire.

- On December 10, 1981, Jackson's Yuma warehouse was totally destroyed by fire. The warehouse was acquired in 1960 for $300,000. At the time of the fire, the warehouse was unencumbered by any mortgage; it was insured against fire with Eagle for $300,000; and it had a value of $500,000. The policy contained an 80% coinsurance clause.

- On December 26, 1981, Jackson's Rye City garage was damaged by fire. At the time of the fire, the garage had a value of $250,000 and was unencumbered by any mortgage. The fire caused $60,000 damage to the garage, which was constructed in 1965 at a cost of $50,000. In 1975 Jackson expanded the capacity of the garage at an additional cost of $50,000. When the garage was constructed in 1965, Jackson insured the garage against fire for $50,000 with Eagle, and this policy was still in force on the date of the fire. When the garage was expanded in 1975, Jackson obtained $100,000 of additional fire insurance coverage from Queen Insurance Company. Each policy contains an 80% coinsurance clause and a standard pro-rata clause.

Required:
Answer the following, setting forth reasons for any conclusions stated.

1. How much of the fire loss relating to the Parksdale plant will be recovered from Eagle?
2. How will such recovery be distributed between Second National and Jackson?
3. How much of the fire loss relating to the Yuma warehouse will be recovered from Eagle?
4. How much of the fire loss relating to the Rye City garage will be recovered from the insurance companies?
5. What portion of the amount recoverable in connection with the Rye City garage loss will Queen be obligated to pay?

A. 1. The recoverable loss is determined by reference to the following formula:

$$\frac{\text{Insurance carried}}{\text{Insurance required}} \times \text{the amount of the loss}$$

where the insurance required is defined as the value of the property at the time of the loss multiplied by the coinsurance percentage. Applying the foregoing formula, the amount of the loss recovered is as follows:

$$\frac{\$600,000}{\$1,000,000 \times .8} \times \$200,000 = \$150,000$$

2. The $150,000 will be distributed as follows: $106,000 to Second National and $44,000 to Jackson. This is because Second National's insurable interest equals the extent of its mortgage outstanding, which is limited to debt outstanding plus accrued interest, and is paid first. The remaining $44,000 would then be paid to Jackson.
3. Jackson will recover $300,000—the face amount of the policy. The coinsurance clause does not apply to a total loss.
4. Jackson will recover $45,000. The formula for determination of the total amount recoverable under the 80% coinsurance clause is as follows:

$$\frac{\$150,000}{\$250,000 \times .8} \times \$60,000 = \$45,000$$

5. Jackson will recover $30,000 from Queen. This amount is determined as follows:

$$\frac{\$100,000 \text{ (Queen's coverage)}}{\$150,000 \text{ (Total coverage)}} \times \$45,000 = \$30,000$$

11/82

Q. 2. During January 1972 Cragsmoore, one of Foley's employees, negligently dropped a lighted cigar on some packing material, which caught fire and totally destroyed the warehouse and the goods stored therein. The warehouse and contents were covered by a $2 million fire insurance policy that contains a 90% coinsurance clause. The loss was subsequently appraised at $2.5 million.

Foley seeks to recover for the loss. Adams denies any and all liability; or, in the alternative, claims that it is not obligated to pay the full $2 million.

Required

What can Foley recover? Explain.

A. $2 million. One of the risks assumed by an insurer is the negligence of the insured, including its employees. Thus, despite Cragsmoore's negligence, Foley can recover for the destruction of its warehouse and the goods stored therein: In addition, the coinsurance clause does not apply to a total destruction of the insured property. Hence, Foley will recover the face amount of the policy. If Adams pays Foley, Adams will be subrogated to any rights Foley would have against Cragsmoore.

11/72

Q.   3.   You have been assigned to review the insurance coverage as of June 30, 1972, of Foley & Co., a partnership. As part of your work you inspect the correspondence file with Foley's insurance agent. The file reveals that Foley has filed a number of claims with Adams Insurance that remain unpaid. You extracted the following facts from the correspondence file:

Foley dispatched an order on November 11, 1971, to Western Computer Co. accompanied by its check in full payment for 1,000 computer components to be shipped by boat, f.a.s. Vessel at Western's home port. The parts were labeled, packed, crated, and picked up for delivery to the pier. On the way to the pier, the truck caught fire and the goods were completely destroyed. Foley sent a claim to Adams for recovery under its blanket insurance policy, which covers "all goods in Foley's possession, owned by it, or to which it had any legally recognized insurable interest."

Adams denies liability on the policy, claiming:

a. The risk of loss had not passed to Foley.

b. Foley did not have any legally recognized insurable interest.

Required

Is Adams correct in either of its contentions? Explain.

A.   Yes as to risk of loss. No as to insurable interest. Since the contract was f.a.s. Vessel at Western's home port the risk of loss remains with Western until the goods arrive and are unloaded at that point. However, the Uniform Commercial Code provides for "an insurable interest in the purchaser of goods upon identification of existing goods to the contract." Thus, under the facts presented, identification to the contract having been clearly made, Foley can recover from Adams for any insured loss. If Adams pays Foley, Adams will be subrogated to any rights Foley would have against Western.

11/72

Q.   4.   Anderson loaned the Drum Corporation $60,000. The loan was secured by a first mortgage on Drum's land and the plant thereon. Anderson independently procured a fire insurance policy for $60,000 on the mortgaged property from the Victory Insurance Company. Six years later when the mortgage had been amortized down to $52,000, the plant was totally destroyed by a fire caused by faulty electrical wiring in the rear storage area.

Required

Answer the following, setting forth reasons for any conclusions stated.

1. Anderson seeks recovery of $60,000 from the Victory Insurance Company. How much will it collect?

2. Upon payment by Victory Insurance Company, what rights does Victory have?

A.   1.   Anderson's insurable interest equals the extent of the mortgage debt outstanding. Thus, his recovery is limited to the $52,000 debt outstanding plus accrued interest on the debt, but the total recovery cannot exceed $60,000, the maximum coverage under the policy.

2. Upon payment, Victory is subrogated to the rights of Anderson and will succeed to Anderson's rights to receive payments under the terms of the mortgage and mortgage bond. If Drum Corporation fails to continue the payments, Victory may foreclose on the mortgage.

11/76

Q. 5. An employee of Carter Corporation negligently dropped a match into some waste material that was awaiting removal by the refuse collector from Carter's plant. The resulting fire spread to the plant and totally destroyed it. The plant and its contents were worth $180,000 at the time of the fire.

Carter's plant building and contents were insured for $200,000 against fire loss by Phoen Fire & Casualty Co. In a separate fire policy Phoen insured Carter's plant for $150,000 to Alpha Bank, which had held a $150,000 first mortgage on Carter's plant. The unpaid principal on the mortgage was $100,000. The mortgage contained an acceleration clause that provided that substantial damage to the property by fire or other casualty would cause the entire unpaid principal to become due and payable.

Carter has filed a fire loss claim with Phoen under its fire insurance policy, and Alpha Bank has filed a claim with Phoen under its policy. Phoen has declined to pay Carter on its fire loss claim, asserting that Carter's negligence voided the policy.

Required
1. Discuss the merits of Phoen's contentions as to its obligations under the policy with Carter.
2. Assuming it has no defense against the fire loss claims by Carter and Alpha, how mauch will Phoen ultimately have to pay on its policies to Carter and Alpha Bank? Explain.
3. Would Phoen be liable on the policy to Alpha Bank if the mortgage on Carter's plant had been fully paid prior to the fire but Alpha Bank had nevertheless continued its policy with Phoen in effect?

A. 1. The negligence of Carter or of its employees would be no defense on Carter's fire policy with Phoen since such policies, ordinarily, insure against loss even when caused by the negligence of the insured. If the fire loss were occasioned by active wrongdoing of the insured, the policy would have been breached. However, on the facts given, there was no active wrongdoing by Carter and, hence, the insurer must pay the claim.
2. Phoen will have to pay Alpha Bank $100,000 on its policy with Alpha, that being the unpaid balance due Alpha on its mortgage at the time of the loss. After Phoen pays Alpha, Phoen will become subrogated to Alpha's claim in that amount against Carter on the mortgage. By virtue of the acceleration clause in the mortgage, this claim became immediately enforceable at the time of the loss. Carter's actual loss from the fire was $180,000. Although Carter carried insurance in the amount of $200,000, it cannot recover more than its actual loss, or $180,000. Moreover, since, as discussed above, Phoen would be subrogated to Alpha's claim against Carter on the mortgage in the amount of $100,000, Phoen would thus ultimately be required to pay Carter $80,000.
3. No. To enforce a claim under a policy of property insurance (such as a fire insurance policy), the insured must have an insurable interest in the property at the time the loss is suffered. The interest of a creditor in the security for his debt is an insurable interest. Hence, so long as any part of Alpha's mortgage loan remained unpaid it had, to that extent, an insurable interest in Carter's plant. This interest ceased, however, when the mortgage debt was fully paid. Thus, Alpha would have no enforceable claim under its policy with Phoen if, prior to the loss, Carter's mortgage had been fully paid. In such a case, however, Alpha would be entitled to a refund of premiums it had paid for the period subsequent to extinguishment of the mortgage debt.

11/69

Practice Questions

Q. 1. Marvel Enterprises, Inc., contracted to buy Jonstone's factory and warehouse. The contract provided that if title did not pass to Marvel prior to October 1, 1974, Marvel would have the right to possession on that date pending conveyance of title upon delivery of the deed. The contract also provided that the purchase price was to be adjusted depending upon the actual acreage conveyed as determined by an independent survey. This provision was subject to a further stipulation: the maximum purchase price would not exceed $450,000 nor be less than $425,000 as long as the survey did not reveal major variances nor render title unmarketable.

All the requisite paperwork was not in order by October 1, 1974, and Marvel exercised its option to take possession on that date. Concurrently, Marvel obtained a fire insurance policy on the factory and warehouse effective October 1, 1974. The closing was finally scheduled for October 17, 1974. The survey confirmed the acreage described in the contract of sale, and Marvel tendered the balance of the purchase price on October 17, 1974. During the interim period, however, the factory and warehouse were totally destroyed by fire and Marvel seeks to recover on its fire insurance policy. The insurance company denies liability.

Required

Discuss Marvel's rights to recover from the insurance company.

Q. 2. Skidmore Trucking Company decided to expand its operations into the warehousing field. After examining several available properties, it decided to purchase a carbarn for $100,000 from a local bus company and to convert it into a warehouse. The standard real estate purchase contract was signed by the parties. The contract obligated Skidmore to pay the seller on an apportioned basis for the prepaid premiums on the existing fire insurance policy ($100,000 extended coverage). The policy expired 2 years and 1 month from the closing date.

At the closing the seller duly assigned the fire insurance policy to Skidmore in return for the payment of the apportioned amount of the prepaid premiums; but Barton W. Broxbury, the attorney for Skidmore, failed to notify the insurance company of the change in ownership.

Skidmore took possession of the premises and after extensive renovation began to use the building as a warehouse. Soon afterward one of Skidmore's employees negligently dropped a lighted cigarette into a trash basket and started a fire that totally destroyed the building.

Required

What are the legal problems and implications of these facts? Discuss.

Q. 3. Able and Baker are equal shareholders of the Alt Manufacturing Company, Inc., which owned a garage and storage facility that was used in its business. Title to this real property was recorded in the corporate name. Able and Baker purchased a fire insurance policy covering the building. They took out this policy in their own names as owners, rather than in the name of the Corporation, and personally paid the premiums due. The face value of the policy was $40,000, and it contained the standard 80% co-insurance clause. Filmore, an employee of the Corporation, negligently dropped his cigarette into a refuse receptacle and started a fire. The building was totally destroyed as a result of the fire. Subsequently Able and Baker assigned their rights under the policy to the Corporation. The fair market value of the property was admitted by all parties to be $100,000. The Corporation engaged a local CPA firm to examine its financial statements. During the audit a question has arisen as to how the insurance claim on the property should be treated. The Corporation asserts that on the basis of the facts, which are undisputed, the claim should be valued at the full face value of the policy, i.e., $40,000. The insurer denies all liability on the basis of (1) title being in the Corporation and not in the parties insuring and/or (2) the negligence of the Corporation's agent in causing the fire. As an alternative argument, the insurer asserts that even if it were found liable on the fire insurance policy, the amount recoverable is limited by the 80% coinsurance clause.

Required

1. In the absence of an assignment of their rights, were Able and Baker entitled to collect on the fire insurance policy? Explain.
2. Does the insurer's defense of negligence on the part of the Corporation's agent preclude recovery by the Corporation? Explain.
3. Assume that the insurance company is liable.
   (a) How does the co-insurance clause function and what is the purpose of this clause?
   (b) Will the co-insurance clause limit the amount of the Corporation's recovery? Explain.
4. Assume that the insurance company has satisfied a judgment obtained against it on the above claim. Will the insurance company have any rights against anyone to recover the amount paid? Explain.

Practice Objective Questions

Instructions 1–10

Select the *best* answer for each of the following items. Mark only one answer for *each* item. Answer all items. Your grade will be based on your total correct answers.

1. Which of the following statements *best* describes the insurable interest requirement?
   a. It is a historical anachronism and has little or no validity in modern times.
   b. It is identical for all types of insurance.
   c. It has been abolished by most modern insurance legislation in respect to fire insurance.
   d. At a minimum, it must exist at the time of the loss in respect to property insurance.

2. The usual fire insurance policy does *not*
   a. Have to meet the insurable interest test if this requirement is waived by the parties.
   b. Permit assignment of the policy prior to loss without the consent of the insurer.
   c. Provide for subrogation of the insurer to the insured's rights upon payment of the amount of the loss covered by the policy.
   d. Cover losses caused by the negligence of the insured's agent.

3. Peters leased a restaurant from Brady with all furnishings and fixtures for a period of five years with an option to renew for two additional years. Peters made several structural improvements and modifications to the interior of the building. He obtained a fire insurance policy for his own benefit insuring his interest in the property for $25,000. The restaurant was totally destroyed by an accidental fire. Peters seeks recovery from his insurer. Subject to policy limits, which of the following is correct?
   a. Peters is entitled to recover damages to the extent of the value of his leasehold interest.
   b. Peters is entitled to recover for lost profits due to the fire even though the policy is silent on the point.
   c. Peters must first seek redress from the owner before he is entitled to recover.
   d. Peters will *not* recover because he lacks the requisite insurable interest in the property.

4. Margo, Inc., insured its property against fire with two separate insurance companies, Excelsior and Wilberforce. Each carrier insured the property for its full value, and neither insurer was aware that the other had also insured the property. The policies were the standard fire insurance policies used throughout the United States. If the property is totally destroyed by fire, how much will Margo recover?
   a. Nothing, because Margo has engaged in an illegal gambling venture.
   b. The full amount from both insurers.
   c. A ratable or pro rata share from each insurer, *not* to exceed the value of the property insured.
   d. Only 80% of the value of the property from each insurer because of the standard coinsurance clause.

5. Stein bought an office building valued at $200,000. The fire insurance policy contained a 100% coinsurance clause. Stein insured the building for $120,000. Subsequently, a fire caused damage of $40,000 to the building. Which of the following is the correct amount Stein will recover?
   a. $40,000.
   b. $24,000.
   c. $13,333.
   d. Nothing because the building was *not* insured for 100% of its value.

6. Nabor, Inc., purchased a three-year fire insurance policy from the Fidelity Insurance Company covering its factory and warehouse. Which of the following statements is correct as a general rule of insurance law?
   a. The policy will *not* cover the intentional destruction of the property by a third party.
   b. The policy will *not* cover the destruction of the property if it is caused by the gross negligence of an employee of Nabor.
   c. If Nabor sells the insured property to a third party and assigns the insurance policy to the buyer, it continues in effect.
   d. If Nabor sells the insured property, but retains the fire insurance policy, it will *not* be able to collect on the policy in the event of its destruction by fire.

7. The partnership of Cox & Hayes, CPAs, is a medium-sized accounting firm. The senior staff member, Walton, is the office manager. The office building is owned by the partnership and title is duly recorded in the partnership name. With regard to life and property insurance, which of the following is true?

    a. Only the partnership, *not* the partners, has an insurable interest in the lives of the partners.

    b. The partnership does *not* have an insurable interest in the life of Walton because he is *not* a partner.

    c. Each individual partner has an insurable interest in the partnership property even though title to the property is in the partnership name.

    d. Only the partnership can insure the firm's office building against property damage.

8. Wexford Furniture, Inc., is in the retail furniture business and has stores located in principal cities in the United States. Its designers created a unique cocktail table. After obtaining prices and schedules, Wexford ordered 2,000 tables to be made to its design and specifications for sale as a part of its annual spring sales promotion campaign. Which of the following represents the earliest time Wexford will have an insurable interest in the tables?

    a. At the time the goods are in Wexford's possession.

    b. Upon shipment of conforming goods by the seller.

    c. When the goods are marked or otherwise designated by the seller as the goods to which the contract refers.

    d. At the time the contract is made.

9. Adams Company purchased a factory and warehouse from Martinson for $150,000. Adams obtained a $100,000 real estate mortgage loan from a local bank and was required by the lender to pay for the cost of title insurance covering the bank's interest in the property. In addition, Adams was required to obtain fire insurance sufficient to protect the bank against loss due to fire. The coinsurance factor has been satisfied. Under these circumstances, which of the following is correct?

    a. Adams can purchase only $50,000 of title insurance since it already obtained a $100,000 title policy for the bank equal to the bank loan.

    b. The bank could *not* have independently obtained a fire insurance policy on the property because Adams has legal title.

    c. If Adams obtained a $150,000 fire insurance policy which covered its interest and the bank's interest in the property and there is an estimated $50,000 of fire loss, the insurer will typically be obligated to pay the owner and the bank the amounts equal to their respective interests as they may appear.

    d. If Adams obtained a $100,000 fire insurance policy covering the bank's interest and $150,000 covering his own interest, each would obtain these amounts upon total destruction of the property.

10. Marcross Corporation owns a fleet of taxicabs it has insured with the Countrywide Insurance Company against liability and collision. Nabor, one of its drivers, deliberately backed one of the cabs into two other parked cabs in the corporation's garage after a heated dispute with the garage manager. While waiting for a traffic signal, another Marcross cab was hit in the rear by a negligently driven truck. Each cab involved had damages in excess of the minimum deductible.

    a. Marcross can recover against Countrywide for damages to all the cabs less the minimum deductible.

    b. Countrywide has *no* rights against Nabor.

    c. General creditors of Marcross could insure Marcross' cabs against collision and other types of loss because in the event of bankruptcy the creditors would have to resort to the corporation's property to satisfy their claims.

    d. Marcross must first sue the negligent truck driver, or his principal, for damages to its cab before it can collect against Countrywide.

II

An Illustrative Examination and Answers and a Practice Examination for the Candidate

Illustrative Examination and Answers in Business Law*

(Commercial Law)

Administered the first week of November and May of each year; 8:30 AM and 12:00 PM.

NOTE TO CANDIDATES: Suggested time allotments are as follows:

All questions are required:	Estimated Minimum	Minutes Maximum
No. 1	110	130
No. 2	15	20
No. 3	15	20
No. 4	15	20
No. 5	15	20
Total	170	210

---

*The attempt here is to construct realistic, whole examinations based upon the *AICPA Revised Content Specification Outlines,* effective May 1986. The above examination and the practice examination that follows have been created by your authors from pre-1980 AICPA examination questions. In respect to the content and the allocation, these questions are in conformity with what you might encounter in the May 1986 examination, based upon the AICPA Revised Content Specification Outline.

INSTRUCTIONS TO CANDIDATES

(Disregard of these instructions may be considered as indicating inefficiency in accounting work.)

1. You must arrange the papers in numerical order of the questions. If more than one page is required for an answer, write "continued" at the bottom of the page. Number pages consecutively. For instance, if 12 pages are used for your answers, the objective answer sheet is page 1 and your other pages should be numbered 2 through 12.
2. Answer **all** objective-type items on the printed answer sheet provided for that purpose. It is to your advantage to attempt all questions even if you are uncertain of the answer. You are likely to get the highest score if you omit no answers. Since objective items are computer-graded, your comments and calculations associated with them are not considered. Be certain that you have entered your answers on the objective answer sheet before the examination time is up.
3. A CPA is continually confronted with the necessity of expressing opinions and conclusions in written reports in clear, unequivocal language. Although the primary purpose of the examination is to test the candidate's knowledge and application of the subject matter, the ability to organize and present such knowledge in acceptable written language will be considered by the examiners.

Number 1 (Estimated time—110 to 130 minutes)

Instructions
Select the **best** answer for each of the following items. Use a soft pencil, preferably No. 2, to blacken the appropriate circle on the separate printed answer sheet to indicate your answer. **Mark only one answer for each item. Answer all items.** Your grade will be based on your total correct answers.

The following is an example of the manner in which the answer sheet should be marked:

Item
99. The text of the letter from Bridge Builders, Inc., to Allied Steel Co. follows:

> We offer to purchase 10,000 tons of No. 4 steel pipes at today's quoted price for delivery two months from today. Your acceptance must be received in five days.

> Bridge Builders intended to create a (an)
> a. Option contract.
> b. Unilateral contract.
> c. Bilateral contract.
> d. Joint contract.

Answer Sheet

99.

Items to be Answered
1. Who among the following can personally qualify as a holder in due course?
   a. A payee.
   b. A reacquirer who was not initially a holder in due course.
   c. A holder to whom the instrument was negotiated as a gift.
   d. A holder who had notice of a defect but who took from a prior holder in due course.

2. The Mechanics Bank refused to pay a check drawn upon it by Clyde, one of its depositors. Which of the reasons listed below is **not** a proper defense for the bank to assert when it refused to pay?
   a. The bank believed the check to be an overdraft as a result of its misdirecting a deposit made by Clyde.
   b. The required indorsement of an intermediary transferee was missing.
   c. Clyde had orally stopped payment on the check.
   d. The party attempting to cash the check did not have proper identification.

3. Your client, Globe, Inc., has in its possession an undated instrument which is payable 30 days after date. It is believed that the instrument was issued on or about August 10, 1980, by Dixie Manufacturing, Inc., to Harding Enterprises in payment of goods purchased. On August 13, 1980, it was negotiated to Desert Products, Inc., and thereafter to Globe on the 15th. Globe took for value, in good faith and without notice of any defense. It has been learned that the goods shipped by Harding to Dixie are defective. Which of the following is correct?
   a. Since the time of payment is indefinite, the instrument is nonnegotiable and Globe can **not** qualify as a holder in due course.
   b. By issuing an undated instrument payable 30 days after date, Dixie was reserving the right to avoid liability on it until it filled in or authorized the filling in of the date.
   c. Since the defense involves a rightful rejection of the goods delivered, it is valid against Globe.
   d. Globe can validly fill in the date and will qualify as a holder in due course.

4. A CPA's client has an instrument which contains certain ambiguities or deficiencies. In construing the instrument, which of the following is **incorrect?**
   a. Where there is doubt whether the instrument is a draft or a note, the holder may treat it as either.
   b. Handwritten terms control typewritten and printed terms, and typewritten terms control printed terms.
   c. An instrument which is payable only upon the happening of an event that is uncertain as to the time of its occurrence is payable at a definite time if the event has occurred.
   d. The fact that the instrument is antedated will not affect the instrument's negotiability.

5. Smith buys a TV set from the ABC Appliance Store and pays for the set with a check. Later in the day Smith finds a better model for the same price at another store. Smith immediately calls ABC trying to cancel the sale. ABC tells Smith that they are holding him to the sale and have negotiated the check to their wholesaler, Glenn Company, as a partial payment on inventory purchases. Smith telephones his bank, the Union Trust Bank, and orders the bank to stop payment on the check. Which of the following statements is correct?
   a. If Glenn can prove it is a holder in due course, the drawee bank, Union Trust, must honor Smith's check.
   b. Union Trust is **not** bound or liable for Smith's stop payment order unless the order is placed in writing.
   c. If Union Trust mistakenly pays Smith's check two days after receiving the stop order, the bank will **not** be liable.
   d. Glenn can **not** hold Smith liable on the check.

6. Marshall Franks purchased $1,050 worth of inventory for his business from Micro Enterprises. Micro insisted on the signature of Franks' former partner, Hobart, before credit would be extended. Hobart reluctantly signed. Franks delivered the following instrument to Micro:

January 15, 1980

We, the undersigned, do hereby promise to pay to the order of Micro Enterprises, Inc., One Thousand and Fifty Dollars ($1,050.00) on the 15th of April, 1980.

Marshall Franks
Marshall Franks

Norman Hobart
Norman Hobart

Memo:
N. Hobart signed as an
accommodation for Franks

Franks defaulted on the due date. Which of the following is correct?

a. The instrument is nonnegotiable.

b. Hobart is liable on the instrument but only for $525.

c. Since it was known to Micro that Hobart signed as an accommodation party, Micro must first proceed against Franks.

d. Hobart is liable on the instrument for the full amount and is obligated to satisfy it immediately upon default.

7. Rapid Delivery, Inc., has in its possession the following instrument which it purchased for value.

March 1, 1980

Thirty days from date, I, Harold Kales, do hereby promise to pay Ronald Green four hundred dollars and no cents ($400.00). This note is given for value received.

Harold Kales
Harold Kales

Which of the following is correct?

a. The instrument is negotiable.

b. The instrument is nonnegotiable, and therefore Rapid has obtained no rights on the instrument.

c. Rapid is an assignee of the instrument and has the same rights as the assignor had on it.

d. The instrument is nontransferable on its face.

8. Harrison obtained from Bristow his $11,500 check drawn on the Union National Bank in payment for bogus uranium stock. He immediately negotiated it by a blank indorsement to Dunlop in return for $1,000 in cash and her check for $10,400. Dunlop qualified as a holder in due course. She deposited the check in her checking account in the Oceanside Bank. Upon discovering that the stock was bogus, Bristow notified Union National to stop payment on his check, which it did. The check was returned to Oceanside Bank, which in turn debited Dunlop's account and returned the check to her. Which of the following statements is correct?

a. Dunlop can collect from Union National Bank since Bristow's stop payment order was invalid in that the defense was only a personal defense.

b. Oceanside's debiting of Dunlop's account was improper since she qualified as a holder in due course.

c. Dunlop can recover $11,500 from Bristow despite the stop order, since she qualified as a holder in due course.

d. Dunlop will be entitled to collect only $1,000.

9. An otherwise valid negotiable bearer note is signed with the forged signature of Darby. Archer, who believed he knew Darby's signature, bought the note in good faith from Harding, the forger. Archer transferred the note without indorsement to Barker, in partial payment of a debt. Barker then sold the note to Chase for 80% of its face amount and delivered it without indorsement. When Chase presented the note for payment at maturity, Darby refused to honor it, pleading forgery. Chase gave proper notice of dishonor to Barker and to Archer. Which of the following statements **best** describes the situation from Chase's standpoint?

a. Chase can **not** qualify as a holder in due course for the reason that he did **not** pay face value for the note.

b. Chase can hold Barker liable on the ground that Barker warranted to Chase that neither Darby nor Archer had any defense valid against Barker.

c. Chase can hold Archer liable on the ground that Archer warranted to Chase that Darby's signature was genuine.

d. Chase can **not** hold Harding, the forger, liable on the note because his signature does **not** appear on it and thus, he made no warranties to Chase.

10. Hargrove lost some stock certificates of the Apex Corporation which were registered in his name, but which he had indorsed in blank. Flagg found the securities and sold them through a brokerage house to Waldorf. Apex, unaware of Hargrove's problem, transferred them to Waldorf. Hargrove is seeking to recover the securities or damages for their value. Which of the following is correct?

a. The stock in question is transferable but Waldorf takes subject to Hargrove's claim of title.

b. Waldorf is a holder in due course of a negotiable instrument and therefore will prevail.

c. Apex is liable for wrongfully transferring Hargrove's stock to Waldorf.

d. Waldorf qualifies as a bona fide purchaser and acquires the stock free of Hargrove's adverse claim.

11. Base Electric Co. has entered an agreement to buy its actual requirements of copper wiring for six months from the Seymour Metal Wire Company and Seymour Metal has agreed to sell all the copper wiring Base will require for six months. The agreement between the two companies is

a. Unenforceable because it is too indefinite.

b. Unenforceable because it lacks mutuality of obligation.

c. Unenforceable because of lack of consideration.

d. Valid and enforceable.

12. Gibbeon Manufacturing shipped 300 designer navy blue blazers to Custom Clothing Emporeum. The blazers arrived on Friday, earlier than Custom had anticipated and on an exceptionally busy day for its receiving department. They were perfunctorily examined and sent to a nearby warehouse for storage until needed. On Monday of the following week, upon closer examination, it was discovered that the quality of the linings of the blazers was inferior to that specified in the sales contract. Which of the following is correct insofar as Custom's rights are concerned?

a. Custom can reject the blazers upon subsequent discovery of the defects.

b. Custom must retain the blazers since it accepted them and had an opportunity to inspect them upon delivery.

c. Custom's only course of action is rescission.

d. Custom had no rights if the linings were of merchantable quality.

13. The Balboa Custom Furniture Company sells fine custom furniture. It has been encountering difficulties lately with some customers who have breached their contracts after the furniture they have selected has been customized to their order or the fabric they have selected has been cut or actually installed on the piece of furniture purchased. The company therefore wishes to resort to a liquidated damages clause in its sales contract to encourage performance or provide an acceptable amount of damages. Regarding Balboa's contemplated resort to a liquidated damages clause, which of the following is correct?

a. Balboa may not use a liquidated damages clause since it is a merchant and is the preparer of the contract.

b. Balboa can simply take a very large deposit which will be forfeited if performance by a customer is not made for any reason.

c. The amount of the liquidated damages stipulated in the contract must be reasonable in light of the anticipated or actual harm caused by the breach.

d. Even if Balboa uses a liquidated damages clause in its sales contract, it will nevertheless have to establish that the liquidated damages claimed did not exceed actual damages by more than 10%.

14. Fernandez is planning to attend an auction of the assets of Cross & Black, one of his major competitors who is liquidating. In the conduct of the auction, which of the following rules applies?

a. Such a sale is without reserve unless the goods are explicitly put up with reserve.

b. A bidder may retract his bid at any time until the falling of the hammer.

c. The retraction of a bid by a bidder revives the previous bid.

d. If the auction is without reserve, the auctioneer can withdraw the article at any time prior to the fall of the hammer.

15. Joseph Manufacturing, Inc., received an order from Raulings Supply Company for certain valves it manufactured. The order called for prompt shipment. In respect to Joseph's options as to the manner of acceptance, which of the following is **incorrect?**

a. Joseph can accept only by prompt shipment since this was the manner indicated in the order.

b. The order is construed as an offer to enter into either a unilateral or bilateral contract and Joseph may accept by a promise of or prompt shipment.

c. If Joseph promptly ships the goods, Raulings must be notified within a reasonable time.

d. Joseph may accept by mail, but he must make prompt shipment.

16. Which of the following requirements must be met for modification of a sales contract under the Uniform Commercial Code?

   a. There must be consideration present if the contract is between merchants.

   b. There must be a writing if the original sales contract is in writing.

   c. The modification must satisfy the Statute of Frauds if the contract as modified is within its provisions.

   d. The parol evidence rule applies and thus a writing is required.

17. Barstow Hardware Company received an order for $850 of assorted hardware from Flanagan & Company. The shipping terms were F.O.B. Mannix Freight Line, seller's place of business, 2/10, net/30. Barstow packed and crated the hardware for shipment and it was loaded upon Mannix Freight's truck. While the goods were in transit to Flanagan, Barstow learned that Flanagan was insolvent in the equity sense (unable to pay its debts in the ordinary course of business). Barstow promptly wired Mannix Freight's office in Pueblo, Colorado, and instructed them to stop shipment of the goods to Flanagan and to store them until further instructions. Mannix complied with these instructions. Regarding the rights, duties, and liabilities of the parties, which of the following is correct?

   a. Barstow's stoppage in transit was improper if Flanagan's assets exceeded its liabilities.

   b. Flanagan is entitled to the hardware if it pays cash.

   c. Once Barstow correctly learned of Flanagan's insolvency, it had no further duty or obligation to Flanagan.

   d. The fact that Flanagan became insolvent in no way affects the rights, duties, and obligations of the parties.

18. Marsh and Lennon entered into an all inclusive written contract involving the purchase of a tract of land. Lennon claims that there was a contemporaneous oral agreement between the parties which called for the removal by Marsh of several large rocks on the land. Marsh relies upon the parol evidence rule to avoid having to remove the rocks. Which of the following is correct?

   a. The parol evidence rule does **not** apply to contemporaneous oral agreements.

   b. Since the statute of frauds was satisfied in respect to the contract for the purchase of the land, the parol evidence rule does **not** apply.

   c. Since the oral agreement does not contradict the terms of the written contract, the oral agreement is valid despite the parol evidence rule.

   d. The parol evidence rule applies and Lennon will be precluded from proving the oral promise in the absence of fraud.

19. Perone was a member of Cass, Hack & Perone, a general trading partnership. He died on August 2, 1980. The partnership is insolvent, but Perone's estate is substantial. The creditors of the partnership are seeking to collect on their claims from Perone's estate. Which of the following statements is correct insofar as their claims are concerned?

   a. The death of Perone caused a dissolution of the firm, thereby freeing his estate from personal liability.

   b. If the existing obligations to Perone's personal creditors are all satisfied, then the remaining estate assets are available to satisfy partnership debts.

   c. The creditors must first proceed against the remaining partners before Perone's estate can be held liable for the partnership's debts.

   d. The liability of Perone's estate can **not** exceed his capital contribution plus that percentage of the deficit attributable to his capital contribution.

20. The partnership agreement of one of your clients provides that upon death or withdrawal, a partner shall be entitled to the book value of his or her partnership interest as of the close of the year preceding such death or withdrawal and nothing more. It also provides that the partnership shall continue. Regarding this partnership provision, which of the following is a correct statement?

   a. It is unconscionable on its face.

   b. It has the legal effect of preventing a dissolution upon the death or withdrawal of a partner.

   c. It effectively eliminates the legal necessity of a winding up of the partnership upon the death or withdrawal of a partner.

   d. It is **not** binding upon the spouse of a deceased partner if the book value figure is less than the fair market value at the date of death.

21. Watson decided to withdraw from the Sterling Enterprises Partnership. Watson found Holmes as a prospective purchaser and his successor as a partner in the partnership. The other partners agreed to admit Holmes as a general partner in Watson's place. As a part of the agreement between Watson and Holmes, Holmes promised to satisfy any

prior partnership debts for which Watson might be liable. What potential liability does Holmes or Watson have to firm creditors?

a. Holmes has no liability for the obligations arising before he entered the partnership.

b. Holmes is liable for the obligations arising before he entered the partnership, but only to the extent of partnership property.

c. Holmes is fully liable to firm creditors for liabilities occurring before and after his entry into the partnership.

d. Watson's liability to firm creditors has been extinguished.

22. One of your audit clients, Major Supply, Inc., is seeking a judgment against Danforth on the basis of a representation made by one Coleman, in Danforth's presence, that they were in partnership together doing business as the D & C Trading Partnership. Major Supply received an order from Coleman on behalf of D & C and shipped $800 worth of goods to Coleman. Coleman has defaulted on payment of the bill and is insolvent. Danforth denies he is Coleman's partner and that he has any liability for the goods. Insofar as Danforth's liability is concerned, which of the following is correct?

a. Danforth is **not** liable if he is **not** in fact Coleman's partner.

b. Since Danforth did **not** make the statement about being Coleman's partner, he is **not** liable.

c. If Major Supply gave credit in reliance upon the misrepresentation made by Coleman, Danforth is a partner by estoppel.

d. Since the "partnership" is operating under a fictitious name (the D & C Partnership) a filing is required and Major Supply's failure to ascertain whether there was in fact such a partnership precludes it from recovering.

23. In the course of your audit of James Fine, doing business as Fine's Apparels, a sole proprietorship, you discovered that in the past year Fine had regularly joined with Charles Walters in the marketing of bathing suits and beach accessories. You are concerned whether Fine and Walters have created a partnership relationship. Which of the following factors is the **most** important in ascertaining this status?

a. The fact that a partnership agreement is **not** in existence.

b. The fact that each has a separate business of his own which he operates independently.

c. The fact that Fine and Walters divide the net profits equally on a quarterly basis.

d. The fact that Fine and Walters did **not** intend to be partners.

24. Ms. Walls is a limited partner of the Amalgamated Limited Partnership. She is insolvent and her debts exceed her assets by $28,000. Goldsmith, one of Walls' largest creditors, is resorting to legal process to obtain the payment of Walls' debt to him. Goldsmith has obtained a charging order against Walls' limited partnership interest for the unsatisfied amount of the debt. As a result of Goldsmith's action, which of the following will happen?

a. The partnership will be dissolved.

b. Walls' partnership interest must be redeemed with partnership property.

c. Goldsmith automatically becomes a substituted limited partner.

d. Goldsmith becomes in effect an assignee of Walls' partnership interest.

25. Wallers and Company has decided to expand the scope of its business. In this connection, it contemplates engaging several agents. Which of the following agency relationships is within the Statute of Frauds and thus should be contained in a signed writing?

a. An irrevocable agency.

b. A sales agency where the agent normally will sell goods which have a value in excess of $500.

c. An agency for the forthcoming calendar year which is entered into in mid-December of the prior year.

d. An agency which is of indefinite duration but which is terminable upon one month's notice.

26. A power of attorney is a useful method of creation of an agency relationship. The power of attorney

a. Must be signed by both the principal and the agent.

b. Exclusively determines the purpose and powers of the agent.

c. Is the written authorization of the agent to act on the principal's behalf.

d. Is used primarily in the creation of the attorney-client relationship.

27. Agents sometimes have liability to third parties for their actions taken for and on behalf of the principal. An agent will **not** be personally liable in which of the following circumstances?

a. If he makes a contract which he had no authority to make but which the principal ratifies.

b. If he commits a tort while engaged in the principal's business.

    c. If he acts for a principal which he knows is nonexistent and the third party is unaware of this.

    d. If he acts for an undisclosed principal as long as the principal is subsequently disclosed.

28. Mayberry engaged Williams as her agent. It was mutually agreed that Williams would **not** disclose that he was acting as Mayberry's agent. Instead he was to deal with prospective customers as if he were a principal acting on his own behalf. This he did and made several contracts for Mayberry. Assuming Mayberry, Williams or the customer seeks to avoid liability on one of the contracts involved, which of the following statements is correct?

    a. Williams has **no** liability once he discloses that Mayberry was the real principal.

    b. Mayberry must ratify the Williams contracts in order to be held liable.

    c. The third party may choose to hold either Williams or Mayberry liable.

    d. The third party can avoid liability because he believed he was dealing with Williams as a principal.

29. Park Manufacturing hired Stone as a traveling salesman to sell goods manufactured by Park. Stone also sold a line of products manufactured by a friend. He did **not** disclose this to Park. The relationship was unsatisfactory and Park finally fired Stone after learning of Stone's sales of the other manufacturer's goods. Stone, enraged at Park for firing him, continued to make contracts on Park's behalf with both new and old customers that were almost uniformly disadvantageous to Park. Park, upon learning of this, gave written notice of Stone's discharge to all parties with whom Stone had dealt. Which of the following statements is **incorrect?**

    a. Park can bring an action against Stone to have him account for any secret profits.

    b. Prior to notification, Stone retained some continued authority to bind Park despite termination of the agency relationship.

    c. New customers who contracted with Stone for the first time could enforce the contracts against Park if they knew that Stone had been Park's salesman but were unaware that Stone was fired.

    d. If Park had promptly published a notification of termination of Stone's employment in the local newspapers and in the trade publications, he would **not** be liable for any of Stone's contracts.

30. Michaels appointed Fairfax as his agent. The appointment was in writing and clearly indicated the scope of Fairfax's authority and also that Fairfax was **not** to disclose that he was acting as an agent for Michaels. Under the circumstances

    a. Fairfax is an agent coupled with an interest.

    b. Michaels must ratify any contracts made by Fairfax on behalf of Michaels.

    c. Fairfax's appointment had to be in writing to be enforceable.

    d. Fairfax has the implied and apparent authority of an agent.

31. In the course of an examination of the financial statements of Control Finance Company for the year ended September 30, 1980, the auditors learned that the company has just taken possession of certain heavy industrial equipment from Arrow Manufacturing Company, a debtor in default. Arrow had previously borrowed $60,000 from Control secured by a security interest in the heavy industrial equipment. The amount of the loan outstanding is $30,000. Which of the following is correct regarding the rights of Control and Arrow?

    a. Control is **not** permitted to sell the repossessed equipment at private sale.

    b. Arrow has **no** right to redeem the collateral at any time once possession has been taken.

    c. Control is **not** entitled to retain the collateral it has repossessed in satisfaction of the debt even though it has given written notice to the debtor and he consents.

    d. Arrow is **not** entitled to a compulsory disposition of the collateral.

32. The Jolly Finance Company provides the financing for Triple J Appliance Company's inventory. As a part of its sales promotion and public relations campaign, Jolly Finance placed posters in Triple J's stores indicating that Triple J is another satisfied customer of Jolly and that the goods purchased at Triple J are available through the financing by Jolly. Jolly also files a financing statement which covers the financed inventory. Victor Restaurants purchased four hi-fi sets for use in its restaurants and had read one of the Jolly posters. Triple J has defaulted on its loan and Jolly Finance is seeking to repossess the hi-fi sets. Which of the following is correct?

    a. Jolly has a perfected security interest in the hi-fi sets which is good against Victor.

    b. Victor's knowledge of the financing arrangement between Jolly and Triple J does **not** affect its rights to the hi-fi sets.

    c. Jolly's filing was unnecessary to perfect its security interest in Triple J's inventory since it was perfected upon attachment.

     d. The hi-fi sets are consumer goods in Victor's hands.

33. The Gordon Manufacturing Company manufactures various types of lathes. It sold on credit 25 general-use lathes to Hardware City, a large retail outlet. Hardware City sold one of the lathes to Johnson for use in his home repair business, reserving a security interest for the unpaid balance. However, Hardware City did **not** file a financing statement. Johnson's creditors are asserting rights against the lathe. Which of the following statements is correct?

     a. The lathe is a consumer good in Johnson's hands.

     b. No filing was necessary to perfect a security interest in the lathe against Johnson's creditors.

     c. Gordon Manufacturing could assert rights against the lathe sold to Johnson in the event Hardware City defaults in its payments.

     d. The lathe was inventory in both Gordon and Hardware's hands and is equipment in Johnson's, and both Gordon and Hardware City must file to perfect their interests.

34. The Town Bank makes collateralized loans to its customers at 1% above prime on securities owned by the customer, subject to existing margin requirements. In doing so, which of the following is correct?

     a. Notification of the issuer is necessary in order to perfect a security interest.

     b. Filing is a permissible method of perfecting a security interest in the securities if the circumstances dictate.

     c. Any dividend or interest distributions during the term of the loan belong to the bank.

     d. A perfected security interest in the securities can only be obtained by possession.

35. Bass, an automobile dealer, had an inventory of 40 cars and 10 trucks. He financed the purchase of this inventory with County Bank under an agreement dated July 7 that gave the bank a security interest in all vehicles on Bass' premises, all future acquired vehicles, and the proceeds thereof. On July 11, County Bank properly filed a financing statement that identified the collateral in the same way that it was identified in the agreement. On October 1, Bass sold a passenger car to Dodd for family use and a truck to Diamond Company for its hardware business. Which of the following is correct?

     a. The security agreement may **not** provide for a security interest in future acquired vehicles even if the parties agree.

     b. The passenger car sold by Bass to Dodd continues to be subject to the security interest of the County Bank.

     c. The bank's security interest is perfected as of July 7, despite the fact it was **not** filed until July 11.

     d. The security interest of the County Bank does **not** include the proceeds from the sale of the truck to Diamond Company.

36. Retailer Corp. was in need of financing. To secure a loan, it made an oral assignment of its accounts receivable to J. Roe, a local investor, under which Roe loaned Retailer on a continuing basis, 90% of the face value of the assigned accounts receivable. Retailer collected from the account debtors and remitted to Roe at intervals. Before the debt was paid, Retailer filed a petition in bankruptcy. Which of the following is correct?

     a. As between the account debtors and Roe, the assignment is **not** an enforceable security interest.

     b. Roe is a secured creditor to the extent of the unpaid debt.

     c. Other unpaid creditors of Retailer Corp. who knew of the assignment are bound by its terms.

     d. An assignment of accounts, to be valid, requires the debtors owing the accounts to be notified.

37. The Secured Transactions Article of the Code recognizes various methods of perfecting a security interest in collateral. Which of the following is **not** recognized by the Code?

     a. Filing.

     b. Possession.

     c. Consent.

     d. Attachment.

38. Which of the following is included within the scope of the Secured Transactions Article of the Code?

     a. The outright sale of accounts receivable.

     b. A landlord's lien.

     c. The assignment of a claim for wages.

     d. The sale of chattel paper as a part of the sale of a business out of which it arose.

39. The Securities Exchange Act of 1934 requires that certain persons register and that the securities of certain issuers be registered. In respect to such registration under the 1934 Act, which of the following statements is **incorrect**?

    a. All securities offered under the Securities Act of 1933 also must be registered under the 1934 Act.

    b. National securities exchanges must register.

    c. The equity securities of issuers, which are traded on a national securities exchange, must be registered.

    d. The equity securities of issuers having in excess of $1 million in assets and 500 or more stockholders which are traded in interstate commerce must be registered.

40. Of the following securities transactions, which is exempt from federal securities regulation?

    a. An offering of $100,000 of corporate bonds.

    b. The sale of $1 million of limited partnership interests.

    c. A secondary offering of stock that had been previously registered.

    d. The sale of $500,000 of common stock to a single sophisticated purchaser for investment purposes.

41. Marvel Corporation has decided to make an offering of its securities to raise additional capital. It plans to issue 30,000 shares of its common stock at $20 a share and to restrict the offer to its existing stockholders, customers, employees, retired employees, and relatives of such people. The securities will be offered to fewer than 500 people, and it is expected that only 300 people will actually make purchases. The Marvel Corporation does business in a tri-state area.

    a. A registration statement need not be filed with the Securities and Exchange Commission because the amount of the transaction is less than $1 million.

    b. No registration is required because the number of people who will purchase the shares is small and select.

    c. Marvel must file a registration statement since the offering is a public offering involving interstate commerce.

    d. If the 30,000 shares are treasury stock for which a registration statement previously had been filed, no additional registration is required.

42. Which of the following statements concerning the scope of Section 10(b) of the Securities Exchange Act of 1934 is correct?

    a. In order to come within its scope, a transaction must have taken place on a national stock exchange.

    b. It applies exclusively to securities of corporations registered under the Securities Exchange Act of 1934.

    c. There is an exemption from its application for securities registered under the Securities Act of 1933.

    d. It applies to purchases as well as sales of securities in interstate commerce.

43. Which of the following statements is correct regarding qualification for the private placement exemption from registration under the Securities Act of 1933?

    a. The instrumentalities of interstate commerce must **not** be used.

    b. The securities must be offered to **not** more than 35 persons.

    c. The minimum amount of securities purchased by each offeree must not be less than $100,000.

    d. The offerees **must** have access to or be furnished with the kind of information that would be available in a registration statement.

44. The Foreign Corrupt Practices Act of 1977 prohibits bribery of foreign officials. Which of the following statements correctly describes the Act's application to corporations engaging in such practices?

    a. It only applies to multinational corporations.

    b. It applies to all domestic corporations engaged in interstate commerce.

    c. It only applies to corporations whose securities are registered under the Securities Exchange Act of 1934.

    d. It applies only to corporations engaged in foreign commerce.

45. The Marquis Trust has been properly created and it qualifies as a real estate investment trust (REIT) for federal income tax purposes. As such, it will

    a. Be taxed as any other trust for income tax purposes.

    b. Have been created under the Federal Trust Indenture Act.

    c. Provide limited liability for the parties investing in the trust.

    d. Be exempt from the Securities Act of 1933.

46. Anderson agreed to purchase Parker's real property. Anderson's purchase was dependent upon his being able to sell certain real property that he owned. Anderson gave Parker an instrument for the purchase price. Assuming the instrument is otherwise negotiable, which one of the statements below, written on the face of the instrument, will render it nonnegotiable?

a. A statement that Parker's cashing or indorsing the instrument acknowledges full satisfaction of Anderson's obligation.

b. A statement that payment of the instrument is contingent upon Anderson's sale of his real property.

c. A statement that the instrument is secured by a first mortgage on Parker's property and that upon default in payment the entire amount of the instrument is due.

d. A statement that the instrument is subject to the usual implied and constructive conditions applicable to such transactions.

47. Gilgo has entered into a contract for the purchase of land from the Wicklow Land Company. A title search reveals certain defects in the title to the land to be conveyed by Wicklow. Wicklow has demanded that Gilgo accept the deed and pay the balance of the purchase price. Furthermore, Wicklow has informed Gilgo that unless Gilgo proceeds with the closing, Wicklow will hold Gilgo liable for breach of contract. Wicklow has pointed out to Gilgo that the contract says nothing about defects and that he must take the property "as is." Which of the following is correct?

a. Gilgo can rely on the implied warranty of merchantability.

b. Wicklow is right in that if there is **no** express warranty against title defects, none exists.

c. Gilgo will prevail because he is entitled to a perfect title from Wicklow.

d. Gilgo will win if the title is **not** marketable.

48. Marks is a commercial tenant of Tudor Buildings, Inc. The term of the lease is five years and two years have elapsed. The lease prohibits subletting, but does **not** contain any provision relating to assignment. Marks approached Tudor and asked whether Tudor could release him from the balance of the term of the lease for $500. Tudor refused unless Marks would agree to pay $2,000. Marks located Flint who was interested in renting in Tudor's building and transferred the entire balance of the lease to Flint in consideration of his promise to pay Tudor the monthly rental and otherwise perform Marks' obligations under the lease. Tudor objects. Which of the following statements is correct?

a. A prohibition of the right to sublet contained in the lease completely prohibits an assignment.

b. The assignment need **not** be in writing.

c. The assignment does **not** extinguish Marks' obligation to pay the rent if Flint defaults.

d. The assignment is invalid without Tudor's consent.

49. James Gordon decided to create an inter vivos trust for the benefit of his grandchildren. Gordon wished to bypass his own children and to provide an independent income for his grandchildren. He did not, however, wish to completely part with the assets he would transfer to the trust. Therefore, he transferred the assets to the York Trust Company in trust for the benefit of his grandchildren irrevocably for a period of 21 years. In relation to the Gordon trust and the rights and duties of the parties in respect to it.

a. Such a trust is quite useful in skipping generations and tying up the ownership of property, since its duration can be potentially infinite.

b. The trust is **not** recognized as a legal entity for tax purposes, thus Gordon must include the trust income with his own.

c. York has legal title to the trust property, the grandchildren have equitable title, and Gordon has a reversionary interest.

d. If the trust deed is silent on the point, York must **not** sell or otherwise dispose of the trust assets without Gordon's advice and consent.

50. Paul Good's will left all of his commercial real property to his wife Dorothy for life and the remainder to his two daughters, Joan and Doris, as tenants in common. All beneficiaries are alive and over 21 years of age. Regarding the rights of the parties, which of the following is a correct statement?

a. Dorothy may **not** elect to take against the will and receive a statutory share instead.

b. The daughters **must** survive Dorothy in order to receive any interest in the property.

c. Either of the daughters may sell her interest in the property without the consent of their mother or the other daughter.

d. If only one daughter is alive upon the death of Dorothy, she is entitled to the entire property.

51. Larson is considering the creation of either a lifetime (inter vivos) or testamentary (by his will) trust. In deciding what to do, which of the following statements is correct?

    a. If the trust is an inter vivos trust, the trustee must file papers in the appropriate state office roughly similar to those required to be filed by a corporation to qualify.

    b. An inter vivos trust must meet the same legal requirements as one created by a will.

    c. Property transferred to a testamentary trust upon the grantor's (creator's) death is **not** included in the decedent's gross estate for federal tax purposes.

    d. Larson can retain the power to revoke an inter vivos trust.

52. An executor named in a decedent's will

    a. Must consent to serve, have read the will, and be present at the execution of the will.

    b. Need **not** serve if he does **not** wish to do so.

    c. Must serve without compensation unless the will provides otherwise.

    d. Can **not** be the principal beneficiary of the will.

53. Bernard Manufacturing, Inc., owns a three-story building which it recently purchased. The purchase price was $200,000 of which $160,000 was financed by the proceeds of a mortgage loan from the Cattleman Savings and Loan Association. Bernard immediately procured a standard fire insurance policy on the premises for $200,000 from the Magnificent Insurance Company. Cattleman also took out fire insurance of $160,000 on the property from the Reliable Insurance Company of America. The property was subsequently totally destroyed as a result of a fire which started in an adjacent loft and spread to Bernard's building. Insofar as the rights and duties of Bernard, Cattleman, and the insurers are concerned, which of the following is a correct statement?

    a. Cattleman Savings and Loan lacks the requisite insurable interest to collect on its policy.

    b. Bernard Manufacturing can only collect $40,000.

    c. Reliable Insurance Company is subrogated to Cattleman's rights against Bernard upon payment of Cattleman's insurance claim.

    d. The maximum amount that Bernard Manufacturing can collect from Magnificent is $40,000, the value of its insurable interest.

54. Real Life Insurance Company has refused to pay on a $50,000 term life insurance policy taken out by Dodson. The circumstances surrounding Dodson's procuring the policy are as follows: Maxwell, an acquaintance of Dodson's, contacted him one day and asked him if he would like to make $100. Dodson said, "Sure, as long as it is easy money." Maxwell assured Dodson that the only thing Dodson had to do was sign an application for insurance, submit to a physical, name Maxwell as the benificiary, and subsequently assign the policy to Maxwell. Maxwell paid Dodson the $100 and reimbursed him for the premium. Two years after taking out the policy, Dodson died. Maxwell presented the policy to Real Life for payment and it refused to pay. Which of the following is correct?

    a. Real Life must pay the $50,000 to Maxwell since he is the beneficiary.

    b. Dodson's estate is entitled to the $50,000 proceeds of the life insurance policy.

    c. Maxwell will recover the $50,000 since the policy was assigned to him.

    d. Maxwell will recover nothing in that he lacked an insurable interest in Dodson's life.

55. Morse is seeking to collect on a property insurance policy covering certain described property which was destroyed. The insurer has denied recovery based upon Morse's alleged lack of an insurable interest in the property. In which of the situations described below will the insurance company prevail?

    a. The property has been willed to Morse's father for life and, upon his father's death, to Morse as the remainderman.

    b. The insured property does **not** belong to Morse, but instead to a corporation which he controls.

    c. Morse is **not** the owner of the insured property but a mere long-term lessee.

    d. The insured property belongs to a general trade debtor of Morse and the debt is unsecured.

56. Which of the following represents the basic distinction between a bilateral contract and a unilateral contract?

    a. Specific performance is available if the contract is unilateral whereas it is **not** if the contract is bilateral.

    b. There is only one promise involved if the contract is unilateral whereas there are two promises if the contract is bilateral.

    c. The statute of frauds applies to a bilateral contract but **not** to a unilateral contract.

    d. The rights under a bilateral contract are assignable whereas rights under a unilateral contract are **not** assignable.

57. The usual fire insurance policy does **not**

    a. Have to meet the insurable interest test if this requirement is waived by the parties.

   b. Provide for subrogation of the insurer to the insured's rights upon payment of the amount of the loss covered by the policy.

   c. Cover losses caused by the negligence of the insured's agent.

   d. Permit assignment of the policy prior to loss without the consent of the insurer.

58. Ichi Ban Mopeds, Inc., is a Japanese manufacturer which has a manufacturing facility in the United States. United States business comprises ten percent (10%) of the sales of Ichi Ban of which four percent (4%) is manufactured at its United States facility. Under these circumstances

   a. Ichi Ban is exempt from state workmen's compensation laws.

   b. Ichi Ban is exempt from the Fair Labor Standards Act provided it is governed by comparable Japanese law.

   c. Ichi Ban is subject to generally prevailing federal and state laws applicable to American employees with respect to its employees at the United States facility.

   d. Ichi Ban could legally institute a policy which limited promotions to Japanese-Americans.

59. Harris was engaged as a crane operator by the Wilcox Manufacturing Corporation, a company complying with state worker's compensation laws. Harris suffered injuries during regular working hours as a result of carelessly climbing out on the arm of the crane to make an adjustment. While doing so, he lost his balance, fell off the arm of the crane and fractured his leg. Wilcox's safety manual for the operation of the crane strictly forbids such conduct by an operator. Wilcox denies any liability, based upon Harris' gross negligence, his disobedience and a waiver of all liability signed by Harris shortly after the accident. Wilcox further asserts that Harris is **not** entitled to worker's compensation because he is a skilled worker and is on a guaranteed biweekly salary. Which of the following is a correct statement insofar as Harris' rights are concerned?

   a. If he elects to sue under common law for negligence, his own negligence will result in a denial of recovery.

   b. Harris is **not** entitled to worker's compensation because he is **not** an "employee."

   c. Harris is **not** entitled to recovery because his conduct was a clear violation of the safety manual.

   d. Harris waived his rights by signing a waiver of liability.

60. Which of the following is a correct statement regarding the federal income tax treatment of social security tax payments and retirement benefits?

   a. The employer's social security tax payments are **not** deductible from its gross income.

   b. Social security retirement benefits are fully includable in the gross income of the retiree if he earns an amount in excess of certain established ceilings.

   c. Social security retirement benefits are excludable from the retiree's gross income even if the retiree has recouped all he has contributed.

   d. The employee's social security tax payments are deductible from the employee's gross income.

Number 2 (Estimated time—15 to 20 minutes)

Part a. The Dexter Corporation has not paid a dividend since 1970 on its 7% noncumulative preferred stock. In the years 1970–1973 the company had net losses which threatened to impair its financial position. Since 1974 the company has had earnings sufficient to pay the preferred stock dividend. In fact, earnings have gradually increased since 1974, and by 1976 Dexter had recouped all losses which occurred in the years 1970–1973. During the years 1974–1979 the profits were credited to retained earnings.

   The funds were neither committed to physical plant or equipment nor did the board indicate that it had long range plans calling for such a commitment. Preferred shareholders had complained at board meetings regarding the repeated passing over of preferred dividends. The board's actions were explained on the grounds of pessimism about the company's and the economy's outlook and therefore, the need to build up adequate additional reserves to provide for the possibility of future losses. The board's outlook during the time in question could properly be categorized as one of pessimism and conservatism.

On January 15, 1980, the board decided to pay the 7% dividend on the preferred stock and a large dividend on the common stock. The preferred shareholders were irate. A group of preferred shareholders have commenced a suit seeking an injunction against Dexter and its board of directors prohibiting the payment of dividends on the common stock unless it first pays dividends on the noncumulative preferred for previous years to the extent that the corporation had net earnings available for payment.

Required

Answer the following, setting forth reasons for any conclusions stated.

    Will the preferred shareholders prevail?

Part b. The directors of Despard & Company, Inc., are considering several alternatives to their usual declaration of a cash dividend. The cost of borrowing money has become prohibitive and the directors would prefer to retain the cash to further the corporation's expansion plans. The following possibilities have been suggested:

- A dividend to each shareholder consisting of 60% treasury stock and 40% cash.
- A stock dividend declared and paid in its own authorized and unissued $1.00 par value common shares.
- A 2-for-1 split-up of the issued shares of the $1.00 par value common shares. Par value would be changed from $1.00 to $0.50.

Required

Answer the following, setting forth reasons for any conclusions stated.

1. Separately analyze and discuss the legal impact of each of these possibilities from the standpoint of the corporate requirements (ignore accounting entries) that must be met and the effect that each would have upon the stated capital of the corporation.
2. What is the federal income tax effects or implications to the shareholder as to each of the above possibilities?
3. What is the federal income tax consequence if the corporation continuously elects **not** to pay any cash dividends?

Number 3 (Estimated time—15 to 20 minutes)

Part a. Hardaway Lending, Inc., had a four-year $800,000 callable loan to Superior Metals, Inc., outstanding. The loan was callable at the end of each year upon Hardaway's giving 60 days written notice. Two and one-half years remained of the four years. Hardaway reviewed the loan and decided that Superior Metals was no longer a prime lending risk and it therefore decided to call the loan. The required written notice was sent to and received by Superior 60 days prior to the expiration of the second year. Merriweather, Superior's chief executive officer and principal shareholder, requested Hardaway to continue the loan at least for another year. Hardaway agreed, provided that an acceptable commercial surety would guarantee $400,000 of the loan and Merriweather would personally guarantee repayment in full. These conditions were satisfied and the loan was permitted to continue.

The following year the loan was called and Superior defaulted. Hardaway released the commercial surety but retained its rights against Merriweather and demanded that Merriweather pay the full amount of the loan. Merriweather refused, asserting the following:

- There was no consideration for his promise. The loan was already outstanding and he personally received nothing.
- Hardaway must first proceed against Superior before it can collect from Merriweather.
- Hardaway had released the commercial surety, thereby releasing Merriweather.

Required

Answer the following, setting forth reasons for any conclusions stated.
   Discuss the validity of each of Merriweather's assertions.

Part b. In connection with the audit of One-Up, Inc., a question has arisen regarding the validity of a $10,000 purchase money security interest in certain machinery sold to Essex Company on March 2nd. Essex was petitioned into bankruptcy on May 1st by its creditors. The trustee is seeking to avoid One-Up's security interest on the grounds that it is a preferential transfer, hence voidable. The machinery in question was sold to Essex on the following terms: $1,000 down and the balance plus interest at 9% to be paid over a three-year period. One-Up obtained a signed security agreement which created a security interest in the property on March 2nd, the date of the sale. A financing statement was filed on March 10th.

Required

Answer the following, setting forth reasons for any conclusions stated.

1. Would One-Up's security interest in the machinery be a voidable preference?
2. In general, what are the requirements necessary to permit the trustee to successfully assert a preferential transfer and thereby set aside a creditor's security interest?

Number 4 (Estimated time—15 to 20 minutes)

Part a. Whitlow & Company is a brokerage firm registered under the Securities Exchange Act of 1934. The Act requires such a brokerage firm to file audited financial statements with the SEC annually. Mitchell & Moss, Whitlow's CPAs, performed the annual audit for the year ended December 31, 1979, and rendered an unqualified opinion, which was filed with the SEC along with Whitlow's financial statements. During 1979 Charles, the president of Whitlow & Company, engaged in a huge embezzlement scheme that eventually bankrupted the firm. As a result substantial losses were suffered by customers and shareholders of Whitlow & Company, including Thaxton who had recently purchased several shares of stock of Whitlow & Company after reviewing the company's 1979 audit report. Mitchell & Moss' audit was deficient; if they had complied with generally accepted auditing standards, the embezzlement would have been discovered. However, Mitchell & Moss had no knowledge of the embezzlement nor could their conduct be categorized as reckless.

Required

Answer the following, setting forth reasons for any conclusions stated.

1. What liability to Thaxton, if any, does Mitchell & Moss have under the Securities Exchange Act of 1934?
2. What theory or theories of liability, if any, are available to Whitlow & Company's customers and shareholders under the common law?

Part b. Jackson is a sophisticated investor. As such, she was initially a member of a small group who was going to participate in a private placement of $1 million of common stock of Clarion Corporation. Numerous meetings were held among management and the investor group. Detailed financial and other information was supplied to the participants. Upon the eve of completion of the placement, it was aborted when one major investor withdrew. Clarion then decided to offer $2.5 million of Clarion common stock to the public pursuant to the registration requirements of the Securities Act of 1933. Jackson subscribed to $300,000 of the Clarion public stock offering. Nine months later, Clarion's earnings dropped significantly and as a result the stock dropped 20% beneath the offering price. In addition, the Dow Jones Industrial Average was down 10% from the time of the offering.

Jackson has sold her shares at a loss of $60,000 and seeks to hold all parties liable who participated in the public offering including Allen, Dunn, and Rose, Clarion's CPA firm. Although the audit was performed in conformity with generally accepted auditing standards, there were some relatively minor irregularities. The financial statements of Clarion Corporation, which were part of the registration statement, contained minor misleading facts. It is believed by Clarion and Allen, Dunn and Rose, that Jackson's asserted claim is without merit.

Required
Answer the following, setting forth reasons for any conclusions stated.

1. Assuming Jackson sues under the Securities Act of 1933, what will be the basis of her claim?
2. What are the probable defenses which might be asserted by Allen, Dunn, and Rose in light of these facts?

Number 5 (Estimated time—15 to 20 minutes)

Part a. Fennimore owned a ranch which was encumbered by a 7% mortgage held by the Orange County Bank. As of July 31, 1980, the outstanding mortgage amount was $83,694. Fennimore decided to sell the ranch and engage in the grain storage business. During the time that he was negotiating the sale of the ranch, the bank sent out an offer to several mortgagors indicating a 5% discount on the mortgage if the mortgagors would pay the entire mortgage in cash or by certified check by July 31, 1980. The bank was doing this in order to liquidate older unprofitable mortgages which it had on the books. Anyone seeking to avail himself of the offer was required to present his payment at the Second Street branch on July 31, 1980. Fennimore, having obtained a buyer for his property, decided to take advantage of the offer since his buyer was arranging his own financing and was not interested in assuming the mortgage. Therefore, on July 15th he wrote the bank a letter which stated: "I accept your offer on my mortgage, see you on July 31, 1980, I'll have a certified check." Fennimore did not indicate that he was selling the ranch and would have to pay off the full amount in any event. On July 28, the bank sent Fennimore a letter by certified mail which was received by Fennimore on the 30th of July which stated: "We withdraw our offer. We are over subscribed. Furthermore, we have learned that you are selling your property and the mortgage is not being assumed." Nevertheless, on July 31 at 9:05 in the morning when Fennimore walked in the door of the bank holding his certified check, Vogelspiel, a bank mortgage officer, approached him and stated firmly and clearly that the bank's offer had been revoked and that the bank would refuse to accept tender of payment. Dumbfounded by all this, Fennimore nevertheless tendered the check, which was refused.

Required
Answer the following, setting forth reasons for any conclusions stated.
    In the eventual lawsuit that ensued, who will prevail?

Part b. Austin wrote a letter and mailed it to Hernandez offering to sell Hernandez his tuna canning business for $125,000. Hernandez promptly mailed a reply acknowledging receipt of Austin's letter and expressing an interest in purchasing the cannery. However, Hernandez offered Austin only $110,000. Later Hernandez decided that the business was in fact worth at least the $125,000 that Austin was asking. He therefore decided to accept the original offer tendered to him at $125,000 and telegraphed Austin an unconditional acceptance at $125,000. The telegram reached Austin before Hernandez' prior letter, although the letter arrived later that day. Austin upon receipt of the telegram telegraphed Hernandez that as a result of further analysis as to the worth of the business, he was not willing to sell at less than $150,000. Hernandez claims a contract at $125,000 resulted from his telegram. Austin asserts either that there is no contract or that the perchase price is $150,000.

Required

Answer the following, setting forth reasons for any conclusions stated.
    If the dispute goes to court, who will prevail?

Answers to Business Law Illustrative Examination

Answer 1 (60 points)

1. a	16. c	31. d	46. b
2. a	17. b	32. b	47. d
3. d	18. d	33. d	48. c
4. c	19. b	34. d	49. c
5. c	20. c	35. c	50. c
6. d	21. c	36. a	51. d
7. c	22. c	37. c	52. b
8. c	23. c	38. a	53. c
9. b	24. d	39. a	54. d
10. d	25. c	40. d	55. d
11. d	26. c	41. c	56. b
12. a	27. a	42. d	57. d
13. c	28. c	43. d	58. c
14. b	29. d	44. b	59. a
15. a	30. d	45. c	60. c

Answer 2 (10 points)

Part a.

No. The stock in question was noncumulative preferred. The relationship of the preferred shareholders to the corporation is essentially contractual and the stock certificate is, in fact, the contract. The contract agreed to by the owners of this preferred stock was essentially that if the board of directors passed over the declaration of the preferred dividend in a given year or years, it would not accumulate but would be lost. Whether or not to declare a dividend is within the discretion of the board. Its judgment is not overridden by the courts unless there is dishonesty or a clear abuse of discretion. The fact that there were earnings sufficient to pay preferred dividends after 1973, that the funds were not actually expended for purchase of physical plant or property, or that the earnings were not being accumulated for the purpose of expansion are not sufficient to persuade a court to grant the injunction. Although the board was pessimistic and conservative, that would not be an abuse of their discretion. The Model Business Corporation Act states that "the board of directors of a corporation may, from time to time, declare . . . dividends," thus retaining discretion in the board regarding dividend declaration. In conclusion, the law respects the business judgment of directors in determining whether to declare dividends. The board is afforded wide discretion in such matters, and, unless there is an abuse of such discretion, a court will not interfere with its judgment.

Part b.

1. The payment of a dividend partially out of treasury stock and partially in cash poses few problems. There are few restrictions, limitations, or requirements regarding the use of treasury stock as a dividend. The general requirements, that the board may not declare a dividend when the corporation is insolvent or where the dividend will render it such, are not a barrier here. The facts do not indicate a restriction in the articles of incorporation; therefore, the partial treasury stock dividend may be paid. Stated capital is not affected in any way, and the Model Business Corporation Act merely indicates that dividends may be declared and paid in a corporation's own treasury shares. The 40% cash dividend is subject to the foregoing solvency and restriction requirements. In addition, a cash dividend may be declared and paid only out of the unreserved and unrestricted earned surplus of the corporation.

A corporation may declare and pay a stock dividend in its authorized and unissued shares out of any unreserved and unrestricted surplus. When the share dividend has a par value, such shares must be issued at not less than their par value and, at the time such dividend is paid, an amount of surplus equal to the aggregate par value of the shares to be issued as a dividend must be transferred to stated capital.

The act allows a split-up or division of the issued shares of any class into a greater number of the same class without increasing the stated capital of the corporation. This is not to be construed as a share dividend within the meaning of the act. The effect of a share split is to increase the number of shares without changing the stated capital and to allocate the par equally among the increased number of shares issued and outstanding after the share split. However, because the par value of the shares must be reduced, the articles of incorporation must be amended by vote of the shareholders.

2. The Internal Revenue Code exemption from taxation of stock dividends and stock splits would apply to the foregoing situations; there are exceptions to this favorable treatment, but none would appear germane based upon the particular facts stated. However, the shareholder must allocate basis (typically cost) for the shares originally owned to the total number of shares owned after the stock dividend or split. To the extent that the payment is out of earnings and profits, the only taxable dividend would be the 40% payment in cash. Such income is ordinary income subject to an 85% dividend exclusion to a corporate shareholder or a $100 dividend exclusion to a noncorporate shareholder.

3. The Internal Revenue Code contains a provision aimed at the unreasonable accumulation of earnings and profits. There is a $150,000 credit against the amounts permitted to be accumulated. Accumulations must be retained only for the reasonable needs of the business. Where little or no dividends are paid by a corporation there is always the danger that the accumulations may be wholly or partly unreasonable. It would not appear that the accumulations provisions pose a significant danger here in light of the ambitious expansion plans that would normally constitute a *bona fide* business purpose.

Answer 3 (10 points)

Part a.
The first two defenses asserted by Merriweather are invalid. The third defense is partially valid.

Consideration on Hardaway's part consisted of foregoing the right to call the Superior Metals loan. The fact that the loan was already outstanding is irrelevant. By permitting the loan to remain outstanding for an additional year instead of calling it, Hardaway relinquished a legal right, which is adequate consideration for Merriweather's surety promise. Consideration need not pass to the surety; in fact, it usually primarily benefits the principal debtor.

There is no requirement that the creditor first proceed against the debtor before it can proceed against the surety, unless the surety undertaking expressly provides such a condition. Basic to the usual surety undertaking is the right of the creditor to proceed immediately against the surety. Essentially, that is the reason for the surety.

Hardaway's release of the commercial surety from its $400,000 surety undertaking partially released Merriweather. The release had the legal effect of impairing Merriweather's right of contribution against its cosurety (the commercial surety). Thus, Merriweather is released to the extent of ⅓ [$400,000 (commercial surety's guarantee)/ $1,200,000 (the aggregate of the cosureties's guarantees)] of the principal amount ($800,000), or $266,667.

Part b.
1. No. The Bankruptcy Reform Act of 1978 has not only modified the requirements for establishing a voidable preference, it has also specified transactions that do not constitute preferences. One such transaction is the creditor's taking a security interest in property acquired by the debtor as a contemporaneous exchange for new value given to the debtor to enable him to acquire such property (a purchase money security interest). The security interest must be perfected (filed) within 10 days after attachment. The act is in harmony with the secured transactions provisions of the Uniform Commercial Code. Thus, One-Up has a valid security interest in the machinery it sold to Essex.

2. The Bankruptcy Reform Act of 1978 does not require that the creditor have knowledge or reasonable cause to believe the debtor is insolvent in the bankruptcy sense. Instead, under the act, where such insolvency exists on or within ninety days before the filing of the petition, knowledge of insolvency by the transferee need not be established. The act also assumes that the debtor's insolvency is presumed if the transfer alleged to be preferential is made within 90 days. Finally, the time period in which transfers may be set aside is 90 days unless the transferee is an "insider." If the

transfer is to an insider, the trustee may avoid transfers made within one year prior to the filing of the petition. Thus, the trustee may avoid as preferential any transfer of property of the debtor that is
- To or for the benefit of a creditor.
- For or on account of an antecedent debt owed by the debtor before such transfer was made.
- Made while the debtor was insolvent in the bankruptcy sense (however, if the transfer is made within 90 days, the debtor's insolvency is presumed).
- Made on or within 90 days of the filing of the petition (or if made after the 90 days but within one year prior to the date of the filing of the petition and the transfer was to an "insider," it may be set aside if the transferee had reasonable cause to believe the debtor was insolvent at the time of the transfer).
- Such that it enables the creditor to receive more than he would if it were a straight liquidation proceeding.

The bankruptcy act contains a lengthy definition of the term "insider" that includes common relationships that the transferee has to the debtor, which, in case of an individual debtor, could be certain relatives, a partnership in which he is a general partner, his fellow general partners, or a corporation controlled by him.

Answer 4 (10 points)

Part a.

1. In order for Thaxton to hold Mitchell & Moss liable for his losses under the Securities Exchange Act of 1934, he must rely upon the antifraud provisions of Section 10(b) of the Act. In order to prevail Thaxton must establish that
   - There was an omission or misstatement of a material fact in the financial statements used in connection with his purchase of the Whitlow & Company shares of stock.
   - He sustained a loss as a result of his purchase of the shares of stock.
   - His loss was caused by reliance on the misleading financial statements.
   - Mitchell & Moss acted with scienter.

     Based on the stated facts, Thaxton can probably prove the first three requirements cited above. To prove the fourth requirement, Thaxton must show that Mitchell & Moss had knowledge (scienter) of the fraud or recklessly disregarded the truth. The facts clearly indicate that Mitchell & Moss did not have knowledge of the fraud and did not recklessly disregard the truth.

2. The customers and shareholders of Whitlow & Company would attempt to recover on a negligence theory based on Mitchell & Moss' failure to comply with GAAS. Even if Mitchell & Moss were negligent, Whitlow & Company's customers and shareholders must also establish either that—
   - They were third party beneficiaries of Mitchell & Moss' contract to audit Whitlow & Company, *or*
   - Mitchell & Moss owed the customers and shareholders a legal duty to act without negligence.

     Although recent cases have expanded a CPA's legal responsibilities to a third party for negligence, the facts of this case may fall within the traditional rationale limiting a CPA's liability for negligence; that is, the unfairness of imputing an indeterminate amount of liability to unknown or unforeseen parties as a result of mere negligence on the auditor's part. Accordingly, Whitlow & Company's customers and shareholders will prevail only if (1) the courts rule that they are either third-party beneficiaries or are owed a legal duty and (2) they establish that Mitchell & Moss was negligent in failing to comply with generally accepted auditing standards.

Part b.

1. The basis of Jackson's claim will be that she sustained a loss based upon misleading financial statements. Specifically, she will rely upon Section 11(a) of the Securities Act of 1933, which provides the following:

   > In case any part of the registration statement, when such part became effective, contained an untrue statement of a material fact or omitted to state a material fact required to be stated therein or necessary to make the statements therein not misleading, any person acquiring such security (unless it is proved that at the time of such acquisition he knew of such untruth or omission) may, either at law or in equity, in any court of competent jurisdiction, sue . . . every accountant . . . who has with his consent been named as having prepared or certified any part of the registration statement. . . .

To the extent that the relatively minor irregularities resulted in the certification of materially false or misleading financial statements, there is potential liability. Jackson's case is based on the assertion of such an untrue statement or omission coupled with an allegation of damages. Jackson does not have to prove reliance on the statements nor the company's or auditor's negligence in order to recover the damages. The burden is placed on the defendant to provide defenses that will enable it to avoid liability.

2. The first defense that could be asserted is that Jackson knew of the untruth or omission in audited financial statements included in the registration statement. The act provides that the plaintiff may not recover if it can be proved that at the time of such acquisition she knew of such "untruth or omission."

Since Jackson was a member of the private placement group and presumably privy to the type of information that would be contained in a registration statement, plus any other information requested by the group, she may have had sufficient knowledge of the facts claimed to be untrue or omitted. If this be the case, then she would not be relying on the certified financial statements but upon her own knowledge.

The next defense assertable would be that the untrue statement or omission was not material. The SEC has defined the term as meaning matters about which an average prudent investor ought to be reasonably informed before purchasing the registered security. For Section 11 purposes, this has been construed as meaning a fact that, had it been correctly stated or disclosed, would have deterred or tended to deter the average prudent investor from purchasing the security in question.

Allen, Dunn, and Rose would also assert that the loss in question was not due to the false statement or omission; that is, that the false statement was not the cause of the price drop. It would appear that the general decline in the stock market would account for at least a part of the loss. Additionally, if the decline in earnings was not factually connected with the false statement or omission, the defendants have another basis for refuting the causal connection between their wrongdoing and the resultant drop in the stock's price.

Finally, the accountants will claim that their departure from generally accepted auditing standards was too minor to be considered a violation of the standard of due diligence required by the act.

Answer 5 (10 points)

Part a.

Orange County Bank will prevail. The fact situation poses a classic illustration of a withdrawal of an offer to enter into a unilateral contract. The bank's offer to Fennimore called for the performance of an act (the actual paying of the mortgage), not a promise to pay it, as the means of acceptance. The language in the offer is clear and unambiguous, providing a 5% discount on a mortgage if the mortgagor would pay the entire mortgage in cash or by certified check by July 31, 1980, at the Second Street branch of the bank. Thus, the bank's letter was an offer to enter into a unilateral contract that required the performance of the act as the authorized and exclusive means of acceptance. Fennimore's promise to perform the act was ineffectual in creating a contract. Contract law generally provides that offers may be revoked at any time prior to acceptance; even if the bank revoked its offer the instant before the purported acceptance, it was a timely revocation and the acceptance was too late. The tender of performance would also be of no avail since notice of revocation had been received on the 30th.

In this situation, strict common law rules would deny the creation of a contract. Some states, in recognition of the hardship of such results, have adopted what is known as the *restatement of contracts* rule. This modification of the common law rule in respect to the unilateral contract rule holds that the unilateral promise in an offer calling for an act becomes binding as soon as part of the requested performance actually has been rendered or a proper tender of performance has been made. The courts have required substantial action on the part of the offeree, which does not appear to be present here.

The fact that Fennimore was selling his property and did not disclose the fact that he would have to pay the mortgage off in any event is immaterial. There was no material misrepresentation of fact made by him, hence his action was not fraudulent nor did he misrepresent. He was silent. Additionally, the fact that the bank was using the sale as a reason for terminating the offer was immaterial.

Part b.

Hernandez will prevail. An offer is not effective until communicated to the offeree. The same rule applies to counteroffers including a change in the price, as occurred here. Therefore, a counteroffer is not effective until received by Austin, the original offeror. Hernandez's counteroffer does not destroy the offer until it is received. Thus, Hernandez's telegram, which accepted Austin's offer and arrived ahead of Hernandez's letter containing the counteroffer, is effective in creating a binding contract.

This rule applies even if Hernandez had mailed a letter that unequivocally accepted Austin's offer and that would have been effective upon dispatch. The general rule that an acceptance is effective when dispatched is subject to an exception that is designed to prevent entrapment of an offeror who is misled to his disadvantage by an offeree who attempts to take two inconsistent positions. Thus, when an offeree first rejects an offer, then subsequently accepts it, the subsequent acceptance will be considered effective upon dispatch by an authorized means only if it arrives prior to the offeror's receipt of the rejection. If the rejection arrives first, the original offeror may treat the attempted acceptance as a counteroffer which he is free to accept or not. Were this not the rule, an offeror who, upon reciept of a rejection, in good faith changed his position (that is, sold the goods to another customer), could find himself having sold the same goods twice.

Practice Examination In Business Law

(Commercial Law)

Administered the first week of November and May of each year; 8:30 AM and 12:00 PM

NOTE TO CANDIDATES: Suggested time allotments are as follows:

All questions are required:	Estimated Minimum	Minutes Maximum
No. 1	110	130
No. 2	15	20
No. 3	15	20
No. 4	15	20
No. 5	15	20
Total	170	210

INSTRUCTIONS TO CANDIDATES

(Disregard of these instructions may be considered as indicating inefficiency in accounting work.)

1. You must arrange the papers in numerical order of the questions. If more than one page is required for an answer, write "continued" at the bottom of the page. Number pages consecutively. For instance, if 12

pages are used for your answers, the objective answer sheet is page 1 and your other pages should be numbered 2 through 12.

2. Answer all objective-type items on the printed answer sheet provided for that purpose. It is to your advantage to attempt all questions even if you are uncertain of the answer. You are likely to get the highest score if you omit no answers. Since objective items are computer-graded, your comments and calculations associated with them are not considered. Be certain that you have entered your answers on the objective answer sheet before the examination time is up.

3. A CPA is continually confronted with the necessity of expressing opinions and conclusions in written reports in clear, unequivocal language. Although the primary purpose of the examination is to test the candidate's knowledge and application of the subject matter, the ability to organize and present such knowledge in acceptable written language will be considered by the examiners.

Number 1 (Estimated time—110 to 130 minutes)

Instructions

Select the **best** answer for each of the following items. Use a soft pencil, preferably No. 2, to blacken the appropriate circle on the separate printed answer sheet to indicate your answer. **Mark only one answer for each item. Answer all items.** Your grade will be based on your total correct answers.

The following is an example of the manner in which the answer sheet should be marked:

Item

99. The text of the letter from Bridge Builders, Inc., to Allied Steel Co. follows:

> We offer to purchase 10,000 tons of No. 4 steel pipes at today's quoted price for delivery two months from today. Your acceptance must be received in five days.
>
> Bridge Builders intended to create a (an)
> a. Option contract.
> b. Unilateral contract.
> c. Bilateral contract.
> d. Joint contract.

Answer Sheet

99.

Items to be Answered

1. Lantz sold his moving and warehouse business, including all the personal and real property used therein, to Mallen Van Lines, Inc. The real property was encumbered by a duly-recorded $300,000 first mortgage upon which Lantz was personally liable. Mallen acquired the property subject to the mortgage but did **not** assume the mortgage. Two years later, when the outstanding mortgage was $260,000, Mallen decided to abandon the business location because it had become unprofitable and the value of the real property was less than the outstanding mortgage. Mallen moved to another location and refused to pay the installments due on the mortgage. What is the legal status of the parties in regard to the mortgage?
   a. Mallen breached its contract with Lantz when it abandoned the location and defaulted on the mortgage.
   b. Mallen took the real property free of the mortgage.
   c. If Lantz pays off the mortgage, he will be able to successfully sue Mallen because Lantz is subrogated to the mortgagee's rights against Mallen.

    d. Lantz must satisfy the mortgage debt in the event that foreclosure yields an amount less than the unpaid balance.

2. The federal bankruptcy act contains several important terms. One such term is "insider." The term is used in connection with preferences and preferential transfers. Which among the following is **not** an "insider?"

    a. A secured creditor having a security interest in at least 25% or more of the debtor's property.

    b. A partnership in which the debtor is a general partner.

    c. A corporation of which the debtor is a director.

    d. A close blood relative of the debtor.

3. Which of the following requirements is **not** necessary in order to have a security interest attach?

    a. There must be a proper filing.

    b. The debtor must have rights in the collateral.

    c. Value must be given by the creditor.

    d. Either the creditor must take possession or the debtor must sign a security agreement which describes the collateral.

4. In respect to obtaining a purchase money security interest, which of the following requirements must be met?

    a. The property sold may only be consumer goods.

    b. Only a seller may obtain a purchase money security interest.

    c. Such a security interest must be filed in all cases to be perfected.

    d. Credit advanced to the buyer must be used to obtain the property which serves as the collateral.

5. Vista Motor Sales, a corporation engaged in selling motor vehicles at retail, borrowed money from Sunshine Finance Company and gave Sunshine a properly executed security agreement in its present and future inventory and in the proceeds therefrom to secure the loan. Sunshine's security interest was duly perfected under the laws of the state where Vista does business and maintains its entire inventory. Thereafter, Vista sold a new pickup truck from its inventory to Archer and received Archer's certified check in payment of the full price. Under the circumstances, which of the following is correct?

    a. Sunshine must file an amendment to the financing statement every time Vista receives a substantial number of additional vehicles from the manufacturer if Sunshine is to obtain a valid security interest in subsequently delivered inventory.

    b. Sunshine's security interest in the certified check Vista received is perfected against Vista's other creditors.

    c. Unless Sunshine specifically included proceeds in the financing statement it filed, it has **no** rights to them.

    d. The term "proceeds" does **not** include used cars received by Vista since they will be resold.

6. Barton Corporation and Clagg Corporation have decided to combine their separate companies pursuant to the provisions of their state corporation laws. After much discussion and negotiation, they decided that a consolidation was the appropriate procedure to be followed. Which of the following is an **incorrect** statement with respect to the contemplated statutory consolidation?

    a. A statutory consolidation pursuant to state law is recognized by the Internal Revenue Code as a type of tax-free reorganization.

    b. The larger of the two corporations will emerge as the surviving corporation.

    c. Creditors of Barton and Clagg will have their claims protected despite the consolidation.

    d. The shareholders of both Barton and Clagg must approve the plan of consolidation.

7. Mark Corporation is a moderate-sized closely held corporation which is 80% owned by Joseph Mark. The remaining 20% of stock is owned by Mark's wife, sons, daughter, and parents. One son, David Mark, who recently graduated from business school, has been hired by the corporation as financial vice president at a salary of $60,000 per year. Other members of the family are either officers or directors of the corporation and are all generously compensated. Joseph Mark is paid $300,000 as Chairman of the Board and Chief Executive Officer. The corporation is profitable, solvent, and meeting all claims as they become due. Who of the following would have standing to attack the reasonableness of the salary payments?

    a. The creditors of the corporation.

    b. The attorney general of the state in which Mark is incorporated.

    c. The Internal Revenue Service.

    d. The Securities and Exchange Commission.

8. The Board of Directors of Wilcox Manufacturing Corporation, a publicly held corporation, has noted a significant

drop in the stock market price of its 7% preferred stock and proposes to purchase some of the stock. The proposed purchase price is substantially below the redemption price of the stock. The Board has decided to acquire 100,000 shares of said preferred stock and either place it in the treasury or retire it. Under these circumstances, which of the following is a correct statement?

a. The corporation will realize a taxable gain as a result of the transaction.

b. The preferred stock so acquired must be retired and may **not** be held as treasury stock.

c. The corporation may **not** acquire its own shares unless the articles of incorporation so provide.

d. Such shares may be purchased by the corporation to the extent of unreserved and unrestricted earned surplus available therefore.

9. A major characteristic of the corporation is its recognition as a separate legal entity. As such it is capable of withstanding attacks upon its valid existence by various parties who would wish to disregard its existence or "pierce the corporate veil" for their own purposes. The corporation will normally be able to successfully resist such attempts **except** when

a. The corporation was created with tax savings in mind.

b. The corporation was created in order to insulate the assets of its owners from personal liability.

c. The corporation being attacked is a wholly owned subsidiary of its parent corporation.

d. The creation of and transfer of property to the corporation amounts to a fraud upon creditors.

10. Bunker Industries, Inc., ceased doing business and is in bankruptcy. Among the claimants are employees seeking unpaid wages. The following statements describe the possible status of such claims in a bankruptcy proceeding or legal limitations placed upon them. Which one is an **incorrect** statement?

a. They are entitled to a priority.

b. If a priority is afforded such claims, it **cannot** exceed $2,000 per wage earner.

c. Such claims **cannot** include vacation, severance, or sick-leave pay.

d. The amounts of excess wages **not** entitled to a priority are mere unsecured claims.

11. Carr owns 100 acres of undeveloped land on the outskirts of New Town. He bought the land several years ago to build an industrial park in the event New Town grew and prospered. The land was formerly used for grazing and truck gardening. A subsequent inspection revealed that several adjacent landowners recently had been using a short cut across his land in order to reach a newly constructed highway. Which of the following is a correct statement?

a. There is a danger that the adjacent landowners will obtain title by adverse possession.

b. Since Carr has properly recorded his deed, the facts do **not** pose a problem for him.

c. There is a danger that an easement may be created.

d. Since the adjacent landowners are trespassers, Carr has nothing to fear.

12. Golden Enterprises, Inc., entered into a contract with Hidalgo Corporation for the sale of its mineral holdings. The transaction proved to be *ultra vires*. Which of the following parties, for the reason stated, may properly assert the *ultra vires* doctrine?

a. Golden Enterprises to avoid performance.

b. A shareholder of Golden Enterprises to enjoin the sale.

c. Hidalgo Corporation to avoid performance.

d. Golden Enterprises to rescind the consummated sale.

13. Grandiose secured an option to purchase a tract of land for $100,000. He then organized the Dunbar Corporation and subscribed to 51% of the shares of stock of the corporation for $100,000, which was issued to him in exchange for his three-month promissory note for $100,000. Controlling the board of directors through his share ownership, he had the corporation authorize the purchase of the land from him for $200,000. He made no disclosure to the board or to other shareholders that he was making a $100,000 profit. He promptly paid the corporation for his shares and redeemed his promissory note. A disgruntled shareholder subsequently learned the full details of the transaction and brought suit against Grandiose on the corporation's behalf. Which of the following is a correct statement?

a. Grandiose breached his fiduciary duty to the corporation and must account for the profit he made.

b. The judgment of the board of directors was conclusive under the circumstances.

c. Grandiose is entitled to retain the profit since he controlled the corporation as a result of his share ownership.

d. The giving of the promissory note in exchange for the stock constituted payment for the shares.

14. Destiny Manufacturing, Inc., is incorporated under the laws of Nevada. Its principal place of business is in California and it has permanent sales offices in several other states. Under the circumstances, which of the following is correct?

   a. California may validly demand that Destiny incorporate under the laws of the state of California.

   b. Destiny must obtain a certificate of authority to transact business in California and the other states in which it does business.

   c. Destiny is a foreign corporation in California, but **not** in the other states.

   d. California may prevent Destiny from operating as a corporation if the laws of California differ regarding organization and conduct of the corporation's internal affairs.

15. Mask stole one of Bloom's checks. The check was already signed by Bloom and made payable to Duval. The check was drawn on United Trust Company. Mask forged Duval's signature on the back of the check and cashed the check at the Corner Check Cashing Company which in turn deposited it with its bank, Town National Bank of Toka. Town National proceeded to collect on the check from United. None of the parties mentioned was negligent. Who will bear the loss assuming the amount **cannot** be recovered from Mask?

   a. Bloom.

   b. Duval.

   c. United Trust Company.

   d. Corner Check Cashing Company.

16. Plimpton subscribed to 1,000 shares of $1 par value common stock of the Billiard Ball Corporation at $10 a share. Plimpton paid $1,000 upon the incorporation of Billiard and paid an additional $4,000 at a later time. The corporation subsequently became insolvent and is now in bankruptcy. The creditors of the corporation are seeking to hold Plimpton personally liable. Which of the following is a correct statement?

   a. Plimpton has **no** liability directly or indirectly to the creditors of the corporation since he paid the corporation the full par value of the shares.

   b. As a result of his failure to pay the full subscription price, Plimpton has unlimited joint and several liability for corporate debts.

   c. Plimpton is liable for the remainder of the unpaid subscription price.

   d. Had Plimpton transferred his shares to an innocent third party, neither he nor the third party would be liable.

17. Which of the following provisions is a part of the Social Security law?

   a. Social Security benefits must be fully funded and payments, current and future, must constitutionally come only from Social Security taxes.

   b. Upon the death of an employee prior to his retirement, his estate is entitled to receive the amount attributable to his contributions as a death benefit.

   c. A self-employed person must contribute an annual amount which is less than the combined contributions of an employee and his or her employer.

   d. Social Security benefits are taxable as income when they exceed the individual's total contributions.

18. At age 66, Jonstone retired as a general partner of Gordon & Co. He no longer participates in the affairs of the partnership but does receive a distributive share of the partnership profits as a result of becoming a limited partner upon retirement. Jonstone has accepted a part-time consulting position with a corporation near his retirement home. Which of the following is correct regarding Jonstone's Social Security situation?

   a. Jonstone's limited partner distributive share will be considered self-employment income for Social Security purposes up to a maximum of $10,000.

   b. There is **no** limitation on the amount Jonstone may earn in the first year of retirement.

   c. Jonstone will lose $1 of Social Security benefits for each $1 of earnings in excess of a statutorily permitted amount.

   d. Jonstone will be subject to an annual earnings limitation until he attains a stated age which, if exceeded, will reduce the amount of Social Security benefits.

19. Gomer developed a fraudulent system whereby he could obtain checks payable to the order of certain repairmen who serviced various large corporations. Gomer observed the delivery trucks of repairmen who did business with the corporations, and then he submitted bills on the bogus letterhead of the repairmen to the selected large corporations. The return envelope for payment indicated a local post office box. When the checks arrived, Gomer

would forge the payees' signatures and cash the checks. The parties cashing the checks are holders in due course. Who will bear the loss assuming the amount **cannot** be recovered from Gomer?

a. The defrauded corporations.

b. The drawee banks.

c. Intermediate parties who indorsed the instruments for collection.

d. The ultimate recipients of the proceeds of the checks even though they are holders in due course.

20. Monrad is contemplating making a contract for the purchase of certain real property. Which of the following is **incorrect** insofar as such a contract is concerned?

a. It must meet the requirements of the statute of frauds.

b. If the agreement is legally consummated, Monrad could obtain specific performance.

c. The contract is nonassignable as a matter of law.

d. An implied covenant of marketability applies to the contract.

21. Yeats Manufacturing is engaged in the manufacture and sale of convertible furniture in interstate commerce. Yeats' manufacturing facilities are located in a jurisdiction which has a compulsory workmen's compensation act. Hardwood, Yeats' president, decided that the company should, in light of its safety record, choose to ignore the requirement of providing workmen's compensation insurance. Instead, Hardwood indicated that a special account should be created to provide for such contingencies. Basset was severely injured as a result of his negligent operation of a lathe which accelerated and cut off his right arm. In assessing the potential liability of Yeats, which of the following is a correct answer?

a. Federal law applies since Yeats is engaged in interstate commerce.

b. Yeats has **no** liability, since Basset negligently operated the lathe.

c. Since Yeats did **not** provide workmen's compensation insurance, it can be sued by Basset and cannot resort to the usual common law defenses.

d. Yeats is a self-insurer; hence it has **no** liability beyond the amount of the money in the insurance fund.

Items 22 and 23 are based on the following information:

Martin is the trustee of the Baker Trust which has assets in excess of $1 million. Martin has engaged the CPA firm of Hardy & Fox to prepare the annual accounting statement for the allocation of receipts and expenditures between income and principal. The trust indenture provides that "receipts and expenses are to be allocated to income or principal according to law."

22. Which of the following receipts should be allocated to income?

a. Rights to subscribe to shares of the distributing corporation.

b. Sale of rights to subscribe to shares of the distributing corporation.

c. A 2% stock dividend.

d. Rights to subscribe to shares of another corporation.

23. Which of the following receipts from real property should be allocated to principal?

a. An unexpected payment of nine months' arrears in rental payments.

b. A six-month prepayment of rent.

c. Insurance proceeds for the destruction of a garage on one of the properties.

d. Interest on a purchase money mortgage arising from the sale of a parcel of the trust's real property.

24. Carter wished to obtain additional working capital for his construction company. His bankers indicated that they would be willing to lend the company $50,000 if the bank could obtain a first mortgage on the real property belonging to the business. Carter reluctantly acquiesced and mortgaged all his real property to secure repayment of the loan. Unknown to the bank one portion of the real property was already mortgaged to Johnson for $30,000, but Johnson had neglected to record the mortgage. The bank promptly recorded its mortgage. Which of the following is correct regarding the rights of the parties?

a. Johnson's failure to record makes the mortgage invalid against Carter.

b. The bank's mortgage will have a priority over Johnson's mortgage.

c. Both mortgagees would share the proceeds from any foreclosure on a pro rata basis.

d. The bank will be deemed to have notice of Johnson's mortgage and will take subject to the mortgage.

25. In the process of negotiating the sale of his manufacturing business to Grand, Sterling made certain untrue statements which Grand relied upon. Grand was induced to purchase the business for $10,000 more than its true

value. Grand is **not** sure whether he should seek relief based upon misrepresentation or fraud. Which of the following is a correct statement?

a. If Grand merely wishes to rescind the contract and get his money back, misrepresentation is his **best** recourse.

b. In order to prevail under the fraud theory, Grand must show that Sterling intended for him to rely on the untrue statements; whereas he need **not** do so if he bases his action on misrepresentation.

c. Both fraud and misrepresentation require Grand to prove that Sterling knew the statements were false.

d. If Grand chooses fraud as his basis for relief, the statute of frauds applies.

26. Ford bought a used typewriter for $625 from Jem Typewriters. The contract provided that the typewriter was sold "with all faults, as is, and at the buyer's risk." The typewriter broke down within a month. Ford took it back to Jem, and after prolonged arguing and negotiating, Jem orally agreed to reduce the price by $50 and refund that amount. Jem has reconsidered his rights and duties and decided **not** to refund the money. Under the circumstances, which of the following is correct?

a. The disclaimer of the implied warranties of merchantability and fitness is invalid.

b. The agreement to reduce the price is valid and binding.

c. Jem's promise is unenforceable since Ford gave **no** new consideration.

d. Since the contract as modified is subject to the statute of frauds, the modification must be in writing.

27. The Astor Bank and Trust Company is the trustee of the Wayne Trust. A significant portion of the trust principal has been invested in AAA rated public utility bonds. Some of the bonds have been purchased at face value, some at a discount, and others at a premium. Which of the following is a proper allocation of the various items to income?

a. The income beneficiary is entitled to the entire interest without dilution for the premium paid but is **not** entitled to the proceeds attributable to the discount upon collection.

b. The income beneficiary is entitled to the entire interest without dilution and to the proceeds attributable to the discount.

c. The income beneficiary is only entitled to the interest less the amount of the premium amortized over the life of the bond.

d. The income beneficiary is entitled to the full interest and to an allocable share of the gain resulting from the discount.

28. Marblehead Manufacturing, Inc., contracted with Wellfleet Oil Company in June to provide its regular supply of fuel oil from November 1 through March 31. The written contract required Marblehead to take all of its oil requirements exclusively from Wellfleet at a fixed price subject to an additional amount **not** to exceed 10% of the contract price and only if the market price increases during the term of the contract. By the time performance was due on the contract, the market price had already risen 20%. Wellfleet seeks to avoid performance. Which of the following will be Wellfleet's **best** argument?

a. There is **no** contract since Marblehead was **not** required to take any oil.

b. The contract fails because of lack of definiteness and certainty.

c. The contract is unconscionable.

d. Marblehead has ordered amounts of oil unreasonably disproportionate to its normal requirements.

29. Two Uniform Commercial Code concepts relating to secured transactions are "attachment" and "perfection." Which of the following is correct in connection with the similarities and differences between these two concepts?

a. They are mutually exclusive and wholly independent of each other.

b. Satisfaction of one automatically satisfies the other.

c. Attachment relates primarily to the rights against the debtor and perfection relates primarily to the rights against third parties.

d. It is **not** possible to have a simultaneous attachment and perfection.

30. Merchant is in serious financial difficulty and is unable to meet current unsecured obligations of $25,000 to some 15 creditors who are demanding immediate payment. Merchant owes Flintheart $5,000 and Flintheart has decided to file an involuntary petition against Merchant. Which of the following is necessary in order for Flintheart to validly file?

a. Flintheart must be joined by at least two other creditors.

b. Merchant must have committed an act of bankruptcy within 120 days of the filing.

    c. Flintheart must allege and subsequently establish that Merchant's liabilities exceed Merchant's assets upon fair valuation.

    d. Flintheart must be a secured creditor.

31. Target Company, Inc., ordered a generator from Maximum Voltage Corporation. A dispute has arisen over the effect of a provision in the specifications that the generator have a 5,000 kilowatt capacity. The specifications were attached to the contract and were incorporated by reference in the main body of the contract. The generator did **not** have this capacity but instead had a maximum capacity of 4,800 kilowatts. The contract had a disclaimer clause which effectively negated both of the implied warranties of quality. Target is seeking to avoid the contract based upon breach of warranty and Maximum is relying on its disclaimer. Which of the following is a correct statement?

    a. The 5,000 kilowatt term contained in the specifications does **not** constitute a warranty.

    b. The disclaimer effectively negated any and all warranty protection claimed by Target.

    c. The description language (5,000 kilowatts) contained in the specifications is an express warranty and has **not** been effectively disclaimed.

    d. The parol evidence rule will prevent Target from asserting the 5,000 kilowatt term as a warranty.

32. Williamson purchased from Dilworth Hardware a new lathe for his home workshop for cash. Two weeks later, Williamson was called by the Easy Loan Company. Easy explained to Williamson that it had been financing Dilworth's purchases from the manufacturers and that to protect its interest it had obtained a perfected security interest in Dilworth's entire inventory of hardware and power tools, including the lathe which Williamson bought. Easy further explained that Dilworth had defaulted on a payment due to Easy, and Easy intended to assert its security interest in the lathe and repossess it unless Williamson was willing to make payment of $200 for a release of Easy's security interest. If Williamson refuses to make the payment, which of the following statements is correct?

    a. Williamson will **not** take free of Easy's security interest if he was aware of said interest at the time he purchased the lathe.

    b. Even if Williamson had both actual notice and constructive notice via recordation of Easy's interest, he will prevail if Easy seeks to repossess the lathe.

    c. Easy's security interest in the lathe in question is invalid against all parties unless its filing specifically described and designated the particular lathe Williamson purchased.

    d. Williamson must pay the $200 or the lathe can be validly repossessed and sold to satisfy the amount Dilworth owes Easy and any excess paid to Williamson.

33. Buyer ordered goods from Seller. The contract required Seller to deliver them f.o.b. Buyer's place of business. Buyer inspected the goods, discovered they failed to conform to the contract, and rightfully rejected them. In the event of loss of the goods, which of the following is a correct statement?

    a. Seller initially had the risk of loss and it remains with him after delivery.

    b. Risk of loss passes to Buyer upon tender of the goods f.o.b. Buyer's place of business.

    c. Buyer initially had the risk of loss, but it is shifted to Seller upon rightful rejection.

    d. If Seller used a public carrier to transport the goods to Buyer, risk of loss is on Buyer during transit.

34. Milgore, the vice president of Deluxe Restaurants, telephoned Specialty Restaurant Suppliers and ordered a made-to-order dishwashing unit for one of its restaurants. Due to the specifications, the machine was **not** adaptable for use by other restauranteurs. The agreed price was $2,500. The machine was constructed as agreed but Deluxe has refused to pay for it. Which of the following is correct?

    a. Milgore obviously lacked the authority to make such a contract.

    b. The statute of frauds applies and will bar recovery by Specialty.

    c. Specialty can successfully maintain an action for the price.

    d. Specialty must resell the machine and recover damages based upon the resale price.

35. Hapless is bankrupt. In connection with a debt owed to the Suburban Finance Company, he used a false financial statement to induce it to loan him $500. Hapless is seeking a discharge in bankruptcy. Which of the following is a correct statement?

    a. Hapless will be denied a discharge of any of his debts.

    b. Even if it can be proved that Suburban did **not** rely upon the financial statement, Hapless will be denied a discharge either in whole or part.

    c. Hapless will be denied a discharge of the Suburban debt.

d. Hapless will be totally discharged despite the false financial statement.

36. Dilworth provided collateral to Maxim to secure Dilworth's performance of an obligation owed to Maxim. Maxim also obtained the Protection Surety Company as a surety for Dilworth's performance. Dilworth has defaulted and Protection has discharged the obligation in full. Which of the following is the correct legal basis for Protection's assertion of rights to the collateral?

   a. Promissory estoppel.

   b. Exoneration.

   c. Indemnification.

   d. Subrogation.

37. Pure Food Company packed and sold quality food products to wholesalers and fancy food retailers. One of its most popular items was "southern style" baked beans. Charleston purchased a large can of the beans from the Superior Quality Grocery. Charleston's mother bit into a heaping spoonful of the beans at a family outing and fractured her jaw. The evidence revealed that the beans contained a brown stone, the size of a marble. In a subsequent lawsuit by Mrs. Charleston, which of the following is correct?

   a. Mrs. Charleston can collect against Superior Quality for negligence.

   b. Privity will **not** be a bar in a lawsuit against either Pure Food or Superior Quality.

   c. The various sellers involved could have effectively excluded or limited the rights of third parties to sue them.

   d. Privity is a bar to recovery by Mrs. Charleston, although her son may sue Superior Quality.

38. Martha Supermarkets ordered 1,000 cases of giant pitted olives from Grove Packers and Wholesalers. The olives were to be packed, labelled and shipped in 30 days. The payment terms were 2/10, net/30 upon delivery. After the order was nearly ready for shipment, Grove learned that Martha was **not** paying its debts as they became due. Martha insisted on delivery according to the terms of the contract. Which of the following is correct?

   a. Upon discovery of Martha's financial condition, Grove was relieved from any duty under the contract.

   b. Martha has the right of performance since it was **not** insolvent in the bankruptcy sense.

   c. Grove must perform but it is entitled to demand cash.

   d. The terms of the contract provided credit to Martha and Grove is bound by it.

39. Nolan Surety Company has agreed to serve as a guarantor of collection (a form of conditional guaranty) of the accounts receivable of the Dunbar Sales Corporation. The duration of the guarantee is one year and the maximum liability assumed is $3,000. Nolan charged the appropriate fee for acting in this capacity. Which of the following statements **best** describes the difference between a guarantor of collection and the typical surety relationship?

   a. A guaranty need **not** be in writing provided the duration is less than a year.

   b. The guarantor is **not** immediately liable upon default; the creditor must first proceed against the debtor.

   c. A guaranty is only available from a surety who is a compensated surety.

   d. A guaranty is only used in connection with the sale of goods which have been guaranteed by the seller.

40. Waldorf's last will and testament named Franklin as the executor of the will. In respect to Franklin's serving as executor, which of the following is correct?

   a. He serves without compensation unless the will provides otherwise.

   b. He is at liberty to purchase the estate's property the same as any other person dealing at arm's length.

   c. Waldorf must have obtained Franklin's consent in writing to serve as executor.

   d. Upon appointment by the court, he serves as the legal representative of the estate.

41. Simpson and Thomas made separate contracts of suretyship with Allan to guarantee repayment of a $12,000 loan Allan made to Parker. Simpson's guarantee was for $12,000 and Thomas' for $8,000. In the event Simpson pays the full amount ($12,000), what may he recover from Thomas?

   a. Nothing since their contracts were separate.

   b. $4,800.

   c. $6,000.

   d. $8,000.

42. Moncrief is a surety on a $100,000 obligation owed by Vicars to Sampson. The debt is also secured by a $50,000 mortgage to Sampson on Vicars' factory. Vicars is in bankruptcy. Moncrief has satisfied the debt. Which of the following is a correct statement?

   a. Moncrief is a secured creditor to the extent of the $50,000 mortgage and a general creditor for the balance.

b. Moncrief would not be entitled to a priority in bankruptcy, even though Sampson could validly claim it.

c. Moncrief is only entitled to the standing of a general creditor in bankruptcy.

d. Moncrief is entitled to nothing in bankruptcy since this was a risk he assumed.

43. Newton is an employee of the Black Motor Company. She is covered to the extent of $50,000 by a group term life insurance policy which covers all the full-time employees of Black. She pays no premiums on the policy. Regarding the legal and tax aspects of this policy, which of the following is a correct statement?

a. Black is **not** entitled to a deduction for the premiums paid on the policy.

b. Newton must include the annual premium to purchase the $50,000 policy in her gross income.

c. Newton is obligated to name the Black Motor Company as the contingent beneficiary.

d. The policy is canceled upon her terminating her employment unless she elects to pay the premiums herself at the nongroup rate.

44. Cornwith agreed to serve as a surety on a loan by Super Credit Corporation to Fairfax, one of Cornwith's major customers. The relationship between Fairfax and Super deteriorated to a point of hatred as a result of several late payments on the loan. On the due date of the final payment, Fairfax appeared 15 minutes before closing and tendered payment of the entire amount owing to Super. The office manager of Super told Fairfax that he was too late and would have to pay the next day with additional interest and penalties. Fairfax again tendered the payment, which was again refused. It is now several months later and Super is seeking to collect from either Cornwith or Fairfax or both. What are Super's rights under the circumstances?

a. It cannot collect anything from either party.

b. The tender of performance released Cornwith from his obligation.

c. The tender of performance was too late and rightfully refused.

d. Cornwith is released only to the extent that the refusal to accept the tender harmed him.

45. At his death, Filmore owned a $100,000 life insurance policy on his life in which he designated his wife as the beneficiary. The insurer paid the proceeds of the policy directly to Mrs. Filmore after his death. Which of the following is a correct statement?

a. If Filmore's will designates a person other than his wife to receive the proceeds of the insurance policy, such a designation will not be valid.

b. Upon receipt of the proceeds, Mrs. Filmore will have received $100,000 of taxable income, but income averaging is permitted.

c. The insurance proceeds are **not** includible in Filmore's estate for federal estate tax purposes.

d. Filmore, having designated his wife as the beneficiary of the policy, could **not** change the beneficiary unless she died or they were divorced.

46. Dupree buys and sells merchandise at wholesale. She is concerned with her insurance coverage on her purchases. Her desire is to insure the property at the earliest possible time legally permitted. Which of the following times or circumstances correctly indicates the earliest time permissible?

a. At the time the goods are identified to the contract.

b. When title to the goods has passed to her.

c. When she has received possession of the goods.

d. At the time the contract is made whether or not the goods are identified.

47. Rollo Trading Corporation insured its 15 automobiles for both liability and collision. Poindexter, one of its salesmen, was in an automobile accident while driving a company car on a sales trip. The facts clearly reveal that the accident was solely the fault of Connors, the driver of the other car. Poindexter was seriously injured, and the automobile was declared a total loss. The value of the auto was $2,850. Which of the following is an **incorrect** statement regarding the rights and liabilities of Rollo, its insurer, Poindexter, and Connors?

a. Rollo's insurer has **no** liability whatsoever since the accident was the result of Connors' negligence.

b. Rollo's insurer is liable for $2,850, less any deductible, on the collision policy, but will be subrogated to Rollo's rights.

c. Rollo's insurer must defend Rollo against any claims by Poindexter or Connors.

d. Poindexter has an independent action against Connors for the injuries caused by Connors' negligence.

48. Hazard & Company was the owner of a building valued at $100,000. Since Hazard did not believe that a fire would result in a total loss, it procured two standard fire insurance policies on the property. One was for $24,000 with the

Asbestos Fire Insurance Company and the other was for $16,000 with the Safety Fire Insurance Company. Both policies contained standard pro rata and 80% coinsurance clauses. Six months later, at which time the building was still valued at $100,000, a fire occurred which resulted in a loss of $40,000. What is the total amount Hazard can recover on both policies and the respective amount to be paid by Asbestos?

    a. $0 and $0.
    b. $20,000 and $10,000.
    c. $20,000 and $12,000.
    d. $40,000 and $20,000.

49. A group of real estate dealers has decided to form a Real Estate Investment Trust (REIT) which will invest in diversified real estate holdings. A public offering of $10,000,000 of trust certificates is contemplated. Which of the following is an **incorrect** statement?

    a. Those investing in the venture will **not** be insulated from personal liability.
    b. The entity will be considered to be an "association" for tax purposes.
    c. The offering must be registered under the Securities Act of 1933.
    d. If the trust qualifies as a REIT and distributes all its income to the investors, it will **not** be subject to federal income tax.

50. Mullins created a trust pursuant to her last will and testament which named her husband as the life income beneficiary and her children as the remaindermen. She is dead. Which of the following does **not** apply to the above-described trust?

    a. It is a testamentary trust.
    b. The husband has the right to appoint the ultimate beneficiaries.
    c. The children have a vested interest in the trust.
    d. The trustee owes a fiduciary duty to both the husband and the children.

51. Under the Securities Act of 1933, an accountant may be held liable for any materially false or misleading financial statements, including an omission of a material fact therefrom, provided the purchaser

    a. Proves reliance on the registration statement or prospectus.
    b. Proves negligence or fraud on the part of the accountant.
    c. Brings suit within four years after the security is offered to the public.
    d. Proves a false statement or omission existed **and** the specific securities were the ones offered through the registration statement.

52. Taylor is the executive Vice President for Marketing of Reflex Corporation and a member of the Board of Directors. Based on information obtained during the course of his duties, Taylor concluded that Reflex's profits would fall by 50% for the quarter and 30% for the year. He quietly contacted his broker and disposed of 10,000 shares of his Reflex stock at a profit, some of which he had acquired within six months of the sale. In fact, Reflex's profits did **not** fall, but its stock price declined for unrelated reasons. Taylor had also advised a friend to sell her shares and repurchase the stock later. She followed Taylor's advice, sold for $21, and subsequently repurchased an equal number of shares at $11. A shareholder has commenced a shareholder derivative action against Taylor and the friend for violation of the Securities Exchange Act of 1934. Under these circumstances, which of the following is correct?

    a. Taylor is **not** an insider in relation to Reflex.
    b. Taylor must account to the corporation for his short-swing profit.
    c. Taylor and the friend must both account to the corporation for their short-swing profits.
    d. Neither Taylor nor the friend has incurred any liability under the 1934 act.

53. Which of the following is exempt from registration under the Securities Act of 1933?

    a. First mortgage bonds.
    b. The usual annuity contract issued by an insurer.
    c. Convertible preferred stock.
    d. Limited partnership interests.

54. Glick was the owner of a factory valued at $100,000. He procured a fire insurance policy on the building for $40,000 from Safety Insurance Company, Inc. The policy contained an 80% coinsurance clause. The property was totally destroyed by fire. How much will Glick recover from the insurance company?

    a. $20,000.

    b. $32,000.

    c. $40,000.

    d. Glick will recover nothing because he did **not** meet the coinsurance requirements.

55. Which of the following is a correct statement concerning the similarities of a limited partnership and a corporation?

    a. Shareholders and limited partners may both participate in the management of the business and retain limited liability.

    b. Both are recognized for federal income tax purposes as taxable entities.

    c. Both can only be created pursuant to a statute and each must file a copy of their respective certificates with the proper state authorities.

    d. Both provide insulation from personal liability for all of the owners of the business.

56. Magnus Real Estate Developers, Inc., wanted to acquire certain tracts of land in Marshall Township in order to build a shopping center complex. To accomplish this goal, Magnus engaged Dexter, a sophisticated real estate dealer, to represent them in the purchase of the necessary land without revealing the existence of the agency. Dexter began to slowly but steadily acquire the requisite land. However, Dexter made the mistake of purchasing one tract outside the description of the land needed. Which of the following is correct under these circumstances?

    a. The use of an agent by Magnus, an undisclosed principal, is manifestly illegal.

    b. Either Magnus or Dexter may be held liable on the contracts for the land, including the land that was **not** within the scope of the proposed shopping center.

    c. An undisclosed principal such as Magnus can have **no** liability under the contract since the third party believed he was dealing with Dexter as a principal.

    d. An agent for an undisclosed principal assumes **no** liability as long as he registers his relationship to the principal with the clerk of the proper county having jurisdiction.

57. Charleston, Inc., had its warehouse destroyed by fire. Charleston's property was insured against fire loss by the Conglomerate Insurance Company. An investigation by Conglomerate revealed that the fire had been caused by a disgruntled employee whom Charleston had suspended for one month due to insubordination. Charleston seeks to hold its insurer liable for the $200,000 loss of its warehouse. Which of the following is correct insofar as the dispute between Charleston and the Conglomerate Insurance Company?

    a. Since the loss was due to the deliberate destruction by one of Charleston's employees, recovery will be denied.

    b. Conglomerate must pay Charleston, but it will be subrogated to Conglomerate's rights against the wrongdoing employee.

    c. The fact that the employee has been suspended for one month precludes recovery against Conglomerate.

    d. Arson is excluded from the coverage of most fire insurance policies, and therefore Conglomerate is **not** liable.

58. On March 11, Vizar Sales Corporation telegraphed Watson Company:

> "Will sell 1,000 cases of coffee for $28 a case for delivery at our place of business on April 15. You may pick them up at our loading platform."

Watson telegraphed its acceptance on March 12. On March 20, coffee prices rose to $30 a case. Vizar telegraphed Watson on March 21 that it repudiated the sale and would **not** make delivery. The telegram was received by Watson on March 22 when the price was $32; Watson could have covered at that price but chose not to do so. On April 15 the coffee was selling at $35 a case. Watson tendered $28,000 to Vizar and indicated it was ready to take delivery. Vizar refused to deliver. What relief, if any, is Watson entitled to?

    a. Specific performance, because it made a valid tender of performance.

    b. Nothing, because it failed to cover.

    c. Damages of $4,000 (the difference between the contract price and the fair market value at the time Watson learned of the breach).

    d. Damages of $7,000 (the difference between the contract price and the fair market value at the time delivery should have been made).

59. Master Corporation, a radio and television manufacturer, invited Darling Discount Chain to examine several odd lots of discontinued models and make an offer for the entire lot. The odd lots were segregated from the regular

inventory but inadvertently included 15 current models. Darling was unaware that Master did not intend to include the 15 current models in the group. Darling made Master an offer of $9,000 for the entire lot, which represented a large discount from the normal sales price. Unaware of the error, Master accepted the offer. Master would **not** have accepted had it known of the inclusion of the 15 current models. Upon learning of the error, Master alleged mistake as a defense and refused to perform. Darling sued for breach of contract. Under the circumstances, what is the status of the contract?

a. There is **no** contract since Master did not intend to include the 15 current models in the group of radios to be sold.

b. The contract is voidable because of a unilateral mistake.

c. The contract is voidable because of a mutual mistake.

d. There is a valid and binding contract which includes the 15 current-model radios.

60. Lally sent Queen Supply Company, Inc., a telegram ordering $700 of general merchandise. Lally's telegram indicated that immediate shipment was necessary. That same day Queen delivered the goods to the Red Freight Company. The shipment was delayed due to a breakdown of the truck which was transporting the goods. When the merchandise did **not** arrive as promptly as expected, Lally notified Queen that it revoked the offer and was purchasing the goods elsewhere. Queen indicated to Lally that the merchandise had been shipped the same day Lally had ordered it and Lally's revocation was **not** good. Which of the following statements **best** describes the transaction?

a. The statute of frauds will be a defense on any action by Queen to enforce the contract.

b. Prompt shipment of the merchandise by Queen constituted an acceptance.

c. Lally's revocation of the offer was effective since Lally had **not** received a notice of acceptance.

d. Lally's order was an offer to Queen to enter into a bilateral contract which could be accepted only by a promise.

Number 2 (Estimated time—15 to 20 minutes)

Part a. Marcall is a limited partner of Guarcross, a limited partnership, and is suing a CPA firm which was retained by the limited partnership to perform auditing and tax return preparation services. Guarcross was formed for the purpose of investing in a diversified portfolio of risk capital securities. The partnership agreement included the following provisions:

> The initial capital contribution of each limited partner shall not be less than $250,000; no partner may withdraw any part of his interest in the partnership, except at the end of any fiscal year upon giving written notice of such intention not less than 30 days prior to the end of such year; the books and records of the partnership shall be audited as of the end of the fiscal year by a certified public accountant designated by the general partners; and proper and complete books of account shall be kept and shall be open to inspection by any of the partners or his or her accredited representative.

Marcall's claim of malpractice against the CPA firm centers on the firm's alleged failure to comment, in its audit report, on the withdrawal by the general partners of $2,000,000 of their $2,600,000 capital investment based on back-dated notices, and the lumping together of the $2,000,000 withdrawals with $49,000 in withdrawals by limited partners so that a reader of the financial statement would not be likely to realize that the two general partners had withdrawn a major portion of their investments.

The CPA firm's contention is that its contract was made with the limited partnership, not its partners. It further contends that since the CPA firm had no privity of contract with the third-party limited partners, the limited partners have no right of action for negligence.

Required

Answer the following, setting forth reasons for any conclusions stated.

Discuss the various theories Marcall would rely upon in order to prevail in a lawsuit against the CPA firm.

Part b. Farr & Madison, CPAs, audited Glamour, Inc. Their audit was deficient in several respects:

• Farr and Madison failed to verify properly certain receivables which later proved to be fictitious.

- With respect to other receivables, although they made a cursory check, they did not detect many accounts which were long overdue and obviously uncollectible.
- No physical inventory was taken of the securities claimed to be in Glamour's possession, which in fact had been sold. Both the securities and cash received from the sales were listed on the balance sheet as assets.

There is no indication that Farr & Madison actually believed that the financial statements were false. Subsequent creditors, not known to Farr & Madison, are now suing based upon the deficiencies in the audit described above. Farr and Madison moved to dismiss the lawsuit against it on the basis that the firm did not have actual knowledge of falsity and therefore did not commit fraud.

Required
Answer the following, setting forth reasons for any conclusions stated.
    May the creditors recover without demonstrating Farr & Madison had actual knowledge of falsity?

Number 3 (Estimated time—15 to 20 minutes)

Part a. Jane Anderson offered to sell Richard Heinz a 10-acre tract of commercial property. Anderson's letter indicated the offer would expire on March 1, 1980, at 3:00 P.M. and that any acceptance must be received in her office by that time. On February 29, 1980, Heinz decided to accept the offer and posted an acceptance at 4:00 P.M. Heinz indicated that in the event the acceptance did not arrive on time, he would assume there was a contract if he did not hear anything from Anderson in five days. The letter arrived on March 2, 1980. Anderson never responded to Heinz's letter. Heinz claims a contract was entered into and is suing thereon.

Required
Answer the following, setting forth reasons for any conclusions stated.
    Is there a contract?

Part b. Betty Monash was doing business as Victory Stamp Company. She sold the business as a going concern. The assets of the business consist of an inventory of stamps, various trade fixtures which are an inherent part of the business, a building which houses the retail operation, goodwill, and miscellaneous office equipment. On the liability side, there are numerous trade accounts payable and a first mortgage on the building.

Joe Franklin purchased the business. In addition to a cash payment, he assumed all outstanding debts and promised to hold Monash harmless from any and all liability on the scheduled debts listed in the contract of sale.

Required
Answer the following, setting forth reasons for any conclusions stated.
    What is the legal relationship of Monash, Franklin, and the creditors to each other after the consummation of the sale with respect to the outstanding debts of the business?

Number 4 (Estimated time—15 to 20 minutes)

On July 1, 1974, Martin Hayes signed a promissory note that was made payable to the order of Jones Fabricating, Inc., for $10,000, plus 8% interest, payable 90 days from date. On the front of the note above his signature Hayes wrote: "Subject to satisfactory delivery of goods purchased this date. Delivery to be made no later than July 31, 1974."

Jones' president indorsed the note on behalf of the corporation and transferred it to Acme Bank in consideration of the bank's crediting $9,800 against a $20,000 debt owed to the bank by Jones Fabricating.

When the due date arrived, the bank asked Hayes to pay, but Hayes refused, saying that Jones had not delivered the goods he had bargained for in giving the note. The next day Acme Bank gave notice of dishonor to Jones.

Required
Answer the following, setting forth reasons for any conclusions stated.

1. Is the note negotiable commercial paper? Explain.
2. Assuming the note is nonnegotiable paper, can Acme Bank collect the amount due from Hayes if Hayes can prove that the goods he bargained for were not delivered? Explain.
3. Assuming the note is negotiable, can Acme Bank successfully collect from Hayes? Explain.
4. Assuming the note is negotiable and that Acme Bank is a holder in due course, can Acme successfully sue Jones Fabricating to collect the proceeds of the note? Explain.

Number 5 (Estimated time—15 to 20 minutes)

Part a. Vogel, an assistant buyer for the Granite City Department Store, purchased metal art objects from Duval Reproductions. Vogel was totally without express or apparent authority to do so, but believed that his purchase was a brilliant move likely to get him a promotion. The head buyer of Granite was livid when he learned of Vogel's activities. However, after examining the merchandise and listening to Vogel's pitch, he reluctantly placed the merchandise in the storeroom and put a couple of pieces on display for a few days to see whether it was a "hot item" and a "sure thing" as Vogel claimed. The item was neither "hot" nor "sure" and when it didn't move at all, the head buyer ordered the display merchandise repacked and the entire order returned to Duval with a letter that stated the merchandise had been ordered by an assistant buyer who had absolutely no authority to make the purchase. Duval countered with a lawsuit for breach of contract.

Required
Answer the following, setting forth reasons for any conclusions stated.
    Will Duval prevail?

Part b. Foremost Realty, Inc., is a real estate broker that also buys and sells real property for its own account. Hobson purchased a ranch from Foremost. The terms were 10% down with the balance payable over a 25-year period. After several years of profitable operation of the ranch, Hobson had two successive bad years. As a result, he defaulted on the mortgage. Foremost did not want to foreclose, but instead offered to allow Hobson to remain on the ranch and suspend the payment schedule until Foremost could sell the property at a reasonable price. However, Foremost insisted that it be appointed as the irrevocable and exclusive agent for the sale of the property. Although Hobson agreed, he subsequently became dissatisfied with Foremost's efforts to sell the ranch and gave Foremost notice in writing terminating the agency. Foremost has indicated to Hobson that he does not have the legal power to do so.

Required
Answer the following, setting forth reasons for any conclusions stated.
    Can Hobson terminate the agency?

Part c. Whipple, Ryan, and Lopez decided to pool their assets and talents in a partnership. The partnership was to provide management consulting services. The partnership agreement provided the following:
* All policy questions regarding the scope, nature, billings, size, and future expansion of the business are to be decided by a majority vote of the partners. Each partner shall be bound by the decision reached.
* Since each party to this agreement has discontinued a profitable individual business at great financial sacrifice, it is mutually agreed that this partnership shall be irrevocable for a period of five years from the date of execution.

For the first year things went smoothly for the partnership. The relationship of the partners was amicable as they integrated the three separate businesses into one. However, in the middle of the second year, policy disputes began to arise. In virtually every instance, Ryan and Lopez opposed Whipple on matters of expansion and billing rates. At the end of the second year, Whipple announced "he had had enough." He indicated that the ultraconservative thinking of his partners was deplorable and he could not remain in the partnership under the circumstances. He immediately resigned as a partner, reestablished his own business, and actively competed with the partnership. Many of his former clients followed him.

Required

Answer the following, setting forth reasons for any conclusions stated.

What recourse, if any, do Ryan and Lopez, or the partnership, have against Whipple?

APPENDIX

Revised AICPA Business Law Content Specification Outline

Introductory Note: Presented below in its entirety is the official AICPA *Content Specification Outline for Business Law*. The original version of the Content Specifications was revised by deleting large parts of the original specifications, shifting the location of others, and making some additional changes. The net result is the *Revised Content Specification Outline*. This is effective for the May 1986 exam. Each individual area or topic is presented as a lead-in to the 17 chapters of the book.

I. The CPA and the Law (10%)
  A. Common Law Liability to Clients and Third Persons
  B. Federal Statutory Liability
    1. Securities Acts
    2. Internal Revenue Code
  C. Workpapers, Privileged Communication, and Confidentiality
II. Business Organizations (20%)
  A. Agency
    1. Formation and Termination
    2. Liabilities of Principal
    3. Disclosed and Undisclosed Principals
    4. Agency Authority and Liability
  B. Partnerships and Joint Ventures
    1. Formation and Existence
    2. Liabilities and Authority of Partners and Joint Owners
    3. Allocation of Profit or Loss
    4. Transfer of Interest
    5. Termination, Winding Up, and Dissolution
  C. Corporations
    1. Formation, Purposes, and Powers
    2. Stockholders, Directors, and Officers
    3. Financial Structure, Capital, and Dividends
    4. Merger, Consolidation, and Dissolution

    D. Estates and Trusts
       1. Formation and Purposes
       2. Allocation Between Principal and Income
       3. Fiduciary Responsibilities
       4. Distributions and Termination
III. Contracts (15%)
    A. Offer and Acceptance
    B. Consideration
    C. Capacity, Legality, and Public Policy
    D. Statute of Frauds
    E. Statute of Limitations
    F. Fraud, Duress, and Undue Influence
    G. Mistake and Misrepresentation
    H. Parol Evidence Rule
    I. Third Party Rights
    J. Assignments
    K. Discharge, Breach, and Remedies
IV. Debtor-Creditor Relationships (10%)
    A. Suretyship
       1. Liabilities and Defenses
       2. Release of Parties
       3. Remedies of Parties
    B. Bankruptcy
       1. Voluntary and Involuntary Bankruptcy
       2. Effects of Bankruptcy on Debtor and Creditors
       3. Reorganizations
V. Government Regulation of Business (10%)
    A. Regulation of Employment
       1. Federal Insurance Contributions Act
       2. Federal Unemployment Tax Act
       3. Worker's Compensation Acts
    B. Federal Securities Acts
       1. Securities Registration
       2. Reporting Requirements
       3. Exempt Securities and Transactions
VI. Uniform Commercial Code (25%)
    A. Commercial Paper
       1. Types of Negotiable Instruments
       2. Requisites for Negotiability
       3. Transfer and Negotiation
       4. Holders and Holders in Due Course
       5. Liabilities, Defenses, and Rights
       6. Discharge
    B. Documents of Title and Investment Securities
       1. Warehouse Receipts
       2. Bills of Lading
       3. Issuance, Transfer, and Registration of Securities

Index

Note: This index is primarily based upon the Revised Content Specification Outlines.